HANDBOOK ON OCEAN POLITICS & LAW

HANDBOOK ON OCEAN POLITICS & LAW

JAMES C. F. WANG

GP

Greenwood Press

NEW YORK • WESTPORT, CONNECTICUT • LONDON

Library of Congress Cataloging-in-Publication Data

Wang, James C. F.
Handbook on ocean politics and law / James C. F. Wang.
p. cm.
Includes bibliographical references and index.
ISBN 0–313–26434–1 (alk. paper)
1. Maritime law. 2. Marine resources conservation—Law and legislation. 3. Ocean bottom (Maritime law) I. Title.
JX4411.W36 1992
341.4'5—dc20 91–10532

British Library Cataloguing in Publication Data is available.

Library of Congress Catalog Card Number: 91–10532
ISBN: 0–313–26434–1

First published in 1992

Greenwood Press, 88 Post Road West, Westport, CT 06881
An imprint of Greenwood Publishing Group, Inc.

Printed in the United States of America

The paper used in this book complies with the Permanent Paper Standard issued by the National Information Standards Organization (Z39.48–1984).

10 9 8 7 6 5 4 3 2 1

Copyright Acknowledgments

Every reasonable effort has been made to trace the owners of copyright materials in this book, but in some cases this has proven impossible. The author and publisher will be glad to receive information leading to more complete acknowledgments in subsequent printings of the book and in the meantime extend their apologies for any omissions.

Contents

Illustrations

FIGURES

TABLES

Preface

For more than two decades, from the 1960s to the 1980s, there has been a cascade of literature on the evolution of the new law of the sea and on the multifarious uses of the oceans. These voluminous studies were inspired and stimulated by the seabed debate in the United Nations General Assembly in the 1960s, which eventually led to the convening of the Third United Nations Conference on the Law of the Sea in 1974–1982. Studies on ocean affairs encompass a wide range of subject matter, from ocean boundary delimitation and disputes to fishery conservation and management to seabed mineral resources exploitation and exploration. Taken as a whole, they are multidisciplinary in nature. Thus there is a need for a single-volume reference handbook to provide accurate, comprehensive and timely background information and analysis on these multifaceted subjects for libraries, universities, governmental and nongovernmental agencies concerned with global ocean affairs.

This handbook is arranged in five parts: a global overview on the physical features of the oceans; a brief survey of international conferences on the uses of the oceans and the evolution of international principles on the law of the sea; ocean resources and their economic and political management for both living and nonliving resources, including seabed mining; ocean environmental protection and pollution prevention; and ocean uses such as military, navigation and transport, and marine scientific research.

The handbook contains a number of features. First, it incorporates in the various topical surveys and analyses the salient portions of the 1982 Law of the Sea Convention. In addition, whenever appropriate, pertinent reference is made to all major international conventions that have dealt with global ocean or marine affairs. Third, there are numerous charts and tables, which provide useful supplements to the handbook text. Finally, as a convenient guide to users, each chapter includes useful reference notes listing pertinent studies on the various subjects. The appendix includes a chronological list of international conventions and treaties on the law of the sea, the status of the 1982 UN Convention on the Law of the Sea and its ratifications (as of May 1990), a list of bilateral agreements on maritime boundary delimitation and recent court decisions, national legislation and exclusive economic zones, selected bilateral fishery agreements, coastal state requirements for foreign fishing, and a directory of selected nongovernmental international organizations concerned with ocean affairs. In addition, an extensive bibliographical volume is being prepared to be used in conjunction with this handbook.

The preparation of this book would not have been possible without the help of a number of persons. First, I must acknowledge my indebtedness to ocean affairs scholars whose works are cited in the text and in the chapter notes. Also, I owe a debt of gratitude to Catherine Tignac for her invaluable assistance throughout the years I have been teaching a course on ocean politics and working on this project. Also, my thanks to Edith Worsencroft for helping with typing and checking the manuscript. Last, and certainly not the least, is my profound personal appreciation to Mildred Vasan, Senior Editor for Social and Behavioral Sciences at Greenwood, for her encouragement, guidance and patience in the preparation of this handbook.

Abbreviations

ACOPS	Advisory Committee on Oil Pollution of the Sea (British)
AJIL	American Journal of International Law
ASROC	Anti-submarine Rockets
ASW	Anti-submarine Warfare
ATCPs	Antarctic Treaty Consultative Parties
CENTO	Center Treaty Organization
CEP	Caribbean Environmental Programme
CEP News	Caribbean Environmental Programme News
CLC	Civil Liability Convention, 1969 (International Convention on Civil Liabilities for Oil Pollution)
COW	Crude oil washing
CRISTAL	Contract Regarding Interim Supplement to Tanker Liability for Oil Pollution, 1971
dwt	dead weight tonnage
EEC	European Economic Community
EEZ	Exclusive Economic Zone
EFZ	Exclusive Fishery Zone
FAO	Food and Agriculture Organization
IAEA	International Atomic Energy Agency
IATTA	Inter-American Tropical Tuna Commission
ICBM	Intercontinental Ballistic Missiles
ICCAT	International Convention for the Conservation of Atlantic Tuna, 1969
ICES	International Council for the Exploration of the Sea
ICJ	International Court of Justice

ICSU	International Council of Scientific Union
ILO	International Labor Organization
IMCO	Intergovernmental Maritime Consultative Organization, 1948–1981
IMLI	International Maritime Law Institute at Malta University
IMO	International Maritime Organization
IMO News	International Maritime Organization News
IMS	International Marine Science
INMARSAT	International Maritime Satellite Organization
IOC	Intergovernmental Oceanographic Commission
IOZP	Indian Ocean Zone of Peace
IWC	International Whaling Commission
LL/GDS	Landlocked and Geographically Disadvantaged States
LOS Convention 1982	Law of the Sea Convention, 1982
LOT	"Load on Top"
MAD	Magnetic Depth Sonar
MARPOL	International Convention for the Prevention of Pollution from Ships, 1973
MSR	Marine Scientific Research
MSY	Maximum Sustainable Yield
NEAFC	North East Atlantic Fishery Commission
NIEO	New International Economic Order
OAS	Organization of American States
ODAS	Ocean Data Acquisition System
OPANAL	Treaty for the Prohibition of Nuclear Weapons in Latin-America, 1967
OPOL	Offshore Pollution Liability Agreement, 1975
PPM	Parts-per-million
SCOR	Scientific Committee on Ocean Research
SIPRI	Stockholm International Peace Research Institute
SLBM	Submarine-launched Ballistic Missiles
SLOC	Sealanes of communication
SOLAS	Convention for Safety of Life at Sea, 1974
SOSUS	Sound Surveillance System
SPNFZ	South Pacific Nuclear Free Zone Treaty
TAC	Total allowable catch
TIAS	Treaties and Other International Acts Series
TOVALOP	Tanker Owners' Voluntary Agreement Concerning Liability for Oil Pollution, 1969

UNCLOS I	First United Nations Conference on the Law of the Sea, 1958
UNCLOS II	Second United Nations Conference on the Law of the Sea, 1960
UNCLOS III	Third United Nations Conference on the Law of the Sea, 1973–1982
UNCTAD	United Nations Conference on Trade and Development
UNEP	United Nations Environmental Programs
UNGAOR	United Nations General Assembly Official Records
UNTS	United Nations Treaty Series
VDS	Variable Depth Sonar
WIPO	World Intellectual Property Organization

CHAPTER 1

The World's Oceans and Their Physical and Geographical Features

In the olden days, one spoke of the ''seven seas''—the bodies of salt water that cover 71 percent of the earth's surface. However, today's oceanographers refer only to three great oceans of the world, in terms of their dimensions: the Atlantic, the Pacific and the Indian oceans. All other bodies of water are marginal—enclosed or semi-enclosed—seas connected to, or considered tributaries of, the great oceans. The dimensions and locations of the world's oceans and seas are listed in Table 1.1 and Figure 1.1.

In one sense the whole world can be seen as one enormous ocean if, by turning the map of the globe upside down, one views it from the vantage of the South Pole where the world's three great oceans meet in the southern, or marine, hemisphere. And the ocean waters do mix. One example is the cold Antarctic waters that are heavier than the surface waters of other oceans—the heavier Antarctic waters slide under the waters of other surrounding oceans. Oceanographers have pointed out that the cold Antarctic water can be found north of the equator.

The Pacific is the world's largest, coldest and deepest ocean. It occupies about 166 million square kilometers, or approximately one-third of the earth's total surface area. Its mean depth is about 4,000 meters. (The Mariana Trench, off the island of Guam, is measured at a depth of 11,000 meters.) The Pacific contains a volume of more than 576 million cubic kilometers of water. Water temperature of the Pacific is about 3.36°C, and the salinity content is about 34.6 percent. The Pacific is so vast that it could contain all of the world's land masses or continents within its area. Near the equator the Pacific extends and spreads to 17,700 kilometers—halfway around the world. To the east of the Pacific lie the American continents, and to the west Asia and Australia. To the north the Pacific is connected by the Bering Strait with the Arctic Ocean. In many ways, the Pacific can be a violent ocean where fearsome storms occur and frequent earthquakes, caused by erupting volcanic islands, disturb the tranquility of its

Table 1.1
Dimensions of the Oceans and Marginal Seas

Body of Water	Area		Mean Depth		Volume	
	thousands of kilometers^2	thousands of miles^2	meters	feet	thousands of kilometers^3	thousands of miles^3
Oceans						
Arctic	14,090	5,440	1,205	3,954	17,000	4,100
North Pacific	83,462	32,225	3,858	12,658	322,000	77,200
South Pacific	65,521	25,298	3,891	12,766	254,900	61,150
North Atlantic	46,772	18,059	3,285	10,778	153,600	36,850
South Atlantic	37,364	14,426	4,091	13,423	152,800	36,660
Indian	81,602	31,507	4,284	14,056	349,600	83,870
Antarctic (Southern)	32,249	12,451	3,730	12,238	120,300	28,860
Tributaries to the Arctic Ocean						
Norwegian Sea	1,383	534	1,742	5,716	2,408	578
Greenland Sea	1,205	465	1,444	4,738	1,740	417
Barents Sea	1,405	542	229	751	322	77
White Sea	90	35	89	292	8	2
Kara Sea	883	341	118	387	104	25
Laptev Sea	650	251	519	1,703	338	81
East Siberian Sea	901	348	58	190	53	13
Chukchi Sea	582	225	88	289	51	12
Beaufort Sea	476	184	1,004	3,294	478	115
Baffin Bay	689	266	861	2,825	593	142
Tributaries to the North Atlantic						
North Sea	600	232	91	299	55	13
Baltic Sea	386	149	86	282	33	8
Mediterranean Sea	2,516	971	1,494	4,902	3,758	902
Black Sea	461	178	1,166	3,826	537	129
Caribbean Sea	2,754	1,063	2,491	8,173	6,860	1,646
Gulf of Mexico	1,543	596	1,512	4,961	2,332	559
Gulf of Saint Lawrence	238	92	127	417	30	7
Hudson Bay	1,232	476	128	420	158	38
Tributary to the South Atlantic						
Gulf of Guinea	1,533	592	2,996	9,830	4,592	1,102

Tributaries to the Indian Ocean						
Red Sea	450	174	558	1,831	251	60
Persian Gulf	241	93	40	131	10	2
Arabian Sea	3,863	1,492	2,734	8,970	10,561	2,534
Bay of Bengal	2,172	839	2,586	8,485	5,616	1,347
Andaman Sea	602	232	1,096	3,596	660	158
Great Australian Bight	484	187	950	3,117	459	110
Tributaries to the North Pacific						
Gulf of California	177	68	818	2,684	145	35
Gulf of Alaska	1,327	512	2,431	7,976	3,226	774
Bering Sea	2,304	890	1,598	5,243	3,683	884
Sea of Okhotsk	1,590	614	859	2,818	1,365	327
Sea of Japan	978	378	1,752	5,748	1,713	411
Yellow Sea	417	161	40	131	17	4
East China Sea	752	290	349	1,145	263	63
Sulu Sea	420	162	1,139	3,737	478	115
Celebes Sea	472	182	3,291	10,798	1,553	373
Tributaries to Both the North and South Pacific						
South China Sea	3,685	1,423	1,060	3,478	3,907	937
Makassar Strait	194	75	967	3,173	188	45
Molukka Sea	307	119	1,880	6,168	578	139
Ceram Sea	187	72	1,209	3,967	227	54
Tributaries to the South Pacific						
Java Sea	433	167	46	151	20	5
Bali Sea	119	46	411	1,348	49	12
Flores Sea	121	47	1,829	6,001	222	53
Savu Sea	105	41	1,701	5,581	178	43
Banda Sea	695	268	3,064	10,053	2,129	511
Ceram Sea	187	72	1,209	3,967	227	54
Timor Sea	615	237	406	1,332	250	60
Arafura Sea	1,037	400	197	646	204	49
Coral Sea	4,791	1,850	2,394	7,855	11,470	2,752

Source: *Academic American Encyclopedia* (Princeton, N.J.: Areta Publishing Company, Inc., 1981), vol. 14, p. 326. Used by permission.

Figure 1.1
Map of Major Oceans, Seas and Continents

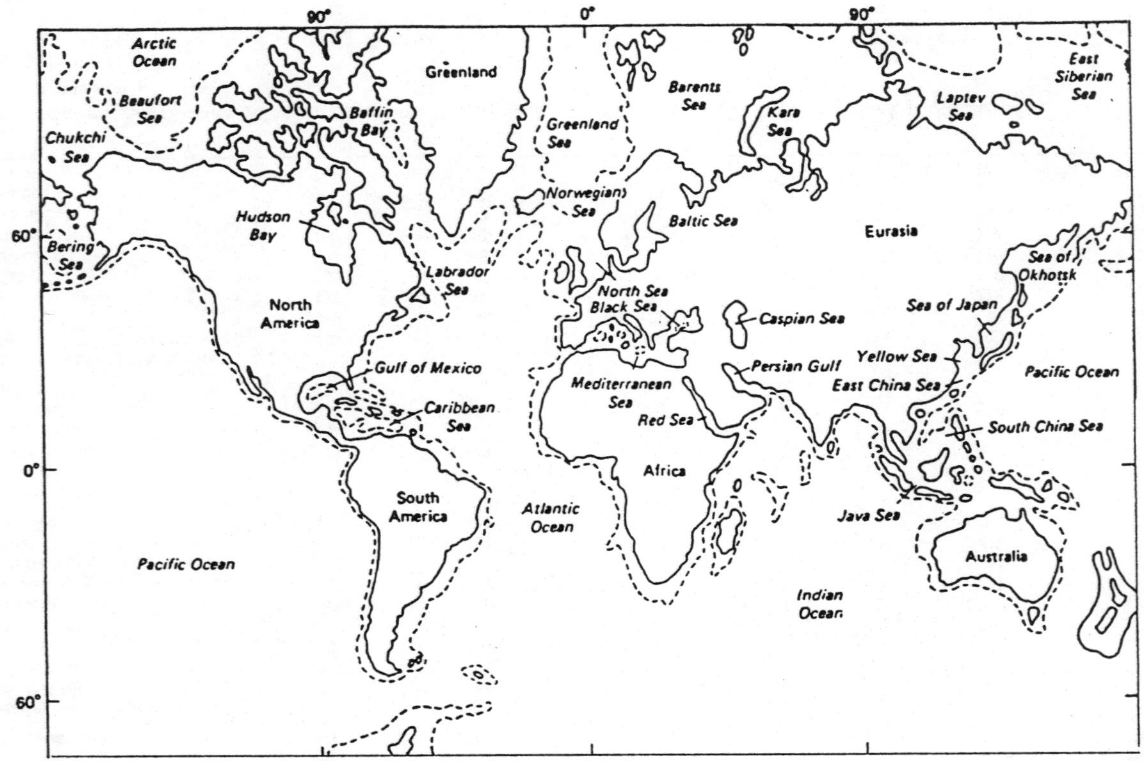

Note: Dashed lines indicate the expansion of ocean space by new ocean regions, such as the 200-mile EC zones.
Source: David A. Ross, *Opportunities and Uses of the Ocean* (New York: Springer-Verlag, 1978), p. 6. Used by permission.

waters. The Pacific Ocean is commonly divided into North, Central and South Pacific segments.

The Atlantic Ocean was named by the Romans after the Atlas Mountains of North Africa. Its area is about 83 million square kilometers, approximately one-half the size of the Pacific, or about one-sixth of the earth's surface. The mean depth of the Atlantic is more than 3,700 meters. (The Puerto Rico Trench is measured at a depth of about 8,600 meters.) Water temperature is about 3.72°C and salinity is about 34.7 percent. The Atlantic Ocean contains a volume of more than 300 million cubic kilometers of water. The North Atlantic is surrounded by marginal or semi-enclosed seas, such as the Baltic, Black, Mediterranean and North seas. The South Atlantic is bounded by West Africa, eastern and southern America and Antarctica. Millions of kilograms of sediments from some of the great rivers of the world—the Mississippi, the Amazon and the Congo—empty annually into the North Atlantic.

The third largest, the Indian Ocean, is slightly smaller than the Atlantic, about 81.6 million square kilometers, covering about 14 percent of the earth's surface. The mean depth of the Indian Ocean is about 4,200 meters. Monsoons from the Arabian Sea blow across the Indian Ocean to the Indian subcontinent in a southwesterly direction during the wet summer, and from land to the ocean in a northeasterly direction in the dry winter. The Indian Ocean is shaped like a triangle and is bound or enclosed by the Indian subcontinent, eastern Africa and northwest Australia. It has been the traditional trade route between Asia and Europe. It serves as a depository of sediments emptied into it by the Indian subcontinent's three rivers—the Ganges, the Indus and the Brahmaputra.

The Arctic Ocean is the smallest and shallowest of all oceans, covering only 14 million square kilometers. Its mean depth is about 1,200 meters. It sits at the far north of the world, north of 66°33'03'' north latitude. The Arctic is covered by an ice mass most of the year. It has long been believed that this ice mass is stationary, but in reality, the Arctic ice is in constant motion and breaks into ice floes of varying size—from the effects of currents, wind and tidal conditions.[1] The Arctic ice mass contains about 90 percent of all the world's snow and ice. The Arctic Ocean basin is bordered by the Soviet Union, Sweden, Norway, Iceland, Greenland, the United States and Canada. The North Pole is located about 300 kilometers from the Arctic center. The Arctic Ocean connects to the Pacific Ocean via the Bering Strait and to the Atlantic by the Greenland and Norwegian Seas.

Parenthetically it needs to be mentioned here that the 1982 Law of the Sea Convention paid special attention to the Arctic Ocean. Initiated by the Canadian delegation, under Article 234, the Third United Nations Conference on the Law of the Sea (hereafter UNCLOS III) negotiations granted the coastal states bordering the Arctic Ocean the authority to adopt and enforce laws and regulations for the prevention and control of marine pollution by vessels in the Arctic:

Article 234: Ice-covered areas

Coastal States have the right to adopt and enforce nondiscriminatory laws and regulations for the prevention, reduction and control of marine pollution from vessels in ice-covered areas within the limits of the exclusive economic zone, where particularly severe climatic conditions and the presence of ice covering such areas for most of the year create obstructions or exceptional hazards to navigation, and pollution of the maritime environment could cause major harm to or irreversible disturbance of the ecological balance. Such laws and regulations shall have due regard to navigation and the protection and preservation of the marine environment based on the best available scientific evidence.

The Antarctic Ocean surrounds the continent of Antarctica. It has been called "the southern ocean" by geographers, for the waters of the Antarctic are really the southern portions of the Atlantic, Pacific and Indian oceans converging at Antarctica. It encompasses 32 million square kilometers and occupies about 20 percent of the total area of the world's oceans. Since the 1957 International Geophysical Year (IGY), nations interested in demilitarization and marine resources conservation for Antarctica have made continuing efforts to establish a special ocean regime. This is evidenced by the 1959 Antarctic Treaty, which came into force in 1961; the 1980 Convention for the Conservation of Antarctic Marine Living Resources, which came into force in 1982; and the draft treaty on Antarctic mineral resources.[2]

This chapter serves as a general introduction to the physical geography of the oceans. It provides a brief sketch of their main physical and geographic features that have meaning or relevance to the principles and rules formulated for universal acceptance at the Law of the Sea conferences. It begins with a discussion on the abyssal plain, one of the deepest parts of oceans, occupying about 40 percent of the deep seabed floor. An important feature of the ocean, in terms of both living and nonliving mineral resources, is the continental margin, which consists of the continental shelf, the slope and the rise. The continental margin has been the primary area in the ocean for intensive offshore energy exploration. Mineral resources have also been found on the continental margins surrounding the world's oceans, exclusive of the fact that 90 percent of the world's living resources are located on the continental shelf.

Several geographical features of the ocean are also discussed in this chapter, for they pose international problems and need more precise definitions in order to resolve disputes. The bay is one of these geographic features that lack precise criteria for definition. The historic usage of coastal bays, claimed by some twenty states, from time to time has been subject to contest requiring equitable and peaceful resolution. Estuaries in the coastal zone contain supplies of nutrient-rich phytoplanktons, which serve as a major source of food for many species of fish. More important, coastal zone water pollution has become a serious marine environmental problem as sewage sludge, heavy metals (mercury) and pesticides are dumped into the ocean by way of estuaries. Finally, there is a brief discussion of the marginal or semi-enclosed seas with respect to their legal definitions and national claims to their resources by coastal states bordering them.

Figure 1.2
Major Submarine Topography

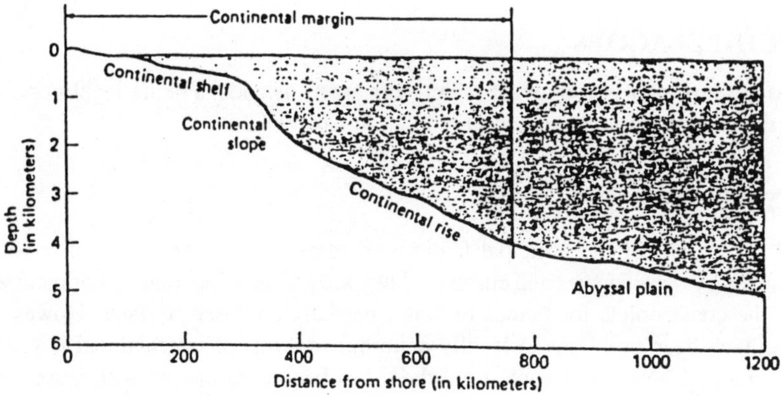

Source: J. J. Bhatt, *Oceanography: Exploring the Planet Ocean* (New York: Van Nostrand, 1978), p. 59. Used by permission.

ABYSSAL PLAINS AND ABYSSAL HILLS

At a depth of three to six kilometers, the abyssal plain is one of the deepest parts of the ocean floor, and it is one of the flattest parts of the earth's crust.[3] The abyssal plains occupy about 40 percent of the ocean floor. They occur most often in the Atlantic Ocean, but less commonly in the Indian Ocean and are rarer in the Pacific where they are found in the narrow, elongated bottoms of the trenches. The progression from continental shelf to ocean floor is shown in the simple cross section in Figure 1.2.

Abyssal plains owe their origin to the large supply of land sediment that is buried or accumulated in deep depressions or flat areas. The abyssal plains commonly occur more often in the Atlantic Ocean and the Indian Ocean, where rivers bring sediment from lands but rarely in the Pacific.

When the ocean floor contains areas of low relief, usually 300–600 meters and three to ten kilometers in diameter, these are called abyssal hills. These hills, more evident in the Pacific, are said to be formed by material resulting from tectonic or volcanic activity in the crust under the oceans.

Samples of sediments obtained from the abyssal plains of the Atlantic show beds of sand, silt and clay. There are few species of living resources found on the flat, smooth abyssal plains, except crustaceans in mobile form with long legs and slow biological reproductive processes.

Significance. The importance of the abyssal plain lies in the types of minerals found on the deep ocean floor: the usual sand, red clay, carbonated oozes, and manganese nodules. As mentioned in Chapter 6, as research and development intensifies for this portion of the ocean floor, deep water drilling for petroleum may provide an additional source of offshore energy for the future.

ARCHIPELAGOES

An archipelago is a body of water with many islands. For its legal concept see the section on archipelagic principles in Chapter 3.

BAYS

Bays are one of the principal features of the shoreline, the result of erosion activities by ocean waves and currents. They are physical indentations or recesses into the coast, inlets for bodies of water partially enclosed by land. However, there have been problems in legally defining, in terms of international law, the meaning of "bay." For some time there has been controversy with respect to the necessary criteria for defining an indentation on the coast as a "bay." The matter was not settled until the 1958 First United Nations Conference on the Law of the Sea (UNCLOS I). Article 7(1) of the Convention on the Territorial Sea and the Contiguous Zone provides the following definitions: "a bay is a well-marked indentation whose penetration is in such proportion to the width of its mouth as to contain landlocked waters and constitute more than a mere curvature of the coast. An indentation shall not, however, be regarded as a bay unless its area is as large as, or larger than, that of the semi-circle whose diameter is a line drawn across the mouth of that indentation." It is further provided in the article that "if the distance between low water marks at the entrance of the bay is less than or equal to twenty-four nautical miles, a closing line must be drawn by making the enclosed waters internal waters."

If the distance is greater than twenty-four nautical miles, Article 7(5) provides the rule that "a straight baseline of twenty-four miles shall be drawn within the bay in such a manner as to enclose the maximum area of water that is possible with a line of that length."

This definition and these rules of measurement for a bay, which were contained in Article 7 of the 1958 Convention on the Territorial Sea and the Contiguous Zone, appeared word for word in Article 10 of the 1982 LOS Convention.

Significance. While the geological and geographical definition of a coastal feature such as a bay is rather simple and uncomplicated, its legal and political implications have been quite enigmatic. Bays, as a coastal feature, need a more precise definition from a legal point of view because controversies have developed involving fishery rights and the historic uses of the bays by coastal states. Until 1958 there was no generally accepted agreement on the criteria for recognizing a coastal indentation as a bay and designation of the lengths of a closing line across a bay. Two fishery disputes—the 1910 North Atlantic Coast Fisheries and the 1951 Anglo-Norwegian Fishery cases—centered on the lack of recognized definition and rules for determining what is a bay.

More vexing still is the problem of "historic bays of long usage by a coastal state."[4] Neither Article 7 of the 1958 Convention on the Territorial Sea and the Contiguous Zone nor Article 10 of the 1982 LOS Convention applies to the "historic bays" such as the Bay of Fundy and Hudson's Bay (Canada), Chesapeake Bay and Delaware Bay (United States), Gulf of Baja California (Mexico), Gulf of Sidra (Libya), Bay of Gdansk (Poland), Skjaergaard (Norway), Gulf of Riga and Bay of Peter the Great (Soviet Union), and Gulf of Pohai (China). Originally developed by the United Nations Secretariat study in 1962 and applied by the U.S. Supreme Court in *United States v. Louisiana* (1969) and *United States v. Alaska* (1975), these criteria provide that a coastal state may claim title to a bay on historic grounds if it can demonstrate that it has claimed such body of water for a long period of time and that such claim has been accepted by other states. Some twenty states today claim historic bays.

There are some forty to fifty bays—Gulf of Aqaba (Arab–Israel), Bay of Figuier (France–Spain), and Passamaquoddy Bay (Canada–United States), to name a few—that are bordered by two or more coastal states and are in a special category of treatment by customary international law. These bays cannot be closed by a line drawn across the mouths of the waterways, but instead by a baseline of low-water mark around the shores of the bay.[5]

CONTINENTAL MARGIN (RISE, SHELF AND SLOPE)

A continental margin is that portion of the solid earth's surface adjacent to land, but underlying a coastal plain that extends seaward.[6] It generally consists of a shelf, a slope and a rise, as seen in the cross section in Figure 1.3.

Geologically, the continental margin is considered to be an integral part of the continent that became submerged under the sea after the glacial epoch in the earth's history. Along with the deep sea (abyssal plains and ridges), it represents another major topographic feature of the ocean. The percentage distribution of the ocean's topographic features of the continental margin and the deep sea is seen in Table 1.2.

The *continental rise* is a surface at the base of the continental margin at depths of 1,500 to 4,000 meters gently sloping to the flat abyssal plain. It is made up of thick deposits from land-based sediments, which in turn are carried down the continental slope by underwater landslides and earthquakes. As seen in Table 1.2, continental rises are few in the Pacific owing to the trenches that store or trap the slurries of sediment and water from the slopes. In the Atlantic, Indian and Arctic oceans, continental rises may be as wide or wider than 600 kilometers. The continental rise links the seabed to the continental slopes; it begins where the slope ends and continues outward until it meets the seabed.

The geological definition of the *continental shelf* is that it is the extension or prolongation of the adjacent land mass that gently slopes seaward from the tide water to a depth of 150–200 meters. To put it another way: geologically speaking, continental shelves are land masses whose edges lie beneath the sea; shelves are

Figure 1.3
General Characteristics of the Continental Margin

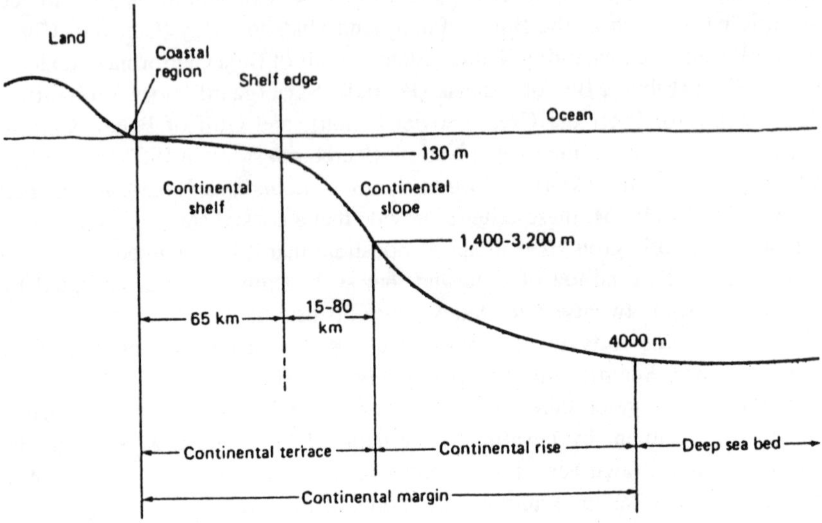

Source: Ross, *Opportunities and Uses of the Ocean*, p. 12. Used by permission.

the submerged edges of the continent. While the average depth may be 200 meters, the width may vary considerably to an average of about sixty-five kilometers. Shelves comprise about 7.6 percent of the total ocean areas of the world. As a new international legal concept, the continental shelf definition is fraught with political controversy and legal complexities, as discussed in Chapter 3.

The *continental slope* is a much steeper portion of the submerged land mass that extends from the edge of the continental shelf to the deep sea floor at a depth of 1,000 to 3,000 meters. Its boundary with the continental shelf is well marked by its steep slope of four to five degrees, resembling a straight mountain front. At the depth of the continental slope there is no light penetrating the water and there is little or no plant life. Here one finds deep sea canyons and trenches, which serve as channels for slurries of sediments and water to create turbidity when these materials become dislodged from the continental shelf.

Significance. The continental margin, which is comprised of the continental rise, shelf and slope, is the major subsea area for offshore petroleum exploration. In fact, the continental shelf may contain the prospect or potential of 1,000 billion barrels of crude oil. On-shore oil production in the Persian Gulf and the Gulf of Mexico has been extended to offshore. Oil drilling in the North Sea is done on the continental shelves bordering the United Kingdom and the Netherlands. Oil discovery and drilling on the continental slope and the continental rise have proven to be promising.[7] Vast reservoirs of natural gas are being

Table 1.2
Percentage of Major Topographic Features in the Main Oceans and Adjacent Seas

	Continental Margin*		Deep Sea			
Oceans and Adjacent Seas	Continental Shelves and Slopes	Continental Rise and Partially Filled Sedimentary Basins	Abyssal Plains	Oceanic Ridges	Other Areas	Percent of Total Ocean
Pacific and adjacent seas	13.1	2.7	43.0	35.9	6.3	50.1
Atlantic and adjacent seas	17.7	8.0	39.3	32.3	2.7	26.0
Indian and adjacent seas	9.1	5.7	49.2	30.2	5.8	20.5
Arctic and adjacent seas	68.2	20.8	0	4.2	6.8	3.4
Percent of total ocean in each group	15.3	5.3	41.8	32.7	4.9	100.0

*The continental margin has an area of about 74.5 million square kilometers (28.8 million square miles).
Source: Ross, *Opportunities and Uses of the Ocean*, p. 13. Used by permission.

Figure 1.4
The Mineral Resources of the Ocean

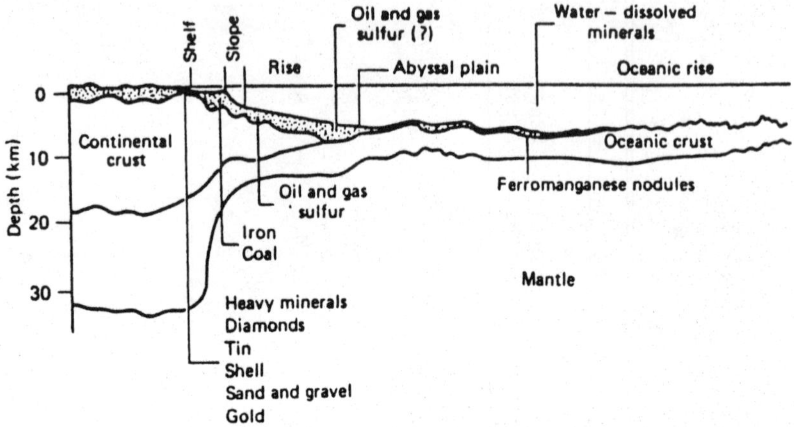

Source: Luc Cuyvers, *Ocean Uses and Their Regulation* (New York: Wiley, 1984), p. 52. Copyright © 1984 by Luc Cuyvers. Reprinted by permission of John Wiley & Sons, Inc.

exploited on the continental margin. Mineral resources, such as manganese, iron, gold and tin, have been found on the continental margins of the world as shown in Figure 1.4.

In addition, 90 percent of the ocean's living resources are to be found on the continental shelf. In short, the waters above the continental margin are the most fertile areas for living resources in the oceans, for there is an abundance of living organisms, such as mollusks, which are needed as a food source for the fish.

DELTAS

A delta is formed by river sediments deposited at the mouth of a river. The name came from the Greek letter "Δ," used by Herodotus in the fifth century B.C. to designate the triangular delta formed by the Nile. A delta can also be shaped like a fan, such as the Rhine delta. Many of the world's seaports are built on deltas: Alexandria, Calcutta, Shanghai and Venice, for instance. The locations of the world's major deltas are shown in Figure 1.5.

Significance. Since rivers carry nutrients in their sediments, which are conducive to offshore organic growth in the form of hydrocarbons, river deltas contain offshore oil and gas accumulations in basins of heavy, thick sediments that extend from land into the offshore areas along a coast.

ESTUARIES

An estuary is a semi-enclosed body of water that connects a river to the sea; within this body of water tidal movements intermix and dilute fresh runoffs from

Figure 1.5
Locations of the Major River Deltas in the World

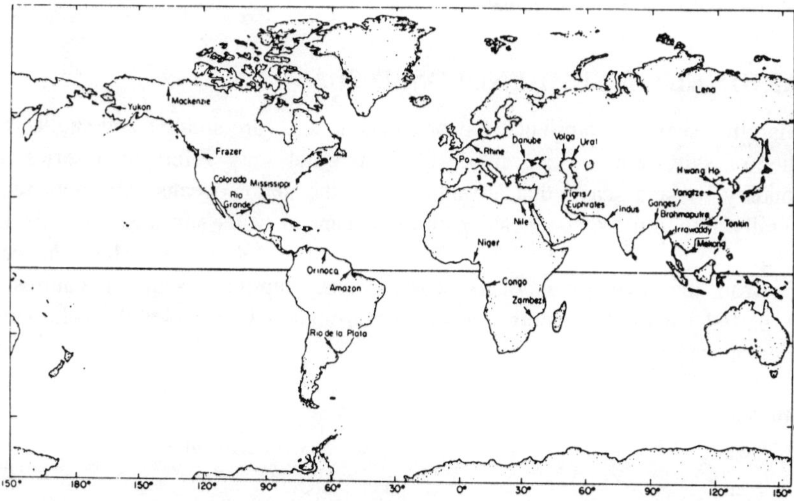

Source: Ross, *Opportunities and Uses of the Ocean*, p. 128. Used by permission.

the river with seawater. There is a higher rate of concentration of sediments in an estuary due to the land runoffs carried by the river into the sea. Estuaries are of four types:[8]

1. Drowned river valley estuaries formed during the Ice Age when glaciers began to thaw, causing a rising sea level to flood the lowlands. An example is Chesapeake Bay.
2. Fjords, found in Norway, Greenland, Alaska and Antarctica.
3. Bar-built estuaries, drowned river valleys closed to the sea by the building up of a barrier.
4. Tectonic activity or ocean crustal movement causing sea-level changes to form basins into which rivers on land discharge their sediments.

Significance. Estuaries are coastal areas where river runoff deposits a rich environment of nutrients. Thus, nutrient-rich phytoplankton found in the estuaries serves as a major source of food supply to zooplankton, fish and shellfish. Most estuaries are in coastal zones where a high productivity of organisms can be found to provide valuable living resources.

On the other hand, also to be found in the estuaries is pollution of coastal zone waters caused by intensified industrial activity and growing population in these regions; many of the world's largest cities are on estuaries. Sewage sludge, phosphates, heavy metals such as mercury, and pesticides are dumped into the ocean via estuaries. (For a detailed discussion on land-based pollution of the ocean, see Chapters 8 and 9.) Due to these human activities which affect the estuary environment, it becomes necessary for coastal states to adopt coastal zone management arrangements.

MARGINAL OR SEMI-ENCLOSED SEAS

Marginal seas, or semi-enclosed or adjacent seas, are smaller and shallower bodies of salt water.[9] Geographically, ''marginal sea'' refers to a series of secondary ''island seas'' that are adjacent to the major oceans. Marginal seas generally abut and are connected with the oceans at water surface, but at depth are bounded by submarine ridges—for instance, the Yellow Sea. Marginal seas differ from the great oceans of the world in size, depth and seafloor features.

A partial list of the twenty-five or so marginal seas includes the following bodies of water:

Arctic Sea
Baltic Sea
Black Sea
Caribbean Sea
Celebes Sea
Coral Sea
Irish Sea
Mediterranean Sea
North Sea
Norwegian/Greenland Sea
Persian Gulf
Red Sea
Sea of Japan
South China Sea
Sulu Sea
Yellow Sea

Significance. Taken as a whole, the semi-enclosed or marginal seas occupy a considerable area of the world's ocean space and are bordered by a large number of nations. For all of these nations bordering the semi-enclosed seas, living resources from the seas alone represent a major source of livelihood. For instance, the annual average catch for these Baltic states—Sweden, Denmark, Finland, Poland and the Baltic republics of the Soviet Union—has been estimated to be more than 400,000 metric tons per year. For the North Sea nations of the United Kingdom, France, Belgium, Netherlands, Germany, and Norway, the estimated annual catch has been at least 3.3 million metric tons per year.

The problem is basically definition: What constitutes a semi-enclosed sea for the purpose of reducing national claims over the resources and closing off of the seas for use by others created by the establishment of the 200-nautical-mile exclusive economic zone? The 1982 LOS Convention provides both a definition and a requirement for states bordering enclosed or semi-enclosed seas to seek cooperation in the conservation and management of living resources, the protection of the marine environment and scientific research. Part IX of the 1982 LOS Convention contains the following provisions concerning enclosed and semi-enclosed seas:

Article 122: Definition

For the purposes of this Convention, ''enclosed or semi-enclosed sea'' means a gulf, basin or sea surrounded by two or more States and connected to another sea or the ocean by a narrow outlet or consisting entirely or primarily of the territorial seas and exclusive economic zones of two or more coastal States.

Article 123: Co-operation of States bordering enclosed or semi-enclosed seas

States bordering an enclosed or semi-enclosed sea should co-operate with each other in the exercise of their rights and in the performance of their duties under this Convention. To this end they shall endeavour, directly or through an appropriate regional organization:

(a) to co-ordinate the management, conservation, exploration and exploitation of the living resources of the sea;

(b) to co-ordinate the implementation of their rights and duties with respect to the protection and preservation of the marine environment;

(c) to co-ordinate their scientific research policies and undertake where appropriate joint programmes of scientific research in the area;

(d) to invite, as appropriate, other interested States or international organizations to co-operate with them in furtherance of the provisions of this article.

MID-OCEAN RIDGES, SEAMOUNTS, SUBMARINE CANYONS AND TRENCHES

For the three major oceans of the world—the Atlantic, Indian and Pacific—mid-ocean ridges are in fact submarine mountain ranges. It has been estimated that the total length of the mid-ocean ridge system is 750,000 kilometers. The Mid-Atlantic Ridge, discovered in the 1960s, lies almost exactly equidistant between the continents on either side and has an elevation of 2,000 meters above its floor. The Mid-Atlantic Ridge extends 60,000 kilometers—almost around the world. Figure 1.6 shows a map of the submarine mountain systems.

Seamounts are volcanic peaks under the ocean surface below 1,000 meters. Sometimes the seamounts are flat-topped and are known as *guyots*. The Pacific may have as many as 10,000 seamounts or guyots. At one time, guyots may have been former islands that sank below sea level.

Trenches under the ocean are depressions or canyons as deep and steep as the North American Grand Canyon. These are the deepest areas of the ocean floor. They are commonly found in the Pacific. The Mariana Trench (reached by two scientists, Jacques Piccard and Don Walsh, in the *Trieste* in 1960) is 11,022 meters deep; it may be a result of the interaction between sediments with turbidity current and earthquakes under the ocean. Some of the deep ocean trenches are the direct continuation of land canyons. These deep sea trenches are major features associated with or confined to the continental margins. Recently a submarine canyon was discovered off the coast of Puna on the Island of Hawaii; it

Figure 1.6
The World's Ocean Ridge System

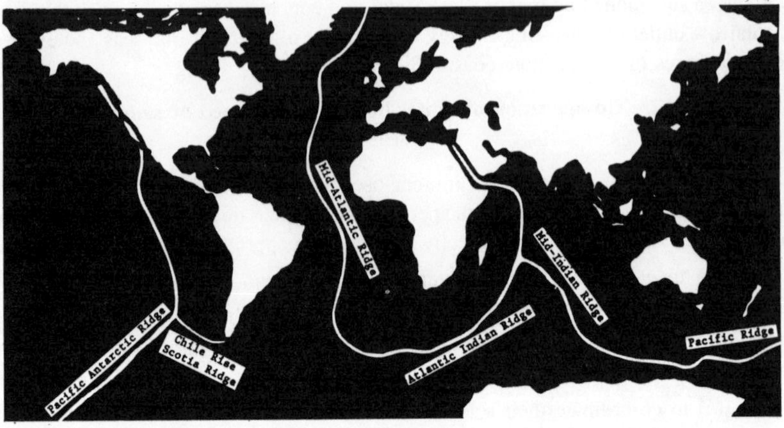

Source: Bhatt, *Oceanography: Exploring the Planet Ocean*, p. 62. Used by permission.

is at a depth of 6,000 meters and is twelve kilometers wide and thirty kilometers in length.

Significance. While mid-ocean ridges and seamounts may be of significant interest only to geologists or geographers, their importance may lie in deposits of carbonhydrates in the trenches and canyons. The Deep Sea Drilling Project has been drilling about 7,000 meters in the Mariana Trench in the Pacific for a possible energy (oil) resource. In addition, a cobalt-rich manganese crust on or near the seamounts has been discovered off the coast of Hawaii and the East Pacific Rise by University of Hawaii marine scientist Alexander Malahoff, who has reported mineral formation along mid-ocean ridge segments at a depth of 1,600 meters. Thus, these physical features on the ocean floor have economic and international legal implications.

NOTES

1. Willy Ostreng, *The Soviet Union in the Arctic Waters: Security Implications for the Northern Flank of NATO*, Occasional Paper No. 36 (Honolulu: The Law of the Sea Institute, University of Hawaii, 1987), p. 19. Also see Dennis M. Egan and David W. Orr, "Sea Control in the Arctic: A Soviet Perspective," *Naval War College Review* 41, no. 2 (Spring 1988): 51–80.

2. The proceedings of two workshops of the Law of the Sea Institute held in Seoul, Korea, 30 June–3 July 1981, and 3–6 July 1984, edited by Choon-ho Park and Jae Kyu Park, in *The Law of the Sea: Problems from the East Asian Perspective* (Honolulu: The Law of the Sea Institute, University of Hawaii, 1987). It contains two articles on the Antarctic: Daniel Cheever, "Problems of Antarctic Resources," pp. 116–120; and Lee Kimball, "Antarctic Issues Today," pp. 524–535. Also see Douglas M. Johnston, ed.,

"Arctic Ocean Issues in the 1980s," Proceedings of workshop, 10–12 June 1981, of the Law of the Sea Institute, University of Hawaii, 1982, pp. 1–57. For a discussion of the contemporary legal status of Antarctica, see Christopher C. Joyner, "Antarctica and the Law of the Sea: Rethinking the Current Legal Dilemmas," *San Diego Law Review* 18, no. 3 (April 1981): 415–422; and Christopher Joyner and Sudhir K. Chapra, *The Antarctic Legal Regime* (New York: Graham & Trotman, 1988). For a recent article updating Antarctica development, see Christopher C. Joyner, "Antarctica and the Indian Ocean States: The Interplay of Law, Interests and Geopolitics," *Ocean Development and International Law* 21, no. 1 (1990): 41–70.

3. For information on this and other sections of the ocean basin, consult J. J. Bhatt, *Oceanography: Exploring the Planet Ocean* (New York: Van Nostrand, 1978), pp. 57–71; Harold V. Thurman, *Introductory Oceanography* 2nd ed. (Columbus, Ohio: Merrill, 1978), pp. 65–101; David A. Ross, *Opportunities and Uses of the Ocean* (New York: Springer Verlag, 1978), pp. 5–36; Luc Cuyvers, *Ocean Uses and Their Regulation* (New York: Wiley, 1984), pp. 1–19; and Brian J. Kinner and Karl K. Turekian, *Man and the Ocean* (Englewood Cliffs, N.J.: Prentice-Hall, 1973), pp. 1–23.

4. See David L. Larson, ed., *Major Issues of the Law of the Seas* (Durham: The University of New Hampshire, 1976), pp. 19–22; and J.R.V. Prescott, *The Maritime Boundaries of the World* (London: Methuen, 1985), pp. 51–60 and 260–261.

5. Prescott, *The Maritime Political Boundaries*, pp. 53–56 and 61–62.

6. Information on the physical aspects of the continental margin (rise, shelf and slope) is culled from the books cited in note 3, as well as the following standard reference sources: *Academic American Encyclopedia* (Princeton, N.J.: Arête, Inc., 1981), vol. 14, pp. 321–333; *Chambers Encyclopedia* (New York: Pergamon, 1967), pp. 172–176; *Collier's Encyclopedia*, vol. 18, 1988, pp. 59–63; *The New Encyclopedia Britannica* (Chicago: Encyclopedia Britannica, Inc., 1984), vol. 1, pp. 41–42 and pp. 470–473; *McGraw-Hill Encyclopedia* (New York: McGraw-Hill, 1977), pp. 103, 139–144 and 327–328; and *The World Book Encyclopedia* (Chicago: World Book, 1988), vol. 14, pp. 656–669.

7. See Ross D. Ecker, ed. "The Continental Margin: From High Seas to Enclosure," *The Enclosure of Ocean Resources: Economics and the Law of the Sea* (Stanford, Calif.: Hoover Institute Press, 1979), pp. 20–58; Cuyvers, *Ocean Uses and Their Regulation*, pp. 51–66; Ross, *Opportunities and Uses of the Ocean*, pp. 103–155; and Kurt Michael Shusterich, *Resources Management and the Ocean: The Political Economy of Deep Seabed Mining* (Boulder, Colo.: Westview Press, 1982).

8. See note 6.

9. See Larson, ed., *Major Issues of the Law of the Seas*, pp. 199–200, 204–206 and 209–212; and Prescott, *The Maritime Political Boundaries of the World*, pp. 88–89. Also see Lewis M. Alexander, "Special Circumstances: Semi-enclosed Seas," in Gamble and Pontecorvo, eds., *Law of the Sea: Emerging Regime of the Oceans* (Cambridge, Mass.: Ballinger, 1973), pp. 158 and 213.

CHAPTER 2

International Conferences on the Uses of the Oceans

Multilateral international conferences on the uses of the sea were held long before the convening of the United Nations Law of the Sea Conferences (1958, 1960, 1974–1982) or the 1930 Hague Conference on the codification of international law. In fact, more than sixty international conferences were held from 1884 to 1957. They produced sixty-four multilateral conventions dealing with specific and technical aspects of marine affairs, from the protection of submarine cables to salvage at sea. The proliferation of international conferences, which produced a multitude of multilateral treaties from 1884 to 1983, can be seen in the following summary of conventions and protocols, based on the chronological listing of treaties contained in *The Law of the Sea: Multilateral Treaties Relevant to the United Nations Convention on the Law of the Sea*: thirty-six instruments for 1884–1944, twenty-eight for 1946–1957, thirty-six for 1958–1966 and sixty-two for 1967–1983.[1] Thus, a total of 162 multilateral conventions and protocols, together with the comprehensive 1982 LOS Convention, constitute a large part of the law of the sea. A chronological listing of these multilateral treaties is found in Appendix I.

Prior to the end of World War II, international conventions, the result of multilateral conferences called to address the problems of common concern, dealt with the technical aspects of seamen's welfare (employment, age, sickness and wages); navigation (free navigation of the Suez Canal and the 1921 Barcelona Convention on the regime of navigable waterways); and shipping (bills of lading, collision at sea, salvage, and vessel liability, immunity and tonnage). The oldest multilateral treaty was the 1884 Convention on the Protection of Submarine Cables. Specific conventions were also concluded to prohibit the transport of opium or other dangerous drug substances, and slavery or slave trade. However, a major international conference on the development of the law of the sea during this period was the 1930 Hague Conference on the Codification of International Law, which will be discussed separately in this chapter. It must

Table 2.1
International Conventions Concluded on the Uses of the Oceans, 1946–1957

Subject Matter	Conventions	Protocols
Collision	2	1
E.E.C. formation	1	-
Fisheries conservation and regional commissions on whales, lobsters and seals	8	7
Oil pollution at sea	1	-
Safety of life at sea	1	-
Sanitary regulations	2	-
Seamen's welfare	7	-
Ships: arrest and tonnage	2	-
Slavery	1	-
Stowaway	1	1
UN organization formation (IMO, WHO)	2	-
Total	28	9

Source: *Multilateral Treaties Relevant to the United Nations Convention on the Law of the Sea*, Office of the Special Representative of the Secretary-General for the Law of the Sea, United Nations, 1985.

be noted here that the Hague Conference was considered to be the first attempt sponsored by the League of Nations to codify some aspects of international law, such as nationality and territorial waters.

From the end of World War II to the eve of convening the 1958 First United Nations Conference on the Law of the Sea (UNCLOS I), a total of twenty-eight international agreements were concluded by multilateral negotiation on fishery conservation and management, seamen's welfare, sanitary regulations, stowaways and oil pollution at sea (see Table 2.1).

Prior to the convening of the UNCLOS I in 1958, three key international concerns seem to have dominated the law of the sea activities in the postwar period from 1946 to 1957: fisheries conservation and management, including regional fishery organization; seamen's welfare; and shipping concerns. Prominent among international multilateral agreements was the 1946 International Convention for the Regulation of Whaling, signed and ratified by the then leading whaling nations: the Netherlands, Norway, the Union of Soviet Socialist Republics, the United Kingdom and the United States. Equally significant was the Convention for the High Seas Fisheries of the North Pacific Ocean at the Tripartite Fisheries Conference at Tokyo in 1951–1952 by the United States, Canada and Japan. For the first time an international conference sponsored by the International Maritime Consultative Organization addressed the marine pollution problem and produced the International Convention for the Prevention of Pollution of the Sea by Oil (May 12, 1954). Chapters 4 and 8 provide detailed information and analysis about these fishery and marine pollution conventions.

The most important law of the sea conferences were the 1958 UNCLOS I and 1960 UNCLOS II, both held in Geneva. (Both will be discussed as separate topics in this chapter.) For this period, fisheries conventions for conservation and man-

Table 2.2
International Conventions Concluded on the Uses of the Oceans, 1958–1965

Subject Matter	Conventions	Protocols
Antarctic	1	-
Broadcasts	1	-
Carriage of passengers by sea	1	1
Collision	1	-
Fishermen: identity, medical, wages	6	-
Fisheries: conservation and management	4	-
Load line	2	-
Narcotic drugs	1	1
Navigation: traffic	6	-
Nuclear energy and ships with test liability	4	2
Safety at sea	1	-
Satellite and tele-communication	2	1
Transit trade of landlocked	1	-
UNCLOS I (1958)	5	-
Total	36	5

Source: *Multilateral Treaties Relevant to the United Nations Convention on the Law of the Sea.*

agement still dominated international concern. In addition to the 1958 Convention on Fishing and Conservation of the Living Resources of the High Seas, seamen's welfare continued to be an important concern that accounted for at least six conventions dealing with seafarers' national identity, medical care, age and wages. Navigational concerns were also very evident in this period. In addition, significant meetings were the 1960 Convention on Third Party Liability of Nuclear Energy, the 1962 Brussels Convention on the Liability of Operation of Nuclear Ships and the 1963 Vienna Convention on Civil Liability for Nuclear Damage (see Table 2.2).

By the time the United Nations General Assembly began to debate on seabed exploitation and exploration in the mid–1960s, more international multilateral conferences were convened to address a host of new problems (see Table 2.3). While fisheries conventions concluded during the period still dominated international concern (see Chapter 4), marine environmental protection and pollution of the sea by oil and air (transboundary) influenced the conclusion of no less than twenty-four international conventions. Among these were the 1969 Agreement for Cooperation in Dealing with Pollution of the North Sea by Oil, the 1971 agreement by Denmark, Finland, Norway and Sweden on Pollution of the Sea by Oil, the 1971 establishment of an International Fund for Compensation for Oil Pollution Damage, the 1972 London Ocean Dumping Convention, and the 1973 International Convention for the Prevention of Pollution from Ships (see Chapter 8 for detailed discussion).

Table 2.3
International Conventions Concluded on the Uses of the Oceans, 1967–1968

Subject Matter		Conventions	Protocols
Archaeological and cultural heritage		3	-
Animal protection		1	-
Collision		1	-
Endangered species of wild flora and fauna		1	-
Fisheries: conservation and management		10	2
Health regulations		1	-
INTELSTAT and other telecommunications		3	-
International organization		1	-
Maritime claims of liability		1	-
Marine environment protection		10	3
Marine lien and mortgage		1	-
Marine search and rescue		1	-
Narcotic drugs		1	-
Nuclear waste, etc.		4	-
Passenger luggage		1	-
Pollution by oil and air		12	10
Safety of life at sea		1	1
Seamen's welfare		6	-
Shipping		1	-
Space launch rescue		1	-
	Total	62	16

Source: *Multilateral Treaties Relevant to the United Nations Convention on the Law of the Sea*.

Of equal international concern in this period was the disposal of nuclear waste and placement of nuclear weapons on the seabed. Two international conventions were concluded to address this concern: the 1971 Treaty on Prohibition of the Emplacement of Nuclear Weapons on the Seabed and the 1971 Brussels Convention on Civil Liability in the Field of Maritime Carriage of Nuclear Material. (See also Chapter 8 for a detailed analysis of these conventions.)

This chapter provides a brief discussion and analysis of the 1930 Conference for the Codification of International Law of the Sea (1958), the Second United Nations Conference on the Law of the Sea (1960), and the Third United Nations Conference on the Law of the Sea (1974–1982). For ready reference, Appendix I will provide a chronological listing of multilateral treaties as prepared by the United Nations. The present status, as of May and December 1990, of signatures and ratifications to the 1982 Law of the Sea Convention can be found in Appendix II.

1930 LEAGUE OF NATIONS CONFERENCE FOR THE CODIFICATION OF INTERNATIONAL LAW (HAGUE CONFERENCE)

With a great deal of good intentions and idealism the League of Nations Assembly requested in September 1924 that the League's Council convene a special Committee of Experts for the purpose of codifying international law. This action seemed particularly necessary because of the tension that had built up between those nations that adhered to the concept of free use of the sea and those that wanted to expand further the enclosure or division of the ocean. A subcommittee of the Committee of Experts was assigned the task of dealing with one of the eleven subjects: the question of territorial seas.[2] The subcommittee resorted to a questionnaire. Enclosed in the questionnaire was a draft scheme establishing a coastal zone of three marine miles from the low-water mark of the coast as territorial sea. The questionnaire also asked the governments to respond to the question of the exploitation of the products of the sea.

In the spring of 1927 responses to the questionnaire began to arrive at the League of Nations in Geneva. Twenty-five nations—including the United Kingdom, Germany, the United States and Japan—felt it desirable to have a convention to codify the law of the territorial seas; twenty-two states—including France, Italy and the United States—favored a convention on the question of exploitation of sea products.

Upon recommendation of the Committee of Experts, the League Assembly in 1927 proceeded to convene an international conference on three subjects: nationality, state responsibility and the territorial sea delimitation. A preparatory commission was formed to prepare various drafts on the subjects for discussion by the international conference. In the preparation of these subjects, the League's Committee of Experts had used the assistance of Harvard Law School faculty, who developed comprehensive research, known as the Harvard Research, on state practices with regard to the territorial seas. The preparatory commission also drafted its own document, known as the "Basis of Discussion."

Delegates from forty-eight states—including nine non-League members—attended the Hague Conference from March 13 to April 13, 1930. The Conference was organized into committees which required a two-thirds majority for approval of any draft articles and a simple majority for adoption at the conference plenary sessions.[3] While there was some general agreement on the proposition for delimiting the territorial seas, there was strong opposition to the establishment of a contiguous zone beyond the three-mile territorial sea. Swarztrauber summarized that there were divergent positions with respect to the extent of the territorial sea:[4]

3-mile zone only (9)

Australia
Canada
Denmark
India
Japan
Netherlands
United Kingdom
Union of South Africa
United States of America

3-mile zone with contiguous zone (8)

Belgium
Chile
Egypt
Estonia
France
Germany
Irish Free State
Poland

4-mile zone only (4)

Finland
Iceland
Norway
Sweden

6-mile zone only (6)

Brazil
Colombia
Italy
Romania
Uruguay
Yugoslavia

6-mile zone with contiguous zone (5)

Cuba
Latvia
Persia
Spain
Turkey

Thus, on the question regarding the width of the territorial sea, at the 1930 Hague Conference seventeen nations were in favor of a three-mile zone, four for a four-mile zone, and eleven for a six-mile zone. But, a majority of delegates, representing thirty-seven states, agreed not to vote on any proposals. The Final Act of the 1930 Hague Conference contained articles on the legal status of the territorial sea as a belt of the sea which formed a part of the coastal state's territory. This included the air space above and the seabed and the subsoil without defining the seaward extent. The legal status of the territorial sea also recognized innocent passage of foreign vessels.[5]

As far as codifying the divergent views on the width of the territorial sea and the purposes of the contiguous zone were concerned, the 1930 Hague Conference failed completely. It might be argued that had there not been strong opposition by Great Britain regarding the contiguous zone, there might have been agreement regarding the three-mile territorial sea.[6] However, the political reality at the time—as dominated by the world's major maritime powers—was for a narrow territorial sea beyond which was the high seas ruled by the traditional principle of the freedom of the seas. This concept was not seriously challenged until the latter part of the twentieth century when the combined forces of technological development and increased human uses of sea resources mandated a concerted attempt to delimit or control the ever-expanding movement for enclosure of the oceans by coastal states. From this point on there evolved a set of new concepts (see Chapter 3) regarding the coastal states' jurisdictional claims over the oceans. These concepts changed fundamentally the law of the sea that had existed and had been practiced by states at the time of the 1930 Hague Conference.

THE FIRST UNITED NATIONS CONFERENCE ON THE LAW OF THE SEA (1958)

The single most significant event that affected both the direction and the scope of the law of the sea in the aftermath of World War II was the Truman Proclamation of 1945, which triggered a chain reaction of unilateral claims by coastal states to enclose the oceans. Certainly one of the motivating forces for calling a new international conference on the law of the sea was to address the mounting controversy among nations on the meaning, limits and legal status of the continental shelf doctrine embodied in the Truman Proclamation. By 1952, when the Latin American countries made a 200-mile claim in the Santiago Declaration for fishery and other resources purposes, it was patently clear that a new international attempt must be made to seek agreement and cooperation, not only on the continental shelf concept, but also on a host of related law of the sea issues, such as the delimitation of coastal states' claims on the territorial sea and the contiguous zone, fisheries controversies and the preservation of freedom of the sea in the regime of high seas beyond national jurisdiction.

As early as 1950 the International Law Commission of the Legal Department in the United Nations Secretariat began preparation for UNCLOS I (1958). They were assisted appreciably by a group of experts in the drafting of some seventy articles dealing with the continental shelf, territorial seas, the contiguous zones and coastal states' jurisdiction over fisheries.[7]

The 1958 UNCLOS I was held in Geneva from February 24 to April 28, attended by eighty-seven nations (if Syria and Egypt are counted separately). The real work of the conference was done by four issue-specific committees: territorial sea and contiguous zone, the high seas, fisheries, and the continental shelf. After two months of work, the 1958 UNCLOS I at Geneva produced four separate conventions: the Convention on the Territorial Sea and the Contiguous Zone, the Convention on the High Seas, the Convention on Fishing and Conservation of Living Resources of the High Seas, and the Convention on the Continental Shelf.

THE SECOND UNITED NATIONS CONFERENCE ON THE LAW OF THE SEA (1960)

The failure in 1958 to reach agreement on the breadth or extent of the territorial sea and the contiguous zone provided the rationale for convening in 1960 a second law of the sea conference by the United Nations—a recommendation to the United Nations Secretary-General that was unanimously endorsed in a concluding resolution by the 1958 UNCLOS I.

The UNCLOS II (1960) was convened from March 17 to April 26 and was attended by delegates from eighty-eight nations. Various proposals were introduced advocating a variety of ranges for the territorial sea and contiguous zones for fishing.[8] After some intensive negotiation and the withdrawal of a number of these proposals, the conference focused its discussion on the following:

1. A joint United States–Canada proposal, which advocated a six-mile territorial sea and a twelve-mile contiguous zone for fishing, with a proviso for historic fishing rights in the zone for ten years.[9]
2. The eighteen-nation-sponsored proposal for a twelve-mile territorial sea or a fishing zone of the same, supported by the Soviet Union. The eighteen-nation proposal failed for adoption by the Committee of the Whole.[10]
3. The Icelandic proposal for a coastal state's preferential right to fish in areas adjacent to the fishing zone.[11]

The joint United States–Canada and the Icelandic proposals were defeated in a vote of the plenary session of the conference, the former by only one vote short of the required two-thirds majority: 54–28, with five abstentions.[12]

Significance. For a second time the nations failed to agree on the breadth of the territorial waters and the extent of a contiguous zone. In spite of this failure at the 1960 UNCLOS, a possible consensus emerged, for by then twenty-six states took the position in favor of a twelve-mile territorial sea (including fishing), and twenty-nine states adhered to the idea of a three-to-ten-mile territorial sea, but claiming twelve miles for fishing.

Table 2.4
Increased Membership of Afro-Asian Nations at UNCLOS

Region	1958-1960	1973-1974
Asia	24	41
Africa	6	41
Latin-America	20	24
Communist-Soviet orbit	10	12
West and others	26	29

Source: Ann L. Hollick, *U.S. Foreign Policy and the Law of the Sea* (Princeton, N.J.: Princeton University Press, 1981), p. 249. Reprinted by permission of Princeton University Press.

THE THIRD UNITED NATIONS CONFERENCE ON THE LAW OF THE SEA (1974–1982)

When the twenty-fifth session of the United Nations General Assembly was convened in New York in the fall of 1970, it was a different world from that of 1958 and 1960. In the first place, there was an increase in the number of sovereign states fully participating as members of the United Nations. A glance at Table 2.4 shows the increased numerical strength of the Afro-Asian-Latin American group, united at least ideologically for a share of the world's distribution of wealth and resources.

Thus, by the 1970s, as compared to 1958–1960, membership in the United Nations had increased phenomenally—by about 59 percent. The combined numerical strength of the African-Asian-Latin American nations totaled more than the two-thirds majority needed for decision making in the United Nations proceedings. The numerical majority was by no means cohesive on all issues, but it stood for the view of the developing world with a "myriad of complex and changing goals."[13]

Second, when Malta's Arvid A. Pardo made his 1967 speech in the United Nations calling for a declaration and treaty on the peaceful use, in the interest of mankind, of seabed resources beyond national jurisdiction, it was evident that undersea technology had reached the point of making deep-seabed mineral resources accessible. To the vast majority of the developing Third World nations, the seabed was the last frontier for mankind to tap the rich resources found there. But they also were keenly aware that without the technology, or the sharing of advanced undersea technology for deep seabed exploration and exploitation, they would be deprived of the economic benefits. The concern of the developing world about the uses and ownership of the sea was basically motivated by the acceptance of the view that technology was "a panacea for their economic ills."[14] Thus, the debate over the seabed at the United Nations in the late 1960s emerged for developing nations as a top priority on the agenda at any multilateral diplomatic conference regarding the oceans.

Third, the failure of the 1958 and 1960 Conferences on the Law of the Sea to agree on the breadth of the territorial sea and contiguous zones merely aggravated the continued unilateral extension of national sovereignty over fishing grounds. This, in turn, created tension and conflict over the traditional uses of the oceans. By the 1970s nations began to realize that these unilateral extensions of the ocean enclosure movement represented only "simplistic and chauvinistic solutions" to global problems that demanded international cooperation. Related to the territorial sea issue was the desire of maritime powers to secure unimpeded transit through, over and under straits for international navigation. Also there was concern about the exercise of naval power as national claims over territorial seas expanded, ranging from 3 to 6 to 12 and then to 200 miles (by Latin American nations). The need for international agreement on the territorial sea and related issues became more urgent in the 1970s than it had been in 1958 or 1960.

At the time of UNCLOS I (1958) and UNCLOS II (1960), the world had just begun to be aware of the problems of ocean pollution from land and from vessels. At the 1972 Conference on the Human Environment, held in Stockholm, the question was raised as to the ocean's vulnerability to the endless amount of toxic and nonbiodegradable waste being dumped into the "ocean sink." There was also the legal question of responsibility for damage done to the coast and shorelines by spillage of crude oil from supertankers, as in the case of the *Torrey Canyon*. As the uses of the oceans multiplied in the 1970s, there was widespread concern among coastal states over the need for acceptable uniform standards for marine environment protection is a global problem that requires international cooperation.

It was against this background that, in the midst of debate in the Committee on the Peaceful Uses of the Seabed and the Ocean Floor Beyond the Limits of National Jurisdiction (the Seabed Committee), the General Assembly adopted Resolution 2750 (XXV) on December 17, 1970, by a vote of 106 to 7, with six abstentions. This resolution called for the convening of the Third United Nations Conference, UNCLOS III, in 1973 and identified the issues to be discussed at the conference:

> A broad range of related issues including those concerning the regions of the high seas, the continental shelf, the territorial seas (including the question of international straits) and contiguous zone fishing and conservation of the living resources of the high seas (including the question of the preferential rights of coastal states), the preservation of marine environment (including *inter alia*, the prevention of pollution) and scientific research.[15]

The United Nations Seabed Committee was designated as the preparatory committee for UNCLOS III. It held three sessions in 1971 for a total of nine weeks, and two sessions in 1972, a total of eleven weeks of work. For each year the sessions were held alternately in New York and Geneva. By 1971 the United Nations Seabed Committee membership had expanded from its original forty-two (in the late 1960s) to ninety-one. In implementing General Assembly Resolution 2750-C (XXV), the Committee was divided into three subcommittees

Table 2.5
Number of Meetings Held by the Seabed Subcommittees and Working Groups Preparatory to UNCLOS III, 1971–1973

Year	Subcommittee I (Seabed Regime)	Subcommittee II (Conference Agenda)	Subcommittee III (Marine Environment)
1971	31	23	14
1972	30	23	18
1973	67*	32	55**

*Pinto working group was the center of activities for Subcommittee I.
**Including twenty-eight meetings of the working group on marine pollution and ten meetings for working groups on scientific research.
Source: Hollick, *U.S. Foreign Policy and the Law of the Sea*, pp. 243–248. Reprinted by permission of Princeton University Press.

for work on these topics: (1) drafting articles on the international regime for the seabed, (2) developing a list of agenda items for the conference, and (3) preparing draft articles on issues of marine environmental protection and marine scientific research. Table 2.5 enumerating meetings conducted during the three-year period gives a "bird's-eye" view of the extent of preparatory work done by the Seabed Committee and its subcommittees.

The results of the preparatory work up to 1973 were uneven. Ann Hollick pointed out that the texts produced were reflections of the "disagreements among delegates" amended with the form of alternative suggestions in brackets.[16] The size of the agenda for the conference recommended by the preparatory group was large (a total of twenty-five items) and was considered to be a barrier to negotiation. As was the case at the 1960 United Nations Seabed debate, there emerged even at the preparatory stage as many as eight "political coalitions" which consumed an enormous amount of negotiation time.[17]

At its twenty-eighth session (November 16, 1973), the United Nations General Assembly adopted Resolution 3067 authorizing the convening of the Third United Nations Conference on the Law of the Sea (UNCLOS III). For the next nine years, excluding the years of Seabed Committee debate and preparation for the conference, a total of eleven official sessions were held, culminating in the opening for signature on December 10, 1982, at Montego Bay, Jamaica. In the words of Jávier Pérez de Cuellar, Secretary-General of the United Nations, there was established "a new legal order for ocean space." The 1982 Law of the Sea Convention, "a constitution for the oceans," was the product of nine years of continuous negotiations, consultation and bargaining between nations with varied concerns for the uses of the oceans. The very first day on which the convention was opened for signature (December 10, 1982) 119 nations signed the document, an unprecedented event in the annals of international conferences. As a background for understanding, a brief summary will be provided in the following pages of the negotiations at UNCLOS III.

Table 2.6
UNCLOS III Official Sessions, 1973–1981

Session	Weeks
First Session - 1973 - December 3-15, New York	2
Second Session - 1974 - June 20-August 29, Caracas	10
Third Session - 1975 - March 17-May 9, Geneva	8
Fourth Session - 1976 - March 15-May 7, New York	8
Fifth Session - 1976 - August 2-September 17, New York	7
Sixth Session - 1977 - May 23-July 15, New York	8
Seventh Session - 1978 - March 28-May 19, Geneva	8
August 21-September 15, New York	4
Eighth Session - 1979 - March 19-April 27, Geneva	6
July 16-August 24, New York	6
Ninth Session - 1980 - February 27-April 3, New York	5
July 28-August 29, Geneva	5
Tenth Session - 1981 - March 7-April 17, New York	6
Eleventh Session - 1982 - March 9-April 30, New York	8
Total	91

Source: Hollick, *U.S. Foreign Policy and the Law of the Sea*, p. 285. Reprinted by permission of Princeton University Press.

The Third United Nations Conference on the Law of the Sea (1973–1982) spent a total of ninety-one weeks in its eleven official sessions. This excluded the time consumed by informal consultations, negotiations and coalition building between and among the various political groups. Table 2.6 lists the official sessions.

Instead of a recapitulation of the lengthy and complex negotiations for the nine-year period, the following highlights are briefly summarized in chronological order: the Caracas session, 1974; the Informal Single Negotiating Text (ISNT), 1975; the Revised Single Negotiating Text (RSNT), 1976; the Informal Composite Negotiation Text (ICNT, 1977–1979) and the Draft Convention on the Law of the Sea (Informal Text), 1980.

The Caracas Session, 1974

The second session of UNCLOS III convened in Caracas from June 20 to August 29, 1974. It was convened mainly as a negotiation session regarding substantive issues on the law of the sea. However, it was beset at the outset by two major obstacles, which remained throughout the nine-year period of the UNCLOS III. First, the number of participants in the conference had increased from 91 when the United Nations Seabed debate began in the 1960s to a staggering 137 when the Caracas session convened in June 1974. Much of the time consumed by procedural debates at Caracas was the result of size.[18]

The other problems at the Caracas session were the size of the agenda and the complexity of the issues to be dealt with at such a multilateral conference. At the Caracas round of negotiations, the virtual impossibility of drafting a single comprehensive text on the law of the sea was obvious. Yet, what came out of this session seemed to set the style, the tone and, more important, the agreement on how conference decisions were to be made. The dispute that centered on the question of conference decision making was further complicated by clashes between the political groupings: the African, Asian and Latin American regional groups, the developed Western nations and the landlocked and shelf-locked groups. The traditional two-thirds majority rule for major substantive decisions, as practiced in the United Nations General Assembly, became inoperable because reality dictated that consent of all participants would be necessary if a universal law of the sea were to be accepted and implemented as part of state practice. In its first session in New York, the Seabed Committee had recommended conclusively the so-called gentlemen's agreement—all substantive issues must be decided by consensus or by voting only "until all efforts at consensus have been exhausted."[19]

Some of the more important procedural questions at Caracas were the requirement for voting (Rule 37) and the required majority for the adoption of the final convention (Rule 39).[20] The conference president, Ambassador Amerasinghe of Sri Lanka, consumed a considerable amount of time in informal consultation and negotiation with the various groups, particularly the Group of 77 (the developing African, Asian and Latin American nations), which wanted a majority rule, and the developed states, which insisted on consensus. Final agreements were obtained without voting, provided that (1) for all substantive decisions a two-thirds majority was required of those present and voting, and (2) the developed states had the recourse not to sign the convention because of reservations or objections to certain portions of the convention.

Following the practice of the United Nations Seabed Committee, which had served as the preparatory organ for UNCLOS III from 1971–1973, the Caracas session maintained the system of three substantive committees for handling the complex set of law of the sea issues: Committee I on deep-seabed mining; Committee II on territorial sea and transit through straits, the economic zone of the fisheries, and the continental shelf issues; and Committee III on marine environmental protection, transfer of technology and scientific research issues.

Key issues that emerged in Committee I at Caracas revolved around the question of who may exploit the international seabed area beyond national jurisdiction. The United States, along with other developed nations, advocated a weak international authority with power to issue mining licenses. The Group of 77, the Third World nations, favored a strong international monopoly controlling production limits, price controls and seabed exploitation for the benefit of developing nations. The committee was able to produce a draft on the seabed regime with alternative suggestions. Further negotiations were required, as the committee delegated much of the work to a negotiating working group which consisted of six subgroups.[21] The working group met six times and devoted its efforts to the issue of who may exploit the seabed area, but little else.[22] It was also the "most politically volatile forum of discussion in Caracas."[23] Part of the reason for the existence of such a political forum in Committee I might have been the less divisiveness among the Group of 77 nations in contrast to their lack of cohesiveness in Committee II concerning coastal jurisdictions.

Although there was general agreement for a twelve-mile territorial sea among the participating nations at Caracas, the issue, or acceptance of it, was conditioned by the related issue of unimpeded transit through straits. The latter position was favored by the developed states, but opposed by the straits states and the Arab bloc on grounds of national security, shipping and control over environmental problems. These divergent views were reflected in the United Kingdom proposal, advocating free passage through straits for all nations,[24] and the Oman proposal, which asked for coastal states' rights to regulate navigational activities in the straits, including control over pollution and nuclear submarines.[25] Unimpeded passage through straits represented the highest priority to the maritime developed states, while the developing states were adamant in their demand for increased coastal state authority as an important ideological requirement.

On the complex issue of a resource zone, Committee II received 120 positions from 110 delegations, with seventy-three nations (61 percent) favoring resources, scientific research and pollution control. Forty-one nations (34 percent) took the position of not favoring an economic zone.[26] On the issue of the continental shelf, of the sixty-one states presenting positions, thirty-five (57 percent) preferred a limit of 200 miles; nineteen (31 percent) wanted the continental margin as the distance limit.[27] However, acceptance of the 12-mile territorial sea and the 200-mile economic zone were conditioned upon agreement over the more difficult issues of free transit through straits, the outer limit of the continental shelf, the right of the landlocked and geographically disadvantaged states to ocean resources and the recognition of the rights and jurisdiction of coastal states.

The Informal Single Negotiating Text, 1975–1976

As the basis for future negotiation, a preparatory text, known as the Informal Single Negotiating Text (ISNT), was produced at the end of the third session of UNCLOS III, which was held in Geneva in the spring of 1975.[28] The ISNT represented a summary or assessment by chairmen of the three conference committees of the issues and the possible compromises among delegates since Caracas. By placing the responsibility on the chairmen, delegates felt free to accept or "disavow" their negotiation positions later or to submit amendments to the draft. This procedure permitted the formation of a large number of negotiation groups, which could undertake the drafting of various texts as basis for negotiation in committees. Under the leadership of Chairman Christopher Pinto (Sri Lanka), Committee I on the deep seabed was able to produce a working draft of twenty-five articles regarding exploitation guidelines and machinery for seabed mining. The original text was subsequently altered by Chairman Paul Engo

(Cameroon), who took the Group of 77 position for control of seabed mining by an international authority.[29]

Committee II took up the issues of economic zone and continental shelf. A key draft regarding the former was prepared by the Evensen Group in favor of the coastal states' position, but it encountered stiff opposition from the Group of 77 (see Chapter 13) and the landlocked and the geographically disadvantaged groups over access to fisheries resources. Likewise, on the continental shelf issue, from among proposed texts drafted by many regional groups, Chairman Reynaldo Galindo Pohl (El Salvador) had the latitude to choose the one that lent support to the coastal states' interests. The text was distributed on the last day of the third session as a basis for future negotiation. Committee III produced a negotiating text regarding marine pollution that granted flag states enforcement power for violations. On the whole, as pointed out by Ann Hollick, the ISNT[30] "reflected the personal biases and political concerns of the individual chairmen," with varying degrees of satisfaction for the competing groups.[31]

The Revised Single Negotiating Text (RSNT)

The fifth and sixth session of UNCLOS III, held in New York in the spring and fall of 1976 and 1977, produced a revised negotiating text.[32] This text reflected the committee chairmen's assessments on a broad range of law of the sea issues that were negotiated at numerous informal and private meetings by competing groups among the delegations. A notable compromise that emerged from these informal meetings was the provision in the RSNT for a parallel system. Under this arrangement, the Enterprise, an operating arm of the international seabed authority, would exist alongside the state and multinational corporations engaged in deep-seabed mining (see Chapter 7).

Committee II delegates reviewed the articles drafted in the ISNT of the previous year and retained most of them. There was some dissatisfaction expressed by the landlocked and geographically disadvantaged states over their rights to access to resources in the economic zone. These objections were made to the draft articles prepared by the Evensen Group the previous year. Because of the numerical strength of the landlocked group, a total of fifty-one nations in the committee, the Evensen Group was forced to make some accommodation to them regarding their access to the economic zone resources. The landlocked and geographically disadvantaged bloc was also active in forming an alliance with coastal states to insist on transit rights, a 200-mile limit for the continental shelf, revenue sharing of resources on the continental margin beyond the 200 miles, and preferential fishing rights. On the issue of deep seabed mining there was an impasse at the negotiations in 1976. As one participant at the negotiations in New York commented, the RSNT proved "to be the most important document" on the law of the sea since the 1958 Geneva Convention.[33] To the end of 1976, agreements on a number of issues had been made even though there had been no vote taken and decisions were by consensus only. The revised text represented only the formal and informal discussions that had been held in New York. In the note by the president of the conference, the RSNT was "to serve purely as a procedural device and only provide a basis for negotiation without affecting either the status of proposals already made by delegations or the right of delegations to submit amendments or introduce new proposals."[34]

Informal Composite Negotiating Text (ICNT)

At the end of the sixth session, May 24 to July 15, 1977, a compact and comprehensive treaty text with 300 clauses was produced for the first time.[35] The issue of deep-seabed mining machinery dominated the session. Based on Evensen's negotiations with various groups, Committee I Chairman Paul Engo revised the Evensen Draft (Evensen Texts) conditioning private and state enterprise access to seabed mining upon mandatory technology transfer to the international seabed authority. The United States objected to this key draft provision, even though it retained the United States favored parallel system. It also provided for a review of the Enterprise every five years and of the international seabed authority every twenty years. The ICNT proposed a twelve-mile territorial sea, a contiguous zone and a continental shelf extending beyond 200 miles, but agreement could not be reached on access to fishery resources by a neighboring coastal state or the right of access to the sea by landlocked states. Under the ICNT coastal states had the right to enact legislation regulating pollution by foreign ships within their territorial seas.

The seventh session was convened in Geneva (March 28 to May 19, 1978) and New York (August 21 to September 15, 1978); it continued revision and negotiation on the various articles in the ICNT. At this session a major confrontation took place over the final text revision responsibility that resulted in placing the responsibility for reflecting the view of major law of the sea issues with the committee chairman. (The government that President H. Shirley Amerasinghe represented had by this time changed from Ceylon to Sri Lanka, thus casting some doubt as to whether he still represented his delegation to the conference.) The procedural wrangling took two weeks of negotiating time and was finally resolved by a conference vote, with most Latin American delegations opposed, reconfirming his representation. The conference decided to adopt a "collegiate system" or a collective responsibility by both committee chairmen and the conference president for any revisions to the ICNT.

The conference was then organized into seven groups for negotiation on the major unresolved issues such as seabed authority (resource policy, financial arrangement and structure), rights of landlocked and geographically disadvantaged states to living resources of the economic zone, dispute settlement with respect to coastal states' rights in the economic zone, definition for the outer limits of the continental shelf and the question of revenue sharing beyond the 200-mile limit.[36] Major disagreements in the ICNT by now had been limited to three key issues: fishery access for landlocked and geographically disadvantaged states, definition of the outer limit of the continental shelf and the question of revenue sharing beyond the 200-mile limit.[37] At the end of the seventh session prospects for a consensus on a comprehensive treaty on the law of the sea seemed to be improving.

When the eighth session concluded in New York in the summer of 1979, developed and developing states had moved closer to agreement in their divergent positions on the parallel system for deep-seabed mining. This and the matter of voting procedure for the council in the governance of the international seabed were the remaining unresolved issues. The uninterrupted negotiations at the eighth session produced a revision of the ICNT.[38] As reported by Bernard H. Oxman, the ICNT/Rev. 1 recorded "the completion of the informal negotiations" on the drafting of a comprehensive treaty on the law of the sea.[39] Oxman listed four "substantive results" at the 1979 session:

1. Draft texts on access to fishery resources by landlocked and surplus fisheries in the economic zone for neighboring coastal states
2. New text on definition of the outer limits of the continental shelf and revenue sharing when the shelf extends beyond 200 miles
3. Amendments on deep-seabed mining that included financial arrangements for the international seabed authority, and settlement of disputes
4. The establishment of a preparatory commission to draft rules and regulations for deep seabed mining[40]

Further textual revisions were made by the committee chairmen and the conference president at the ninth session, which met in New York in the spring of 1980 and resumed in Geneva in the summer.[41] Except for resolutions on the preparatory commission for the international seabed authority and more work on the boundaries or limits for the economic zone and the continental shelf, a comprehensive draft treaty was now ready for a round of changes. A deadline for completion was set, with 1981 as the target date.

When the tenth session of UNCLOS III met in New York and Geneva in the spring and summer of 1981, an informal text on the Draft Convention on the Law of the Sea was placed before the conference for possible final approval.[42] However, that did not occur. The United States, under the new Reagan administration, wanted a policy review of the comprehensive draft treaty. The Law of the Sea conference merely adjourned its sessions pending such a review by the United States government. Strong criticisms and reactions were generated toward the United States as a result of this move for a policy review.[43] Nine specific concerns were raised in the policy review conducted by the United States government. In the testimony by James L. Malone, Chief U.S. negotiator at the Law of the Sea Conference, before the Subcommittee on Oceanography, Committee on Merchant Marine and Fisheries, U.S. House of Representatives, on April 28, 1981, the following objections were raised that the draft convention:

1. places burdensome international regulations on seabed mining
2. establishes a supernational mining entity, the Enterprise
3. compels the sale of technology on deep seabed mining from private companies to the Enterprise
4. limits manganese nodule production from deep-seabed mining sites
5. creates a one-man one-vote procedure in the Assembly, making it a "supreme organ"
6. provides uncertainty by the review process in deep seabed mining provisions
7. imposes revenue-sharing obligations on deep-seabed mining on the continental shelf beyond the 200 miles
8. lacks provisions for protecting investment made in deep seabed mining
9. makes it possible for national liberation movements, such as the Palestinian Liberation Organization, to receive a share of revenue from the Authority[44]

The Law of the Sea conference continued its work with a textual review of the draft convention, article by article.

After the six years of preparation and eight years of negotiation and bargaining by some 150 delegates, the eleventh session of the UNCLOS III met in New York from March 9 to April 30, 1982, ready to take action on the final draft of a comprehensive treaty on the law of the sea. The session began with the introduction of last-minute amendments, a total of thirty-one sets of major changes to the draft convention, including those submitted by the United States government. In the last ten days of the conference, President Koh of Singapore sought compromises without success between the Group of 77 and the United States government on the deep-seabed mining provisions.

On April 30, 1982, at the request of the United States the draft convention and four resolutions were put to a vote that resulted in 130 nations voting in favor, 17 abstaining and 4 voting against (Israel, Turkey, United States and Venezuela). On December 10, 1982, the Law of the Sea Convention was signed by 119 nations at Montego Bay, Jamaica.

Significance. The 1982 LOS Convention has provided, for the first time in human history, a comprehensive legal framework for all uses of the oceans. As of May 1990, 156 nations had affixed their signatures to the convention, and as of December 1990 a total of 45 nations have ratified the convention, which requires 60 ratifications for entry into force. (For the current status of the 1982 LOS Convention, see Appendix II.) The worldwide support by the community of nations for the 1982 LOS Convention has been possible largely because of the treaty provisions that had been negotiated, over the span of fifteen years, to accommodate the major interests of all states. This is one of the most important and enduring merits of the new comprehensive Law of the Sea Convention. The convention does more than codify the existing international customary law on the uses of the oceans. It provides new concepts and new legal principles that are designed to accommodate the competing interests of states, even though some of these compromises lack precision and certitude, as well as neglect issues such as military uses, polar regions and non-module resource recovery.

In the words of Jávier Pérez de Cuellar, Secretary-General of the United Nations, the 1982 LOS Convention

> contains generally acceptable solutions with respect to maritime spaces under the sovereignty and jurisdiction of states, the rational utilization of living and non-living resources, the rights of land-locked states, the promotion of marine scientific research as an instrument for the economic and social development of all peoples, the conservation of the marine environment, respect for the freedoms which have traditionally been observed in so far as the community as a whole is concerned and the settlement by peaceful means of disputes concerning ocean space.[45]

Only time will tell whether the comprehensive charter for the oceans will in the end serve the world community interests.

There is a possibility that the 1982 LOS Convention may come into force in the next two or three years when the sixtieth ratification or accession is deposited with the United Nations.[46] But the forty-five instruments of ratification, about three-quarters of the required sixty, have been deposited mainly by small Third World developing nations: Africa, twenty-four states; Asia and Pacific, nine states; Latin America and Caribbean, ten states; Europe and Mediterranean, two states.

In a survey conducted by David L. Larson, thirty-nine of the total eighty-nine states returning the questionnaire responded that they plan to ratify the convention in the foreseeable future.[47] However, their eventual ratification of the 1982 LOS Convention may depend on variables such as when the United States, United Kingdom and Germany accede to Part XI pertaining to deep-seabed mining, or when the Group of 77 is willing to renegotiate the section on deep-seabed mining, or when the Preparatory Commission completes its work on the International Seabed Authority (see Chapter 7).[48]

Of the major ocean users only Iceland has ratified the Convention (June 21, 1985). From the perspectives of foreign and ocean policy, Canada, another major ocean user and a major player at the UNCLOS III negotiations, has adopted the "wait-and-see" policy, while waiting until the Preparatory Commission has devised an acceptable deep-seabed mining system for the International Seabed Area.[49] While 1992 could be the target date for the sixtieth ratification to be deposited, as predicted by both Satya Nandan, the Director for the Law of the Sea Affairs in the UN Secretariat, and David L. Larson,[50] there seems to be no useful purpose for convening a fourth United Nations Conference on the Law of the Sea.[51]

NOTES

1. Published by the Office of the Special Representative of the Secretary-General for the Law of the Sea, United Nations, 1985.

2. See *First Session of the Committee of Experts for the Progressive Codification of International Law*, League of Nations, 14.

3. See Manley O. Hudson, "The First Conference for the Codification of International Law," *American Journal of International Law* (July 1930): 449–466.

4. Sayre A. Swarztrauber, *The Three-Mile Limit of Territorial Sea* (Annapolis, Md.: Naval Institute Press, 1972), p. 138.

5. *Final Act, Conference for the Codification of International Law* (The Hague: League of Nations, March–April 1930), pp. 184–185.

6. See Swarztrauber, *The Three-Mile Limit of Territorial Sea*, p. 138.

7. Ann L. Hollick, *U.S. Foreign Policy and the Law of the Sea* (Princeton, N.J.: Princeton University Press, 1981), pp. 128–135.

8. UN Doc. A/Conf. 19/C.1/L.10, April 8, 1960.

9. UN Doc. A/Conf. 19/C.1/L.10, April 8, 1960.

10. UN Doc. A/Conf. 19/C.1/L.2/Rev. 1, April 11, 1960.

11. UN Doc. A/Conf. 19/C.1/L.7, April 6, 1960.

12. Hollick, *U.S. Foreign Policy and the Law of the Sea*, p. 158.

13. See John King Gamble, Jr., "Bloc Thinking Accelerating Pluralism?" in Francis T. Christy, Jr., et al., eds., *Law of the Sea: Caracas and Beyond* (Cambridge, Mass.: Ballinger, 1975), p. 4.

14. Ibid., p. 6.

15. See UN Doc. A/8097 (1970), which contains General Assembly Resolution 2750-C (XXV), p. 46, December 17, 1970.

16. Hollick, *U.S. Foreign Policy and the Law of the Sea*, p. 248.

17. Ibid., p. 250.

18. Edward Miles, "An Interpretation of the Caracas Proceedings," in Christy, ed., *Law of the Sea: Caracas and Beyond*, p. 40. Also see Ann L. Hollick, "LOS III: Prospect and Problems," *Columbia Journal of International Law* 14, no. 1 (1975): 105; and idem., *U.S. Foreign Policy and the Law of the Sea*, p. 288.

19. UN Doc. A/Conf. 62/30 and A/Conf. 62/WP.2, June 25, 1974.

20. For a discussion on these rules, see Miles, "An Interpretation of the Caracas Proceedings," pp. 47–55.

21. Ibid., p. 72.

22. Ibid., pp. 72–73.

23. Hollick, *U.S. Foreign Policy and the Law of the Sea*, p. 290.

24. UN Doc. A/Conf. 62/C.II/L.3, July 3, 1974.

25. UN Doc. A/Conf. 62/C.II/L.16, July 23, 1974.

26. See Miles, "An Interpretation of the Caracas Proceedings," pp. 77–79.

27. Ibid., p. 79.

28. See UN Doc. A/Conf. 62/WP.8, Pts. I-III, May 7, 1975, and *Third United Nations Conference on the Law of the Sea*, Official Records, vol. 4, Documents, pp. 137–181.

29. UN Doc. A/Conf. 62/WP.8, Pt. I, May 7, 1975.

30. UN Doc. A/Conf. 62/WP.8, Pts. I-III, May 7, 1975.

31. Hollick, *U.S. Foreign Policy and the Law of the Sea*, p. 312.

32. *Third United Nations Conference on the Law of the Sea*, Official Records, vol. 5, Documents, pp. 125–185. The text is designated in UN Doc. A/Conf. 62/WP.8/Rev. 1, May 6, 1976.

33. See Bernard H. Oxman, "The Third UNCLOS: The 1976 New York Sessions," *American Journal of International Law* 71, no. 2 (1976): 247.

34. UN Doc. A/Conf. 62/WP. 8/Rev. 1, May 6, 1976, which can be found in *Third United Nations Conference on the Law of the Sea*, Official Records, vol. 5, p. 125.

35. UN Doc. A/Conf. 62/WP.10, July 20, 1977, in *Third United Nations Conference on the Law of the Sea*, Official Records, vol. 8.

36. See Bernard H. Oxman, "The Third UNCLOS: The Seventh Session, 1978," *American Journal of International Law* 73, no. 1 (January 1979): 8–24.

37. Ibid., pp. 6–7.

38. UN Doc. A/Conf. 62/WP.10/Rev. 1, April 28, 1979 (known as ICNT/Rev. 1).

39. Bernard H. Oxman, "The Third UNCLOS: The Eighth Session (1979)," *American Journal of International Law* 74, no. 1 (January 1980): 5.

40. Ibid., pp. 3–5 and 6–28.

41. UN Doc. A/Conf. 62/WP. 10/Rev.2, August 11, 1980, and A/Conf. 62/WP. 10/Rev. 3, August 27, 1980.

42. UN Doc. A/Conf. 62/WP. 10/Rev. 3, August 27, 1980.

43. See Bernard H. Oxman, "The Third UNCLOS: The Tenth Session, 1981," *American Journal of International Law* 76, no. 1 (January 1982): 2–5.

44. Ibid., pp. 9–10; and Bernice R. Kleid, "Recent Developments in the Law of the Sea, 1980–1981," *San Diego Law Review* 19, no. 3 (April 1982): 635–636. Also see James L. Malone, "Who Needs the Sea Treaty?" *Foreign Policy*, no. 54 (Spring 1984), pp. 44–63. A reply to Malone's article was made by Elliot L. Richardson, Special U.S. Representative to the Law of the Sea Conference, 1977–1980, in *Foreign Policy*, no. 55 (Summer 1984), pp. 178–182.

45. *The Law of the Sea: Official Text of the United Nations Convention on the Law of the Sea with Annexes and Index* (New York: St. Martin's, 1983), p. xxxi. The original text for the Convention is found in UN Doc. A/Conf. 61/121, October 27, 1982. It is printed in UN Documents, Official Records, *The Third United Nations Conference on the Law of the Sea*, vol. 17, Summary of Records, Resumed Eleventh Session: New York, 22–24 September 1982. Final Part of Eleventh Session and Conclusion of Conference, Montego Bay, 6–10 December 1982, pp. 151–221 and 139–150.

46. See Satya N. Nandan, "The 1982 U. N. Convention on the Law of the Sea: At a Cross Road," *Ocean Development and International Law* 20, no. 5 (1989): 515–518.

47. David L. Larson, "When Will the U.N. Convention on the Law of the Sea Come into Effect?" *Ocean Development and International Law* 20, no. 2 (1989): 178–179.

48. Ibid., p. 179.

49. See Ted L. McDorman, "Will Canada Ratify the Law of the Sea Convention?" *San Diego Law Review* 25, no.3 (August–September 1988): 578.

50. Nandan, "The 1982 U.N. Convention on the Law of the Sea: At a Cross Road," pp. 515–518; and Larson, "When Will the U.N. Convention on the Law of the Sea Come into Effect?" pp. 178–179.

51. Edward L. Miles, "Preparation for UNCLOS IV?" *Ocean Development and International Law* 19, no. 5 (1988): 421–430. Also see Elisabeth Mann Borgese, Mahinda Perera and Aldo Chircop, "The UN Convention on the Law of the Sea: The Cost of Ratification," *Ocean Yearbook* 8 (New York: The University of Chicago Press, 1990), 1–17.

CHAPTER 3

Development of International Principles

This chapter primarily concerns the development of the law of the sea principles, the rules governing access to and the common uses of the oceans. The maritime principles—excluding those that are basically within the purview of private maritime matters such as marine insurance, salvage and collision—to be discussed here deal with the legal and political questions of coastal states' maritime boundaries (zones) and their demand for access to the ocean resources. The development of these law of the sea principles has been influenced, to a large extent, by a combination of economic, political, military and, in recent years, ideological considerations in international relations.

We begin the chapter with a brief sketch of the historical background for the development of the law of the sea principles in order to set the stage for a more detailed discussion on their current status as reflected in the 1982 Law of the Sea Convention. First, the very idea of the sea as common property for all to use had its origin in the juridical writings of Marcianus. In the second century, the Roman jurist advanced the proposition that the sea was *communis omnium naturali jure*, or common to all as a part of the natural law. By the sixth century the concept was codified in Roman law. While the Roman Empire accepted the legal status of the sea as common property for all, nonetheless it declared in the "Theory of Glassators" that it exercised effective control, but not outright ownership, over the Mediterranean Sea. This exercise of Roman jurisdiction over the adjacent sea was made for two purposes: to extend Caesar's power onto the sea and to suppress piracy.

The extension of state sovereignty from land to sea was continued as an accepted practice during the Middle Ages as commerce and trade began to develop in the Mediterranean. By the twelfth and the thirteenth centuries, the Italian city-states, particularly Venice and Genoa, competed with each other for domination over the Mediterranean and Adriatic waters, which provided the connecting link with trade routes to the Far East. By A.D. 1269 Venice was in a position to levy tributes on vessels that sailed into the Adriatic. Then Genoa claimed sovereignty over the Ligurian Sea until the seventeenth century when its warships began stopping Spanish vessels bound for Naples. The Scandinavian countries in the north also imposed their control over adjacent waters: Denmark over the Baltic, Norway over the sea routes to Iceland and Greenland, and Sweden over the Gulf of Bothnia. The English claimed the English Channel and parts of the North Sea. The exploits of Prince Henry the Navigator in the fifteenth century enabled Portugal to explore the coast of west Africa. Through a papal bull, Pope Nicholas V granted Portugal the "exclusive and permanent rights" to that part of Africa. Portuguese jurisdiction over other parts of Africa and the sea routes to the Arabian Sea and Indian Ocean came later as a result of the exploration by Bartholomew Diaz and Vasco Da Gama, who sailed around the Cape of Good Hope. By their reaching the east coast of Africa, a new all-ocean route to the lucrative trade with the Orient was opened up.

Extension of state sovereign control over the ocean and the areas beyond reached a new stage when, under Spanish sponsorship, Christopher Columbus discovered the New World in A.D. 1492. Spain's claim was immediately challenged by the Portuguese king, John II. To avert a military confrontation between the Portuguese and Spanish sovereigns, Pope Alexander VI intervened as a mediator. A line of demarcation was drawn under which, through a series of papal bulls, overseas lands in the Southern Hemisphere were to be granted to each as exclusive possessions. These were soon legitimatized in 1494 by the Treaty of Tordesillas. Under this treaty, a longitudinal line was drawn to award all overseas land possessions west of Cape Verde Island to Spain (Central and South America, most of the Pacific and the Philippines), and all overseas land east of the island to Portugal (Brazil, Africa, India and the East Indies). The Treaty of Tordesillas was a benchmark event in that it was a formal treaty drawn up by two powerful European maritime powers for the specific purpose of dividing the ownership of the oceans and the land possessions lying beyond into exclusive jurisdictions. Even more important, the treaty granted exclusive navigational rights and trade privileges covering an enormous span of ocean space to Spain and Portugal. Each nation was to enjoy navigational rights in each other's jurisdiction.

Soon other nations in Europe saw the enormous economic benefits derived from the Spanish exploitation of the rich resources in the New World and the Portuguese monopoly of the lucrative trade of spices, sugar and tobacco in the East Indies. This was the beginning of the era of what Giulio Pontecorvo would call the period of "opportunity" and "abundance."[1]

The exclusive control of the Southern Hemisphere by Spain and Portugal led to challenges by other European maritime powers, particularly the Dutch and the English, who wanted a share of the lucrative trade. This ushered in another stage of development, one of the most important, in the evolution of the law of the sea principles. As other European maritime powers rushed to the seas seeking trade and profit, they challenged the doctrine of *mare clausum* (closed sea) imposed by Spain and Portugal to keep others out. After becoming independent in 1581 following a protracted war of resistance against Spain, and taking advantage of the rather ineffective occupation of Portugal by Spain, the Dutch took over the Portuguese possessions in the East Indies. After defeating the Spanish Armada in 1588, the British, along with the French, began exploring the east coast of North America, which was nominally under Spanish rule in the seventeenth century.[2]

The Treaty of The Hague (1596) and the Treaty of Westminster (1598) made the English and Dutch the undisputed new rulers of the seas. During this period, the early seventeenth century, there emerged in the writings of publicists—jurists on maritime matters—some of the most important legal treatises on the law of the sea. The concept of *mare clausum* (closed sea), imposed by the Spanish-Portuguese domination after 1494, was confronted by a new argument—the concept of *mare liberum* (open sea) and the freedom of the high seas. As Pontecorvo pointed out, the English and Dutch strategy for an open sea was motivated more by economic considerations than by anything else: "In a competitive world freedom of access was cheaper than paying the cost of ownership and protection of a wide array of distant assets."[3] The concept of *mare liberum*, an open and accessible sea for all, was conceived by Grotius (Hugo De Groot) in his legal brief in defense of the seizure of a Portuguese galleon in the Strait of Malacca. Grotius, retained by the Dutch East Indies Company, argued that every nation had the natural and God-given right to travel and trade by the use of the oceans. The oceans, in Grotius's view, were the property of no one (*res nullius*), but the common property of all (*res communis*). To Grotius, no one, be it a nation or an individual, possessed private ownership rights over the oceans. Military clashes ensued between the competing European maritime powers.

Grotius's doctrine of *mare liberum* gained recognition gradually, in part through the demonstration of the combined military (naval) might of the British, Dutch, French and Germans in their contest for power against Spain and Portugal. Out of this economic, political and military contest between and among the European powers, a body of international principles was developed and accepted in state practices over the next centuries, including the freedom of the oceans (mostly for navigation and fishing) and the concept of neutrality in war. These developments culminated in the Declaration of Paris in 1856.

While the doctrines of open access to the sea and the freedom of the seas prevailed from the time of Grotius in the seventeenth century to the nineteenth century, state practices permitted the right of coastal states to claim exclusive national sovereignty and control over a narrow belt with varying distances along their coasts. This was the concept of the territorial sea, later expanded to contiguous zone for customs, immigration and sanitation purposes. The concept of the territorial sea was defended by John Selden and Cornelius van Bynkershoek in that it was permissible or possible for a coastal state to control and to own a small zone of three to four nautical miles beyond its land area.[4] Thus, from the seventeenth to the nineteenth century, the "twin pillars" of the freedom of the seas and coastal jurisdiction over territorial waters became well established in state practices. However, the ocean regime existing then was mainly as "open ocean system," reflecting the eras of "opportunity and abundance," backed up by a "mercantile economic system and organization" of the European maritime powers for the exploitation of seemingly inexhaustible resources.[5]

For three centuries, from the seventeenth to the end of the nineteenth, the uses of the oceans were dominated by two key traditional principles of the open sea and national claims over a narrow belt of waters from the shore. What had been developed, mainly by state practices, were rights and duties of states on the high seas, as well as within the limited maritime boundary or zonal arrangements. Before World War II international concerns were focused mainly on the codification of the existing state practices on the uses of the oceans and attempts to delimit maritime boundaries. The prevailing concern of the nations before World War II was in seeking means to expand the ocean enclosure and to resolve problems that arose from disputes over extension of maritime boundaries from the coast. (Bilateral agreements on delimitation of maritime boundaries before World War II were small in number, as seen in Appendix III. Bilateral agreements proliferated after the end of the war.)

Three important factors in the postwar period contributed to new development in the law of the sea: the rapid advancement in ocean technology, the emergence of new nations from the old colonial empires and the increased demand for ocean resources. Not only did these factors create the need to reevaluate traditional law of the sea principles, but they also required new rules to govern the new uses of the oceans. For instance, the 1945 Truman Proclamation introduced a new continental shelf doctrine. The use of new technology to explore resources, such as oil and gas, lying offshore underneath several hundred meters of water made this new doctrine essential. The proclamation triggered a series of unilateral claims from a number of Latin American nations and among the newly independent nations in Africa and Asia. Postwar advances in fishing technology also made it possible to fish far away from shore for a lengthy period of time and to catch entire stocks of fisheries which, in turn, contributed to resource depletion or overfishing. Living resources of the ocean could no longer be considered inexhaustible as they had been since the time of Grotius. Ocean resources, under increasing worldwide population pressure, had not only become scarce, but could be depleted if conservation measures were not taken at the proper time. Worldwide population pressure and the need for protein food reinforced the need for expanded ocean enclosures as claimed by coastal states, many of them newly independent, in order to keep others out of their unilaterally established zones of jurisdiction. These developing nations (111 of them in the world today) lacked the technology to explore the resources within their zones of jurisdiction. Instead, they demanded technological transfer from the advanced maritime nations. In addition, developing Third World nations also insisted on a share of the wealth to be obtained from possible exploration and exploitation of the resources from the continental shelf and the deep seabed. Exploration and exploitation of both living and nonliving resources through new advanced ocean technology, such as super oil takers, also created concerns for marine environmental protection in case of oil spills and for rational conservation management of the living resources. Thus, during the 1960s and 1970s a need became increasingly apparent for new law of the sea principles dealing with the continental shelf and the deep seabed (as the common heritage of mankind)—a revival or reemphasis in the twentieth century of some of the traditional concepts developed by Grotius in the seventeenth century.

The new development in the law of the sea at the end of World War II was marked by tense "cold war" and political rivalry between capitalist West and socialist East, led by the two superpowers—the United States and the Soviet Union. While the Soviet Union generally tended to support the ideological positions advanced by Third World nations, at the law of the sea conferences it joined the ranks of the developed maritime powers on issues relating to military concerns, such as innocent passage and transit through straits. In the 1960s and 1970s, the main emphasis in development of the law of the sea principles focused on the uses of the oceans. Major questions to be resolved concerned access to explore and exploit ocean resources on the seabed beyond the limits of national jurisdiction, on the management of living resources, and finally on distribution of the ocean's wealth, which lies beyond the limits of national jurisdiction, among the nations, particularly the developing and geographically disadvantaged nations.

In this chapter, specific topics on the law of the sea principles will be arranged alphabetically. These concepts fall into two types: the traditional "open ocean system" principles of the high seas, territorial sea, contiguous zone, innocent passage, hot pursuit and transit through straits, on the one hand; and the new principles of archipelagic waters, common heritage of mankind, continental shelf, and the exclusive economic zone, on the other. To use Pontecorvo's description, traditional law of the sea principles, which assumed "opportunity" and "abundance," emphasized freedom of the high seas. The new law of the sea principles stress expanded enclosure of the ocean space with agreed upon "limits" in a period of "scarcity." In addition, pressures have come from the developing Third World nations for the new concepts of sharing deep seabed wealth, under the doctrine of "common heritage of mankind," and for the new doctrine of archipelagic waters for mid-ocean states.

ARCHIPELAGIC PRINCIPLE

Article 46: Use of terms

For the purpose of this Convention:

(a) "archipelagic State" means a State constituted wholly by one or more archipelagos and may include other islands;

(b) "archipelago" means a group of islands, including parts of islands, interconnecting waters and other natural features which are closely inter-related that such islands, waters and other natural features form an intrinsic geographical, economic and political entity, or which historically have been regarded as such.

While the general geographic definition of an archipelago refers to a large body of water with many islands, the legal concept of an archipelago and its political implications are rather complex. Its evolution as a principle in the law of the sea is of recent origin. At the heart of the archipelagic concept is the question of delimitation of the territorial waters for an archipelago in mid-ocean: should each island have its own territorial water or must the island groups be treated as a whole? What about the waters within the archipelago? International attempts to codify and delimit the territorial waters of an archipelago were not conclusive before the 1950s. The 1930 Hague Conference, while determining that every island had its own territorial waters, failed to agree on the legal status of waters within the archipelagos.

Prior to the 1958 Geneva Conference on the Law of the Sea, the failure of the 1930 Hague Conference to delimit the waters between island groups of an archipelago opened the doors for unilateral claims by two mid-ocean states: the Philippines and Indonesia. In 1955 the Philippine government took the position that "all waters around, between and connecting the different islands of the Philippine Archipelago, irrespective of their width or dimension, were necessary appurtenances of its land territory, forming an integral part of the national and inland waters, subject to the exclusive sovereignty of the Philippines."[6] Indonesia, on December 13, 1957, declared "its land, waters and people to be inseparable, linked to each other; the survival of the Indonesian nation depended on the unity of these three elements."[7] It declared further that Indonesia's waters must not become "pockets of so-called 'high seas,' open to activities which might endanger the Country's unity, security, and territorial integrity."[8] These positions were enacted legislatively as part of national law by the Philippines in 1960 and Indonesia in 1961. At the 1958 Conference on the Law of the Sea, maritime powers were confronted with the new concept of a special archipelagic regime. Their opposition to the new concept, as advocated by the Philippines and Indonesia, was based on the grounds that it would result in (1) an expansion of internal waters into the high seas, and (2) a loss or erosion of traditional navigational rights to shipping routes on the high seas and through many international passageways. The maritime powers wanted the right of free passage through the archipelagic waters. Although the 1958 Convention on the Territorial Sea and Contiguous Zone skirted the main issue for a special archipelagic regime, it did recognize the International Court of Justice (ICJ) judgment in the 1951 Anglo-Norwegian Fisheries case that a coastal archipelago may draw a straight baseline around its outermost points to allow it to "tie" to the mainland (Article 4).[9] Figure 3.1 demonstrates the application of the straight baseline as applied to Indonesia and the Philippines.

By the 1960s a number of new factors had entered the international scene that

Figure 3.1
Archipelagic Concept and Southeast Asia

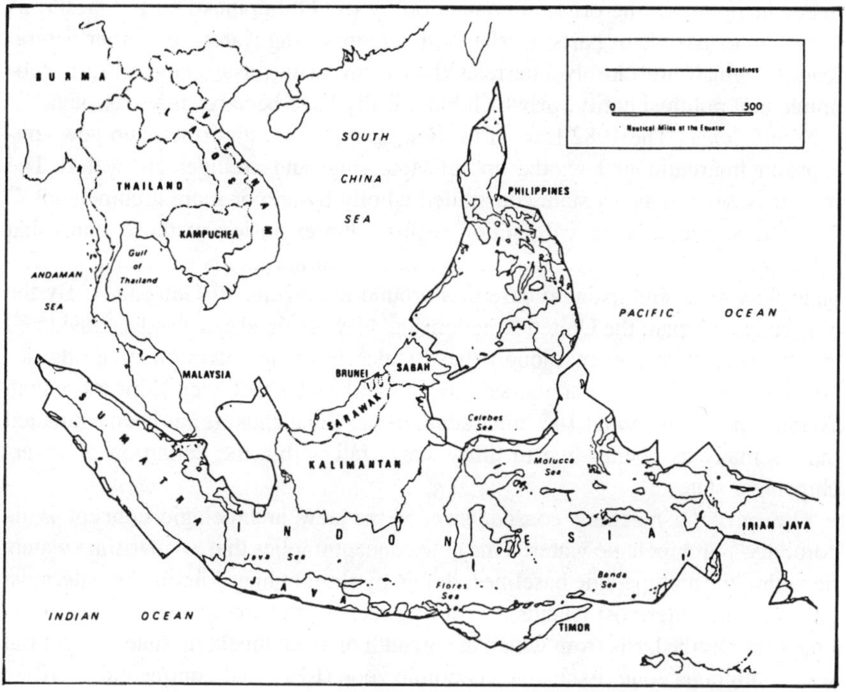

Source: Lee Yong Leng, "The Archipelagic Concept and Its Impact on Southeast Asia," *Singapore Journal of Tropical Geography* 4, no. 1 (1983), p. 37. Used by permission.

strengthened the position taken by the Philippines and Indonesia for international recognition of the new concept of a special mid-ocean archipelagic regime. One was the emergence of new states on mid-ocean archipelagos in the Pacific Ocean, the Indian Ocean and the Caribbean. When the United Nations General Assembly took up the seabed debate in the late 1960s, the Philippines and Indonesia were joined by Fiji, Tonga and Mauritius in demanding the establishment of a new fundamental principle applicable to an archipelagic state.[10] A major concern of the world's maritime powers was the right of innocent passage through international straits, such as Gibraltar, Hormuz, and Malacca. In order to secure free and innocent passage through international straits, maritime powers with nuclear-powered ocean-going navies had to make concessions to the demands of the Philippines, Indonesia, Fiji, Mauritius and the Bahamas for acceptance of a special archipelagic regime. The result of the intense negotiations at Caracas, Geneva and New York by the Third United Nations Conference on the Law of the Sea (UNCLOS III) was Article 46 of the 1982 Law of the Sea Convention (hereafter referred to as LOS Convention). For the first time since the 1930 Hague Conference on the codification of international law, this article established the concept of an "archipelagic state" as "a state constituted wholly by one or more archipelagos and may include other islands." An archipelago is now defined, in line with the original contention by the Philippines and Indonesia, as "a group of islands or parts of islands, interconnecting waters and other natural features which are closely interrelated to form an intrinsic geographical, economic and political entity, or which historically have been regarded as such."[11]

Significance. The 1982 Law of the Sea Convention established two new concepts in international law: the archipelagic state and archipelagic water. The former is defined as "a state constituted wholly by one or more archipelagos." The acceptance of such a definition requires the exclusion of those states that possess noncoastal archipelagos. Under this definition, neither Portugal nor Ecuador can draw archipelagic baselines around the Azores or Galápagos. By the new concept Japan, the United Kingdom and New Zealand can also be considered archipelagic states, even though these states have no intention of doing so. However, Ecuador has maintained navigational routes that keep ships more than 70 miles north and about 145 miles south of the Galápagos. It has been estimated that as many as twenty-five to thirty states fall within the definition of an archipelagic state.

The most far-reaching consequence of the new archipelagic concept is its corollary—archipelagic water. This new concept implies that all maritime waters lie within the archipelagic baselines, drawn by straight lines joining the outermost points of the outermost islands and drying reefs of the archipelago. These baselines serve as the basis from which the breadth of an archipelagic state's territorial sea, contiguous zone, exclusive economic zone (EEZ) and continental shelf are measured. In essence, recognition of the archipelagic state and its waters promotes further erosion of the traditional high seas concept. An archipelagic state can enjoy sovereignty rights over its waters, air space, seabed and subsoil. Thus, as seen in Figure 3.1, an archipelagic state, like the Philippines or Indonesia, can expand its jurisdiction over vast areas of the ocean.

In exchange for a greatly expanded ocean space under the new archipelagic concept, the archipelagic states acquiesced to demands from the world's major maritime powers for a guarantee of traditional navigational and air routes rights. These include innocent passage by user states through archipelagic waters and international straits, subject to the designated archipelagic sealane up to fifty nautical miles in width. When archipelagic states have designated their archipelagic sealanes, potential controversies and disputes exist between them and user states, such as the United States, which are not parties to the 1982 Law of the Sea Convention. Archipelagic states must recognize the traditional fishery rights and other legitimate activities of adjacent neighboring states. They must also honor existing rights to which they have bilaterally agreed. The creation of a special regime for archipelagic states, whether or not it increases the size of an exclusive economic zone, now universally accepted as an important provision in the 1982 Law of the Sea Convention, produced an enormous "psychological feeling" in island states such as Fiji, the Philippines and Indonesia. So far, Fiji is the only state that, as an archipelagic state, has drawn closing lines for delimitation of its internal waters in accordance with the right provided under Article 50 of the 1982 LOS Convention.

COMMON HERITAGE

Of the new principles introduced during the long negotiation for a comprehensive convention on law of the sea in the 1970s and early 1980s, common heritage must be considered the most novel, and, at the same time, the most controversial concept incorporated in the 1982 multilateral treaty. When the common heritage of mankind concept was first introduced in the United Nations in November 1967 by the Maltese delegate, Dr. Arvid Pardo, the international community was only beginning to be aware of the possibilities for exploration and exploitation of the nonliving resources in the deep seabed and the implications for mankind.

It took three years of debate in the United Nations General Assembly seabed committee to produce, on December 17, 1970, the Declaration of Principles governing the exploration and exploitation of the seabed resources in the high seas beyond national jurisdiction. A key provision in the declaration was the expression, "The seabed and ocean floor, and the subsoil thereof, beyond the limits of national jurisdiction, as well as the resources of the area, are the common heritage of mankind."[12]

Major points from the 1970 Declaration of Principles were incorporated into Articles 1, 133 and 136 of the 1982 LOS Convention. The 1982 LOS Convention stated that all solid, liquid or gaseous mineral resources on the seabed and ocean floor and subsoil thereof, beyond the limits of national jurisdiction, are "the common heritage of mankind."

There was considerable debate over the meaning of the term "common heritage of mankind." Some saw it more as a set of ideological, moral and political expressions than as a legal doctrine. The opponents of common heritage of mankind argued that the seabed has long been accepted as a part of the high seas and, under the principle of *res nullius*, was "common to all because it was the property of no one." It was contended that under *res nullius*, whichever state captured and controlled the sea or a part of it acquired the ownership, or the exclusive use, of the sea. It was a "first come, first served" proposition.

Proponents of the common heritage concept argued that the original purposes for establishing a special international regime for the seabed were

1. to "prevent the total division of ocean space among the states"
2. to ensure "nondiscriminatory resource management and conservation"
3. to promote "equitable distribution of benefits" from the seabed to all states.[13]

It was felt that a new concept was needed to fill a "jurisdictional void" regarding the high seas under *res nullius* that said, "if you find it, you keep it." Thus, the concept of common heritage contains specific principles that govern the seabed, as provided in the 1970 Declaration of Principles:

1. the seabed area beyond national jurisdiction is not subject to appropriation by any state or person
2. no state can make a claim for the exercise of sovereign rights over the seabed
3. benefits derived from the exploration and exploitation of the seabed shall be shared equitably for all developing nations under international management
4. there is to be no infringement on freedom of access, use and navigation
5. the use of the seabed must be for peaceful purposes
6. states are to promote international cooperation in scientific research on the seabed
7. exploration and exploitation of the area's resources must be carried out for the benefit of mankind
8. the area beyond the national jurisdiction must be reserved for peaceful purposes
9. there shall be established an international machinery for orderly and rational management of the area's resources
10. states shall promote international cooperation in scientific research by peaceful purposes in the area
11. there shall be appropriate measures for cooperation in prevention of pollution in the area
12. states shall pay due regard to the rights and legitimate interests of coastal states
13. there shall be respect for the legal status of waters superjacent to the area
14. states shall have responsibility to ensure that activities in the area shall be carried out in conformity with the international regime to be established
15. parties to any dispute relating to activities in the area and its resources shall resolve such dispute by peaceful means and procedures agreed upon in the international regime to be established

Significance. Under the 1982 LOS Convention, the concept of common heritage is intended to annul or revoke the traditionally accepted principle of open and free access for anyone to the resources on the seabed on the basis of "first come, first served," so long as it does not impede freedom of navigation. Seabed resources, under the common heritage concept, are to be regulated and developed by an internationally established entity for the benefit of mankind and are to be shared with less developed nations in the world (see Chapter 7). Thus, the common heritage concept is aimed in part at redressing the inequity between the rich, technologically advanced nations and the poor, less developed Third World, insofar as the exploitation of seabed resources is concerned. As new technology is developed to exploit the mineral resources, particularly the poly-metallic manganese nodules, the common heritage principle is designed to forestall competition among major maritime powers for increased control of the ocean floor. It is hoped that by placing the seabed beyond national jurisdiction, a Klondiketype rush for seabed resources would be mitigated. In many respects the common heritage concept does represent an ideological and moral expression by the Third World nations.

The common heritage concept is also intended to address the twentieth-century reality that resources of the sea are no longer inexhaustible, as Grotius once claimed. Ample evidence is available on the overfishing and the possibility of depleting the mineral resources on the ocean floor. Ocean pollution and waste dumping have become serious problems for coastal states in recent years. If the traditional freedom of the seas is not supplemented by new concepts to meet changing conditions, "a regime of waste or disorder on the high seas may ensue."[14] Embodied in the common heritage concept is the need for international cooperation in rational ocean resources management, conservation and protection against ocean pollution.

The common heritage concept has been controversial. It is not yet considered to be an established international legal principle. While the United States, along with 108 nations in the United Nations, has endorsed the 1970 Declaration of the Common Heritage Principle governing the seabed, the United States has refused to sign the 1982 LOS Convention, primarily because the Convention restricts access to seabed resources and calls for establishment of international machinery to control and regulate exploitation of seabed resources. The acceptance of common heritage as a general principle by major maritime powers in 1970 was a "concession" to Third World nations in exchange for a guarantee of the freedom of transit over major international waterways.[15]

Although the common heritage principle does contain some ambiguities, it is now a part of the 1982 LOS Convention. In time the treaty itself will become a part of customary international law. As one legal scholar explains it: "Customary international law arises when nations conform their actions to a consistent pattern of action because of a collective feeling that they are obliged by law to act in such a manner."[16] Thus, in the final analysis, the common heritage principle and the provisions governing the seabed resources contained in the 1982 LOS Convention will in time have to be recognized and observed by all, including those states that failed to sign the Convention.

CONTIGUOUS ZONE

Article 33: Contiguous zone

1. In a zone contiguous to its territorial sea, described as the contiguous zone, the coastal State may exercise the control necessary to:

(a) prevent infringement of its customs, fiscal, immigration or sanitary laws and regulations within its territory or territorial sea;

(b) punish infringement of the above laws and regulations committed within its territory or territorial sea.

2. The contiguous zone may not extend beyond 24 nautical miles from the baselines from which the breadth of the territorial sea is measured.

A contiguous zone is a belt of water adjacent to, but extending seaward beyond, the territorial sea; in this zone the coastal state exercises a certain special jurisdiction for the enforcement of customs, immigration and health laws. It has also been the practice of coastal states to declare such a contiguous zone for defense and security purposes.

The contiguous zone concept developed in the beginning of the eighteenth century when Great Britain enforced a series of so-called Hovering Acts intended to prevent smuggling.[17] The smuggler's vessels, laden with dutiable goods, were hovering off the coast and waiting to come ashore while evading customs authorities. Under the Hovering Acts, customs officers were given power to visit and search vessels at various distances from shore, as determined by port authorities. The distances varied between three or five miles to more than thirty miles from the shore. As smuggling increased, the British Parliament first extended customs jurisdictions to twenty-four miles and then in 1802 to a zone of one hundred leagues, or about 300 miles. The Hovering Acts were repealed by 1876, and Parliament limited customs jurisdiction in the Custom Consolidation Act to a nine-mile zone for British vessels and a three-mile zone for foreign vessels. The British had adhered to the three-mile limit by refusing to accept a zone of twelve miles in the name of the freedom of navigation.

Recent practices of the United States in the use of the contiguous zone have been influenced by the need to enforce the Prohibition Act (1919), the Tariff Act (1922) and the Anti-smuggling Act (1935) and for defense in the Pacific prior to the attack on Pearl Harbor.[18] The "Defensive Sea Areas" (1939–1941), extending about 1,000 miles into the sea, were declared by executive order just prior to World War II. Contiguous zones, known as "Maritime Control Areas," in normal times could be established extending into large areas of the high seas for self-defense. The 1922 Tariff Act provided a zone of twelve miles to permit federal agents to "inspect, search and examine" any vessel for violation of the Volstead Act in the sale and transportation of intoxicating liquor. The repeal of Prohibition in 1933 did not abrogate the right to exercise customs jurisdiction on the high seas. In 1935 the United States Congress passed the Anti-smuggling Act, which established mobile "customs enforcement areas" of varying size within which United States customs agents could search and seize vessels hovering fifty to sixty miles off the coast. In short, practices of states before the 1930s had extended their national jurisdiction over areas, or zones, of water offshore by specialized regulations for specific purposes. For instance, the Aircraft Defense Identification Zone extended 500 nautical miles offshore and provided jurisdiction over aircraft that intended to land within the United States.[19]

The use of the term "contiguous zone" appeared first in the 1930 Hague Codification Conference: "the coastal states may exercise control necessary to prevent infringement of customs and sanitary regulations, and security interference by foreign ships within its territory or territorial waters in a zone of the high seas adjacent to territorial waters.'' Such control must not be exercised more than 12 nautical miles from the coast.[20] A decade after the Hague Conference, an increasing number of nations had unilaterally declared or legislated a contiguous or supplementary zone to meet a variety of claimed special needs. Table 3.1 gives examples of state practices on the uses of a contiguous zone before 1958.

When the 1958 United Nations Conference on the Law of the Sea convened in Geneva, two concerns dominated the debate over the question of the breadth of the territorial area and the contiguous zone: military security and fishery rights. General proposals on the special fishery zone, ranging from six to twelve miles, were not adopted. But, through hard bargaining at the conference, a general agreement was reached among the participating states that a contiguous zone be recognized and delimited. The results were incorporated in Article 24 of the 1958 Convention on the Territorial Sea and the Contiguous Zone. Article 24 provided that the coastal state may exercise the control necessary to (1) prevent infringement of its customs, fiscal, immigration or sanitary regulations within its territory or territorial sea; and (2) punish violation or infringement of these regulations committed within the territorial sea. However, the 1958 Convention also recognized that the zone was a part of the high seas and limited to twelve nautical miles measured from the baseline of the territorial sea. A Polish amendment to include violations of security as one of the specific purposes for which a contiguous zone could be established was defeated by the conference as a whole; it lacked the required two-thirds majority vote (thirty-three to twenty-seven with fifteen abstentions). Article 24 of the 1982 Law of the Sea Convention adopted almost the same language as the 1958 Convention, except that the contiguous zone was doubled to ''twenty-four nautical miles from the baseline from which the breadth of the territorial sea is measured'' (Article 33). By July 1988, twenty-two nations had claimed a contiguous zone of twenty-four nautical miles and nine had claimed less than twenty-four nautical miles, as shown in Table 3.2.

Significance. The acceptance of the contiguous zone and the delimitation of its breadth from the territorial sea by the 1958 Convention on the Territorial Sea and the Contiguous Zone and the 1982 Law of the Sea Convention simply reaffirmed coastal states' special claims for the right to enforce violations of prescribed regulations within their territorial sea. However, under these conventions coastal states have no jurisdiction to take action against offenses committed within the contiguous zone, since this zone is considered a part of the high seas. Controversy of this type may have to be solved by the rules of ''reasonableness'' and ''equity.''[21]

Despite the delimitation of a contiguous zone of not more than twenty-four nautical miles by the 1982 LOS Convention, there is still considerable confusion regarding the breadth of the contiguous zone. In order to preserve the sanctity of the freedom of navigation, some states—the United Kingdom is one—have

Table 3.1
Miscellaneous State Contiguous Zone Claims (1930–1940)

State	Extent	Purpose of Claim	Means and Date of Implementation
Bulgaria	6 miles	Territorial Waters	Decree-Law of 25 August 1935
China	12 miles	Customs	Customs Preventive Law of 19 June 1934
Colombia	20 kilometers	Customs	Customs Law of 19 June 1931
Cuba	5 miles	Sanitation	General Law on Fisheries of 28 March 1936
Czechoslovakia	12 miles	Anti-smuggling	Treaty with Finland, 21 March 1936
Denmark	12 miles	Anti-smuggling	Act No. 316 of 28 November 1935
Dominican Republic	3 leagues	Naval security area	Law No. 55 of 27 December 1938
Ecuador	15 miles	Fishing	Decree No. 607 of 29 August 1934
El Salvador	12 miles	Police and scrutiny	Law of Navigation and Marine of 23 October 1933
Finland	6 miles	Customs	Customs Regulation of 8 September 1939
France	20 kilometers	Fishing (Indo-China)	Presidential Decree of 22 September 1936
Greece	6 miles	Territorial seas	Law No. 230 of 17 September 1936
Guatemala	12 miles	Port authority	Regulations of 21 April 1939
Honduras	12 miles	Territorial seas	Constitution of 28 March 1936
Hungary	12 miles	Anti-smuggling	Treaty with Finland of 23 November 1932
Iran	6 miles	Territorial waters	Act of 19 July 1934
	12 miles	Marine supervision zone	
Italy	12 miles	Customs	Customs Law No. 1424 of 25 September 1940
Lebanon	20 kilometers	Customs	Order No. 137/LR of 15 June 1935
Norway	10 miles	Customs	Royal Resolution of 28 October 1932
Poland	12 miles	Customs	Customs Law of 27 October 1933
Romania	6 miles	Territorial seas	Royal Decree No. 296 of 7 February 1934
Syria	20 kilometers	Customs	Customs Code of 15 June 1935
United Kingdom	1 hour sail	Customs	Treaty with Finland of 13 Octoeber 1933
U.S.S.R.	12 miles	Air space sovereignty	Air Code of 7 August 1935
Venezuela	12 miles	Security, customs, sanitation	Presidential Decree of 15 September 1939

Source: Sayre A. Swarztrauber, *The Three-Mile Limit of Territorial Sea* (Annapolis, Md.: Naval Institute Press, 1972), p. 148. Used by permission.

Table 3.2
Extent of the Contiguous Zone

Areas with 24-mile Limit		Areas with Limit Less than 24 Miles	
Antigua and Barbuda	24	Bangladesh	18
Burma	24	Egypt	18
Chile	24	Finland	6
Democratic Kampuchea	24	Gambia	18
Democratic Yemen	24	Saudi Arabia	18
Dominica	24	Sudan	18
Dominican Republic	24	Trust Territory of the Pacific	18
France	24	United States of America	12
Gabon	24	Venezuela	3
Ghana	24	Total with less than 24-mile limit: 9	
India	24		
Madagascar	24		
Malta	24		
Morocco	24		
Pakistan	24		
Saint Lucia	24		
Senegal	24		
Sri Lanka	24		
St. Kitts	24		
St. Vincent	24		
Vanuatu	24		
Viet Nam	24		
Total with 24-mile limit: 22			

Source: Office for Ocean Affairs and the Law of the Sea, *Law of the Sea Bulletin*, no. 11 (United Nations, July 1988), p. 50.

claimed no contiguous zone. Many other states, both parties and nonparties to the 1982 LOS Convention, have exceeded the twenty-four-nautical-mile limit in claiming the contiguous zone. Others have expressed their adherence to either Article 24 of the 1958 Convention or the 1982 LOS Convention. Many states who are parties to the 1958 and/or the 1982 LOS Conventions have repealed the hundreds of statutes extending their national jurisdiction for enforcement in the contiguous zones, which were designed for special purposes not enumerated in the conventions. These zones extended far beyond the limit (twenty-four nautical miles) in the high seas. Many Latin American states have made extensive claims in terms of both distance and jurisdiction in the establishment of their contiguous zones, a sort of "creeping jurisdiction." Special contiguous zones for security or self-defense, extending hundreds and even thousands of miles from the shore, were enacted during World War II or in crisis situations and have remained in effect. For instance, during the 1940s the United States' special contiguous zone for security purposes proclaimed an extension of 1,200 miles into the high seas; it remains in effect to this day. India, Pakistan and South Yemen have claimed security as a purpose for establishing their contiguous zones. On August 1, 1977, North Korea established a fifty-nautical-mile military maritime boundary measured from a claimed straight baseline from which the territorial sea is drawn in the Sea of Japan. (The United States protested the line on January 4, 1990.) A contiguous zone for security and self-defense has become part of international customary law. There have been incidents in which coastal states wished to proclaim and enforce contiguous zones on the high seas for control of electronic reconnaissance by foreign vessels; examples are the cases of the *Pueblo* and *Mayaguez*.

Finally, it may be argued that the establishment of the EEZ, of which the contiguous zone is a part, may make the contiguous zone redundant. The contiguous zone is still regarded as a very important concept. In the first place, it has provided the rationale behind the establishment of the EEZ. It has also served as a legal framework for coastal states to establish ocean pollution control and environmental protection on the high seas. The contiguous zone concept is by no means outdated. It is one of the special regimes in the law of the sea.

CONTINENTAL SHELF

Article 76: Definition of the continental shelf

1. The continental shelf of a coastal State comprises the sea-bed and subsoil of the submarine areas that extend beyond its territorial sea throughout the natural prolongation of its land territory to the outer edge of the continental margin, or to a distance of 200 miles from the baselines from which the breadth of the territorial sea is measured where the outer edge of the continental margin does not extend up to that distance. . . .

3. The continental margin comprises the submerged prolongation of the land mass of the coastal State, and consists of the sea-bed and subsoil of the shelf, the slope and the rise. It does not include the deep ocean floor with its oceanic ridges or the subsoil thereof.

4. (a) For the purposes of this Convention, the coastal State shall establish the outer edge of the continental margin wherever the margin extends beyond 200 nautical miles from the baselines from which the breadth of the territorial sea is measured.

From the days of Grotius in the seventeenth century to the 1940s, the classic international law principle rested on the two basic assumptions of unimpeded navigation on the high seas and the seemingly inexhaustible living resources (fisheries). The legal doctrine of the continental shelf represents a far-reaching departure from this principle. Claims for the seabed resources beneath the high seas date back to the 1811 British exclusion of foreign fishing in pearl beds outside the territorial waters of Ceylon, the 1839 British-Franco agreement to exclude oyster fishing over Ganville Bay, and the 1942 British-Venezuelan agreement to divide the submarine areas of the Gulf of Paria. The most serious challenge to the Grotian concept of the freedom of the seas came in the fall of 1945 when President Harry Truman of the United States issued a proclamation laying claim to the mineral rights of the continental shelf.

The 1945 Truman Proclamation was motivated by the need for the United States federal government to own and control offshore energy resources, such as oil and gas. It not only marked the birth of a new doctrine on the continental shelf, but also triggered a chain reaction of unprecedented unilateral claims by coastal states around the world. The Truman Proclamation did not define the extent or limit of the continental shelf. An accompanying press release stated that the continental shelf referred to the submerged land contiguous to the continental shelf United States which is covered by 100 fathoms, or 200 meters, of water. The subsequent unilateral claims made by other coastal states between 1945 and 1957 created a labyrinth of national jurisdictions beyond the traditional territorial waters. The 1947 claim made by Chile and Peru for a zone 200 nautical miles from their coasts was the key point endorsed by the 1952 Santiago Declaration. In fact, the Latin American states had declared a 200-nautical-mile territorial sea within which exclusive national jurisdiction over all natural resources would be exercised.

In 1958 the United Nations called for an international conference to address, among many other law of the sea problems, the mounting controversy over the meaning, limits and legal status of the new continental shelf doctrine. One of the first objectives at the 1958 UNCLOS I in Geneva was to limit the continental shelf to a depth of 200 meters (600 feet). This was accomplished by Article 1 of the 1958 Convention on the Continental Shelf, which defined the shelf as "the seabed and subsoil of the submarine area adjacent to the coast but outside the area of the territorial sea, to a depth of 200 meters." However, Article 1 also permitted the extension of the continental shelf to "where the depth of the superjacent water admits of exploitation of the natural resources of the said area." In other words, a coastal state's claim over its continental shelf could go beyond the 200 meter limit to any depth where technical capabilities allowed it. This definition, contained in Article 1 of the 1958 Convention on the Continental Shelf, was not only imprecise, but was drafted in favor of those technologically advanced nations that were in the process of developing the capability to go beyond the depth limit of 200 meters. At any rate, 200-meter depth limit for the continental shelf was only an interim measure within the then technical ability on deep seabed exploration, for by 1973 the *Glomar Explorer* was already probing deep seabed mineral resources in the Pacific to a depth of 4,000 meters, or 12,000 feet.

The 1982 LOS Convention defines the continental shelf in Article 76(1) as "the seabed and subsoil of the submarine areas that extend beyond its territorial sea throughout the natural prolongation of its land territory to the outer edge of the continental margin, or to a distance of 200 nautical miles from the baseline from which the breadth of the territorial sea is measured." While the 1958 Continental Shelf Convention employed an open-ended definition by using the test of exploitability as the criterion, the 1982 LOS Convention's definition of the continental shelf comprises the entire continental margin: the shelf proper (averaging about 100 meters), the slope (about 1,500 to 3,000 meters), and the rise (descends to the level of seabed at about 3,500 to 5,000 meters). The continental margin constitutes about 20 percent of the sea floor where one finds both living and nonliving resources of the sea. The continental margin also is defined in the 1982 LOS Convention as "comprising the submerged prolongation of the land mass of the coastal state," thus reaffirming the 1969 ruling made by the International Court of Justice in the North Sea Continental Shelf cases, which defined the continental shelf as "a natural prolongation of island territory into and under the sea," to consist of "the seabed and subsoil of the shelf, the slope, and the rise, but to exclude the deep ocean floor."[22]

The 1982 LOS Convention attempts to resolve the controversy, developed before 1958, with respect to the outer limits of the continental shelf. One aspect of the controversy is the fact that many states, including the United Kingdom and the United States, have continental margins that extend beyond the 200-mile limit; all of them claim resources found there. Article 76(5) of the 1982 LOS Convention states that coastal states can extend their claim of the shelf beyond the outer edge of the continental margin, but not beyond 350 nautical miles from the shore, except in shallow areas or where "the thickness of sedimentary rock is at least one percent of the shortest distance from such point to the foot of the continental slope." Then a line can be drawn one hundred nautical miles beyond the area where the ocean depth reaches 2,500 meters. Figure 3.2 is a simplified diagram illustrating the many possible definitions of continental shelf.[23] Under Article 84, coastal states must establish the outer limits of their continental shelf and continental margin boundary as laid down in Article 76(8) and report such information and data to the International Commission on the Limits of the Continental Shelf set up under Annex II to the 1982 LOS Convention.

Under Article 77 of the 1982 LOS Convention, a coastal state has only limited sovereign rights over the shelf when it is exploring and exploiting the natural

Figure 3.2
Definition of the Continental Shelf

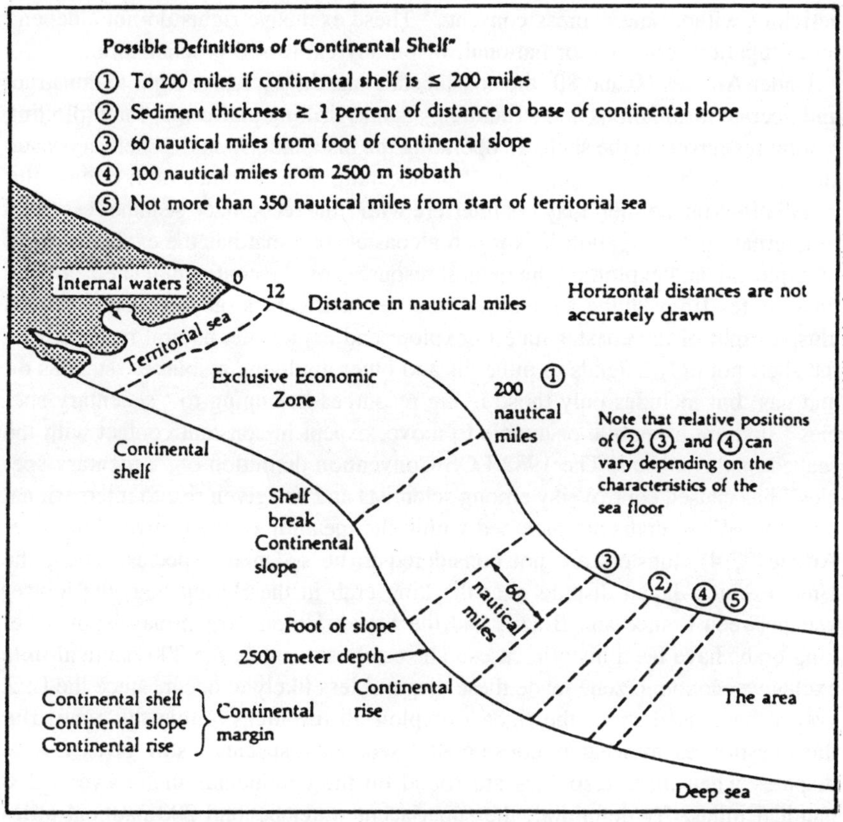

The major divisions of the ocean under the UNCLOS III treaty. The numbers refer to possible definitions of the continental shelf: (1) to 200 miles if the continental shelf is < 200 miles; (2) sediment thickness ⩾ 1 percent of the distance to the foot of the continental slope; (3) 60 nautical miles from the foot of the continental slope; (4) 100 nautical miles from the 1500-meter isobath; and (5) not more than 350 nautical miles from the inner boundary of the territorial sea. Note that the relative position of 2, 3 and 4 can vary depending on the characteristics of the sea floor. (Horizontal distances are not accurately drawn.)

Source: David A. Ross, "Ocean Science: Its Place in the New Order of the Ocean," in *The New Order of the Oceans: The Advent of a Managed Environment*, Giulio Pontecorvo, ed. (New York: Columbia University Press, 1986), p. 71. Copyright © 1986, Columbia University Press, New York. Used by permission.

resources there; otherwise it may not assert ownership rights over the shelf. Ownership consists only of exclusive franchise rights for exploring and exploiting purposes. Thus, the shelf is not a part of the coastal state's territory. However, the exclusive right over the shelf for exploring and exploiting the seabed resources gives the coastal state the right to prevent any other state to "undertake these activities without the express consent." These exclusive rights do not "depend on occupation, effective or national, or on any expressed proclamation."

Under Articles 60 and 80, the coastal state has the exclusive right to construct and operate installations and structures, such as drilling platforms, for exploiting natural resources on the shelf. In operating the installations on the shelf, a coastal state may establish a "safety zone" of not more than 500 meters in radius. But installations on the shelf may not interfere with "the recognized sealanes essential to international navigation." Nor can a coastal state that has the exclusive right of exploring and exploiting the natural resources on the continental shelf prevent other states from laying submarine pipelines and cables on the shelf. The exclusive right of the coastal state to explore and exploit the natural resources on the shelf not only extends to minerals and other nonliving resources, such as oil and gas, but includes only those living resources belonging to "sedentary species" that are immobile or unable to move, except in constant contact with the seabed or the subsoil. The 1982 LOS Convention definition of "sedentary species" has caused controversy among scientists and has given rise to international disputes. While crabs are included within the meaning of the Convention under Article 77(4), lobsters are not considered to be sedentary species. Thus, the United States–Japan dispute over the king crab in the Bering Sea, the lobster war between France and Brazil, and the Soviet Union–Argentina dispute over king crabs have been historic cases. The establishment of the 200-nautical-mile exclusive economic zone made these disputes less likely to occur, since the EEZ grants the coastal states the right to exploit all resources within the zone. But the question as to what is considered "sedentary species" still gives rise to disputes when these resources are found on the continental shelf beyond 200 nautical miles. By definition, the superjacent water beyond 200 nautical miles is a part of the high seas. If fish found there are sedentary species, the coastal state does not have the exclusive right to exploit. However, if they are nonsedentary, they are then governed by the principle of the freedom of fishing on the high seas.

For nonliving resources on the continental shelf beyond 200 nautical miles, Article 82(2) of the 1982 LOS Convention requires the coastal state to make an annual payment or "contribution-in-kind" within the first five years of production to the International Seabed Authority amounting to 1 percent of the value or volume of production at a site. Then the rate of payment increases "by one percent for each subsequent year until the twelfth year and shall remain seven percent thereafter." The contributions so collected must be distributed to all states-parties to the Convention on the basis of "equitable sharing criteria" and with due consideration for the developing nations of the world. As of July 1988, the extent of the continental shelf claimed by various nations is as shown in Table 3.3.[24]

Significance. The most difficult political problem raised by the continental shelf concept has been the question of dividing the shelf between coastal states with opposite or adjacent coasts. The legal language of the 1958 Continental Shelf Convention states that "where the same continental shelf is adjacent to the territories of two or more states whose coasts are opposite each other," "adjacent" means uninterrupted contact between the coast and the shelf. Article 6 of the 1958 Convention provides that in case of dispute, the states shall determine the boundary line by agreement. If no such agreement is possible, then the principle of the equidistance is applied. Under this principle a boundary line is drawn from each disputing state's territorial sea baseline so that the distance is the same—the median line through the middle of the water between the coastal states. The 1958 Continental Shelf Convention also provides for a situation whereby the boundary line may deviate from the "equidistance principle" because of "special circumstances" that need to be taken into consideration. In short, the 1958 Continental Shelf Convention provides the principles of "equidistance plus special circumstances" in settling boundary delimitation disputes between coastal states with opposite and adjacent shelves. Generally, the equidistance line is the tool most often used in dispute settlement.

However, the principle of "equidistance plus special circumstances" was not applied in the 1969 North Sea Continental Shelf cases by the International Court of Justice (ICJ), which dealt with delimitation of the coastline of West Germany and the adjacent states of Denmark and the Netherlands. The ICJ ruled that the "equidistance" rule was not obligatory, but urged agreement through negotiation between the littoral states on the customary law of equity "in such a way as to leave as much as possible to each party all those parts of the continental shelf that constitutes a natural prolongation of its land territory into and under the sea without encroachment on the mutual prolongation of the land territory of the other."[25] In the end, under the agreement West Germany obtained a larger share of the shelf, stretching to the middle of the North Sea, than it would have if the pure equidistance principle had been applied.

Two other cases (the 1977 arbitral decision regarding the Anglo-French continental shelf and the 1982 case concerning the continental shelf between Libya and Tunisia) were rendered on the principle of equity.[26] The criticism of these rulings has been that too much emphasis had been placed on the length of the coastline or its irregularity, but not much consideration had been given in these rulings to the population, scarcity of land resources and importance of continental shelf resources to the coastal states.[27] The 1982 LOS Convention contained in Article 83(1) the provision that delimitation of the shelf between states with opposite or adjacent coasts shall be made by agreement "on the basis of international law . . . in order to achieve an equitable solution." During the interim, Article 83(3) asked that a "provisional arrangement of a practical nature" be arranged so as "not to jeopardize or hamper the reading of the final agreement."

Table 3.3
Extent of the Continental Shelf

a.	<u>Exploitability criteria</u>	
	Philippines	EXP
b.	<u>Continental margin criteria</u>	
	Bangladesh	CM
c.	<u>200 nautical miles criteria</u>	
	Cote d'Ivoire	200 nm
	Ghana	200 nm
	Peru	200 nm
	Chile*	200/350 nm
d.	<u>200 nautical miles or 100 nautical miles from the 2,500-meter isobath criteria</u>	
	Ecuador**	200 nm/100 nm from 2,500 m isobath
	Madagascar	200 nm/100 nm from 2,500 m isobath
e.	<u>200 meters depth plus exploitability criteria</u>	
	Albania	200 m/EXP
	Argentina	200 m/EXP
	Australia	200 m/EXP
	Bahamas	200 m/EXP
	Bulgaria	200 m/EXP
	Canada	200 m/EXP
	Colombia	200 m/EXP
	Costa Rica	200 m/EXP
	Cyprus	200 m/EXP
	Democratic Kampuchea	200 m/EXP
	Denmark	200 m/EXP
	Egypt	200 m/EXP
	Fiji	200 m/EXP
	Finland	200 m/EXP
	France	200 m/EXP
	German Democratic Republic	200 m/EXP
	Germany, Federal Republic of	200 m/EXP
	Greece	200 m/EXP
	Guatamala	200 m/EXP
	Haiti	200 m/EXP
	Honduras	200 m/EXP
	Israel	200 m/EXP
	Italy	200 m/EXP
	Jamaica	200 m/EXP
	Kenya	200 m/EXP
	Malaysia	200 m/EXP
	Malta	200 m/EXP
	Mexico	200 m/EXP
	Netherlands	200 m/EXP
	Nigeria	200 m/EXP
	Norway	200 m/EXP
	Papua New Guinea	200 m/EXP
	Poland	200 m/EXP
	Portugal	200 m/EXP
	Romania	200 m/EXP
	Sierra Leone	200 m/EXP
	South Africa	200 m/EXP

Table 3.3 (Continued)

e.	200 meters depth plus exploitability criteria	
	Spain	200 m/EXP
	Sudan	200 m/EXP
	Sweden	200 m/EXP
	Thailand	200 m/EXP
	Tonga	200 m/EXP
	Trinidad and Tobago	200 m/EXP
	Ukrainian SSR	200 m/EXP
	United Kingdom	200 m/EXP
	United States	200 m/EXP
	Uruguay	200 m/EXP
	USSR	200 m/EXP
	Venezuela	200 m/EXP
	Yugoslavia	200 m/EXP
	Total with 200 meters depth plus exploitability criteria: 50	
f.	Breadth (200 nautical miles or outer edge of the continental margin criteria)	
	Burma	200 nm/CM
	Cook Islands	200 nm/CM
	Democratic Yemen	200 nm/CM
	Dominican Republic	200 nm/CM
	Guyana	200 nm/CM
	Iceland	200 nm/CM
	India	200 nm/CM
	Mauritania	200 nm/CM
	Mauritius	200 nm/CM
	New Zealand	200 nm/CM
	Pakistan	200 nm/CM
	Senegal	200 nm/CM
	Seychelles	200 nm/CM
	Sri Lanka	200 nm/CM
	Saint Lucia	200 nm/CM
	Vanuatu	200 nm/CM
	Viet Nam	200 nm/CM
	Total with breadth (200 nm) or outer edge of the continental margin criteria: 17	

Note: m/EXP - meter exploitation
nm/CM - nautical mile/continental margin
*350 nautical miles applies to Sala y Gomez and Easter Island.
**100 nautical miles from the 2,500-metre isobath applies to the Galápagos Islands.
Source: *Law of the Sea Bulletin*, no. 11 (July, 1988), pp. 54–56.

Several states, notably Turkey and Venezuela, and to some extent Thailand, considered these provisions unacceptable and unworkable for reaching any agreement on disputed claims of opposite or adjacent continental shelves. There are fifty continental shelf boundary delimitation treaties in existence, and in a number of them the boundary line has been drawn and dictated by the need for economic exploitation of the resources on the continental shelf on a shared basis in a form

Table 3.4
Opposite States Separated by a Continuous Continental Margin More than 400 Nautical Miles Wide, Which Can Be Entirely Claimed

Australia (Heard Island) and Antarctica[1]
United Kingdom (Falkland Island Dependencies) and Antarctica[2]
Sri Lanka and India
Australia (Lord Howe Island) and New Zealand
Australia and France (New Caledonia)
Fiji and Vanuatu or France (New Caledonia)[3]
United Kingdom and Iceland
India and Oman
Denmark (Greenland) and the Soviet Union
Canada and the Soviet Union[4]

[1] This boundary would only be necessary if Australia's claim to Antarctica was not sustained.
[2] This boundary would only be required if Britain's claim to Antarctica was not sustained.
[3] The uncertainty recorded here results from a dispute between France and Vanuatu over the ownership of Hunter and Matthew islands.
[4] It is not clear whether claims to Lomonosov Ridge would be excluded by the convention.
Source: J.R.V. Prescott, *The Maritime Political Boundary of the World* (New York: Methuen, 1985), p. 101. Used by permission.

of a joint arrangement. Examples are the 1976 Frigg gas deposit between Norway and the United Kingdom, the 1969 Persian Gulf resources exploitation between Abu Dhabi and the United Kingdom, and the 1974 joint agreement for the exploitation of resources in the Korean Strait between South Korea and Japan.[28] According to J.R.V. Prescott, who provided Table 3.4, there are several cases involving opposite coastal states that are separated by a continuous continental margin more than 400 nautical miles wide that could be disputed by both states.

The continental shelf doctrine in the 1982 LOS Convention permits the coastal states to claim exclusive jurisdiction for exploration and exploitation of both living and nonliving resources on the seabed and the subsoil of the continental shelf. It allocates, in essence, a large part of the high seas to adjacent coastal states. The doctrine marked the beginning of the process of indefinite expansion in national claims over the ocean space. On the one hand, it minimizes the traditional concept of *res communis*, which expresses the proposition of the sea and the seabed as not subject to appropriation by any state, open and accessible to all. Under the continental shelf doctrine only the area that is beyond the shelf is considered *res communis*. On the other hand, the doctrine of the continental shelf differentiates the seabed on the continental shelf as *res nullius*—that is, the seabed, like land, is capable of being acquired but subject only to development (exploration and exploitation). Furthermore, such exclusive right is not the same as sovereign right—that is, it does not depend on occupation or expressed proclamation as was traditionally the case. In short, the new continental shelf doctrine combines both concepts of *res communis* and *res nullius*; they coexist when it comes to appropriation of the coastal state's resources on the continental shelf, but with common or joint ownership by all states over the area beyond 200 nautical miles. The coexistence of these two traditional concepts in the 1982 LOS Convention sections dealing with the continental shelf represents a political compromise between the demands of the developed nations, which supported *res nullius*, and the large number of Third World developing nations who adhered to *res communis*.

The new continental shelf doctrine points up clearly the crucial importance of the technological capabilities of industrialized nations to explore and exploit the seabed resources on the shelf. While the continental shelf doctrine has opened up, in a geological sense, the entire continental margin to the abyssal plain on the deep seabed, this will enhance the accessibility and acquisition by many coastal states of the new uses of the high seas. For other states, particularly those African states with a very narrow continental shelf, the doctrine is of limited benefit. Some coastal states have very broad continental margins and others have none at all. For thirty-one states that have margins extending beyond the 200-nautical-mile distance, the continental shelf doctrine, as stated in the 1982 LOS Convention, is both politically and economically important. It is more desirable to have some form of international rules that will help guide activities on the continental shelf, even though the language in the 1982 LOS Convention provisions may give rise to future disputes.[29]

EXCLUSIVE ECONOMIC ZONE (EEZ)

Article 55: Specific legal regime of the exclusive economic zone

The exclusive economic zone is an area beyond and adjacent to the territorial sea, subject to the specific legal regime established in this Part, under which the rights and jurisdiction of the coastal State and the rights and freedoms of other States are governed by the relevant provisions of this Convention.

Article 57: Breadth of the exclusive economic zone

The exclusive economic zone shall not extend beyond 200 nautical miles from the baselines from which the breadth of the territorial sea is measured.

The origin of the exclusive economic zone concept grew from a combination of factors. In the first place, technological revolution since the end of World War II had enabled people to exploit the energy (oil and gas) and mineral resources (manganese nodules) on the continental shelf and the seabed extending seaward from the traditional coastal state territorial sea. Second, fishing technology had expanded so rapidly that some stocks of living resources once considered inexhaustible had become depleted or almost extinct due to overfishing. Another important pressure for the establishment of a legal fishery regime and an exclusive economic development zone was the proliferation of unilateral national claims by the developing Third World nations over a vast expanse of water, traditionally a part of the high seas. This proliferation of claims had been inspired and encouraged by the 1945 Truman Proclamation, which asserted national jurisdiction over the continental shelf of the United States. Admittedly, a large portion of these unilateral claims were motivated by the desire of many Latin American and African countries to amend the "abuses" or "injustice" found in some of the traditional law of the sea concepts, such as freedom of the seas. In 1971 one African state alleged that the freedom of the seas principle was being "used as a license to deplete the developing countries of their resources."[30] Thus, the political and economic pressure for an equitable distribution of the wealth of the oceans by resource-poor Third World nations generated the original concept of an exclusive economic zone. As a novel idea in the law of the sea, the exclusive economic zone was as much political and economic as it was ideological in the classic setting of "haves" versus "have nots."

An immediate response to the 1945 Truman Proclamation was made by Mexico and Argentina in 1945 and 1946 when they claimed their own national jurisdiction over the resources in their respective continental shelves. In 1947 Chile and Peru followed suit by declaring jurisdiction over all resources in a 200-nautical-mile zone. Chile's unilateral action was believed to have been motivated by considerations for protecting its whaling operations, establishing a security zone of 200 nautical miles, and for control over fisheries on the superjacent waters of its narrow continental shelf to a seaward limit of 200 nautical miles.[31] The early archetype of the present-day exclusive economic zone was contained in the 1952 Santiago Declaration of Chile, Ecuador and Peru (CEP) for a maritime zone extending 200 nautical miles seaward from their coasts. Their justification was that their people must have access to the necessary protein food and the need for economic development.

Most Latin American nations had reservations about the 1958 Continental Shelf Convention because it was concerned primarily with mineral and energy resources and only secondarily with fisheries in the shelf's superjacent waters. More importantly, as it was pointed out in the discussion on the continental shelf, the 1958 Convention's imprecise definition of the "exploitability" criterion for national claims over the shelf was biased in favor of technologically developed nations.[32] Even more objectionable to the Latin American nations, particularly the CEP group, was that the 1958 Continental Shelf convention granted only "preferential rights" to coastal states in regulating fisheries on the shelf; the licensing system made it possible for the increasingly large distant-water fishing fleets to operate within another nation's coastal waters. While the 1970 Montevideo and Lima Declarations introduced more specifically the limits for a new maritime zone, the 1972 Santo Domingo Declaration by ten Caribbean nations advocated a plan that is very close to the present day 200-nautical-mile EEZ concept. The ten Caribbean nations agreed to:[33]

1. a zone not to exceed 200 nautical miles from the territorial sea, or "patrimonial sea," to be established that would provide coastal states sovereign rights over all renewable and nonrenewable resources on the seabed and the subsoil

2. the right of coastal states to regulate scientific research and to take preventive action on pollution within their zone
3. the retention of the freedom of navigation and overflight enjoyed by all states, as well as for cable and pipeline laying in the submarine space.

The Latin American and the Caribbean states had advanced the idea of a "patrimonial sea," meaning sovereign rights of coastal states over all resources found in the waters and on the seabed and its subsoil over an area adjacent to the territorial sea. African and Asian states organized the Asian-African Legal Consultative Committee in their preparation for the seabed debate scheduled for 1972–1973 called by the United Nations General Assembly. In its 1971 Colombo session it submitted a proposal, made by the delegate from Kenya (Professor Frank X. Njenga), calling for formulation of "a possible basis for a just and equitable accommodation of competing interests of developing coastal states and maritime powers."[34] Kenya was opposed to any future international conferences on the law of the sea being used by developed nations "in their search for empires," without considering the interests of the developing nations. The Kenya representative said that "irresponsible" freedom of fisheries in adjacent waters of territorial seas had led to fishery stock depletion and extinction. Thus, it was argued, a wider belt of water, one measuring 200 nautical miles, should be recognized so as to include almost all of the continental shelf to a depth of 200 meters for an exclusive fishery and conservation zone beyond the traditional territorial waters of coastal states.[35]

This proposal was later refined by a Seminar of African Experts at Yaoundé (Cameroon) in June 1972. For the first time, the term "economic zone" was used to include not only all coastal states, but landlocked states as well. (The word "exclusive" was added later on in the seabed debate to denote coastal states' rights to enact legislation for resources exploitation and protection against pollution within their economic zones).[36] When the UNCLOS III began its Caracas session in 1974, there were at least two main proposals for the establishment of a new special ocean regime: the Latin American Caribbean "patrimonial sea" idea and the African economic zone concept, endorsed by the Organization of African Unity (OAU) in Addis Ababa in April 1973. Two primary differences emerged in these proposals. One concerned the continental shelf: in the Latin American Caribbean proposal a continental shelf regime and a separate "patrimonial sea" existed side by side, whereas under the African proposal, the "economic zone" included most of the world's continental shelf. The second difference concerned the rights of landlocked and geographically disadvantaged states set forward in the African proposal. Fourteen of the then existing fifty African states were landlocked, had narrow coastlines, or were facing closed or semi-closed seas. The Santo Domingo Declaration made no reference to this right.

Developed nations, represented by the United States, Japan and the Soviet Union, at first expressed opposition to the emerging concept of an economic zone because they saw it as an overextension of coastal states' rights beyond the traditional territorial sea. In their initial opposition, they cited freedom of navigation and their preference for wide-ranging naval mobility. Specifically, the United States would recognize the coastal states' right to explore and exploit only seabed resources, but not fisheries. Instead, the United States advanced the controversial "species approach" (discussed in detail in Chapter 5) and less restrictive use of coastal states' power to permit scientific research. At Caracas (1974) the concept of an economic zone received wide support from a majority of Third World nations. By July 1974 the United States' initial opposition to the concept began to soften when it expressed its willingness to accept the 200-nautical-mile economic zone as a part of the "comprehensive package" in a *quid pro quo* for guaranteeing free navigation rights and unimpeded transit through straits. But many Third World nations, known as the Group of 77, insisted on stronger coastal rights within the proposed economic zone. The deadlock was broken when an informed group of legal experts, the Evensen Group, chaired by Norway's Jens Evensen, provided one of the "great compromises" of UNCLOS III. They proposed combining the key provisions of the competing interest groups at the conference: an economic zone of not more than 200 nautical miles from the territorial sea within which the coastal state would enjoy sovereign rights for the purposes of exploration, exploitation and management of all the natural resources, coastal jurisdiction over scientific research, and the right of pollution control. All other states would enjoy the traditional high seas rights, characterized by freedom of navigation, overflight, and laying of cables and pipelines. Evensen's draft became a part of the Informal Single Negotiating Text (ISNT), the basic negotiation draft for the participants in the Geneva session (1975) of UNCLOS III.[37] It was then that the word "exclusive" was inserted, creating the "EEZ."

Since the adoption of the concept by the 1982 LOS Convention, the number of states endorsing the 200-nautical-mile EEZ has grown steadily. By 1982, there were fifty-five states declaring an EEZ; the total number rose to seventy-four by January 1988. This is not to be confused with the fishery zone (EFZ)—for instance, the United States declared an exclusive fishery management zone in the Magnuson Fishery Management and Conservation Act in 1977, but did not declare an EEZ until March 1983 (see Chapter 4). The United States has refused to sign the 1982 LOS Convention because of the disputed deep-seabed-mining provisions, but concedes that the rest of the 1982 LOS Convention provisions on traditional uses of oceans "generally confirm existing ocean laws and practices and balance fairly the interests of all states."[38] On March 10, 1983, President Ronald Reagan proclaimed a United States EEZ that is contiguous to the territorial sea and extends 200 nautical miles into the high seas.[39]

Part V (Articles 55–75) of the 1982 LOS Convention deals with the EEZ in terms of legal regime, rights of coastal and other states in the zone, treatment of different species of fisheries found in the zone, and conservation measures for the utilization of fisheries. This section will focus on the legal status and the rights and duties of coastal and other states. Fishery management and utilization within the EEZ will be discussed separately in Chapters 4 and 5.

Legal Status of the EEZ

There is a conceptual controversy with respect to the legal status of the EEZ. The controversy stems from the lack of a precise definition of the EEZ in Article 55. On the one hand, maritime powers sometimes argue that the zone is still a part of the high seas, even though special rights have been granted to the coastal states for exploitation and exploration of the natural resources found there. This viewpoint was endorsed by the 1984 International Maritime Consultative Organization (IMCO) conference in Chicago. On the other hand, others argue that, since the convention grants substantial rights to the coastal states, it is inconceivable to view the EEZ as a part of the high seas. The EEZ is not a traditional territorial sea, since many features of the high sea principles do prevail in the zone. Thus, the exclusive economic zone must be viewed as a *sui generis* ocean space, a "specific legal regime" that is neither the territorial sea nor the high seas.[40] It is actually a "transitional zone" between the territorial sea and the high seas, within which a centralized management is required of the coastal states for the conservation and use of natural resources. In other words, it is a "halfway house" between the high seas regime and "an ecosystem management" that requires international cooperation. In declaring the EEZ for the United States, President Reagan proclaimed the sovereign rights of the United States for the purposes of "exploring, exploiting, conserving and managing natural resources." He then declared that "the EEZ remains an area beyond the territorial sea of the United States in which all states enjoy the high seas freedom of navigation, overflight, and the laying of submarine cables and pipelines."[41] The intentional omission of a clear definition in Article 55 of the 1982 LOS Convention seems to imply that the EEZ is a "special legal regime" that is altogether different from all other ocean regimes: "the coastal state has the sovereign rights but not sovereignty."

Rights and Jurisdiction of Coastal States

Articles 56 of the 1982 LOS Convention provides "sovereign rights" of the coastal states to enact legislation and regulation of exploration, exploitation, management and conservation of fisheries within the 200-mile EEZ. Under Article 56 the coastal states have "the moral and political obligation" to provide rational management of the resources in the EEZ not only for their own population but for the "world community at large." Subsequently, Articles 61 through 68 impose obligations and responsibilities for coastal states on the size of allowable catch, capacity to harvest fisheries, highly migratory species, marine mammals, and sedentary, anadromous and catadromous species. All of these provisions will be discussed in Chapters 4 and 5.

In terms of nonliving resources, Article 56 also provides the coastal states with the same sovereign rights of exploration, exploitation, management and conservation of the natural resources found on the continental shelf, even though the 1982 LOS Convention does not provide any specific provisions. Under Article 56 coastal states possess new rights in other economic activities, such as technological development in generating alternate energy sources from ocean water current and winds. Under Articles 56(1-b) and 60, a set of limited rights is also given to the coastal states for construction of artificial islands, installations and structures.

In erecting these structures, the coastal states may establish ''safety zones'' which shall not exceed 500 meters (1,500 feet) around them, provided due notice and warning are given, and so long as these installations do not interfere with ''the recognized sealanes'' essential to navigation. Other coastal states' sovereign rights provided by Article 56 include marine scientific research and pollution control with the EEZ. These will be discussed in Chapters 8 and 12, respectively.

Since the EEZ is still a part of the high seas, certain traditional rights are reserved in the EEZ for use by other states. Article 58 and the traditional freedoms contained in Articles 87–115 of the 1982 LOS Convention are applicable if these are not incompatible with the rights in the EEZ. For instance, noncoastal states enjoy freedom of navigation within the EEZ and that freedom is only limited by ''due regard'' for the rights and duties of the coastal states and the laws or regulations imposed by them. In case of conflict, Article 59 stipulates that such disputes must be resolved ''on the basis of equity'' and in the light of all relevant circumstances and the interests of the international community. Some experts suggested that this broad and vague provision will be little help when it comes to dispute settlement within the EEZ between a coastal and a noncoastal state.[43] Oscar Schachter argued that a coastal state may enact conservation and environmental measures, justified on the basis of equity, that will abridge the freedom of navigation by a super oil tanker, a ''high risk'' vessel.[44] Further, disputes may arise concerning naval maneuvers and weapons practice, which traditionally have been considered to come under the purview of navigation, within the EEZ. As the argument goes, since the EEZ is considered to be a part of the high seas, it is reserved for peaceful purposes if such activities as weapons testing are not ''internationally lawful.''[45]

The rules of the high seas, to be discussed shortly, are also applicable in the EEZ. Thus, all states enjoy freedom of overflight in the zone. One possible limitation to the exercise of overflight freedom may be the right of coastal states to erect artificial islands or installations high enough to interfere with low-flying aircraft in the vicinity of these installations. A more serious conflict may arise over whether the rules of the International Civil Aviation Organization (ICAO), which in Article 12 require that all aircraft observe its rules over the high seas, should apply in the EEZ, or whether those of the coastal states that regulate the air space over their own territorial sea should apply. The 1982 LOS Convention does not provide a clear answer to these questions: Is the EEZ a part of the high seas or a territorial sea? Whose rules must aircraft obey during transit within the EEZ: ICAO or the coastal state's regulation?

All states may also enjoy the right to lay submarine cables and pipelines within the EEZ, subject only to the consent of and the conditions laid down by the coastal states. In practice both coastal state and the state that owns the pipeline or cable may exercise joint or concurrent jurisdiction. An example is the 1976 agreement between Norway and the United Kingdom over the Frigg Field Reservoir.

The seventy-four states which had established an EEZ by July 1988 are shown in Table 3.5. In some regions of the world it is not possible for coastal states to claim the full 200-nautical-mile EEZ because it then would overlap with the claims of a neighboring state. Under those conditions, Article 74 of the 1982 LOS Convention requires the concerned states to reach an equitable solution "within a reasonable period of time." Thirty states have agreed that the EEZ boundary is the same as the continental shelf boundary in order to avoid possible disputes that may arise when the two boundaries differ. The 1984 International Court of Justice decision on the case concerning delimitation of the maritime boundaries in the Gulf of Maine for a single boundary dividing the continental shelves and EEZs between the United States and Canada is significant. It not only provided settlement on the United States–Canada maritime boundary dispute in the Gulf of Maine, but it also resolved the conflicting jurisdictional claims over Georges Bank, a major fishing ground, when both nations declared their 200-nautical-mile EFZ in 1977. The case is to be discussed fully in Chapter 4. In June 1990 the United States and the Soviet Union settled their dispute over the 1,600-nautical-mile maritime boundary between Alaska and Siberia by agreeing to accept the 1867 U.S.–Russian Convention line as the maritime boundary along the entire length. The agreement involves transferring resource jurisdiction of one nation or the other. Thus, the agreement places 70 percent of the Bering Sea under United States jurisdiction.

Significance. The establishment of EEZs by seventy-four nations has brought approximately 40 percent of the world's oceans under national jurisdiction for exclusive economic activities that affect living and nonliving resources of the waters superjacent to the seabed and of the seabed and its subsoil. Although the EEZ doctrine was a compromise reached by competing interests that divide the maritime powers and the developing Third World nations, nevertheless it provides a legal justification for coastal states to lay claim over living and nonliving resources off their shorelines. This is particularly important for those coastal states without a continental shelf that must depend heavily on fishery resources. The new EEZ doctrine enables such states to claim a part of the high seas as their exclusive zone for economic activities. The EEZ doctrine widens the coastal states' claim of 200 nautical miles measured from the baseline of their territorial sea once reserved only for maritime powers who possessed sufficient capital and technology to exploit the resources therein.

The EEZ doctrine of coastal states' claim over living and nonliving resources

Table 3.5
Extent of the Exclusive Economic Zone

<u>200-mile limit</u>	
Antigua and Barbuda	200
Bangladesh	200
Barbados	200
Bulgaria	200
Burma	200
Cape Verde	200
Chile	200
Colombia	200
Comoros	200
Cook Islands	200
Costa Rica	200
Côte d'Ivoire	200
Cuba	200
Democratic Kampuchea	200
Democratic People's Republic of Korea	200
Democratic Yemen	200
Djibouti	200
Dominica	200
Dominican Republic	200
Equatorial Guinea	200
Fiji	200
France	200
Gabon	200
Ghana	200
Grenada	200
Guatemala	200
Guinea	200
Guinea-Bissau	200
Haiti	200
Honduras	200
Iceland	200
India	200
Indonesia	200
Kenya	200
Kiribati	200
Madagascar	200
Malaysia	200
Mauritania	200
Mauritius	200
Mexico	200
Morocco	200
Mozambique	200
New Zealand	200
Nigeria	200
Niue	200
Norway	200
Oman	200
Pakistan	200
Philippines	200
Portugal	200
Romania	200
Samoa	200
Sao Tome and Principe	200
Senegal	200

Table 3.5 (Continued)

200-mile limit	
Seychelles	200
Solomon Islands	200
Spain	200
Sri Lanka	200
St. Kitts and Nevis	200
St. Lucia	200
St. Vincent and the Grenadines	200
Suriname	200
Thailand	200
Togo	200
Tonga	200
Trinidad and Tobago	200
Trust Territory of the Pacific Islands	200
Tuvalu	200
Ukrainian SSR	200
United States	200
USSR	200
Vanuatu	200
Venezuela	200
Viet Nam	200

Source: *Law of the Sea Bulletin*, no. 11 (July, 1988), pp. 51–52.

also enlarged the sea-land domain of many coastal states. It has been estimated that "about thirty states stand to gain significantly" by the establishment of the EEZ.[46] The irony is that few of the developing states which initially supported and declared unilaterally for the EEZ have been the main beneficiaries. As shown in Table 3.6, the seven major gainers of the EEZ have been the developed nations of the world.[47]

When the United States declared its 200-nautical-mile EEZ on March 10, 1983, to be contiguous to its territorial sea—including zones contiguous to the territorial sea of the United States, Puerto Rico, Northern Marianas and its other overseas territories and possessions—it established a zone that covers about 2.2 million square nautical miles of ocean. Under the 1983 EEZ declaration, the Hawaiian chain of islands alone gained about 600,000 square nautical miles.

FREEDOM OF THE HIGH SEAS

Article 86: Application of the provisions of this Part

The provisions of this Part apply to all parts of the sea that are not included in the exclusive economic zone, in the territorial sea or in the internal waters of a State, or in the archipelagic waters of an archipelagic State. This article does not entail any abridgement of the freedoms enjoyed by all States in the exclusive economic zone in accordance with article 58.

Table 3.6
States with the Largest Exclusive Economic Zones

Developed States	Developing States	Approximate Area in Square Nautical Miles
1. United States		2,222,000
2. Australia		2,043,300
	3. Indonesia	1,577,300
4. New Zealand		1,409,500
5. Canada		1,370,000
6. Soviet Union		1,309,500
7. Japan		1,126,000
	8. Brazil	924,000
	9. Mexico	831,500
	10. Chile	667,300
11. Norway		590,500
	12. India	587,000
	13. Philippines	551,400
14. Portugal		517,400
	15. Madagascar	376,800
Subtotal, top seven developing states		5,515,300 (34%)
Subtotal, top eight developed states		10,588,200 (66%)
Total, top fifteen states		16,103,500 (100%)

Note: Several newly independent states in the South Pacific with large zones and very small or nonexistent navies are not included. Zones sizes indicated are from baselines to the 200-nm limit (territorial and EEZ). In cases of archipelagic states, archipelagic waters within archipelagic baselines are not included.

Source: U.S. Department of State, Office of the Geographer, *Theoretical Areal Allocations of Seabed to Coastal States Based on Certain U.N. Seabeds Committee Proposals*, International Boundary Study, Series A: Limits in the Seas, no. 46, 12 August 1972 (Washington, D.C.: GPO, 1972); Lewis M. Alexander and Robert D. Hodgson, "The Impact of the 200-Mile Economic Zone on the Law of the Sea," *San Diego Law Review* 12 (April 1975), pp. 574–575; and reprinted in *Ocean Yearbook 3* Elisabeth Mann Borgese and Norton Ginsberg, eds. (Chicago: Univ. of Chicago, 1983), p. 346. By permission of the publisher.

Article 87: Freedom of the high seas

1. The high seas are open to all States, whether coastal or land-locked. Freedom of the high seas is exercised under the conditions laid down by this convention and by other rules of international law. It comprises, *inter alia*, both for coastal and land-locked States:

(a) freedom of navigation;

(b) freedom of overflight;

(c) freedom to lay submarine cables and pipelines, subject to Part VI;

(d) freedom to construct artificial islands and other installations permitted under international law, subject to Part VI;

(e) freedom of fishing, subject to the conditions laid down in section 2;

(f) freedom of scientific research, subject to Parts VI and XIII.

2. These freedoms shall be exercised by all States with due regard for the interests of other States in their exercise of the freedom of the high seas, and also with due regard for the rights under this Convention with respect to activities in the Area.

The high seas doctrine is not only one of the oldest, but also the most fundamental of all the principles in the law of the seas. The seas were not always free and open for all, even though the Roman jurist, Marcianus, had proposed the principle in the second century A.D. In the *Digest of Justinian* Marcianus stated that all men had the right to use the sea for commercial and navigation purposes. During the era of the Roman Empire the sea could be policed or controlled partially, but there was no exclusive ownership.[48] Free use of the ocean was not observed after the collapse of the Roman Empire. During the Middle Ages, Venice exercised dominion over the Adriatic Sea, Sweden claimed the Baltic, Denmark-Norway considered all northern seas their jurisdiction, and England laid claim over a large part of the Atlantic and the North Sea. Thomas W. Fulton painted a chaotic picture of control of the sea in *Sovereignty of the Sea*. There was a state of anarchy so far as navigation and commerce were concerned. Free use of the seas was interrupted by roving pirates and by attacks of "freebooters."[49] Then, with the Treaty of Tordesillas in 1494, Spain placed the Pacific Ocean under its jurisdiction and Portugal claimed the Atlantic and Indian oceans.

For the period from the thirteenth century to the early part of the sixteenth century, large portions of the seas were more or less under the exclusive control of any state capable of exercising its jurisdiction. Here was the beginning of *res nullius*, and the seas were subject to appropriation by anyone. After the discovery of America, in dividing the world and the seas between them, Spain and Portugal denied other European seafaring and trading nations, particularly the Dutch and the English, freedom to use the trading routes and sealanes to the riches of the East Indies and China. In 1580, when Spain protested to England about the exploits of Sir Francis Drake in the Pacific, Queen Elizabeth I answered that the sea was common to all and that no one should have title to the oceans.[50] The very idea of free access to the sea was espoused in jurisdictional terms by the Dutch jurist, Hugo De Groot (Grotius). In his treatise, *De Mare Liberum* (1609), Grotius advanced the proposition that no one could claim sovereignty over the seas, which were too immense for anyone to effectively occupy. The treatise was jurist Grotius's legal brief in defense of the seizure of a Portuguese ship by the Dutch East Indies Company. In addition, Grotius pointed out that there was plenty of room in the ocean for navigation and fishing, then the two major uses of the ocean, and that there was no need to appropriate the high seas as sovereign claims. Oceans, in Grotius's view, could be used by all without loss to anyone. (Grotius's premise of the inexhaustibility of ocean resources is no longer valid in the twentieth century.)

Grotius's concept of free and open access (*res communis*) to the oceans dominated the maritime world for the next 300 years. The only rebuttal to his thesis was advanced by John Selden, who argued in 1635 for *De Mare Clausum*, a nation's right to enclose a portion of the sea and exclude others from fishing in it as England had done with parts of the North Atlantic. Selden rejected the Grotian thesis that the seas were inexhaustible. Instead, he argued that nations had the right to enclose and "regulate" the oceans. But as it became a major maritime power ruling the waves in subsequent centuries, Britain soon abandoned the Selden idea of closed seas. Britain became a staunch supporter of the Grotian concept of open and free seas for all.

In many ways Britain epitomized the essence of freedom of the seas, then limited to navigation, commercial and fishing purposes. By the middle of the nineteenth century, freedom of the high seas, as distinct from a narrow belt of waters where coastal states exercised territorial sovereignty, was a well-established doctrine. The concept was so well accepted that by 1826 the Supreme Court of the United States defined the high seas as "the common highway of all, appropriate to the use of all."[51] There were many court decisions in Great Britain and the United States that upheld the high seas principle. The exercise of sovereign state jurisdiction on the high seas was limited only to piracy and the contiguous zone for customs and immigration. There were not even restrictions for conservation purposes, such as protecting the fur seals in the Bering Sea at the turn of the century. The free and open high seas doctrine worked well as long as the major maritime powers adhered to it and other states supported it. With the expansion of ocean enclosure by the coastal states, the development in ocean technology during the period between the two world wars, and the emergence of new states after World War II, confusion developed as to (1) the definition of the high seas, (2) the meaning and extent of the freedoms of the high seas, and (3) the responsibilities of a flag state on the high seas.

Having failed to delimit the extent of the territorial sea, UNCLOS I in 1958 made an attempt to address these problems concerning the high seas and to codify state practices. "High seas" was defined in the 1958 convention as "all parts of the sea that are not included in the territorial sea or in the internal waters of a state." By the 1970s the above definition needed modification as new claims, in the form of the exclusive economic or preferential fishing zones, were advanced. The 1982 LOS Convention defined the high seas in Article 86 as "all parts of the sea that are not included in the exclusive economic zone, in the territorial sea or in the internal waters of a state, or in the archipelagic waters of an archipelagic state." This represents a significant reduction in the high seas definition. According to one study, the distribution of high seas has been narrowed to sixteen areas in the world. Aside from the largest areas of the Atlantic, Pacific and Arctic oceans, the remaining high seas are "enclaves" surrounded by national waters. More startling is Prescott's conclusion that "there are no high seas in the Mediterranean, Baltic, North, Black and Red Seas, Yellow Sea, South China Sea, East China Sea, the Persian Gulf, and the Sea of Japan."[52] As of 1988, the 200-nautical-mile EEZ claimed by seventy-four states comprised more than 40 percent of the ocean space.

The 1958 Convention on the High Seas listed the traditional four freedoms that should be enjoyed by all states: navigation, fishing, overflight, cable and pipeline laying. The 1982 LOS Convention added two more freedoms: freedom to construct artificial islands and freedom of scientific research on the high seas. As a concession to the African group of nations, it also added a provision, under Article 87, that "the high seas are open to all states, whether coastal or land-locked." The listing of these freedoms of the high seas represents the primary purposes for which states use the high seas.[53] Today, freedom of navigation means the transport of goods and cargo so essential in international commerce and trade, as does the freedom of overflight. Next in importance comes the freedom of fishing. Equally important are the uses of the high seas for security and political purposes, for communications (submarine cables), for scientific research in locating both living and nonliving resources, for recreational and for waste disposal purposes.[54] Article 87(2) of the 1982 LOS Convention also speaks of "due regard" for the interests of other states in the exercise of high seas freedoms, as well as the international ocean regime (the seabed) established under the convention. Cable laying and the construction of artificial islands and installations on the continental shelf may be regulated by the coastal states or with their consent (Articles 78–81). Under Articles 116–120 even the freedom of fishing is subject to treaty arrangements and national laws for the conservation and management of living resources in the areas of the high seas.

Article 88 of the 1982 LOS Convention states that the high seas shall be reserved for peaceful purposes. But testing and naval maneuvers on the high seas are generally acceptable, so long as these are not considered "acts of aggression" as interpreted by the naval powers.[55] State practices call for notification to seafarers to keep out of the areas designated for military exercises. In 1974 Australia and New Zealand filed a protest in the International Court of Justice over French nuclear testing in the Pacific, which they claimed interfered with ships on the high seas. The court did not take up the case because the French terminated the testing. In the opinion of one legal scholar, even though Article 95 of the 1982 LOS Convention grants warships on the high seas "complete immunity from the jurisdictions of any state other than the flag state," governments conducting missile tests on the high seas may be liable to damages to civilian ships or aircraft resulting from the military exercise.[56]

International customary law provides a well-developed set of duties and responsibilities for the flag state on the high seas. These are codified in Articles 91–98 of the 1982 LOS Convention, dealing with ship registration and status, safety at sea, compensation for damages to cables and pipelines, collision and the duty to render assistance for ships in distress on the high seas.

Freedom of the high seas does not mean lawlessness. Three types of unlawful activities are prohibited on the high seas by the 1982 LOS Convention: piracy (Articles 100–107), transport of illicit drugs and slaves (Articles 108 and 99), and unauthorized broadcasting from the high seas (Article 109). In Article 101, the Convention defines piracy as "any illegal acts of violence or detention, or any act of depredation, committed for private ends by the crew or passengers of a private ship or private aircraft," directed on the high seas against another ship or aircraft or against persons or property on board a ship or an aircraft. A warship is permitted to board a foreign ship on the high seas if there are reasonable grounds to suspect unlawful acts of piracy, slave trade or unauthorized broadcasting. However, if the suspicion for boarding a vessel is unfounded, Article 110 provides the injured party compensation for any loss or damage sustained.

Unauthorized broadcasting on the high seas involves unlicensed transmission stations based on foreign vessels on the high seas for "transmitting radio or television broadcasts intended for reception by the general public not in accordance with national regulations." Violators may be arrested and prosecuted by a state which has jurisdiction over the unauthorized broadcasting, even though the unlawful act is committed on the high seas (Article 109). In 1990 the Chinese dissidents, after having escaped from China and exiled in France in the aftermath of the June 4, 1989, Tiananmen Square bloody crackdown, launched a ship with the intention of sailing close to the coast of China, but on international waters, for the purpose of broadcasting messages of democracy and human rights to China. The ship, *Goddess of Democracy*, was refused cooperation and needed assistance by Taiwan, Hong Kong and Japanese authorities on grounds of violation of Article 109 and for fear of Chinese intervention and arrest, a right provided to the state where broadcasting transmission can be received. As a result, the whole effort was abandoned in May 1990.

Significance. The doctrine that the high seas belong to no one and are to be used by all has been generally accepted as an important part of customary international law. The traditional high seas regime has been enforced since the mid-seventeenth century by major maritime powers of the world, who desired then, as they do now, the freedom of their maritime operations on the vast expanse of the open and high seas. The doctrine in its traditional sense has enabled the maritime powers not only to expand their trade routes worldwide, but to acquire their overseas empires. Also, maximation of ocean space open to all has been beneficial to smaller and lesser maritime states as well, for they, too, could enjoy the traditional freedoms of navigation and fishing for the benefit of their people.

The traditional concept of high seas began to be challenged as technological sophistication expanded following World War II. These technological advancements altered the uses of the oceans traditionally guaranteed by freedom of the high seas. For instance, coastal states cannot ignore the consequences of overfishing by depleting the fishery stock under the doctrine of freedom to fish on the high seas. There are now additional responsibilities on the part of the coastal states to expand their national jurisdiction beyond the traditional narrow belt of water from the shoreline comprising the territorial sea and the contiguous zone for the conservation and rational management of the living resources. Coastal states, as well as landlocked and geographically disadvantaged states, want a share of the wealth found on the continental shelf and the deep seabed.

Contemporary claims on the uses of the oceans raise questions about the jurisdictional content and nature of the high seas, and the traditional freedoms closely associated with it. Expansion of national jurisdiction into the high seas created conflicts and uncertainties about the meaning of the high seas doctrine and the traditional high seas freedoms. The 1958 Convention on the High Seas (UNCLOS I) and UNCLOS III were signed and convened because of the urgent need, not only to establish universally accepted rules dealing with conflicting claims over areas beyond coastal-state jurisdiction, but also to accommodate contemporary challenges to the fundamental concept of the high seas and its uses.

While the 1982 LOS Convention reaffirmed the traditional freedom of the high seas, it still leaves room for conflicting interpretation with regard to deep seabed mining beyond the limits of national jurisdiction. For instance, can a sovereign state or a corporation chartered by its nationals have the freedom to mine deep seabed resources beyond the limits of national jurisdiction? There has been a large measure of modification made in the traditional freedom of fishing on the high seas, which is now subject to conservation and management requirements based on the ecosystem of the living resources. While the exclusiveness of the flag-state jurisdiction is still the key principle for the high seas under the 1982 LOS Convention, it nevertheless was excluded from the special EEZ regime but included in the section on archipelagic waters—a case of inconsistency in the application of the high seas definition. Finally, the 1982 LOS Convention has contributed to further erosion of the high seas area by the various enclosure provisions in the treaty: the continental shelf regime, the 200-nautical-mile exclusive economic and fishing zones, and the deep seabed regime for exploration and exploitation of nonliving resources beyond the limits of national jurisdiction.

HOT PURSUIT

As a corollary to the high seas doctrine, the customary rule in international law known as "hot pursuit" refers to the right of a coastal state to apprehend a foreign vessel that is believed to have committed a crime within its territorial waters but has then sailed away onto the high seas. There is the classic case of the *I'm Alone* (1935), a rum-laden vessel intent on engaging in the illegal act of smuggling prohibited by the Volstead Act enacted by the United States Congress. When discovered, the vessel escaped into the high seas, some 200 nautical miles off the coast, whereupon it was sunk by a pursuing United States Coast Guard cutter.[57] Hot pursuit, as a rule in customary international law, had been challenged as a violation of the freedom of the high seas in many disputes. In an attempt to codify this controversial rule in customary international law, the 1958 Convention on the High Seas provided the following rule in Article 23:

> Hot pursuit of a foreign vessel may be made by competent coastal state authorities if there is good reason to believe a law violation has occurred. Such pursuit must commence when the foreign ship is within the pursuing state's territorial sea or the contiguous zone and must be continued into the high seas without any interruption. The right of hot pursuit must cease when the suspected foreign vessel enters the territorial sea of its own state or of a third state.

In the decades following the end of World War II, the hot pursuit doctrine became more controversial, primarily because of its ambiguous position with respect to the contiguous and fishery zones claimed by many coastal states: these zones were generally considered a part of the high seas. A brief summary of a selected number of recent cases may illustrate the problems concerning hot pursuit on the high seas.

In 1952 Peru declared its sovereignty over the sea to a distance of 200 nautical miles from its coast. Two years later, Peru's naval and air units seized five of Aristotle Onassis's whaling vessels flying the Panamanian flag within the declared 200-nautical-mile zone. In the chase, two of the whaling vessels were seized 160 nautical miles off the Peruvian coast and three others were attacked by Peru's naval units some 300 nautical miles offshore. Panama protested that its registered vessels had been attacked by the Peruvian navy and pursued on the high seas, a violation of the doctrine of hot pursuit. During the 1950s and 1960s, there were numerous incidents of seizure by Mexico and Ecuador of American fishing vessels fishing in the 200-nautical-mile zone claimed by these Latin American states. Other more serious incidents involving the right of hot pursuit have occurred. In one case, in 1972 a Soviet survey vessel was detained and interned at port by Indonesia but escaped into the high seas. In 1968 five Soviet trawlers were sighted 120 nautical miles off the coast of Argentina by its aircraft. In a coordinated pursuit Argentine warships were deployed 200 nautical miles from shore and captured two of the five Soviet ships. One captured Soviet ship escaped from armed escort about twenty-five nautical miles off the coast. Argentine warplanes vectored and opened fire on the escaped Soviet vessel on the high seas. In the 1974 *Taiyo Maru* case, involving a Japanese fishing vessel which was fishing within the United States' twelve-mile (three-mile territorial sea plus nine miles) contiguous fishery zone. The United States Coast Guard engaged in hot pursuit into the high seas and made an arrest. The Japanese contested that, under Article 23 of the 1958 Convention on the High Seas, the fishery zone was not a contiguous zone. The U.S. federal court ruled that the United States could establish a fishery conservation zone even though admittedly the fishery zone established by the Bartlet Act was not a contiguous zone; therefore the Court then ruled that hot pursuit could commence there into the high seas. The ruling was criticized by some as "an assault on the freedom of the high seas."[58]

The 1982 LOS Convention extends the coastal state's right of hot pursuit to commence, in addition to the territorial sea and the contiguous zone, from archipelagic waters and the continental shelf, including safety zones around continental shelf installations and special economic zones (Article 111).

It seems, debatably, that hot pursuit does not cease when the offending vessel enters its own EEZ or that of a third state. The right of hot pursuit on the continental shelf implies the exercise by a coastal state of "both legislative and enforcement jurisdiction" on the high seas when the continental shelf is more than 200 nautical miles. Article 111(6) in the 1982 LOS Convention provides basic rules for aircraft engaged in hot pursuit: "The aircraft giving the order to stop must actively pursue the vessel" and "it does not suffice to justify an arrest outside of the territorial sea that the ship was merely sighted by the aircraft."

Significance. Hot pursuit represents the only example in which a coastal state can exercise its national jurisdiction on the high seas. Under the 1982 LOS Convention, hot pursuit is a recognized "enforcement tool" for a coastal state to enforce fishery conservation and management laws, as well as national and international measures for regulating pollution against the ocean environment.

The right of hot pursuit may be aided in the future by the use of more advanced and sophisticated aerial surveillance techniques (satellites) employed to detect possible violations by foreign vessels in the territorial sea in contiguous and special economic zones, and on the continental shelf to a distance of more than 200 nautical miles. In any event, under the 1982 LOS Convention, the exercise of the right of hot pursuit, particularly in the new maritime zones, will make it more defensible for coastal states to enforce their legislative jurisdiction; but it may also give rise to international disputes in the future. A legal officer of the United States Coast Guard points out the need to develop functional procedure standards governing hot pursuit in the light of modern, sophisticated tracking technologies such as observation by radar, underwater sensors and satellites being used nowadays to revolutionize maritime enforcement operations. The traditional concept of hot pursuit was based on the past assumptions of three-mile territorial sea and local fishing.[59]

INNOCENT PASSAGE

Article 17:

Subject to this Convention, ships of all States, whether coastal or land-locked, enjoy the right of passage through the territorial sea.

Article 18: Meaning of passage

1. Passage means navigation through the territorial sea for the purpose of:

   (a) traversing the sea without entering internal waters or calling at a roadstead or port facility outside internal waters; or

   (b) proceeding to or from internal waters or a call at such roadstead or port facility.

2. Passage shall be continuous and expeditious. However, passage includes stopping and anchoring, but only in so far as the same are incidental to ordinary navigation or are rendered necessary by *force majeure* or distress or for the purpose of rendering assistance to persons, ships or aircraft in danger or distress.

Article 19: Meaning of innocent passage

1. Passage is innocent so long as it is not prejudicial to the peace, good order or security of the coastal State. Such passage shall take place in conformity with this Convention and with other rules of international law.

2. Passage of a foreign ship shall be considered to be prejudicial to the peace, good order or security of the coastal State if in the territorial sea it engages in any of the following activities. . . .

While high seas open and accessible to all is an important principle under customary international law, the right of ships of all states to seek passage through the territorial waters of a foreign coastal state without interference is also a fundamental customary rule in navigation, dating to the time of Vattel. For a long time the concept, or notion, of innocent passage needed clear definition. Equally unclear were the rights and duties of the coastal states in regulating innocent passage of vessels through their territorial waters or straits. Also, there was the need to define conditions of innocent passage under which warships could cover territorial waters of another state in order to avoid conflict.

The 1982 LOS Convention provides answers to these uncertainties in state practices with respect to innocent passage. It is sufficient to say here, before these specific provisions are discussed, that negotiation and drafting of the pertinent articles on innocent passage at the UNCLOS III benefited, in a large measure, from the work done at the 1930 Hague Conference and the UNCLOS I in 1958, particularly Articles 14–20 in the Convention on the Territorial Sea and the Contiguous Zone. In the 1982 LOS Convention, innocent passage is defined in Article 18 as navigation through the territorial sea for two main purposes: traversing that part of the sea without entering the internal waters, or calling at a roadstead or port facility outside internal waters, proceeding to or from internal waters or a call at port facilities. Innocent passage must be "continuous and expeditious." This rules out anchoring or hovering in the territorial sea, except when the ship or aircraft is in distress or in danger that requires emergency assistance. In short, the 1982 LOS Convention incorporated the wording as well as the intent of Article 14 in the 1958 Convention on the Territorial Sea and the Contiguous Zone as generally accepted rules in international law. However, Article 19 of the 1982 LOS Convention provides a set of specific, objective criteria for determining when the passage is or is not innocent. The acceptance or incorporation of these specific criteria by which to measure innocent passage must be viewed in the context of the ideological and political contest between the competing interests of the coastal states on the one hand, and the maritime powers' concerns on the other.[60] For the coastal states, a large number of them emergent Third World nations, sovereign integrity and security of territorial waters and contiguous zones are paramount, whereas the maritime powers are more concerned with unimpeded navigational rights of their naval vessels and stress the need for "maximum naval mobility" and the right of their distant-water fishery fleets to sail the vast oceans. Thus, Article 19 represents a delicate balance of divergent interests between the coastal states and the maritime powers.

Article 19(1) defines passage as innocent if it is not prejudicial to the peace, good, order and security of the coastal state. This means, then, that foreign military activities in the territorial sea or the contiguous zone must be prohibited; otherwise coastal states are placed in the vulnerable position of being intimidated or attacked by a foreign naval force. Then Article 19(2) specifies the types of activities by a foreign ship while passing through the territorial waters of a coastal state that are considered to be prejudicial to peace, good, order and security of the coastal state, or noninnocent:

1. the use of force against the coastal state's sovereignty, territorial integrity or political independence or in violation of the United Nations Charter
2. the exercise of weapons of any kind
3. the gathering of information affecting the security or the spread of propaganda
4. the launching, landing or taking on board of any aircraft or of any military device
5. any activities in violation of the coastal state's customs, fiscal, immigration or sanitary laws and regulations
6. willful acts of pollution, any fishing activities, acts that interfere with any system of communication or such facilities and installations of the coastal state
7. any other act that has no direct bearing on passage

Under Article 21, innocent passage through the territorial water can be regulated by the coastal states. The coastal states can enact laws and regulations relating to innocent passage in these areas: navigational safety and traffic; protection of navigational aids, cables, pipelines; the conservation of fisheries; environmental protection and pollution control; scientific research and hydrographic surveys; and for customs, fiscal, navigation and sanitary reasons. For purposes of navigational safety, the coastal states may require foreign ships exercising innocent passage within their territorial sea to observe sealanes designated by the coastal states, particularly those sealanes so designated for tankers, nuclear-powered ships and ships carrying nuclear substances. These ships must, when exercising innocent passage, carry documents and observe regulations established by the coastal states.

The coastal states must also assume responsibility for not hampering the innocent passage of foreign ships through the territorial sea, for example, by imposing requirements that create the effect of denying or impairing the right of innocent passage. Nor can the coastal state discriminate against any ships carrying cargos to, from, or on behalf of another state. It is also the duty of the coastal state to warn others of any hazards to navigation within the territorial sea. Finally, the coastal state can prevent passage that is not innocent or can suspend temporarily a specific area in the territorial sea from passage for reasons of security (Article 25). The coastal state does not have the right to make criminal arrest or conduct criminal investigation on board a foreign ship unless

1. under Article 27, the consequences of the crime extend to the coastal state
2. the nature of the crime is to disturb the peace or good order of the territorial sea
3. a request for local assistance has been made by the shipmaster or by a diplomatic/consular officer of the flag state
4. for taking the necessary measures to suppress illicit drug traffic.

The part of the 1982 LOS Convention on innocent passage that has been subject to uncertainty is innocent or noninnocent passage of warships—an issue of strategic importance to major maritime powers such as the United States, the United Kingdom, France and the Soviet Union. There have been repeated cases of challenges by warships seeking innocent passage through international straits and territorial waters of another state. These cases range from the 1946 dispute over the Corfu Channel between the United Kingdom and Albania to the 1988 ramming of two U.S. cruisers in the Black Sea by Soviet vessels. The United States Navy has steadfastly maintained that the right of innocent passage must be exercised, or it will be lost. There have also been serious incidents of non-innocent passage of unidentified submarines in Norwegian and Swedish waters (1982). The 1982 LOS Convention has not provided clear and unambiguous language in dealing with some of the most recent incidents involving warships in the coastal state's territorial water.

Prior to the mid–1850s, in state practice, there was no specific differentiation between a merchant ship and a warship for innocent passage through territorial waters. A warship was then considered a ''floating extension'' of the sovereign state and thus remained immune from the jurisdiction of other states.[61] By the turn of the century, however, the right of innocent passage for warships became a subject of controversy between those ''jurisdictionalists'' who believed it was the customary right for coastal states to grant warships innocent passage and those ''territorialists'' who viewed that passage by warships could be denied by the coastal states.[62] The ''jurisdictionalist'' view was supported by the International Court of Justice (ICJ) in its 1949 ruling in the Corfu Channel case, in which the court held that it was customary law to allow innocent passage by warships through straits for international navigation.

A decade later the 1958 Convention on the Territorial Sea and the Contiguous Zone reaffirmed the right of innocent passage for warships in the territorial sea.[63] It has been argued that Article 23 of the 1958 Convention permits warships the right of innocent passage by virtue of the fact that it specifically provides sanction for the coastal state to require a warship to leave its territorial sea if the warship does not comply with or disregards the coastal state's regulations concerning passage through the territorial sea.[64] An attempt was made, but failed, at the 1958 Law of the Sea Conference (UNCLOS I) negotiations to require ''prior authorization'' by the coastal states for the right of innocent passage for warships. The attempt to require ''prior authorization'' for a warship's innocent passage in the territorial sea was revived by a number of coastal states at the UNCLOS III, but it also failed. This led to a protest by thirty states, mostly from the Third World, plus Finland and Sweden (for these two states already required prior notification of warship transit through their territorial waters), over the warship transit articles being drafted at the August 1980 general debate of the resumed ninth session of the UNCLOS III.[65]

The 1982 LOS Convention approved separate articles for warships in transit through the territorial sea. Article 30 borrowed the identical wording that appeared in Article 23 of the 1958 Convention, namely, that if a warship does not comply with the coastal state's laws and regulations or disregards requests for compliance made to it, the warship must immediately leave or be expelled from the territorial sea—the last word is the only significant word added by the 1982 LOS Convention. Under Article 20, submarines and other underwater vessels must surface and show their flag when in transit through territorial waters. Thus the 1982 LOS Convention, at least nominally, provides warships with the same rights of transit and innocent passage as it does merchant ships. However, state practices do not seem to have reflected the right of innocent passage for warships as provided in the 1982 LOS Convention. At least twenty-one states have enacted laws that require "prior notice or authorization" for a warship's right to innocent passage in their territorial waters:[66] Albania, Algeria, Brazil, Bulgaria, Burma, Denmark, Dominican Republic, Germany (Democratic Republic), Guyana, India, Maldives, Pakistan, Poland, Romania, Seychelles, Somalia, Sri Lanka, Sudan, Sweden, the Soviet Union and Yemen (P.D.R.).

Significance. The detailed set of criteria contained in the 1982 LOS Convention for determining when a passage is innocent would appear on face value designed to reduce the latitude of coastal states for narrow interpretations on the right of innocent passage. However, the 1982 LOS Convention permits the coastal states to enact legislation and regulations not only for navigational safety and traffic, but for conservation of fisheries and, most important, for pollution control or prevention of environmental threat—a problem posed by oil spills from supertankers plying through straits and the introduction of liquid natural gas (LNG) carriers. Recognition that the coastal states may rule such passage by supertankers and LNG carriers as noninnocent and subject to its regulations has, in reality, altered to a great extent the traditional concept of innocent passage, which generally has meant unlimited passage in the territorial sea.

Coastal state regulations that require "prior authorization" or "prior notice" for a warship's right to innocent passage in the territorial sea seem to contradict or are in conflict with the requirement embodied in Article 24 of the 1982 LOS Convention, which charges the coastal state with the duty not to hamper the innocent passage of foreign ships through its territorial sea. Thus, there is incongruity between a recognized principle in customary international law and state practice. In a rapidly changing world, a world of ICBMs, depleting resources, and competing national claims to the oceans, the traditional right of innocent passage has also undergone some significant alterations in the various provisions of the 1982 LOS Convention. While these new rules may not lessen the chances for conflict, they nevertheless do reflect one of the political realities of the present world: the assertiveness of the numerically strong Third World nations who demand changes in the traditional international law that would benefit them.

In September 1989 the governments of the United States and the Soviet Union entered into an agreement concerning the uniform interpretation of norms governing innocent passage in the territorial sea. The agreement specifies that all ships, including warships, enjoy the right of innocent passage, in accordance with Article 19 of the 1982 LOS Convention, without prior notification or authorization.

STRAITS: REGIME OF TRANSIT PASSAGE THROUGH STRAITS

Article 38: Right of transit passage

1. In straits referred to in article 37, all ships and aircraft enjoy the right of transit passage, which shall not be impeded; except that, if the strait is formed by an island of a State bordering the strait and its mainland, transit passage shall not apply if there exists seaward of the island a route through the high seas or through an exclusive economic zone of similar convenience with respect to navigational and hydrographical characteristics.

2. Transit passage means the exercise in accordance with this Part of the freedom of navigation and overflight solely for the purpose of continuous and expeditious transit of the strait between one part of the high seas or an exclusive economic zone and another part of the high seas or an exclusive economic zone. However, the requirement of continuous and expeditious transit does not preclude passage through the strait for the purpose of entering, leaving or returning from a State bordering the strait, subject to the conditions of entry to that State.

3. Any activity which is not an exercise of the right of transit passage through a strait remains subject to the other applicable provisions of this Convention.

Article 45: Innocent passage

1. The regime of innocent passage, in accordance with Part II, section 3, shall apply in straits used for international navigation:

(a) excluded from the application of the regime of transit passage under article 38, paragraph 1; or

(b) between a part of the high seas or an exclusive economic zone and the territorial sea of a foreign State.

2. There shall be no suspension of innocent passage through such straits.

For international navigation purposes, a strait is defined as a "narrow strip of water connecting two other bodies of water, at least one of which is outside the comprehensive, exclusive competence of any state."[67] Straits are in a sense "bridges" or "crossroads" that connect one ocean with another or the high seas to the territorial water of a state. In many ways "it is the legal status of the waters constituting the strait and their use by international shipping" that determines the rights of a coastal state governing transit through it.[68]

There are as many as 116 straits in the world with varying widths. Some straits may consist partly of territorial sea and partly of high seas. If a strait that connects two other bodies of water is broader than the territorial waters claimed by coastal states on both sides, then a corridor of high seas is provided. Under such a situation no legal problem would arise with respect to unimpeded free navigation, the most basic of all customary rules in international law. Problems do arise if the strait is made up of territorial waters of one or more coastal states. In that case only the right of innocent passage is applicable, subject to temporary suspension by the coastal state. For centuries state practices have permitted the right of innocent passage through those straits, such as the Straits of Gibraltar and Malacca, which are considered important in terms of their geographic location and traffic volume, so long as such passage does not pose a threat to the security of a coastal state. Thus, even if a strait's width is less than the combined breadth of territorial waters claimed by the coastal states on both sides, the right of free transit may still prevail if the strait is indispensable for international navigation.

When the waters of a narrow strait are under the jurisdiction of a coastal state, then the strait becomes a part of the coastal state's territorial water. The width of the Bosphorus and the Dardanelles, which connect the Mediterranean and the Aegean Seas to the Black Sea, is barely one mile, and the waters surrounding the straits are the territorial waters of Turkey. When Turkey controlled the shores of the Black Sea, it exercised rights over transit passage through the straits. By the eighteenth century Russia became a Black Sea power and challenged Turkish sovereignty over the waters. Turkey was forced to enter into a treaty relationship with various European powers to permit free transit passage rights for merchant vessels, not warships, through the Bosphorus and the Dardanelles. In fact, the 1923 Treaty of Lausanne placed the two straits under international control, which to a large extent guaranteed freedom of navigation to and from the Mediterranean, in addition to demilitarizing the waters. This international regulation of transit through the Bosphorus and Dardanelles straits was followed by the 1936 Montreux Convention between eight European nations (Bulgaria, France, Greece, Italy, Romania, Turkey, the Soviet Union, Yugoslavia) and Japan. The Montreux Convention contained these features:

1. free transit passage through the straits by merchant ships in peace and war, so long as Turkey was not a party to the war
2. denial of free passage to warships in time of war, and if Turkey was a belligerent or it felt its security threatened, then free passage must be approved by two-thirds majority of the League of Nations
3. in time of peace, unlimited transit passage rights for warships of all Black Sea powers in single formation
4. a quota system for all non–Black Sea power warships.

In contrast to the Bosphorus and Dardanelles, because of its vital importance to international shipping and navigation, there has been no treaty arrangement that governs transit through the Strait of Gibraltar. As a consequence, there is little legal or political controversy over the right of free transit through the Strait of Gibraltar. In the case of Are Sund that connects the North Sea and the Baltic, at one time Denmark required fees for its use, but in 1857 abandoned that practice in deference to the demands of users that the strait be kept free and accessible to all. In 1881, by a treaty between Chile and Argentina, the Strait of Magellan was made free for navigation by all states and remains free today.

The right of warships to free transit passage through the straits was a matter of legal and diplomatic debate until the 1949 Corfu Channel case. In state practices there was a differentiated treatment between a merchant vessel and a warship. Before the 1936 Montreux Convention, under Turkish national policies, which were influenced at times by other European powers, free warship passage through the Bosphorus and Dardanelles was rarely certain. McDougal and Burke point out that before World War I, as straits became more important and strategic in competitive power politics and relatively less so in commerce, warship access to free transit passage was a crucial consideration in the competing objectives of Russia for excluding foreign warships from the Black Sea, on the one hand, and for gaining access for Russian warships to the Mediterranean, on the other.[69]

The British wanted to exclude the Russian fleet from access to the Mediterranean and the Black seas. The 1936 Montreux Convention represented a change in British policy that sought accommodation as it secured its control and influence over India and Egypt.[70] As mentioned earlier, under the 1936 Montreux Convention, in peacetime warships enjoyed "complete freedom of passage by day and night under any flag, without any formalities or tax or charge whatever." The exception was in time of war when Turkey was a belligerent; then, and only then, the passage of warships was to be controlled by Turkey. Thus it was the established rule in customary international law that in time of peace there must be no obstacle to the right of warships for transit passage through straits. The rule was reaffirmed in the 1949 judgment of the International Court of Justice in the Corfu Channel case.

The 1946 Corfu Channel dispute arose from the British insistence on free transit passage of warships through a body of water that lies between the Greek island of Corfu and the coasts of Greece and Albania, a situation in which parts of the strait fall within the territorial seas of both countries. Two British naval vessels were fired on by Albanian shore batteries when they were in the Albanian part of the strait. The British maintained the right of innocent passage while Albania insisted on "prior notification" and permission. When the British vessels sailed through the strait as a means of testing the Albanian claim to its right, they struck mines that caused casualty to lives and damage to the ships. The case then went to the International Court of Justice (ICJ) for an opinion on the questions of Albanian responsibility and its failure to notify the British of the mine field, as well as the British claim for the right of innocent passage of warships. On the latter issue the ICJ ruled clearly that it was the recognized international custom that "states in times of peace have a right to send their warships through straits used for international navigation between two parts of the high seas without the previous authorization of a coastal state, provided that the passage is innocent.''

The 1949 ruling by the ICJ in the Corfu Channel case was enshrined in the 1958 Convention on the Territorial Sea and the Contiguous Zone. Article 16(4) of the Convention, ratified by forty-four nations, stated that ''There shall be no suspension of the innocent passage of foreign ships through straits which are used for international navigation between one part of the high seas and another part of the high seas or the territorial sea of a foreign state.''[71]

The 1958 Convention left the door ajar in Article 16(1) when it declared that ''the coastal state may take the necessary steps in its territorial sea to prevent passage which is not innocent,'' without specifying what constitutes noninnocent passage. Thus, Article 16(1) could presumably become a license for coastal states to impede passage of nuclear-powered ships or those carrying harmful substances through straits. The 1958 Convention also failed to provide guidelines with respect to overflight by aircraft over the territorial waters of the strait state. By the mid–1960s, as more coastal states claimed unilaterally expanded territorial seas from the traditional breadth of three miles to more than twelve nautical miles, and as national security needs of the maritime powers began to be tied in closely with free access to transit passage through straits, it became obvious that a new regime for the straits had become a major issue from the perspective of major maritime powers in their negotiations in the law of the sea conferences. In Article 3, the 1982 LOS Convention provides for a twelve-nautical-mile zone as the breadth of the territorial sea. As a consequence, 106 of the 116 straits for international navigation are overlapped or closed by twelve-nautical-mile territorial seas, since the widths of these straits are less than twenty-four nautical miles (see Table 3.7).

The issue of unimpeded transit through straits for international navigation was an important issue at the UNCLOS III in the 1970s. The maritime powers had insisted on the right of unimpeded passage through all the straits on grounds of freedom of navigation and the need for their navies to maintain mobility. In addition, the 1958 Convention's provision of innocent passage was inadequate in that it applied to neither aircraft nor submarines in transit through international straits. Both the United States and the Soviet Union negotiated hard on the issue of transit rights through straits. Third World nations, the Group of 77, insisted that the right of innocent passage was sufficient to allow coastal states to regulate international navigation for reasons of national security and pollution control against oil spills from tankers. It was to the maritime power's global strategic advantage to insist on unimpeded transit rights by all vessels and aircraft through the straits. During 1972–1973 there emerged a ''package deal'' under which the United States would accept a twelve-nautical-mile territorial sea if unimpeded passage was guaranteed through, over and under all international straits that overlapped the twelve-nautical-mile territorial boundaries. In addition, along with the ''package deal,'' the United States would be willing to accept a new 200-nautical-mile fishing zone desired by most developing nations.[72]

Table 3.7
Widths of Straits and Channels That Would Be Overlapped by a Twelve-Mile Territorial Sea*

Passage (Clockwise by Regions)	Sovereignty (on Either Side)	Least-Width (Nautical Miles)	Passage (Clockwise by Regions)	Sovereignty (on Either Side)	Least-Width (Nautical Miles)
	Anglo-America (10)			Latin America (12)	
Robeson Channel	Canada/Denmark	10	Turks Island Passage	United Kingdom	13
Strait of Belle Isle	Canada	9	Mouchoir Passage	United Kingdom	23
Jacques Cartier Passage	Canada	15	Virgin Passage	United States	8
Northlumberland Strait	Canada	7	Dominica Channel	France/United Kingdom	16
Santa Barbara Channel	United States	11	Martinique Passage	France/United Kingdom	22
Strait of Juan de Fuca	United States/Canada	9	St. Lucia Channel	France/United Kingdom	17
Hecate Strait	Canada	24	St. Vincent Passage	United Kingdom	23
Unimak Pass	United States	10	Dragon's Mouth	Trinidad and Tobago/Venezuela	6
Shelikof Strait	United States	20	Serpent's Mouth	Trinidad and Tobago/Venezuela	8
Bering Strait	United States/USSR	19	Araba-Paraguana Passage	Netherlands/Venezuela	15
			Estrecho de la Maire	Argentina	16
			Strait of Magellan	Argentina/Chile	2
	Europe (18)			Far East (18)	
Bosporus	Turkey	1	Kuril Strait	USSR	6
Dardanelles	Turkey	1	Estorofu Kaikyo	USSR/USSR Administration	22
Karpathos Strait	Greece	23	Kunashiri Suido	USSR Administration	12
Strait of Messina	Italy	2	Shikotan Suido	USSR Administration	12
Strait between Elba and Italy	Italy	5	Taraku Suido	USSR Administration	6
			Notsuke	Japan/USSR Administration	9

Strait of Bonificio	France/Italy	6
Strait of Gibraltar	Morocco/Spain	8
The Solent	United Kingdom	2
North Channel	United Kingdom	11
Little Minch	United Kingdom	10
North Minch	United Kingdom	20
Pentland Firth	United Kingdom	5
The Hole	United Kingdom	23
Ore Sund	Denmark/Sweden	2
Bornholmsgat	Denmark/Sweden	19
Kalmar Sund	Sweden	2
Entrance to Gulf of Bothnia	Finland/Sweden	17
Entrance to Gulf of Finland	Estonia/Finland	23

Soya Kaikyo	Japan/USSR	23
Tsugara Kaikyo	Japan	10
Western Chosen Strait	Japan/Korea	23
Cheju Haehyop	Korea	12
Maemul Suido	Korea	13
Huksan Chedo	Korea	8
Pohai Strait	China	22
Osumi Kaikyo	Japan	16
Tokara Kaikyo	Japan	22
Penghu Shuitao	China	17
Lema Channel	China/United Kingdom	6
Hainan Strait	China	10

Southeast Asia (26)

Babuyan Channel	Philippines	15
Polillo Strait	Philippines	10
Maqueda Channel	Philippines	4
Verde Island Passage	Philippines	4
San Bernardino Passage	Philippines	8
Mindoro Strait	Philippines	20
Surigao Strait	Philippines	10
Basilan Passage	Philippines	7
Siburu Passage	Philippines	18
Bangka Passage	Indonesia	19
Selat Grehund	Indonesia	10
Koti Passage	Indonesia	10
Serasan Passage	Indonesia	23
Api Passage	Indonesia	16

Oceania (18)

Alalakeiki Channel	United States	6
Kealaikahiki Channel	United States	15
Auau Channel	United States	8
Pailolo Channel	United States	8
Kalohi Channel	United States	8
Kaiwi Channel	United States	22
Kaulakahi Channel	United States	15
Apolima Strait	Western Samoa	4
Indispensable Strait	United Kingdom	19
Manning Strait	United Kingdom	6
Bougainville Strait	United Kingdom	15

Table 3.7 (Continued)

Passage (Clockwise by Regions)	Sovereignty (on Either Side)	Least-Width (Nautical Miles)	Passage (Clockwise by Regions)	Sovereignty (on Either Side)	Least-Width (Nautical Miles)
	Southeast Asia (26)			Oceania (18)	
Selat Ombai	Indonesia/Portugal	16	St. George's Channel	Australia	8
Selat Roti	Indonesia	6			
Selat Sape	Indonesia	8	Goschen Strait	Australia	7
Selat Alas	Indonesia	5	Dampier Strait	Australia	13
Selat Lombok	Indonesia	11	Vitiar Strait	Australia	24
Selat Bali	Indonesia	2	Cook Strait	New Zealand	12
Selat Sunda	Indonesia	12	Banks Strait	Australia	8
Gaspar Strait	Indonesia	8	Floveaux	New Zealand	15
Selat Bangka	Indonesia	8			
Berhala Strait	Indonesia	9		Miscellaneous (4)	
Strait of Malacca (North)	Indonesia/Malaysia	20	Kara Strait	USSR	19
			Palk Strait	Ceylon/India	3
Strait of Malacca (South)	Indonesia/Malaysia	8	Strait of Hormuz	Iran/Muscat & Oman	21
			Bab el Mandeb	France/Yemen	14

Note: For exact geographical situations, consult Lay, Churchill, and Nordquist, *New Directions on the Law of the Sea*, vol. 2 (1973), pp. 885–891.

*Consequently, they must be 24 miles in width or less. There are 106 straits in total which would be overlapped.

Source David L. Larson, ed., *Major Issues of the Law of the Sea* (Durham: The University of New Hampshire, 1976), pp. 133–135. Used by permission.

The 1982 LOS Convention recognized four categories of straits used for international navigation. First, under Article 35(c), is "the legal regime in straits in which passage is regulated in whole or in part by long-standing international conventions in force, specifically relating to such straits." Falling within this category are the Danish Strait (by the 1857 Copenhagen Treaty and the Treaty for Redemption of the Sound Dues); the Bosphorus and the Dardanelles straits (under the 1936 Montreux Convention); the Straits of Magellan (by the 1881 treaty between Argentina and Chile); and the Strait of Gibraltar (by the 1904 Anglo-French Declaration). The second category of straits includes those under Article 36, in which "a strait used for international navigation if there exists through the strait a route through the high seas or through an exclusive economic zone of similar convenience with respect to navigational and hydrographical characteristics" or is more than twenty-four nautical miles wide, where full freedom of navigation and overflight apply (Florida Strait between the United States and Cuba). The third category of straits refers to, under Article 37 and Article 38(1), "straits which are used for international navigation between one part of the high seas or an exclusive economic zone and another part of the high seas or an exclusive economic zone." For this category of straits, which most likely applies to a majority for international navigation, all vessels and aircraft shall enjoy the right of transit passage. However, under Article 38(1), the exception is "if the strait is formed by an island of a state bordering the strait and its mainland" and "if there exists seaward of the island a route through the high seas or through an exclusive economic zone"—the so-called island exception as described by Churchill and Lowe.[73] Thus, straits of Pemba (Pemba Island and Tanzania in East Africa), Messina (Sicily and the Italian mainland) and Corfu (island of Corfu and the Albanian coast) are examples of "island exceptions."

Transit passage is defined by the 1982 LOS Convention as freedom of navigation and overflight solely for the purpose of continuous and expeditious transit. In exercising the right of transit passage, ships and aircraft must

1. proceed without delay through the strait
2. refrain from any threat or use of force against the sovereignty of states bordering the strait
3. comply with accepted international regulations, procedures for safety at sea, including prevention of collisions, and the Rules of the Air established by the International Civil Aviation Organization (ICAO) for aircraft.

States bordering the straits may designate sea lanes and traffic separation schemes, as well as laws for prevention, reduction and control of pollution.

The fourth category of straits is provided for under Article 45: the high seas to territorial sea category—those straits excluded in Article 38(1), the "island exceptions," and those that lie "between a part of the high seas or an exclusive economic zone and the territorial sea of a foreign state." Falling under this category of straits used for international navigation are the Strait of Tiran, Head Harbor Passage, the Strait of Georgia and the Gulf of Honduras, all of which are overlapped by a three-mile territorial sea. For this category there shall be no suspension of innocent passage through such straits, a reaffirmation of the 1949 Corfu Channel ruling by the ICJ and the 1958 Convention on the Territorial Sea and the Contiguous Zone as customary international law governing straits used for international navigation.

Significance. The international navigation regimes on innocent and transit passage through straits established in the 1982 LOS Convention represent compromises for reconciling competing interests. These measures are intended to find a balance in the needs of the world community, not only those of maritime powers for guarantees of meaningful and reasonable high seas usage, but also the understandable concerns of strait states, mostly the developing Third World nations. The principles contained in the transit passage sections uphold the long-standing international convention that regulates international navigation through some of the most important straits of the world. In the words of John Norton Moore, a negotiator on the portions regarding straits, the 1982 LOS Convention on transit passage broadens the Corfu Channel decision by extending ''non-suspendable innocent passage to straits connecting to 'the territorial sea of a foreign state.' ''[74] In fact, Article 45 created a special regime of ''non-suspendable innocent passage rather than mere innocent passage.''[75] Thus, the 1982 LOS Convention both strengthens and improves the regime of innocent passage through the territorial sea. For example, the regulatory competence of the coastal states has been clarified under Article 21 in areas of maritime traffic, safety, cable protection, fishery conservation, pollution prevention, regulation on customs, and sanitation. (The 1958 Convention on the Territorial Sea and the Contiguous Zone failed to deal with the environmental problems associated with innocent passage.) More important, under the 1982 LOS Convention on regime for the straits, the right of overflight by aircraft has been made a general rule of ocean law. But the right of submerged transit through straits, a key point stressed by the maritime powers such as the United Kingdom, the United States and the Soviet Union, is not clear enough under Article 39(1). John Norton Moore's claim of the right of submarines for submerged transit as ''recognized'' by the 1982 LOS Convention may have been based on ''an understanding'' among the negotiators.[76] W. Michael Reisman prefers the text agreed upon at the 1978 Camp David summit meeting of heads of states which dealt with the Middle East crisis: ''The Straits of Tiran and the Gulf of Aqaba are international waterways to be open to all nations for unimpeded and non-suspendable freedom of navigation and overflight.''[77]

Current state practices indicate some disagreement with those provisions on transit passage through straits discussed here. Strait states such as Malaysia, Indonesia and Singapore still assert that they have full ''autonomy'' over the use of the Malacca Strait, including navigation. Article 43 of the 1982 LOS Convention mandates user states and strait states to seek cooperative measures for safety aids. Japan is the only major user state to have cooperated with Malaysia, Indonesia and Singapore in the Strait of Malacca. In the case of the

Singapore Strait, some 61 to 87 percent of the vessels using the strait call at the port of Singapore. This seems to be in conflict with Article 38(2) which calls for continuous and expeditious transit by vessels and aircraft. It is not clear whether the right-of-transit passage is enjoyed only by vessels that do not call at the ports in the straits of Malacca and Singapore.[78] There are uncertainties and ambiguities in the 1982 LOS Convention regarding transit passage for straits, which may encourage dissent on legal grounds by the powers on the Baltic Straits.[79] The unresolved dispute between Chile, Argentina and the British Falkland Islands over the Beagle Channel continues to threaten navigation through the eastern mouth of the Strait of Magellan, as well as the unresolved legal issues related to the Korean Strait, an important ocean passage for South Korea and Japan. South Korea requires prior notification by warships transiting the western portion of the Korean Strait.[80]

TERRITORIAL SEA

Article 3: Breadth of the territorial sea

Every State has the right to establish the breadth of its territorial sea up to a limit not exceeding 12 nautical miles, measured from the baselines determined in accordance with this Convention.

Article 4: Outer limit of the territorial sea

The outer limit of the territorial sea is the line every point of which is at a distance from the nearest point of the baseline equal to the breadth of the territorial sea.

Article 5: Normal baseline

Except where otherwise provided in the Convention, the normal baseline for measuring the breadth of the territorial sea is the low-water line along the coast as marked on large-scale charts officially recognized by the coastal State.

Territorial sea, a term codified at the 1930 Hague Conference, is one of the oldest concepts in the law of the seas. It denotes the idea that the sovereignty, or the territorial jurisdiction, of a coastal state extends to an adjacent belt of water beyond the land territory and internal waters. At various times it has been referred to as "territorial waters," "marginal sea," and "littoral sea." The origin of the territorial sea concept may be traced to the Theory of the Glassators of the ancient Roman Empire for the suppression of piracy at sea and for the extension of Caesar's jurisdiction over the sea.[81] From the fourteenth to the sixteenth centuries jurists such as Bartolus and Gentili advocated ownership of coastal waters adjoining the land.[82] Even Grotius, the advocate for freedom of the seas, *res communis*, implied in his works that it was possible for the coastal state to control, but not own, a small zone beyond the land.[83] By the end of the seventeenth and early eighteenth centuries, the "twin pillars" of freedom of the high seas and sovereignty over an adjacent belt of water beyond the coast were well established in state practices. What caused controversy was not so much the concept of the territorial sea itself, but the numerous, varied and inconsistent national claims over the breadth of the adjacent water off the coast.

While the 1930 Hague Conference on codification failed to reach any agreement on the numerous national claims over the territorial sea, nevertheless it removed doubts concerning the legal status of the territorial sea by defining it: "the territory of a state includes a belt of sea . . . as the territorial sea." Also unsettled were the controversial issues of the methods of delimiting boundaries between opposite and adjacent states; the manner of baseline drawing; the legal status of the seabed, subsoil and airspace of the territorial sea; the treatment of islands and internal waters; and the rights and duties of coastal states. But the most controversial of all these issues regarding the territorial sea has been what constitutes the appropriate breadth of the territorial sea or how far the territorial sea can be extended into the high seas.

Breadth of Territorial Sea

At the heart of the issue has been the desire on the part of coastal states to extend their national jurisdiction to ever-greater distances from the shore in order to exercise coastal jurisdiction over (1) increasingly scarce ocean resources, (2) the growth of shipping traffic, and (3) pollution that poses a threat to a coastal state's environment. The situation that existed before the 1958 UNCLOS I was that the major maritime powers of the world insisted on a narrow territorial sea extending only three miles offshore. The well-established national claim of three miles was accepted by most European states and the United States, as originally attributed to the "cannon-shot" rule, but modified by Scandinavian practices.[84]

Some states claimed a territorial sea of twelve nautical miles and a few nations from Latin America made extensive claims to as far as 200 nautical miles. These territorial sea claims beyond the traditional three-mile limit were made on the basis of national security and economic needs. No fewer than thirteen proposals were introduced at the 1958 UNCLOS I on a variety of limits for the breadth of the territorial sea, ranging from the traditional three to six to twelve nautical miles, coupled by a fishery zone of six to no more than twelve nautical miles. However, none of the proposals received the necessary two-thirds majority vote at the 1958 UNCLOS I. The issue of the breadth of the territorial sea was again a major item for the 1960 UNCLOS II at Geneva. Various formulas on the basis of a territorial, plus a fishing zone, were debated; but only one, proposed jointly by sixteen developing nations for a twelve-nautical-mile limit, came close to adoption by the 1958 conference; it died for a lack of only one vote for the required two-thirds majority. Thus, the pattern of territorial sea claims that existed in 1960 was as follows: twenty-two states claimed three nautical miles, eighteen claimed four to ten nautical miles, eleven claimed twelve nautical miles, and two more than twelve nautical miles.

Between 1967 and 1975, territorial sea claims took a decisive turn in favor of twelve nautical miles. In 1967, about twenty-six nations claimed a twelve-nautical-mile territorial sea. By 1975, the number had increased to fifty-six nations for a twelve-nautical-mile territorial sea. At the same time there was also a significant increase in the number of states that claimed a territorial sea of more than twelve nautical miles, from twelve nations in 1967 to twenty-two nations in 1975.[85] During this period there was a significant change in U.S. policy with regard to the breadth of the territorial sea. John Stevenson, U.S. chief negotiator to the UNCLOS III, spoke publicly about the United States' willingness to revise its traditional policy of three to twelve nautical miles as a "package deal" or as a *quid pro quo* for a guarantee for a free transit passage through international straits, as discussed earlier. Both the United States and the Soviet Union had entered into negotiations in 1967 for an international agreement on a twelve-nautical-mile territorial sea, if free strait transit were guaranteed. By the time the Caracas session of the UNCLOS III was convened in 1973–1974, there was a general consensus favoring an agreement of a twelve-nautical-mile territorial sea breadth, except among the "territorialists" of Latin America (Brazil, Ecuador, Panama, Peru and Uruguay) and the coastal African states who adhered to an extended 200-nautical-mile territorial sea boundary. Their desire was to bring their coastal water under national control to keep out foreign fishing and to prevent pollution by vessels. Article 3 of the 1982 LOS Convention now states, "Every state has the right to establish the breadth of its territorial sea up to a limit not exceeding 12 nautical miles."

State practices on the breadth of the territorial sea since the signing of the 1982 LOS Convention remain diverse.[86] As of July 1988, national claims on the territorial sea are delineated in Table 3.8.

Baseline Measurement

The baseline is the line of points from which the territorial sea is measured.[87] The farther the baseline is from the shore, the more area of territorial sea a coastal state can claim as its national jurisdiction. The baseline is the starting point of a national claim to the sea. Since the seventeenth century two practices, or formulas, have been used to measure or delimit the territorial sea. One is the extreme headland to extreme headland. This method is considered convenient because it can include the deeply cut coast or a coast with a fringe of islands. The other commonly used method is to draw the baseline by following the contour of the coast, the trace parallel.

Until 1951, there was no general agreement among nations as to where the baseline should begin: low-water mark or high tide. In 1951 the continuing dispute over fishing came to a head between the United Kingdom and Norway, which used the headland-to-headland formula for measuring the baseline along its island-fringed coast, in order to keep British fishermen off the Norwegian coast. The United Kingdom took the position that the baseline of Norway's territorial sea should be measured from the low-water mark. In the 1951 Anglo-

Table 3.8
Extent of the Territorial Sea

12-mile limit

Algeria	12
Antigua and Barbuda	12
Bangladesh	12
Barbados	12
Brunei Darussalam	12
Bulgaria	12
Burma	12
Canada	12
Cape Verde	12
Chile	12
China	12
Colombia	12
Comoros	12
Cook Islands	12
Costa Rica	12
Cote d'Ivoire	12
Cuba	12
Cyprus	12
Democratic Kampuchea	12
Democratic People's Republic of Korea	12
Democratic Yemen	12
Djibouti	12
Dominica	12
Egypt	12
Equatorial Guinea	12
Ethiopia	12
Fiji	12
France	12
Gabon	12
Gambia	12
German Democratic Republic	12
Ghana	12
Grenada	12
Guatemala	12
Guinea	12
Guinea-Bissau	12
Guyana	12
Haiti	12
Honduras	12
Iceland	12
India	12
Indonesia	12
Iran (Islamic Republic of)	12
Iraq	12
Israel[5]	12
Italy	12
Jamaica	12
Japan	12
United Arab Emirates[2]	12
United Kingdom	12
USSR	12
Vanuatu	12
Venezuela	12
Kenya	12
Kiribati	12
Kuwait	12
Lebanon	12
Libyan Arab Jamahiriya	12
Madagascar	12
Malaysia	12
Maldives	12
Malta	12
Mauritania	12
Mauritius	12
Mexico	12
Monaco	12
Morocco	12
Mozambique	12
Nauru	12
Netherlands	12
New Zealand	12
Niue	12
Oman	12
Pakistan	12
Papua New Guinea	12
Poland	12
Portugal	12
Republic of Korea	12
Romania	12
Samoa	12
Sao Tome and Principe	12
Saudi Arabia	12
Senegal	12
Seychelles	12
Solomon Islands	12
South Africa	12
Spain	12
Sri Lanka	12
St. Kitts and Nevis	12
St. Lucia	12
St. Vincent and the Grenadines	12
Sudan	12
Suriname	12
Sweden	12
Thailand	12
Tonga	12
Trinidad and Tobago	12
Tunisia	12
Turkey[1]	12
Tuvalu	12
Ukrainian SSR	12
Vietnam	12
Yemen	12
Yugoslavia	12
Zaire	12

Total with 12-mile limit: 106

Table 3.8 (Continued)

Limit less than 12 miles			
Australia	3	Finland	4
Bahamas	3	Norway	4
Bahrain	3	Total with 4-mile limit: 2	
Belize	3		
Denmark	3	Dominican Republic	6
Germany, Federal Republic of[3]	3	Greece	6
Ireland	3	Turkey[4]	6
Jordan	3	Total with 6-mile limit: 3	
Qatar	3		
Singapore	3		
United Arab Emirates[2]	3		
United States	3		
Total with 3-mile limit: 12			
Limit exceeding 12 miles			
Albania	15	Argentina	200
Angola	20	Benin	200
Nigeria	30	Brazil	200
Togo	30	Congo	200
Syrian Arab Republic	35	Ecuador	200
Cameroon	50	El Salvador	200
United Republic of Tanzania	50	Liberia	200
		Nicaragua	200
		Panama	200
		Peru	200
		Sierra Leone	200
		Somalia	200
		Uruguay	200
		Total with 200-mile limit: 13	

[1] Applies to the Mediterranean and Black seas. Turkey also has a 6-mile limit in the Aegean Sea.
[2] The 12-mile limit applies only to Sharga.
[3] A decree was promulgated on 12 November 1984 on the Extension of the Territorial Sea of the Federal Republic of Germany in the North Sea for Preventing Tanker Casualties in the German Bight. See *Law of the Sea Bulletin*, no. 7, April 1986.
[4] Applies to the Aegean Sea. Turkey also has a 12-mile limit in the Mediterranean and Black seas.
[5] On 5 February 1990 Israel extended its territorial sea to 12 miles.
Source: *Law of the Sea Bulletin*, no. 11 (July, 1988), pp. 46–49.

Norwegian Fishery case, the International Court of Justice ruled in favor of Norway by declaring that the baseline measurement drawn across the fjords, the rugged geographic features of the Norwegian coastline, was not contrary to international law, so long as it was conforming to the general direction of the coast. Based on that ruling, the 1958 Convention on the Territorial Sea and the Contiguous Zone states in Article 3 that, "Except where otherwise provided, the normal baseline for measuring the breadth of the territorial sea is the low-water line along the coast as marked on a large-scale chart officially recognized by the coastal state." Then, in Article 5, it provides the exception that when the coast line is indented or if there is a fringe of islands along it, the method of straight line measurement can be used to include harbor works and low-tide elevations.

Both methods for measuring the baseline of the territorial sea were incorporated in the 1982 LOS Convention as Article 5 (normal baseline) and Article 7 (straight baseline). The straight baseline method is designed to link the farther points of the low-water line when the coastal line is deeply indented or there is a fringe if islands along the coast. Article 14 of the 1982 LOS Convention allows a coastal state to use either of these methods, or a mixed method, for measuring the baseline of the territorial sea to meet the special geographic features of the coastal state. Article 7(6) states that the system of straight baseline must not ''cut off'' the territorial sea of another state from the high seas or an exclusive economic zone. All waters on the landward side of the straight baseline for the territorial sea are ''internal waters,'' which are under the full sovereignty of the coastal state according to customary international law. By definition internal waters include harbors, bays and river mouths. However, if the straight baseline has the effect of enclosing the internal water areas not previously considered as such, a right of innocent passage exists in those waters (Article 8).

Rules for Delimiting Opposing or Adjacent Coastlines

Controversies have developed between two states with coastlines facing each other and where the breadth of their territorial sea is twenty-four nautical miles or less. There have been inconsistent state practices for resolving these controversies. The 1927 agreement by the United Kingdom and the Sultan of Johore, and the 1932 Danish-Swedish Declaration over the Oresund, applied the principle of the median line to delimit the territorial sea, a line that is equidistant from opposite points on the coast for each state. (See Appendix IIIA for a list of bilateral agreements on maritime boundary delimitation.) Article 15 of the 1982 LOS Convention adopted the agreed upon rule contained in Article 12 of the 1958 Convention on the Territorial Sea and Contiguous Zone that in the absence of agreement, no state is allowed to extend its territorial sea beyond the median line, every point of which is equidistant from the nearest points on the baselines from which the territorial sea of each is measured. An exception to this rule applies when historic title or other special circumstances of politics, geography or economics require a variance. The median-equidistance rule has also been used in delimiting the territorial seas of adjacent coastal states. The November 20, 1976, boundary delimitation agreement between Colombia and Panama is one such example.

In Articles 17–32, the 1982 LOS Convention does provide the right of innocent passage in the territorial sea, discussed previously in this chapter. But the 1982 LOS Convention failed to resolve the divergent state views and practices concerning the coastal states' rights to apply laws to foreign vessels in transit through the territorial sea. Some contend that a coastal state has jurisdiction over specific matters, such as navigation, customs, sanitation and security, but cannot impose all of its general law.[88] However, others argue that there is no limit imposed on a coastal state to exercise its sovereign rights in the territorial sea, including applying legislative acts to foreign vessels as an integral part of exercising its sovereignty. The United Kingdom has been a consistent upholder of the "plenary jurisdiction" view, tempered at times with exceptions.[89] In Article 21(1) the 1982 LOS Convention specifies the right of the coastal state to adopt laws and regulations on matters of navigational safety, protection of navigational facilities, cables and pipelines, conservation and prevention of infringement of fisheries laws, pollution control, in addition to customs, fiscal, immigration or sanitary laws and regulations of the coastal states. Then in Article 21(4) it requires all foreign ships exercising innocent passage through the territorial sea to comply with all such laws and regulations and all generally accepted international rules on collision prevention at sea.

Significance. The 1982 LOS Convention certainly has accomplished a significant achievement where other law of the sea conferences in the past failed: the general agreement by 106 nations, as of 1988, on the breadth of the territorial sea not to exceed twelve nautical miles. It may be argued that the agreement on the twelve-nautical-mile breadth of the territorial sea was made possible by the United States' willingness to accept it as a trade-off for a guarantee on the right of free transit passage through straits.

Another unique achievement of the 1982 LOS Convention is the agreement on methods for measuring the baseline of the territorial sea in order to resolve maritime boundary disputes. The normal baseline is the low-water line along the coast. For an indented or irregular coast or one where there is a fringe of islands along the coast, a straight baseline joining the appropriate points on the coast is used to measure the territorial sea. It is important to note that, without establishing the baseline to be used by the coastal state, it would not be possible to determine the outer edge of the internal waters, as well as the outer edge of the territorial sea, the contiguous zone, and the exclusive economic zone.

While the breadth of the territorial sea as measured from the baseline has set a uniform standard for common international limits on national maritime claims, in practice the use of the low-water-mark line permits the "widest possible area of sea" to the coastal states. Since the 1982 LOS Convention does not require that there shall be uniform low-water marks on all official charts, a coastal state could presumably select different data for different areas of the coast in determining the lowest water line.

Problems may also arise in the application of Article 15 dealing with the delimitation of territorial waters between opposite and adjacent states. An exception to the equidistance line is provided if there is a historic site or special circumstances that varies the equidistance rule. By defining what constitutes the "historic site" or "special circumstances," any coastal state could refuse the equidistance rule in a disputed maritime boundary delimitation case. There are now sixty states in the world that have definitely proclaimed straight baselines for delimiting their national maritime boundaries.

NOTES

1. Giulio Pontecorvo, ed., *The New Order of the Oceans: The Advent of a Managed Environment* (New York: Columbia University Press, 1986), pp. 1–7.

2. See Sayre A. Swarztrauber, *The Three-Mile Limit of Territorial Sea* (Annapolis, Md.: Naval Institute Press, 1972), pp. 10–22. Also, David L. Larson, ed., *Major Issues of the Law of the Sea* (Durham, N.H.: University of New Hampshire, 1976), pp. 2–4.

3. Pontecorvo, ed. *The New Order of the Oceans*, p. 3.

4. H. Gary Knight, *The Law of the Sea: Documents and Notes* (Baton Rouge: Louisiana State University Law School, 1969), p. 44; and R. R. Churchill and A. V. Lowe, *The Law of the Sea* (Manchester, England: Manchester University Press, 1983), p. 53. Also see John Seldon, *Of the Dominion or Ownership of the Sea* (London: Needham, 1923).

5. Pontecorvo, ed., *The New Order of the Oceans*, pp. 1–7.

6. Position paper prepared by the Philippines for the 1958 United Nations Conference on the Law of the Sea, I. Statement of Jose D. Ingles, Undersecretary of Foreign Affairs, at the Diplomatic Symposium, June 28, 1973: "The Archipelagic Principle," p. 6.

7. *United Nations Third Conference on the Law of the Sea*, Official Records, vol. 3, Summary of Meetings, Caracas, 20 June–29 August 1974, p. 260.

8. Ibid.

9. Text of Article 4 of the 1958 Convention on the Territorial Sea and Contiguous Zone can be found in Gerard J. Mangone, *The Elements of International Law: A Casebook* (Homewood, Ill.: The Dorsey Press, 1963), p. 179.

10. See UN Document A/9021 and A/Conf.62/C.2/L.49 in *Third United Nations Conference on the Law of the Sea*, Official Records, vol. 2, Summary of Meetings, Second Session: Caracas, 20 June–29 August 1974, pp. 262–263.

11. Article 46 of the 1982 LOS Convention.

12. See text of UN General Assembly Resolution 2749 (XXV), 17 December 1970. It can be found in *The Yearbook of the United Nations*, vol. 24 (United Nations: Office of Public Information, 1970), pp. 66–68.

13. Hersch Lauterpacht, "Sovereignty over Submarine Areas," *British Year Book of International Law* 27 (1951), p. 399.

14. R. P. Barston and Patricia Birnie, *The Maritime Dimension* (Boston: Allen and Unwin, 1980), p. 6.

15. For a more thorough discussion on the common heritage principle, see Jon Van Dyke and Christopher Yuen, " 'Common Heritage' v. 'Freedom of the High Seas': Which Governs the Seabed?" *San Diego Law Review* 19, no. 3 (1982): 493–551.

16. Larson, *Major Issues of the Law of the Sea*, p. 38. The quote is a paraphrase of the draft by the Preparatory Committee. For the original text see *Supplement to the American Journal of International Law: Official Documents* 24 (1930): 235.

17. The information on Hovering Acts is culled from Swarztrauber, *The Three-Mile Limit of Territorial Sea*, pp. 50–51 and 70–71.

18. Information on the U.S. state practice on the use of the contiguous zone is also culled from Swarztrauber, *The Three-Mile Limit of Territorial Sea*, pp. 141–146.

19. Ibid.

20. Ibid.

21. See Churchill and Lowe, *The Law of the Sea*, p. 106.

22. Ibid., p. 111; and Stephen J. Murray, ''A Discussion of the World Court's North Sea Judgment,'' *American University Law Journal*, August 1970, p. 480.

23. See David A. Ross, ''Ocean Science: Its Place in the New Order of the Ocean,'' in Pontecorvo, ed., *The New Order of the Oceans*, p. 71.

24. *UN Law of the Sea Bulletin*, no. 11 (July 1988), pp. 54–56.

25. See *International Legal Materials*, no. 797 (1981), p. 803. Also see E. D. Brown, ''The Anglo-French Continental Shelf Case,'' *San Diego Law Review* 16, no. 3 (April 1979): 461–530; and Churchill and Lowe, *The Law of the Sea*, pp. 116–117.

26. See a brief summary of the case in J.R.V. Prescott, *The Maritime Political Boundaries of the World* (London: Methuen, 1985), pp. 101–102.

27. Churchill and Lowe, *The Law of the Sea*, pp. 116–117.

28. Ibid. Also see J.R.V. Prescott, *The Political Geography of the Oceans* (New York: Wiley, 1975), pp. 194–197.

29. Prescott, *The Maritime Political Boundaries of the World*, p. 101.

30. Frank X. Njenga, ''Historical Background of the Evolution of the Exclusive Economic Zone and the Contribution of Africa,'' in Pontecorvo, ed., *The New Order of the Oceans*, p. 130.

31. See Ann L. Hollick, ''A Comment: The Origins of the 200-Mile Offshore Zones,'' *The American Journal of International Law* 71, no. 3 (July 1977): 495.

32. Njenga, ''Historical Background of the Evolution of the Exclusive Economic Zone and the Contribution of Africa,'' p. 135.

33. See *United Nations Legislative Series*, B/16, p. 599.

34. Njenga, ''Historical Background of the Evolution of the Exclusive Economic Zone and the Contribution of Africa,'' p. 135.

35. Ibid.

36. Ibid.

37. See Ann L. Hollick, *U.S. Foreign Policy and the Law of the Sea* (Princeton, N.J.: Princeton University Press, 1981), pp. 306–307 and 323–326.

38. Presidential Proclamation 5030 (March 10, 1983), *U.S. Department of State Bulletin*, June 1983, p. 70.

39. Ibid.

40. Lawrence Juda, ''The Exclusive Economic Zone: Compatibility of National Claims and the UN Convention on the Law of the Sea,'' *Ocean Development and International Law* 16, no. 1 (1986): 324.

41. See *The New York Times*, 11 March 1983, p. A–4. Also see ''U.S. Exclusive Economic Zone (EEZ),'' *GIST*, Department of State, April 1983.

42. *GIST*, Bureau of Public Affairs, Department of State, April 1983.

43. Oscar Schachter, ''Concepts and Realities in the New Law of the Sea,'' in Pontecorvo, ed., *The New Order of the Oceans*, pp. 44–45.

44. Ibid., p. 45.

45. Churchill and Lowe, *The Law of the Sea*, p. 135.

46. Ibid.

47. See *Ocean Yearbook 3* (Chicago: The University of Chicago Press, 1983), p. 346.

48. See Introduction to Chapter 2.

49. Thomas W. Fulton, *The Sovereignty of the Sea* (Edinburgh: William Blackwood, 1911).

50. H. Lauterpacht, *International Law*, 8th ed., vol. 1 (London: Longmans, Green, 1955), p. 583.

51. Mangone, *The Elements of International Law: A Casebook*, p. 173.

52. Prescott, *The Maritime Political Boundaries of the World*, p. 113.

53. Prescott, *The Political Geography of the Oceans*, pp. 211–213.

54. Ibid.

55. Churchill and Lowe, *The Law of the Sea*, pp. 147 and 154 (footnote 1).

56. Interview with Jon Van Dyke, University of Hawaii Richardson School of Law, *The Honolulu Advertiser*, 20 December 1988, p. A–3.

57. Knight, *The Law of the Sea: Documents and Notes*, pp. 110–111.

58. B. A. Siscco, "Hot Pursuit from a Contiguous Zone: An Assault on the Freedom of the High Seas," *San Diego Law Review* 14, no. 4 (1977): 656–680.

59. See Craig H. Allen, "Doctrine of Hot Pursuit: A Functional Interpretation Adaptable to Emerging Maritime Law Enforcement Technologies and Practices," *Ocean Development and International Law* 20, no. 4 (1989): 309–342.

60. F. David Froman, "Unchartered Waters: Non-Innocent Passage of Warships in the Territorial Sea," *San Diego Law Review* 21, no. 3 (June 1984): 638–639; and Peter B. Walker, "What Is Innocent Passage?" *International Law Studies* 61 (1980): 368–369 and 376–383.

61. See *First United Nations Conference on the Law of the Sea*, Official Records, vol. 3, p. 129.

62. D. O'Connell, "The Juridical Nature of the Territorial Sea," *British Yearbook of International Law*, vol. 45 (1971), p. 303.

63. Froman, "Unchartered Waters," p. 636.

64. Ibid.

65. Ibid., pp. 640–641.

66. Froman, "Unchartered Waters," pp. 651–652; and Lewis M. Alexander, "The Ocean Enclosure Movement: Inventory and Prospect," *San Diego Law Review* 20, no. 3 (April 1983): 586–587. For recent change of Soviet Policy with regard to innocent passage of warships, see Lawrence Juda, "Innocent Passage by Warships in the Territorial Sea of the Soviet Union: Changing Doctrine," *Ocean Development and International Law* 21, no. 1 (1990): 111–116. Also see John C. Hill, Jr., "Ocean Law and Superpower Relations: The Bumping of the *Yorktown* and the *Caroon* in the Black Sea," *Virginia Journal of International Law* 29l, no. 3 (Spring 1989): 713–743.

67. Edward Wenk, Jr., *The Politics of the Oceans* (Seattle: University of Washington Press, 1972), p. 175.

68. Churchill and Lowe, *The Law of the Sea*, p. 81.

69. Myres S. McDougal and William T. Burke, *The Public Order of the Oceans: A Contemporary International Law of the Sea* (Norwell, Mass.: Kluwer-Nijhoff, 1987), pp. 200–201.

70. Wenk, *The Politics of the Oceans*, pp. 200–201.

71. Text is to be found in Mangone, *The Elements of International Law: A Casebook*, p. 181.

72. See Hollick, *U.S. Foreign Policy and the Law of the Sea*, pp. 234–236, 271–276 and 305.

73. Churchill and Lowe, *The Law of the Sea*, pp. 81–82.

74. John Norton Moore, "The Regime of Straits and the Third United Nations Conference on the Law of the Sea," *American Journal of International Law* 74 (1980): 114.

75. Ibid.

76. See W. Michael Reisman, "The Regime of Straits and National Security: An

Appraisal of International Law Making,'' *American Journal of International Law* 74 (1980): 71.

77. Ibid., p. 76; and also see U.S. Department of State Publication #8954.

78. See Abu Bakar Jaafar, ''The Changing Legal Status of the Malacca and Singapore Straits,'' in Jon Van Dyke, ed., *Consensus and Confrontation: The U.S. and the Law of the Sea Convention* (Honolulu: The Law of the Sea Institute, University of Hawaii, 1985), pp. 285–291.

79. See Wolfgang Graf Vitzthum, '' The Baltic Straits,'' *The Law of the Sea in the 1980s* (Honolulu: The Law of the Sea Institute, University of Hawaii, 1980), pp. 578–580.

80. See *Ocean Yearbook 6* (Chicago: University of Chicago Press, 1986), pp. 427–431; and Chi-Young Pak, *The Korean Straits* (Dordrecht, The Netherlands: Martinus-Nijhoff, 1988).

81. See Percy Thomas Fenn, Jr., ''Origins of the Theory of Territorial Waters,'' *American Journal of International Law* 20 (July 1926): 465 and 480–481.

82. Ibid., p. 481.

83. See Knight, *The Law of the Sea: Documents and Notes*, p. 44; and Churchill and Lowe, *The Law of the Sea*, p. 53.

84. Wyndham L. Walker, ''Territorial Waters: The Cannon Shot Rule,'' *American Journal of International Law* 22 (1945): 210–231; and H.S.K. Kent, ''The Historical Origin of the Three-Mile Limit,'' *American Journal of International Law* 48 (1954): 53. Also see Swarztrauber, *The Three-Mile Limit of Territorial Sea.*

85. U.S. Department of State Publication No. 36, April 1, 1974.

86. See *The Law of the Sea: Maritime Boundary Agreements (1970–1984)* (United Nations: Office of Ocean Affairs and the Law of the Sea, 1988). For regional aspects of maritime boundary making, see Douglas M. Johnston and Philip M. Saunders, eds. *Ocean Boundary Making: Regional Issues and Development* (London: Croom Helm, 1988); and John P. Craven, Jan Schneider and Carol Stimson, eds., *The International Implications of Extended Maritime Jurisdiction in the Pacific* (Honolulu: The Law of the Sea Institute, University of Hawaii, 1989). For a recent study on East China Sea boundary conflict, see Kendrick F. Royer, ''Japan's East China Sea Ocean Boundaries: What Solutions Can a Confused Legal Environment Provide in a Complex Boundary Dispute?'' *Vanderbilt Journal of Transnational Law* 22, no. 3 (1989): 581–630.

87. See *The Law of the Sea: Maritime Baselines*, nos. i–ii (United Nations: Office of Ocean Affairs and the Law of the Sea, 1987 and 1989).

88. Churchill and Lowe, *The Law of the Sea*, pp. 71–72. For current state practices see *The Law of the Sea: Current Developments in State Practices* (United Nations: Office of the Special Representative of the Secretary-General for the Law of the Sea, 1987).

89. Churchill and Lowe, *The Law of the Sea*, p. 72.

CHAPTER 4

Living Resources: Access, EEZ and Disputes

This chapter focuses on the new legal order for living resources established under the 1982 Law of the Sea Convention. Specifically, this refers to Articles 55–75 on the exclusive economic zone and its conservation management, Articles 116–120 on fishing in the high seas, and Article 51, which deals with fishing rights in archipelagic waters.

The importance of living resources of the oceans as a major international issue lies in the fact that for a number of nations fisheries constitute either a major source of animal protein or source of income. Fisheries are a potential source of food for a large number of developing nations with rapidly growing populations. If the present world population growth continues at the rate of 2 percent per annum, world population would double to more than 7 billion in thirty-five years. Moreover, one-third of the world population is facing either constant malnutrition or starvation. Thus, the sea is a major source of food, and the exploitation of the living marine resources is an important issue in international politics.

Fishery resources must also be seen in two related perspectives. One is the steady increase to more than 92 million metric tons in total world commercial catch as compared to 62 million metric tons in 1970, an increase of 30 million metric tons. This serves as convincing evidence against the argument that the world's total commercial catch might reach a point of stagnation. With full employment of fishery technology and full access to fishery resources, it has been estimated that the world's total catch could reach 200 million metric tons per year.[1] The other significant aspect of the world fishery situation is that the top six leading fishery nations of the world—Japan, the Soviet Union, China, Chile, Peru and the United States—accounted for more than half the world's total catch (by live weight) in 1986, as seen in Figure 4.1.

This fact raises more acutely the problem of access to fishery resources because of the competing demands for the resources by other developing Third World

Figure 4.1
World Commercial Catch by Leading Countries, 1976–1986 (Live Weight)

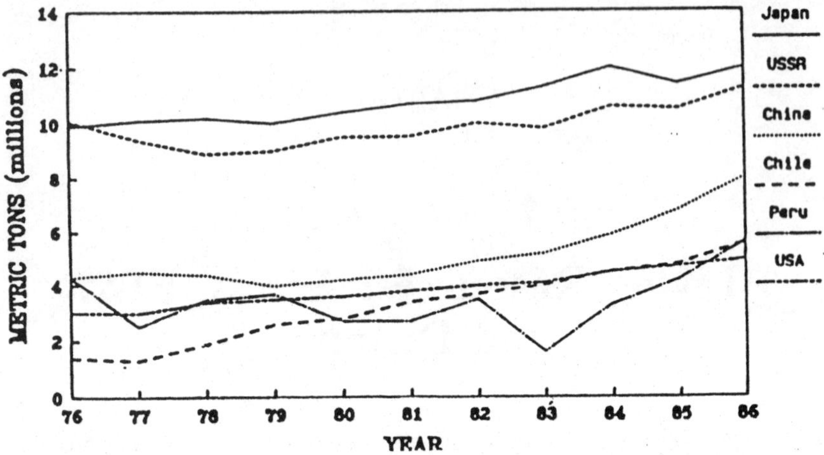

Source: *Fisheries of the United States, 1987: Current Fishery Statistics No. 8077* (Washington, D.C.: Department of Commerce and National Oceanic Atmospheric Administration, May 1988), p. 96.

nations and by landlocked or geographically disadvantaged states. This situation is dealt with in Articles 69 and 70 of the 1982 LOS Convention on the rights of landlocked and geographically disadvantaged states. World fishery resources are not distributed evenly throughout the oceans; the distribution is determined by major currents and the natural up-wellings, which are found only in the ocean areas near the equator, the Arctic, the Antarctic, the Gulf Stream and the Humboldt Current.[2] For fishermen from many of the developing nations, access to fishery resources is limited to within sight of their own shores. They do not have access to other areas where there are abundant fishery resources or to the shores of other nations because they lack modern fishing technology. At the end of World War II, a new development appeared: the ability of fishermen of a few nations to roam the oceans on distant waters with fishing trawlers and factory ships. The development of this technological capability by fishermen from the leading fishery nations placed them in a unique position to gain access not only to major fishery resources of the world, but also to the coasts of small but less technologically developed states. As argued by the Third World nations, the existence of free access to fishery resources was made possible because the doctrine of freedom of the seas for navigation and fishing originated in the seventeenth century and was defended by Grotius. The doctrine was long upheld by the world's leading maritime powers.[3] At the end of World War II, distant-water fleets of Japan, South Korea and the Soviet Union were found in the northwest and northeast waters of the Atlantic, off the coast of Africa and in the northwest Pacific. All of them were equipped with advanced fishing technology, such as freezer trawlers and factory ships. Access to fisheries was open to anyone who had the capability; there was no other recognized rule for control of access to fishing. After all, the oceans were the "natural commons," inexhaustible, inappropriable and nondegradable.

Finally, the combination of economic nationalism and environmental concerns led to the expanded movement for ocean enclosure, the division of ocean space, by coastal states. The 1945 Truman Proclamation paved the way for the rush to establish fishery conservation zones for "the protection and perpetuation of fishery resources." A flood of similar claims was followed by Latin American states demanding extended jurisdiction beyond the traditionally accepted narrow belt of water from the shore. The new ocean enclosure movement began to erode the doctrine of freedom to fish; now the old legal order for freedom to fish was challenged and contested.

The period from the 1960s, when the United Nations seabed debate began, to the convening of the UNCLOS III in the 1970s, was an era characterized by endemic disputes over fishing rights between coastal states in adjacent and opposite waters, accompanied by a wave of unilateral claims for 200-nautical-mile preferential fishery zones. It was indeed an era of "unilateralism" and the gradual breakdown of the 370-year-old freedom of fishing doctrine. The final outcome was the acceptance of a new legal regime for fishing, the claim of exclusive economic and fishery zones up to 200 nautical miles from the coast, in accordance with Article 57 of the 1982 LOS Convention. By 1988 ninety-two nations had established exclusive fishery zones (EFZs) and seventy-four had exclusive economic zones (EEZs). In short, these actions enclosed more than 40 percent of the world's area, which contained more than 90 percent of the world's living resources. For all practical purposes, as one expert so aptly summarized, "the ocean as a commons for living resources has disappeared."[4] Article 55 of the 1982 LOS Convention established a "specific legal regime" of the exclusive economic zone as "an area beyond and adjacent to the territorial sea, subject to the specific legal regime established in this Part, under which the rights and jurisdiction of the Coastal States and the rights and freedoms of other States are governed by the relevant provisions of this Convention." Access to fisheries for other states was limited, mainly to the "surplus" resources as defined and determined by the coastal states in their domestic regulations, or by bilateral agreements for the EEZs and EFZs.

The new legal regime for the fisheries is, in essence, the new "regulated commons" of the oceans if, as maintained by John Craven, "coastal states are willing to provide full access to economically capable nations" for the fishery resources in the zonal arrangement.[5] As discussed later in this chapter, it is within the coastal state's discretionary power to determine the allowable catch, harvest capacity and allocation of surplus to other states. Under these conditions, it is in the interest of coastal states to enter into "equitable" arrangements at bilateral or regional levels to permit foreign vessels to fish for the surplus in the zone.

This chapter offers not only a brief review of the bilateral fishery agreements in terms of the patterns and specific provisions, but also listings of these agreements for ready reference. Appendix V lists 103 selected bilateral fishery agreements concluded from 1975 to 1978, compiled by two experts from the United Nations Food and Agriculture Organization (FAO). Appendix VI lists 104 agreements culled from M. J. Savini's recent study, on a country-by-country basis, of bilateral fishery agreements concluded with other states for the period from 1981 to 1985. The second list of bilateral fishery agreements contains a brief summary of key provisions, which will provide a useful reference to coastal states' requirements for fishing by permit by foreign vessels in the EFZ, as well as catch quotas, gear size, fee payment, quantity to be utilized and other pertinent information regarding access granted to foreign fishing.

The next chapter reviews multilateral agreements for achieving cooperative conservation efforts regulating certain species such as whales, tuna, salmon, seals, herring, halibut and marine mammals. In addition, considerable attention is given to the species-management approach for anadromous (salmon) and catadromous (shrimp) species, cetaceans (whales and small cetaceans), seals and tuna (as highly migratory species), and the controversy that has revolved around the application of the species management approach.

ACCESS TO FISHERIES RESOURCES

For more than 300 years, along with freedom of navigation, freedom to fish was a part of the general concept of freedom of the seas. When he published the treatise *Mare Liberum* in 1609, Grotius's perception of the ocean was one of immense space and inexhaustible resources. By the eighteenth and nineteenth centuries his views became an acceptable part of customary international law, but at the same time, these views were subject to challenges and limitations. Freedom of access to fisheries has become increasingly difficult to uphold because of the realization that living resources in the ocean are not inexhaustible and that fishing stock can be depleted by overfishing.

At first nations generally agreed that coastal states could claim exclusive jurisdiction over fisheries within the narrow belt of ocean known as territorial water; beyond that zone fisheries became "common property" belonging to whoever had the capacity to take advantage of them. For a time, this was a practical solution to the fisheries utilization problem. In the eighteenth and nineteenth centuries controversies over fisheries had been concerned mostly with the problem of delimitation of the territorial waters and the methods for drawing the baseline from which the territorial waters were to be measured: for instance, the 1839 Anglo-French Fisheries Convention, the 1882 North Sea Fisheries Convention, 1901 treaties between Britain and Denmark on fishing near the waters of Iceland, and the 1925 treaty between the United States and Mexico on fishing in the Gulf of Mexico.

World War II produced severe food shortages in many parts of the world.

While fishing suffered during the war, fishery technology made a quantum leap in terms of the ability to locate fishing schools by radar, nylon purse seining and new modernized fishing fleets that could travel long distances. The pressure for animal protein and newly developed fishing technology propelled many coastal states into extending their fishing rights and access beyond the traditional three-mile territorial waters. This brought on confrontations and disputes over the questions of access and claims.

The period from 1945 to 1970 represented a time of bitter disputes over the right of fishing by coastal states, aggravated by the inability among nations to agree on the width of the territorial sea and the controversy over the right of coastal states to claim fishery resources in ever-broadening offshore zones of a fixed distance. At the heart of the issue concerning the breadth of territorial seas has been the demand for exclusive fishing rights by developing coastal states. The 1958 United Nations Conference on the Law of the Sea (UNCLOS I) was convened to address two interrelated problems: holding the line on expanded claims for ''extra-territorial fishing grounds''[6] and permitting the coastal states to adopt cooperative measures for conservation of the living resources on the high seas. On the first, the 1958 UNCLOS I failed to reach any consensus. On the second, it established a set of guidelines, benefited by the expert studies from both the 1955 Rome-based FAO–sponsored International Technical Conference on the Living Resources of the Sea and the International Law Commission on conservative measures for fisheries. Article 1(1) of the 1958 Convention on Fishing and Conservation of Living Resources of the High Seas proclaimed, ''All states have the right for their nationals to engage in fishing in the high seas,'' subject to treaty obligations and interests and rights of coastal states provided in the Convention. To the disappointment of the coastal states, the Convention did not legally provide them with any exclusive right on fisheries beyond the three-nautical-mile limit except, as a way of mitigating the situation, the adoption of a conference resolution which ''recognized'' the coastal states' right to ''preferential requirements'' of adjacent fisheries. The reality was that in 1958 some twenty-three states had already claimed unilateral fishing jurisdiction beyond their territorial seas ranging from 12 to 200 nautical miles. In 1960 a second international attempt was made to delimit the breadth of the territorial sea at twelve nautical miles, augmented by another twelve-nautical-mile fishery zone; both attempts met with defeat at the UNCLOS II in Geneva in 1960, as pointed out in Chapter 3.

During the period from 1960 to 1973, on the eve of the convening of the UNCLOS III, the state of fishing worldwide was characterized by three interrelated developments. There were continued unilateral claims over expanded exclusive fishery jurisdiction beyond the traditional three-nautical-mile limit. One study showed that by 1973 the total number of states with ''extra-territorial'' fishing claims had risen to thirty-two, including twelve that claimed a 200-nautical-mile fishing zone.[7] Since there was no international agreement on the extent of coastal state offshore jurisdiction, the number of fishing incidents and vessel seizures followed by retaliation increased dramatically worldwide.[8] At the same time, unilateral claims of expanded offshore fishing jurisdiction and increased fishing incidents were stimulated by the new threat posed by fishing technological developments—purse sein and distant-water operations—to the developing coastal states' preferential or exclusive right to control their offshore fisheries.

Of particular interest are Articles 116–118 in the 1982 LOS Convention on the freedom of fishing and the limitations imposed on the coastal states' offshore fishery jurisdiction. Article 16 adopted, word-by-word, Article 1 of the 1958 Convention on Conservation of the Living Resources of the High Seas: "All states have the right for their nationals to engage in fishing on the high seas, subject to their treaty obligations and the rights and duties of coastal states interests provided in the convention." Taking Article 116 as a whole, it can be seen that the classic concept of freedom of fishing is not only limited, but can be regulated as well. Articles 117 and 188 mandate the coastal states to seek negotiations at bilateral and regional levels for the conservation of living resources. Article 119 provides that coastal states shall use scientific methods and data on allowable catch to determine maximum sustainable yield and other matters.

Articles 61–69 in the 1982 LOS Convention provided guidelines for conservation and use of living resources in the exclusive fishery areas under the 200-nautical-mile EFZ (see separate section on the topic in this chapter). It is sufficient to say here that, with the establishment of the 200-nautical-mile EEZ, foreign access to fishery resources within the zone is governed by the numerous bilateral fisheries agreements (see Appendix V). Most of these bilateral agreements contain principles that govern foreign vessel access to fisheries within the EFZ.[9] The following is a summary of the principles governing foreign vessel access within the exclusive economic zones:[10]

1. Under Article 61(1) the coastal state "shall determine the allowable catch of the living resources in its exclusive economic zone."
2. Under Article 62(1) the coastal state "shall promote the objective of optimum utilization of the living resources in the exclusive economic zone."
3. Under Article 62(1) the coastal state "shall determine its capacity to harvest the living resources of the exclusive economic zone"; but if the coastal state "does not have the capacity to harvest the entire allowable catch," it must, through bilateral agreements or other arrangements, "give other states access to the surplus of the allowable catch . . . especially in relation to the developing states."

FAO reported that, with the exception of the bilateral agreements concluded by African coastal states, agreements entered into by the most important fishery nations—Canada, Japan, South Korea, the United States, and those by the European Economic Community (EEC)—reflected these general principles for foreign fishing access within the EEZs.[11] Detailed discussion about these principles will be found in the entry on exclusive fishery zones in this chapter.

Significance. With the establishment of the twelve-nautical-mile territorial sea by the 1982 LOS Convention, access to fishing in the area is now reserved exclusively for the coastal state. However, under arrangement by the European Economic Community it is possible for a foreign vessel to gain access to fishing in the territorial sea of another EEC member state. Although the 1982 LOS Convention upholds the classic doctrine for freedom of fishing in the high seas, in practice access to fisheries on the high seas is limited only to those coastal states with sophisticated fishing technology, that is, distant water fleets and freezer trawlers. The formation of an EFZ within the 200-nautical-mile EEZ grants the coastal states exclusive access to fisheries within the zone and access by other states only after the surplus of allowable catch has been determined. There are also specific provisions governing special species, that is, sedentary, high migratory, anadromous and catadromous stocks. Under the 1982 LOS Convention, fishing is now largely regulated by the coastal states, including the access and the right to fish.

BIOLOGICAL AND "RELEVANT ENVIRONMENTAL AND ECONOMIC" FACTORS IN THE MANAGEMENT OF LIVING RESOURCES

In the 1982 LOS Convention the articles on living resources were drafted to reflect ''the biological characteristics of the fish.''[12] The following items provide understanding of some of the key biological bases of living resources management and conservation concepts that were reflected in the Convention.

Fish Stock

A fish stock is said to have ''an inherent reproductive overcapacity''[13] when it can move over to a ''vacant environment'' to grow and recover from any ''natural depletion of its members.''[14] Some fish stock is said to be ''density dependent'' in that further growth is possible when some members are removed by natural causes or fishing, so that there is less competition for good. The result is that a ''fall in stock will result in an increase in recruitment'' by larvae or juveniles joining the adult stock, or an increase in the stock size will reduce recruitment reproduction.[15]

Maximum Sustainable Yield

This refers to a level under stable environmental conditions at which it is possible to procure continuously the largest annual catch or yield from a fishery stock. To determine what is the maximum sustainable yield (MSY), it is necessary to make an estimate based on the best available scientific data. It is a biological measurement test. Churchill and Lowe define maximum sustainable yield as follows: ''There is for each fish stock a level at which it can be fished where the loss to the stock from fishing and natural mortality is balanced by the increase from reproduction.''[16] At that level the same quantity of fish can be caught each year without adversely affecting the total size of the stock.[17]

Article 61(3) and Article 119(1-a) of the 1982 LOS Convention require that states engaging in fishing in the exclusive economic zone and in the high seas undertake proper conservation and management measures designed to ''maintain or restore populations of harvested species at levels which can produce the maximum sustainable yield.'' The problem with advocating the concept of maximum sustainable yield as a goal in fishery conservation is that it is not unanimously accepted among marine biologists, who believe that it is not meaningful to ''formulate conservation objectives in terms of a biological limit upon the yield of fish species.''[18] There are so many factors that affect fluctuation in fish population, with natural features being more decisive than those controlled by man. Barston and Birnie point out that ''the stock size of a fish species depends upon a web of interaction between the species, its environment, its competitors, its predators and diseases, and its food.''[19] Thus, the exercise of determining what is maximum sustainable yield is ''at best a bad guess by frustrated scientists.''[20]

Optimum Yield

While the MSY is primarily a biological mathematical concept, the optimum yield (OY) is a concept that contains a combination of biological and nonbiological factors. Both Articles 61(3) and 119(1-a) require the coastal states to enact conservation and management measures designed to maintain the maximum sustainable yield, ''as qualified by relevant environmental and socio-economic factors,'' including the economic needs of coastal fishing communities and the special requirements of developing states. This provision serves to achieve balance between the biological limit, on the one hand, and the possible adjustment of economic and social factors, on the other.[21] In the Magnuson Fishery Conservation and Management Act, enacted by the U.S. Congress in 1976, optimum yield refers not only to the maximum sustainable yield as modified by relevant ecological, economic or social factors, but also the amount of fish that will provide the greatest overall benefit to the United States.

Overfishing

To a fisherman, overfishing simply means a decline in catch per unit of effort he expends. But to a marine biologist, ''the concept of overfishing relates to the notion of a fishing population in equilibrium with its environment including fishing mortality.''[22] This is explained in a simple equation: C (catch size in one year) = A (stock recruitment and reproduction) + G (stock growth) − M (natural mortality)—this is the equilibrium catch with no change in stock. If the catch (C) is greater than the level ($A + G - M$), then the stock is decreased.[23] Thus, a stock reduction as a result of fishing, which in turn results in an increase in recruitment (reproduction) to a certain size beyond which recruitment will fall, is referred to as overfishing. North Sea herring and California sardines are the examples. Or, to put it another way, overfishing occurs when fishing is beyond or above the maximum sustainable yield (MSY); then the stock size decreases and catch falls of as a result. In order to determine or measure scientifically when overfishing is present for a particular stock, it is necessary to obtain information and data on "fishing intensity, size and composition of the population, and the size and composition of the catch," a difficult and complicated process indeed.[24]

Surplus

Articles 61(1) and 62(1) of the 1982 LOS Convention require the coastal state to provide management measures within its exclusive economic zone in order to ensure that the living resources are "not endangered by overfishing exploitation." Under provisions of the bilateral agreement or regional arrangement, or in accordance with national legislation, after the state has determined the total allowable catch in the zone and its capacity to harvest the living resources, any excess fisheries are the "allowable access to surplus," which may be granted to foreign vessels fishing in the EEZ. At present, state practice does not provide definite procedures for allocating access to surplus to foreign vessels in the EEZs.[25]

In fact, most national laws say little about access to surplus.[26] In a few instances where references are made to access to surplus resources, there is no obligation to do so—such are the national laws of Gambia, Bahamas, Cape Verde, Fiji and New Zealand.[27] However, under national laws of the United States, Mexico and Cuba there is a recognition of access to surplus for foreign vessels fishing within the EEZs.[28] Most bilateral agreements on living resources make specific reference to Articles 61 and 62 of the 1982 LOS Convention.[29]

Total Allowable Catch

The total allowable catch (TAC) is a concept that is an offshoot of the concept of maximum sustainable yield. Its origin came about during the reorganization of the North East Atlantic Fisheries Commission in 1974, under which the regional fishery commission was authorized to set the total catch available for each stock in a given period for the North East Atlantic, thus the TAC system. Each member state for the North East Atlantic Fisheries Commission (NEAFC) was given a quota from the TAC. The objective of the TAC system is to set a limit on catch for a given stock. It has been arranged so that the TAC system has "the advantage of being easy to alter annually" in pelagic fisheries, based on recruitment (reproduction) estimates.[30] Under the Magnuson Fishery Conservation and Management Act, the United States must determine the total allowable level of foreign fishing (TALFF) each year. That is, the portion of the optimum yield of a fishery stock which will not be harvested by U.S. vessels will be negotiated with foreign fishery countries for their share of catch within the U.S. fishery zone. In many respects, the TALFF formula used by the United States is a modified version of the TAC as originally established by the North East Atlantic Fisheries Commission in 1974.

Article 61(1) of the 1982 LOS Convention mandates coastal states to determine the allowable catch of the living resources in the exclusive economic zones. Articles 118 and 119(1) urge coastal states fishing in the high seas to seek cooperative conservation measures by determining the allowable catch for the living resources in the high seas.

The system of TAC in the 1982 LOS Convention has a number of drawbacks. First, a regional fishery commission such as the NEAFC is a politically oriented entity, and as such it often does not adhere to the limit of catch set by a scientific body—NEAFC frequently sets a higher level of allowable catch. Second, member states in the region do not necessarily abide by the total allowable catch set by the regional fishery commission. For example, TAC for cod for the North East Atlantic for 1975 was set by the NEAFC at 810,000 tons, but the actual catch was 834,000 tons, resulting in continued overfishing for cod.[31] Third, under the TAC system the participants tend to encourage ''uneconomic fishing'' by overcapitalizing in terms of equipment and gear in order to take a large share of the total allowable catch as quickly as possible.[32] Finally, both the maximum sustainable yield and the allowable catch systems may be more ''political'' or ''ideological'' than scientific.[33] Holt and Vanderbilt argue that MSY and TAC serve political and ideological functions because they imply that ''if fishermen from one nation do not take all the gift they should not hinder its acceptance by other nations'' if there is a need for the fishery.[34] In practice, what it really means, as far as fishing in the high seas is concerned, is favoring of the technically advanced fishing nations at the expense of the ''newcomers,'' the developing Third World nations.[35]

Significance. Conservation and management of living resources, if they are to be meaningful and effective, must take into account the biological factors of fish stocks. Fisheries are renewable resources, and their biological environment in the long run generally provides a balance between natural mortality and reproduction to allow a stable population. Fishing or catching represents another mortality, besides the natural one, in the otherwise normal equilibrium. Thus, maximum sustainable yield (leaving aside the lack of consensus among marine scientists on the meaning of the term) is a useful guide by which to develop conservation objectives. Open access to living resources, if not regulated, can lead to overfishing and economic waste. Thus, conservation and management schemes are necessary to avoid upsetting the biological equilibrium.

However, it must be pointed out that the 1982 LOS Convention has also considered relevant environmental and socioeconomic needs to be just as important as the biological factors, such as the ''maximum sustainable biological yield,'' in regulating coastal states' living resources. Coastal states' management schemes are the ''means'' of achieving a variety of significant national social, economic and political objectives.[36] Thus, Article 61(3) makes it clear that conservation and management measures ''shall also be designed to maintain or restore populations of harvested species at levels which can produce the maximum sustainable yield, as qualified by relevant environmental and economic factors, including the economic needs to coastal fishing communities and the special requirements of developing states, and taking into account fishing patterns, the interdependence of stocks and any generally recommended international minimum standards, whether subregional, regional or global.''

EXCLUSIVE FISHERY ZONE: CONSERVATION AND MANAGEMENT

Boundary

Article 57 of the 1982 LOS Convention states that a coastal state can declare a fishery zone up to, but not beyond, 200 nautical miles measured from the baseline of the territorial sea. There are 159 independent coastal states in the world today. National claims over fishery jurisdiction declared by coastal states can be seen in Table 4.1.

Exclusive fishery zone is one type of national claim that first appeared in the 1950s to 1960s. Many coastal states made claims over their jurisdiction on fisheries before the convening of the UNCLOS III in the 1970s. In the case of claims to a fishery zone, the coastal states have jurisdiction to exploit, conserve and manage the living resources in their adjacent waters. However, the economic zone established as a result of negotiations at UNCLOS III (1973–1982) authorizes the coastal state to exploit, conserve and manage the living and nonliving resources of the seabed, subsoil and superjacent waters. In other words, the scope of the EEZ is very comprehensive; it allows the coastal states to be responsible for the regulation of energy production from the water currents and winds, as well as the construction of artificial islands and other installations, and scientific research.

The 1982 LOS Convention, under Article 75, requires coastal states declaring claims for the EEZ or EFZ to publish for other states' information the lines of delimitation for the zone as shown on charts of scales and with ''list of geographical coordinates.'' One of the purposes of the above requirement is to provide other states the basis for a protest if the claim is ''overextensive'' or infringes on the high seas or on some other state's EEZ.[37] As Lawrence Juda points out, delimitation of EEZ or EFZ boundaries is a very costly and complex affair. As a result few states have entered into agreement for a fixed international boundary of their EEZ.[38] A case in point is the settlement by the International Court of Justice on a single boundary for the Gulf of Maine between the United States and Canada when their EEZs overlapped.

Table 4.1
National Maritime Claims: Fishing Limits

3 nautical miles (3)

- Bahrain
- Jordan
- Qatar

6 nautical miles (3)

- Greece
- Israel
- Lebanon

12 nautical miles (29)

- Algeria
- Antigua and Barbuda
- Belize
- Bulgaria
- China
- Cyprus
- Egypt
- Equatorial Guinea
- Ethiopia
- Finland
- Iraq
- Italy
- Jamaica
- Kuwait
- Libya
- Monaco
- Romania
- Saint Lucia
- St. Vincent and the Grenadines
- Saudi Arabia
- Singapore
- Sudan
- Trinidad and Tobago
- Tunisia
- Turkey
- Western Samoa
- Yemen (Sanaa)
- Yugoslavia
- Zaire

15 nautical miles (1)

- Albania

25 nautical miles (1)

- Malta

35 nautical miles (1)

- Syria

50 nautical miles (3)

- Cameroon
- The Gambia
- Tanzania

150 nautical miles (3)

- Gabon
- Madagascar
- Senegal

200 nautical miles[1,2] (92)

Angola	176,600	Cuba	105,800
Argentina	339,500	Denmark[3]	426,900
Australia	1,310,900	Djibouti	1,800
The Bahamas	221,400	Dominica	
Bangladesh	22,400	Dominican Republic	78,400
Barbados	48,800	Ecuador	338,000
Belgium	800	El Salvador	26,800
Benin	7,900	Fiji	331,000
Brazil	924,000	France[4]	2,083,400
Burma	148,600	German Democratic Republic	2,800
Canada	857,000	German Federal Republic	11,900
Cape Verde	230,200	Ghana	63,600
Chile	667,300	Grenada	78,000
Colombia	175,900	Guatemala	28,900
Comoros	72,600	Guinea	20,700
Congo	7,200		
Costa Rica	75,500		

Table 4.1 (Continued)

200 nautical miles (continued)			
Guinea-Bissau	43,900	Pakistan	92,900
Guyana	38,000	Panama	89,400
Haiti	46,800	Papua New Guinea	690,000
Honduras	58,600	Peru	229,400
Iceland	252,800	Philippines	520,700
India	587,600	Poland	8,300
Indonesia	1,577,300	Portugal	517,400
Iran	45,400	Sao Tome & Principe	37,400
Ireland	110,900	Seychelles	393,400
Ivory Coast	30,500	Sierra Leone	45,400
Japan	1,126,000	Solomon Islands	325,400
Kampuchea	16,200	Somalia	228,300
Kenya	34,400	South Africa	452,900
Kiribati	770,000	Soviet Union	1,309,500
Korea, North	37,300	Spain	355,600
Korea, South	101,600	Sri Lanka	150,900
Liberia	57,000	Suriname	29,500
Malaysia	138,700	Sweden	45,300
Mauritania	45,000	Thailand	25,000
Mauritius	344,500	Togo	600
Mexico	831,500	Tuvalu (Ukrainian	
Morocco	81,100	SSR)	95,700
Mozambique	163,900	United Arab Emirates	17,300
Nauru	125,700	United Kingdom[5]	520,500
Netherlands	24,700	United States[6]	2,831,400
New Zealand	1,409,500	Uruguay	34,800
Nicaragua	46,600	Vanuatu	
Nigeria	61,500	Venezuela	106,100
Norway	590,500	Vietnam	210,600
Oman	163,800	Yemen (Aden)	160,500
Rectangular-pologonal claim (2)			
Maldives	279,700		
Tonga	173,800		

[1] Boundary situations with neighboring states prevent many states from extending their fishing zones to a full 200 nautical miles.

[2] Numbers represent the approximate area enclosed (n.mi.^{2}).

[3] Includes Greenland and Faroe Islands.

[4] Includes all overseas departments and territories.

[5] Includes Bermuda, British Virgin Islands, the Cayman Islands, the Turks and Caicos islands, Pitcairn, Henderson, Ducie, Oeno islands, St. Helene and Ascension.

[6] Includes Puerto Rico, U.S. Virgin Islands, American Samoa, Guam, Johnson Atoll, Wake Island, Jarvis Island, Kingman Reef, Howland and Baker islands, and the Northern Marianas.

Source: *Maritime Fisheries Review* 44, no. 5 (May 1982): 30.

Conservation and Management Measures within the EFZ

The key provisions for conservation of living resources in the EEZ and EFZ are in Article 61 of the 1982 LOS Convention. Article 61(1) states that the coastal state shall determine the allowable catch of the living resources in the EEZ. Article 61 seems to imply that what shall constitute the allowable catch is within the discretionary power of the coastal state, and Article 297(3-a) provides that a coastal state shall not be obliged to accept any dispute settlement process with respect to the living resources in the EEZ. It goes on to state that such conservation measures as allowable catch, harvest capacity, and the allocation of surpluses to others are the discretionary powers exercised by the coastal state. This seems to mean that the coastal state may establish any level of allowable catch for fisheries within the EEZ or EFZ. However, Article 297(3-b-ii) also provides nonbinding conciliation procedures if "a coastal state has arbitrarily refused to determine, at the request of another state, the allowable catch and its capacity to harvest living resources with respect to stocks which that other state is interested in fishing."

Another general guideline for the conservation of living resources is the requirement in Article 61(3) for maintaining or restoring populations of harvested species at the levels that can produce the MSY. One expert interprets this provision to mean only that the coastal state must consider the environmental and economic interests, but not the requirement "to manage the fishery actually to produce a scientifically determined MSY."[39] This consideration—not requiring the coastal state to determine the yield solely on biological grounds—is practical, for there are many species of fish caught in a given operation within the zone. Article 61(4), which imposes an obligation on coastal states to take measures on the effects of fishing on "species associated with or dependent upon harvested species" in order to protect their overexploitation, requires a great deal of costly scientific investigation and study to generate the needed data. Few coastal states that declared EEZ or EFZ are in a position to undertake such studies.

While Article 62(1) requires the coastal state to promote "the objectives of optimum utilization" of the living resources within the EEZ or EFZ, it does not really obligate it to allocate fishery stocks to other states when its own fishermen cannot take them. In other words, a coastal state can, as part of its discretionary power, set any level of optimum use that is compatible with the "allowable catch" and so long as the harvest level is secured. The coastal state is solely in the position to determine the level of optimum use. Thus, after having determined what the allowable catch is, the coastal state, under Article 62(2), can also fix the harvesting capacity of the living resources and then allocate the surplus available to foreign fishermen. These decisions are not subject to challenge if the coastal state decides not to share the surplus when it is in its interest not to do so. However, in making these decisions the coastal state must keep in mind "the requirements of developing states in the subregion or region in harvesting part of the surplus and the need to minimize economic dislocation" for those countries' fishermen who have habitually fished in the zone or "which have made substantial efforts in research and identification of stocks." It is generally assumed that it would be in the coastal state's interest to permit (for a set fee) foreign vessels to fish for the surplus in the zone. Table 4.2 illustrates the allocation for foreign fishing within the United States' exclusive economic zone under the Magnuson Fishery Conservation and Management Act (MFCMA).

Table 4.2
All Foreign Countries: Catch in the U.S. Exclusive Economic Zone, by Continent and Country, 1987*

Continent and Country	North Atlantic**	Washington Oregon and California	Alaska: Gulf of Alaska	Alaska: Eastern Bering Sea and Aleutian Islands	Total Alaska	Grand Total
Europe:						
European Economic Comm.:						
Italy	33.2	-	-	-	-	33.2
Netherlands	10,928.4	-	-	-	-	10,928.4
Other:						
German Democratic Rep.	18,553.3	-	-	-	-	18,553.3
Poland	-	48,975.4	-	-	-	48,975.4
Asia:						
China	-	5.0	-	-	-	5.0
Japan	-	-	-	67,436.5	67,436.5	67,436.5
Republic of Korea	-	1,412.7	-	1,614.4	1,614.4	3,027.1
Grand Total	29,514.9	50,393.1	-	69,050.9	69,050.9	148,958.9

Note: Excludes tunas and prohibited species. Some fishing years overlap two calendar years.

*Metric tons, round weight.

**Cape Hatteras, North Carolina, northward.

Source: Barbara K. O'Bannon, ed., *Fisheries of the United States, 1987: Current Fishery Statistics No. 8700* (Washington, DC: U.S. Department of Commerce and National Oceanic and Atmospheric Administration, May 1988), p. 28.

Under Article 62(4) concerning foreign vessels permitted to fish for the surplus, the coastal state can regulate their activities by (1) licensing fishermen, vessels and equipment for a fee as payment; (2) establishing or fixing quotas of catch for the species caught; (3) regulating seasons and areas of fishing, sizes and amount of gear or number of vessels; (4) fixing limits for age and size of fish that may be caught; (5) regulating research to be engaged in by fishing vessels; (6) placing observers on board foreign vessels that have the permit to fish; and (7) requiring any enforcement measures.

Article 63 of the 1982 LOS Convention requires the coastal states concerned to agree upon measures of conservation by working with or through the regional fishery commission if a stock or stocks of associated species migrate between two or more EEZs or EFZs or between an EEZ or EFZ and the high seas. However, the management of shared of straddling stocks, such as mackerels and other pelagic species, is interrelated with their allocation, and in these instances joint management and coordination by coastal states is an obligation imposed by Article 63.

What happens when there is failure on the part of coastal and noncoastal states to agree on an acceptable conservation management measure for associated or straddling stocks that travel between the high seas and the EEZ? Here Articles 63 and 116, referring to fishing on the high seas, seem inadequate in settling disputes, as evidenced by the conflicts developed recently concerning the straddling stocks in the Northwest and Southwest Atlantic, Eastern and Southwest Pacific, and the Central Bering Sea, known as the "Doughnut Hole," an international area where the fishing harvest, mostly pollock, has increased from 15,000 metric tons in 1980 to over 1.7 million metric tons in 1987.[40] Edward Miles and William Burke called for submission of the disputes to a compulsory third-party arbitration process if negotiations for multilateral agreement failed.[41] Lourene Miovski, on the other hand, insisted that noncoastal states—Japan, South Korea, China, Taiwan and Poland, in the case of the Central Bering Sea—have a duty under Articles 63, 87 and 116 of the 1982 LOS Convention to negotiate in good faith with the United States and the Soviet Union on conservation management measures for the straddling stocks as a matter of treaty obligation and customary international law.[42]

While Articles 61 and 62 of the 1982 LOS Convention provide broad guidelines in the management of the living resources in a coastal state fishery zone, there is a myriad of state practices in fishery management measures for the EEZs. Two known methods of stock management have been most common in the various state practices within the fishery zones under their jurisdiction. One management method is to control the age and size at first capture and the other is to limit the total fishing effort or catch.[43] An example of the first method is the legal requirement for mesh size in order to allow young fish to escape, most suitable for "pelagic fish which swim in single species shoals."[44] Regulations on minimum size taken for a particular species represent another example of fishery management measure. Introduction of a licensing system to control catch limit for species can also be effective as a conservation and management measure.

Experts in fishery management seem to agree that one basic purpose for the establishment of the EEZs and EFZs has been undoubtedly achieved—that is the control of distant-water fishermen. Most coastal states that have declared the 200-nautical-mile exclusive economic zone have made little commitment on a rational fishery management system.[45] Old problems of waste and overfishing remain, and new problems have also been created since the proliferation of extended jurisdictions to 200 miles from the territorial sea. As a management measure limitations on total catch by quotas within the EEZ, which are set based on either unreliable biological data or deliberate "falsification," have created challenges and "constraint in fishing efforts."[46] There is the problem of enforcement, which is administratively costly for the coastal states—mostly developing Third World countries; it is also financially burdensome. With the establishment of exclusive fishery zones, the question is still left unanswered: How often do fish stocks cross the maritime boundaries?

Thus there is confusion as long as this question cannot be definitely answered with respect to fishery allocation among the coastal states. Joint or international organizational effort is then needed to help develop suitable mechanisms for the conservation and management of transboundary or cross-boundary fisheries. An example has been given that, under the U.S. Magnuson Fishery Conservation and Management Act (1976), in the absence of a joint agreement it is hard to deal with fish that cross the boundary between the United States and Canada or Mexico. There is no international management mechanism for transboundary stocks such as herring.

Lawrence Juda suggests that each coastal state with an EEZ, in addition to providing for boundary delimitation and resources assessment, should set goals with priorities for policymaking, establish institutional machinery for policymaking and administration of the EEZ, and develop strategies to overcome identified problems.[47] Brian Rothschild proposes a set of seven principles of policy development in fishery management: the importance of economic investment in fisheries; the need for developing new arrangements for managing cross-boundary fisheries; increased expenditures for developing new concepts of management and information on stocks; the need to provide more incentive for the private sector and new control strategy by government; the important role of international and regional organizations for effectiveness in fishery management; the formulation of fishery policy as a part of the coastal state's overall development policy; and some rethinking about fisheries management and control.[48]

Significance. The unilateral declaration by coastal states for the enclosure of exclusive jurisdiction of 200 nautical miles for fishery control, intended originally against distant-water fishing, and the eventual inclusion of the concept of EEZ in the 1982 LOS Convention have modified the traditional concept of freedom of fishing under which all can have open access to fishery resources. Parenthetically, it has been maintained that the doctrine of freedom of fishing benefitted the developed nations of the world more than the developing ones. As of July 1988, some ninety-two nations have declared exclusive fishery zones, and seventy-four have declared EEZs. These ocean enclosures occupy more than 40 percent of the world's ocean space which, in turn, contains about 90 percent of the living resources of the world.

Although the 1982 LOS Convention requires the coastal states that claimed the EFZ to enact conservation and management measures for the living resources within and across their 200-nautical-mile zones, fishery control for the EFZ is still beset with management problems that are complex and in many instances regional and international in scope. There has been no suitable shared management mechanism for fish stocks of cross-boundary and transboundary natures. Stock allocation for adjoining coastal states with overlapping fishery zones creates disputes and conflicts. (Also see Appendix IV for EFZs declared.)

To provide the choice of action to be taken in order to gain the benefits, rational management of living resources must be based on solid scientific data and information, in addition to socioeconomic considerations. This is such a complex and costly matter that coastal states, most often developing Third World nations, need technical assistance and transfer of technology. Despite the problems associated with or created by the new ocean regimes, the EEZs and EFZs, coastal states now are in a much better position to use fishery resources to meet their social and economic objectives, if they can enact conservation and management measures for the fisheries.

FISHERY CATCH: SIZE AND DISTRIBUTION

The size of the world's total fishery catch can be seen in three aspects: the total world fishery by countries' commercial catch, world fishery landings by groups of species, and world fishery catch by continent. The Food and Agricultural Organization (FAO) publishes an annual *Yearbook of Fishery Statistics*, which is the major source for such information.

Total world commercial catch in the 1960s was about 60 million metric tons; by 1970 it was close to 62 million; and by the mid–1970s it went down to 59 million metric tons. In 1980, the total world fisheries catch reached over 65 million. Since then there has been a steady increase in world commercial catch, as seen from Table 4.3, provided by the FAO.

In terms of world fishery landings by species groups for the period of 1982–1986, about half of the total world catch consisted of herring, sardines, anchovies, cods and haddocks, and diadromous fishes. Tunas, flounders, halibuts and salmons represent a small percentage of the total as seen in Table 4.4.

Major fishing areas are the three oceans and their adjacent waters: the Pacific, the Atlantic and the Indian. Some fishery catch comes from the island waters of the various continents. For 1983 to 1987 the world commercial catch is listed in Table 4.5.

Table 4.3

World Fisheries: Commercial Catch of Fish, Crustaceans and Mollusks by Countries, 1983–1987[1]

Country	1983[2]	1984[2]	1985[2]	1986[2]	1987
Japan	11,255	12,021	11,409	11,976	11,841
USSR	9,817	10,593	10,523	11,260	11,160
China	5,213	5,927	6,779	8,000	9,346
United States[3]	4,257	4,832	4,786	4,971	5,755
Chile	3,978	4,499	4,804	5,572	4,814
Peru	1,569	3,317	4,136	5,614	4,584
India	2,507	2,862	2,824	2,922	2,893
Republic of Korea	2,400	2,477	2,650	3,103	2,876
Indonesia	2,205	2,276	2,345	2,457	2,630
Thailand	2,260	2,135	2,225	2,536	2,168
Philippines	1,976	1,934	1,865	1,916	1,989
Norway	2,836	2,466	2,119	1,898	1,929
Korea (4)	1,600	1,650	1,700	1,700	1,700
Denmark	1,863	1,846	1,762	1,848	1,696
Iceland	839	1,535	1,680	1,657	1,633
Canada	1,348	1,282	1,418	1,507	1,453
Mexico	1,064	1,104	1,226	1,305	1,419
Spain	1,413	1,440	1,483	1,434	1,393
United Kingdom	840	836	891	850	955
Republic of South Africa	582	554	601	629	902
Vietnam	757	776	808	825	871
France	782	770	850	870	844
Bangladesh	724	754	774	794	815
Brazil	754	835	838	832	793
Burma	588	610	644	687	686
Ecuador	372	883	1,087	1,003	679
Poland	735	719	683	645	671
Turkey	557	567	578	583	626
Malaysia	741	665	632	616	608
Argentina	416	315	406	420	559

Table 4.3 (Continued)

Country	1983[2]	1984[2]	1985[2]	1986[2]	1987
Italy	546	573	583	560	554
Namibia	365	187	186	202	520
Morocco	454	467	473	598	491
Venezuela	231	259	265	314	453
Netherlands	506	432	504	455	435
New Zealand	282	295	305	345	431
Pakistan	343	372	408	416	428
All others	8,641	8,691	8,782	9,084	9,434
Total	77,616	83,756	86,032	92,403	93,034

Note: Statistics for mariculture, aquaculture, and other kinds of farming, etc., except for the United States, are included in country totals. Statistics on quantities caught by recreational fishermen are excluded. Does not include marine mammals and acquatic plants.

[1] Thousand metric tons, live weight.

[2] Revised.

[3] Includes the weight of clam, oyster, scallop and other mollusk shells. This weight is not included in U.S. landings statistics shown elsewhere.

[4] Data estimated by FAO.

Source: FAO, *Yearbook of Fishery Statistics, 1987*, vol. 64, Rome; reprinted in *Fisheries of the United States, 1988: Current Fishery Statistics No. 8800*, May 1989, p. 38.

Table 4.4
World Commercial Catch of Fish, Crustaceans and Mollusks, by Species Groups, 1983–1987[1]

Species Group	1983[2]	1984[2]	1985[2]	1986[2]	1987
Herring, sardines, anchovies, etc.	17,503	19,620	21,100	23,967	22,226
Cods, hakes, haddocks, etc.	11,223	12,258	12,450	13,534	13,703
Miscellaneous marine and diadromous fishes	8,761	8,972	9,281	10,025	10,167
Freshwater fishes	7,586	8,024	8,745	9,490	10,142
Jacks, mullets, sauries, etc.	7,967	8,562	8,013	7,182	7,866
Mollusks	5,960	6,364	6,441	6,546	7,524
Redfish, basses, congers, etc.	4,984	5,448	5,208	5,994	5,732
Crustaceans	3,227	3,250	3,503	3,920	3,975
Mackerel, snoeks, cutlass-fishes, etc.	3,674	4,268	3,828	4,018	3,648
Tunas, bonitos, billfishes, etc.	2,967	3,145	3,179	3,427	3,442
Flounders, halibuts, soles, etc.	1,125	1,191	1,348	1,315	1,279
Salmons, trouts, smelts, etc.	956	914	1,121	1,045	1,033
Shads, milkfishes, etc.	560	739	772	776	826
Sharks, rays, chimaeras, etc.	585	604	618	637	656
River eels	85	98	98	94	92
Sturgeons, paddlefishes, etc.	28	27	26	25	24
Miscellaneous	425	272	301	408	699
Total	77,616	83,756	86,032	92,403	93,034

Note: Does not include marine mammals and aquatic plants.

[1] Thousand metric tons, live weight.

[2] Revised.

Source: FAO, *Yearbook of Fishery Statistics, 1987*, p. 40.

Table 4.5

World Commercial Catch of Fish, Crustaceans and Mollusks, by Major Fishing Areas, 1983–1987

Area	1983[2]	1984[2]	1985[2]	1986[2]	1987
Marine Areas:					
Pacific Ocean and adjacent areas	38,255	43,729	45,720	51,019	49,407
Atlantic Ocean and adjacent areas	25,611	25,348	24,921	24,974	26,084
Indian Ocean and adjacent areas	4,457	4,739	4,766	4,970	5,014
Total	68,323	73,816	75,407	80,963	80,505
Inland Waters:					
Asia	5,884	6,391	7,106	7,714	8,381
Africa	1,556	1,612	1,553	1,676	1,738
USSR	856	881	906	927	988
South America	328	337	327	352	581
Europe	401	413	429	450	469
North and Central America	244	274	274	286	335
Oceania	24	32	30	35	37
Total	9,293	9,940	10,625	11,440	12,529
Grand Total	77,616	83,756	86,032	92,403	93,034

Note: Does not include marine mammals and aquatic plants.

[1] Thousand metric tons, live weight.

[2] Revised.

Source: FAO, *Yearbook of Fishery Statistics, 1987*, p. 39.

The largest fishery catch comes from the Asian continent, about 44 percent of the world's total in 1985. The European continent comes next with about 14.7 percent of the total world catch for 1985. Commercial fish catch, by continent, is shown in Table 4.6.

Significance. The total world fisheries commercial productivity is increasing each year. Since the end of World War II this increase has been estimated at about 7 to 8 percent per year. The top ten leading fishing nations—Japan, Soviet Union, China, Chile, United States, Peru, India, South Korea, Thailand and Norway—accounted for more than half of the world's total commercial catch for 1987. With the present rate of fishing technology development, the world fishery production may increase to 200 million metric tons by the year 2000.

Scientists do not agree on the question of the relationship between living resources of the sea and human population growth to more than 6 billion by 1998. However, Milner Schaefer argues that 200 million metric tons of seafood per year would be sufficient to provide the needed protein requirement for a total world population of 6 billion.[49] On the other hand, a rather pessimistic prediction has been made by William and Paul Paddock that food from the sea would not be able to catch up with the protein needs of an ever-expanding world population.[50] But the puzzling question remains: figures for total world catch have been increasing instead of decreasing despite the establishment of 200-nautical-mile exclusive fishing zones for the purpose of regulating fishing and reducing quotas under license by other coastal states within these zones. It should be noted here that about 40 percent of the total world catch is constituted by cod and herring families, and about 5 percent caught are tuna, salmon and swordfish.

FISHERY: DISPUTES AND AGREEMENTS (BILATERAL AND REGIONAL)

Disputes over fishing among nations with adjacent or opposite waters are as old as some of the principles in customary international law. Fishery disputes between Britain and Iceland and Holland date back to as early as the seventeenth century. Japanese and Korean quarrels over fishery rights in adjacent waters were recorded in 1442. Fishery disputes were endemic in the post–World War II period and tapered off after 1976 when 200-nautical-mile preferential fishery zones became the acceptable state practice. Fishery disputes are still occurring in the world's oceans despite the signing by 159 nations of the 1982 LOS Convention, which authorized the establishment of EEZs.

Causes for fishery disputes are many; following are the most prevalent. First, the assertion has been made by coastal states that fish stock is declining off their coasts and that unilateral measures for enclosure are necessary in order to curtail foreign fishing activities. This has resulted in conflict over the right of freedom of fishing. The classic example was the disagreement between Holland and the United Kingdom over the right to fish herring in the North Sea, which contributed

Table 4.6
World Commercial Catch of Fish, Crustaceans and Mollusks, by Continent, 1983–1987[1]

Continent	1983[2]	1984[2]	1985[2]	1986[2]	1987
Asia	35,085	37,045	37,711	40,697	41,700
Europe	12,797	13,116	12,947	12,693	12,600
South America	7,573	10,377	11,806	14,043	12,236
USSR	9,817	10,593	10,523	11,260	11,160
North and Central America	7,268	7,776	8,158	8,396	9,261
Africa	4,481	4,227	4,257	4,605	5,253
Oceania	595	622	630	709	824
Total	77,616	83,756	86,032	92,403	93,034

Note: Does not include marine mammals and aquatic plants.
[1] Thousand metric tons, live weight.
[2] Revised.
Source: FAO, *Yearbook of Fishery Statistics, 1987*, p. 39.

in part to the Anglo-Dutch Wars in the seventeenth century. One of the many recent examples was the 1984 fishing dispute between Iceland and the United Kingdom when the Icelandic parliament enacted legislation to regulate all fishery operations in waters above the Icelandic continental shelf. This 1948 dispute culminated in the 1974 International Court of Justice decision on the fishery jurisdiction case between Iceland and the United Kingdom, which will be discussed later. One needs to mention here only briefly that there were similar cases of fishing conflicts in the 1950s, 1960s and 1970s. Details of the 1951 United Kingdom versus Norway dispute in the 1969 North Sea Continental Shelf case, and of the 1974 Germany versus Iceland case, will be discussed shortly.

A second major cause of fishery disputes has been the assertion of independent economic nationalism by the newly emerged Third World nations. While these fishery disputes across the world's oceans are, in the main, influenced by the economic factors of providing food and protein for a rapidly rising population, they are ideological as well. The Third World nations have become keenly aware of the disparity in wealth and economic resources measured against the more industrialized West and Japan. Then there is the fact that since there are a number of Third World nations whose offshore fishing grounds are rich and unexploited, their obvious response has been to enclose their waters by extending their exclusive national jurisdiction over fisheries beyond the traditionally recognized limits. For many developing Third World nations offshore living resources are the key economic prize to be fought over against the encroachment, in their view, of the developed nations who possess the sophisticated fishing technology. From an economic point of view, it needs to be pointed out that the world's fishing fleets in 1980 harvested $14.9 billion from exports. The fishing fleets of five developed nations—Canada, Denmark, Japan, Norway and the United States—earned $1 billion each in that year.[51]

Third, beginning in the 1960s, fishing no longer has been confined to fleets operating close to home ports. Instead, distant-water fishing fleets from Japan, the Soviet Union and South Korea operate thousands of miles away from their home ports. These fleets are accompanied by factory ships, which process the fish caught while on long voyages away from land-based processing facilities. Distant-water fishing grounds can now be found in the Northwest and Northeast Atlantic, off Northwest and Southwest Africa, and in the Northwest Pacific. A Japanese distant-water fleet can now fish off the Icelandic coast; a Korean distant-water fleet operates off Southwest Africa; and a Soviet fleet off the coast of Argentina. In one year, 1971, there were eighteen distant-water fishing fleets operating in the fishing grounds from the East Atlantic to West Africa.[52]

Fourth, the need for a coastal state to provide conservation and management measures for its living resources has contributed to the disputes in recent years. Fishing grounds may be declared closed by coastal states whose waters are adjacent to or opposite the resources. Coastal authorities instigate arrests and are then challenged by fishing fleets of the affected nations. Also, as more coastal states declare the 200-nautical-mile EEZ, more incidents of seizures and arrests seem to occur. The very first seizure by the U.S. Coast Guard was on July 9,

1977, under the 200-nautical-mile EFZ established by the Magnuson Fishery Conservation and Management Act, which came into effect on March 1, 1977. It involved a Soviet trawler about 240 nautical miles southeast of Boston and 75 nautical miles within the 200-nautical-mile exclusive fishery zone boundary. The Soviet trawler *Taras Snevechenko* and a factory ship had evidently caught 1.4 metric tons of river herring in excess of the authorized amount allowed by the Magnuson Fishery Conservation and Management Act. During the two-month period after the Act came into effect—from March to April 1977—the U.S. Coast Guard had cited fifty-three Soviet ships for ninety-seven separate violations of the Act.[53] About half of Japan's annual fishery harvest of approximately 10 million metric tons comes from within 200 nautical miles of other countries: 15 percent of Japan's total catch comes from the United States 200-nautical-mile zone, about 20 percent from the Soviet zone, and a substantial portion is also taken from the Canadian 200-nautical-mile zone. As will be discussed later, there has been an ongoing dispute, a "fish war," between the United States and Japan over the salmon fishing rights, particularly on Japanese fishermen's interceptions on the high seas of salmon spawned in Alaskan rivers and streams.

Historically there have been a number of agreements concluded between coastal states and foreign fishing states to resolve fishing disputes. One of the oldest was the 1938 United Kingdom–France agreement concerning dredging for oysters in the waters between the island of Jersey and the French coast. The agreement permitted a three-mile zone on each other's coast for oyster fishing under acceptable rules for gear and identification of fishing vessels on the high seas.[54] Then there was the dispute between Japan and South Korea that erupted in 1952 and 1954 after the latter proclaimed special zones for fishery conservation. By 1965 a compromise was reached by which each side was to recognize the other's exclusive fishing zone of twelve miles and a joint control over fishing by mackerel trawlers. In 1923 there was an agreement between the United States and Canada over halibut in the Alaskan waters; the original agreement was further expanded by agreements in 1932, 1937 and 1953. Also in 1953, after separate protests from the United States, Japan agreed not to fish for salmon spawned in Alaskan rivers and streams, designating an arbitrary dividing line fixed at 175° west longitude. However, disputes over salmon and ground fishing continued to erupt, so that in 1986 the United States and Japan held a series of secret negotiations in Seattle. In the salmon fishing dispute between the United States and Canada, a series of technical agreements dealing with the selection of turf lines along the coasts of Washington, Oregon and British Columbia were negotiated. The 1979 interim agreement concluded between the United States and Canada on fishing stock assignment for the Georges Bank serves as another illustration of cooperative sharing of the living resources for coastal states with adjacent waters. Fish stocks under the interim agreement in the disputed area, the Georges Bank, were to be taken by the following quota or shares: for scallops, Canada 73.35 percent and the United States 26.65 percent; for cod, Canada 17 percent and the United States 83 percent; for haddock, Canada 21 percent and the United States 83 percent; and for herring, Canada 33.3 percent and the United States 66.6 percent.[55]

Since the negotiations began in the Third United Nations Law of the Sea Conferences in the 1970s, there has been a proliferation of agreements concluded by governments for regulating their fishery rights and jurisdictions. These agreements have provided acceptable rules intended for the avoidance of and the settlement of disputes. These rules are to be found in bilateral agreements, multilateral conventions and the decisions of the International Court of Justice (ICJ).

There have been more than 200 bilateral agreements concluded by governments. A partial list of these agreements is provided in Appendix V. They represent a selected list of bilateral agreements concluded since the establishment of the new international regimes of the oceans: the twelve-nautical-mile territorial sea and the 200-nautical-mile EEZ.

In a study by J. B. Carroz and M. J. Savini of the FAO, these bilateral agreements on fisheries tend to fall into three major patterns:[56] replacement of foreign fishing vessels in the EEZ with local fisheries operations; granting of reciprocal fishing rights within the respective EEZ; and proscription of terms and conditions for foreign fishing vessels to operate within the EEZ.[57] Bilateral agreements listed here contain provisions of specific requirements for conservation and management of the living resources: number of vessels to be permitted to operate in the EEZ; limitation of foreign fishing vessels operating in designated areas; catch quota to be observed; gear size; fee payments by foreign vessels authorized to fish within the zone; and fixed quantity for foreign fishing vessels which must land their catches in coastal states' ports.[58] In addition, these bilateral agreements provide rules and regulations on enforcement measures, inspection procedures and seizure procedures of foreign vessels found to be violating rules promulgated by the coastal states that extend jurisdiction to the zone. Few of these bilateral agreements contain specific provisions for dispute settlement regarding the application and interpretation of the agreements concluded between the parties. Several of these bilateral agreements provide consultation, joint commission and fisheries boards for settlement of claims. Bilateral agreement between the EEC and Sweden provides final arbitration as a method of dispute settlement. The 1986 arbitration award on the *La Bretagne* between Canada and France over the fishery rights on the Gulf of St. Lawrence, off the coast of southern Newfoundland (France owns two small islands, Saint Pierre and Miquelon), introduced some interesting interpretations with reference to conservation and management measures by a coastal state under Articles 61 and 62 of the 1982 LOS Convention. The arbitration award ruled, perhaps erroneously in the view of one expert on the law of the sea, that even though Canada can decide how much fish a foreign vessel can take, it cannot prohibit, in this case, freezer-trawlers from processing the catch by filleting.[59]

One of the first multilateral agreements on the regulation of fishing was the 1882 North Sea Fisheries Convention under which the signatory nations of Great

Britain, Germany, Belgium, Denmark, France and Holland proclaimed exclusive fishing rights within three miles from the low-water mark and a ten-mile-wide bay drawn between arbitrarily chosen points. The 1882 North Sea Fisheries Convention was later replaced by a new convention in 1964, the result of a conference in which thirteen European nations participated. The new convention provided an exclusive fishery zone of six miles for the signatory nations. Then a fishing zone for the waters beyond six miles, but not to exceed twelve miles, was to be the exclusive jurisdiction of the coastal states and those nations that had traditionally fished in the waters between 1953 and 1962.

Multilateral agreements on fishery operations or for achieving cooperative conservation efforts have been on the rise in recent years. In a list of international conventions on living resources management prepared by the United Nations in 1985, a total of thirty-seven multilateral agreements have been recorded, including those that deal with the conservation and management of particular species such as whales, tuna, salmon, herring and halibut. The list has been arranged according to region: Antarctica, Arctic, Atlantic, Baltic, Black Sea, Mediterranean, North and South Pacific and Indo-Pacific.[60]

Since the formation of the United Nations at the end of World War II, a number of fishery jurisdiction cases have been referred to the International Court of Justice (ICJ) at The Hague for adjudication. The 1951 Anglo-Norwegian Fishery case was brought to the ICJ on a United Kingdom protest that Norway was entitled to only a four-mile seaward limit of its territorial waters from which the baseline was measured to establish the fishery zone. The ICJ held that Norway's method of measuring straight baselines between the headlands and the outer edge of offshore rocks for determining its fishery zone was valid in accordance with customary international law.[61] The court also held the view that Norway had a historic title to the disputed area for fishing. In other words, the 1951 Anglo-Norwegian Fishery case established the principle that a coastal state can establish, by its historic practice and economic need, an exclusive fishery zone in the adjacent waters along its coast. Based on the decision in the Anglo-Norwegian Fishery case, Iceland and Denmark (on behalf of Greenland) subsequently enacted regulations to close off part of the high seas as their exclusive jurisdiction fishery zones. (Eventually the method of measuring straight baselines to form the territorial seas was incorporated first in the 1958 UNCLOS I, and then it became a part of Article 7 of the 1982 LOS Convention.)

The United Kingdom and Iceland have been embroiled in continuous disputes over fishing rights in waters adjacent to the Icelandic coast. In 1958 the failure of UNCLOS I to reach an agreement on the delimitation of the territorial sea provided Iceland the pretext to claim unilaterally a twelve-mile fishing zone and a series of baselines drawn around Iceland and its fringe islands. Prior to this action in 1946 Iceland had declared exclusive fishing rights in waters above its continental shelf. British fishermen objected to the unilateral enclosure of what was then considered a part of the high seas. Thus, the "fish war" or "cod war" that began two months after the conclusion of the 1958 UNCLOS I lasted more than eighteen months. During that period, the British navy provided escorts for its fishing fleets as it had done a century before in their ongoing fishery disputes with Iceland. The British finally called for a truce on the eve of the convening of the 1960 UNCLOS II, which again failed to reach agreement on the extent and the breadth of the territorial sea.

In 1961 negotiations between Iceland and the United Kingdom reached a tentative ten-year agreement, the Exchange of Notes, which provided (1) discontinuance of fishing by British vessels within the disputed area and limiting of their operations beyond the twelve miles; (2) recognition by the United Kingdom of the right of Iceland to extend exclusive fishing rights for the entire Icelandic continental shelf; (3) that the United Kingdom must be notified of any extension of fishery rights by Iceland and fishery rights by either party to the International Court of Justice.[62]

In 1971 Iceland proclaimed an extension of its fishery jurisdiction to fifty nautical miles and the termination of fishery agreements with both the United Kingdom and West Germany. While insisting on its right to fish beyond the twelve-mile zone, the United Kingdom referred its protest to the ICJ in 1971 in accordance with the 1961 Exchange of Notes between it and Iceland.

After the issuance by the court on August 17, 1972, of an interim order restraining the enforcement of Icelandic regulation intended to prevent fishing by British vessels outside of the twelve-mile zone, the parties resumed negotiations that resulted in another Exchange of Notes in 1973, valid for two years, which limited total yearly catch for British vessels to 130,000 metric tons. The court finally took up the case and ruled on July 25, 1974, that: (1) Iceland, both as a coastal state and as a nation whose livelihood was dependent upon the fishing economy, was entitled to claim preferential fishing right over the disputed area; (2) the United kingdom had "an historic right" of the high seas and "special interests" derived from its long and continued practice of fishing in the disputed areas (these factors tend to limit Iceland's preferential fishing rights); and (3) taking into account these considerations, Iceland could not unilaterally proclaim an arbitrary expansion of the exclusive fishing zone to fifty nautical miles.[63] The court's instruction to both parties was to continue negotiation for "an equitable apportionment" of the living resources in the disputed area.[64] (The ICJ disposed of the fishery jurisdiction case of the Federal Republic of Germany versus Iceland, the companion case to the United Kingdom versus Iceland, in a similar fashion at the same time.)

In the 1984 case of the Delimitation of the Maritime Boundary in the Gulf of Maine Area,[65] several important precedents were established by the ICJ.[66] Instead of the judgment by the fifteen-member ICJ, the parties agreed to use, for the first time, a five-member "special chamber"—a procedure provided for in the ICJ's Statutes to allow greater flexibility in dispute settlement. The Gulf of Maine dispute originated from the 1964 Canadian issuance of oil and gas exploratory permits for the eastern half of the Georges Bank, one of the world's richest fishing grounds. This action was based on Article 6 of the

1958 Continental Shelf Convention concluded at the UNCLOS I. This article, to which both Canada and the United States are signatories, states that if the continental shelf is adjacent to the territories of two or more states whose coasts are opposite each other, the boundary of the continental shelf shall be determined by agreement between them, and in the absence of such agreement, the boundary is the median line. In the case of the continental shelf that is adjacent to the territories of two adjacent states, the boundary line shall be determined by agreement, and in the absence of such agreement, the boundary must be determined by the equidistance principle. On November 5, 1969, the United States officially stated that it refused to recognize the validity of Canadian permits for oil and gas exploration on Georges Bank. Bilateral talks between the two countries in 1970 were unfruitful. Then in 1976 and 1977 the United States and Canada proclaimed the 200-nautical-mile fishery zones that further complicated the dispute. Negotiations were renewed to resolve the dispute and, during the interim, an agreement on fisheries was signed on February 24, 1977, continuing the fishing operation on Georges Bank that existed before their establishment of the 200-nautical-mile special fishery zones. Also by special agreement, in 1981 Canada and the United States submitted the boundary dispute to the ICJ. At that time, the United States claimed 30,000 nautical square miles in the Gulf of Maine and the entire Georges Bank.

The United States claim was based on the principle that the boundary must provide maritime space in proportion to the relevant coastlines of the two countries—the United States coastline being longer than the Canadian—and the continuous extension of the east coast of the United States. Canada, on the other hand, laid claim to over 40 percent of Georges Bank by its modified equidistance line and the economic need of its fishery communities. The ICJ's special chamber of five members rejected both claims and independently advanced its own solution. It argued that the criteria applied in previous continental shelf dispute cases were not really suitable for the delimitation of both the continental shelf in the Gulf of Maine area and the 200-nautical-mile fishery zones affecting Georges Bank. The special chamber preferred to use only the "geometrical methods" based on geographical features of the area as an equitable solution. In effect the special chamber felt it was necessary in this case to delimit both the seabed on the continental shelf in the Gulf of Maine and the superjacent waters by a single boundary line or a multipurpose delimitation rather than a plurality of separate delimitations.[67] The effects of the court's single boundary line were that for the Gulf of Maine, the United States received about two-thirds of the area; for Georges Bank, Canada received about one-sixth of the rich fishing ground, or 1,350 square nautical miles. Included in the area is the Northeast Peak, rich in scallops and a spawning ground for haddock.

Significance. Fishery disputes have been on the wane since the establishment of the 200-nautical-mile fishery zones. The 1982 Law of the Sea Convention, which as of 1991 has not yet come into effect, has influenced to a significant extent the negotiations that produced more than one hundred bilateral fishery agreements for sharing and devising rational cooperative conservation management measures for living resources. As a whole, these bilateral fishery agreements constitute ''a network of rules'' for preventing, as well as solving, fishery disputes. In fact, the rules with respect to fishery disputes continued in the bilateral agreements have been accepted by developed and developing nations in their national legislation dealing with matters of fishery conservation and management. There have also been extensive fishery cooperative arrangements established by a number of multilateral agreements concluded on global, regional and specie management bases as seen in Appendices V and VI.

Significant fishery jurisdiction cases have been brought to the International Court of Justice for adjudication. In the cases of the 1951 Anglo-Norwegian Fishery dispute and the 1975 United Kingdom–Iceland fishery controversy, the court adhered to historic right and economic needs as criteria for an equitable solution. But the 1984 United States–Canada delimitation of the Gulf of Maine case seemed to establish a new approach: the emphasis on coastal geographic (geographic adjacency measure by distance) criterion, but not human activities, in determining an equitable basis for delimiting the continental shelf and the 200-nautical-mile fishery zones with a single boundary line. In the 1984 United States–Canada delimitation of the Gulf of Maine case, the ICJ has formulated a new concept of ''partial fusion or integration'' of two separate ocean regimes—the continental shelf and the 200-nautical-mile fishery zone. This simultaneous delimitation may have a lasting effect on the public order of the fishery regime.[68]

FISHERY: DISTANT-WATER FLEETS

A revolution in fishery operations took place at the beginning of the 1960s that not only altered the way of fishing, but contributed to the development of the new ocean regime known as the 200-nautical-mile exclusive fishing zone. This was the invention of the ''factory equipped freezer stern trawler'' or simply the ''factory trawler'' that catches and processes the fish at sea thousands of miles from home port for months at a time.[69] Captain Harold Saloesen of the United Kingdom, an experienced veteran in the whaling industry before World War II, was credited with the revolutionary design for this method of fishing. Typically, a factory trawler is equipped with a stern ramp, an assembly-line fillet machine, a refrigeration plant and equipment for fish meal processing of non-marketable fish.[70] Soon other fishing nations—West Germany, Norway, Italy, the Netherlands, Belgium, Iceland, Denmark, Poland, Japan, South Korea and the Soviet Union—followed with factory trawlers. By 1974, the Soviet Union had the world's largest fleet of more than 700 factory trawlers, plus factory mother ships, which only process the fish caught by the fishing fleet.

By the time UNCLOS III began its sessions in the mid–1970s, distant-water fishing nations equipped with factory trawlers harvested approximately 50 percent of the fish stock on the west coast of Africa and 100 percent of the total catch

Table 4.7
Long-Range Catch in the Northwest Pacific Ocean, 1976[1]

Fishing Fleet of:	Coastal Waters Adjacent to:			
	USSR	Japan	South Korea	Total
Japan	1,500	-	207	1,707
USSR	-	665	-	665
South Korea	400	-	-	400
Total	1,900	665	207	1,772

[1] In million tons.

Source: Vladimir Kaczynski, *Distant-Water Fisheries: After 200-mile Economic Zone* (Seattle: Institute for Marine Studies, University of Washington, 1982), p. 18. Used by permission.

of all marine species in the southern oceans.[71] In 1975, distant-water fleets accounted for 53 percent of the catch in the Northwest Atlantic and 78 percent in the Northeast Pacific. A typical pattern of overfishing by distant-water fishing fleets has been to concentrate in one area until the fishing stocks begin to decline and then move on to another area to repeat the process. Kaczynski's study showed that for the six-year period from 1971 to 1976, the total catch for herring in the Northwest Atlantic dropped by as much as 56 percent and in the Northeast Atlantic by 40 percent.[72] At the same time, total harvest for South African sardines and Northwest Atlantic apeline increased appreciably. Overexploitation by distant-water fleets caused not only grave concern by coastal fishermen about the need for measures to protect and conserve the living resources, but also economic hardship in terms of loss of revenues for local fishermen. These concerns were eventually translated into protective measures aimed at preventing the distant-water fleets from fishing in the area. A primary motivation for both Canada and the United States to declare a 200-nautical-mile exclusive fishery zone on the Georges Bank in the Gulf of Maine was the concern over the volume of fish stock caught by Soviet and Eastern European distant-water fleets in the area. In 1973, Soviet factory trawlers and mother ships took 42 percent of the total volume of all species caught on the George Banks, and the Eastern European nations took another 30 percent; while for the same year, the United States and Canada harvested only 11 and 9 percent respectively.[73] Increased conflicts between local fishermen and foreign distant-water fleets also occurred in the Northwest Pacific. In 1976, South Korean, Japanese and Soviet distant-water fleets harvested over 2.7 million metric tons of fish in fishing grounds adjacent to other nations' coasts without entering into any bilateral or multilateral agreements between them. Table 4.7 provides a picture of the distant water fleets operating in the Northwest Pacific in 1976.

The 200-nautical-mile EFZ established by the United States and Canada in 1977 reduced the number of fishing vessels of several foreign distant-water fleets, particularly the Soviet Union, by as much as 45 percent in the two nations' fishing grounds.[74] Other distant-water fleets affected were those of Japan, Spain,

South Korea and Poland. However, in 1987 there was a noticeable increase in South Korean distant-water fishing fleets.

Significance. With the establishment of the 200-nautical-mile fishery regime by coastal nations around the world, distant-water factory trawlers are gradually phasing out of service. One no longer sees the concentration of massive factory trawlers on major fishing grounds. Often based on socioeconomic factors rather than surplus catch, licensing by coastal states that placed emphasis on low quotas made it costly to operate these factory trawlers thousands of miles from their home ports. Nowadays the factory trawlers in distant-water fishing are being described as "lumbering dinosaurs."[75] The oil price increases in 1974 and 1978 added to the problems for factory trawlers amidst the expansion of ocean enclosure movement. In 1974, Japan's distant-water fleets caught 43.7 percent of its total distant-water fisheries; by 1977, they accounted for abut 29.9 percent.[76] The decline in distant-water fishing also encouraged development of many coastal states' own offshore fishing.

Overexploitation by factory trawlers equipped with advanced electronic gear has caused significant changes in the type of fish caught as well as the fishing grounds pursued. Today the most caught and consumed fish in the world is Alaskan pollock rather than cod from the North Atlantic. Instead of herring as the most used specie for fishmeal, it is the Peruvian anchoveta, a specie so overfished that its production dropped to barely 2 million tons in the early 1970s from its peak of 13 million tons in the 1960s. Fleets of Soviet, Japanese and South Korean factory trawlers roam the Atlantic, the Indian Ocean and both coasts of Africa. Distant-water fishing has been the important impetus for the development of the 200-nautical-mile fishery zone, which encompasses the continental shelves and slopes, the home of 85 to 95 percent of the world's fishing. These enclosed fishing areas are no longer the "fishing commons" of the oceans or the ocean regime of open access in the classic sense. The phasing out of giant factory trawlers in distant-water fishing, a direct result of the establishment of the 200-nautical-mile exclusive fishery zones, has considerably reduced the intense concentration of fishing for targeted species in the world's major fishing grounds. Now fishing on the worldwide scale is more diffused with a larger number of smaller vessels over "a wider expanse of world oceans."[77]

NOTES

1. See John P. Craven, *The Management of the Pacific Marine Resources: Present Problems and Future Trends* (Boulder, Colo.: Westview Press, 1982), p. 56.
2. Ibid., p. 48.
3. R. P. Anand, "The Politics of a New Legal Order for Fisheries," *Ocean Development and International Law* 11, nos. 3–4 (1982): 268–270.
4. Craven, *The Management of the Pacific Marine Resources*, p. 56.
5. Ibid., p. 58.
6. Lewis M. Alexander, "The Ocean Enclosure Movement: Inventory and Prospects," *San Diego Law Review* 20, no. 3 (April 1983): 569.

7. Ibid., pp. 569–570.

8. See Ann L. Hollick, *U.S. Foreign Policy and the Law of the Sea* (Princeton, N.J.: Princeton University Press, 1981), pp. 162–170.

9. See Jean Carroz and Michele Savine, "The Practice of Coastal States Regarding Foreign Access to Fishery Resources," *Report of Expert Consultation on the Conditions of Access to the Fish Resources of the Exclusive Economic Zones*, FAO Fisheries Report No. 293 (Rome, 11–15 April 1983), pp. 47–51.

10. Ibid., p. 47.

11. Ibid., p. 48.

12. Comments made by Bernard Oxman at a meeting on the background and problems in the drafting of the fishery provisions for the 1982 LOS Convention. See Jon M. Van Dyke, ed., *Consensus and Confrontation: The United States and the Law of the Sea Convention* (Honolulu: The Law of the Sea Institute, University of Hawaii, 1985), p. 394.

13. See R. P. Barston and Patricia Birnie, *The Maritime Dimension* (London: Allen & Unwin, 1980), p. 34. Also see S. J. Holt, "The Food Resources of the Ocean," *Scientific American* 221, no. 3 (September 1969): 2–14.

14. Barston and Birnie, *The Maritime Dimension*, p. 34.

15. Ibid.

16. R. R. Churchill and A. V. Lowe, *The Law of the Sea* (Manchester, England: Manchester University Press, 1983), p. 199.

17. Ibid.

18. Myres S. McDougal and William T. Burke, *The Public Order of the Oceans: A Contemporary International Law of the Sea* (Norwell, Mass.: Kluwer-Nijhoff, 1987), pp. 469 and 475.

19. Barston and Birnie, *The Maritime Dimension*, p. 37.

20. Craven, *The Management of the Pacific Resources*, p. 53.

21. McDougal and Burke, *The Public Order of the Oceans*, pp. 473–475. Also see Craven, *The Management of the Pacific Resources*, pp. 58–61.

22. McDougal and Burke, *The Public Order of the Oceans*, p. 470.

23. Ibid.

24. Ibid., p. 275. Also see Jeremiah J. Sullivan, *Pacific Basin Enterprise and the Changing Law of the Sea* (Lexington, Mass.: D. C. Heath, 1977), pp. 138–142.

25. Gerald K. Moore, *Coastal State Requirements for Foreign Fishing*, Legislative Study No. 21, Rev. 2, FAO (Rome, 1985), pp. 7–9.

26. Ibid., p. 7.

27. Ibid., p. 18.

28. Ibid., pp. 8–9.

29. Ibid., p. 10.

30. Barston and Birnie, *The Maritime Dimension*, p. 39.

31. Churchill and Lowe, *The Law of the Sea*, p. 204.

32. Barston and Birnie, *The Maritime Dimension*, p. 39; and J. A. Crutchfield, "Over-Capitalization of the Fishing Effort," in L. M. Alexander, ed., *The Future of the Sea's Resources* (Kingston, R.I.: University of Rhode Island, 1968), pp. 23–29.

33. S. J. Holt and C. Vanderbilt, "Marine Fisheries," in Elisabeth Mann Borgese and Norton Ginsburg, eds., *Ocean Yearbook 2* (Chicago: The University of Chicago Press, 1980), p. 49.

34. Ibid., p. 50.

35. Ibid.

36. William T. Burke, ''Coastal State Fishery Regulation under International Law: A Comment on the La Bretagne Award of July 17, 1986 (The Arbitration between Canada and France),'' *San Diego Law Review* 25, no. 3 (August–September 1988): 518.

37. Lawrence Juda, ''The EEZ and Ocean Management,'' *Ocean Development and International Law* 18, no. 3 (1987): 314.

38. Ibid., p. 315.

39. William T. Burke, ''The Law of the Sea Convention and Fishing Practices of Nonsignatories with Special Reference to the United States,'' in Van Dyke, ed., *Consensus and Confrontation*, p. 318.

40. See Edward L. Miles and William T. Burke, ''Pressures on the United Nations Convention on the Law of the Sea of 1982 Arising from New Fisheries Conflicts: The Problem of Straddling Stocks,'' *Ocean Development and International Law* 20, no. 4 (1989): 343–357.

41. Ibid., p. 353.

42. See Lourene Miovski, ''Solution in the Convention on the Law of the Sea to the Problem of Overfishing in the Central Bering Sea: Analysis of the Convention Provisions Concerning Fisheries and Enclosed and Semi-Enclosed Seas,'' *San Diego Law Review* 26, no. 3 (August–September 1989): 525–574.

43. Barston and Birnie, *The Maritime Dimension*, p. 38.

44. Ibid.

45. Brian Rothschild, ''Global Fisheries Management: The New Challenge,'' in Douglas M. Johnston and Norman G. Letalik, eds., *The Law of the Sea and Ocean Industry: New Opportunities and Restraints* (Honolulu: The Law of the Sea Institute, University of Hawaii, 1984), p. 332.

46. Ibid., p. 333.

47. Juda, ''The EEZ and Ocean Management,'' pp. 313–324.

48. Rothschild, ''Global Fisheries Management,'' pp. 333–337.

49. Milner Shaefer, ''Economic and Social Needs for Marine Resources,'' in *Ocean Engineering: Goals, Environment, Technology* (New York: Wiley, 1968), pp. 6 and 10.

50. Ibid., p. 71.

51. *The New York Times*, 30 January 1983, p. E–4.

52. J.R.V. Prescott, *Political Geography of the Oceans* (New York: Wiley, 1975), p. 121.

53. *Time*, 25 April 1977, p. 23.

54. Prescott, *Political Geography of the Oceans*, p. 135.

55. See Sang-Myon Rhee, ''The Application of Equitable Principles to Resolve the United States–Canada Dispute over East Coast Fishery Resources,'' *Harvard International Law Journal* 21, no. 3 (Fall 1980): 671.

56. ''The New International Law of Fisheries Emerging from Bilateral Agreements,'' *Marine Policy* 3 (1979): 78–98.

57. Ibid., p. 82.

58. Ibid., pp. 84–88.

59. Burke, ''Coastal State Fishery Regulation under International Law,'' pp. 495–533.

60. See *The Law of the Sea: Multilateral Treaties Relevant to the UN Conference on the Law of the Sea* (United Nations: Office of the Special Representative of the Secretary-General for the Law of the Sea, 1983), pp. 22–32.

61. *ICJ Reports*, 1951, p. 143.

62. See *United Nations Treaty Series*, 397, p. 275.

63. See David L. Larson, *Major Issues of the Law of the Sea* (Durham: University of New Hampshire, 1976), pp. 93–96; and R. P. Barston and Hjalmar W. Hanneson, "The Anglo-Icelandic Fisheries Dispute," *International Relations* 4, no. 6 (November 1974): 559–584. Also see Jeffrey G. Weil, "Law of the Sea—Exclusive Economic Zone: Iceland Accorded Preferential Fishing Rights in Waters Adjacent to Its Coast," *Harvard International Law Journal* 16, no. 2 (Spring 1975): 474–490.

64. Barston and Hanneson, "The Anglo-Icelandic Fisheries Dispute," pp. 580–582; and Larson, *Major Issues of the Law of the Sea*, p. 93. Also see Barston and Birnie, *The Maritime Dimension*, p. 174.

65. *ICJ Reports*, no. 67 (*U.S.A. v. Canada*), 1984.

66. For further discussion of the Gulf of Maine case, see Sang-Myon Rhee, "The Application of Equitable Principles to Resolve the United States–Canada Dispute over East Coast Fishery Resources," pp. 668–683; G. David Nied, "International Adjudication: Settlement of the United States–Canada Maritime Boundary Dispute: Delimitation of the Marine Boundary in the Gulf of Maine Area (*U.S. v. Canada*), 1982, I.C.J. 3 (Constitution of Chamber Order of January 20), *Harvard International Law Journal* 23, no. 1 (Spring 1982): 138–143; L. H. Legault and Blair Hankey, "From Sea to Seabed: The Single maritime Boundary in the Gulf of Maine Case," *American Journal of International Law* 79 (October 1985): 961–991; "World Court Panel Sets Boundary Line for Canada–United States Fishing Zone," *UN Chronicle* 21, nos. 10–11 (12 October 1984): 37–39; Paul D. McHugh, "International Law Delimitation of Maritime Boundaries," *Natural Resources Journal* 25, no. 4 (October 1985): 1025–1038; John Cooper, "Delimitation of the Maritime Boundary in the Gulf of Maine Area," *Ocean Development and International Law* 16, no. 1 (1986): 59–90; Jan Schneider, "The Gulf of Maine Case: The Nature of an Equitable Result," *American Journal of International Law* 79, no. 7 (July 1985): 539–577. Also see an earlier article by Sang-Myon Rhee, "Equitable Solution to the Maritime Boundary Dispute between the United States and Canada in the Gulf of Maine," *American Journal of International Law* 75 (July 1981): 590–628. For the text of judgment, see "Affaire de la Delimitation de la Frontier Maritime dans la Région du Golfe du Maine," *ICJ Report*, 246 (*Canada c. États-Unis d'Amerique*), 12 October 1984. Copy provided by the Ministry of External Affairs of Canada. Also see *International Legal Materials* 23 (1984): 1197–1273.

67. *ICJ Report*, 327, 1984 (paragraph 194).

68. Legault and Hankey, "From Sea to Seabed: The Single Maritime Boundary," p. 990.

69. See William W. Warner, *Distant Water: The Fate of the North Atlantic Fishermen* (Boston: Little, Brown and Company, 1977).

70. Ibid., p. 32.

71. Vladimir Kaczynski, *Distant-Water Fisheries: After 200-Mile Economic Zone* (Seattle: Institute of Marine Studies, University of Washington, March 1982), p. 1.

72. Ibid., p. 8.

73. *The Wall Street Journal*, 15 October 1984, p. 10.

74. Ibid., p. 29.

75. Warner, *Distant Water*, p. 30.

76. See Tsuneo Akaha, *Japan in Global Ocean Politics* (Honolulu: University of Hawaii Press, 1985), p. 21.

77. Warner, *Distant Water*, p. 322.

CHAPTER 5

Living Resources: Regional Fishery Commissions, Marine Mammals Protection and Species Approach

FISHERIES: REGIONAL FISHERY COMMISSIONS

At present there are more than twenty international fisheries commissions.[1] Most of these fisheries commissions were formed at the end of World War II as regional fishery coordinating and regulating bodies. A number of them were established for the conservation and management of particular species, such as whales, seals, salmon, halibut and tuna. Since 1946 some of these regional commissions were formed at the urging of the Food and Agricultural Organization (FAO) to aid developing coastal states in the Indo-Pacific, the Indian Ocean, the Caribbean and the Mediterranean. Those that formed outside the FAO framework are the regional fishery commissions in northern and southeastern Pacific, the Baltic Sea and the Antarctic. At present there are eight regional and species commissions established for the Atlantic Ocean, seven for the Pacific, and one each for the Mediterranean, the Black Sea, the Baltic Sea, the Indian Ocean and Antarctica. The oldest of these regional and specie commissions is the International Whaling Commission (IWC), established by the 1946 International Convention on Whaling. It has a membership of forty-one. The IWC is in fact a global organization for overseeing the conservation and the utilization of whaling resources worldwide (see the section on mammals in this chapter). Another older regional fishery commission is the Indo-Pacific Fishery Commission, formed under the auspices of FAO in 1948. It has a membership of nineteen, and its main functions are to formulate and recommend conservation and management measures, review social and economic aspects of fishing, and conduct research and training. Similar in function and also organized under the aegis of FAO is the 1949 General Fisheries Council for the Mediterranean, which has a membership of nineteen coastal states bordering the Mediterranean and parts of the Black Sea.

In 1949 six coastal states (Canada, France, Japan, Nicaragua, Panama and the United States) of the Eastern Pacific Ocean formed the Inter-American Tropical Tuna Commission for the purpose of gathering and interpreting information on tuna and proposing joint action for tuna conservation. For the period 1952–1953, an active fishery organizing period for the Pacific, four regional and species commissions were formed. The 1952 international convention, with participation by Canada, Japan and the United States, established the International North Pacific Fisheries Commission as a forum for cooperation and for studies on anadromous and non-anadromous species (see species approach section in this chapter). In the same year the North Pacific Fur Seal Commission was formed as the result of an international convention on conservation measures for seals. Canada, Japan, the United States and the Soviet Union were the participants. Also in 1952, the Permanent Commission for the Conference on the Use and Conservation of the Marine Resources of the South Pacific was established by Chile, Colombia, Ecuador and Peru. In 1953 the International Pacific Halibut Commission was formed through a bilateral agreement between Canada and the United States to develop and regulate halibut stock in the North Pacific and the Bering Sea by means of optimum yield permits. In 1979 the South Pacific Forum Fisheries Agency was established with a membership of thirteen South Pacific nations for the purpose of providing fishery management policies, enforcement measures, and reciprocal access arrangements for members in each other's 200-nautical-mile fishery zone.

For the two decades from 1961 to 1982, eight regional commissions were formed in the Atlantic Ocean area. In 1961, by a resolution of FAO conference, the Regional Fisheries Advisory Commission for the Southwest Atlantic was established to develop management measures for the exploitation of marine and inland fishery resources in that region. Argentina, Brazil and Uruguay were its members. For conservation of the tuna population in the Atlantic Ocean, a twenty-one-member (including Japan and South Korea) International Commission for the Conservation of Atlantic Tunas was organized in 1966. A year later, in 1967, by resolution of the FAO Council, a thirty-member (including Japan and South Korea) Fishery Committee for the Eastern Central Atlantic, between Cape Spartel and the Congo River, was formed for developing programs of living resources use. In 1969, the International Commission for the Southeast Atlantic Fisheries was established with a membership of seventeen nations (including Japan, South Korea and Cuba). The commission is empowered to recommend joint actions for closed sessions, size limitation, gear control and total catch limit. Again, in 1973, under the aegis of a resolution by the FAO Council, the Western Central Atlantic Fisheries Commission was formed for developing rational fishery policies and management of living resources for the area. It has a participating membership of twenty-seven including Japan and South Korea. The Northwest Atlantic Fisheries Organization came into being in 1978 as a result of a convention participated in by twelve nations including Japan and the European Economic Community (EEC) for the purpose of optimum use and conservation of fishery resources. In 1980 the new Northeast Atlantic Fisheries Commission (NEAFC) was formed by six European countries, plus the EEC, to replace the old one established by the 1964 Overfishing Convention. To cooperate for rational management of salmon stocks, four Scandinavian nations (Denmark, Iceland, Norway and Sweden), plus Canada, the United States and the EEC, formed the North Atlantic Salmon Conservation Organization to operate in the area north of 36° north latitude. Both the old NEAFC and the new Northeast Atlantic Fisheries Commission were originally created under the 1964 Overfishing Convention.

A mixed Commission for Black Sea Fisheries was formed by the 1959 international convention with Bulgaria, Romania and the Soviet Union participating. It was empowered to enact regulatory measures for catch size, organize information exchange, engage in scientific research about conservation and provide for augmentation of stocks in the Black Sea. Similarly empowered was the 1973 International Baltic Sea Fisheries Commission of seven powers (Denmark, Finland, East Germany, West Germany, Poland, Sweden and the Soviet Union). For the conservation and rational exploitation of Antarctic living resources, a fifteen-member Commission for the Conservation of Antarctic Marine Living Resources was formed with headquarters in Australia.

The 1982 LOS Convention and the establishment of the 200-nautical-mile EEZ have had some impact on the work of the regional fishery commissions. Article 63 of the 1982 LOS Convention provides a broad guideline for those coastal states which have declared a 200-nautical-mile exclusive fishery regime. If fishery stock or stocks of associate species are found within the exclusive economic zones of two or more states, they must seek agreements for the conservation and use of these stocks either directly or through appropriate regional or subregional organizations for intergovernmental cooperation. It provides also for the situation where fishing stocks, other than highly migratory species, may migrate between the EEZ and the high seas, such as those in the North and Southwest Atlantic. In this case the coastal states must agree on the appropriate conservation and management measures or work through the regional fishery commissions to ensure that these measures are in place.

As a consequence, amendments have been introduced and enacted by various regional fishery commissions to meet the changing conditions created by the establishment of the 200-nautical-mile EEZ. Some regional fishery commissions have convened international conferences within their membership for the purpose of providing cooperative conservation and management measures. The Northeast Atlantic Fisheries Commission will be used here as an illustration. This is the new NEAFC, the result of the 1978 London conference called to explore the implication of the 200-nautical-mile EEZ extension. The 1978 London meetings led to signature on the 1980 Convention on Future Multilateral Cooperation in Northeast Atlantic Fisheries, which came into effect on March 17, 1982, for Denmark (for the Faroes Islands), the EEC, East Germany, Iceland, Norway, Sweden and the Soviet Union. (The old NEAFC was formed by the 1959 convention and operated from 1963 to 1977.)

By 1977 the old NEAFC could no longer function as a regional fishery commission, as most of the original members had withdrawn their membership and claimed the 200-nautical-mile EEZ. Under the old framework, it had rather limited regulatory power concerning net mesh size, minimum size for landing catch to protect immature fish and designation of closed seasons and areas to protect spawning fish stocks. Commission recommendations on these regulatory measures were supposed to be binding upon member states, unless they were challenged within a certain fixed period. Often the commission's recommendations were not enforced by the flag states. In 1969 it inaugurated a system of on-board inspection in order to improve enforcement of net and catch size. But the overall enforcement measures of the old NEAFC were considered a failure in that overfishing in the Northeast Atlantic was widespread for many fishery stocks. In the end it had to ban herring fishing altogether in order to conserve the stock. The experience of the old NEAFC demonstrated that regulatory measures limited to the size of nets and minimum fish landing size were not sufficient to prevent overfishing. In 1974 when the old NEAFC adopted and implemented the concept of total allowable catch (TAC) and then divided TAC into quotas for its members, it generally set the limit in excess of that recommended by the scientific panel of biologists, the International Council for the Exploration of the Sea (ICES), established in 1903. Since a member state could merely object to the commission's recommendations, it was not possible for the members to reach agreement on national quotas set for a particular fishery stock.

The new 1980 NEAFC can now make recommendations on fisheries beyond the 200-nautical-mile EEZ of member countries, provided these measures are consistent both within and beyond the limits of national jurisdiction. If so requested, the new commission can recommend conservation management measures for fisheries found within the 200-mile EEZ of its members.

Significance. The overall record of the regional fishery commissions has not been very successful in providing rational conservation and management measures for living resources in the oceans for many reasons. One is the habit of member states in these regional commissions to disagree on proposed regulations for the conservation of fisheries.[2] There has also been a tendency for member states to disregard, for political and economic reasons, scientific advice on catch reductions for the prevention of overfishing of cod and herring in the Atlantic. Third, the regional fishery commissions, by the nature of their constitutions, usually lack effective means for enforcement. Because of the high seas nature of the fish involved, there is frequently unlimited entry by nonmembers into the fishery, thus placing the regional fishery commissions in a position of not being able to control the fishing activities in the area.

In spite of the record of some failures, there is still a role for the regional fishery commissions to play in the new ocean regime of 200-nautical-mile EEZs. Fishery stocks are mobile, and they migrate across these arbitrary ocean enclosures. In many instances, fish stocks—the straddling stocks, for example—must be shared because they are found within two or more EEZs or migrate between the EEZ and the high seas. Therefore, there is a need for intergovernmental cooperation, the intent and purpose of Article 63 of the 1982 LOS Convention. Many states that claimed the 200-nautical-mile EEZ still need scientific information and research on fisheries. And techniques for conservation management still need to be refined, if not innovated anew. Thus more, not less, international and intergovernmental collaboration is needed for rational conservation and management of living resources. Of the 103 states claiming exclusive fishery or economic zones, a vast majority are developing coastal states. Technical assistance in fishery conservation and management are crucial for developing their fisheries. The work of the FAO in relation to the regional fishery commissions is illustrative of the need for international cooperation. Finally, as pointed out by J. E. Carroz of the FAO, conflicting uses of the oceans would most likely generate new problems, which, in turn, would call for "effective fisheries management."[3]

FISHING TECHNOLOGY

The age of technological innovation also extends to ocean fishing, the oldest use of the oceans. Fishing technology refers not only to fishing gear and methods but, as pointed out by J. Scharfe of the Fisheries Department of the FAO, includes vessel design and operation and the application of electronic and acoustical devices such as echo sounders, sonar and netsonde as well.[4] Jon L. Jacobson provides a useful summary of fishing methods in terms of capture and fish location techniques, in addition to types of fishing vessels used for ocean fishing.[5]

According to Jon Jacobson the principal capture methods for today's ocean fishing still rely on the use of rot-resistant nets. The ancient way of hook and line with bait is still being used—horizontal lines strung between floats to capture nonschooling fish such as tuna, marlin and shark. Gill nets, floated on top and weighted down at the bottom to entangle the fish, are also used. The use of the purse seine and otter trawl have contributed immensely to fishing technology advancement.

Purse Seines

This has been a revolutionary fishing technological advancement in recent decades. It is a fish-capturing method by which the purse line draws the net bottom closed after a school of fish has been encircled. In the 1960s large purse seines became the major method of capturing tuna and anchovy. A modern purse seiner is usually a vessel of 1,000 to 2,000 tons, which can spread a huge net in the ocean. The net may be 3,600 feet in length, 600 feet deep and weigh about one ton. American tuna fleets based in San Diego are equipped with purse seines that can easily catch 10,000 yellowfin tuna of forty to seventy pounds each time. It usually takes six hours or more to empty the net. As a result, tuna may die of suffocation and entanglement or become spoiled before they can be refrigerated on board ship. Too often purse seines encircle yellowfin tuna as well as porpoises (air-breathing), which habitually associate and swim with the tuna.

Otter Trawl

This method consists of cone-shaped nets towed behind the vessel. The mouth of the trawl can be opened wide and literally "scoop" fish into the net. It has been used as a device for bottom fishing that passes along the seabed on rollers or for mid-water trawl.

Great strides have been made with respect to fish detection technology. Ocean-going fishing vessels, particularly the distant-water stern trawlers, employ the latest telemeters, such as echo sounders and sonar for finding areas of fish concentration. Use of helicopters and other aircraft as spotters of surface fish is common nowadays. Underwater searches with the aid of laser or satellite detection of fish schools, or the use of sophisticated devices for "fish forecasting," can enhance an increase in catch and thus make fishing economically more profitable.

In terms of fishing vessel technology, the most important development has been the design and equipment for stern factory trawlers used for distant-water fishing. These vessels are designed to catch the greatest quantities of a few species with predictable size, such as cod and herring families, in the North Atlantic; then they process or fillet these fish on board the trawler thousands of miles from home port. Most of these vessels are equipped with up-to-date electronic devices such as radar, depth recorders and telecommunication systems. Jon Jacobson predicted that "computer-assisted fleet dispatch and vessel automation" would soon be on the way toward "the systems approach" for efficiency in fishing.[6]

Significance. The development of sophisticated fishing techniques—the purse seines, fish detection, distant-water trawling by exploiting concentrations of spawning fish—has contributed to overfishing, a concern that led to a unilateral coastal claims before the United Nations Law of the Sea conferences in the 1960s and 1970s. Advancement in fishing technology also has been a factor contributing to the international acceptance of the 200-nautical-mile EEZ. Coastal, regional and international efforts to control "overfishing" have led to more restrictions on season, gear and area for fishing in the oceans. All these restrictions on techniques made it necessary to increase fishing efficiency, which in turn called for increases in investment in ocean fisheries. As Jon Jacobson points out, in the future there might be more "passive gear" instead of "actual gear"—stationary fishing platforms using techniques that depend little on vessels, thus making fishing from vessels an outdated mode. Jacobson laments the fact that the UNCLOS III discussion and the language of the 1982 LOS Convention on the conservation and management of fisheries seemed to rely still on fishing from vessels.[7]

PROTECTION OF MARINE MAMMALS AND CETACEANS

Unlike fishery stocks, marine mammals do not biologically reproduce sufficient recruits to the stock to permit intensive exploitation. In the absence of restrictive measures for conservation, marine mammal species—such as whales, seals and dolphins—may be threatened with extinction. The intensive hunting for whales since 1945, pursued by technologically advanced worldwide whaling industries, almost led to the depletion of sperm and right whales. Not surprisingly, there has been an array of national and international efforts for placing limits on the kill of marine mammals, beginning with the International Fur Sea Conventions in 1911 and the Convention for the Regulation of Whaling in 1931.

The establishment of the 200-nautical-mile EEZ has produced two significant developments in the management of marine mammals. One is the fact that the habitats and migratory range of some marine mammals now lie within the exclusive economic zones of the coastal states. Second, as a consequence, there is a larger concern and realization by the coastal states of the need to provide conservation and management measures for marine mammal protection. A glance at the variety of national legislation dealing with marine mammal protection is illustrative of these concerns:

1. on Antarctic exploitation of marine mammals (France)
2. on establishment of marine sanctuaries (Mexico)
3. on establishment of a moratorium on taking marine mammals (United States)
4. on protecting the seals (Argentina, Canada, the Soviet Union, Uruguay and the United Kingdom)
5. on restrictions on importation of whales and whale products (France, New Zealand and the United Kingdom)
6. on whale killing (Australia, Bahamas, Brazil, Canada, New Zealand and the United Kingdom)

Generally national or municipal legislation is enacted to respond to the states' obligations as parties to regional and international conventions. For instance, the Pelly Amendment to the 1967 Fishermen's Protection Act and the Packwood-Magnuson Amendment to the Magnuson Fishery Conservation and Management Act mandated U.S. sanctions against any nations that "diminish the effectiveness" of any international fisheries conservation program to which the United States is a party. International conventions either specifically or indirectly affecting marine mammals are:

1. The Antarctic Treaty (December 1, 1959)
2. Convention for the Conservation of Antarctic Seals (June 1, 1972)
3. The Interim Convention on Conservation of North Pacific Seals (February 9, 1957)

4. Agreement on the Conservation of Polar Bears (November 15, 1973)
5. Convention on Nature Protection and Wildlife Preservation in the Western Hemisphere (October 12, 1940)
6. International Council for the Exploration of the Seas (September 12, 1964)
7. Inter-American Tropical Tuna Convention (May 31, 1949)
8. International Convention for the Conservation of Atlantic Tuna (May 14, 1966)
9. International Convention for the High Seas Fisheries of the North Pacific Ocean (May 9, 1952)
10. Amended Agreement for the Establishment of the Indo-Pacific Fisheries Council (November 23, 1961)
11. Convention on Future Multilateral Cooperation in the Northwest Atlantic Fisheries (October 24, 1978)

There are three important global treaties that deal directly and specifically with marine mammal protection:

1. Convention on International Trade in Endangered Species of Wild Fauna and Flora (March 3, 1973)
2. International Convention for the Regulation of Whaling (December 2, 1946)
3. Convention on the Conservation of Migratory Species of Wild Animals (June 21, 1979)

Article 65 of the 1982 LOS Convention provides the following guideline for the protection of marine mammals:

> Nothing in this part restricts the right of a coastal State or the competence of an international organization, as appropriate to prohibit, limit or regulate the exploitation of marine mammals more strictly than provided for in this Part. States shall cooperate with a view to the conservation of marine mammals and in the case of cetaceans shall in particular work through the appropriate international organization for their conservation, management and study.

The language in Article 65 has been criticized as deficient and imprecise.[8] For instance, it has been argued that it lacks criteria as to when coastal states or the international organization should determine it is appropriate to take marine mammal conservation measures. Presumably, without clear stipulation, a coastal state could join a weak, pro-whaling organization such as the Permanent Commission for the Exploitation and Conservation of the Marine Resources of the South Pacific—a weakness in Article 65.

Whales

No discussion on marine mammal protection is complete without making some reference to the IWC. The IWC was formed in 1946 under the International

Table 5.1
The International Whaling Commission, 1972–1986: Catch Quota and Membership

Year	Quota	Membership
1972-73	42,500	14 nations: United States, Britain, Mexico, France, Argentina, Australia, Canada, Panama, Denmark, Japan, USSR, Norway, Iceland, South Africa
1973-74	40,979	
1974-75	39,864	15 nations: Brazil joins
1975-76	32,578	
1976-77	28,050	16 nations: New Zealand joins
1977-78	23,520	17 nations: Netherlands joins
1878-79	20,428	
1979-80	15,653	23 nations: Seychelles, Sweden, Chile, Peru, Spain, Korea join
1980-81	14,523	24 nations: Switzerland, Oman join (Panama withdraws)
1981-82	14,233	32 nations: Jamaica, St. Lucia, Dominica, Costa Rica, Uruguay, China, St. Vincent, India, Philippines join (Canada withdraws)
1982-83	12,263	37 nations: Egypt, Kenya, Senegal, Belize, Antigua, Monaco, Germany join (Jamaica, Dominica withdraw)
1983-84	9,390	39 nations: Finland, Mauritius join
1984-85	6,623	
1985-86	0	41 nations: Ireland, Solomon Islands join

Note: Membership recruitment and quota figures were based on information from the International Whaling Commission, 1972–86.

Source: David Day, *The Whale War* (San Francisco: Sierra Club, 1987), p. 97. Used by permission.

Convention for Regulation of Whaling, and has been amended from time to time since then. The preamble to the convention states clearly that its objective is to prevent overexploitation by properly regulating the size of the stocks for a variety of whales: "That it is in the common interest to achieve the optimum level of whale stock as rapidly as possible without causing widespread economic and nutritional distress."[9] Methods for regulating commercial whaling include: the designation of open and closed seasons, protection against possible "commercial extinction" for certain overfished species and yearly bargaining among IWC members for total catch limits. The IWC quota and membership distribution for 1972 to 1986 are given in Table 5.1.

In 1972 the conscience of the world began to voice in a more dramatic way the need for an immediate moratorium on all commercial whaling as reflected by a vote of 50 to 0 at the United Nations Environmental Conference in Stockholm. In the same year the United States enacted the Marine Mammals Protection Act.[10] A key provision in the act was a general moratorium on the "taking" or any action to "harass, hunt, capture or kill, or to attempt to harass, hunt, capture or kill any marine mammal." In subsequent years other actions were taken: (1) the Convention in Trade of Endangered Species, which prohibits international trade of whale products; (2) the United States Endangered Species Act, which prohibits trade of whale products in United States markets; and (3) most important of all, the passage in 1973 of the Pelly Amendment to the United States Fishermen's Act, which provides sanction authority against any nation that engages in fishing operations that "diminish the effectiveness" of any international fisheries conservation program to which the United States is a participant. Under the Pelly Amendment, if a violation is discovered, the president, upon certification by the Secretary of Commerce, may direct the Treasury Secretary to prohibit the importation of fish products of the offending nation.

Significance. Unfortunately, the IWC has no enforcement power over its members to abide by the limit of catch set by the quota (see Table 5.1). A member is bound only to comply voluntarily with the IWC decisions, and too often a member continues to violate the quota table. Before 1972 the IWC was merely a "trade association" or "club" of whaling industries whose main concern was to maintain price stability on an oversupply of whale oil. By the early 1960s, aided by the invention of explosive harpoons and stronger vessels, whaling technology enabled the whalers to drive blue and humpback whales into "commercial extinction." Having reduced the population of baleen whales by intensive hunting in the Antarctic and North Pacific in the 1970s, the whaling industries of many nations then concentrated on the sperm and the minke whale.

After 1972, the IWC made a distinct change in its orientation from that of "commercialization of whales" to one of conservation management of the species. However, annual quota setting was still one of its main activities, and a member could still defy the IWC decision by filing its objections. But now the Pelly Amendment to the United States Fishermen's Act has provided the enforcement "teeth" for the IWC setting of catch quotas. By 1979 the United States Congress further strengthened the Pelly Amendment by passing the Packwood-Magnuson Amendment to the Magnuson Fishery Conservation and Management Act of 1976. This amendment provides that automatic sanctions—the reduction by as much as 50 percent of the fishing allocation right of a foreign country permitted to fish within the United States' 200-nautical-mile fishery conservation zone—are imposed if "nationals of a foreign country, directly or indirectly, conducting fishing operations are engaged in trade or taking which diminishes the effectiveness of the International Convention for the Regulation of Whaling." On a number of occasions, these enforcement procedures were applied against whaling violations. In 1974, Japan and the Soviet Union were forced to accept the 1974–1975 IWC quotas for minke whales after a certification by the United States Secretary of Commerce that they had taken the whales in excess of the IWC quota. In 1978 the Pelly Amendment was used to force Chile, Peru and South Korea—then nonmembers of IWC—to adhere to IWC quotas and join the international organizations. Thus the threat of automatic sanctions by the United States, in accordance with these amendments, has proven to be effective in enforcing IWC decisions and quotas.[11] Also, on-the-scene harassment waged by the Greenpeace organization against whaling operations on the sea created a worldwide outcry against those whaling nations—Japan, Norway, Iceland and the Soviet Union—that culminated in the moratorium, despite a number of setbacks such as the compromise agreement with the Eskimos on the harvest of bowhead whales in the Bering Sea stock.[12] Finally, at the 1982 annual session, the IWC, its membership having grown to thirty-seven nations, passed by a vote of 25–7 a general ten-year moratorium on commercial whaling, to become effective in 1985 with zero quota. The Soviet Union promised to end whaling by 1987, but Japan, Norway, Iceland and South Korea continued harvesting in 1986 under the guise of "scientific whaling." In 1986, Japan killed 2,769 whales under the pretext of scientific research. In 1986, after the United States Supreme Court reversed a lower court ruling to require a certification of violation of the whaling zero quota with U.S. sanctions, Japan agreed to abide by the moratorium on commercial whaling by 1988. Norway and Iceland acceded to the moratorium in 1987 and 1985 respectively. However, in April 1990 *Nisshin Maru No. 3*, a Japanese whaling mother ship, returned to port after killing 330 whales in a four-month hunt in the Antarctic. The kill was done under the pretext that it was a part of a scientific research program, even though the whale meat processed on board the mother ship would be sold as an expensive delicacy in gourmet restaurants in Japan. At the July 1990 Noordwjk (Netherlands) meeting of the International Whaling Commission, Japan threatened to pull out of the commission after its proposal to end the ban on certain types of commercial whaling, mainly the minke, smallest of whales, was defeated. On July 5, 1990, the IWC upheld the 1986 global moratorium on all commercial whale hunting. As of April 1991 Japan's whaling fleet returned from the Antarctic with 327 minke whales killed.

Small Cetaceans

The International Whaling Commission is primarily concerned with the catch quota for the commercial harvest of large cetaceans. Earlier negotiation working papers of the UNCLOS III made no mention of cetaceans. At the June 1977 session the U.S. delegation submitted an amendment to the draft on marine mammals that included the recommendation that states must cooperate in order to protect marine mammals and "to establish an international organization for the protection, conservation and understanding of cetaceans on a global basis."[13] The 1977 statement by the U.S. delegation was amended in the July–August 1979 session of UNCLOS III and became the final version of Article 65 in the 1982 LOS Convention: "States shall cooperate with a view to the conservation of marine mammals and in the case of cetaceans shall in particular work through the appropriate international organization for their conservation, management and study."[14]

There are now in existence sixty species of small cetaceans or whales less than thirty feet in length, including porpoises, dolphins and killer whales. Table 5.2 provides a list of known small cetaceans that do not have international protection.

Significance. There is considerable support for international regulation of small cetaceans to provide the needed protection for conservation and management of these species.[15] Worldwide concern has been focused recently on the "incidental captures" by purse seines and gill nets of a large number of small cetaceans, particularly in the eastern Pacific in connection with commercial fishing of yellowfin tuna. In 1972, before the enactment of the Marine Mammal Protection Act, the United States' share of mortality of porpoises in the eastern Pacific was more than 400,000 per year. According to the Marine Mammal Commission established under the Marine Mammal Protection Act, since 1972 the figures for the capture of and for serious injuries to porpoises have declined significantly from 368,000 in 1972 to 27,736 in 1982.[16]

However, estimated kill and serious injury to porpoises during tuna fishing seemed to have increased in 1981 and 1982 as compared to previous years. In 1986 the United States took a unilateral and unprecedented action of banning American tuna fishing in the eastern tropical Pacific Ocean area after the authorized 20,500 quota for porpoise kill had been met.[17] Tuna importers to the United States must certify that no porpoises were harmed in connection with the tuna catch. But the estimated number of dolphins killed related to commercial fishing worldwide for 1989 was 100,000.[18] The Center for Marine Conservation, a Washington, D.C.–based group, estimated that the coastal spotted dolphin population has been reduced by 60 percent and the eastern spinner dolphin reduced by about 75 percent.[19] A dolphin population reduced by 40 percent is considered to be in need of protection. This has provided impetus for environmental groups in the United States to demand in 1990–91 "dolphin safe" fishing by U.S. and Mexican tuna fishermen.

Cynthia Carlson advocated that the IWC should have a logical role in the international regulation of small cetaceans, as it has made progress since 1977 on the review of small cetaceans.[20] As the killing of large whales is decreasing under the whaling moratorium, and as the take of small cetaceans has been rising, the IWC has also shifted its scientific study to the biology, migration and management of the latter species. The IWC is said to be the appropriate organization for operation of the needed comprehensive management system for all cetaceans.[21] Meanwhile, the U.S. Dolphin Protection and Consumer Information Bill of 1990, proposed legislation before Congress, is designed to reduce the number of dolphins killed annually as part of the tuna-fishing operation. The bill would also ban tuna products imported from those nations using drift nets in the South Pacific after July 1, 1991, and would expand the ban to nations using drift nets anywhere on the high seas as a response to the December 1989 UN General Assembly Resolution on a drift net moratorium.[22]

Seals

When the United States purchased Alaska in 1867, it also acquired the Pribilof Islands in the Bering Sea, the habitat of a herd of some 1.4 million seals whose

Table 5.2
List of Recognized Small Cetaceans

Scientific Name	Recommended Common Name
Balaenoptera acutorostrata	Minke whale
Caperea marginata	Pygmy right whale
Tasmacetus shepherdi	Shepherd's beaked whale
Berardius arnuxii duvernoy	Arnoux's beaked whale
Berardius bairdii stejneger	Baird's beaked whale
Mesoplodon pacificus	Longman's beaked whale
Mesoplodon bidens	Sowerby's beaked whale
Mesoplodon densirostris	Blainville's beaked whale
Mesoplodon europaeus	Gervais' beaked whale
Mesoplodon layardii	Strap-toothed whale
Mesoplodon hectori	Hector's beaked whale
Mesoplodon grayi	Gray's beaked whale
Mesoplodon stejnegri	Stejneger's beaked whale
Mesoplodon bowdoini	Andrew's beaked whale
Mesoplodon mirus	True's beaked whale
Mesoplodon ginkgodens	Ginkgo-toothed beaked whale
Mesoplodon carlhubbsi	Hubb's beaked whale
Ziphius cavirostris	Cuvier's beaked whale
Hyperoodon ampullatus	Northern bottlenose whale
Hyperoodon planifrons	Southern bottlenose whale
Kogia breviceps	Pygmy sperm whale
Kogia simus	Dwarf spern whale
Monodon monoceros	Narwhal
Delphinapterus leucas	White whale (beluga)
Steno bredanensis	Rough-toothed dolphin
Sotalia fluviatilis	Tucuxi
Sousa chinensis	Indo-Pacific hump-backed dolphin
Sousa teuszii	Atlantic hump-backed dolphin
Orcaella brevirostris	Irrawaddy dolphin
Peponsocphala electra	Melon-headed whale
Feresa attenuata	Pygmy killer whale
Pseudorca crassidens	False killer whale
Orcinus orca	Killer whale
Globicephala melaena	Long-finned pilot whale
Globicephala macrorhynchus	Short-finned pilot whale
Lagenorhynchus albirostris	White-beaked dolphin
Lagenorhynchus acutus	Atlantic white-sided dolphin
Lagenorhynchus obscurus	Dusky dolphin
Lagenorhynchus cruciger	Hourglass dolphin
Lagenorhynchus australis	Peale's dolphin
Lagenorhynchus obliquidens	Pacific white-sided dolphin
Lagenorhynchus hosei	Fraser's dolphin
Tursiops truncatus	Bottlenose dolphin
Grampus griseus	Risso's dolphin
Stenella longirostris	Spinner dolphin
Stenella coeruleoalba	Striped dolphin
Stenella attenuata	
Stenella dubia	Spotted dolphins (2 species)
Stenella frontalis	
Stenella plagiodon	
Delphinus delphis	Common dolphin
Lissodelphis peronii	Southern right whale dolphin
Lissodelphis borealis	Northern right whale dolphin

Table 5.2 (Continued)

Scientific Name	Recommended Common Name
Cephalorhynchus heaviside	Heaviside's dolphin
Cephalorhynchus eutropia	Black dolphin
Cephalorhynchus hectori	Hector's dolphin
Cephalorhynchus commersonii	Commerson's dolphin
Phocoena phocoena	Harbour porpoise
Phocoena sinus	Cochito
Phocoena spinipinnis	Burmeister's dolphin
Phocoena dioptrica	Spectacled porpoise
Phocoenoides dalli	Dall's porpoise
Neophocauna phocaenoides	Finless porpoise
Plantanista gangetica	Ganges susu
Plantanista indi	Indus susu
Inia geoffrensis	Boutu
Lipotes vexillifer	White flag dolphin
Pontoporia blainvillei	Franciscana

Source: Cynthia E. Carlson, "The International Regulation of Small Cetaceans," *San Diego Law Review*, 21, no. 3 (1984): 621–622. Copyright 1984 San Diego Law Review Association. Reprinted with the permission of the *San Diego Law Review*.

female furs were then much in demand in women's fashion. The United States exercised exclusive right for the control and preservation of the seal population within the three-mile territorial sea. However, Canadian hunters were not only stationed outside the three-mile limit, but roved the high seas to slaughter the pelagic animals as they swam to and from breeding grounds on the Pribilof Islands. In 1886, United States Coast Guard cutters began to seize Canadian schooners on the high seas on the grounds that fur seals were the property of the United States and that pelagic seal hunting on the high seas was against good public morals. The British response was to refute the existence of "property rights" on seals except the right of possession. The British also argued that seals on the high seas fell within the purview of freedom of the seas.[23]

The dispute over the exclusive right and control of fur seals in the North Pacific finally ended with arbitration in 1892 in Paris. The arbitration tribunal ruled against the United States and drew up a set of regulations for the preservation of the seals that included a seal hunting zone of sixty miles around the Pribilof Islands.[24]

In 1911, after realizing the inadequacy of the existing measure for protecting the declining seal population—by then the herd was estimated at 100,000—a four-power conference (Canada, Japan, Russia and the United States) concluded with the 1911 North Pacific Sealing Convention, which prohibited pelagic sealing. The nomadic herd of seals migrates annually by two routes: south from the Pribilof Islands to Santa Barbara, California, and southwest to northern Honshu and into the Sea of Japan, a migration pattern that covers the waters of Canada, Japan, Russia (the Soviet Union) and the United States. In the spring about 70 to 80 percent of the 1.4 million fur seals in the North Pacific descend on the Pribilof Islands to breed; and the remainder arrive in the islands of Commander,

Robben and the Kuriles (owned now by the Soviet Union but by Japan before 1945). The 1911 four-power conference devised an innovative arrangement in order to compensate for the pledge by Canada and Japan not to engage in "pelagic sealing" (defined in the convention as "killing, taking or hunting in any manner whatsoever of fur seals at sea"). This agreement permitted capture of fur seals only at the end of each harvesting season on islands belonging to the United States and the Soviet Union. The four powers also agreed that the total number of sealskins taken commercially must be shared on a basis of percentage of the gross in number and value, in accordance with the formula provided under Article IX of the 1957 Interim Convention on Conservation of North Pacific Fur Seals.

By the Soviet Union: to Canada—15 percent; to Japan—15 percent

By the United States: to Canada—15 percent; to Japan—15 percent

The 1911 North Pacific Sealing Convention was replaced by the 1957 Interim Convention on the Conservation of North Pacific Fur Seals and has been amended since then by the protocols of 1963 (October 8), 1964 (April 10), 1969 (September 3), 1976 (October 12), 1980 (October 14) and 1981 (July 2). The 1980 Protocol extended the terms of the Interim Convention for four years to 1984, and it has since been extended and revised to 1990.

Significance. While the North Pacific Fur Seal Commission—established by the 1957 Convention on Conservation of North Pacific Fur Seals—does not set annual harvest quotas for the United States or the Soviet Union, through its Scientific Committee under Article V, it does provide safeguards against overharvesting of fur seal stock. This is to be accomplished by monitoring the herd on any island or group of islands to insure that the total population does not fall below the sustainable productivity level. The North Pacific Fur Seal Commission maintains research and study statistics on the fur seal habitat, migration, feeding habits and reproduction. The commission's scientific committee can make a recommendation, if accepted by the parties to the convention, to cease harvesting if "such action is necessary to the well-being of the fur seal populations."[25] The convention has been recognized internationally as a "model" or as a more successful conservation program that has resulted in the recovery of the fur seal from 300,000 in the early 1900s to the present level of 1.4 million herd size. The population is now distributed among each island group as follows:[26]

Island Group	**Jurisdiction by**	**Number of Seals**
Pribilof Islands	USA	975,000
Commander Islands	USSR	325,000
Robben Islands	USSR	84,000

Middle Kurile Islands	USSR	54,000
San Miguel Island	USA	4,000
	Total	1,442,000

However, on the Atlantic side, the Canadian government has permitted the kill of 180,600 adult seals for 1989–1990 under pressure from Newfoundland fishermen whose main argument was that the seals are consuming scarce fish, an assertion repudiated by Greenpeace and biologists.[27]

THE SPECIES APPROACH

The species approach implies that a coastal state has control over coastal anadromous stocks that spawn in fresh water (e.g., salmon), coexistent with the range of each species and international management of highly migratory species such as tuna. In the 1970s a basic U.S. fishery policy was that different species of fish stock be treated differently. The species approach adopted by the United States was an attempt to balance and accommodate the conflicting demands of U.S. fishery industries on the Atlantic and Pacific coasts.[28] The species approach was presented by the United States to the 1971 United Nations Seabed Committee debate as a part of the United States' position on the territorial sea and international straits.[29] By 1974 when UNCLOS III convened in New York and Caracas amidst widespread pressure by nations for a 200-nautical-mile fishery zone, the United States officially presented a revised version of the species approach to include the following provisions:[30]

1. Coastal states would have conservation and management jurisdiction over coastal stocks within the economic zone.
2. Coastal states would also have preferential rights over anadromous stocks, and fishing for such species on the high seas would be prohibited except with the consent of the state of origin.
3. Coastal states would not have the preferential right to migratory species, and the use of highly migratory species (tuna) must be arranged by international or regional cooperation.

The Nixon administration was then under pressure by the U.S. tuna fishing industry to provide protection for its distant-water fleets off the west coast of Latin America, and by the demands of New England coast fishermen for an exclusive 200-nautical-mile fishery zone to keep out the distant-water fleets of other nations. In the second committee of the Caracas session of UNCLOS III, the species approach received various degrees of support from Ireland, Australia,

New Zealand and Canada, which submitted their own proposals on the treatment of anadromous and highly migratory species.[31]

By 1976 when the Magnuson Fishery Conservation and Management Act was enacted by the U.S. Congress, the species approach was incorporated in Section 102. It states that the United States has exclusive fishery management authority over "all anadromous fish throughout the migratory range of each species beyond the fishery conservation zone, except when in a foreign nation's territorial sea or fishery conservation zone to the extent such jurisdictions are recognized by the United States" and that there is "no fishery management authority over highly migratory species."[32] Five articles in the 1982 LOS Convention reflected the species approach in essence, if not in wording: Article 64 on highly migratory species, Article 65 on marine mammals, Article 66 on anadromous stocks, Article 67 on catadromous stocks and Article 68 on sedentary species.

Anadromous Species

Anadromous species belong to a diverse group of fish consisting of more than a thousand species known as the salmoniforms in fresh water and the oceans. The largest in size are members of the *Salmonidae* that include the Pacific King salmon (Chinook), the Danube and the Siberian salmons. The life cycle of salmon, for instance, is anadromous in that it spawns in fresh water or streams but migrates to the sea for feeding and maturation. Thus, anadromous fish such as salmon are completely dependent on unpolluted freshwater rivers for growth during the first four years of their lives before migrating for thousands of miles through several states to the sea. When fully grown in the sea, they return to the river or stream in which they were spawned. (The homing instinct is said to have been guided by the sense of smell, celestial navigation and detection of gravity.) In the open sea anadromous stocks such as salmon are found in the coastal states' 200-nautical-mile exclusive economic zones and also in areas beyond the maritime boundary in the high seas beyond national jurisdiction. The strongest argument for the coastal state of origin to have the jurisdiction in the conservation and management of anadromous species is that any industrial development or pollution in the rivers would affect the migration pattern of the parent fish upstream, and, as a consequence, it would also affect the young fish downstream in terms of the stock's reproduction and supply. Thus, it becomes necessary for the state of origin of the anadromous fish to impose stringent regulations on the use of the fresh water and controlled capture by specific allocation on the high seas. In short, under Article 66 of the 1982 LOS Convention, the states in whose rivers anadromous stocks originate must have the primary jurisdiction for the conservation and management of such stocks. Under Article 66(2), the state of origin shall have the right to regulate anadromous stock "in all waters landward of the outer limits of its exclusive economic zone." Also under Article 66(2), the state of origin may establish, in consultation with other interested states, total allowable catches (TAL) for stocks originating in its rivers. In accordance with Article 66(4), "In cases where anadromous stocks migrate into or through the waters landward of the outer limits of EEZ of a state other than the state of origin, such state shall cooperate with the state of origin with regard to the conservation and management of such stocks." They must make the appropriate arrangements through regional organizations for the implementation of Article 66. Under Article 63(3-a), other states may have access to anadromous fish stock by entering into an appropriate agreement with the state of origin "with due regard to the conservation requirement and the needs of the state of origin in respect of these stocks."

An example of a bilateral cooperation on the conservation of anadromous salmon is the Convention for Protection, Preservation and Extension of the Sockeye Salmon Fisheries of the Fraser River System, signed by Canada and the United States in 1930, which became effective in 1937. The principal motivating factor behind the convention was the population decline of the sockeye (red) salmon of the Fraser River in British Columbia, which was caused by the building of a railroad (in addition to intensive fishing). In this case the sockeye salmon returning to the Fraser River to spawn must pass through American waters as well. The convention established the International Pacific Salmon Fisheries Commission (IPSFC) whose main task was to adopt a conservation policy. The policy was based on an eight-year scientific study, which was aimed at producing a maximum sustainable yield (catch) for the fish stock in trouble. The convention was amended in 1957 to include the Fraser River runs of the pink, as well as sockeye, salmon. By the 1960s and 1970s the United States–Canada joint conservation and management program for anadromous salmon stocks experienced many problems and uncertainties as a result of the unilateral national claims for the extension of fishery zones. The salmon dispute was further aggravated by the U.S. court decision to grant Native Americans a portion of the Fraser River sockeye salmon runs.[33] Formal negotiations on the salmon issue between the United States and Canada produced the bilateral agreement of April 1970, which provided the reciprocal right to fishermen of both nations to continue fishing for salmon in the traditional areas under national jurisdiction. This bilateral agreement was extended in 1972, but reduced the reciprocal areas of fishing. It was extended again to April 1977 when both the United States and Canada established their respective 200-nautical-mile exclusive fishery zones. Joint agreements during the period from 1970 to 1977 were concerned mainly with policies for reducing interceptions by American fishermen catching sockeye (pink) salmon bound for the Fraser River, and Canadian harvest of King (Chinook) salmon bound for Alaska, Washington and Oregon. In 1982 a draft agreement was concluded, which was intended to replace the 1930 convention with a new Pacific salmon commission. It was proposed that "a new joint management scheme" and authority be established in order to prevent overfishing in the areas from the Columbia River to Alaska. The United States–Canada Salmon Treaty, signed in Ottawa on January 28, 1985, which terminated the original 1930 convention, was the result of fifteen years of formal negotiations between Canada and the United States. The new joint Pacific Salmon Commission came into being after the new treaty came into force on August 13, 1986.

One of the main tasks of the new joint Pacific Salmon Commission is to determine future allocation of five salmon stocks, particularly the King (Chinook) salmon. The joint commission is also responsible for regulating the salmon catch by setting rules for interception on the high seas; it also must develop arrangements for equitable sharing of the salmon stock between the United States and Canada. The 1986 United States–Canada bilateral agreement on Pacific salmon covers the waters of the northwest United States, British Columbia and southeast Alaska. Management authority of the new Pacific Salmon Commission includes limitation and prohibition in the taking and interception of Chinook, Coho, the Fraser River Sockeye and Pink salmon in any waters designated by the 1986 convention. The Pacific Salmon Commission is composed of four members each from Canada and the United States. The U.S. members are represented by designated officials from Alaska, Oregon or Washington, one representative for the Indian tribes of Idaho, Oregon and Washington, and one nonvoting federal official. There have been problems and frustrations in the first three years of implementing the 1986 Convention on Pacific Salmon for the commission seems to have focused on short-term solutions of allocation of the fishery resources instead of plans for the salmon production increase and protection of the salmon habitat.[34]

Salmon has also figured prominently in the United States–Japan fishery relationship. Alaskan salmon had been under restrictive conservation measures adopted in 1892 and 1924. Under the White Act, the Bureau of Fisheries had the full power over Alaskan fishing. Then prior to World War II, Japanese salmon fishing fleets appeared in Bristol Bay, a spawning ground for Alaskan salmon. After repeated American protests, United States–Japanese negotiations began, which produced a bilateral agreement whereby Japan agreed to refrain from fishing in the Bristol Bay area. In 1952 a tripartite agreement was reached between the United States, Canada and Japan to resolve the problems and disputes over salmon fishing. This was the 1952 International Convention for the High Seas Fisheries of the North Pacific. Under the 1952 convention Japan agreed not to exploit fish stocks beyond the level of their maximum sustainable yield, which in practice meant that North American salmon were reserved only for American and Canadian fishermen. As a way of protecting Bristol Bay salmon stock, Japanese were not permitted to fish west of 175° west longitude.[35] Later it was discovered that the North American salmon intermingled with Asian salmon in waters west of the line.[36] In 1957 and 1958, through the authority of the INPFC, established by the 1952 conventions, the United States sought without success to ban all fishing in waters where North American salmon were found. Then in 1958 the United States threatened to close down fishing in Bristol Bay entirely if Japan continued to "overfish" salmon in the area. There had been a drastic decline in salmon runs in Bristol Bay, a circumstantial evidence nonetheless.

Negotiations resumed in January 1986 between the United States and Japan to resolve the continuing salmon fishery dispute. Much of the dispute centered on Japanese interception of salmon in the high seas before their return to Alaskan waters and the use of Japanese drift nets stretching thirty miles across the ocean, which caught immature salmon spawned in American rivers. American negotiators pushed for a reduction of Japanese catch of North American salmon on the high seas during their return to Alaskan streams. Research scientists from the United States estimated that Japanese salmon fleets each year intercepted about 1 million salmon bound for United States waters, causing economic hardship for communities in western Alaska. The United States contended that a reduction of Japan's catch to a third of that level would help to assure the survival of North American salmon. Japan claimed that its fleets intercepted only 100,000 per year. In the negotiations the United States linked the salmon issue with a threat to reduce further the allocation for Japan's share of Alaskan bottom fish, such as flounder, sole and cod, within the United States' 200-nautical-mile zone from over 500,000 metric tons to only 10,000.[37] Japan then responded that it would boycott U.S. seafood, which could have meant an economic loss to Alaska of as much as $270 million in 1984–1986. In March 1986, the United States and Japan finally reached an agreement on North American salmon fishing.[38] The terms adopted by the joint International North Pacific Fisheries Commission of the United States, Canada and Japan on April 8–9, 1986, provided the following:

1. Japan's driftnet salmon fishing on the high seas in the Bering Sea between Alaska and north of the Aleutian Islands would be phased out in eight years, or by 1994.
2. The land-based (the eastern boundary of Japan's fishing in the North Pacific area) salmon fishery in the North Pacific Ocean would be moved thirty-five miles westward by one degree to 174° east to reserve the harvesting for American fishermen and, at the same time, conserve the stock, which tend to concentrate in the area.
3. As an enforcement measure, Japan must provide six patrol vessels to monitor the land-based fishing area on the eastern side of the boundary, in cooperation with the U.S. enforcement activities.[39]

Significance. The 1982 LOS Convention on anadromous species, such as salmon, grants the state of origin the exclusive jurisdiction over the conservation and management of the anadromous stock. At the same time, the 1982 LOS Convention mandates the coastal states, in whose zones anadromous fish migrate, the obligation to enter into agreement with the state of origin to ensure conservation and management of such species in the open high seas beyond the national jurisdiction. As a consequence this results in a reservation of the harvest of the anadromous species for the state of origin. This is another example of how the classic doctrine of the freedom of access to fishery resources in the high seas has been modified. The provision in Article 66 of the 1982 LOS Convention indicates that the management and conservation of anadromous stock is a matter for the spawning state as well as other interested coastal states.

Catadromous Species

The life cycle for catadromous species is the reverse of the anadromous fish stocks in that they spawn in the sea for feeding and growing and then migrate to the streams and fresh ponds on land and return to the sea to complete the cycle. Shrimps are one of the catadromous species. Article 67 in the 1982 Law of the Sea Convention provides that:

1. A coastal state in whose water catadromous species spend the greater part of their life cycle shall have responsibility for the management of these species and shall ensure the ingress and egress of migrating fish.
2. Harvesting of catadromous species shall be conducted only in waters landward of the outer limits of exclusive economic zones. When conducted in exclusive economic zones, harvesting shall be subject to this article and the other provisions of this Convention concerning fishing in these zones.
3. In cases where catadromous fish migrate through the exclusive economic zone of another state, whether as juvenile or maturing fish, the management, including harvesting, of such fish shall be regulated by agreement between the state mentioned in paragraph 1 and the other state concerned. Such agreement shall ensure the rational management of the species and take into account the responsibilities of the state mentioned in paragraph 1 for the maintenance of these species.

Traditionally U.S. fishermen harvested shrimp in Mexican waters in the Gulf of Mexico. However, the immediate effect of the establishment of the EEZ by both Mexico and the United States since 1976 and 1977 has been the eventual phasing out of U.S. fishing activities in the Mexican EEZ by 1990. This would enhance Mexican export of shrimp to the U.S. markets but would be detrimental to U.S. shrimp fishermen from Texas and Florida. Illegal shrimp operations by United States shrimpers in Mexican waters and seizures of U.S. shrimp trawlers by Mexico have been on the increase.[40] Bilateral negotiations continued in 1984 between the two countries, but to this date have not produced new bilateral agreements.

Significance. As in the case of anadromous species such as salmon, Article 67 grants the state of origin, or the coastal state in whose waters the catadromous species such as shrimp "spend the greater part of their life cycle" the major responsibility for the management of the species. In essence, the 200-nautical-mile EEZ claimed by the state of origin in practice results in the exclusion from harvest of migrating catadromous species by other coastal states, unless there is an arrangement to the contrary. The state of origin controls "the ingress and egress of the migrating fish." Thus, the special treatment of catadromous and anadromous species, together with the establishment of the 200-nautical-mile

EEZ, serves to modify the principle of the freedom of fishing as an essential part of the freedom of the seas. This permits the coastal states, a majority of them developing states of the Third World, "to become masters in their own houses in the waters close to their shores."[41]

Sedentary Species

For a discussion and definition of the term and its meaning, see the Continental Shelf section in Chapter 3. What needs to be emphasized here is that Article 77 does provide exclusive right to the coastal states over nonliving as well as living resources on the continental shelf; thus it is debatable as to whether high seas freedom of fishing is applicable to the sedentary species lying immobile on the subsoil of the continental shelf. When the definition of Article 77(4) on sedentary species is applied to the dispute for the central Bering Sea "Doughnut Hole" area, the continental shelf claimed by both the United States and the Soviet Union would give these two coastal states "sovereign rights" over the sedentary species on the central Bering Sea continental shelf and the imposition of conservation and management measures for these species, as argued by Lourene Miovski, the legal advisor to NOAA.[42]

TUNA: HIGHLY MIGRATORY SPECIES

One major characteristic of tuna is their migratory mode of existence. Typically they complete transoceanic migration in a matter of months. (Tagged skipjack tuna migrate through the entire Pacific Ocean and the yellowfin tuna travel thousands of miles.) Thus, tuna migrate through the 200-nautical-mile EEZ of many coastal states and through the high seas beyond national jurisdictions. This behavior affects the coastal state conservation and management programs. Another characteristic of tuna is their importance to the economy of many coastal states as a favorite food item for human consumption. Also, tuna seems to be plentiful and can be found in many regions of the world; this makes tuna an important commercial fishery to a number of nations. For the newly independent nations in the South Pacific, tuna fishing and processing industries constitute the most important means of generating employment, income and government revenue.

As an important commercial fishery there are five major species of tuna: albacore, bigeye, bluefin, skipjack and yellowfin in the Atlantic and eastern Pacific. In terms of catch, almost 70 percent of total world harvest is caught in the Pacific. Of the Pacific tuna caught, skipjack and yellowfin tuna constitute the major species.

The 1982 LOS Convention established a category of fishery, the highly migratory species (HMS), for special treatment. The text of Article 64 provides:

Article 64: Highly Migratory Species

1. The coastal State and other States whose nationals fish in the region for the highly migratory species listed in Annex I shall cooperate directly or through appropriate international organizations with a view to ensuring conservation and promoting the objective of optimum utilization of such species throughout the region, both within and beyond the exclusive economic zone. In regions for which no appropriate international organization exists, the coastal State and other states whose nationals harvest these species in the region shall cooperate to establish such an organization and participate in its work.

2. The provisions of paragraph 1 apply in addition to the other provisions of this Part.

Annex I to the 1982 LOS Convention contains a list of fishery stock considered highly migratory that includes all species of tuna and those species which are related to tuna, such as marlin, billfish and swordfish, as well as some small cetaceans.

ANNEX I. HIGHLY MIGRATORY SPECIES

1. Albacore tuna: *Thunnus alalunga*
2. Bluefin tuna: *Thunnus thynnus*
3. Bigeye tuna: *Thunnus obesus*
4. Skipjack tuna: *Katsuwonus pelamis*
5. Yellowfin tuna: *Thunnus albacares*
6. Blackfin tuna: *Thunnus atlanticus*
7. Little tuna: *Euthynnus alletteratus; Euthynnus affinis*
8. Southern bluefin tuna: *Thunnus maccoyii*
9. Frigate mackerel: *Auxis thazard; Auxis rochei*
10. Pomfrets: Family *Bramidae*
11. Marlins: *Tetrapturus angustirostris; Tetrapturus belone; Tetrapturus pfluegeri; Tetrapturus albidus; Tetrapturus audax; Tetrapturus georgei; Makaira mazara; Makaira indica; Makaira nigricans*
12. Sailfishes: *Istiophorus platypterus; Istiophorus albicans*
13. Swordfish: *Xiphias gladius*
14. Sauries: *Scomberesox saurus; Cololabis saira; Cololabis adocetus; Scomberesox saurus scombroides*
15. Dolphin: *Coryphaena hippurus; Coryphaena equiselis*
16. Oceanic sharks: *Hexanchus griseus; Cetorhinus maximus;* Family *Alopiidae; Rhincodon typus;* Family *Carcharhinidae*; Family *Sphyrnidae*; Family *Isurida*
17. Cetaceans: Family *Physeteridae;* Family *Balaenopteridae*; Family *Balaenidae*; Family *Eschrichtiidae*; Family *Monodontidae*; Family *Ziphiidae;* Family *Delphinidae*

There has been some controversy with respect to the meaning of Article 64. On the one hand, it has been argued that the article places no restrictions on the coastal state's authority to regulate tuna within the 200-nautical-mile EEZ and that it ''merely requests'' the coastal states and other distant-water nations to cooperate on tuna conservation and management measures.[43] Others argue that it is even doubtful whether a regional fishery organization has the authority to be responsible for tuna conservation and management as stated in Article 64, for there was no general ''consensus'' among the nations to accept the proviso of the term ''highly migratory species'' at the negotiations for the Law of the Sea Conference. In their study of the South Pacific Forum Fisheries Agency, Van Dyke and Heftel point out that the language of Article 64 is mandatory: that coastal states and distant-water fishing nations shall cooperate directly or through appropriate international organizations in the conservation of highly migratory species and shall cooperate to establish appropriate international organizations in regions where none exist.[44]

The mandatory nature of Article 64 is further reinforced by Article 56, which requires the coastal state to pay due regard to the rights of other states in declaring the 200-nautical-mile EEZ, and Article 61, which mandated all nations to be responsible for the conservation and management of the living resources.[45] Certainly there is some general agreement among marine biologists that there must be international or regional cooperation by all states in order to ensure the successful management and conservation of the living resources. But the unclear language of Article 64 on the management authority by international organizations over highly migratory species seems to contradict Article 56,which grants the coastal states sovereign rights over all marine resources (living and nonliving) within the 200-nautical-mile EEZ without any exception. Added to this textual contradiction in the 1982 LOS Convention is the insistence on the part of the United States, as reflected in its 1976 Magnuson Fishery Conservation and Management Act, in refusing to recognize exclusive jurisdiction of coastal states over such highly migratory species as tuna.

Following is a summary of recent state practices with respect to the conservation and management of tuna in different regions of the oceans.

Northwest Atlantic. Bluefin tuna frequents the northwest Atlantic. It spawns in the Gulf of Mexico and the Mediterranean and migrates to the north to feed. Bluefin tuna is the major fishery resource within the 200-nautical-mile zone for the northeastern United States. Abut 25 percent of the total annual harvest weight is taken within the zone. As the tuna resources in the northwest Atlantic became critical, the 1969 International Convention for the Conservation of Atlantic Tunas (ICCAT) was signed by twenty nations and came into effect in 1969. In 1981, the ICCAT recommended a moratorium on bluefin tuna in the northwest Atlantic.

South and southwest Pacific. The most significant cooperative effort in tuna conservation and management for the South Pacific was the Convention on the South Pacific Forum Fisheries Agency in 1979 by the seventeen South Pacific Forum members of Australia, Belau, Cook Islands, Federated States of Micronesia, Fiji, Kiribati, Marshall Islands, Nauru, New Zealand, Niue, Papua New

Guinea, Solomon Islands, Tonga, Tuvalu, Vanuatu and Western Samoa.[46] It excludes from membership in the agency all dependent territories, metropolitan powers such as the United States or the United Kingdom, and distant-water fishing nations such as Japan or Taiwan. The agency does not have the authority to regulate; it is a service, not a management, agency for collecting data for members, as well as for rendering assistance in the fishery access agreement negotiations with major fishery nations (United States, Japan and the Soviet Union) outside of the 200-nautical-mile zones of some twelve independent nations in the South Pacific. Under Article 64 of the 1982 LOS Convention, coastal states in the South Pacific Forum Fishery Agency claim to enjoy full sovereign rights over highly migratory species, since none of the distant-water fishing nations are members of the regional organization for tuna conservation and management. Nonmember nations fishing in the South Pacific region must register to fish in the area. The agency is empowered to require distant-water fishing nations to provide needed data for tuna management or face the likelihood of no surplus allocation.[47] The United States' tuna industry, the American Tunaboat Association, has been able to conclude bilateral agreements with the Federated States of Micronesia, Belau, Kiribati and the Marshall Islands (see Appendix VI). These access agreements recognize the coastal states' management authority over all living resources, including tuna (mostly skipjack and yellowfin), and permit licenses on a fee basis for U.S. west coast tuna fishing vessels within the 200-nautical-mile zones.[48]

The practice of coastal states in the South Pacific has focused on negotiation with distant-water fishing nations with the aim of forcing the latter to recognize the island states' sovereignty over tuna within their EEZs. Many of these bilateral agreements contain provisions for technological transfer and skills in tuna fishing, as well as scientific research needed to preserve tuna resources. Typically tuna fishing licenses are granted in exchange for the transfer of fishing technology and capital.[49] The South Pacific agency has been able to render valuable negotiation services to members in concluding access agreements with distant-water fishing nations.[50]

Eastern Pacific. Post–World War II expansion in tuna fishing in the eastern Pacific began as market demand for canned tuna increased. Fishing fleets dominated by American purse seiners roamed freely south and west from Baja California to the equator. Coastal Latin American states sold bait fish licenses to tuna vessels. An increase in tuna catch, as well as an increase in demand for bait fish, led to concerns over the effects on tuna stock in the eastern Pacific. These concerns led to the formation in 1950 of the Inter-American Tropical Tuna Commission (IATTC), under the 1949 (May 31) convention concluded between Costa Rica and the United States,[51] but open also to nations in the eastern Pacific, since the convention covered "the waters of the Eastern Pacific Ocean."[52] As pointed out by James Joseph, when coastal states claimed only a very narrow belt of water as a fishery zone, the IATTC's management style was "on an open access, competitive, first-come, first-served basis"; it permitted U.S. tuna fishermen to take as much as 90 percent of the total catch in the eastern Pacific.[53] Then by the 1960s, as more Latin American countries led by Chile, Ecuador and Peru opted for extended national jurisdiction over their living resources, problems over seizure of U.S. tuna vessels became a common occurrence resulting in reduced catch of yellowfin tuna for the California-based tuna fleets. The IATTC's overall quota, on the basis of open access for the eastern Pacific, became the focus of criticism by Latin American nations that led to the demands for special national quotas and allocation. Thus from 1969 on the IATTC had assigned special quotas of 6,000 tons to each country. Later the special national quota was increased to 13,000 tons in 1976 and 26,000 tons in 1978 for Mexico, in order to induce that nation to cooperate in the overall conservation program for yellowfin tuna. When their attempt to restructure the IATTC failed, Mexico and Costa Rica withdrew from the regional organization in 1978 and 1979 respectively. Mexico also extended its jurisdiction on tuna within its 200-nautical-mile zone and seized American vessels which fished in the zone. In 1980 Mexico also terminated its fishing agreements with the United States. After 1981, negotiations between the United States and Costa Rica and Panama produced the 1983 Eastern Pacific Ocean Tuna Fishing Agreement, which came into effect in 1983. In that year Guatemala and Honduras also became parties to the agreement.[54]

The 1983 Eastern Pacific Ocean Tuna Fishing Agreement is an interim agreement on the conservation and management of tuna. It does not replace the IATTC, which continues to have responsibilities in research and study for tuna and porpoise in the eastern Pacific. Key provisions of the agreement are as follows:[55]

1. An international licensing system for fishing tuna in the Eastern Pacific Ocean (Article IV)
2. Vessel license fee is set for $60 per net registered ton as a minimum and will increase incrementally to a maximum of $100 (Paragraphs A-D of Protocol)
3. Fees collected shall be disbursed to the coastal states, after a deduction of not more than 10 percent for administrative cost, in proportion to the amount of tuna taken within the 200 nautical miles
4. An area known as yellowfin conservation and regulatory area (CYRA), originally established by the IATTC (see Figure 5.1), of over 2 million square miles, extending from California to Chile, except those areas within 200 nautical miles of states not parties to the Agreement and those areas within twelve nautical miles of the contracting parties. In order to fish in the CYRA area, the parties must agree to require their tuna vessels to possess an international license (Article II-B)
5. Enforcement measures of fines, sanctions and reciprocal port inspection are to be adopted in the national laws of the respective parties to the Agreement (Article VI)

Significance. As discussed at the beginning of this section on the "species approach," the principle rationale for special treatment of "highly migratory species" was the interest of several coastal states in the tuna industry and the

Figure 5.1
Eastern Pacific Yellowfin Tuna Regulatory Area

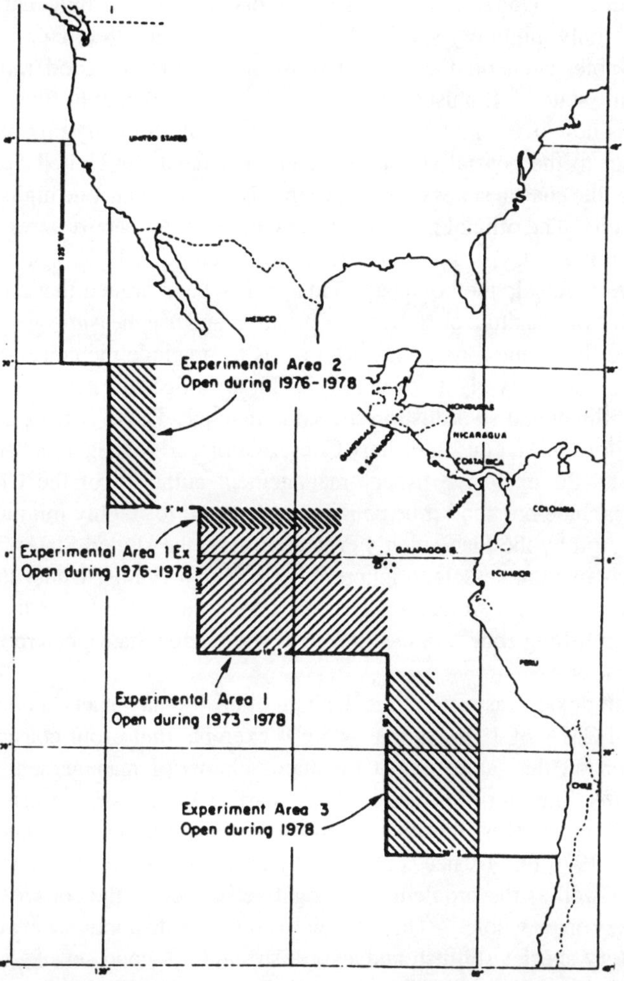

Source: Jon Van Dyke and Susan Heftel, "Tuna Management in the Pacific: An Analysis of the South Pacific Forum Fisheries Agency," *University of Hawaii Law Review* 3, no. 1 (1981): 22. Used by permission.

migratory pattern of tuna, which travels across the oceans and in and out of the 200-nautical-mile EEZ.[56] William Burke argues that Article 64 requires both coastal and long-distance fishing states to cooperate in the conservation and optimum use of the highly migratory species "both within the EEZ and in the region beyond" as provided for in Articles 61 and 62 of the 1982 LOS Convention.[57] Burke also takes the position that the special treatment for "highly migratory species" in Article 64 invokes Article 87 on freedom of fishing on the high seas and Article 116 on the right of nationals of all states in fishing on the high seas, subject to treaty obligations and the interests and duties of the coastal states.[58] Under Articles 116–119 distant-water fishing nations, when fishing "highly migratory species" such as tuna beyond the EEZ, must observe the allowable catch on the high seas by negotiating in good faith with the neighboring states.[59] It must be noted that practically all nations (the total number of states is now over eighty) adopt the practice that all highly migratory species are subject to the coastal states' jurisdiction, except the United States, which insists that the coastal states do not have the right to regulate one highly migratory species, tuna. The official position of the United States seems to rest on the fact that tuna do not stay or reside in the 200-nautical-mile EEZ of a coastal state; they migrate outside the boundary. Thus, it has been argued that a coastal state cannot possibly institute objective conservation and use measures for tuna. While the United States interprets Article 64 so as to preclude the coastal states from exercising regulatory rights over tuna as highly migratory, it nonetheless does not treat billfish and swordfish in the same manner. Thus, Title 1, Section 103, of the 1976 U.S. Magnuson Fishery Conservation and Management Act (FCMA) states that "the exclusive fishery management authority of the United States shall not include nor shall it be construed to extend to, highly migratory species of fish." And by the Fishermen's Protective Act, the United States protects and encourages its tuna vessels to ignore other nation's claims. Under the domestic law (the Fishermen's Protective Act), vessels of the United States that are seized in a foreign fishing zone, not recognized by the United States, can receive federal funds for losses.

The paradoxical aspect of the United States' tuna fishery policy, as contained in FCMA of 1976, is that while it exempts tuna from coastal exclusive jurisdiction, at the same time it maintains claims of management rights over other highly migratory species such as marlin, swordfish, sailfish, shark and dolphin. Some suggest that the exclusion of tuna from coastal states' jurisdiction in the 1976 FCMA needs revision by removing the contradictions and inequities, as well as the problems and negative impact on the conservation of the tuna fishery as a whole.[60] The artificial (political) distinction between one set of migratory species (billfish and swordfish) and a second set of "highly" migratory species (all tuna) makes it difficult to promote international conservation and management in the western and southern Pacific which, in the final analysis, is the aim of both the 1982 LOS Convention and the United States' own Magnuson Fishery Conservation and Management Act. The United States' interpretation of Article 64 as excluding tuna from national jurisdiction would impede the formation of a regional international management agreement for tuna in the South Pacific. In 1990 the U.S. House of Representatives approved legislation (HR 2061) to amend the Magnuson Fishery Conservation and Management Act by extending United States jurisdiction to include tuna stocks within the United States exclusive economic zone, and the U.S. Senate followed the action a few weeks later.[61]

NOTES

1. See J. E. Carroz, ''Institutional Aspects of Fishery Management under the New Regime of the Oceans,'' *San Diego Law Review* 21, no. 3 (June 1984): 513–540; R. R. Churchill and A. V. Lowe, *The Law of the Sea* (Manchester, England: Manchester University Press, 1983), pp. 203–205; R. P. Barston and Patricia Birnie, *The Maritime Dimension* (London: Allen and Unwin, 1980), pp. 40–44; and C. H. Cushing, ''The Atlantic Fisheries Commissions,'' *Marine Policy* 1, no. 3 (1977): 230–236.

2. See Churchill and Lowe, *The Law of the Sea*, p. 204; and Barston and Birnie, *The Maritime Dimension*, pp. 42–43.

3. Carroz, ''Institutional Aspects of Fishery Management,'' p. 531.

4. J. Scharfe, ''Interrelations between Fishing Technology and the Coming International Fishery Regime,'' in Francis T. Christy, Jr., Thomas A. Clingan, Jr., John King Gamble, Jr., H. Gary Knight and Edward Miles, eds. *Law of the Sea: Caracas and Beyond* (Cambridge, Mass.: Ballinger, 1975), p. 260.

5. Jon L. Jacobson, ''The Future Fishing Technology and Its Impact on the Law of the Sea,'' in *Law of the Sea: Caracas and Beyond*, pp. 238–242.

6. Ibid., p. 240.

7. Ibid., p. 244; and Scharfe, ''Interrelations between Fishing Technology and the Coming International Fishery Regime,'' p. 262.

8. See James A. R. Nofziger, ''Global Conservation and Management of Marine Mammals,'' *San Diego Law Review* 17, no. 3 (April 1980): 607–609.

9. See 161 *United States Treaty Series*, 74, 1953.

10. See Public Law No. 92–522; and also see David C. Slade, ''Back to the Drawing Board: Fourth Amendment Rights and the Marine Mammals Protection Act,'' *Ocean Development and International Law* 16, no. 1 (1986): 91–101. For a related view on foreign vessel search and seizure on the high seas and the Fourth Amendment, see Kimberly A. Strang, ''Foreign Search and Seizure: The Fourth Amendment at Large,'' *San Diego Law Review* 25, no. 3 (August–September 1988): 609–630.

11. See *American Cetacean Society v. Malcolm Baldridge*, Civil Action No. 84–3414, U.S. District Court, District of Columbia; and *Memorandum Opinion of the Honorable Charles R. Richey, U.S. District Judge*, Civil Action No. 84–3314, March 13, 1984.

12. See Honorable Don Bonker, ''U.S. Policy and Strategy in the International Whaling Commission: Sinking or Swimming?'' *Ocean Development and International Law* 10, nos. 1–2 (1981): 41–91. Also see Nofziger, ''Global Conservation and Management of Marine Mammals,'' pp. 604–605.

13. Nofziger, ''Global Conservation and Management of Marine Mammals,'' pp. 610–612.

14. See UN Document A/Conf.62/WP.10/Rev.3, 1980. Also see Cynthia E. Carlson, ''The International Regulation of Small Cetaceans,'' *San Diego Law Review* 21, no. 3 (June 1984): 602–605.

15. Carlson, ''The International Regulation of Small Cetaceans,'' pp. 602–605; and E. Mitchell, *Porpoises, Dolphins and Small Whales Fisheries of the World: Status and Problems* 8 (IUCN Monograph No. 3, 1975).

16. Carlson, ''International Regulation of Small Cetaceans,'' p. 594. For a discussion of the unilateral use by the United States Marine Mammal Protection Act for further international protection of cetaceans, see Laura L. Lones, ''The Marine Mammal Pro-

tection Act and International Protection of Cetaceans: A Unilateral Attempt to Effectuate Transnational Conservation,'' *Vanderbilt Journal of Transnational Law* 22, no. 4 (1989): 997–1028.

17. See 51 *Federal Register*, 32, 1986, p. 786.

18. The figure is taken from Beverly Beyette, ''Dolphin Policy Irks Fishermen,'' Los Angeles Times Service as reprinted in *The Sunday Honolulu Star Bulletin and Advertiser*, 27 May 1990, p. B–6. An estimated figure of dolphins killed annually worldwide ranges from 100,000 to 200,000, as provided by *The Honolulu Advertiser*, 13 April 1990, p. A–1.

19. ''Will a Dolphin Save Your Life?'' Center for Marine Conservation, 1725 De Sales Street, N.W., Washington, D.C. 20036, January 1990.

20. Carlson, ''International Regulation of Small Cetaceans,'' pp. 596–599.

21. Ibid., pp. 618–619.

22. For text of the General Assembly Resolution adopted on 22 December 1989, on the drift-net moratorium, see *Law of the Sea Bulletin*, no. 15 (May 1990), pp. 15–17. For analysis on the drift-net problem see Douglas M. Johnston, ''The Driftnet Problem in the Pacific Ocean: Legal Considerations and Diplomatic Options,'' *Ocean Development and International Law* 21, no. 1 (1990): 5–39.

23. See Thomas A. Bailey, *A Diplomatic History of the American People* (New York: Appleton-Century-Crofts, 1946), pp. 446–449.

24. Ibid., p. 448.

25. See *1980 Protocol Amending Interim Convention on the Conservation of North Pacific Fur Seals* (U.S. Senate, 97th Congress, 1st session, 20 May 1981), p. 4.

26. Ibid., p. 10. Also see *Draft Environmental Impact Statement on the Interim Convention Conservation of North Pacific Fur Seals*, Departments of State and Commerce, October 1983, p. 14.

27. See Kevin Cox, ''Fisherman Say Seal Herds Are Gobbling Up the Fish,'' *Toronto Globe and Mail*, as reprinted in *The Honolulu Star Bulletin*, 28 February 1990, p. A–14.

28. See Finn Laursen, *Superpower at Sea: U.S. Ocean Policy* (New York: Praeger, 1983), pp. 67–72; and Ann L. Hollick, *U.S. Foreign Policy and the Law of the Sea* (Princeton, N.J.: Princeton University Press, 1981) pp. 268–270.

29. See UN Document A/AC.138/SC.II/L.4.

30. UN Document A/Conv.62/C.2/L.47 in UNCLOS III, *Official Records*, vol. 3, pp. 223–224.

31. UN Documents A/Conf.62/C.2/L.41; A/Conf.62/C.2/L.57/Rev.1; and A/Conf.62/C.2/L.81. Also see UNCLOS III, *Official Records*, vol. 2, pp. 181, 190 and 224.

32. See William Gordon, ''Management of Living Resources: Challenge of the Future,'' *Comparative Marine Policy: Perspectives from Europe, Scandinavia, Canada and the United States*, Center for Ocean Management Studies, University of Rhode Island (Brooklyn, N.Y.: J. F. Bergin, 1981), p. 148, D (Sec. 102).

33. Marc L. Miller and Charles F. Broches, ''U.S. Fishery Negotiations with Canada and Mexico,'' *Ocean Development and International Law* 14, no. 4 (1985): 427–432.

34. See Marlyn Twitchell, ''Implementing the U.S.–Canada Pacific Salmon Treaty: The Struggle to Move from Fish Wars to Cooperative Fishery Management,'' *Ocean Development and International Law* 20, no. 4 (1989): 409–428. Also see Jere Van Dyk, ''Long Journey of the Pacific Salmon,'' *National Geographic* 178, no. 1 (July 1990): 3–37.

35. See Barbara Johnson and Frank Langdon, "Two Hundred Mile Zones: The Politics of North Pacific Fishers," *Pacific Affairs* 49, no. 1 (Spring 1976): 9–10; Myres S. McDougal and William T. Burke, *The Public Order of the Oceans: A Contemporary International Law of the Sea* (Norwell, Mass.: Kluwer-Nijhoff, 1987) pp. 735–736 and 929–945; and Julian V. Minghi, "The Conflict of Salmon Fishing Politics in the North Pacific," *Pacific Viewpoint* 2 (1961): 59–86.

36. Johnson and Langdon, "Two Hundred Mile Zones," p. 10.

37. See *Department of State Bulletin*, March 1986, p. 42.

38. Ibid.

39. See *Department of State Bulletin*, June 1986, p. 74.

40. Miller and Broches, "U.S. Fishery Negotiations with Canada and Mexico," P. 440.

41. R. P. Anand, "The Politics of a New Legal Order for Fisheries," *Ocean Development and International Law* II, nos. 3–4 (1982): 268–270.

42. "Solution in the Convention on the Law of the Sea to the Problem of Overfishing in the Central Bering Sea: Analysis of the Convention, Highlighting the Provisions Concerning Fisheries and Enclosed and Semi-Enclosed Seas," *San Diego Law Review* 26, no. 3 (August–September 1989): 556.

43. Edward Miles, "An Interpretation of the Geneva Proceedings, Part III," *Ocean Development and International Law* 10, no. 3 (1976).

44. Jon Van Dyke and Susan Heftel, "Tuna Management in the Pacific: An Analysis of the South Pacific Forum Fisheries Agency," *University of Hawaii Law Review* 3, no. 1 (1981): 53. Also see Camillus Narokobi, "The Tuna Issue: The South Pacific and the U.S.," in Jon Van Dyke, ed., *Consensus and Confrontation: The United States and the Law of the Sea Convention*, (Honolulu: The Law of the Sea Institute, University of Hawaii, 1985), pp. 371–372.

45. Van Dyke and Heftel, "Tuna Management in the Pacific," p. 53.

46. Ibid., pp. 1–65. For latest membership of the South Pacific Forum Fisheries Agency, see David J. Doulman, "In Pursuit of Fisheries Cooperation: The South Pacific Forum Fisheries Agency," *University of Hawaii Law Review* 10, no. 1 (Summer 1988): 137–138.

47. Van Dyke and Heftel, "Tuna Management in the Pacific," p. 53.

48. Ibid. And also see George Kent, *The Politics of Pacific Island Fisheries* (Boulder, Colo.: Westview, 1980).

49. Camillus Narokobi, "The Tuna Issue," pp. 372–373.

50. David J. Doulman, "In Pursuit of Fisheries Cooperation," pp. 138 and 150.

51. See U.S. TIAS 2044; UST 230; and USTS 3.

52. See Hollick, *U.S. Foreign Policy and the Law of the Sea*, pp. 73–74. Also see James Joseph, "Management of Tuna Fisheries in the Eastern Pacific Ocean," in Edward L. Miles and Scott Allen, eds., *The Law of the Sea and Ocean Development Issues in the Pacific Basin* (Honolulu: The Law of the Sea Institute, University of Hawaii, 1983), pp. 147–154.

53. Joseph, "Management of Tuna Fisheries in the Eastern Pacific Ocean," p. 148.

54. See *Eastern Pacific Ocean Tuna Fishing Agreement*, message from the President of the United States, 12 May 1983.

55. Ibid.

56. See William T. Burke, "Highly Migratory Species in the New Law of the Sea," *Ocean Development and International Law* 14, no. 3 (1984): 274–275.

57. Ibid., pp. 281–283.
58. Ibid., pp. 284–285.
59. Ibid., p. 287.
60. See Susan O'Malley Wade, ''A Proposal to Include Tunas in the U.S. Fishery Jurisdiction,'' *Ocean Development and International Law* 16, no. 3 (1986): 225–293. Also see letter to Senator Packwood from Wadsworth Y. H. Yee, Chairman of Western Pacific Management Council, dated 16 March 1983.
61. See *Oceans Policy News*, May 1990, p. 4; and *The Honolulu Star Bulletin*, 2 June 1990, p. A–4.

CHAPTER 6

Nonliving Resources: Offshore Oil and Strategic Minerals

The increasing importance of nonliving ocean resources can be seen from the following simple statistics: during the period 1960–1971 offshore hydrocarbon production of crude oil and natural gas represented only 5 percent of the world's total production, but by 1985–1986 the overall production of these marine resources had reached close to one-third of the total. When offshore drilling for oil and gas began in Texas and Louisiana in the 1930s and 1940s, the sites for these offshore resources were located mostly in swamps and shallow water a few miles from the shore. Now, in the 1990s, offshore exploitation of hydrocarbons has moved to the continental rise hundreds of miles from the coast and at a drilling depth of thousands of meters. Floating drilling platforms and artificial islands on the high seas and in the frigid Arctic Ocean are now common sights in the ocean space.

During the epic scientific voyage of the H.M.S. *Challenger* in 1872 discovery was made of golfball-sized nodules on the sea floor of the Atlantic, Pacific and Indian oceans, but their usefulness as a potential mineral resource was not recognized until the 1950s. The value of manganese nodules as a new source of mineral deposits escalated as prices for the traditional land-based metals soared when industrialized nations became heavily dependent upon those land-based supplies from the more politically volatile Third World nations. This marked the beginning of a new discovery in uses of the ocean: deep-seabed mineral resources.[1] For much of the late 1960s and throughout the 1970s, world attention and publicity seemed to have been focused on the new economic opportunities, as well as the legal and political problems, generated by the possibility of deep-seabed mining.

This chapter begins with the topic of deep-water drilling for oil and gas at a distance of more than 1,000 meters offshore. A total of more than twenty-seven deep-water holes have been drilled by oil companies from a number of nations. While the cost of deep-water drilling involving floating platforms, submersibles and specially designed drill ships has been considered rather high, the potential for deep-water oil and gas mining could double the current world estimate of energy resources. More significantly, drilling for hydrocarbons has now reached the continental margins at a depth of at least 1,000 meters, which constitutes more than 80 percent of the ocean area.

A brief, but concise, survey of the ocean's nonfuel resources is presented in the second section of this chapter: the mineral resources of the ocean. Five selected mineral resources are discussed, accompanied by a reference table of the recent estimates of their deposit availability. These are calcium carbonate, manganese nodules, marine polymetallic sulfides (MPS) and cobalt crust, phosphorite, and sand and gravel. Attention is paid to the political and economic significance of the potential for deep seabed mining of the manganese nodules. These considerations led to the drafting of those provisions in the 1982 LOS Convention for international management—including production control, licensing by the International Seabed Authority, and the parallel approach (see Chapter 7).

Current scientific research and experimentation on ocean thermal energy conversion (OTEC) represent one of the most exciting events in marine research. Its potential for generating abundant and inexpensive energy from ocean water is unparalleled. However, jurisdictional conflicts may arise in the future when OTEC sites and plants are located on the high seas. Sixty equatorial nations could make OTEC economically feasible because of the coastal ocean water temperature differences that would be suitable for energy conversion. The legal and political problems for OTEC seem to be the lack of a precise definition within the meaning of Articles 60 and 80 of the 1982 LOS Convention for placing OTEC plants on the high seas.

The increasing importance of offshore oil and gas production—the hydrocarbons, which may constitute almost half of the world's total oil and gas production in the 1990s and beyond—is presented and discussed in this chapter under the topic of offshore oil and gas. The up-to-date figures for offshore fuel resources presented here point to the underlying reasons why new ocean regimes or ocean enclosure arrangements have been endorsed by the 1982 LOS Convention. New legal concepts, such as continental shelf and exclusive economic zone, have awarded the coastal states jurisdiction within 200 nautical miles from their coastlines where offshore energy resources are to be found.

Under Article 57 the exclusive economic zones could encompass more than 35 percent of the ocean area; and under Article 76 the continental shelf regime, without a precise seaward limit, could constitute as much as one-third of the ocean space. Unfortunately, the nonliving resources on the continental shelf and in the exclusive economic zone in many instances are found in overlapped areas claimed by the coastal states. In accordance with Article 83 of the LOS Convention, overlapping claims for the exploitation and exploration of nonliving resources on the continental shelf have been resolved in some cases by bilateral agreements. These bilateral arrangements for boundary delimitation of the continental shelf often call for joint development of these nonliving resources on a sharing basis.

Finally, there is discussion in this chapter on the question of strategic minerals for industrial and defense purposes. Many of the hard strategic minerals, such as manganese, cobalt, titanium and chromium, have been provided by land-based suppliers in politically volatile areas of the world. The basic argument, advanced mainly by the United States, is that Western industrialized nations, plus Japan, are heavily dependent upon imports of these mineral resources from overseas; the alternatives to their predicament lie either in the stockpiling of the strategic minerals, or in finding another source of supply, or in substitution. The mining of ocean mineral resources from the deep seabed has figured prominently as a viable alternative. The euphoria of mining hard minerals from the deep seabed waned considerably in the 1980s as new substitutes—plastics, aluminum and tin—came on the scene, filling the need for imported minerals. In reality, deep seabed mining has become less attractive as an enterprise, primarily because of the cost in terms of heavy investment in research and development followed by insignificant returns as a business venture. These disadvantages are compounded by uncertainty with respect to the legal status of deep seabed mining under Part XI of the 1982 LOS Convention and the alternate ocean regime established by the Reciprocal States Agreement.

DEEP-WATER OIL

This section deals with drilling under the prospect of finding oil and gas deposits in very deep water of more than 1,000 meters depth beyond the offshore areas.[2] Under the Deep Sea Drilling Project (DSDP), the *Glomar Challenger* has drilled over 7,000 meters in the Marianas Trench of the Pacific. For the period from 1976 to 1983, twenty-seven deep-water holes of more than 1,000 meters depth had been drilled by oil companies for potential oil production (see Table 6.1).

It must be remembered that the central ocean region, which comprises over 77 percent of the world's total marine area, is covered by deep water. Hollis D. Hedberg lists three deep-water regions where petroleum accumulation may be discovered.[3] First, there is the greater central ocean region where the sediments are thin with low organic carbon content; thus the prospects for petroleum accumulation are not favorable. However, methane hydrate accumulations have been found in drill sites near the continental margin. Second is the continental margin region, with a variety of geological features with promising petroleum prospects because of the thickness in sediments and presence of source rocks. Hedberg reports that 51 of the 140 DSDP continental margin drill sites showed evidence of hydrocarbons.[4] And finally, the forty semi-enclosed seas of the continental margin seem to be the best prospective sites for petroleum mining, as they are close to land and are fed by large rivers that provide the continental margins with an accumulation of marine organic matter. Continental shelves of

Table 6.1
Petroleum Industry Holes Drilled in Water Depths More than 1,000 Meters

Year	Country	Company & Well Name	Water Depth
1976	Thailand	Esso--W9-E-1	1,055 m
1977	Spain	Eniepsa--Anl	1,151 m
1978	Congo	Getty	1,325 m
	French Guinea	Esso--FG-2-1	1,250 m
	Suriname	Esso--A-2-1	1,160 m
	Spain	Hispanoil, Eniepsa	1,144 m
1979	Canada	Texaco, Shell, et al.--Blue	1,486 m
	Spain	Eniepsa--Gabriel B-24	1,399 m
	Spain	Getty, Grumete--C-1X	1,353 m
	Australia	Esso Australia--Zeewulf 1	1,195 m
	Australia	Phillips--Mercury 1X	1,142 m
	Canada	Esso Res.--EVG C-60	1,108 m
	Australia	Esso Australia--Resol-1	1,087 m
	Suriname	Elf, Shell, Eurafrep--A21	1,201 m
1980	Britain, Rockall Trough	BNOC--163/6-1	1,374 m
	Australia	Esso Australia--Vinck 1	1,373 m
	Australia	Esso Aust.--N.W. Shelf	1,373 m
	Australia	Esso Aust.--Exmouth Plat.	1,363 m
	Australia	Esso Aust.--E. Exmouth Plat.	1,183 m
	Australia	Phillips--Exmouth Plat.	1,178 m
	Australia	Esso Aust.--Sirius 1	1,173 m
	Mauritania	Hispanoil--Ras al Baida Al	1,119 m
1981	Australia	Phillips--Exmouth, Saturn 1X	1,177 m
1982	Spain	Getty, Tarragona, Grumete--F-1X	1,067 m
	France	Total, Elf, Esso--GLP-1	1,715 m
1983	France	Total, Elf, Esso--GLP-2 (proposed)	1,200 m
	United States	Shell--Atlantic coast (proposed)	2,073 m

Source: Hollis D. Hedberg, "Deep Water Petroleum Prospects of the Oceans and Seas," *Oceanus* 26, no. 3 (Fall 1983): 10. Used by permission.

many of the semi-enclosed seas, such as the Gulf of Mexico, Persian Gulf, Caribbean Sea, Mediterranean Sea, Caspian Sea and North Sea, have already become the sites of petroleum production. The United States Geological Survey has estimated that the Gulf of Mexico contains an oil deposit of 22 billion barrels. More than 75 percent of the area of the central Gulf of Mexico lies under a water depth exceeding 3,000 meters.

Drilling a well for oil prospecting in deep water of more than 1,000 meters is a very costly enterprise; it involves erecting platforms, submersibles and drill ships designed for drilling in deep waters. Besides the cost factor, ranging from a low estimate of $30 million to a high of $100 million for drilling one well from 1,200 to over 2,000 meters, drilling technology is in a state of constant refinement. One example is the directional drill for producing several wells with a single platform, as seen in Figure 6.1.

Significance. While the legal problem of coastal state jurisdiction over the

Figure 6.1
Directional Drilling

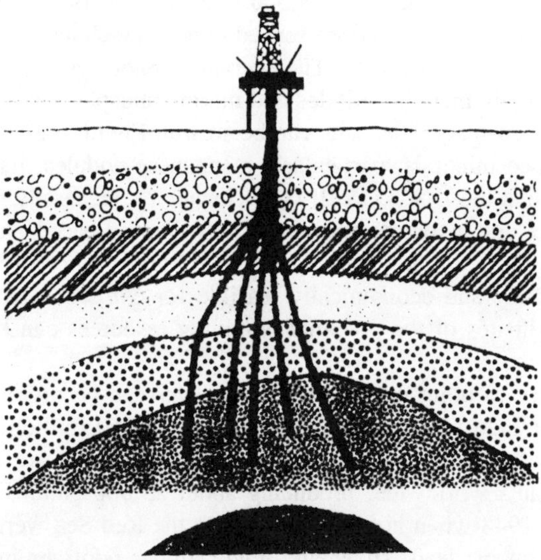

Directional drilling is often used to produce several wells from a single offshore platform without moving the equipment. (Provided by Petroleum Extension Service, University of Texas at Austin)

Source: Hedberg, "Deep Water Petroleum Prospects of the Oceans and Seas," p. 13. Used by permission.

mineral resources of the continental margin in relation to the 1982 LOS Convention will be discussed separately in this chapter, the significant implication of deep-water drilling for petroleum lies in the enormous prospects for additional sources of energy beyond what offshore drilling now provides (constituting only 25 percent of oil and 18 percent of gas production). As pointed out earlier, offshore waters of more than 1,000 meters depth constitute more than 80 percent of the world's ocean area. Offshore deep-water drilling could potentially double the present world estimates of offshore oil and gas deposits. There is every expectation that the twenty-first century will see all of the continental margins being made accessible for oil and gas exploitation. To a larger extent that accessibility will be dependent upon favorable technological improvement and the clarification of international legal restraints or limitations.

OCEAN MINERAL RESOURCES

This section concerns itself primarily with deep seabed deposits of nonfuel mineral materials. James M. Broadus classifies these nonfuel seabed minerals into two major types: (1) those minerals obtainable from deposits in shallow coastal waters of less than 200 meters depth, and (2) those that can be extracted from abyssal or sea floor depths of 3,500 to 5,500 meters.[5]

The first category of nonfuel deep-seabed minerals includes sand, gravel phosphorites, tin and sulfur deposits. The second category consists of manganese nodules, marine polymetallic sulfides and marine phosphorites. The location of these nonfuel deep-seabed deposits can be seen in Figure 6.2.

Nonfuel seabed minerals, particularly manganese nodules, have become the center of debate at the UNCLOS III (see Chapter 7). Generally speaking, these seabed deposits are in demand commercially if land-based supplies become exhausted, and therefore they are considered a future source of revenue if they are technologically and economically feasible for extraction from the seabed. The overall estimates of the potential nonliving resources can be see in Table 6.2.

It is necessary to point out that, if fresh water can be produced for human consumption or industrial use by desalination, the 350 million cubic miles of ocean water is the most useful nonliving resource. There are more than 700 desalination plants worldwide, producing about 25,000 gallons of fresh water per day. Since 1948 when hot brines (mud) in the Red Sea were discovered to contain zinc, copper, lead, silver and gold, similar pools or muds have been found elsewhere in the Pacific Ocean and the Red Sea. Related to the hot brines are the deep-sea brown muds on the ocean floor containing a possible volume of 30 million cubic kilometers of aluminum and iron deposits. Barite, the ore of barium sulfate ($BaSO_4$), a whitish malleable metallic element, has been mined on the continental margin in Alaska. On the continental margins off the coast of the United States, titanium and zirconium deposits have been recovered.

Calcium Carbonate (Shell)

In its pure form, calcium carbonate is known as aragonite ($CaCO_3$) and is usually identified with calcite in crystalline form in limestone. One recovery on the continental margin of the Bahamas led to an estimate of a possible reserve there of 70 to 90 billion tons. Lime in calcium carbonate is used in agriculture, as well as for cement in construction. It has been estimated that over one-third of the deep-sea floor is covered with sediments of calcium carbonate.

Manganese Nodules

Manganese nodules are "a form of pelagic sedimentation" on the deep ocean floor.[6] These are manganese-dioxide grains, mostly golfball or potato size, one-half millimeter in diameter and ten to fifteen centimeters in thickness. Some are found to be a large cannonball-sized solid manganite—the largest, recovered 2,400 kilometers north of Hawaii, weighed fifty-five kilograms.[7] There are still many unanswered questions about the formation of these nodules on the deep

Figure 6.2
Major Oceanic Mineral Sites

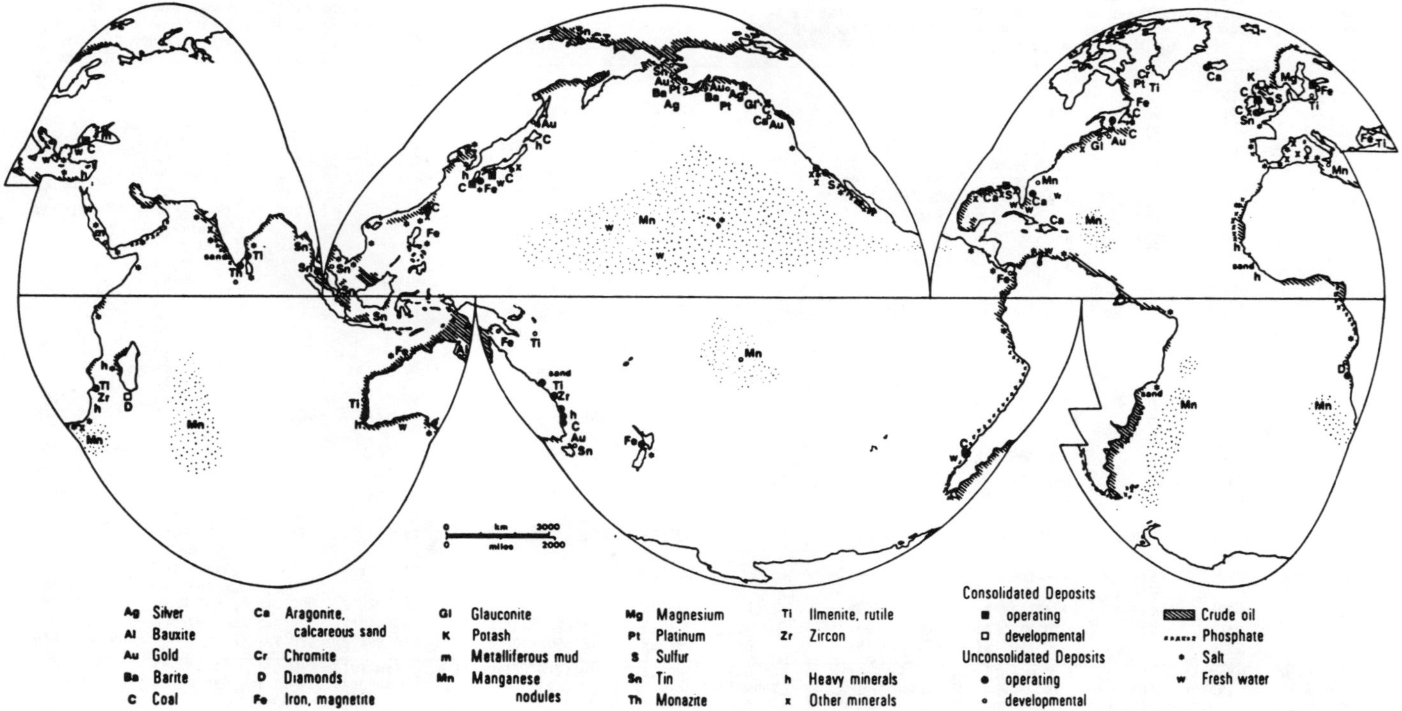

Source: Reprinted from R. H. Charlier, ''Other Ocean Resources,'' in *Ocean Yearbook 1*, Elisabeth Mann Borgese and Norton Ginsburg, eds. (Chicago: University of Chicago Press, 1978), p. 188. Used by permission.

Table 6.2
Seabed Materials in World Perspective (MT = Metric Tons)

Seabed deposits	Material commodity	Seabed production (10^3MT)	World mine production (10^3 MT)	Estimated average price ($ in millions)	Seabed revenues[a] ($ in millions)	World revenues[b] ($ in millions)	Seabed share of world revenues[c] (%)	Seabed reported potential resources (10^3 MT)	World onshore resources (10^3 MT)	Seabed comparison to world resources[d] (%)	Resource life index[e] (years)	Projected onshore depletion by year 2030[f] (%)
Hydrocarbons[g]	Crude oil	788,834	2,788,913	70	55,218	195,224	28	>61,429,000	181,857,000	34	65	185
	Natural gas	246,670	1,296,405	95	23,434	123,158	19	>60,000,000	228,214,000	26	176	45
Sand and gravel	Sand and gravel	112,300	7,620,480	3	334	22,861	1	665,778,000	very large	small	long	
	Industrial sand		181,440	14		2,540		large	very large	small	long	
Shell	Calcium carbonate	16,667	1,666,667	6	100	10,000	1	90,000,000	very large	small	long	
Sulfur	Sulfur	381	54,000	105	40	5,670	<1	27,125[h]	5,000,000	<1	93	120
Barite	Barite		5,652	31		175		2,087[h]	453,600	<1	80	
Phosphorite	Phosphate rock		159,000	24		3,816		7,939,000	129,500,000	6	814	12
Mineral placers	Tin	28	201	6,614	185	1,329	14	2,500	34,500	7	172	105
	Rutile		356	364		130		13,060	181,440	7	510	
	Ilmenite		4,187	49		205		230,500	907,200	25	217	
	Titanium[i]		90	12,236		1,101						40
	Zirconium		709	182		129		29,040	54,432	53	77	
	Hafnium		<<1	231,483		17		290	544	53	7,452	
	Yttrium		<1	35,020		14		[3,450[h]]	172		430	
	Thorium		2	35,850		72			5,168		2,584	
	Chromite		9,616	42		404		30,158[h]	32,659,200	<1	3,396	1
	Gold		1	10,600,000		10,600		<1[h]	72	<1	72	443
	Silver		12	206,667		2,480			743		62	295
	Platinum		<<1	9,000,000		1,980		<<1[h]	99	<<1	446	13
Nodules and Crusts	Platinum[j]							2-3		2-3		
	Cobalt		32	25,353		811		6,000- 24,000	10,886	55-220	340	
	Nickel		745	5,026		3,744		53,000- 131,000	129,730	27-101	174	77
	Manganese		23,406	141		3,300		706,000-2,600,000	10,886,400	6- 24	465	17
	Copper		7,805	1,475		11,512		29,000- 108,000	1,600,000	2- 7	205	86
Massive sulfides	Copper[k]							5,000- 216,000		<1- 14		
	Zinc		6,560	893		5,858		11,000- 518,000	1,800,000	<1- 29	274	47
	Lead		3,350	419		1,4[illegible]4			1,400,000		418	46

a Seabed production times estimated average price
b World mine production times estimated average price
c Seabed revenues times 100, divided by world revenues
d Seabed reported potential resources times 100, divided by world onshore resources
e World onshore resources divided by world mine production
f Based on low growth case for developing economics
g Hydrocarbons in metric tons of oil equivalent
h Seabed estimate for the United States only; the number in brackets [3,450] is for U. S. seabed monazite deposits yttrium and thorium
i Titanium resources are included in rutile and ilmenite resources
j See numbers directly above in Mineral Placers for platinum
k See numbers directly above in Nodules and Crusts for copper

Source: James M. Broadus, "Seabed Materials," *Science* 235 (20 February 1987): 854. Copyright 1987 by AAAS. Used by permission.

ocean floor. But this much is known: Organic particles, such as plant or animal, or inorganic particles of volcanic material settling through the sea water, act as agents of accretion by extracting manganese and other metallic substances from the sea water. The nucleic crust of the nodules contains nickel, copper, manganese and cobalt. Based on a survey of only 3 percent of the world's ocean floor, it is estimated that manganese nodules appear in the deep seabed sediments of all oceans, particularly the Pacific and Indian oceans (see Figure 6.3).

Thus, it has been discovered that on the seabed floor there lie great quantities of nodules rich in iron and manganese that can be extracted for commercial uses. The composition of ore-grade manganese nodules recovered southeast of Hawaii is as follows (by dry weight): Manganese, 25–30 percent; iron, 6 percent; nickel, 1.5 percent; copper, 1.3 percent; and cobalt, 0.25 percent.[8]

Studies have shown that the Pacific Ocean, particularly the Clarion-Clipperton area in the north-central Pacific, seems to contain the largest concentration of manganese nodules, estimated at 1.5 trillion tons, with a possible annual renewal rate of 10 million tons (see Figure 6.3).[9] Manganese nodules are the important mineral resource of the deep seabed to be exploited in the International Seabed Area beyond the limits of national jurisdiction, which is to be managed, regulated and controlled by the International Seabed Authority. While the mining and processing system is still in the development stage, the general approach can be seen in Figure 6.4.

Marine Polymetallic Sulfides (MPS) and Cobalt Crust

Lately, undersea research scientists have discovered deposits of sulfide and hydrothermal mineral formation on the ocean floor in the Galápagos, Juan de Fuca Ridge and East Pacific Rise.[10] On the Hawaiian Ridge undersea scientists have observed submarine hydrothermal activities associated with "hot spot" volcanoes, such as the growing undersea Loihi volcano just south of the island of Hawaii. Malahoff reports the observation of mineral formation along the volcanic mid-ocean ridge segments at a depth of 1,600 meters on the Juan de Fuca Ridge and the East Pacific Rise. High temperature volcanic magma heats the seawater on the ocean floor to form a new "cap rock" of basalt sheets, rich in iron and manganese. Metallic elements, when leached from the basalt by heated seawater, form the polymetallic sulfides.[11] This newly discovered marine mineral resource, the metallic content in the sulfides from the ocean floor, is said to be variably distributed as follows: Sulfur, 40 percent; iron, 20 percent, copper, 20 percent; and zinc, up to 20 percent.[12]

Another new marine scientific discovery is the cobalt-rich manganese crust on the surface of ancient submarine volcanic terrain or seamounts on the ocean floor adjacent to Hawaii. As reported by Malahoff, the rate of accumulation of this manganese crust on the seamount is estimated to be a few millimeters per million years.[13] Seamount deposits, rich in cobalt, are found within the 200 nautical miles of the Hawaiian EEZ, as seen in Figure 6.5.

Figure 6.3
North Pacific Manganese Nodule Zone

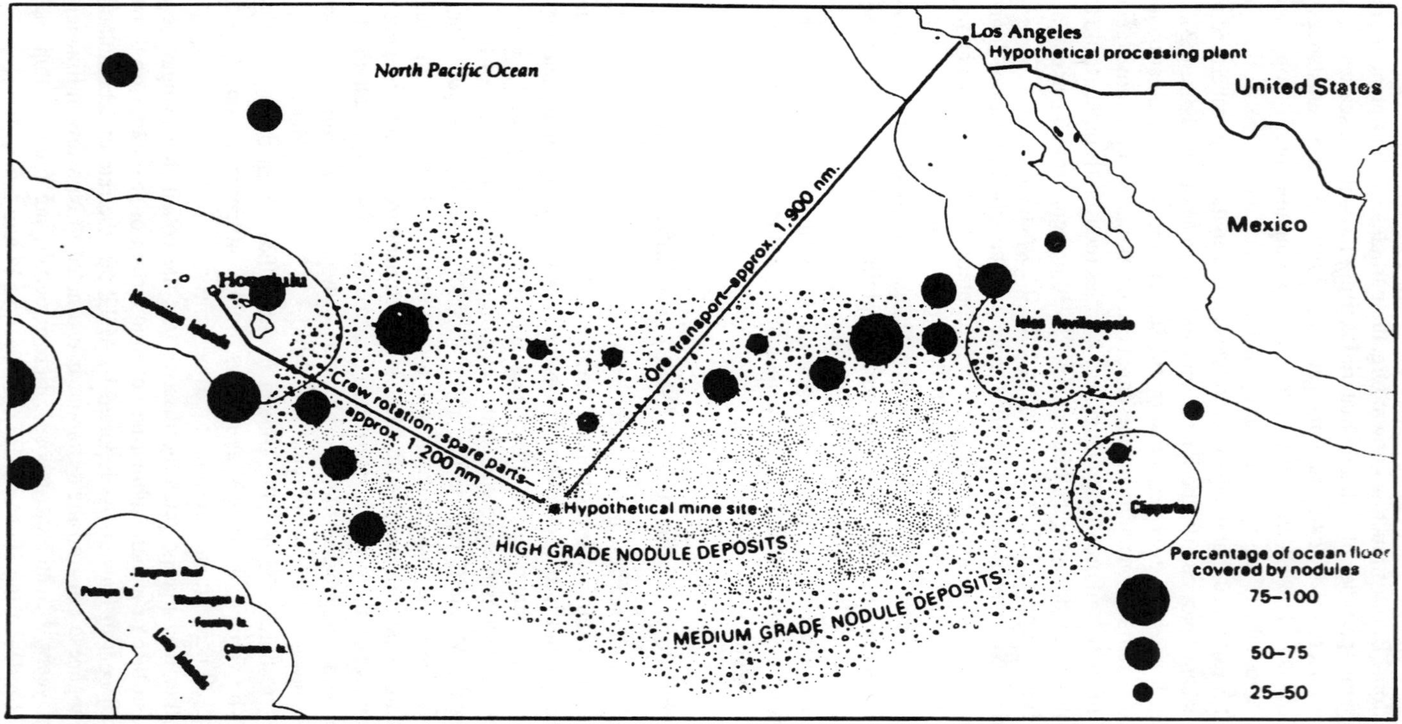

Source: John P. Craven, *The Management of Pacific Marine Resources: Present Problems and Future Trends* (Boulder, Colo.: Westview Press, 1982), p. 30. Used by permission.

Figure 6.4
Manganese-Nodule Mining and Processing System

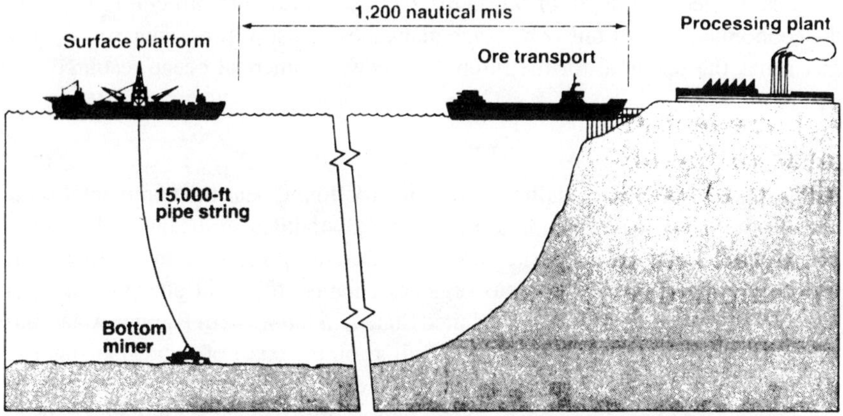

Source: *Far Eastern Economic Review* 29 (March 1984): 71. Used by permission.

Figure 6.5
Delineation of the U.S. Exclusive Economic Zone around the Hawaiian Islands

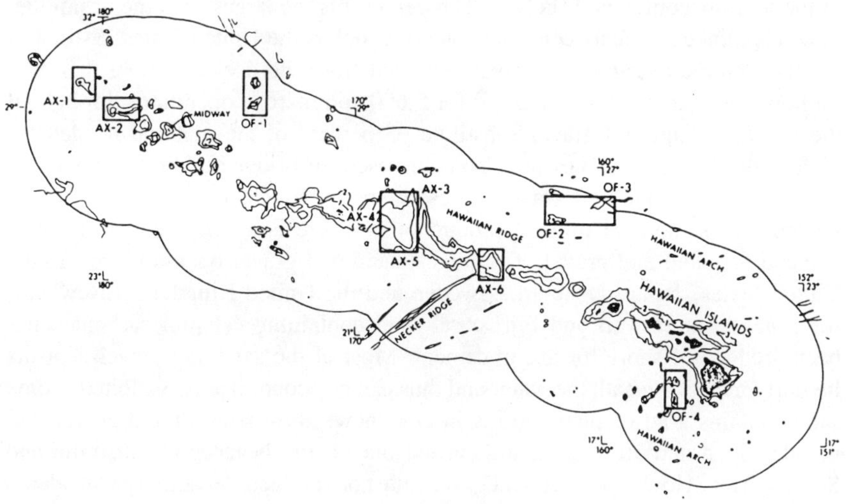

Note: Rectangles indicate areas where cobalt-rich manganese crust has been sampled to date. OF–4 is located over the site of the Hawaiian Seamounts. Contour values: 1000

Source: Alexander Malahoff, ''Polymetallic Sulfides and Cobalt Crust: New Mineral Resources of the Ocean Floor?'' in *The Developing Order of the Oceans*, Robert B. Krueger and Stefan A. Riesenfeld, eds. (Honolulu: The Law of the Sea Institute, University of Hawaii, 1985), p. 302. Used by permission.

Cobalt-rich manganese crust can now be found in waters at a depth of 1,000 to 3,000 meters, technologically an easier range to mine than those manganese nodules located at a depth of 5,000 meters. At present it is difficult to estimate the economic value of this cobalt-rich manganese crust; it is possible to say only that it has the potential for the future as a new commercial ocean resource.

Phosphorite

Phosphorites are nonmetallic clumps of sand found near the continental shelf at a depth of less than a hundred meters. These nodules are heavy rocks on the continental slopes. Phosphorite has been used as potassium in fertilizers. It consists of sand, some calcareous organic remains and fossil phosphorite. It is found on the southern coast of the United States, in the western Pacific, Australia, Japan and parts of southern Africa, as well as on the coast of India. Phosphorite deposits are estimated to be about 200 million tons worldwide, far exceeding the demand for agricultural needs. Total phosphorite deposit it estimated at from 7.9 million to 30 billion tons.

Sand and Gravel

For some time the ocean has supplied a vast amount of building material in the form of sand and gravel. It has been estimated that they compose 70 percent of the world's continental shelves. This represents the largest volume of nonfuel minerals mined for many countries, one of which is the United States. Estimates put the volume of sand and gravel extracted from the ocean at more than 900 million tons, valued at $1.6 billion, for 5,600 commercial operations throughout the world.[14] Sand and gravel constitute 95 percent of the material needed for highway construction. They are also being used for bridge building and housing in urban areas. Sand and gravel represent about 10 percent of the value of all United States' nonfuel mineral production.[15] There is a continuing worldwide demand for sand and gravel. The largest sand and gravel operations are in the United States, Japan, Denmark, Sweden and the United Kingdom. Elsewhere, for instance in Hawaii and Fiji, coral sand containing calcium carbonate has been dredged offshore for use in cement. Most of the sand and gravel deposits lie thirty meters beneath the water and thus can be economically exploited. Some sand contains gold or platinum (as in Goodnews Bay, Alaska) and gravel diamonds. Such activities are being carried out on the beaches of Australia and South Africa. However, sand and gravel must be dredged, an activity considered harmful to the shoreline marine environment.

Significance. Analysis of the subject of the ocean's nonfuel minerals will focus on the manganese nodules in relation to deep seabed mining and as the central controversial concern at the UNCLOS III. In the first place, the political and economic significance of manganese nodules, the deep sea minerals most likely to be exploited in the foreseeable future, lies in their importance as hard and strategic minerals for industrial uses. Nickel is used as a high-temperature steel alloy for jet engines, and manganese is vital in steel manufacture. When iron is converted to steel, manganese is added to cleanse it of sulfur. Copper is used as an electrical conductor in all electrical instruments. Cobalt is a must for the aircraft industry in jet engine blades, and it is also used as an alloy to toughen steel and as a necessary element for high-temperature resistance in missiles and jet engines.[16]

Most industrialized nations must rely on land-based suppliers for these strategic minerals. Almost 97 percent of U.S. needs for the expensive cobalt must be imported from Zaire, Canada, Norway and Finland. Of U.S. industrial manganese 95 percent is imported from Brazil, Gabon, Zaire and South Africa. In 1977 the United States spent $2 billion to import these minerals. It has been estimated that 1 percent of the known deep-seabed manganese nodules could supply the world industrial needs for manganese, nickel and copper for fifty-five years. For an industrialized developed nation such as the United States mining of deep-seabed manganese resources would mean possible self-sufficiency. Assuming that deep-seabed mining production is commercialized in the future, three mines in the Pacific could reduce its import of manganese by 12 percent, copper by 41 percent and nickel by 54 percent.

At present African nations play a dominant role in world cobalt mining production, producing 69 percent of the world's total (see Table 6.3).[17] For the land-based suppliers of these hard minerals, deep-seabed mining production could have a serious impact on their economies in the form of reduced revenues. In a note from the chairman of the First Committee in UNCLOS III in 1974, it was pointed out that:

> 4. . . . the impact of sea-bed production would be most evident in the drastic redistribution of production and production revenues which would result if compared with current patterns of production and trade. Gross revenues presently accruing to developing countries from cobalt production amount to approximately $95 million annually in terms of 1970 prices. By 1980, if there were no production from the sea-bed, this latter amount is projected to increase to $240 million, again at 1970 prices. In the event of sea-bed production, however, developing countries' revenues would be less, between $120–$220 million for 1980, depending on the level of sea-bed production assumed.
>
> 5. The national revenue loss to developing countries in the event of sea-bed production is thus projected, for 1980, to be in the region of $19 to $120 million at 1970 prices, depending on the assumptions made. Under these same assumptions, the revenue accruing to sea-bed production in 1980 would be $16 to $100 million, at 1970 prices, while developed countries' revenues would remain substantially unchanged in the region of $10 million.[18]

The political impact for the developed countries is that when manganese nodule recovery from deep-seabed mining becomes fully operational, there will be a secure supply of these hard minerals for industrial needs without a dependence on developing land-based producers. In this context the land-based developing

Table 6.3
World Cobalt Mine Production, 1978; and Capacity 1978, 1979 and 1985*

	Production in 1978**	Capacity 1978	Capacity 1979	Capacity 1985
North America				
Canada	2,720	3,600	3,600	5,000
Cuba	3,600	3,600	3,600	4,000
Total	6,320	7,200	7,200	9,000
Europe:				
Finland	2,858	2,900	3,000	3,500
USSR	4,300	4,400	4,400	4,500
Total	7,158	7,300	7,400	8,000
Africa				
Botswana	576	600	600	1,000
Morocco	2,500	2,500	2,500	2,500
South Africa	200	200	200	500
Zaire	29,320	35,000	35,000	42,000
Zambia	3,822	4,000	6,000	12,000
Total	36,418	42,300	44,300	58,000
Oceania				
Australia	3,000	3,000	3,500	4,000
New Caledonia	340	500	500	2,000
Philippines	2,626	2,800	2,800	3,000
Total	5,966	6,300	6,800	9,000
World Total***	55,862	63,100	65,700	84,000

* Thousand pounds.
** Estimated recovered cobalt content.
*** Data may not add to total shown because of independent rounding.
Source: William P. Pendley, "The U.S. Will Need Seabed Minerals," *Oceanus* 25, no. 3 (Fall 1982): 15. Used by permission.

states, members of the Group of 77, insisted that production control be exercised by the International Seabed Authority, possible adverse effects of deep-seabed mining on the economies of the developing nations be continuously reviewed, and the Authority's executive organ, the Council, develop a system of compensation for economic assistance to those land-based supplier nations that might suffer the ill effects.

OCEAN THERMAL ENERGY CONVERSION

The basic concept behind ocean thermal energy conversion, known as OTEC, is deceptively simple: the use of a new technology to produce energy (electricity) from the interaction between cold deep-ocean water and warm surface water in the tropical ocean.[19] The energy derives from a generator, rotated by a turbine, which in turn is powered by the expansion of heated ammonia as the working fluid. Cold ocean water pumped from a depth of several thousand meters through a pipe connected to a barge or a platform is then mixed with the warmer surface

Figure 6.6
An OTEC Closed-Cycle System

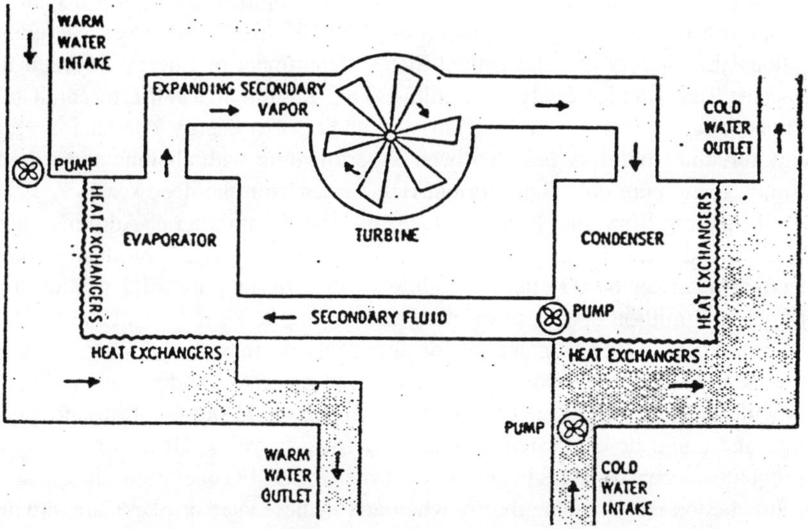

Source: Robert Cohen, "Ocean Thermal Gradients," *Oceanus* 22, no. 4 (Winter 1979–80): 13. Used by permission.

water from the tropical ocean to trigger the reaction, which creates a perpetual cycle of electrical energy (seen in Figure 6.6).

By generating energy from the sea, OTEC offers a number of unique advantages as an alternate energy source.[20] First, there is no need to burn fossil fuel, but instead, reliance is on the ocean's ability to store solar energy. Second, it is "ecologically benign" and causes no environmental problems. The United States Department of Energy has pointed out that more than sixty equatorial nations could make OTEC economically feasible because there is a temperature variation of 40° Fahrenheit between the cold deep-ocean water and warm surface water off their coasts.[21] There is, however, some concern about potential ammonia spills.

At present a small OTEC plant has been constructed by Japan's Kyushu Electric Power Company in Okinawa; it is designed to produce fifty kilowatts. Experimental testing plants have been established in the Gulf of Mexico and in Hawaii by the United States Department of Energy. Under the Ocean Thermal Energy Conversion Research and Development and Demonstration Act (Public Law No. 96–310, 94 Stat. 941, 1980), the United States Congress authorized stations in the Gulf of Mexico and United States islands for development of a comprehensive program in the design, construction and operation of OTEC.[22] Hawaii was selected for three major OTEC seawater experiments: the Mini-OTEC, OTEC–1 and the Seacoast Test Facility (STF).[23]

In 1974 the State Legislature of Hawaii established the Natural Energy Laboratory of Hawaii (NELH) for developing OTEC research facilities on a 320-acre site on shorefront property at Ke-ahole Point on the west side of the island of Hawaii. In 1978 the Seacoast Test Facility Development Group was organized to establish onshore OTEC test facilities at NELH. In the same year, Argonne National Laboratory and the United States Department of Energy awarded the Seacoast Test Facility funds for a mini-OTEC station. In 1980 a research laboratory was built at Ke-ahole Point. (In addition to energy conversion from seawater, the laboratory has also been experimenting with abalone and salmon farming using pure cold, but nutrient-rich, water from the deep sea.)

Information from the National Oceanic and Atmospheric Administration (NOAA) indicates that a 400 megawatt OTEC facility could produce enough electric power for 60,000 families while saving consumption of 2 million tons of coal or 6 million barrels of oil per year.[24]

Significance. OTEC's potential for abundant and inexpensive energy generation is an exciting experiment in a new use of the ocean and its water. This is particularly important in view of the fact that the world supply of oil and gas is finite and could be exhausted within thirty to forty years. However, if any of the equatorial coastal states begin to select sites for OTEC operation, the question of jurisdiction may become thorny when and if these sites or plants are situated on the high seas. Since there is no international organization which has the authority to provide regulations for OTEC plants on the high seas, one writer has suggested the need for developing international regulations governing OTEC.[25] Another suggestion has been to define OTEC devices on the high seas the same as any other oceanborne devices, such as vessels or fixed installations. However, the modern technology that has been developed for OTEC may need a new uniform definition fitting the uses generated by OTEC.

Under articles of the 1982 LOS Convention, one of the enumerated freedoms of the high seas is the "freedom to construct artificial islands and other installations under international law." OTEC plants constructed on the high seas cannot be regulated by a coastal state, except by the state in which it is registered. Likewise, the freedoms of the high seas permit any nation to exploit the natural resources, including activities such as OTEC, so long as they do not interfere with the exercise of high seas freedoms by other states. In a case whereby an OTEC-like device is erected on the continental shelf of a given coastal state for research or commercial purposes, if the device itself is located on the high seas, Articles 60 and 80 of the 1982 LOS Convention seem to authorize a coastal state the exclusive right to construct and operate artificial islands, installations and structures.

OFFSHORE OIL AND GAS

Since 1937, when the first complete offshore oil well was drilled off the coast of Louisiana, there has been a phenomenal growth in the quantities of these energy sources produced from the ocean. In 1973, in preparation for the UNCLOS III, the United Nations Secretariat published a study that estimated the ultimate

Table 6.4
World Production of Crude Oil, Total and Offshore*

Year	World Production	Offshore Production	Offshore as % of World
1973	55,212.70	10,067.28	18.2
1974	56,772.00	9,268.62	16.3
1975	53,850.00	8,278.36	15.4
1976	57,210.00	9,431.91	16.5
1977	56,567.00	11,436.75	20.2
1978	60,337.00	11,480.75	19.0
1979	62,768.00	12,491.93	19.9
1980	59,812.00	13,587.49	22.7
1981	55,886.20	13,664.61	24.5
1982	53,191.00	13,541.25	25.5
1983	53,259.00	13,791.04	26.7
1984	54,090.00	15,311.50	28.3
1985	53,391.00	15,128.33	28.0
1986	55,801.00	13,478.78	24.2

Note: 6,998 barrels of crude petroleum approximately equal 1.0 metric ton (ASTM–1P Petroleum Measurement Tables).

*Barrels per day in thousands.

Source: *Offshore*, June 20, 1977, 1978, 1979, 1980, 1981, 1982, 1983, July 20, 1984, and May 1986 and 1987, as reprinted in *Ocean Yearbook 7*, Elisabeth Mann Borgese and Norton Ginsburg, eds. (Chicago: University of Chicago Press, 1988), p. 566. Used by permission.

recoverable reserves for offshore oil and gas to be 114.8 billion barrels.[26] By the time the 1982 LOS Convention was signed, world offshore oil and natural gas production had increased enormously, as seen in Tables 6.4 to 6.7.

By 1984–1985 the world's total offshore oil production had reached over 15 million barrels per day, about 28 percent of the world's total oil production. The largest amount of offshore oil extracted from the ocean was in the Middle East–Persian Gulf region; for 1985 it constituted more than one-third of the world's total offshore oil production of 15.1 million barrels per day. The next largest volume was taken from the West European region, mostly from the North Sea oil drilling by the United Kingdom, which produced 73 percent of the region's total daily offshore volume of about 4 million barrels for 1985. Then came the Latin American region with 3.3 million barrels per day, more than half of which came from Mexico's offshore operations.

The world's total annual production of offshore natural gas reached almost 12.5 trillion cubic feet in 1985, about 20 percent of the total world annual natural gas production of 62.7 trillion cubic feet. As seen in Table 6.7, the United States produced more than 12.7 billion cubic feet per day of offshore natural gas, or about one-third of the world's 34 billion cubic feet per day and just slightly more than produced by the eight Western European nations in 1985–1986. In terms of individual countries' offshore natural gas production, following the United States in 1985 were the United Kingdom (5,826 million cubic feet per day), Norway (2,910 million cubic feet per day), Venezuela (1,693 million cubic

Table 6.5
World Production of Natural Gas, Total and Offshore*

Year	World Production	Offshore Production	Offshore as % of World
1973	56,992.3	7,697.0	13.5
1974	47,253.3	8,088.7	17.1
1975	47,029.9	9,932.1	20.3
1976	50,407.5	10,847.0**	21.5
1977	53,883.7	6,663.3**	12.4
1978	53,859.5	9,509.0**	17.8
1979	57,194.6	9,369.0**	16.4
1980	58,636.4	10,160.9**	17.3
1981	57,816.0	10,085.1**	17.4
1982	55,893.9	10,326.7**	18.5
1983	55,066.5	10,360.1**	18.8
1984	59,932.3	12,196.8**	20.4
1985	62,721.4	12,451.4**	19.9
1986	63,603.2	12,348.6	19.4

*Cubic feet, in billions.

**Based on extrapolation from average daily rate.

Source: *Basic Petroleum Data Book* for 1973–1975, *Oil and Gas Journal* and *Offshore* for 1976–1986; reprinted in *Ocean Yearbook 7*, Borgese and Ginsburg, eds. (Chicago: Univ. of Chicago, 1988), p. 569. Used by permission.

feet per day), the Netherlands (1,528 million cubic feet per day), and the Soviet Union (1,520 million cubic feet per day).

Significance. Mining of hydrocarbons (oil and gas) from the ocean has become increasingly important, for by the year 2000 offshore oil wells will be expected to produce 24 million barrels per day worldwide, amounting to almost one-half of the total world oil production. The continental shelf areas of the United States alone contain 3.5 billion barrels of oil and 36 trillion cubic feet of offshore natural gas. Estimated hydrocarbon reserves for the Indian Ocean range from 37 to 371 billion barrels of oil and 35 to 1,253 trillion cubic feet of natural gas. In short, offshore hydrocarbons will constitute the bulk of the world's energy needs in the future.

In the mid–1970s total world offshore oil production was worth $40 billion, four times as much as the value of living resources from the ocean. These facts alone indicate clearly why delicate negotiations developed at the UNCLOS III and subsequently the concept of coastal state jurisdiction over ocean regimes such as the continental shelf and the EEZ within 200 nautical miles from the coast was legally endorsed. These are the best potential areas for offshore petroleum production.

OVERLAPPING NATIONAL CLAIMS OVER PROPERTY RIGHTS TO NONLIVING RESOURCES

To a large extent the race for mining of hydrocarbons (oil and gas) and for hard minerals (manganese crust, manganese nodules and polymetallic sulfides)

Table 6.6
Offshore Crude Oil Production, by Region and Country*

Area and Country	1970	1975	1980	1984	1985	1986	1985-86 % Change
Total	7,532.0	8,278.4	13,587.5	15,209.5**	15,143.3**	13,478.8**	-11.0
Anglo-America:							
U.S.A.	1,557.0	909.6	1,038.1	1,216.0	1,250.0	1,257.0***	0.6
Latin America:							
Brazil	8.0	19.0	73.0	313.0	375.4	376.0	0.2
Chile				23.0	22.1	11.3	-49.1
Mexico	35.0	45.0	500.2	1,793.4	1,703.0	1,700.0	- 0.2
Peru		28.9	29.9	26.0	113.0	116.6	3.1
Trinidad & Tobago	76.0	174.0	166.5	137.5	135.7	127.8	- 5.8
Venezuela	2,460.0	1,737.1	1,095.6	1,100.0	951.1	900.0	- 5.4
Sub-total	2,579.0	2,004.0	1,865.2	3,392.9	3,300.3	3,231.6	- 2.1
Western Europe:							
Denmark		3.3	6.6	46.7	52.4	55.1	5.1
Greece				26.1	26.4	27.2	3.0
Italy	12.0	10.4	6.3	22.9	28.2	8.9	-68.3
The Netherlands				32.0	23.9	20.7	-13.5
Norway		189.6	628.8	725.1	755.9	780.6	3.3
Spain		32.9	31.2	44.8	49.1	36.1	-26.5
United Kingdom		83.0	1,650.0	2,479.2	2,548.6	2,236.6	-12.2
Sub-total	12.0	319.2	2,322.9	3,376.8	3,484.5	3,165.1	- 9.2
Socialist Eastern Europe:							
USSR	258.0	228.0	200.0	168.0	165.0	165.0***	0.0
Near East:							
Abu Dhabi	269.0	462.7	1,322.0	340.0***	281.0	265.0	- 5.7
Divided Zone		315.1	403.0	320.0	266.0	266.0	0.0
Dubai	70.0	249.3	344.9	346.9	322.2	330.6	2.6
Egypt	257.0	165.0	390.3	712.1	743.1	589.6	-20.7
Iran	322.0	481.2	150.0		610.6	505.0	-17.3
Qatar	172.0		247.6	202.1	196.0	158.0	-19.4

Table 6.6 (Continued)

Area and Country	1970	1975	1980	1984	1985	1986	1985-86 % Change
Ras al Khaimah					9.1	11.1	21.5
Saudi Arabia	1,251.0	1,385.8	2,958.0	2,100.0***	1,505.9	1,107.0	-26.5
Sharjah		38.4	10.0	5.9	5.9	8.6	46.1
Tunisia		43.0	43.6	35.8	29.7	6.1	-79.4
Sub-total	2,341.0	3,140.5	5,769.4	4,062.8	3,969.5	3,247.0	-18.2
Sub-Saharan Africa:							
Angola/Cabinda	96.0	143.2	99.0	175.0	170.0	185.6	9.2
Cameroon				150.0	133.0	125.0	- 6.0
Congo		37.3	27.0	117.5	114.4	115.0	0.5
Gabon	29.0	179.9	177.9	130.0***	112.8	105.0	- 6.9
Ghana			2.0	0.8	2.0	0.3	-85.0
Ivory Coast			5.8	22.0	22.0	19.5	-11.5
Nigeria	275.0	431.3	579.1	385.7	415.9	289.5	-30.4
Zaire			21.6	26.8	17.6	16.6	- 5.7
Sub-total	400.0	791.7	910.4	1,007.8	987.7	856.5	-13.3
South Asia:							
India			142.1	432.0	614.0	621.0	1.1
East Asia:							
China			2.0	2.0	2.5	1.0	-60.0
Japan	3.0	0.9	1.6	4.0	0.8	1.4	72.5
Sub-total	3.0	0.9	3.6	6.0	3.3	2.4	-27.3
Southeast Asia:							
Brunei	146.0****	141.2	192.2	116.0	98.8	98.7	- 0.1
Indonesia		246.4	533.0	543.3	483.0	391.9	-18.9
Malaysia		84.5	280.3	439.4	279.5	20.9	-92.5
Philippines			4.0	10.6	8.5	7.8	- 7.8
Thailand				8.0	13.4	15.9	19.0
Sub-total	146.0	472.1	1,009.5	1,117.3	883.2	535.2	-39.4
Australasia:							
Australia	216.0	412.5	323.2	420.0	474.1	384.1	-19.0
New Zealand			3.2	10.1	11.9	14.0	17.6
Sub-total	216.0	412.5	326.4	430.1	486.0	398.1	-18.1

* Barrels per day, in thousands.

** Subtotals do not equal total because of rounding.

*** Estimate.

**** Brunei/Malaysia combined production.

Source: Offshore and *Oil and Gas Journal*; reprinted in *Ocean Yearbook 7*, Borgese and Ginsburg, eds. (Chicago: Univ. of Chicago, 1988), pp. 567–568. Used by permission.

Table 6.7
Offshore Natural Gas Production, by Region and Country*

Area and Country	1970	1975	1980	1984	1985	1986	1985-86 % Change
Total	10,315.1	20,967.0	27,838.0	33,330.6**	34,113.3	33,831.9	- 0.8
Anglo-America:							
U.S.A.	8,591.8	11,664.3	14,703.7	12,440.0	12,781.0	11,917.0	- 6.8
Latin America							
Brazil		25.4	100.0	221.0	235.0	215.0	- 8.5
Colombia			64.7	176.0	219.0	127.0	-42.0
Mexico			25.0***	1,002.5	937.0	950.0	1.4
Peru	64.7	77.0					
Trinidad & Tobago	11.0	123.0	420.0	350.0	346.0	0.6	-99.8
Venezuela				1,693.0	1,693.0	1,510.0	-10.8
Sub-total	75.7	225.0	609.7	3,442.5	3,430.0	2,802.6	-18.3
Western Europe:							
Denmark				90.0	200.0	462.0	131.0
Greece				3.0	7.0	5.0	-28.6
Ireland			125.0	223.1	230.3	230.0	- 0.1
Italy			22.0	408.1	414.7	415.1	0.1
The Netherlands		186.0	1,170.0	1,528.1	1,537.7	1,480.0	- 3.8
Norway		16.5	2,426.0	2,976.0	2,910.0	3,011.0	3.5
Spain				26.6	26.0	26.0	0.0
United Kingdom	1,086.3	3,600.0	3,610.0	5,560.0	5,826.0	5,600.0	- 3.9
Sub-total	1,086.3	3,802.5	7,353.0	10,814.9	11,151.7	11,229.1	0.7
Socialist Eastern Europe:							
U.S.S.R.		774.0	1,225.0	1,520.0	1,475.0	1,300.0	-11.9
Near East:							
Abu Dhabi			1,434.0	414.0	372.0	315.0	-15.3
Egypt			57.9	116.0	112.0	110.0	- 1.8
Oman				52.0	48.0	35.1	-26.9
Saudi Arabia	494.8	3,825.4	0.0****				
Qatar				92.2	97.3	0.0	-100.0
Sub-Total	494.8	3,825.4	1,491.9	674.2	629.3	460.1	-26.9

Table 6.7 (Continued)

Area and Country	1970	1975	1980	1984	1985	1986	1985-86 % Change
Sub-Saharan Africa:							
Angola				268.0	275.0	271.0	- 1.5
Congo				3.0	3.0	3.0	0.0
Gabon				0.1	0.3		
Ghana			6.0				
Nigeria		314.0	500.0	493.0	487.0	475.0	- 2.5
Sub-total		314.0	506.0	764.1	765.3	749.0	- 2.1
East Asia:							
Japan			47.7	27.0	26.0	55.0	111.5
South Asia:							
India			2.7	246.0	243.0	240.6	- 1.0
Southeast Asia:							
Brunei			984.8	900.0	833.0	815.0	- 2.2
Indonesia		158.8	440.0	872.0	757.0	663.7	-12.3
Malaysia				400.0	486.0	1,440.3	196.4
Thailand				256.0	346.0	341.9	- 1.2
Sub-total		158.8	1,424.8	2,428.0	2,422.0	3,260.9	34.6
Australasia:							
Australia	60.5	203.0	388.0	638.0	677.0	1,448.6	114.0
New Zealand			84.0	336.0	513.0	369.0	-28.1
Sub-total	60.5	203.0	472.0	974.0	1,190.0	1,817.6	52.7

* Cubic feet per day, in millions.

** Subtotals do not equal total because of rounding.

*** Estimate.

**** All gas flared.

Source: *Offshore* and *Oil and Gas Journal*; reprinted in *Ocean Yearbook 7*, Borgese and Ginsburg, eds. (Chicago: Univ. of Chicago, 1988), pp. 570–571. Used by permission.

Table 6.8
Dimension of Ocean Space Encompassed by Ocean Regimes Established in the 1982 LOS Convention

Ocean Regime	By 1982 LOS Convention	Ocean Space Encompassed (In Square Miles)
Territorial Sea (12 nautical miles)	Article 3	2,000,000
Continguous Zone (12 nautical miles)	Article 33	2,000,000
Exclusive Economic Zone (200 nautical miles)	Article 57	32,000,000, or 35.4% of the ocean
Continental Shelf	Article 76	No numerical seaward limit, but constitutes one-third of ocean space

Source: John Warren Kindt, *Marine Pollution and the Law of the Sea* (Buffalo, N.Y.: William S. Hein, 1986), pp. 1424–1425. Used by permission.

from the ocean will be centered on the continental shelf and 200 nautical miles beyond. John Warren Kindt gives the dimensions of ocean space encompassed by the various ocean regimes established under the 1982 LOS Convention (see Table 6.8).[27]

Certainly the exploitation and exploration of the ocean's nonliving resources—hydrocarbons and hard minerals—will be extended farther seaward to 200 nautical miles and beyond. What complicates the situation is that these nonliving resources are to be found on the continental shelf and in the EEZ in some overlapping areas claimed by the coastal states. Thus, as the race for these nonliving resources extends and expands, disputes are bound to arise. There are many overlapping claims already existing in many regions of the world. Listed here, with brief comments, is a selected enumeration of overlapping claims for the exploration and exploitation of nonliving resources.[28]

Thailand–Malaysia

Northwest of the Malay Basin is a triangular overlap where natural gas has been discovered.[29] Complicating the overlap is the Vietnamese claim of a continental shelf that encompasses the northwestern portion of the area claimed by both Malaysia and Thailand. While the boundary is still being negotiated by Malaysia and Thailand, a joint authority was established in 1979 (February 21) by both governments to exploit jointly the seabed resources in the overlapped area.

South Korea–Japan–Taiwan

All three nations have made overlapping claims for the continental shelf between Taiwan and Japan over the oil resources found there.[30] The overlapping claim was further complicated by the dispute of the Diaoyutai (Senkaku) Islands between Japan and Taiwan. In 1970 a three-power (Japan, South Korea and Taiwan) agreement was reached to exploit oil jointly in the overlapping area pending further boundary settlement by negotiation. The People's Republic of China protested, so the agreement was invalidated. In 1978, Japan and South Korea entered into a joint agreement to develop oil production in the overlapping area.

Kuwait–Saudi Arabia

This dispute is centered on the ownership of three islands (Kubbar, Qaruh and Umm Al Maradim) off the northeastern portion of the Saudi Arabian peninsula.[31] In 1965 the two nations jointly agreed to divide the zone equally for petroleum resource development.

Iceland–Norway

This dispute between Norway and Iceland was over the continental shelf rights to the Jan Mayen Island.[32] On May 28, 1980, an agreement was reached under which Iceland agreed to seek conciliation regarding the dividing line for the continental shelf. In 1982 both Iceland and Norway accepted the recommendation by a conciliation commission for joint development of oil and gas production in the overlapping claim area.

Fiji–Tonga

An overlapping claim for 4,860 nautical square miles of water and seabed and Tonga's claim to Minerva Reefs would increase its claims by an additional 56,500 nautical square miles to Fiji's 18,500 nautical square miles.[33]

New Caledonia–Vanuatu

An overlapping claim for ownership of Hunter and Matthew islands—about 53,800 nautical square miles of seabed—is in dispute between the two island groups.[34]

There are many other disputes or claims over the property rights to the nonliving resources on opposite or adjacent continental shelves and in EEZs: Greece–Turkey over the East Aegean Sea; Norway–Soviet Union over Spitsbergen in the Barents Sea; United Kingdom–Denmark over the Rockall Island; Spain–Morocco over the Mediterranean, and Egypt–Israel over the Gulf of Suez.

Significance. It has been pointed out in Chapter 3 that Article 83(1) of the 1982 LOS Convention provides that the delimitation of the continental shelf between states with opposite or adjacent coasts shall be made through bilateral agreements on the basis of "an equitable solution." The article also encourages disputing coastal states to make "provisional arrangements of a practical nature" pending final solution. There are some fifty continental shelf boundary delimitation treaties now in existence, and the key principle for a number of these agreements has been recognition of the need for economic exploitation of the resources on the continental shelf on a shared basis in the form of joint arrangements for development. Examples are the Thailand–Malaysia, South Korea–Japan, Kuwait–Saudi Arabia and Iceland–Norway agreements. In short, joint arrangements for developing the resources in overlapping and disputed areas of the continental shelf and the EEZ seem to be a practical, sensible method of settling the offshore property rights disputes, particularly for mining facilities in developing offshore oil and gas production in order to meet the mounting demands for these resources in the future.[35]

STRATEGIC MINERALS

In the early 1980s an alarm was sounded around the world's industrialized nations, particularly in the United States, that land-based supplies for some minerals such as manganese, cobalt, titanium, platinum and chromium (all considered strategic for industrial and military uses) were either soon to be exhausted or under control of politically volatile developing nations of the Third World. The crux of the argument then was that most of the industrialized nations of the West, plus Japan, were heavily dependent upon imports of these strategic minerals. Thus, if the industrialized nations were to avoid being blackmailed and subjecting themselves to price extortion by land-based exporters of these strategic minerals, it was necessary, as a national policy, to embark on two alternative actions: either to stockpile these critical minerals or to find suitable substitutes through new inventions or discovery (from the seabed deposits).[36] Four of the strategic metals—chromium, cobalt, manganese and platinum—were considered highly critical to defense and arms race programs because of their use as high-strength alloys for aircraft engines and missile manufacture. For example, the building and deployment of 200 land-based intercontinental ballistic missiles (ICBMs) would need 10,000 tons of aluminum, 2,500 tons of chromium, 150 tons of titanium and 24 tons of beryllium, in addition to an enormous amount of steel and cement.[37] Major land-based suppliers for these four strategic minerals are Brazil, Gabon, Zaire, Zambia, South Africa and the Soviet Union.[38] Industrialized countries of the West, plus Japan, consume more than two-thirds of the land-based annual production of these strategic minerals.

Prospects for mining the deep-seabed minerals in order to bridge the claimed strategic minerals gap loomed larger when the United Nations General Assembly in 1967 took up the debate regarding a declaration and treaty concerning reserving for peaceful purposes in the interests of mankind the deep seabed resources beyond the limits of national jurisdiction—the original proposal was made by Malta. The Maltese Initiative (see Chapter 7) and the General Assembly Seabed Committee debate paved the way for convening the 1974 UNCLOS III at Caracas and Geneva. By then world attention and publicity focused on developing the appropriate technology for extracting manganese nodules from the ocean floor by a number of multinational deep seabed mining consortia engaged in prospecting polymetallic nodules. In 1982 UNCLOS III produced the LOS Convention, which, in Part XI, established the International Seabed Area (on the seabed and ocean floor beyond the limits of national jurisdiction) as the exclusive area for the exploitation and exploration of deep seabed resources for the benefit of mankind.

Significance. The euphoria over mining strategic minerals for industrial and defense use from the deep seabed abated somewhat in the mid–1980s. There were many reasons for the declining enthusiasm for deep-seabed mining of strategic and hard minerals. First, mining has always been a risky business venture, and deep-seabed mining is more hazardous than mining on land, for it requires heavy capital investment, as discussed in Chapter 7. When the return on the investment has been estimated by experts to be rather small or unprofitable, not only is enthusiasm dampened for deep-seabed mining, but so is the amount of venture capital available for ocean mining research and development decreased. Second, in the 1980s, worldwide prices for land-based metal have been low, and the market price for most metals has fallen behind the production cost. For instance, it takes more than $3.50 to produce a ton of nickel whose average price is not more than $2.30 per ton.[39] Third, the alarm issued in the 1970s and early 1980s over the possible depletion of land-based mineral supplies has become difficult to sustain, primarily because of the invention of substitutes to take the place of the traditional hard minerals such as copper or lead. Metals are being replaced increasingly by plastics and aluminum or tin.[40] Fourth, the importance of deep-seabed manganese nodules had possibly been exaggerated in the late 1970s. In fact, deep-seabed mineral resources available beyond the limits of national jurisdiction represent only 5 to 10 percent of the mineral wealth of the oceans.[41] Finally, the uncertainty that surrounds the legal status of the deep-seabed mining regime, as provided by Part XI of the 1982 LOS Convention and the Mini-Treaty regime (see Chapter 7), would have some important bearing on the increasing risk of financing deep seabed mining.

NOTES

1. For discussions on deep seabed mining see the following: Roderick D. Ogley, *Internationalizing the Seabed* (Brookfield, Vt.: Gower, 1985); Ross D. Eckert, *The Enclosure of Ocean Resources: Economics and Law of the Sea* (Stanford, Calif.: Hoover Institute Press, 1979), pp. 20–83 and pp. 214–258; David L. Larson, "Deep Seabed Mining: A Definition of the Problem," *Ocean Development and International Law* 17,

no. 4 (1986): 271–308; Lee Kimball, "Turning Points in the Future of Deep Seabed Mining," *Ocean Development and International Law* 17, no. 4 (1986): 367–398; William B. Jones, "Risk Assessment: Corporate Ventures in Deep Seabed Mining outside the Framework of the UN Convention on the Law of the Sea," *Ocean Development and International Law* 16, no. 4 (1986): 341–351; William C. Brewer, Jr., "The Prospect for Deep Seabed Mining in a Divided World," *Ocean Development and International Law* 14, no. 4 (1985): 363–381; Ambassador William B. Jones, "The International Seabed Authority without U.S. Participation," *Ocean Development and International Law* 12, nos. 3–4 (1983): 151–171; and Kurt Michael Shusterich, *Resource Management and the Oceans: The Political Economy of Deep Seabed Mining* (Boulder, Colo.: Westview Press, 1982), pp. 133–159. For additional references, see Notes to Chapter 7.

2. This entry is based on an article by Hollis D. Hedberg, "Deep-Water Petroleum Prospects of the Oceans and Seas," *Oceanus* 26, no. 3 (Fall 1983): 9–16. Also see *Oil and Gas Technologies for the Arctic and Deepwater*, Office of Technology Assessment, U.S. Congress (Washington, D.C.: U.S. Government Printing Office, 1985).

3. Hedberg, "Deep-Water Petroleum Prospects of the Oceans and Seas," pp. 13–14.

4. Ibid., p. 13.

5. "Seabed Materials," *Science* 230 (20 February 1987): 853–860.

6. See John L. Mero, *The Mineral Resources of the Sea* (Amsterdam: Elsevier, 1965), p. 127.

7. Ibid., p. 135.

8. G. Ross Heath, "Manganese Nodules: Unanswered Questions," *Oceanus* 25, no. 3 (Fall 1982): 37–41.

9. See Charles Finchman and William Van Rensburg, *Bread upon the Water: The Developing Law of the Sea* (Forest Grove, Ore.: Turtledove 1980), p. 108. Figures are based on UN Economic and Social Council Report, UN Doc. E/4680, 2 June 1969.

10. See Alexander Malahoff, "Polymetallic Sulfides and Cobalt Crusts: New Mineral Resources of the Ocean Floor?" in Robert B. Krueger and Stefan A. Riesenfeld, eds., *The Developing Order of the Oceans* (Honolulu: Law of the Sea Institute, University of Hawaii, 1985), pp. 279–304.

11. Ibid., pp. 275–277.

12. Ibid., pp. 282–283.

13. Ibid., p. 295.

14. Michael J. Cruickshank and Harold D. Hess, "Marine Sand and Gravel Mining," *Oceanus* 19, no. 1 (Fall 1985): 32–44. Also see R. H. Charlier, "Other Ocean Resources," in Elisabeth Mann Borgese and Norton Ginsburg, eds., *Ocean Yearbook 1* (Chicago and London, University of Chicago Press, 1978), pp. 197–199.

15. Cruickshank and Hess, "Marine Sand and Gravel Mining," p. 32.

16. Shusterich, *Resource Management and the Oceans*, p. 212.

17. See William P. Pendley, "The U.S. Will Need Seabed Minerals," *Oceanus* 25, no. 3 (Fall 1982): 15.

18. Third United Nations Conference on the Law of the Sea, *Official Records*, vol. 3, p. 156.

19. For a selected list of works on OTEC, see the following: Emery, "Toward a Viable Legal Regime for Ocean Thermal Energy Conversion: Some Principles and Priorities," *ASILS International Law Journal* 4, no. 25 (1980); FY 1979 Authorization Hear-

ings: Hearings before the Subcommittee on Advanced Energy Technologies and Energy Conservation, Research Development and Demonstration of the House Committee on Science and Technology, 95th Congress, 2nd Session (1978); Hurwood, "Ocean Thermal Energy: Potentials and Pitfalls," *Ocean Development and International Law* 10, no. 13 (1981); Joseph, "Legal Issues Confronting the Exploitation of Renewable Sources of Energy from the Oceans," *California Western International Law Journal* 11, no. 387 (1981); Keith, "Laws Affecting the Development of Ocean Resources in Hawaii," *University of Hawaii Law Review* 4, no. 222 (1981); Keith, "State and Federal Regulation of OTEC Plants in Hawaii," *Solar Law Report* 2, no. 491 (1980); Keith, "Laws Affecting the Development of Ocean Thermal Energy Conversion in the United States," *University of Pittsburgh Law Review* 43, no. 1 (1981); Krueger and Yarema, "New Institutions for New Energy Technology: The Case of Ocean Thermal Energy Conversion," *Southern California Law Review* 54, no. 767 (1981); Nanda, "The Legal Framework for the Development of Ocean Thermal Energy Conversion (OTEC)," *San Diego Law Review* 19, no. 385 (1982); Nanda, "Ocean Thermal Energy Conversion (OTEC) Development under U.S. and International Law and Institutions," *Denver Journal of International Law and Policy* 8, no. 239 (1979); National Oceanic and Atmospheric Administration, U.S. Department of Commerce, *Ocean Thermal Energy Conversion: Final Environmental Impact Statement (1981)*; "The Ocean Thermal Energy Conversion Act of 1980," *Georgia Journal of International and Comp. Law* 11, no. 192 (1981); "Ocean Thermal Energy Conversion: Hearings on H.R. 6154 before the Subcommittee on Oceanography and the Subcommittee on Merchant Marine of the House Committee on Merchant Marine and Fisheries, 96th Congress, 1st and 2nd Sessions (1979–1980); Comment, "Ocean Thermal Energy Conversion on the High Seas: Toward an International Regulatory Regime," *San Diego Law Review* 18, no. 473 (1981); "OTEC Projects Promise Electricity by 1990s," *Chemical and Engineering News*, 16 July 1979; Reisman, Key International Legal Issues with Regard to Ocean Thermal Energy Conversion Systems," *California Western International Law Journal* 11, no. 425 (1981); Walker and Bloom, "Ocean Thermal Energy Conversion: The Codification of a Potential Technology," *Vanderbilt Journal of Transnational Law* 14, no. 509 (1981); Whitmore, "OTEC: Electricity from the Ocean," *Technology Review*, October 1978.

20. See Gary Alan Hecker, "Ocean Thermal Energy Conversion on the High Seas: Toward an International Regulatory Regime," *San Diego Law Review* 18, no. 3 (April 1981): 477–478; and John Warren Kindt, *Marine Pollution and the Law of the Sea*, 4 vols. (Buffalo, N.Y.: William S. Hein, 1985), pp. 1756–1757.

21. See Brian Gorman, "OTEC: The Sleeping Giant," *NOAA Magazine* (Fall 1981): p. 5.

22. See Myron H. Nordquist and Kent U. Keith, "Ocean Energy and Industrialization: Development Strategies for Pacific Island," a paper presented at the 15th Annual Conference, Law of the Sea Institute.

23. For a list of news articles concerning OTEC in Hawaii, see: R. Leuma Schwenke, "OTEC Plant Takes a Step toward Isles," *The Honolulu Advertiser*, 26 January 1980, p. A–3; "OTEC Mooring System Launched off Big Island," *The Honolulu Star-Bulletin*, 27 February 1980, p. B–12; Sandra S. Oshiro, "$10.5 Million Okd by Panel to Lure U.S. OTEC Project," *The Honolulu Advertiser*, 1 March 1980, p. A–15; "Inouye Bill Would Make OTEC Eligible for Aid," *The Honolulu Advertiser*, 28 March 1980, p. A–7; Sanford Zalburg, "Getting Electricity from the Ocean Feasible but Cost Now Prohibitive," *The Honolulu Advertiser*, 30 March 1980, p. F–1; Barbara Hastings, "Advocates

Stress Value of OTEC in Testimony before Senate Panel,'' *The Honolulu Advertiser*, 11 April 1980, p. A–5; Harry Whitten, ''OTEC for Islands: Electricity, Food and Jobs Are Possible,'' *The Honolulu Star-Bulletin*, 11 April 1980, p. A–2; Stu Glauberman, ''OTEC Pipe on Ocean Floor Being Sought,'' *The Honolulu Star-Bulletin*, 1 May 1980, p. A–2; ''Scientists Studying Methods to Salvage Mini-OTEC Pipe,'' *The Honolulu Star-Bulletin*, 8 May 1980, p. B–1; ''OTEC's Prospects to Serve Oahu,'' *The Honolulu Star-Bulletin*, 21 May 1980, p. A–18; ''Ariyoshi Stumps for OTEC,'' *The Honolulu Advertiser*, 3 June 1980, p. D–16; David Shapiro, ''Ariyoshi Sees OTEC in Our Future,'' *The Honolulu Star-Bulletin*, 3 June 1980, p. A–5; Harry Whitten, ''Public Can Inspect OTEC Test Vessel,'' *The Honolulu Star-Bulletin*, 3 July 1980; Barbara Vobejda, ''Sea Energy Vessel Is Dedicated Here,'' *The Sunday Advertiser and Star-Bulletin*, 6 July 1980, p. A–3; ''OTEC Bill Awaits Carter's Okay,'' *The Honolulu Advertiser*, 22 July 1980; David Shapiro, ''House Oks $75 Million in New OTEC Funding,'' *The Honolulu Star-Bulletin*, 21 July 1980; ''Ocean Currents Plague OTEC Platform Mooring,'' *The Honolulu Star-Bulletin*, 23 July 1980; ''Energy Converter Ship Is Due Here,'' *The Honolulu Star-Bulletin*, 8 October 1980; ''OTEC's Giant Plumbing Job Starts Today,'' *The Honolulu Star-Bulletin*, 1 November 1980; Barbara Hastings, ''Lack of Funds Mothballs Award-winning Mini-OTEC,'' *The Honolulu Advertiser*, 7 November 1980; ''OTEC System Being Tested,'' *The Honolulu Star-Bulletin*, 15 November 1980.

24. Gorman, ''OTEC: The Sleeping Giant,'' p. 9.

25. Comment, ''Ocean Thermal Energy Conversion on the High Seas: Toward an International Regulatory Regime,'' pp. 492–501.

26. UN Doc. A/AC.138/87, 4 June 1973.

27. Kindt, *Marine Pollution and the Law of the Sea*, pp. 1424–1425.

28. For recent studies of ocean boundary developments, see Douglas M. Johnston and Phillip M. Saunders, eds., *Ocean Boundary Making: Regional Issues and Developments* (London: Croom Helm, 1988); and John P. Craven, Jan Schneider and Carol Stimson, eds. *The International Implications of Extended Marine Jurisdiction in the Pacific* (Honolulu: The Law of the Sea institute, University of Hawaii, 1989).

29. Choon-ho Park, ''Boundary Delimitation in the South China Sea,'' Douglas M. Johnston, Edgar Gold, Phiphat Tangsubkul, eds., *International Symposium on the New Law of the Sea in Southeast Asia* (Halifax, N.S.: Dalhousie Ocean Studies Program, 1983), pp. 131–145. Also see Sang-Myon Rhee and James MacAulay, ''Ocean Boundary Issues in East Asia: The Need for Practical Solutions,'' in Johnston and Saunders, eds., *Ocean Boundary Making*, pp. 75, 80 and 82–83.

30. See Mark J. Valencia, ''Taming Troubled Waters: Joint Development of Oil and Mineral Resources in Overlapping Claim Areas,'' *San Diego Law Review* 23, no. 3 (May–June 1986): 668–669. Also see Rhee and MacAulay, ''Ocean Boundary Issues in East Asia,'' pp. 84–87.

31. Valencia, ''Taming Troubled Waters,'' p. 669; and Ian Townsend Gault, ''Offshore Boundary Delimitation in the Arabian/Persian Gulf,'' in Johnston and Saunders, eds., *Ocean Boundary Making*, pp. 204–223.

32. Valencia, ''Taming Troubled Waters,'' p. 669; and Susan J. Rolston and Ted L. McDroman, ''Maritime Boundary Making in the Arctic Region,'' in Johnston and Saunders, eds., *Ocean Boundary Making*, pp. 32–37.

33. Valencia, ''Taming Troubled Waters,'' p. 664.

34. Ibid., p. 665; and also see J.R.V. Prescott, ''Maritime Boundaries and Issues in

the Southwest Pacific Ocean,'' in Johnston and Saunders, eds., *Ocean Boundary Making*, pp. 268 and 278.

35. See Rhee and MacAulay, ''Ocean Boundary Issues in East Asia,'' pp. 100–101.

36. See Herbert E. Meyer, ''How We're Fixed for Strategic Minerals,'' *Fortune Magazine*, 8 February 1981, pp. 68–70; Tony Velocci, ''Minerals: The Resource Gap,'' *Nation's Business* 68, no. 10 (October 1980): 33–38; and ''Raw Materials,'' *The UNESCO Courier*, March 1982, pp. 16–17.

37. ''Raw Materials,'' p. 16.

38. See Meyer, ''How We're Fixed for Strategic Minerals,'' pp. 69–70. Also see ''Foreign Metals: An Achilles' Heel for the U.S.,'' *U.S. News and World Report*, 18 March 1985, p. 74.

39. Alexander J. Krem, ''Financing Ocean Mineral Developments: Feasible under What Terms?'' in Robert B. Krueger and Stefan A. Riesenfeld, eds., *The Developing Order of the Oceans* (Honolulu: The Law of the Sea Institute, University of Hawaii, 1987), p. 321.

40. Ibid., pp. 320–321.

41. Conrad Welling, ''A View from the Industry,'' in Jon M. Van Dyke, ed., *Consensus and Confrontation: The United States and the Law of the Sea Convention* (Honolulu: The Law of the Sea Institute, University of Hawaii, 1985), p. 235.

CHAPTER 7

Deep-Seabed Mining

Technologically speaking, since the 1960s the very prospect of being able to explore deep-seabed mineral resources has created high expectations of new wealth for the world. At the same time, a myriad of ideological, economic and legal issues have been raised. The establishment of a legal regime for the exploitation and exploration of deep-seabed resources under the 1982 LOS Convention, the result of more than nine years of arduous negotiation in Geneva and New York, has been and still is an intense controversy. It is controversial not only because the United States has refused to sign the multilateral convention on the ground that Part XI, the provisions that deal with the exploration of seabed resources and the machinery for governing the International Seabed Area (hereafter called the Area), is flawed and incomplete, but also because the new international ocean regime leaves open many unresolved problems. A consequence of the controversy is the formation of an alternative seabed mining regime by the United States and seven European nations, plus Japan, under the 1984 Provisional Understanding Regarding Deep Seabed Matters. Thus, there are now two competing ocean regimes for seabed mining in the Area, the existence of which would ultimately create confusion and instability for seabed mining as a whole.

This chapter provides background reference and analysis on three interrelated aspects of seabed mining. One, what sort of regime has the 1982 LOS Convention created? The chapter reviews the purposes for creating the International Seabed Area (the seabed and ocean floor and subsoil thereof beyond the limits of national jurisdiction): peaceful uses and the exploration and exploitation of the resources including solid, liquid or gaseous minerals on the seabed. The definition of the Area is rather imprecise until the full implementation of the seabed machinery (the International Seabed Authority) for regulating the Area under Article 76 of the Convention can be explained and the origins of its controversial aspects can be traced. Two, detailed reference will be made concerning the legal status of the Enterprise, the operating arm of the Authority, under the parallel system, which is a compromise negotiated by the United States to offer the opposing ideological camps (the developed and the developing Third World) an opportunity to split the difference. Specific reference to the 1982 LOS Convention will also be made with regard to the complex system of financial arrangements for the Authority and its Enterprise. Three, implications and capacity for dispute settlement, through a law of the sea tribunal, between the miners and mining contractors, states, and multinational consortia, a unique feature for the Authority, are carefully documented and discussed.

A focal point in the seabed mining controversy has been the problem of acceptance by the conflicting camps (developed and developing nations) over the fundamental principle governing seabed mining activities. The roots of the lack of agreement lie in the legal meaning and validity of Article 136, which was based on the various United Nations General Assembly resolutions adopted from 1967 to 1970: the concept of common heritage of mankind for the seabed beyond the limits of national jurisdiction. For one thing, the concept for the new "law of the seabed" is controversial because, as the developed states argue, it challenges the traditional principle of freedom of the seas under which a state or a multilateral consortium is free to mine the seabed resources so long as such mining activities do not violate the interests of other coastal states. There is an ongoing debate over the distinction between the assertion of exclusive right to mine the seabed versus the right to seabed claim.

Questions have also been raised as to whether General Assembly resolutions represent a "law-creation process" and are thus morally and legally binding. Related to the legal issue on the fundamental principles for seabed mining, this chapter discusses the role of the Group of 77 in influencing and forcing compromises during seabed negotiation, the significance of the Maltese initiative, and the moratorium resolution on seabed mining pending the establishment of an international seabed regime.

Several other topics are discussed in order to pinpoint some of the sources of difficulties and conflict in the deep seabed mining provisions of the 1982 LOS Convention: the nature of the mineral resources; the multinational consortia engaged in seabed mining; the accommodations made to alleviate the fears of the industrialized nations over matters such as access, application and registration for mining sites for pioneer investors; the review conference; transfer of technology; and the work of the Preparatory Commission for the seabed authority. Finally, reference will be made to the implications of the reciprocal state arrangement under the Provisional Understanding and of the enactment of unilateral national legislation, such as the United States' 1980 Deep Seabed Hard Mineral Resource Act, on the 1982 LOS Convention's seabed mining provisions in the area beyond the limits of national jurisdiction. The question arises as to the legal status of mining licenses granted under unilateral national legislation, but not recognized internationally.

The International Seabed Area beyond the limits of national jurisdiction is the global commons that requires international management for the eventual orderly and efficient exploitation of deep-seabed mineral resources. The ideological aspect of the controversy and the industrialized nations' fear for the lack of decision-making power can be mitigated and removed as the Preparatory Commission begins its work.

All in all, there are seventeen sections in this chapter on deep seabed mining: the Area, the Arusha Understanding (for resolving overlapping claims before registration as "pioneer investor"), the multinational consortia, the Enterprise, financial arrangements, fundamental principles on seabed exploitation, the Authority, the Maltese initiative, moratorium resolution, the parallel system, pioneer investors, Preparatory Commission, reciprocal state arrangement (the mini-treaty), the review conference, dispute settlement, transfer of technology and unilateral national legislation for seabed mining.

THE AREA

Article 1 of the 1982 LOS Convention defines the Area as the "seabed and ocean floor and subsoil thereof, beyond the limits of national jurisdiction." Deep ocean floor, the seabed, covers about 56 percent of the earth's surface. Large portions of deep seabed are found underlying the Atlantic, Pacific, Indian and Arctic oceans. Most, if not all, of the seabed in the other seas, from the Baltic to the Sulu, is subject to national claims. A fundamental question to be raised here is: What are the limits of national jurisdiction beyond which there is established, by the 1982 LOS Convention, a new ocean regime known as the Area?

By examining the work of the 1958 Continental Shelf Convention and the preparatory studies made by the International Law Commission, which drafted the original version of the 1958 convention, Theodore G. Kronmiller concluded, "there is an area of the seabed beyond the limits of national jurisdiction."[1] In the seabed debates in the United Nations General Assembly in the 1960s and 1970s practically all member states expressed the view that under the 1958 Continental Shelf Convention there existed a "spatial limit" to what a coastal state could claim over the seabed and the subsoil thereof.[2] J.R.V. Prescott also points out that the "minimum boundary of the deep seabed will lie 200 nautical miles," measured from a coastal state's baseline, if the continental margin is narrower than 200 nautical miles.[3] In other words, the maximum seaward limit of 200 nautical miles has been the standard claim made by coastal states for exclusive resource zones. Beyond this limit lies the seabed and the subsoil thereof not subject to national jurisdiction.[4] (Also see other sections in this chapter on Fundamental Principles, Financial Arrangement, International Seabed Authority, The Maltese Initiative, and Manganese Nodules.)

Significance. The importance of the seabed area lies in the mineral deposits, particularly the polymetallic manganese nodules, present in large quantities on the ocean floor (see Figure 7.1). The Area, as now defined by the 1982 LOS

Figure 7.1
Potential Ocean Mining Area

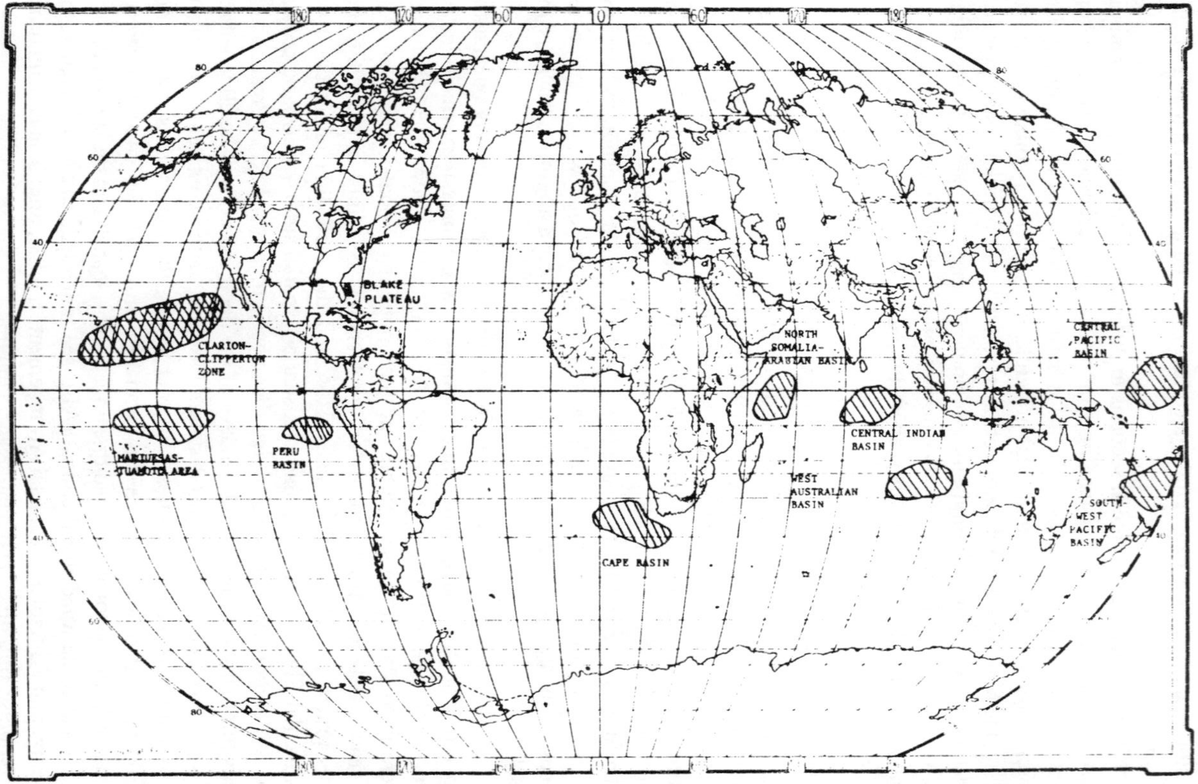

Source: Kurt Michael Shusterich, *Resource Management and the Ocean: The Political Economy of Deep Seabed Mining* (Boulder, Colo.: Westview Press, 1982), p. 15. Used by permission.

Figure 7.2
The Clarion-Clipperton Region

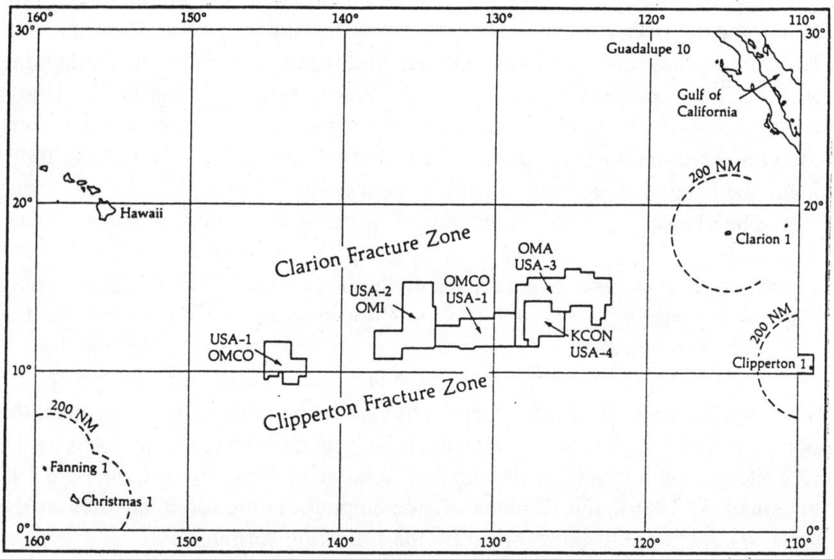

Source: Marne A. Dubs, "Minerals of the Deep Sea Myth and Reality," in *The New Order of the Oceans: The Advent of a Managed Environment*, Giulio Pontecorvo, ed. (New York: Columbia University Press, 1986), p. 119. Copyright © 1986, Columbia University Press, New York. Used by permission.

Convention, establishes a new international seabed regime for two essential purposes: peaceful uses of the seabed (Article 141) and exploration and exploitation of the "resources"—all solid, liquid and gaseous minerals—on the seabed (Articles 150–155) for the "benefit of mankind." While the definition for the International Seabed Area is imprecise, it does provide a wide ocean space, 200 nautical miles seaward from a coastal state's baseline, as an area that is beyond national jurisdiction. What this means is that the mineral resources on which the new international ocean regime must rely exclusively are the polymetallic manganese nodules in the Pacific (see Figure 7.2) and Indian Oceans. The revenue derived must be governed by the principle of the common heritage of mankind or for the benefit of the developing states. The Area may eventually become more precisely defined as coastal states go through the process of making specific declarations concerning the limits for the outer edge of their continental margins, as provided in Article 76. As projected by Arvid Pardo, the process may take as long as ten years from the date that the 1982 LOS Convention takes effect. Until then, the definition of the precise Area beyond the limits of national jurisdiction may have to be postponed. This postponement may in turn hinder considerably the planning for the seabed mining activities of the Authority.

ARUSHA UNDERSTANDING

In its effort to register mining investors in the Area, the Preparatory Commission for the International Seabed Authority, established under Resolution II, Final Act of the 1982 LOS Convention, discovered a number of overlapping claims. When "pioneer investors" from France, Japan and the Soviet Union applied to register for specific mining sites in the Pacific, four deep-seabed mining consortia representing investors from Belgium, Canada, West Germany, Italy, Japan, the United Kingdom and the United States also applied for the same areas. The chairman for the Preparatory Commission, Joseph Warioba of Tanzania, invited the applicants to a meeting in Arusha, Tanzania, in February 1986 to work out a set of procedures for resolving the controversy on the overlapping claims for the mining sites in the Clarion-Clipperton Zone in the central Pacific. The result of the meeting at Arusha was a set of procedural "understandings," known as the Arusha Understanding, which allocated equal sites in the central Pacific mining areas for France, Japan, the Soviet Union and the Enterprise (the mining operating arm of the International Seabed Authority). As adopted by the Preparatory Commission in its summer session in New York (August 11 to September 5, 1986), the disputes of overlapping claims for mine sites in the central Pacific were to be resolved by the following formula:[5]

10. Applicants who do not have practical problems and do not make voluntary advance relinquishments of areas shall be deemed to have complied with requirements for relinquishment under Resolution II, paragraph 1(e) upon registration, provided that the total pioneer area allocated to them does not exceed 75,000 sq. km.

11. The Preparatory Commission shall allocate according to the procedures specified in Resolution II, paragraph 3, to applicants who are not deemed to have complied with the requirements of Resolution II, paragraph 1(e), under paragraphs 9 and 10 above, an area necessary to ensure that each such applicant shall have a pioneer area not exceeding 75,000 sq. km. after the relinquishment of areas in accordance with Resolution II, paragraph 1(e).

12. The relinquished areas, referred to in paragraph 9, shall remain deposited with the Preparatory Commission and will be reserved to form part of the application areas of potential applicants qualified to apply as pioneer investors under Resolution II, paragraph 1(a)(ii), until the Convention enters into force.

13. The General Committee shall make its decisions relating to the designation of the areas to be reserved for the Authority and the allocation of pioneer areas covered by revised applications of the first group of applicants in accordance with the following:

> 1.(a) The area to be designated in respect of each application as an area to be reserved for the conduct of activities by the Authority through the Enterprise or in association with developing countries shall be not less than one half of the total area applied for by each applicant. In the case where an applicant has relinquished over 75,000 sq. km. under paragraph 9 above, the area to be reserved for the Authority may be reduced, but in any case it shall not be less than 75,000 sq. km.

(b) The areas to be reserved for the Authority in respect of each application shall be of equal estimated commercial value to the respective areas allocated to each applicant.

(c) Applicants with overlapping claims, namely France, Japan and the USSR, shall contribute portions of areas in the northeast Pacific Ocean covered by their respective revised applications that will constitute part of the area to be reserved for the Authority. The areas so contributed may be incorporated in any area for which the Enterprise may wish to submit a plan of work and together they shall be of equal estimated commercial value to at least the average estimated commercial value of the three areas of up to 52,300 sq. km. to be allocated to the pioneer investors pursuant to paragraph 13(2).

(d) The contribution to be made by the three applicants for this purpose shall be as follows:

(i) *France* – an area totalling 20,000 sq. km. adjacent to its presently overlapping area with the Soviet Union;

(ii) *Japan* – an area totalling 17,300 sq. km. adjacent to its presently overlapping area with the Soviet Union;

(iii) *Soviet Union* – an area totalling 15,000 sq. km., 14,549 sq. km. of which will be from within its presently overlapping areas with France and with Japan and 451 sq. km. which it obtains from France following adjustment of claims between the two applicants.

2. The total area to be allocated to each applicant shall not exceed 75,000 sq. km. after any relinquishment of areas referred to in paragraphs 9, 10 and 11 has been made. For the purpose of allocation, each applicant may indicate in its application portions of its application area up to a limit of 52,300 sq. km. that shall form part of the total area to be allocated to it by the Commission. In addition to the areas indicated by the applicants, the Commission shall allocate, in accordance with resolution II, paragraph 3, an area from their respective application areas necessary to complete the total area to be allocated to each applicant.

3. Notwithstanding the foregoing the registration of India as a pioneer investor shall be made in conformity with resolution II. However, India, like other applicants, if it so wishes, will identify in its application area an area totalling 52,300 sq. km. for incorporation in the area of up to 150,000 sq. km. to be allocated to it as a pioneer area. The provisions on relinquishment in Resolution II, paragraph 1(e), shall apply to the allocated area.

(Also see sections on Pioneer Investors, Preparatory Commission, and Reciprocating State Agreements.)

Significance. In 1984 the Preparatory Commission adopted the Understanding on Resolution of Conflicts among Applicants for Registration as Pioneer Investors, an attempt to resolve conflicts by exchanging pioneer area coordinates, identification of overlaps and initiation of discussions known as ''nonpoaching'' agreements. However, because of the size of the mining sites claimed, the understanding was not specific enough to resolve the conflict on overlapping claims between France and the Soviet Union in the Clarion-Clipperton mining area in the central Pacific. Also, the Soviet claim overlapped the claims of the multinational mining consortia as potential "pioneer investors" and licensees under the international deep seabed mining regime. The importance of the Arusha Understanding seems to be that it provided a way of breaking out of the impasse between the interests of the four multinational mining consortia as potential pioneer investors and the first group of investor applicants. Thus the overlapped area between the Soviet claim and the potential applicants' (see entry topic Consortia) would be relinquished as a reserve to be held by the Preparatory Commission. It cannot be overemphasized that the conflict resolution process developed and contained in the Arusha Understanding has enabled deep seabed mining to begin. For without such a process to resolve the overlapping claims, there would be no "security of tenure" for the mining enterprises "to prevent claim jumping" and to make major mining investments.[6]

In its report on the Fifth Session held in Kingston, Jamaica, from March 30 to April 16, 1987, the Preparatory Commission stated that "under the Arusha Understanding, France and the USSR, along with Japan and the USSR, agreed to relinquish areas before Resolution II required them to do so, in order to meet certain practical problems as well as to facilitate the resolution of conflicts between the claims of the Soviet Union and some of the potential applicants. In addition, the three applicants were to contribute areas adjacent to the overlapping areas to compose a mine site for the Authority."[7] The most important point concerning the Arusha Understanding is that by the summer of 1987 it cleared the way for the registration of pioneer investors, with India as the first; and by December 17, 1987, three more governments were also registered as pioneer investors: France, Japan and the Soviet Union.

CONSORTIA: FOR DEEP-SEABED MINING

Article 153–2(b) of the 1982 LOS Convention provides for seabed mining enterprises of both state and private commercial companies (in addition to the International Seabed Authority's Enterprise) engaging in mining activities in the Area. Since 1974 a number of multinational deep seabed mining consortia have been organized to engage in prospecting and research activities on polymetallic nodules. These are pioneer investors, defined by Resolution II, Final Act of the 1982 LOS Convention, as those who had spent before January 1, 1983, at least $30 million in pioneer deep-seabed activities, such as research and engineering development of polymetallic nodules. These privately organized international mining consortia have the right to apply to the Preparatory Commission for registration as pioneer investors and receive an area reserved for conducting activities in the international seabed area so designated (see separate section in this chapter).

There are, at present, six major international consortia engaged in seabed mining. These mining groups are privately owned and comprise some of the largest mining companies in the world (see Table 7.1).

In Resolution II–1(a)(ii) Annex 1, Final Act of the 1982 LOS Convention, four of the multinational consortia listed in Table 7.1 were designated as pioneer investors. They were originally identified by the United Nations Department of International Economic and Social Affairs: Kennecott Consortium (KCON), Ocean Mining Associates (OMA), Ocean Management, Inc. (OMI), and Ocean Minerals Company (OMC).[8] These four pioneer mining consortia are well-known multinational corporations from the states mentioned in paragraph 1(a)(ii) of Resolution II, Final Act of the 1982 LOS Convention: Belgium, Canada, West Germany, Italy, Japan, the Netherlands, the United Kingdom and the United States. The other two are consortia formed exclusively by national corporations of France and Japan. In addition to the six consortia mentioned here, Resolution II, paragraph 1(a)(i) also extended pioneer investors category to India and the Soviet Union. (Also see separate sections in this chapter on Arusha Understanding, Parallel System, Pioneer Investors and Reciprocating States Agreement.)

Significance. Resolution II, Final Act of the 1982 LOS Convention, was enacted primarily to meet the demands of the six consortia listed here. These six multinational consortia on deep-seabed mining, as of the mid–1980s, had already invested substantially for a total of more than one-half billion U.S. dollars. As pioneer investors, they enjoy the site protection and tenure under the Convention. Since they represent the major deep-seabed mining companies from the West, plus Japan, their contributions in terms of financial and technical resources are crucial in the eventual establishment and work of the International Seabed Authority. However, West Germany, the United Kingdom and the United States failed to sign the 1982 LOS Convention. Therefore, some legal uncertainty has been created about the four consortia's rights to participate in seabed mining activities in the Area, unless some changes are made in their corporate composition, such as the withdrawal or transfer of interest of the nonsignatory states' components from the consortia. These legal uncertainties for the status of the consortia as pioneer investors in seabed mining in the Area may also affect their ability to secure the necessary financing from investment banking institutions.

THE ENTERPRISE

Article 170: The Enterprise

1. The Enterprise shall be the organ of the Authority which shall carry out activities in the Area directly, pursuant to article 153, paragraph 2(a), as well as the transporting, processing and marketing of minerals recovered from the Area.

2. The Enterprise shall, within the framework of the international legal personality of the Authority, have such legal capacity as is provided for in the Statute set forth in Annex

Table 7.1
Major International Deep Sea Mining Consortia

Consortium	Country	Stake (%)	Mining Technology	Year Formed	Estimated Expenditure	Area (km²)
1. Ocean Mining Assoc. (OMA)						
U. S. Steel	U.S.	25	Dredge	1974	$130 million	60,000
Union Miniere	Belgium*	25	device			
Sun Oil Co.	U.S.	25	with			
SAMIN	Italy	25	airlift			
*Deepsea Ventures, Inc. is the service contractor and is owned by OMA partners.						
2. Ocean Management, Inc. (OMI)						
INCO	Canada	25	Dredge	1975	$100 million	135,000
SEDCO	U.S.	25	device			
AMR Group:			with			
Preusagg A.G.	West		hydraulic or			
Metallgesellschaft A.G.	Germany		airlift			
Salzgitter A.G.						
DOMCO Group	Japan					
(led by Sumitomo)		25				
3. Ocean Minerals Co. (OMCO)						
Lockheed	U.S.	30	Dredge	1977	$120 million	160,000
Standard Oil of Indiana			device with			
(AMCO Minerals)	U.S.	30	hydraulic			
Royal Dutch Shell		30	lift			
(Billiton Intl. Metals)	U.K./ Holland					
Royal Bos Kalis Westminster	Holland	10				
4. Kennecott Consortium (KCON)	U.S.	40	Dredge device with	1974	$ 50 million	173,000
Noranda Exploration, Inc.	Canada	12	hydraulic lift			
Consolidated Gold Fields	U.K.	12				
Rio Tinto-Zinc, Ltd.	U.K.	12				
British Petroleum	U.K.	12				
Mitsubishi Corporation	Japan	12				
5. Afernod						
Centre National pour l'Exploitation des Oceans (CNEXO)	France	20	Unspecified: Studying dredge and	1974	$ 50 million	300,000
Commissariat a l'Energie Atomique (CEA)	France	20	continuous line bucket;			
Bureau de Recherches Geologiques et Minieres	France	20	possible future use			
Societe Metallurgique Nouvelle/Societe Le Nickel	France	20	of robot submersibles			
Chantiers de France Dunkerque	France	20				
6. Deep Ocean Resources Development (DORD)						
An association between Japanese industry and government. Includes 35 Japanese companies, three from Mitsubishi Group, four from Mitsui Group, six from Nippon Group, four from Sumitomo Group and C. Itoh, Dowa Mining, Furukawa, Kanematsu-Gosho, Kyokuyo, Marubeni, Nichimen, Nissho-Iwai, and Toyo Menka.	Japan	N/A	Exploration carried out by Metal Mining Agency, a semi-commercial entity linked to MITI of the Japanese government; cooperative arrangement with Geological Survey to use vessel Hakurei-Mauru, survey on southern Hawaiian seas.	1982	$ 86 million	168,000-287,500

Sources: Based on figures from J. K. Amsbaugh, Ocean Mining Associates, H. Enzer, U.S. Department of the Interior and industry correspondence. Kurt Michael Shusterich, *Resource Management and the Ocean* (Boulder, Colo.: Westview Press, 1982), pp. 75–76. The table is found in Daniel L. Larson, "Deep Seabed Mining: A Definition of the Problem," *Ocean Development and International Law* 17, no. 4 (1986): 283–285. Figures on year formed, estimated expenditure and area claimed are based on J. M. Broadus and Porter Hoagland III, "Conflict Resolution in the Assignment of Area Entitlements for Seabed Mining," *San Diego Law Review* 21, no. 3 (1984): 556–562, copyright 1984 San Diego Law Review Association. Reprinted with the permission of the *San Diego Law Review*.

IV. The Enterprise shall act in accordance with this Convention and the rules, regulations and procedures of the Authority, as well as the general policies established by the Assembly, and shall be subject to the directives and control of the Council.

3. The Enterprise shall have its principal place of business at the seat of the Authority.

4. The Enterprise shall, in accordance with article 173, paragraph 2, and Annex IV, article 11, be provided with such funds as it may require to carry out its functions, and shall receive technology as provided in article 144 and other relevant provisions of this Convention.

The Enterprise is the operating arm of the International Seabed Authority for the purpose of "mining for Third World financial advantages," to use the words of one of the key negotiators at the UNCLOS III Geneva and New York sessions.[9] As an operating arm of the Authority, the Enterprise can, under Article 170(1), engage in activities of transporting, processing and marketing of minerals recovered from the seabed in the Area. It is in the main an autonomous body operating in accordance with "sound commercial principles," as well as the rules and regulations governing the Authority's principal organs. The Enterprise can receive seabed mining technology and funding in carrying out its mining functions.

Legal Status and Capacity

Under Article 170(2) the Enterprise is considered to possess a distinct legal capacity "within the framework of the international legal personality of the Authority." In Annex IV to the Final Act on the Statute of the Enterprise, the operating arm of the Authority can exercise the normal "privileges and immunities" in the territories of the states which were parties to the 1982 LOS Convention. Article 13 in Annex IV stipulates further that the Enterprise shall have the "legal capacity" to act as a corporate entity and to enter into contractual arrangements and be sued under certain conditions.

Article 13: Legal status, privileges and immunities

1. To enable the Enterprise to exercise its functions, the status, privileges and immunities set forth in this article shall be accorded to the Enterprise in the territories of States Parties. To give effect to this principle the Enterprise and States Parties may, where necessary, enter into special agreements.

2. The Enterprise shall have such legal capacity as is necessary for the exercise of its functions and the fulfillment of its purposes and, in particular, the capacity:

(a) to enter into contracts, joint arrangements or other arrangements, including agreements with States and international organizations;

(b) to acquire, lease, hold and dispose of immovable and movable property;

(c) to be a party to legal proceedings.

3. (a) Actions may be brought against the Enterprise only in a court of competent jurisdiction in the territory of a State Party in which the Enterprise:

(i) has an office or facility;

(ii) has appointed an agent for the purpose of accepting service or notice of process;

(iii) has entered into a contract for goods or services;

(iv) has issued securities; or

(v) is otherwise engaged in commercial activity.

(b) The property and assets of the Enterprise, wherever located and by whomsoever held, shall be immune from all forms of seizure, attachment or execution before the delivery of final judgment against the Enterprise.

4. (a) The property and assets of the Enterprise, wherever located and by whomsoever held, shall be immune from requisition, confiscation, expropriation or any other form of seizure by executive or legislative action.

(b) The property and assets of the Enterprise, wherever located and by whomsoever held, shall be free from discriminatory restrictions, regulations, controls and moratoria of any nature.

(c) The Enterprise and its employees shall respect local laws and regulations in any State or territory in which the Enterprise or its employees may do business or otherwise act.

(d) States Parties shall ensure that the Enterprise enjoys all rights, privileges and immunities accorded by them to entities conducting commercial activities in their territories. These rights, privileges and immunities shall be accorded to the Enterprise on no less favourable a basis than that on which they are accorded to entities engaged in similar commercial activities. If special privileges are provided by States Parties for developing States or their commercial entities, the Enterprise shall enjoy those privileges on a similarly preferential basis.

(e) States Parties may provide special incentives, rights, privileges and immunities to the Enterprise without the obligation to provide such incentives, rights, privileges and immunities to other commercial entities.

5. The Enterprise shall negotiate with the host countries in which its offices and facilities are located for exemption from direct and indirect taxation.

6. Each State Party shall take such action as is necessary for giving effect in terms of its own law to the principles set forth in this Annex and shall inform the Enterprise of the specific action which it has taken.

7. The Enterprise may waive any of the privileges and immunities conferred under this article or in the special agreements referred to in paragraph 1 to such extent and upon such conditions as it may determine.

Despite the argument presented by the Group of 77 at the ninth session of the UNCLOS III negotiations in New York (March 3 to April 14, 1980) that the Enterprise need not make payment to the International Seabed Authority or pay national taxation,[10] Article 10 in Annex IV (the Statute of the Enterprise) states that it must make payments to the Authority the same as other private contractors, but is given an exemption for the first ten years:

Article 10: Allocation of net income

1. Subject to paragraph 3, the Enterprise shall make payments to the Authority under Annex III, article 13, or their equivalent.

2. The Assembly shall, upon the recommendation of the Governing Board, determine what portion of the net income of the Enterprise shall be retained as reserves of the Enterprise. The remainder shall be transferred to the Authority.

3. During an initial period required for the Enterprise to become self-supporting, which shall not exceed 10 years from the commencement of commercial production by it, the Assembly shall exempt the Enterprise from the payments referred to in paragraph 1, and shall leave all of the net income of the Enterprise in its reserves.

As far as taxation is concerned, Article 13(5) in Annex I on immunities and privileges exempts the Enterprise from direct and indirect national taxation by most nations in which its offices and facilities are located. Furthermore, the Enterprise is not liable ''for acts or obligations of the Authority or make the Authority liable for the acts or obligations of the Enterprise,'' as stipulated under Article 2, Annex IV on the Statute of the Enterprise. However, the Enterprise is subject to suit under Article 13(3), Annex IV, in the territory of a state party to the 1982 LOS Convention.

Governing Board: Functions and Power

Governing structure for the Enterprise is deceptively simple: A Governing Board and a Director-General who heads an administrative staff. The fifteen-member Governing Board is elected by the Authority's Assembly for a four-year term and can be reelected with due regard to membership rotation. Once elected to the Governing Board, to ensure integrity and independence, members are to act in their personal capacity, not on instructions from their governments. Decisions of the Governing Board are made by a majority vote with one vote for each member. In case of conflict of interest, a member must refrain from voting.

Functions and powers of the Enterprise's Governing Board are detailed in Article 6, Annex IV, to the Final Act:

(a) to elect a Chairman from among its members;

(b) to adopt its rules of procedure;

(c) to draw up and submit formal written plans of work to the Council in accordance with article 153, paragraph 3, and article 162, paragraph 2(j);

(d) to develop plans of work and programmes for carrying out the activities specified in article 170;

(e) to prepare and submit to the Council applications for production authorizations in accordance with article 15, paragraphs 2 to 7;

(f) to authorize negotiations concerning the acquisition of technology, including those provided for in Annex III, article 5, paragraph 3(a), (c) and (d), and to approve the results of those negotiations;

(g) to establish terms and conditions, and to authorize negotiations, concerning joint ventures and other forms of joint arrangements referred to in Annex III, articles 9 and 11, and to approve the results of such negotiations;

(h) to recommend to the Assembly what portion of the net income of the Enterprise should be retained as its reserves in accordance with article 160, paragraph 2(f), and article 10 of this Annex;

(i) to approve the annual budget of the Enterprise;

(j) to authorize the procurement of goods and services in accordance with article 12, paragraph 3, of this Annex;

(k) to submit an annual report to the Council in accordance with article 9 of this Annex;

(l) to submit to the Council for the approval of the Assembly draft rules in respect of the organization, management, appointment and dismissal of the staff of the Enterprise and to adopt regulations to give effect to such rules;

(m) to borrow funds and to furnish such collateral or other security as it may determine in accordance with article 11, paragraph 2, of this Annex;

(n) to enter into any legal proceedings, agreements and transactions and to take any other actions in accordance with article 13 of this Annex;

(o) to delegate, subject to the approval of the Council, any non-discretionary powers to the Director-General and to its committees.

The Director-General for the Enterprise is elected for a fixed term of five years by the Authority's Assembly, upon recommendation of the Council and the Governing Board, in accordance with Article 7 of Annex IV. The person so elected is responsible for "the organization, management, appointment and dismissal of the staff for the Enterprise. He participates *ex officio* without vote in the meetings of the Authority's Assembly and Council on matters related to the Enterprise." Presumably, the Director-General must prepare an annual report to the Authority's Council on the Enterprise's financial profits and losses. (Also see separate sections in this chapter on Area, Financial Arrangement, Parallel System, and the Preparatory Commission.)

Significance. The Enterprise, as the operating arm of the Authority, is not only the result of a compromise created under the parallel system, but an international mining entity subsidized by and in competition with the other authorized seabed mining entities in the Area. The section of the agreement creating the Enterprise is one of the most controversial on seabed mining. The opponents of the 1982 LOS Convention have objected to it as burdensome and biased in favor of the ideological and economic aims of the Third World developing states. Moreover, as an international mining concern, the Enterprise would, if it were fully realized, have claims on the seabed mining sites, funding, and activities equal to the combined total of all competing private consortia and state-sponsored mining concerns authorized to operate in the Area. The Enterprise gains a technological advantage under the 1982 LOS Convention because it requires other private mining concerns which are licensed to operate in the Area to sell mining technology to the operating arm of the Authority ten years from the commencement of commercial production—an obligation imposed on other deep-seabed mining companies. Thus, when one considers all these features for the Enterprise plus the additional feature that its initial capitalization is the cost of developing one mine site—half of which is guaranteed by state parties and the other half is interest-free loans—the Authority's mining operating arm is a most unusual entity indeed.

FINANCIAL ARRANGEMENTS FOR THE AUTHORITY AND THE ENTERPRISE

There are elaborate financial arrangements for both the International Seabed Authority and its operating arm, the Enterprise. First, Article 13, Annex III, Final Act of the 1982 LOS Convention, provides for three types of "fees" or payments to be made by approved deep-seabed mining contractors to the Authority: an application fee, an annual fixed fee, and a production charge only or in combination with profit sharing from the net proceeds within a year from the commencement of commercial production of deep seabed mineral resources.

Under Article 13(2) the application fee is levied to cover the administrative cost of processing a miner's application:

> 2. A fee shall be levied for the administrative cost of processing an application for approval of a plan of work in the form of a contract and shall be fixed at an amount of $US 500,000 per application. The amount of the fee shall be reviewed from time to time by the Council in order to ensure that it covers the administrative cost incurred. If such administrative cost incurred by the Authority in processing an application is less than the fixed amount, the Authority shall refund the difference to the applicant.

Some nations, particularly the European Economic Community group, considered the application fee to be rather high, but accepted the $500,000 figure under pressure from the United States and the Third World developing nations. The amount may be reduced or adjusted if the actual administrative cost is less than that amount, or it may be periodically reviewed by the Council for the International Seabed Authority.

The second type of payment by mining contractors to the Authority is the fixed annual fee as prescribed in Article 13(3):

3. A contractor shall pay an annual fixed fee of $US 1 million from the date of entry into force of the contract. If the approved date of commencement of commercial production is postponed because of a delay in issuing the production authorization, in accordance with article 151, the annual fixed fee shall be waived for the period of postponement. From the date of commencement of commercial production, the contractor shall pay either the production charge or the annual fixed fee, whichever is greater.

To the potential deep-seabed mining investor the annual fixed fee of U.S.$1 million is a "front-end load" charged without regard to whether a venture is profitable—this has been the United States delegation's position.[11] As a front-end payment, it has been considered a financial burden imposed on the deep-seabed miners before production begins.[12]

The third type of payment to the Authority consists of a mixed system of production charges: a form of royalty payment based on gross revenue from the sales of the processed metals traded in the international market or a production charge in combination with a scheme of profit sharing of net proceeds. Articles 13(4) and (5) represent a compromise, worked out by Ambassador Koh of Singapore, to reflect two different economic approaches: centralized socialistic and market oriented. In Article 13(4) the compromise provided a contract with a choice of two systems:

4. Within a year of the date of commencement of commercial production, in conformity with paragraph 3, a contractor shall choose to make his financial contribution to the Authority by either:

(a) paying a production charge only; or

(b) paying a combination of a production charge and a share of net proceeds.

5. (a) If a contractor chooses to make his financial contribution to the Authority by paying a production charge only, it shall be fixed at a percentage of the market value of the processed metals produced from the polymetallic nodules recovered from the area covered by the contract. This percentage shall be fixed as follows:

(i) years 1–10 of commercial production	5 percent
(ii) years 11 to the end of commercial production	12 percent

(b) The said market value shall be the product of the quantity of the processed metals produced from the polymetallic nodules extracted from the area covered by the contract and the average price for those metals during the relevant accounting year, as defined in paragraphs 7 and 8.

Thus, if a contractor for deep-seabed mining in the Area chooses the single royalty payment system, it must abide by Article 13(5) in two stages based on "the passage of time," rather than on the rate of return: a fixed 5 percent of the market value of the processed metal recovered in the Area in the first ten years and then an increase to 12 percent from year 11 to the end of the commercial production. As explained by Ambassador Koh, the method of production charge only would financially help the Authority in the early years and ensure a steady flow of revenue regardless of profitability of the contractor's project.[13] The considerations for the Authority's financial well-being finally prevailed, rather than those of the very heavy burden imposed on the contractor.

Highly complex financial arrangements have been designed for a deep-seabed mining operator to make payments to the Authority via a mixed or combined production charge or royalty payment, plus profit sharing of the net proceeds. Article 13(6) provides a detailed payment arrangement as an alternate method:

6. If a contractor chooses to make his financial contribution to the Authority by paying a combination of a production charge and a share of net proceeds, such payments shall be determined as follows:

(a) The production charge shall be fixed at a percentage of the market value, determined in accordance with subparagraph (b), of the processed metals produced from the polymetallic nodules recovered from the area covered by the contract. This percentage shall be fixed as follows:

(i) first period of commercial production	2 percent
(ii) second period of commercial production	4 percent

If, in the second period of commercial production, as defined in subparagraph (d), the return on investment in any accounting year as defined in subparagraph (m) falls below 15 percent as a result of the payment of the production charge at 4 percent, the production charge shall be 2 percent instead of 4 percent in that accounting year.

There is no time or duration specified in the progression from the first stage of 2 percent to the second stage of a higher charge of 4 percent, a heavy financial burden for a contractor. Rather, the progression is determined by a formula at a point at which a contractor's development costs "are fully recovered by his surplus," outlined by Article 13(6)(d)(i-ii):

(d)(i) The first period of commercial production referred to in subparagraphs (a) and (c) shall commence in the first accounting year of commercial production and terminate in the accounting year in which the contractor's development costs with interest on the unrecovered portion thereof are fully recovered by his cash surplus, as follows:

In the first accounting year during which development costs are incurred, unrecovered development costs shall equal the development costs less cash surplus in that year. In each subsequent accounting year, unrecovered development costs shall equal the unrecovered development costs at the end of the preceding accounting year, plus interest thereon at the rate of 10 percent per annum, plus development costs incurred in the current accounting year and less contractor's cash surplus in the current accounting year. The accounting year in which unrecovered development costs become zero for the first time shall be the accounting year in which the contractor's development costs with interest on the unrecovered portion thereof are fully recovered by his cash surplus. The contractor's cash surplus in any accounting year shall be his gross proceeds less his operating costs and less his payments to the Authority under subparagraph (c).

(ii) The second period of commercial production shall commence in the accounting year following the termination of the first period of commercial production and shall continue until the end of the contract.

The Authority's share of net proceeds from a deep-seabed mining contractor is governed by the "attributable net proceeds" (ANP). Article 13(6)(e) states that the "attributable net proceeds" formula is calculated by the combination of the "development cost ratio" and "the pre-determined constant ratio" of not more than 25 percent of total net proceeds in the commercial production of the three processed metals of cobalt, copper and nickel:

(e) "Attributable net proceeds" means the product of the contractor's net proceeds and the ratio of the development costs in the mining sector to the contractor's development costs. If the contractor engages in mining, transporting polymetallic nodules and production primarily of three processed metals, namely, cobalt, copper and nickel, the amount of attributable net proceeds shall not be less than 25 percent of the contractor's net proceeds. Subject to subparagraph (n), in all other cases, including those where the contractor engages in mining, transporting polymetallic nodules, and production primarily of four processed metals, namely, cobalt, copper, manganese and nickel, the Authority may, in its rules, regulations and procedures, prescribe appropriate floors which shall bear the same relationship to each case as the 25 percent floor does to the three-metal case.

In accordance with a fixed incremental schedule as defined in article 13(6)(c)(ii), a tax system is then imposed on the contractors when "the Authority's share of the net proceeds" is taken out of that portion of the contractor's net proceeds attributable to the mining operation of the deep seabed resources in the Area covered by the contract with the Authority:

(ii) The Authority's share of attributable net proceeds shall be determined in accordance with the following incremental schedule:

Portion of attributable net proceeds	*Share of the Authority*	
	First period of commercial production	*Second period of commercial production*
That portion representing a return on investment which is greater than 0 percent, but less than 10 percent	35 percent	40 percent

That portion representing a return on investment which is 10 percent or greater, but less than 20 percent	42.5 percent	50 percent
That portion representing a return on investment which is 20 percent or greater	50 percent	70 percent

Article 13(6) also provides specific definitional concepts for the various accounting terms used to calculate the Authority's tax system to be imposed on the contractors. The following key definitions are presented here for reference purposes:

(f) "Contractor's net proceeds" means the contractor's gross proceeds less his operating costs and less the recovery of his development costs as set out in subparagraph (j).

(g) (i) If the contractor engages in mining, transporting polymetallic nodules and production of processed metals, "contractor's gross proceeds" means the gross revenues from the sale of the processed metals and any other monies deemed reasonably attributable to operations under the contract in accordance with the financial rules, regulations and procedures of the Authority.

(ii) In all cases other than those specified in subparagraphs (g) (i) and (n)(iii), "contractor's gross proceeds" means the gross revenues from the sale of the semi-processed metals from the polymetallic nodules recovered from the area covered by the contract, and any other monies deemed reasonably attributable to operations under the contract in accordance with the financial rules, regulations and procedures of the Authority.

(h) "Contractor's development costs" means:

(i) all expenditures incurred prior to the commencement of commercial production which are directly related to the development of the productive capacity of the area covered by the contract and the activities related thereto for operations under the contract in all cases other than that specified in subparagraph (n), in conformity with generally recognized accounting principles, including, *inter alia*, costs of machinery, equipment, ships, processing plant, construction, buildings, land, roads, prospecting and exploration of the area covered by the contract, research and development, interest, required leases, licences and fees; and

(ii) expenditures similar to those set forth in (i) above incurred subsequent to the commencement of commercial production and necessary to carry out the plan of work, except those chargeable to operating costs.

(i) The proceeds from the disposal of capital assets and the market value of those capital assets which are no longer required for operations under the contract and which are not sold shall be deducted from the contractor's development costs during the relevant accounting year. When these deductions exceed the contractor's development costs the excess shall be added to the contractor's gross proceeds.

(j) The contractor's development costs incurred prior to the commencement of commercial production referred to in subparagraphs (h) (i) and (n)(iv) shall be recovered in 10 equal annual installments from the date of commencement of commercial production. The contractor's development costs incurred subsequent to the commencement of commercial production referred to in subparagraphs (h)(ii) and (n)(iv) shall be recovered in 10 or fewer equal annual installments so as to ensure their complete recovery by the end of the contract.

(k) "Contractor's operating costs" means all expenditures incurred after the commencement of commercial production in the operation of the productive capacity of the area covered by the contract and the activities related thereto for operations under the contract, in conformity with generally recognized accounting principles, including, *inter alia*, the annual fixed fee or the production charge, whichever is greater, expenditures for wages, salaries, employee benefits, materials, services, transporting, processing and marketing costs, interest, utilities, preservation of the marine environment, overhead and administrative costs specifically related to operations under the contract, and any net operating losses carried forward or backward as specified herein. Net operating losses may be carried forward for two consecutive years except in the last two years of the contract in which case they may be carried backward to the two preceding years.

(1) If the contractor engages in mining, transporting of polymetallic nodules, and production of processed and semi-processed metals, "development costs of the mining sector" means the portion of the contractor's development costs which is directly related to the mining of the resources of the area covered by the contract, in conformity with generally recognized accounting principles, and the financial rules, regulations and procedures of the Authority, including, *inter alia*, application fee, annual fixed fee and, where applicable, costs of prospecting and exploration of the area covered by the contract, and a portion of research and development costs.

(m) "Return on investment" in any accounting year means the ratio of attributable net proceeds in that year to the development costs of the mining sector. For the purpose of computing this ratio the development costs of the mining sector shall include expenditures on new or replacement equipment in the mining sector less the original cost of the equipment replaced.

Financial Arrangements for the Enterprise

Article 11(1), Annex IV, Final Act, provides five main sources of funding for the Enterprise:

1. The funds of the Enterprise shall include:

   (a) amounts received from the Authority in accordance with article 173, paragraph 2(b);

   (b) voluntary contributions made by States Parties for the purpose of financing activities of the Enterprise;

   (c) amounts borrowed by the Enterprise in accordance with paragraphs 2 and 3;

(d) income of the Enterprise from its operations;

(e) other funds made available to the Enterprise to enable it to commence operations as soon as possible and to carry out its functions.

As governed by Article 11(2), Annex IV, it is obvious that the Enterprise must rely on external borrowing during its initial operating years:

2. (a) The Enterprise shall have the power to borrow funds and to furnish such collateral or other security as it may determine. Before making a public sale of its obligations in the financial markets or currency of a State Party, the Enterprise shall obtain the approval of that State Party. The total amount of borrowings shall be approved by the Council upon the recommendation of the Governing Board.

(b) States Parties shall make every reasonable effort to support applications by the Enterprise for loans on capital markets and from international financial institutions.

Article 11(3)(a) and (b) provide for the steps to be taken in financing the Enterprise's very first mine site:

3. (a) The Enterprise shall be provided with the funds necessary to explore and exploit one mine site, and to transport, process and market the minerals recovered therefrom and the nickel, copper, cobalt and manganese obtained, and to meet its initial administrative expenses. The amount of the said funds, and the criteria and factors for its adjustment, shall be included by the Preparatory Commission in the draft rules, regulations and procedures of the Authority.

Notice that this paragraph refers to only one mining site for recovering four metals (nickel, copper, cobalt and manganese), and the funds are to be used "to meet its initial administrative expenses." The amount needed for operating the Enterprise's first mining site is left unspecified; it is to be determined later by the Preparatory Commission when it proceeds to draft the rules and regulations for the Authority. Resolution I of UNCLOS III establishes such a commission and states that the dollar amount is to be fixed by it allowing for adjustment to realistically reflect the cost involved. This was the agreement reached in the New York session between the Group of 77 and the developed industrialized states.[14]

In case of a shortfall and indebtedness, Article 11(3)(b) and (c) provide the following remedies:

(b) All States Parties shall make available to the Enterprise an amount equivalent to one half of the funds referred to in subparagraph (a) by way of long-term interest-free loans in accordance with the scale of assessments for the United Nations regular budget in force at the time when the assessments are made, adjusted to take into account the States which are not members of the United Nations. Debts incurred by the Enterprise in raising the other half of the funds shall be guaranteed by all States Parties in accordance with the same scale.

(c) If the sum of the financial contributions of States Parties is less than the funds to be provided to the Enterprise under subparagraph (a), the Assembly shall, at its first session, consider the extent of the shortfall and adopt by consensus measures for dealing with this shortfall, taking into account the obligation of States Parties under subparagraphs (a) and (b) and any recommendations of the Preparatory Commission.

The key provision in Article 11(3)(b) is the United Nations budget contribution assessment scale set by the United Nations General Assembly on the basis of a member state's population and per capita income. A separate assessment scale, based on the United Nations budget contribution formula, under Article 3(b), will have to be drawn up by the Authority for the Enterprise for all state parties to the 1982 LOS Convention. There are, based on United Nations experience, two problems inherent in the assessment formula. One is that a number of industrialized nations, such as the United States, the Soviet Union and France, pay a large share of the budget assessment to the annual United Nations budget. At present the United States is assessed to pay 25 percent of the total United Nations budget and is not a signatory to the 1982 LOS Convention. The second problem is the arrears or debt payment of membership assessment. For instance, the United States, after payment of $188 million of its arrears in the fall of 1988, was still behind about $520 million in its assessment payment. Nonparticipation by the United States and the practice of nonpayment or arrears in assessment by other United Nations members will eventually mean a possible shortfall or indebtedness for the Enterprise's operations. However, under Article 11(3)(e), state parties to the 1982 LOS Convention may "provide debt guarantees" in addition to those provided under the formula for assessment; or "in lieu of debt guarantees, a state party may make a voluntary contribution to the Enterprise in an amount equivalent to the portion of the debt which it would otherwise be liable to guarantee."

Article 11(3)(d), however, sees to it that contributions will be made available to the Enterprise whenever needed:

(d)(i) Each State Party shall, within 60 days after the entry into force of this Convention, or within 30 days after the deposit of its instrument of ratification or accession, whichever is later, deposit with the Enterprise irrevocable, non-negotiable, non-interest-bearing promissory notes in the amount of the share of such State Party of interest-free loans pursuant to subparagraph (b).

(ii) The Board shall prepare, at the earliest practicable date after this Convention enters into force, and thereafter at annual or other appropriate intervals, a schedule of the magnitude and timing of its requirements for the funding of its administrative expenses and for activities carried out by the Enterprise in accordance with article 170 and article 12 of this Annex.

(iii) The States Parties shall, thereupon, be notified by the Enterprise, through the Authority, of their respective shares of the funds in accordance with subparagraph (b), required for such expenses. The Enterprise shall encash such amounts of the promissory notes as may be required to meet the expenditure referred to in the schedule with respect to interest-free loans.

(iv) States Parties shall, upon receipt of the notification, make available their respective shares of debt guarantees for the Enterprise in accordance with subparagraph (b).

Under the scheme outlined by Article 11(3)(d), each state party to the 1982 LOS Convention must deposit with the Enterprise "irrevocable, non-negotiable, non-interest-bearing promissory notes" equal to its share of interest-free loans. The Enterprise's administration shall prepare an annual financial schedule for administrative expenses and mining activities. The promissory notes can be cashed in by the Enterprise to meet its expenditure needs.

In case of default of loan payments, the Enterprise must follow these procedures prescribed under Article 11(3)(f):

(f) Repayment of the interest-bearing loans shall have priority over the repayment of the interest-free loans. Repayment of interest-free loans shall be in accordance with a schedule adopted by the Assembly, upon the recommendation of the Council and the advice of the Board. In the exercise of this function the Board shall be guided by the relevant provisions of the rules, regulations and procedures of the Authority, which shall take into account the paramount importance of ensuring the effective functioning of the Enterprise and, in particular, ensuring its financial independence.

The last two sentences were added at the New York sessions to satisfy the concern expressed by the developed states, which demanded a fixed schedule of repayment after the tenth year of the Enterprise's mining production.[15] (Also see separate sections in this chapter on the Area, the Enterprise, Fundamental Principles, Parallel System, International Seabed Authority, and Pioneer Investors.)

Significance. The annual fixed fee of U.S.$1 million charged contractors by the Authority has been viewed as a front-end payment by the industrialized states, particularly voiced by the United States at the final negotiation sessions. The compromise reached on the tax system in Article 13(6)(c)(ii) provides the contractor a low rate of tax payable to the Authority when the return on investment in seabed mining is low and, conversely, a higher rate of tax for the Authority when the investment return is high. In any event, only real profit of a contractor's operation is taxed. As some experts point out, "the maximum effective marginal tax is 17.5%—equal to a 70% rate applied to 25% of the net profit of an integrated operation."[16] Thus, it has been argued that these payment arrangements to the Authority "compare favorably" with those made in many land-based mining operations in industrialized countries.[17] The tax system of the 1982 LOS Convention becomes even more attractive when considering tax credits allowed on the payments by the contractor's parent government.[18]

Taking the entire financial arrangement for the Authority as a whole, Ambassador Koh of Singapore, chairman for the negotiation on finances, estimated that the maximum revenue from one seabed mining contract could be U.S.$1 billion in a twenty-year period, or about $40 million per year.[19] There have been two other expert studies made on the methods of calculating the Authority's revenue, which would place the total revenue over a twenty-five-year period at $981 million for each authorized mining site in the Area. These calculations were based on the formula provided under Article 13(6) for a mixed system that combined production charge and net proceeds sharing.[20] However, a West German calculation estimated that the studies might be too optimistic.[21]

There is some ambiguity in both Annex III of the Statute (Basic Conditions) and Annex IV (The Enterprise) as to whether the Enterprise, the operating arm of the Authority, must pay the application fee and the annual fixed payment to the Authority in accordance with Article 13 of Annex IV for all contractors in the Area. Article 10(1), Annex IV, on the one hand, requires the Enterprise to make payments to the Authority under Article 13, Annex III. However, on the other hand, in Article 10(2), Annex IV it is stipulated that

> 2. The Assembly shall, upon the recommendation of the Governing Board, determine what portion of the net income of the Enterprise shall be retained as reserve of the Enterprise. The remainder shall be transferred to the Authority.

On the assumption that the Enterprise would have the same costs and revenues as other commercial contractors in the Area and that its revenues would be for international improvement of the developing nations, one estimate puts the Enterprise contribution to the Authority at $52 million annually.[22]

In conclusion, financial arrangements for the Authority, the Enterprise, and the revenues expected under the 1982 LOS Convention, including Annexes III and IV of the Final Act, are merely assumptions under the most favorable international conditions for the mining operations in the Area. These assumptions, optimistic at best, do not take into account a number of difficulties which may well arise if and when deep seabed operation in the Area does begin by the end of the century or in the 1990s. These difficulties, or possible hindrances to the actual mining operations in the Area, are:

1. Deep seabed revenues by the Authority might not be sufficient to compensate for the loss of foreign exchange earnings of land-based developing states as a result of ocean mining (UNTAD estimates put the losses for land-based developing countries in foreign exchange earnings for copper at $2.3 billion for the year 2000, $1.1 billion for cobalt, and $3.8 billion for nickel)
2. The changing political and economic conditions in the 1990s
3. The uncertainty in legal status with respect to ocean mining.[23]

All these may deter capital investment from bankers, which in turn may delay commercial operation to beyond the 1990s. Furthermore, it may well be the case that ocean mining might begin first in areas within national jurisdiction, not in the Area after all.

FUNDAMENTAL PRINCIPLES FOR THE AREA

Article 136, Section 2, Part XI of the 1982 LOS Convention on the international seabed regime states briefly that ''the Area and its resources are the common heritage of mankind.'' Then in subsequent Articles 137–149, the legal status and general conduct, peaceful use, equitable sharing, rights of coastal states, transfer of technology, scientific research, protection of the marine environment and the effective participation of developing states in the Area are enumerated. These articles, which express the principles governing the Area, are basically derived from various United Nations General Assembly resolutions from 1967 to 1970. As discussed in Chapter 2, the most significant of these resolutions has been the 1970 declaration of principles governing the seabed, adopted by the General Assembly on December 17, 1970, by a vote of 108 for, none against, and 14 abstentions. (The text of the United Nations General Assembly declaration on the general principles governing the seabed is summarized in Chapter 3 under the heading ''Common heritage of mankind.'') However, it will be necessary to review briefly all related articles in Part XI in order to determine the meaning and implication of the fundamental principles governing the uses of the seabed area in accordance with the 1982 LOS Convention.

Article 136 refers to the concept of common heritage of mankind as the fundamental governing principle for the seabed area. It is said that when it was originally proposed by Malta in 1967 the article was deliberately drafted to be a vague and general expression in order to avoid a repetitious ideological debate on the concept.[24] Until it has been universally accepted as a legally binding concept, common heritage of mankind is a controversial principle that is intended to establish, through its application in the 1982 LOS Convention, ''the institutional and legal framework and machinery to give the concept practical shape and form.''[25]

Application of the common heritage of mankind principle is limited to that part of the Area as defined in Article 1(1): ''The seabed and ocean floor and subsoil thereof, beyond the limits of national jurisdiction,'' or the outer limits of the legal continental shelf. Seabed resources which are the common heritage of mankind refer to ''all solid, liquid or gaseous mineral resources *in situ* in the Area at or beneath the seabed, including polymetallic.'' In short, the common heritage of mankind concept in Article 136 embodies the following key elements now recognized by a large number of states, signatories to the 1982 LOS Convention:

1. As long as the concept applies to the international seabed beyond the limits of national jurisdiction, no nation can appropriate the Area's resources.

2. All nations, however, must share not only the benefits derived from the exploitation of the resources, but the management as well.
3. The Area must be reserved for peaceful purposes.[26]

Article 137: Legal status of the Area and its resources

1. No State shall claim or exercise sovereignty or sovereign rights over any part of the Area or its resources, nor shall any State or natural or juridical person appropriate any part thereof. No such claim or exercise of sovereignty or sovereign rights nor such appropriation shall be recognized.

2. All rights in the resources of the Area are vested in mankind as a whole, on whose behalf the Authority shall act. These resources are not subject to alienation. The minerals recovered from the Area, however, may only be alienated in accordance with this Part and the rules, regulations and procedures of the Authority.

3. No State or natural or juridical person shall claim, acquire or exercise rights with respect to the minerals recovered from the Area except in accordance with this Part. Otherwise, no such claim, acquisition or exercise of such rights shall be recognized.

As a logical consequence of the common heritage of mankind principle, Article 137 declares that seabed resources are "common property" and as such no state can exercise sovereign claim over any part of the Area or its resources. Similarly, no state or natural or juridical person (a multinational corporation, for instance) has the right to appropriate such resources in the Area. This provision runs smack into the competing assertion that a state can exercise the right of freedom of the high seas under the doctrine of *res nullius*, which admits the right or lawfulness of a state or a private enterprise to exploit the seabed resources unilaterally. For instance, Deep Sea Venture, Inc., the service contractor owned by the consortium Ocean Mining Associates (OMA), deposited its exclusive claim on deep-seabed discovery and mining rights on November 15, 1974, with the United States government and requested diplomatic protection for its investment. The United States Department of State responded by taking the position that, while the freedom of the high seas does not include exclusive exploitation or exploration rights, mining in the Area may proceed as a freedom of the high seas under existing international law. The American position was not shared by a number of developed states.[27] While the textual language of Article 137(1) prohibits recognition of any state's claim or the exercise of sovereignty rights over the Area or its resources, controversy will inevitably arise if a seabed mining enterprise of a nonparty to the 1982 LOS Convention chooses to contest the legal status of Article 137 by claiming its rights under the freedom of the high seas.

Article 138 reaffirms the principles of the United Nations Charter as basic rules of conduct in relations between states in the Area:

The general conduct of states in relation to the Area shall be in accordance with the provisions of this Part, the principles embodied in the Charter of the United Nations and other rules of international law in the interests of maintaining peace and security and promoting international cooperation and mutual understanding.

As though such reaffirmation is not sufficient, Article 141 makes it abundantly clear that "the Area shall be open to use exclusively for peaceful purpose by all states, whether coastal or landlocked, without discrimination and without prejudice to the other provisions of this Part."

Article 139: Responsibility to ensure compliance and liability for damage

1. States Parties shall have the responsibility to ensure that activities in the Area, whether carried out by States Parties, or state enterprises or natural or juridical persons which possess the nationality of States Parties or are effectively controlled by them or their nationals, shall be carried out in conformity with this Part. The same responsibility applies to international organizations for activities in the Area carried out by such organizations.

2. Without prejudice to the rules of international law and Annex III, article 22, damage caused by the failure of a State Party or international organization to carry out its responsibilities under this Part shall entail liability; States Parties or international organizations acting together shall bear joint and several liability. A State Party shall not however be liable for damage caused by any failure to comply with this Part by a person whom it has sponsored under article 153, paragraph 2(b), if the State Party has taken all necessary and appropriate measures to secure effective compliance under article 153, paragraph 4, and Annex III, article 4, paragraph 4.

3. States Parties that are members of international organizations shall take appropriate measures to ensure the implementation of this article with respect to such organizations.

Article 139 establishes the principle of the responsibility of a state and any international institution, other than the Enterprise or the Authority, for compliance with the Convention's provisions in carrying out its activities in the Area and its liability for damages caused by any failure to discharge the responsibilities. In other words, a state that is a party to the Convention and is also a sponsor for an international consortium engaged in seabed mining in the Area is responsible and liable for damages for failure to discharge the responsibilities contained in Part XI of the Convention.

Article 140: Benefit of mankind

1. Activities in the Area shall, as specifically provided for in this Part, be carried out for the benefit of mankind as a whole, irrespective of the geographical location of States, whether coastal or land-locked, and taking into particular consideration the interests and needs of developing States and of peoples who have not attained full independence or other self-governing status recognized by the United Nations in accordance with General Assembly resolution 1514 (XV) and other relevant General Assembly resolutions.

2. The Authority shall provide for the equitable sharing of financial and other economic benefits derived from activities in the Area through any appropriate mechanism, on a non-discriminatory basis, in accordance with article 160, paragraph 2(f)(i).

Article 140 contains one specific item of controversy: The very concept of sharing the benefits with not only the developing Third World nations, but with "peoples who have not attained full independence or other self-governing status recognized by the United Nations," particularly the Declaration on the Granting of Independence of Colonial Countries and Peoples, General Assembly Resolution 1514 (XV). Thus, the second paragraph in Article 140 provides for the "equitable sharing of financial and other economic benefits" on a "non-discriminatory basis, in accordance with article 160, paragraph (2)(f)(i)," which mandates the special consideration of the "interests and needs of developing States and of peoples who have not attained full independence or other self-governing status." Article 140 is in contradiction to Article 82(4), which limits distribution of payments or contributions to "state parties to this convention" and includes only developing states, "particularly the least developed and the landlocked," with respect to the exploitation of the continental shelf beyond 200 nautical miles. In spite of this inherent conflict, the intention of Article 140 is clear: benefits from seabed activities in the Area are for mankind as a whole, not merely limited to sovereign states parties to the LOS Convention, but including self-governing as well as non-self-governing territories under colonial administration and, finally, national liberation movements.

Article 142: Rights and legitimate interests of coastal States

1. Activities in the Area, with respect to resource deposits in the Area which lie across limits of national jurisdiction, shall be conducted with due regard to the rights and legitimate interests of any coastal State across whose jurisdiction such deposits lie.

2. Consultations, including a system of prior notification, shall be maintained with the State concerned, with a view to avoiding infringement of such rights and interests. In cases where activities in the Area may result in the exploitation of resources lying within national jurisdiction, the prior consent of the coastal State concerned shall be required.

3. Neither this Part nor any rights granted or exercised pursuant thereto shall affect the rights of coastal States to take such measures consistent with the relevant provisions of Part XII as may be necessary to prevent, mitigate or eliminate grave and imminent danger to their coastline, or related interests from pollution or threat thereof or from other hazardous occurrences resulting from or caused by any activities in the Area.

Article 142 provides basic guidelines with respect to deep seabed resources lying both in the Area and within the limits of a national jurisdiction. In such a case, activities in the Area "shall be conducted with due regard to the rights and legitimate interests of any coastal state across whose jurisdiction such deposits lie." It mandates the international seabed regime to maintain consultation, or prior notification, in order to obtain prior consent from the coastal state in cases where activities in the Area may infringe on the rights of the coastal state for resources within its national jurisdiction. Coastal states, under Article 142(3), can take measures to "prevent, mitigate or eliminate grave and imminent danger to their coastline" and for pollution control.

Article 143 grants both the international seabed regime, the Authority, and the state parties to the LOS Convention and right to undertake marine scientific research concerning the Area and its resources:

Article 143: Marine scientific research

1. Marine scientific research in the Area shall be carried out exclusively for peaceful purposes and for the benefit of mankind as a whole, in accordance with Part XIII.

2. The Authority may carry out marine scientific research concerning the Area and its resources, and may enter into contracts for that purpose. The Authority shall promote and encourage the conduct of marine scientific research in the Area, and shall co-ordinate and disseminate the results of such research and analysis when available.

3. States Parties may carry out marine scientific research in the Area. States Parties shall promote international co-operation in marine scientific research in the Area by:

(a) participating in international programmes and encouraging co-operation in marine scientific research by personnel of different countries and of the Authority;

(b) ensuring that programmes are developed through the Authority or other international organizations as appropriate for the benefit of developing States and technologically less developed States with a view to:

(i) strengthening their research capabilities;

(ii) training their personnel and the personnel of the Authority in the techniques and applications of research;

(iii) fostering the employment of their qualified personnel in research in the Area;

(c) effectively disseminating the results of research and analysis when available, through the Authority or other international channels when appropriate.

The key to Article 143 is that it permits all marine scientific research activities so long as these are "exclusively for peaceful purposes and for the benefit of mankind as a whole." States parties to the Convention may engage in such scientific research in the Area, but are obligated to promote international co-operation and programs designed to aid developing Third World nations in strengthening their research capabilities, training of research personnel and disseminating research findings and analyses.

Significance. Several comments may be offered to show the controversial aspects of the governing principles on the seabed. First, collectively speaking, these fundamental principles governing the Area have become the basis of the new law of the seabed that challenges the traditional principle of the freedom of the seas. During the UNCLOS III negotiations, it was argued in the Northcut Ely opinion that, under the principle of freedom of the seas, a sovereign state or a corporation chartered by its nationals is free to mine the seabed resources, so long as the mining activities conducted on the deep seabed do not violate the interests of other coastal states. One must note that the assertion of exclusive right to deep-seabed claims is not the same as exclusive right to mine resources on the continental shelf and the continental margin. The latter rights have already been subsumed under the new legal concept for the continental shelf.

Second, these fundamental principles governing the international seabed regime derived mainly from the numerous United Nations General Assembly resolutions since the mid–1960s when debate on the seabed began. As resolutions, they have no binding effect in international law, contrary to some of the assertions made by spokesmen for the Third World. However, as collective expressions of the world community-at-large, these new principles enunciated in the United Nations General Assembly resolutions may "constitute part of a broader law-creating process."[28]

Third, it may be argued that in view of future developments in international law, it is possible that these governing principles for the international seabed regime may become, in due time, part of customary international law.

And, finally, these fundamental principles represent the intractable ideological and philosophical confrontation between the Western industrialized states, on the one hand, and the numerically powerful Third World developing nations, on the other. The very concepts of the common heritage of mankind and the equitable sharing of the proceeds of seabed mining for the benefit of the developing world have been considered by the critics as "a threat to basic principles of Western economic and political philosophy."[29]

However, in the view of one proponent, leaving aside the discourses made by the Third World diplomats at the UNCLOS III, the new concepts for the international seabed regime marked a new beginning, a "breakthrough" in international relations:

> Here is an opening to industrial cooperation between the North and the South based not on aid but on sharing. . . . The International Seabed Authority, Utopian dream of twenty years ago, is now a fact of international law. Something has been moving.[30]

INTERNATIONAL SEABED AUTHORITY

Exploitation and exploration of resources from the seabed and the subsoil thereof beyond the limits of national jurisdiction was to be governed by an international seabed regime, known as the international Seabed Authority (hereafter referred to as the Authority), in accordance with Article 136 of the 1982 LOS Convention. Membership in the Authority comprises all states parties to the Convention, as well as observers at the UNCLOS III who sign the Final Act. (At this writing 155 sovereign states have signed the Convention, and 140 have signed the Final Act; and these states/territories have observer status: Netherlands Antilles, Trust Territory of the Pacific Islands, plus the European Economic Community and four national liberation movements.)

Article 157(1) states in general terms the purpose of the Authority as "the organization through which states parties shall, in accordance with this part, organize and control activities in the Area, particularly with a view to administering the resources of the Area.'' Article 157(2) states that the Authority's process and functions are ''those expressly conferred upon it by this Convention,'' which are extremely complex, and ''incidental powers'' implied as necessary for the exercise of those powers with respect to activities in the Area. Articles 157(3) and (4) point to the traditional sovereign equality concept as the basic principle for all members as far as membership rights and benefits are concerned.

Article 158 establishes four main organs for the Authority: the Assembly, a Council, a Secretariat and the Enterprise, the operating arm of the Authority.

Under Article 159, the Assembly is made up of all members of the Authority, with each having one vote. On matters of procedure, a majority vote of those present and voting shall suffice, but on substantial matters, a two-thirds majority is required. A question is treated as one of substance unless otherwise decided by a two-thirds vote in the Assembly. A vote of substance may be deferred by the President of the Assembly to allow a ''cooling-off period'' of not more than five calendar days. Or a vote may be postponed upon the request of at least one-fourth of the members pending an advisory opinion from the Seabed Disputes Chamber of Deputies of the International Tribunal for the convention.

Article 160(1) states that the Assembly is ''the supreme organ'' of the Authority and is empowered to set general policies. Then in Article 160(2) a list of specific functions and powers are enumerated:

(a) to elect the members of the Council in accordance with article 161;

(b) to elect the Secretary-General from among the candidates proposed by the Council;

(c) to elect, upon the recommendation of the Council, the members of the Governing Board of the Enterprise and the Director-General of the Enterprise;

(d) to establish such subsidiary organs as it finds necessary for the exercise of its functions in accordance with this Part. In the composition of these subsidiary organs due account shall be taken of the principle of equitable geographical distribution and of special interests and the need for members qualified and competent in the relevant technical questions dealt with by such organs;

(e) to assess the contributions of members to the administrative budget of the Authority in accordance with an agreed scale of assessment based upon the scale used for the regular budget of the United Nations until the Authority shall have sufficient income from other sources to meet its administrative expenses;

(f) (i) to consider and approve, upon the recommendation of the Council, the rules, regulations and procedures on the equitable sharing of financial and other economic benefits derived from activities in the Area and the payments and contributions made pursuant to article 82, taking into particular consideration the interests and needs of developing States and peoples who have not attained full independence or other self-governing status. If the Assembly does not approve the recommendations of the Council, the Assembly shall return them to the Council for reconsideration in the light of the views expressed by the Assembly;

(ii) to consider and approve the rules, regulations and procedures of the Authority, and any amendments thereto, provisionally adopted by the Council pursuant to article 162, paragraph 2 (o)(ii). These rules, regulations and procedures shall relate to prospecting, exploration and exploitation in the Area, the financial management and internal administration of the Authority, and, upon the recommendation of the Governing Board of the Enterprise, to the transfer of funds from the Enterprise to the Authority;

(g) to decide upon the equitable sharing of financial and other economic benefits derived from activities in the Area, consistent with this Convention and the rules, regulations and procedures of the Authority;

(h) to consider and approve the proposed annual budget of the Authority submitted by the Council;

(i) to examine periodic reports from the Council and from the Enterprise and special reports requested from the Council or any other organ of the Authority;

(j) to initiate studies and make recommendations for the purpose of promoting international co-operation concerning activities in the Area and encouraging the progressive development of international law relating thereto and its codification;

(k) to consider problems of a general nature in connection with activities in the Area arising in particular for developing States, as well as those problems for States in connection with activities in the Area that are due to their geographical location, particularly for land-locked and geographically disadvantaged States;

(l) to establish, upon the recommendation of the Council, on the basis of advice from the Economic Planning Commission, a system of compensation or other measures of economic adjustment assistance as provided in article 151, paragraph 10;

(m) to suspend the exercise of rights and privileges of membership pursuant to article 185;

(n) to discuss any question or matter within the competence of the Authority and to decide as to which organ of the Authority shall deal with any such question or matter not specifically entrusted to a particular organ, consistent with the distribution of powers and functions among the organs of the Authority.

The executive organ for the Authority is the Council. As a result of intensive debate and negotiation among the developing Third World nations and the industrialized developed states at the UNCLOS III, the Council has a complex formula for allocating its membership of thirty-six, distributed as follows under Article 161(1):

1. The Council shall consist of 36 members of the Authority elected by the Assembly in the following order:

(a) four members from among those States Parties which, during the last five years for which statistics are available, have either consumed more than 2 percent of total world consumption or have had net imports of more than 2 percent of total world imports of the commodities produced from the categories of minerals to be derived from the Area, and in any case one

State from the Eastern European (Socialist) region, as well as the largest consumer;

(b) four members from among the eight States Parties which have the largest investments in preparation for and in the conduct of activities in the Area, either directly or through their nationals, including at least one State from the Eastern European (Socialist) region;

(c) four members from among States Parties which on the basis of production in areas under their jurisdiction are major net exporters of the categories of minerals to be derived from the Area, including at least two developing States whose exports of such minerals have a substantial bearing upon their economies;

(d) six members from among developing States Parties, representing special interests. The special interests to be represented shall include those of States with large populations, States which are land-locked or geographically disadvantaged, States which are major importers of the categories of minerals to be derived from the Area, States which are potential producers of such minerals, and least developed States;

(e) eighteen members elected according to the principle of ensuring an equitable geographical distribution of seats in the Council as a whole, provided that each geographical region shall have at least one member elected under this subparagraph. For this purpose, the geographical regions shall be Africa, Asia, Eastern European (Socialist), Latin America and Western European and Others.

In addition, Article 161(2) requires that the Council membership must ensure representation of landlocked and geographically disadvantage states in reasonable proportion to their representation in the Assembly. Coastal states that are not qualified as members under Article 161(1)(a–d), or as major consumers/importers, or as large investors, or as major net exporters must also have some representation on the Council. Members of the Council are elected for a term of four years and serve on a rotation basis; that is, the term of one-half of the members of each group shall serve for only two years after the first election. Each member of the Council shall have one vote. On procedural issues, a simple majority of members present and voting prevails. But on substantive issues, three separate sets of decision-making formula are provided by Article 161(8)(b), (c) and (d): specified two-thirds majority, three-fourths majority, and by consensus. Decisions on questions of substance arising under provisions of Article 162, paragraph 2, subparagraphs (f), (g), (h), (i), (n), (p), (v) and Article 191 require a two-thirds majority, which must include a majority of the Council members:

(f) enter into agreements with the United Nations or other international organizations on behalf of the Authority and within its competence, subject to approval by the Assembly;

(g) consider the reports of the Enterprise and transmit them to the Assembly with its recommendations;

(h) present to the Assembly annual reports and such special reports as the Assembly may request;

(i) issue directives to the Enterprise in accordance with article 170;

(n) make recommendations to the Assembly, on the basis of advice from the Economic Planning Commission, for a system of compensation or other measures of economic adjustment assistance as provided in article 151, paragraph 10;

(p) review the collection of all payments to be made by or to the Authority in connection with operations pursuant to this Part;

(v) notify the Assembly upon a decision by the Sea-Bed Disputes Chamber in proceedings instituted under subparagraph (u), and make any recommendations which it may find appropriate with respect to measures to be taken.

Article 161 concerns the Sea-Bed Disputes Chamber's right to render advisory opinions.

Matters which fall under provisions of Article 162(2) require a three-fourths majority, which must also include a majority of the Council members:

(a) supervise and co-ordinate the implementation of the provisions of this Part on all questions and matters within the competence of the Authority and invite the attention of the Assembly to cases of non-compliance;

(b) propose to the Assembly a list of candidates for the election of the Secretary-General;

(c) recommend to the Assembly candidates for the election of the members of the Governing Board of the Enterprise and the Director-General of the Enterprise;

(d) establish, as appropriate, and with due regard to economy and efficiency, such subsidiary organs as it finds necessary for the exercise of its functions in accordance with this Part. In the composition of subsidiary organs, emphasis shall be placed on the need for members qualified and competent in relevant technical matters dealt with by those organs provided that due account shall be taken of the principle of equitable geographical distribution and of special interests;

(e) adopt its rules of procedure including the method of selecting its president;

(1) exercise control over activities in the Area in accordance with article 153, paragraph 4, and the rules, regulations and procedures of the Authority;

(r) submit the proposed annual budget of the Authority to the Assembly for its approval;

(s) make recommendations to the Assembly concerning policies on any question or matter within the competence of the Authority;

(t) make recommendations to the Assembly concerning suspension of the exercise of the rights and privileges of membership pursuant to article 185;

(u) institute proceedings on behalf of the Authority before the Sea-Bed Disputes Chamber in cases of non-compliance;

(w) issue emergency orders, which may include orders for the suspension or adjustment of operations, to prevent serious harm to the marine environment arising out of activities in the Area;

(x) disapprove areas for exploitation by contractors or the Enterprise in cases where substantial evidence indicates the risk of serious harm to the marine environment;

A three-fourths majority vote of the Council is also required on matters concerning expansion of its subsidiary bodies under Article 163(2), borrowing power of the Assembly under Article 174(3), and financial arrangements for the Enterprise under Article 11 of Annex IV.

In addition there are matters of importance for the Council to decide by what is known as "consensus," meaning "the absence of any formal objection" within two weeks of submission of a proposal or a veto power by a member of the Council on matters under Article 162(2), subparagraphs (m) and (o):

(m) take, upon the recommendation of the Economic Planning Commission, necessary and appropriate measures in accordance with article 150, subparagraph (h), to provide protection from the adverse economic effects specified therein;

(o) (i) recommend to the Assembly rules, regulations and procedures on the equitable sharing of financial and other economic benefits derived from activities in the Area and the payments and contributions made pursuant to article 82, taking into particular consideration the interests and needs of the developing States and peoples who have not attained full independence or other self-governing status;

(ii) adopt and apply provisionally, pending approval by the Assembly, the rules, regulations and procedures of the Authority, and any amendments thereto, taking into account the recommendations of the Legal and Technical Commission or other subordinate organ concerned. These rules, regulations and procedures shall relate to prospecting, exploration and exploitation in the Area and the financial management and internal administration of the Authority. Priority shall be given to the adoption of rules, regulations and procedures for the exploration for and exploitation of polymetallic nodules. Rules, regulations and procedures for the exploration for and exploitation of any resource other than polymetallic nodules shall be adopted within three years from the date of a request to the Authority by any of its members to adopt such rules, regulations and procedures in respect of such resource. All rules, regulations and procedures shall remain in effect on a provisional basis until approved by the Assembly or until amended by the Council in the light of any views expressed by the Assembly;

Also, "consensus" must be applied to the adoption of any amendment to Part XI of the 1982 LOS Convention on the Area.

The Council is empowered to establish subsidiary organs. Article 163 names two such organs: an Economic Planning Commission and a Legal and Technical Commission. Both bodies have a membership of fifteen elected for a five-year term by the Council. In Article 164 the Economic Planning Commission is charged with responsibility for: reviewing the trends and factors affecting the supply, demand and prices of seabed minerals derived from the Area; making studies of adverse effects of seabed mining on the economies of the developing nations; and proposing to the Council a "system of compensation or other measures of economic assistance for developing states which suffer adverse effects caused by activities in the Area." Under Article 165 the Legal and Technical Commission has extensive jurisdiction on the following: reviewing formal written plans of work in the Area; supervising activities in the Area; preparing and recommending assessment for environmental protection and implications of activities in the Area; recommending a monitoring program on pollution of the marine environment; helping the Council in proceedings before the Seabed Dispute Chamber; recommending disapproval of activities engaged in by contractors or the Enterprise on risk of serious harm to the marine environment; and calculating production ceilings and issuing production authorizations.

The Authority's administrative staff, the Secretariat, is headed by a Secretary-General. Under Article 166 he is elected by the Authority's Assembly for a four-year term and may be reelected. The Secretariat is essentially a scientific and technical staff with international character and responsible only to the Authority. (Also see separate sections in this chapter on the Area, Arusha Understanding, Consortia, the Enterprise, Financial Arrangements, Fundamental Principles, Maltese Initiative, Moratorium Resolution, Pioneer Investors, and Preparatory Commission.)

Significance. The provisions in the 1982 LOS Convention on the International Seabed Authority as presented here reflect the compromises achieved between two powerful negotiation groups at UNCLOS III: the developing states of the Third World (the Group of 77) and the industrialized developed states (the West, plus Japan). The structure of the Authority and the powers entrusted in the organs established under it for deep-seabed mining are forceful evidence of the compromises and underlying conflicts between these two political groups.

First, Article 157 established an international organization and "monopoly" through which states parties to the Convention are permitted to organize and control activities in the Area. This means that no one can engage in seabed mining in the Area without entering into a contractual arrangement with the Authority. Disputes may arise as to the extent of the Authority's control over "activities." Are "activities" limited only to those related to exploitation and exploration of seabed mineral resources? Negotiation history does show the conflict over definition expressed by the developing states, which favored "all" activities, and the developed states, which sought to limit the Authority's activities to those related only to seabed resources.[31] Article 1(3) of the 1982 LOS Convention defines the meaning of "activities" as "All activities of exploration for, and exploitation of, the resources of the Area." This limitation of the Authority's power over resources-related activities in the Area is clear evidence of the developing states' concession to the developed nations.

Compromise is also evident in the very structural setup for the Authority, which balances the powers of the Assembly and the Council. The developing nations can control the Assembly on the one-nation, one-vote basis because of their numerical majority, but it is only the general policymaking organ of the Authority. In fact, the executive power in policy implementation rests in the Council, whose membership is not based on the numerical strength of the Group of 77 but on a representation formula of mineral consumption, investment in the Area, production, and other "special interests." Thus, the Council must decide whether, where and under what conditions exploitation takes place in the Area. It decides what company's work plan is to be approved. It controls the Authority's budget and the power of budget formulation process for the Assembly's approval. The Council exercises influence over other organs of the Authority through the process of candidate selection or recommendation for their executive officers. While it may be argued that the Group of 77 could exercise control in the Council by its numerical strength, as suggested in two recent studies, presumably the West could obtain eight or nine seats on the Council, three or four seats for the Soviet bloc, and twenty-four or twenty-five for the developing nations.[32]

In its three-tiered voting system on most important questions for the Authority, the "consensus" or unanimity rule would provide the necessary safeguard to protect the industrialized nations' interests. On matters that require three-fourths vote, the West needs only one or two additional votes to its total of eight or nine votes in the thirty-six-member Council to block any decision considered harmful to the interests of the more advanced industrialized nations.

MALTESE INITIATIVE

The Maltese Initiative refers to a *note verbale* submitted August 17, 1967, by Dr. Arvid Pardo, the representative of Malta to the United Nations, for inclusion as an agenda item in the 1967 General Assembly. It was entitled "Declaration and treaty concerning the reservation for peaceful purposes of the seabed and of the ocean floor, underlying the seas beyond the limits of present national jurisdiction, and the use of their resources in the interests of mankind."[33] In an explanatory memorandum, Pardo proposed:

> that the time has come to declare the sea-bed and the ocean floor a common heritage of mankind and that immediate steps should be taken to draft a treaty embodying, *inter alia*, the following principles:
>
> (a) the sea-bed and ocean floor, underlying the seas beyond the limits of present national jurisdiction, are not subject to national appropriation in any manner whatsoever; . . .
>
> (c) The use of the sea-bed and of the ocean floor, underlying the seas beyond the

limits of present national jurisdiction, and their economic exploitation shall be undertaken with the aim of safeguarding the interests of mankind. The net financial benefits derived from the use and exploitation of the sea-bed and of the ocean floor shall be used primarily to promote the development of poor countries.

Thus, a bold initiative was officially launched for an international regime for the seabed governed and controlled by an international body for the benefit of mankind. This move inspired and stimulated a host of subsequent United Nations debates and actions which finally culminated in the signing of the 1982 LOS Convention. It may well be pointed out that the idea of sharing the benefits from the seabed resources for mankind as a whole was advanced by others preceding the Maltese Initiative of August 17, 1967. For instance, United States President Lyndon B. Johnson declared in July 1966 that "Under no circumstances, we believe, must we ever allow the prospects of a rich harvest of mineral wealth to create a new form of colonial competition among the maritime nations. We must be careful to avoid a race to grab and hold the lands under the high seas; for the ocean bottoms are, and remain, the legacy of all human beings."[34]

The Maltese proposal formed the basis for the first of the many United Nations General Assembly resolutions regarding the seabed. Resolution 2340 (XXII), adopted on December 18, 1967, established an ad hoc committee to study the peaceful uses of the seabed beyond the limits of national jurisdiction. From then until the end of 1976, over a period of a decade, the United Nations General Assembly adopted ten resolutions dealing with the various aspects of the seabed:

1. A/Res/2467 (XXIII)	21 December 1968
2. A/Res/2574 (XXIV)	15 December 1969
3. A/Res/2749 (XXV)	17 December 1970
4. A/Res/2750 (XXV)	17 December 1970
5. A/Res/2881 (XXVI)	21 December 1971
6. A/Res/3029 (XXVII)	18 December 1972
7. A/Res/3067 (XXVIII)	16 November 1973
8. A/Res/3334 (XXIX)	17 December 1974
9. A/Res/3483 (XXX)	12 December 1975
10. A/Res/3163 (XXXI)	10 December 1976

Also, one needs to mention here that in Resolution 2750(XXV) of December 17, 1970, adopted by a vote of 106 to 7 with six abstentions, the United Nations General Assembly called for the convening of a third conference on the Law of the Sea that

would deal with the establishment of an equitable international regime including an international machinery for the area and the resources of the seabed and ocean floor, and the subsoil thereof, beyond the national jurisdiction and use of these resources in the interest of mankind.

(Also see separate sections in this chapter on the Area, Fundamental Principles, Group of 77, and the Moratorium Resolution.)

Significance. The significance of the Maltese Initiative, a historic event in the annals of the law of the sea, lies in its impact on the involvement of the United Nations and its members in the new subject of international control of the deep seabed beyond national jurisdiction, separate from the codification of conflicting national boundary claims to the oceans. The Maltese proposal developed a new but controversial concept of the common heritage of mankind over the mineral wealth on the ocean floor. This concept served to provide the link between sharing deep-seabed wealth with the Third World developing nations and the "New International Economic Order," which called for price stabilization of primary commodities and the reduction and cancellation of debts incurred by the poor Third World nations. The euphoria over the sharing of deep-seabed mineral wealth on the part of the developing nations has also brought into sharp focus the ideological conflict between the Third World and the industrialized developed countries, as revealed in the debates in the United Nations Law of the Sea Conferences.

Finally, the Maltese Initiative provided both the impetus and the legal rationale for the need to establish a cooperative organization to control, manage and operate an international area reserved specifically for the benefit of mankind. The Maltese proposal became, in the end, the focal point in the seabed debate from the mid–1960s to the conclusion of UNCLOS III in 1982. The key ideas contained in the Maltese Initiative have now been enshrined in Part XI of the 1982 LOS Convention, the section which the United States refuses to endorse without modification, a position shared to some degree by Germany and Great Britain.

THE MORATORIUM RESOLUTION

On December 15, 1969, the United Nations General Assembly adopted Resolution 2574-D(XXIV), known as the "Moratorium Resolution," which declared, pending the establishment of an international regime for the seabed beyond the limits of national jurisdiction, that

> (a) states and persons, physical or juridical, are bound to refrain from all activities of exploitation of the resources of the area of the seabed and ocean floor, and the subsoil thereof, beyond the limits of national jurisdiction; b) no claim to any part of that area or its resources shall be recognized.

It was this particular resolution, prohibiting any further seabed mineral exploitation pending the establishment of an international seabed regime, that clearly separated the developed nations from the developing nations of the Third World. Although the vote of the General Assembly plenary on the "Moratorium Resolution" was sixty-two for, twenty-eight against, with twenty-eight abstentions, those voting against the resolution included Australia, Canada, France, Japan, the Netherlands, Norway, the Soviet Union, the United Kingdom and the United States.

It was argued by representatives of a number of developing nations, particularly by some Latin American states, such as Brazil, Chile and Mexico, that any mining activities on the deep seabed by the developed states before the establishment of an international seabed regime was "unlawful" and contrary to the intent of Resolution 2340(XXII) adopted on December 18, 1967. In part, this resolution states:

> the importance of preserving the seabed and the ocean floor, and the subsoil thereof, beyond the limits of national jurisdiction, from actions and uses which might be detrimental to the common interests of mankind.[35]

The United States argued that all United Nations General Assembly resolutions have no binding legal effect.[36] The United Kingdom and the Soviet Union expressed the view that not only should the General Assembly not modify existing international law by resolutions, but that to prohibit exploitation on the seabed infringed on the "freedom of the open seas."[37] (Also see separate sections in this chapter on the Area, Consortia, Fundamental Principles, Group of 77, International Seabed Authority and Maltese Initiative.)

Significance. In spite of the objection to and nonbinding effect of the Moratorium Resolution raised by the developed countries, continued references were made in a number of subsequent United Nations General Assembly resolutions, most notably Resolution 3029 (XXVII) of December 18, 1972. Even more significant are the divergent views reflected by the developed and developing nations on the applicability of the traditional freedom of the seas. The developed nations held firmly to the view that deep seabed exploitation was a "reasonable use of the high seas"; the developing nations clung to the view that the Moratorium Resolution must be legally binding upon all states and that the principle of the high seas was inapplicable as far as the deep seabed was concerned. The practical result of the Moratorium Resolution at the time of its adoption by the General Assembly was that it had no influence on seabed mining activities except for its "psychological effect" for the developing states.[38] But, as pointed out by Kronmiller and Smith, scholars seemed to hold the view that the Moratorium Resolution had no legal binding effect.[39]

PARALLEL SYSTEM

At the UNCLOS III negotiation sessions there was extensive debate on the key question of who must be given access to exploit the mineral resources in the Area. The developing nations, the Group of 77, supported the unitary system—that is, the International Seabed Authority must have the exclusive or sole right to deep-seabed mining beyond the limits of national jurisdiction on behalf of all nations for the benefit of mankind. The developed industrialized states, on the other hand, held firmly to the view, at least initially, that anyone, a state or an international mining consortium, could have the access to mine the seabed resources and that the International Seabed Authority should merely serve as an "international claim office" processing applications and issuing licenses. Attempts were made at these negotiations to bring the two divergent viewpoints closer in the form of a compromise. In the spring of 1976, a compromise proposal, known as the "parallel system," emerged. On the one side, the Authority's operating arm, the Enterprise, was to engage directly in mining operations in the Area, and on the other hand, access was to be given to state enterprises and private corporations qualified for seabed mining and licensed by the Authority.[40] The compromise was not acceptable to the Group of 77 and an impasse was reached at the ends of the fifth and sixth sessions in the spring of 1977. It was not until the seventh session, which began on March 28, 1978, in Geneva, that the impasse was broken with the acceptance by both sides of the framework contained in Article 153 of the 1982 LOS Convention. The parallel or "dual" system of exploitation in the Area is provided for in Article 153(2), which states that

> 2. Activities in the Area shall be carried out as prescribed in paragraph 3:
>
> (a) by the Enterprise, and
>
> (b) in association with the Authority by States Parties, or state enterprises or natural or juridical persons which possess the nationality of States Parties or are effectively controlled by them or their nationals, when sponsored by such States, or any group of the foregoing which meets the requirements provided in this Part and in Annex III.

In order to meet the demands of the developed states that qualified miners be given access to seabed mining in the Area, qualifications to entitle an applicant to engage in exploitation activities had to be clearly specified. Thus, Article 4 of Annex III, on basic conditions of prospecting and exploitation, was drafted to determine who is qualified and by what criteria a prospective miner is to receive a mining contract from the Authority, along with the Enterprise:

Article 4: Qualifications of applicants

1. Applicants, other than the Enterprise, shall be qualified if they have the nationality or control and sponsorship required by article 153, paragraph 2(b), and if they follow the procedures and meet the qualification standards set forth in the rules, regulations and procedures of the Authority.

2. Except as provided in paragraph 6, such qualification standards shall relate to the

financial and technical capabilities of the applicant and his performance under any previous contracts with the Authority.

3. Each applicant shall be sponsored by the State Party of which it is a national unless the applicant has more than one nationality, as in the case of a partnership or consortium of entities from several States, in which event all States Parties involved shall sponsor the application, or unless the applicant is effectively controlled by another State Party or its nationals, in which event both States Parties shall sponsor the application. The criteria and procedures for implementation of the sponsorship requirements shall be set forth in the rules, regulations and procedures of the Authority.

4. The sponsoring State or States shall, pursuant to article 139, have the responsibility to ensure, within their legal systems, that a contractor so sponsored shall carry out activities in the Area in conformity with the terms of its contract and its obligations under this Convention. A sponsoring State shall not, however, be liable for damage caused by any failure of a contractor sponsored by it to comply with its obligations if that State Party has adopted laws and regulations and taken administrative measures which are, within the framework of its legal system, reasonably appropriate for securing compliance by persons under its jurisdiction.

5. The procedures for assessing the qualifications of States Parties which are applicants shall take into account their character as States.

6. The qualification standards shall require that every applicant, without exception, shall as part of his application undertake:

(a) to accept as enforceable and comply with the applicable obligations created by the provisions of Part XI, the rules, regulations and procedures of the Authority, the decisions of the organs of the Authority and terms of his contracts with the Authority;

(b) to accept control by the Authority of activities in the Area, as authorized by this Convention;

(c) to provide the Authority with a written assurance that his obligations under the contract will be fulfilled in good faith;

(d) to comply with the provisions on the transfer of technology set forth in article 5 of this Annex.

Paragraph 3 specifically applies to a deep-seabed mining consortium with several states as partners. In such cases all states involved must sponsor the application for license from the Authority; or if the applicant is in effect controlled by another state, both states must sponsor the application. (Also see separate sections in this chapter on the Area, Arusha Understanding, the Enterprise, Group of 77, International Seabed Authority and Pioneer Investors.)

Significance. Suggested originally by Henry Kissinger and negotiated by Elliot Richardson, the parallel system was the compromise that broke the deadlock at the UNCLOS III over the access to deep-seabed mining. It offered the ideologically opposing camps—the industrialized developed states and the Third World developing states as represented by the Group of 77—a proposal to "split the difference" by allowing, on the one hand, the private corporations and state enterprises of the developed states to mine the Area under the Authority's license and, on the other hand, the Enterprise to mine for the benefit of mankind. In addition, the compromise contains the understanding of a series of "package deals" for both sides. In return for private corporations having access to deep seabed mining in the Area under international license, the developing states were assured transfer of mining technology and capital available for the Enterprise to operate. In an attempt to ensure against any adverse effects on the economies of the land-based producers of strategic minerals, by agreeing to make access possible for private corporations and state enterprises of the industrialized nations, the Group of 77 obtained the privilege to write protective clauses regarding seabed mining production into the 1982 LOS Convention.

More important, a compromise in the form of a parallel system paved the way for overall agreement and acceptance of a comprehensive law of the sea convention under which free transit through international straits was guaranteed, as well as preservation of sea lanes through archipelagic waters and high sea freedoms within national claims. All of these are matters of vital interest to developed nations, particularly the United States, for it is better to have a comprehensive law of the sea convention than none at all—at least that was the view of the U.S. negotiators at that time.

PIONEER INVESTORS

As a way of enticing the major industrialized states to continue negotiating on some of the key provisions dealing with the exploitation and exploration of the deep seabed mineral resources and, at the same time, of providing safeguards for the heavy investments already made by the international deep seabed mining consortia, a set of compromise resolutions were adopted as part of the Final Act for the 1982 LOS Convention.

First, for the purpose of providing a forum for continued negotiation on the seabed, the Preparatory Commission for the International Seabed Authority was entrusted with the task of formulating rules, regulations and procedures for the Authority. Second, for the purpose of providing safeguards for those industrialized and/or international mining consortia which had already made heavy investments in deep seabed mining activities, a set of guidelines governing a special regime for the so-called pioneer investors was established under Resolution II, Annex I, of the Final Act.

There were three types of pioneer investors named in paragraph 1(a) of Resolution II:

> (a) "pioneer investor" refers to:
>
> (i) France, India, Japan and the Union of Soviet Socialist Republics, or a state enterprise of each of those States or one natural or juridical person which possesses the nationality of or is effectively controlled by each of those States, or their nationals, provided that the State concerned signs the

> Convention and the State or state enterprise or natural or juridical person has expended, before 1 January 1983, an amount equivalent to at least $US 30 million (United States dollars calculated in constant dollars relative to 1982) in pioneer activities and has expended no less than 10 percent of that amount in the location, survey and evaluation of the area referred to in paragraph 3 (a);
>
> (ii) four entities, whose components being natural or juridical persons, possess the nationality of one or more of the following States, or are effectively controlled by one or more of them or their nationals: Belgium, Canada, the Federal Republic of Germany, Italy, Japan, the Netherlands, the United Kingdom of Great Britain and Northern Ireland, and the United States of America, provided that the certifying State or States sign the Convention and the entity concerned has expended, before 1 January 1983, the levels of expenditure for the purpose stated in subparagraph (i);
>
> (iii) any developing State which signs the Convention or any state enterprise or natural or juridical person which possesses the nationality of such State or is effectively controlled by it or its nationals, or any group of the foregoing, which, before 1 January 1985, has expended the levels of expenditure for the purpose stated in subparagraph (i);

For the first type of pioneer investors, in addition to France and Japan, India and the Soviet Union are included, plus a state enterprise of each of the four states and "one natural or juridical person possessing the nationality of, or effectively controlled by, each of the four states named or its nationals." To be eligible as a pioneer investor under the first type, the following requirements must be met before registration approval is given:

1. The state so named must sign the 1982 LOS Convention.
2. At least U.S.$ 30 million must have been spent on pioneer activities before January 1, 1983.
3. No less than 10 percent of the amount had been spent in the location, survey and evolution of the mine site to be registered.

A second type of prospective pioneer investor refers exclusively to the four well-known international mining consortia of Kennecott Consortium, Ocean Mining Associates, Ocean Management Incorporated and Ocean Minerals Company, all controlled by one or more of the following eight states: Belgium, Canada, the Federal Republic of Germany, Italy, Japan, the Netherlands, the United Kingdom and the United States. To qualify as a registered pioneer investor, each of the four entities must be certified by a state that has signed the 1982 LOS Convention. Based on statements made by the various delegations at the conference, in the case of a consortium controlled by four different states, the interpretation seemed to imply that the signature of only one state would be sufficient.[41] The refusal by the United States, the Federal Republic of Germany and the United Kingdom to sign the 1982 LOS Convention may in the future create some legal complications for this category of pioneer investors. As is the case with the first type of pioneer investor, certification must be provided to show that these four entities have spent at least U.S.$ 30 million before January 1, 1983, in pioneer deep-seabed mining activities.

The third type of pioneer investors to be registered includes those developing states or any state enterprise of such states or any natural or juridical person possessing the nationality of or being effectively controlled by them or their nationals or ''any group of the foregoing.'' To qualify for registration under this category of pioneer investor, the concerned developing state must be a signatory to the 1982 LOS Convention and provide evidence of expenditure of no less than U.S.$ 30 million before January 1, 1985. However, Brazil has requested the Preparatory Commission to extend the January 1, 1985, date, and thus the date set forth in Resolution II may no longer hold.[42]

Pioneer Activities

Entities registered as pioneer investors are permitted to engage in pioneer activities on the deep seabed in the Area as defined in paragraph 1(b), Resolution II, Annex I, of the Final Act:

> (b) ''pioneer activities'' means undertakings, commitments of financial and other assets, investigations, findings, research, engineering development and other activities relevant to the identification, discovery, and systematic analysis and evaluation of polymetallic nodules and to the determination of the technical and economic feasibility of exploitation. Pioneer activities include:
>
> (i) any at-sea observation and evaluation activity which has as its objective the establishment and documentation of the nature, shape, concentration, location and grade of polymetallic nodules and of the environmental, technical and other appropriate factors which must be taken into account before exploitation;
>
> (ii) the recovery from the Area of polymetallic nodules with a view to the designing, fabricating and testing of equipment which is intended to be used in the exploitation of polymetallic nodules;

These activities of exploitation and exploration must be approved by the Preparatory Commission upon submission of a plan of work by a registered pioneer investor.

Pioneer Area and Allocation

The Preparatory Commission has the responsibility to (1) make allocations of one pioneer area for each pioneer investor to conduct exclusively pioneer activities and (2) designate an area reserved for use by the Authority. Paragraph 1(e) of Resolution II, Annex I, defines the pioneer areas as:

(e) ''pioneer area'' means an area allocated by the Commission to a pioneer investor for pioneer activities pursuant to this resolution. A pioneer area shall not exceed 150,000 square kilometres. The pioneer investor shall relinquish portions of the pioneer area to revert to the Area, in accordance with the following schedule:

(i) 20 per cent of the area allocated by the end of the third year from the date of the allocation;

(ii) an additional 10 per cent of the area allocated by the end of the fifth year from the date of the allocation;

(iii) an additional 20 per cent of the area allocated or such larger amount as would exceed the exploitation area decided upon by the Authority in its rules, regulations and procedures, after eight years from the date of the allocation of the area or the date of the award of a production authorization, whichever is earlier;

Thus a pioneer investor is allowed to work in only one pioneer area that does not exceed 150,000 square kilometers. Furthermore, a pioneer investor must set aside or relinquish, over a period of eight years from the date of allocation by the Preparatory Commission, 50 percent of the total area to the international Area for use by the International Seabed Authority. (The international Area is defined by the 1982 LOS Convention as the seabed and its subsoil thereof beyond the limits of national jurisdiction.)

Plan of Work Approval

A pioneer investor is not permitted to engage in commercial processing of deep-seabed mining in the allocated pioneer area unless its plan of work has been approved by the Preparatory Commission. Paragraph 8, Resolution II, Annex I established a procedure for approval of a plan of work which has been submitted by a pioneer investor:

(a) Within six months of the entry into force of the Convention and certification by the Commission in accordance with paragraph 11, of compliance with this resolution, the pioneer investor so registered shall apply to the Authority for approval of a plan of work for exploration and exploitation, in accordance with the Convention. The plan of work in respect of such application shall comply with and be governed by the relevant provisions of the Convention and the rules, regulations and procedures of the Authority, including those on the operational requirements, the financial requirements and the undertakings concerning the transfer of technology. Accordingly, the Authority shall approve such application.

(b) When an application for approval of a plan of work is submitted by an entity other than a State, pursuant to subparagraph (a), the certifying State or States shall be deemed to be the sponsoring State for the purposes of Annex III, article 4, of the Convention, and shall thereupon assume such obligations.

(c) No plan of work for exploration and exploitation shall be approved unless the certifying State is a Party to the Convention. In the case of the entities referred to in

Table 7.2
Status of State Composition of International Consortia

	Composition of	
	Signatory States	Non-Signatory States
1. Kennecott Consortium (KCON)	Canada Japan	United Kingdom United States
2. Ocean Mining Associates (OMA)	Belgium Italy	United States
3. Ocean Management, Inc. (OMI)	Canada Japan	Federated Republic of Germany United States
4. Ocean Minerals Company (OMC)	Netherlands	United States

Source: E. D. Brown, *Seabed Energy and Mineral Resources and the Law of the Sea* (Gaithersburg, Md.: Graham and Trotman, 1985), chapter 7, p. 13. Used by permission.

paragraph 1 (a) (ii), the plan of work for exploration and exploitation shall not be approved unless all the States whose natural or juridical persons comprise those entities are Parties to the Convention. If any such State fails to ratify the Convention within six months after it has received a notification from the Authority that an application by it, or sponsored by it, is pending, its status as a pioneer investor or certifying State, as the case may be, shall terminate, unless the Council, by a majority of three fourths of its members present and voting, decides to postpone the terminal date for a period not exceeding six months.

A plan of work submitted by a registered pioneer investor is a form of contract between it and the Authority. The contract must be submitted for approval within six months of the entry into force of the 1982 LOS Convention and be accompanied by a certification from the Preparatory Commission that the pioneer investor has complied with the provisions under Resolution II. Paragraph 8(c) makes it clear that the plan of work cannot be approved unless all the certifying states sign the 1982 LOS Convention. Thus, the failure of the Federal Republic of Germany, the United Kingdom and the United States to sign the 1982 LOS Convention would permit registration, but prevent the four international deep seabed mining consortia's work plans from being approved, since each consortium has at least one controlling state that has not acceded to the Convention before such application is to be made. At the time of writing, the status of the state composition of the four international consortia in relation to the 1982 LOS Convention is laid out in Table 7.2.[43]

Suggestions have been made with respect to the ways by which the requirement under paragraph 8(c) could be circumvented.[44] For instance, a nonsignatory state may withdraw from the consortium by transferring its interests to the other controlling state signatories to the Convention. However, paragraph 10(a–c), Resolution II, seems to offer a better method for the four international deep-seabed mining consortia to circumvent the restriction set forth in paragraph 8(c):

10. (a) Any rights acquired by entitied or natural or juridical persons which possess the nationality of or are effectively controlled by a State or States whose status as certifying

State has been terminated, shall lapse unless the pioneer investor changes its nationality and sponsorship within six months of the date of such termination, as provided for in subparagraph (c).

(b) A pioneer investor may change its nationality and sponsorship from that existing at the time of its registration as a pioneer investor to that of any State Party to the Convention which has effective control over the pioneer investor in terms of paragraph 1(a).

(c) Changes of nationality and sponsorship pursuant to this paragraph shall not affect any right or priority conferred on a pioneer investor pursuant to paragraphs 6 and 8.

Thus, in the case of any of the four international consortia, registration for pioneer investor status can be certified by the signatory states by changing its nationality or sponsorship. But for the work plans to be approved, it will be necessary for the nonsignatory states—Federal Republic of Germany, the United Kingdom and the United States—either to withdraw from the composition or to have their interests transferred to the signatory states, as provided in paragraph 10(c), Resolution II.

Production Authorization

There is established an order of priority for commercial production in deep seabed mining, as provided in paragraph 9 (a–g), Resolution II of the Final Act:

9. (a) In the allocation of production authorizations, in accordance with article 151 and Annex III, article 7, of the Convention, the pioneer investors who have obtained approval of plans of work for exploration and exploitation shall have priority over all applicants other than the Enterprise which shall be entitled to production authorizations for two mine sites including that referred to in article 151, paragraph 5, of the Convention. After each of the pioneer investors has obtained production authorization for its first mine site, the priority for the Enterprise contained in Annex III, article 7, paragraph 6, of the Convention shall apply.

(b) Production authorizations shall be issued to each pioneer investor within 30 days of the date on which that pioneer investor notifies the Authority that it will commence commercial production within five years. If a pioneer investor is unable to begin production within the period of five years for reasons beyond its control, it shall apply to the Legal and Technical Commission for an extension of time. That Commission shall grant the extension of time, for a period not exceeding five years and not subject to further extension, if it is satisfied that the pioneer investor cannot begin on an economically viable basis at the time originally planned. Nothing in this subparagraph shall prevent the Enterprise or any other pioneer applicant, who has notified the Authority that it will commence commercial production within five years, from being given a priority over any applicant who has obtained an extension of time under this subparagraph.

(c) If the Authority, upon being given notice, pursuant to subparagraph (b), determines that the commencement of commercial production within five years would exceed the production ceiling in article 151, paragraphs 2 to 7, of the Convention, the applicant shall hold a priority over any other applicant for the award of the next production authorization allowed by the production ceiling.

(d) If two or more pioneer investors apply for production authorizations to begin commercial production at the same time and article 151, paragraphs 2 to 7, of the Convention, would not permit all such production to commence simultaneously, the Authority shall notify the pioneer investors concerned. Within three months of such notification, they shall decide whether and, if so, to what extent they wish to apportion the allowable tonnage among themselves.

(e) If, pursuant to subparagraph (d), the pioneer investors concerned decide not to apportion the available production among themselves they shall agree on an order of priority for production authorizations and all subsequent applications for production authorizations will be granted after those referred to in this subparagraph have been approved.

(f) If, pursuant to subparagraph (d), the pioneer investors concerned decide to apportion the available production among themselves, the Authority shall award each of them a production authorization for such lesser quantity as they have agreed. In each case the stated production requirements of the applicant will be approved and their full production will be allowed as soon as the production ceiling admits of additional capacity sufficient for the applicants involved in the competition. All subsequent applications for production authorizations will only be granted after the requirements of this subparagraph have been met and the applicant is no longer subject to the reduction of production provided for in this subparagraph.

(g) If the parties fail to reach agreement within the stated time period, the matter shall be decided immediately by the means provided for in paragraph 5(c) in accordance with the criteria set forth in Annex III, article 7, paragraphs 3 and 5, of the Convention.

The production priority order is reserved first for the Enterprise, which is entitled to two mining sites in the Area, as provided under Article 151. The Enterprise's initial production is for a quantity of 38,000 metric tons of nickel. Then production authorization will be given to each pioneer investor within thirty days of notification to the Authority that it will begin commercial production within five years. Pioneer investors must adhere to the production ceiling provided in Article 151 (2–7). If commercial production exceeds the required ceiling limit, production authorization will be delayed, but "the application shall hold a priority over any applicant for the award of the next production authorization allowed by the production ceiling."

When more than two pioneer investors apply for commercial production at the same time and if, under Article 151 (2–7), the production ceiling would not permit all such production to begin simultaneously, the parties involved must make arrangements to apportion the allowable tonnage among themselves within three months of notification by the Authority. And, under paragraph 9(g), if the parties fail to reach an agreement on the apportionment of production ceiling, the dispute must be referred, under paragraph 5(c), Resolution II, Annex I, Final Act for binding arbitration in accordance with United Nations (UNCITRAL) Arbitration Rules.

Registration as Pioneer Investor

Registration of a pioneer investor can begin as soon as the Preparatory Commission is ready to function—that is, upon signature of or accession to the 1982 LOS Convention by fifty states in accordance with Resolution I, Annex I of the Final Act. Paragraph 2 of Resolution II then provides that:

> 2. As soon as the Commission begins to function, any State which has signed the Convention may apply to the Commission on its behalf or on behalf of any state enterprise or entity or natural or juridical person specified in paragraph 1(a) for registration as a pioneer investor. The Commission shall register the applicant as a pioneer investor if the application:
>
> (a) is accompanied, in the case of a State which has signed the Convention, by a statement certifying the level of expenditure made in accordance with paragraph 1(a), and, in all other cases, a certificate concerning such level of expenditure issued by a certifying State or States; and
>
> (b) is in conformity with the other provisions of this resolution, including paragraph 5.

Thus, a signatory state may apply on its own behalf or on behalf of any of the prospective pioneer investors for registration with the Preparatory Commission if, first of all, conditions set forth in paragraph 2(a) are met. Then the applicant must also satisfy the requirements contained in paragraph 5(a–d) on resolution of overlapping claims and conflicts in the pioneer areas:

> 5. (a) Any State which has signed the Convention and which is a prospective certifying State shall ensure, before making applications to the Commission under paragraph 2, that areas in respect of which applications are made do not overlap one another or areas previously allocated as pioneer areas. The States concerned shall keep the Commission currently and fully informed of any efforts to resolve conflicts with respect to overlapping claims and of the results thereof.
>
> (b) Certifying States shall ensure, before the entry into force of the Convention, that pioneer activities are conducted in a manner compatible with it.
>
> (c) The prospective certifying States, including all potential claimants, shall resolve their conflicts as required under subparagraph (a) by negotiations within a reasonable period. If such conflicts have not been resolved by 1 March 1983, the prospective certifying States shall arrange for the submission of all such claims to binding arbitration in accordance with UNCITRAL Arbitration Rules to commence not later than 1 May 1983 and to be completed by 1 December 1984. If one of the States concerned does not wish to participate in the arbitration, it shall arrange for a juridical person of its nationality to represent it in the arbitration. The arbitral tribunal may, for good cause, extend the deadline for the making of the award for one or more 30-day periods.
>
> (d) In determining the issue as to which applicant involved in a conflict shall be awarded all or part of each area in conflict, the arbitral tribunal shall find a solution which is fair

and equitable, having regard, with respect to each applicant involved in the conflict, to the following factors:

(i) the deposit of the list of relevant co-ordinates with the prospective certifying State or States not later than the date of adoption of the Final Act or 1 January 1983, whichever is earlier;

(ii) the continuity and extent of past activities relevant to each area in conflict and to the application area of which it is a part;

(iii) the date on which each pioneer investor concerned or predecessor in interest or component organization thereof commenced activities at sea in the application area;

(iv) the financial cost of activities measured in constant United States dollars relevant to each area in conflict and to the application area of which it is a part; and

(v) the time when those activities were carried out and the quality of activities.

On August 17, 1987, and again on December 17, 1987, the General Committee of the Preparatory Commission, acting on behalf of the Preparatory Commission, registered India as the first pioneer investor in the International Seabed Area and approved respectively applications of France, Japan and the Soviet Union as the other three pioneer investors.[45]

Locations of the approved regions for pioneer investors of France and Japan are shown in Figures 7.3 and 7.4. The Clarion-Clipperton Region in the Pacific can be seen in Figure 7.2.

India made its declaration for registration as a pioneer investor under Resolution II on August 4, 1987. The application was reported by the Group of Experts on December 4, 1987. The Indian application area is in the central Indian Ocean beyond the limits of national jurisdiction of any state and has no overlapping claims.[46] It is an area totaling 300,000 square kilometers in the central Indian Ocean. Metal content for the Indian declared area consists of nickel, manganese and cobalt.[47] An illustration map for the international seabed area now reserved for India in the central Indian Ocean is provided in Figure 7.5.

In the case of the Soviet Union, the application was made on behalf of *Yuzhmorgeologiya* for registration as a pioneer investor. It was approved by the Group of Experts between November 23 and December 4, 1987, to cover a total of 300,000 square kilometers in the Clarion-Clipperton Zone in the north Pacific in two regions. The area reserved for the Soviet Union's *Yuzhmorgeologiya* contains varying degrees of high and low nodule abundance of nickel, manganese and cobalt.[48] A map of the Soviet Union's reserved area is presented in Figure 7.6.

In each of the four applications, information is recorded to indicate:

1. the identify of the applicant and of the certifying state
2. the date of signature of the Convention by the certifying state and the date of receipt of the application and any revision thereto

Figure 7.3
Locations of Areas Registered on December 17, 1987, with the Preparatory Commission from Application of France

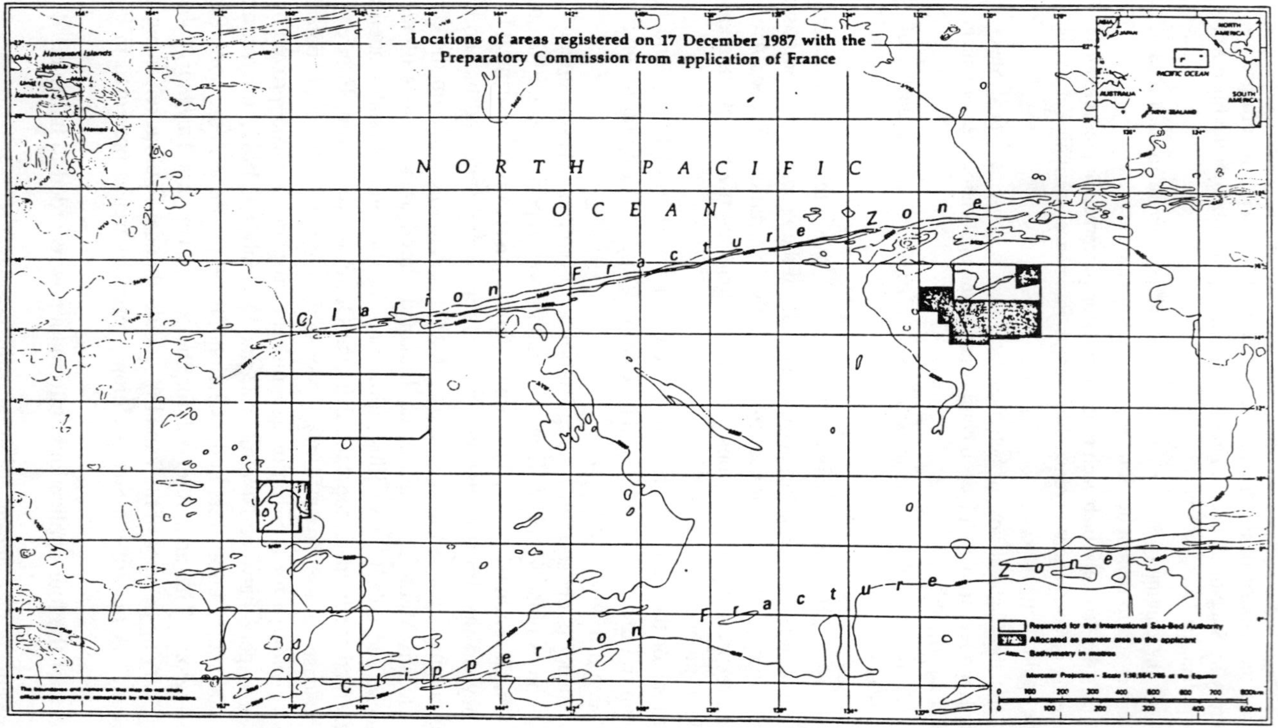

Source: *Law of the Sea Bulletin, Special Issue II: Registration of Pioneer Investors in the International Seabed Area in Accordance with Resolution II of the Third United Nations Conference on the Law of the Sea* (United Nations: Office of Ocean Affairs and the Law of the Sea, April 1988), p. 39.

Figure 7.4
Locations of Areas Registered on December 17, 1987, with the Preparatory Commission from Application of Japan

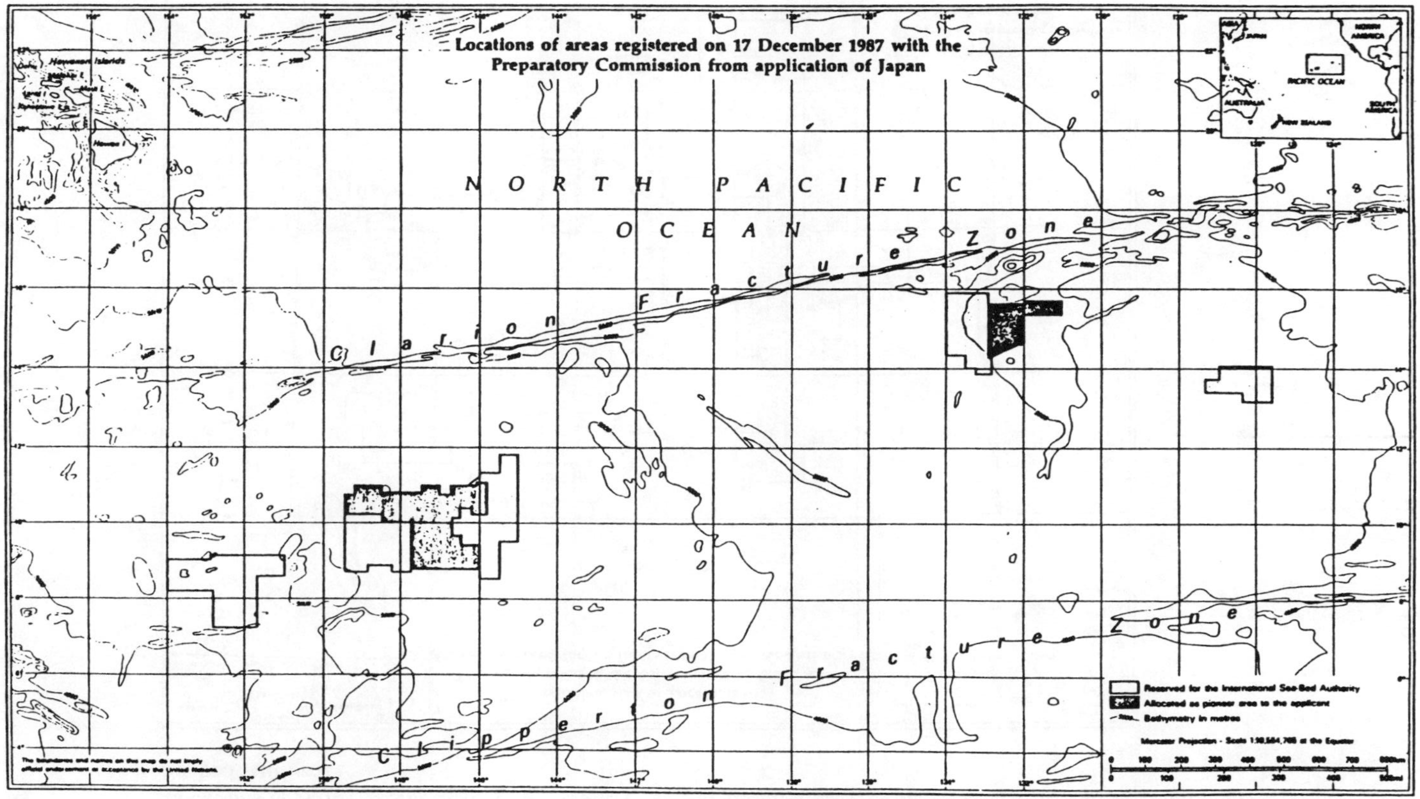

Source: *Law of the Sea Bulletin, Special Issue II*, p. 94.

Figure 7.5
Locations of Area A, Allocated to the Government of India, and Area B, Reserved for the International Seabed Authority

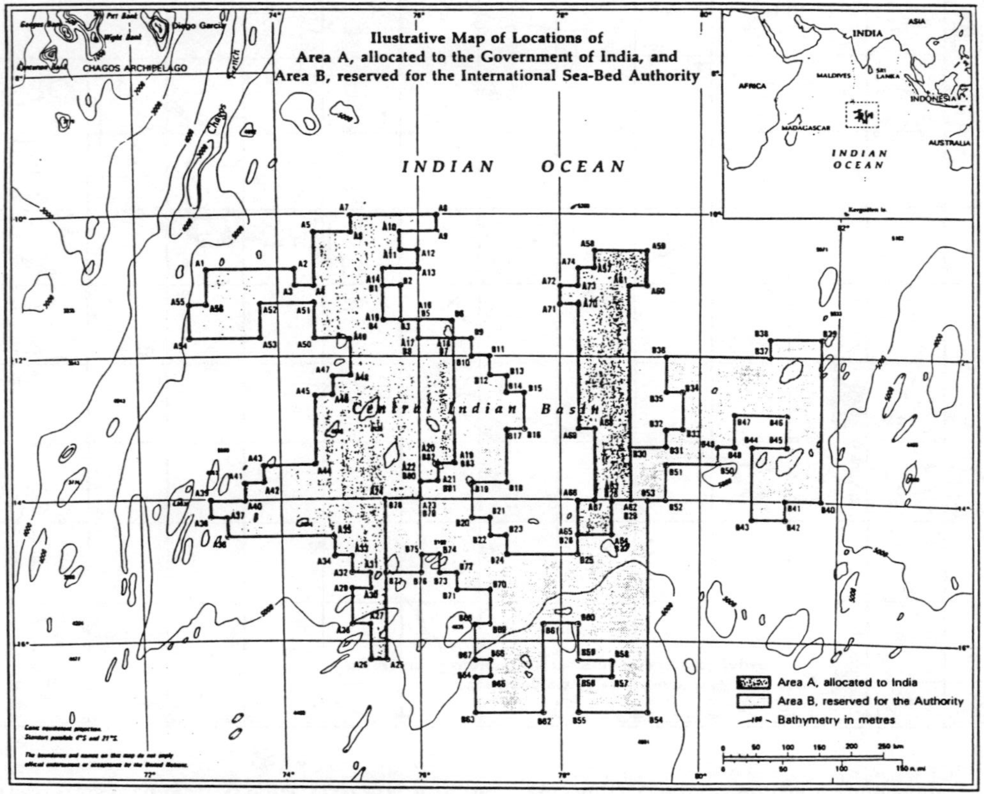

Source: *Law of the Sea Bulletin, Special Issue II*, p. 63.

Figure 7.6
Locations of Areas Registered on December 17, 1987, with the Preparatory Commission from Application of the Soviet Union

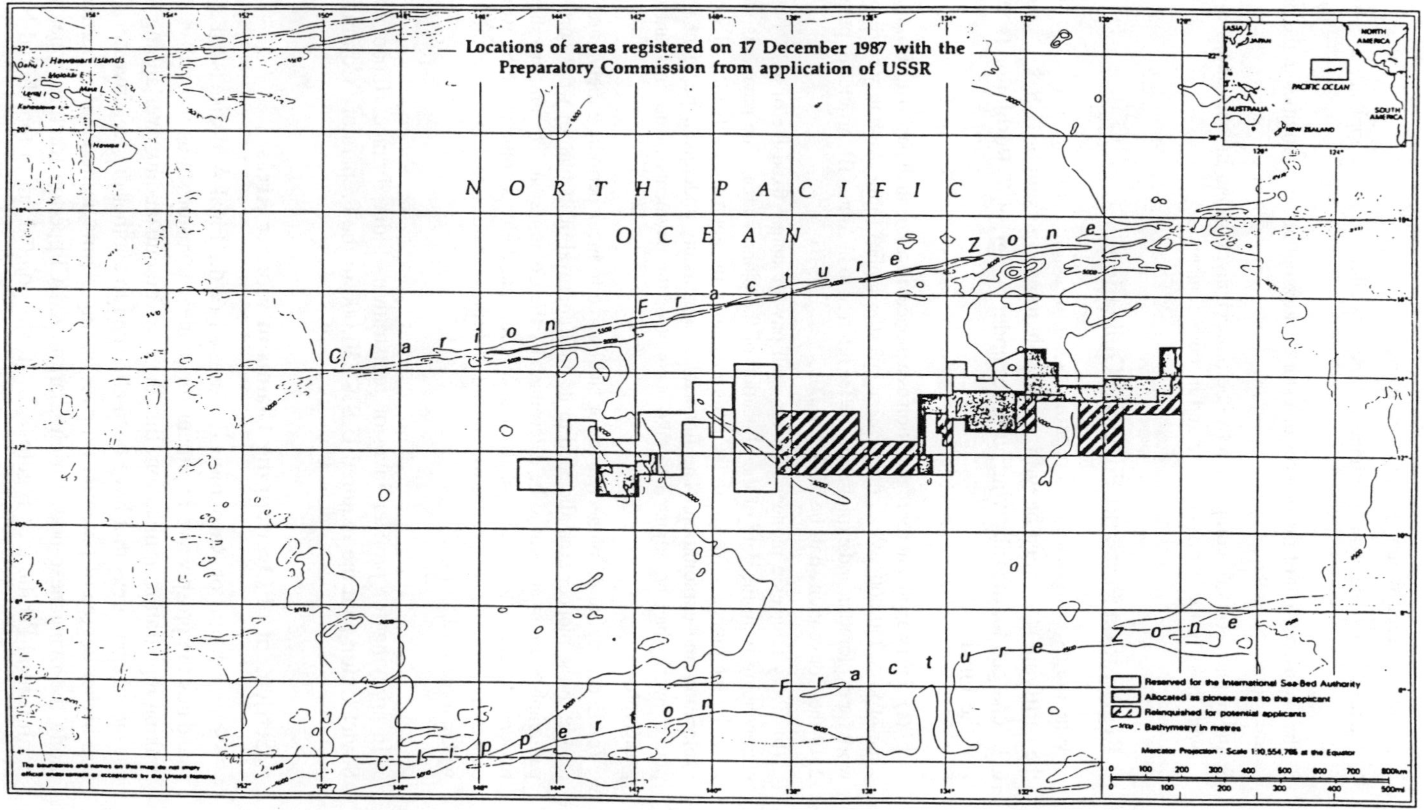

Source: *Law of the Sea Bulletin, Special Issue II*, p. 129.

3. the date of registration as a pioneer investor
4. the precise geographical coordinates of the area allocated to the applicant as a pioneer area
5. the exclusive right of the pioneer investor to carry out pioneer activities in the pioneer area allocated to it
6. the requirements of compliance by the pioneer investor and its obligations together with those of the certifying state and its commitments.

Registration Fees and Financial Obligations

When registering with the Preparatory Commission for pioneer investor status, the certifying state must be willing and able to pay the sum of U.S.$ 1.5 million to be charged for the following purposes under paragraph 7, Resolution II, Annex I of the Final Act:

> 7. (a) Every applicant for registration as a pioneer investor shall pay to the Commission a fee of $US 250,000. When the pioneer investor applies to the Authority for a plan of work for exploration and exploitation the fee referred to in Annex III, article 13, paragraph 2, of the Convention shall be $US 250,000.
>
> (b) Every registered pioneer investor shall pay an annual fixed fee of $US 1 million commencing from the date of the allocation of the pioneer area. The payments shall be made by the pioneer investor to the Authority upon the approval of its plan of work for exploration and exploitation. The financial arrangements undertaken pursuant to such plan of work shall be adjusted to take account of the payments made pursuant to this paragraph.
>
> (c) Every registered pioneer investor shall agree to incur periodic expenditures, with respect to the pioneer area allocated to it, until approval of its plan of work pursuant to paragraph 8, of an amount to be determined by the Commission. The amount should be reasonably related to the size of the pioneer area and the expenditures which would be expected of a *bona fide* operator who intends to bring that area into commercial production within a reasonable time.

In applying for pioneer investor registration, India, France, Japan and the Soviet Union paid the required U.S.$ 250,000 to the Preparatory Commission.

Settlement of Overlapping Claims in Pioneer Areas

Paragraph 5(a) of Resolution II, Annex I of the Final Act, discussed earlier, mandates the prospective applicant for pioneer investor status to certify, before making registration application, that there are no outstanding overlapping claims for the pioneer areas that have been allocated to another pioneer investor. There is a higher degree of potential for overlapping claims in the Pacific, particularly along the manganese-nodule-rich Clarion and Clipperton fracture zones in the north central Pacific (see Figure 7.2). It was pointed out in the United Nations report that "nodules lie in a monolayer, and therefore the claims sites must be extensive in two directions."[49] Furthermore, under paragraph 1(e), Resolution II, cited earlier, for each pioneer investor there is a maximum area limit of 150,000 square kilometers for each site. There is also the requirement for the prospective pioneer investor to submit two sites of equal commercial value, with one reserved for the Enterprise, the operating arm of the Authority, in accordance with the parallel system.

In December 1984 the four states—France, India, Japan and the Soviet Union—applied for pioneer investor status. It was discovered then that there were overlapping claims between France and Japan and the Soviet Union in the northeastern Pacific. In addition the Soviet Union site also overlapped with sites for three of the four international consortia. France and Japan resolved their conflict by negotiation; but the extensive overlapping claims of the Soviet Union site were not resolved until arrangements were made under the February 7, 1986, Arusha Understanding:

> Under the Arusha Understanding, France and the USSR, and Japan and the USSR, agreed to divide equally the respective areas of overlaps. They also agreed to relinquish areas before Resolution II required them to do so in order to resolve certain practical problems as well as to facilitate the resolution of conflicts between the claims of the USSR and some of the potential applicants. In addition, the three applicants were to contribute areas adjacent to the overlapping areas to compose a mine-site for the Authority. As a departure from Resolution II, all applicants were able to be allowed to identify an area of up to 52,300 square kilometers each for incorporation by the Preparatory Commission in the area to be allocated respectively to the applicants.[50]

(Also see separate sections in this chapter on the Area, Arusha Understanding, Consortia, the Enterprise, Parallel System, International Seabed Authority and Settlement of Disputes.)

Significance. The establishment of the pioneer investor regime is more than a compromise; it is a "grandfather clause" to protect the interests of seabed miners who had already made heavy investment in nodule recovery.[51] Resolution II, Annex I of the Final Act—under which the pioneer investor regime is established—is also intended to provide stability and certainty, two essential elements for continued development in the ocean mining industry, a new mining industry with high risk and heavy investment. Stability and certainty are ensured by the recognition of the exclusive rights for the seabed miners as pioneer investors to engage in mining activities in the Area.

The pioneer investor regime provides a strict requirement that overlapping claims for mine sites must be resolved through a system of conflict resolutions, including binding arbitration, before the registration is approved. This requirement would eliminate conflicting claims. Furthermore, as pioneer investors in the Area, they have priority over other applicants, except the Enterprise, for production authorization over two mining sites. The glaring disadvantage for the pioneer investor is the registration fee of $250,000, plus an annual fixed fee of

U.S.$ 1 million. However, these financial burdens could be lightened by tax credits extended to miners by the parent or sponsoring state.

A major problem for the pioneer investor regime is that in each of the four multinational consortia as pioneer investors there is one controlling state (the United States) that has not signed the 1982 LOS Convention and has refused to participate in the Preparatory Commission's work in drafting detailed rules and regulations for the work of the Authority. Until there is some alteration in the composition of sponsoring states in each of the four multinational consortia, their work plans or contracts with the Authority may not be approved. Paragraph 8(c), Resolution II prohibits a nonsignatory state as a sponsoring party to a consortium to receive contract approval for mining activities in the Area.

PREPARATORY COMMISSION

Resolution I, Annex I, of the Final Act to the 1982 LOS Convention establishes a Preparatory Commission for the International Seabed Authority and the International Tribunal for the Law of the Sea. A major function of the commission is to draft rules and recommend budgets for the Authority, in addition to implementing a system designed to protect the pioneer investors. In many respects, the commission is a device used not only to carry out the preparatory work for the establishment of the seabed Authority, but also to induce or entice membership by those states (particularly the United States) that have refused to sign the 1982 LOS Convention because of the issues of security and tenure of mine sites. It was hoped that these nonsignatory states would continue their participation in the drafting of rules and regulations for the Authority, thereby alleviating their fears and reducing their apprehensions.[52] The resolution allowed the signatories of the Final Act to take part as observers without vote in the discussion of the Preparatory Commission. The Federal Republic of Germany, the United Kingdom and the United States, which are signatories to the Act, would be included. In fact, the industrialized nations initially wanted to sign the Final Act in order to participate fully in the Preparatory Commission.[53]

Other responsibilities of the Preparatory Commission contained in Resolution I are as follows:

Annex I

Resolution I: Establishment of the Preparatory Commission for the International Sea-Bed Authority and for the International Tribunal for the Law of the Sea

The Third United Nations Conference on the Law of the Sea,

Having adopted the Convention on the Law of the Sea which provides for the establishment of the International Sea-Bed Authority and the International Tribunal for the Law of the Sea,

Having decided to take all possible measures to ensure the entry into effective operation without undue delay of the Authority and the Tribunal and to make the necessary arrangements for the commencement of their functions,

Having decided that a Preparatory Commission should be established for the fulfillment of these purposes,

Decides as follows:

1. There is hereby established the Preparatory Commission for the International Sea-Bed Authority and for the International Tribunal for the Law of the Sea. Upon signature of or accession to the Convention by 50 States, the Secretary-General of the United Nations shall convene the Commission, and it shall meet no sooner than 60 days and no later than 90 days thereafter.

2. The Commission shall consist of the representatives of States and of Namibia, represented by the United Nations Council for Namibia, which have signed the Convention are acceded to it. The representative of signatories of the Final Act may participate fully in the deliberations of the Commission as observers but shall not be entitled to participate in the taking of decisions.

3. The Commission shall elect its Chairman and other officers.

4. The Rules of Procedure of the Third United Nations Conference on the Law of the Sea shall apply *mutatis mutandis* to the adoption of the rules of procedure of the Commission.

5. The Commission shall:

(a) prepare the provisional agenda for the first session of the Assembly and of the Council and, as appropriate, make recommendations relating to items thereon;

(b) prepare draft rules of procedure of the Assembly and of the Council;

(c) make recommendations concerning the budget for the first financial period of the Authority;

(d) make recommendations concerning the relationship between the Authority and the United Nations and other international organizations;

(e) make recommendations concerning the Secretariat of the Authority in accordance with the relevant provisions of the Convention;

(f) undertake studies, as necessary, concerning the establishment of the headquarters of the Authority, and make recommendations relating thereto;

(g) prepare draft rules, regulations and procedures, as necessary, to enable the Authority to commence its functions, including draft regulations concerning the financial management and the internal administration of the Authority;

(h) exercise the powers and functions assigned to it by resolution II of the Third United Nations Conference on the Law of the Sea relating to preparatory investment;

(i) undertake studies on the problems which would be encountered by developing land-based producer States likely to be most seriously affected by the production of minerals derived from the Area with a view to minimizing their difficulties and helping them to make the necessary economic adjustment, including studies on the establishment of a compensation fund, and submit recommendations to the Authority hereon.

6. The Commission shall have such legal capacity as may be necessary for the exercise of its functions and the fulfillment of its purposes as set forth in this resolution.

7. The Commission may establish such subsidiary bodies as are necessary for the exercise of its functions and shall determine their functions and rules of procedure. It may also make use, as appropriate, of outside sources of expertise in accordance with United Nations practice to facilitate the work of bodies so established.

8. The Commission shall establish a special commission for the Enterprise and entrust to it the functions referred to in paragraph 12 of resolution II of the Third United Nations Conference on the Law of the Sea relating to preparatory investment. The special commission shall take all measures necessary for the early entry into effective operation of the Enterprise.

9. The Commission shall establish a special commission on the problems which would be encountered by developing land-based producer States likely to be most seriously affected by the production of minerals derived from the Area and entrust to it the functions referred to in paragraph 5 (i).

10. The Commission shall prepare a report containing recommendations for submission to the meeting of the States Parties to be convened in accordance with Annex VI, article 4, of the Convention regarding practical arrangements for the establishment of the International Tribunal for the Law of the Sea.

11. The Commission shall prepare a final report on all matters within its mandate, except as provided in paragraph 10, for the presentation to the Assembly at its first session. Any action which may be taken on the basis of the report must be in conformity with the provisions of the Convention concerning the powers and functions entrusted to the respective organs of the Authority.

12. The Commission shall meet at the seat of the Authority if facilities are available; it shall meet as often as necessary for the expeditious exercise of its functions.

13. The Commission shall remain in existence until the conclusion of the first session of the Assembly, at which time its property and records shall be transferred to the Authority.

14. The expenses of the Commission shall be met from the regular budget of the United Nations, subject to the approval of the General Assembly of the United Nations.

15. The Secretary-General of the United Nations shall make available to the Commission such secretariat services as may be required.

16. The Secretary-General of the United Nations shall bring this resolution, in particular paragraphs 14 and 15, to the attention of the General Assembly for necessary action.

After having met the requirement laid down in paragraph 1 of Resolution I—the deposit of the fiftieth signatory state for the 1982 LOS Convention—the Preparatory Commission held its first session to begin its organized work on March 15, 1983, with 125 members and 28 observers at Kingston, Jamaica, for the first session, from August 15 to September 9, 1983. At the first session the Preparatory Commission elected by consensus Joseph Warioba of Tanzania as its president. It formed four special committees dealing with these substantive topics:

1. the problem of adverse economic effects on land-based procedures from seabed mining
2. rules and regulations for the Enterprise and its entry into operation
3. a mining code
4. preparation for the establishment in Hamburg of the International Tribunal for the Law of the Sea.

A general committee of thirty-six members, based on regional representation, was also formed to serve as a steering group; the committee was chaired by President Warioba.

Since 1983 there has been an annual session of the Preparatory Commission whose work has been focused on the implementation of Resolution II, Annex I, Final Act, the application for mining sites by pioneer investors. In its 1987 session significant progress was made in resolving the overlapping claims made by France, Japan and the Soviet Union. It also made the decision to approve the following applications for registration as pioneer investors: India, France, Japan and the Soviet Union. (Also see separate sections in this chapter on the Area, Arusha Understanding, Pioneer Investors, Settlement of Disputes and Unilateral National Legislation.)

The Preparatory Commission issued its report on the seventh session held in the spring and fall of 1989.[54] The session in 1989 failed to reach agreement on the obligations to be carried out by the four approved Registered Pioneer Investors (France, Japan, India and the Soviet Union). The session was beset by factionalized groupings revolving around the controversial issues over deep-seabed mining in the Area. In addition to the Group of 77 and the group of Registered Pioneer Investors, there were at least three other groups of nations participating at the Preparatory Commission annual sessions: The Friends of the Conference of 11 nations (Australia, Austria, Canada, Denmark, Finland, Iceland, Ireland, New Zealand, Norway, Sweden, and Switzerland), the European Economic Community, the Group of Six industrialized nations (Belgium, the Federal Republic of Germany, Italy, Japan, Netherlands, and the United Kingdom), the Group of Potential Applicants for pioneer investor status (Belgium, Canada, Italy, the Federal Republic of Germany, and the United Kingdom), the Eastern European Group, and China.

The eighth session of the Preparatory Commission convened in Kingston, Jamaica, from March 5 to 30, 1990, attended by seventy-nine state members and four observers. While agreement has yet to be reached, informal discussions could lead to compromise with regard to pioneer investor obligations provided in Resolution II, Final Act, to the 1982 LOS Convention.[55] These obligations involve the registration and annual fixed fee, as well as agreement by the pioneer investors to incur periodic expenditures before the plan of work is approved, the actual carrying out of exploration in the mine site reserved first for the Enterprise, training of personnel for the Enterprise, and the transfer of technology. The resumed eighth session met in New York for the last two weeks of August 1990.

Significance. The UNCLOS III purpose for adopting Resolution I, Annex I of the Final Act was twofold. One was to postpone discussion and debate on the actual implementation of those provisions under Part XI on the new international seabed regime. The delegates were under pressure in the early spring of 1982 to conclude a finished document for accession by the states. There was considerable disagreement raised by the Western industrialized nations on the various provisions for the Area and the powers of the Authority. It was possible that the Preparatory Commission for the new international seabed regime could provide the avenue through which some of the objectionable and flawed (in the view of a number of key Western industrialized nations) seabed provisions might be modified or corrected in the process of drafting the rules, regulations and procedures for the Authority. It was expected that the United States would take an active part in the Preparatory Commission and thus would be in a position to exert its influence on a universally acceptable set of rules for the Authority. Unfortunately, this was not in reality even a possibility, as the United States, the United Kingdom and the Federal Republic of Germany chose not to participate in the Preparatory Commission sessions that commenced in March 1983.

As Bernard Oxman points out, the importance of the Preparatory Commission lies in the fact that it is the body that will "interpret, clarify, and apply the Convention text with greater precision."[56] Specifically, the Preparatory Commission must, before the Convention comes into effect after the deposit of the sixtieth ratification by a signatory state, draft a mining code and establish the International Tribunal for the Law of the Sea for settlement of disputes among signatory states and miners. The successful registration of four pioneer investors by the Preparatory Commission in 1987 augurs well for the awaited event of deep-seabed mining in the Area.

Thus, in many respects, the Preparatory Commission represents not only a concession to the developed states, but serves as an "interim regime" for implementing the provisions of the 1982 LOS Convention on deep-seabed mining in the Area that is beyond the limits of national jurisdiction. It may become a permanent organization should the Law of the Sea Convention fail to come into force for lack of the required ratification. In that case, the Preparatory Commission, in an analogy illustrated by Elisabeth Mann Borgese, might play the role of the General Agreement on Tariff and Trade (GATT), in the absence of a permanent international trade organization, as a "guardian" and a "vehicle" for the development of the law of the sea.

RECIPROCATING STATES AGREEMENT (RSA) OR REGIME OR "MINI-TREATY"

The term "reciprocating states" refers to those industrialized sates, led by the United States, that have disagreed with the principles and operation of the International Seabed Authority, established under Part XI of the 1982 LOS Convention. Subsequently they have either enacted unilateral national legislation concerning deep-seabed mining beyond the limits of national jurisdiction or concluded reciprocal agreements of understanding among themselves with respect to mining licenses, permits or priorities of rights for the recovery of polymetallic nodules from the deep seabed.

The concept of reciprocal recognition of deep seabed mining rights originated when the United States Congress passed the Deep Seabed Hard Mineral Resources Act of 1980 (Public Law 96–283, June 28, 1980). Section 118 of this Act provides:

Section 118: Reciprocating states

(a) DESIGNATION.—The Administrator, in consultation with the Secretary of State and the heads of other appropriate departments and agencies, may designate any foreign nation as a reciprocating state if the Secretary of State finds that such foreign nation—

(1) regulates the conduct of its citizens and other persons subject to its jurisdiction engaged in exploration for, and commercial recovery of, hard mineral resources of the deep seabed in a manner compatible with that provided in this Act and the regulations issued under this Act, which includes adequate measures for the protection of the environment, the conservation of natural resources, and the safety of life and property at sea, and includes effective enforcement provisions;

(2) recognizes licenses and permits issued under this title to the extent that such nation, under its laws, (A) prohibits any person from engaging in exploration or commercial recovery which conflicts with that authorized under any such license or permit and (B) complies with the date for issuance of licenses and the effective date for permits provided in section 102(c)(1)(D) of this Act;

(3) recognizes, under its procedures, priorities of right, consistent with those provided in this Act and the regulations issued under this Act, for applications for licenses for exploration or permits for commercial recovery, which applications are made either under its procedures or under this Act; and

(4) provides an interim legal framework for exploration and commercial recovery which does not unreasonably interfere with the interests of other states in their exercise of the freedoms of the high seas, as recognized under general principles of international law.

The United States' initiative and negotiation among key Western industrialized countries (which have an interest in deep-seabed mining) produced two agreements that served as the basis for an alternate deep-seabed mining regime or "mini-treaty," alongside the International Seabed Authority created under the 1982 LOS Convention.

The first agreement was concluded on September 2, 1982, entitled "Agreement Concerning Interim Arrangements Relating to Polymetallic Nodules of the Deep Seabed." It was signed by France, the Federal Republic of Germany, the United

Kingdom and the United States. The interim agreement expresses two basic objectives:

1. to resolve overlapping claims among the parties in an orderly manner
2. to make sure that there are deep-seabed areas available for operation by other states under customary international law (in other words, the freedom of the high seas)

In short, the interim agreement was intended to stake out international claims or simply to prevent ''claim jumping'' on deep-seabed mining sites already solicited by the international consortia. In one of the preambulary paragraphs, the interim agreement was said to be intended ''for avoiding overlap in the areas claimed for future pioneer activities in the deep seabed,'' and for carrying out seabed mining activities in ''an orderly and peaceful manner.''[57] The agreement also established a consultation procedure for resolving conflicts between parties to the agreement over the claimed areas.

As if to provide further momentum for the initial success in forming an alternate international deep seabed regime, President Ronald Reagan urged in his statement of March 1983 that efforts should be made ''to work with 'like-minded' countries to develop a framework, free from unnecessary political and economic restraints for exploration and exploitation of the deep seabed when conditions warrant.''[58]

Following the 1982 interim agreement and the statement by President Reagan, negotiations to produce a second agreement were conducted among those states that possessed both the technology and the investment capital for deep-seabed mining. This arrangement, known as the ''Provisional Understanding Regarding Deep Seabed Matters,'' was signed in 1984 by eight nations: Belgium, France, the Federal Republic of Germany, Italy, Japan, the Netherlands, the United Kingdom and the United States.[59] The provisional understanding of seven industrialized nations from the West, plus Japan, has been termed as a ''non-poaching'' agreement, with each party promising to respect the other parties' mining claims on the seabed:[60]

Provisional Understanding Regarding Deep Seabed Matters

1. (1) No Party shall issue an authorization in respect of an application, or seek registration, for an area included:

(a) within an area which is covered in another application filed in conformity with the agreements for voluntary conflict resolution reached on 18 May 1983 and 15 December 1983 and being still under consideration by another Party;

(b) within an area claimed in any other application which has been filed in conformity with national law and this Agreement,

(i) prior to the signature of this Agreement, or

(ii) earlier than the application or request for registration in question, and which is still under consideration by another Party; or

(c) within an authorization granted by another Party in conformity with this Agreement.

(2) No Party shall itself engage in deep seabed operations in an area for which, in accordance with this paragraph, it shall not issue an authorization or seek registration.

3. Each Party shall immediately notify the other Parties of each application for an authorization which it accepts, including application for an authorization which it accepts, including applications already received, and of each amendment to such an application. Each Party shall also immediately notify the other Parties after it has taken action subsequently with respect to an application or any action with respect to an authorization.

4. No Party shall authorize, or itself engage in, exploitation of the hard mineral resources of the deep seabed before 1 January 1988.

5. (1) The Parties shall consult together:

(a) prior to the issuance of any authorization or before themselves engaging in deep seabed operations or seeking registration for an area;

(b) with regard to any arrangements between one or more Parties and another State or States for the avoidance of overlapping in deep seabed operations; . . .

(2) The relevant Parties shall consult together in the event that two or more applications are filed simultaneously.

6. (1) To the extent permissible under national law, a Party shall maintain the confidentiality of the coordinates of application areas and other proprietary or confidential commercial information received in confidence from any other Party in pursuance of cooperation in regard to deep seabed operations. In particular:

(a) the confidentiality of the coordinates of application areas shall be maintained until any overlap involving such an area is resolved and the relevant authorization is issued; and

(b) the confidentiality of other proprietary or confidential commercial information shall be maintained in accordance with national law as long as such information retains its character as such.

(2) Denunciation or other action by a Party pursuant to paragraph 14 of this Agreement shall not affect the Parties' obligations under this paragraph.

In addition to guarantee of each party's unimpeded access to the deep-seabed mining site, in paragraph 3 the Provisional Understanding requires that the parties notify each other immediately upon the approval of authorization for deep-seabed mining activities in a site to avoid "multiple authorization for a single site." As stipulated in paragraph 5(1), the parties are also obligated to consult together prior to authorization for deep-seabed mining and, most important of all, on any arrangement that involves overlapping in deep seabed operations. In paragraph 6(1), the Provisional Understanding also mandates confidentiality of the coordinates (location and size) of the mining areas claimed in the application for authorization of operation, as well as confidentiality "of other proprietary or confidential commercial information" in accordance with national law.

The Provisional Understanding also provides for settlement of disputes by conflict resolution. The recommended procedure for resource to binding arbitration is outlined in paragraph 10:

10. The Parties shall settle any dispute arising from the interpretation or application of this Agreement by appropriate means. The Parties to the dispute shall consider the possibility of recourse to binding arbitration and, if they agree, shall have recourse to it.

As a part of the ''nonpoaching'' agreement, at the very outset there is a stipulation in paragraph 1(a) that no authorization shall be issued in an area where there are overlapping claims contained in ''agreements for voluntary conflict resolution'' between the six multinational consortia of *Association Française Pour l'Étude et la Recherche des Nodules*, Deep Ocean Resources Development Co., Ltd., Kennecott Consortium, Ocean Mining Associates, Ocean Minerals Company, and Ocean Management, Inc.

In a memorandum on implementation, the parties to the Provisional Understanding agreed on eligibility, standards and administrative requirements:[61]

Eligibility

(1) Each party will issue or transfer an authorization only to applicants:

(a) which are financially and technologically qualified to conduct the proposed deep seabed operations;

(b) which comply with all requirements of the Party's national law; and

(c) whose deep seabed operations will be carried out in accordance with the standards prescribed below.

Standards

3. (1) Each Party will take all necessary measures so that deep seabed operations under its control:

(a) are conducted with reasonable regard to the interests of other States in the exercise of the freedom of the high seas;

(b) will include efforts to protect the quality of the environment and will not result in significant adverse effects on the environment;

(c) have due regard for the prevention of waste and the future opportunity for the commercial recovery of the unrecovered balance of the hard mineral resources in the authorization area;

(d) do not adversely affect the safety of life and property at sea in accordance with generally accepted international standards;

(e) are conducted diligently by maintaining a reasonable level of operation based on the size of area and other relevant factors; and

(f) are monitored for their effects on the environment.

(2) In accordance with its national law each Party will ensure that persons subject to its jurisdiction minimize interference with any activity authorized under an authorization issued by another Party.

(3) Each Party will cooperate in developing measures, consistent with its national law, needed to implement the provisions of the Agreement and of this Memorandum so that, in general function and effect, these measures are compatible with, comparable to, and as effective as those established by the other Parties.

Administrative Requirements

4. To enforce effectively the standards described in paragraph 3 of this Memorandum, each Party will employ, as appropriate, measures such as: imposing reasonable penalties for violation of requirements; placing observers on vessels to monitor compliance; suspending, revoking, or modifying authorizations; and, issuing orders in an emergency to prevent a significant adverse effect on the environment or to preserve the safety of life and property at sea.

(Also see separate entries in this chapter on Consortia, Fundamental Principles and Unilateral National Legislation.)

Significance. The fundamental purposes for the enactment of both the Interim Agreement of 1982 and the Provisional Understanding of 1984 were

1. to provide the industrialized nations of the West, plus Japan, unimpeded access to mining in the deep seabed
2. to avoid overlapping claims for mining sites in the event of a lack of agreement on an international regime for deep seabed mining at the UNCLOS III

While these arrangements were considered interim and temporary, they soon became an alternate regime for deep seabed operations, since the Federal Republic of Germany, the United Kingdom and the United States refused to sign the 1982 LOS Convention over Part XI on the International Seabed Authority. The continued existence of the Reciprocal States Agreement alongside of an International Seabed Authority provided by the 1982 Convention creates a certain amount of instability for deep seabed mining as a whole. There have been strong objections and opposition to the Reciprocal States Agreement as "mini-treaties." While one of the avowed purposes of these agreements is to prevent "claim jumping" or "poaching," the agreements, particularly the Provisional Understanding, contain no control over or no protection against poaching by nonmember states on mining sites claimed only by the eight signatory parties to the Provisional Understanding. Because of the possible counterclaims and uncertainty with respect to security of tenure for the mining sites under the Provisional Understanding, it would be a "risky" venture for banks to make substantial investment on such deep-seabed mining operations.[62] In addition, there is the strong possibility of a legal challenge by the nonparties to the Provisional Understanding. The last presiding officer for the UNCLOS III, Ambassador Tommy T. B. Koh, of Singapore, offered the chilling thought:

> If the United States does engage in seabed mining through an alternative regime, I will challenge it by bringing an action to the International Court of Justice.

> . . . I hold the view that if the question were put to an authoritative judicial body, such as the International Court of Justice, whether a reciprocating regime is compatible with existing international law, the court is likely to rule against the treaty.[63]

One authority on seabed mining concluded that the Provisional Understanding is not only incompatible with the international regime established by the 1982 LOS Convention, but it "amounts to a breach of both the letter and spirit of the United Nations Convention."[64]

James L. Malone, the U.S. Assistant Secretary for Oceans and International Environment and Scientific Affairs, replied to the above criticisms:

> I find irreproachable and entirely consistent with international law the proposition that sovereign states may conclude an agreement the purpose of which is to avoid conflict and waste, promote rational and orderly development of the seabeds, further the rule of law, and be controlling among them in the absence of any other binding international instrument in force to which they are parties and which treats the same issue. I believe the conclusion of this provisional understanding is a significant and responsible step forward in the field of international affairs and the conduct of foreign relations. I also believe the understanding to be the only realistic and workable approach to deep seabed mining beyond the limits of national jurisdiction which has, to date, been achieved or which is likely to be achieved within the coming decade.[65]

REVIEW CONFERENCE

Two types of review are called for in the 1982 LOS Convention dealing with the international regime for the deep seabed: a general and systematic review and a specified review conference on the operation of the International Seabed Authority.

First, the periodic review:

> **Article 154: Periodic review**
>
> Every five years from the entry into force of this Convention, the Assembly shall undertake a general and systematic review of the manner in which the international regime of the Area established in this Convention has operated in practice. In the light of this review the Assembly may take, or recommend that other organs take, measures in accordance with the provisions and procedures of this Part and the Annexes relating thereto which will lead to the improvement of the operation of the regime.

Periodic review provided under Article 154 is limited and nonspecific insofar as the activities or operation of the international regime are concerned. The interval for such periodic review is every five years from the date of entry into force of the Convention. It is to be undertaken by the Assembly under Part XI.

The review conference to be called by the Assembly is quite different in scope and more controversial in terms of its negotiable-legislative history with respect to the purposes, objectives, and the possible impact of changes recommended by the review conference on the international seabed regime that rests on the parallel system.[66] Specifics about the review conference are contained in Article 155:

Article 155: The Review Conference

1. Fifteen years from 1 January of the year in which the earliest commercial production commences under an approved plan of work, the Assembly shall convene a conference for the review of those provisions of this Part and the relevant Annexes which govern the system of exploration and exploitation of the resources of the Area. The Review Conference shall consider in detail, in the light of the experience acquired during that period:

(a) whether the provisions of this Part which govern the system of exploration and exploitation of the resources of the Area have achieved their aims in all respects, including whether they have benefited mankind as a whole;

(b) whether, during the 15-year period, reserved areas have been exploited in an effective and balanced manner in comparison with non-reserved areas;

(c) whether the development and use of the Area and its resources have been undertaken in such a manner as to foster healthy development of the world economy and balanced growth of international trade;

(d) whether monopolization of activities in the Area has been prevented;

(e) whether the policies set forth in articles 150 and 151 have been fulfilled; and

(f) whether the system has resulted in the equitable sharing of benefits derived from activities in the Area, taking into particular consideration the interests and needs of the developing States.

2. The Review Conference shall ensure the maintenance of the principle of the common heritage of mankind, the international regime designed to ensure equitable exploitation of the resources of the Area for the benefit of all countries, especially the developing States, and an Authority to organize, conduct and control activities in the Area. It shall also ensure the maintenance of the principles laid down in this Part with regard to the exclusion of claims or exercise of sovereignty over any part of the Area, the rights of States and their general conduct in relation to the Area, and their participation in activities in the Area in conformity with this Convention, the prevention of monopolization of activities in the Area, the use of the Area exclusively for peaceful purposes, economic aspects of activities in the Area, marine scientific research, transfer of technology, protection of the marine environment, protection of human life, rights of coastal States, the legal status of the waters superjacent to the Area and that of the air space above those waters and accommodation between activities in the Area and other activities in the marine environment.

3. The decision-making procedure applicable at the Review Conference shall be the same as that applicable at the Third United Nations Conference on the Law of the Sea. The Conference shall make every effort to reach agreement on any amendments by way of consensus and there should be no voting on such matters until all efforts at achieving consensus have been exhausted.

4. If, five years after its commencement, the Review Conference has not reached agreement on the system of exploration and exploitation of the resources of the Area, it may decide during the ensuing 12 months, by a three-fourths majority of the States Parties, to adopt and submit to the States Parties for ratification or accession such amendments changing or modifying the system as it determines necessary and appropriate. Such amendments shall enter into force for all States Parties 12 months after the deposit of instruments of ratification or accession by three fourths of the States Parties.

5. Amendments adopted by the Review Conference pursuant to this article shall not affect rights acquired under existing contracts.

In the first place, there must be a review conference fifteen years from January 1 of the year in which the earliest deep-seabed mining operation begins in the Area. Thus, if commercial nodule mining operation commences in 1995 or 2000, a review conference must be convened by the Assembly in 2010 or 2015. The original idea of a review conference was said to have been suggested by United States Secretary of State Henry Kissinger as a way to ensure the continued competitiveness of the Enterprise.[67]

Second, the review conference must consider, in the light of the experience gained during the fifteen-year period, the following six areas of concern:

1. the aims achieved by the international regime governing the Area's resource exploration and exploitation, including the benefits for mankind
2. comparative review on the effectiveness of exploitation of seabed resources in both the reserved and nonreserved areas
3. the extent for fostering a healthy world economy by use of the Area
4. the prevention of ''monopolization of activities''
5. the fulfillment of policies contained in Articles 150 and 151 with respect to the rational management of the Area's resources, revenues of the Authority, technological transfer and price stabilization of minerals
6. the extent of equitable revenue sharing derived from the Area's activities in meeting the needs of the developing states

Third, decision making or recommendation for change and amendment at the review conference must be made not only by consensus, but is not to be open-ended or free-wheeling. The review conference must ensure no fundamental alteration to the basic principles established in Part XI of the 1982 LOS Convention and the Annexes, such as the common heritage of mankind, equitable exploitation of the Area's resources for benefit of all the developing countries, peaceful uses, transfer of technology, marine environmental protection, and scientific research. However, state parties to the review conference have five years within which to reach consensus or unanimous agreement on changes and amendments to deep seabed mining operations under Part XI of the 1982 LOS Convention. If, after the twentieth year of commercial mining in the Area, no consensus or unanimity on changes is reached, Article 155(4) calls for a ''constitutional convention'' during the ensuing twelve months to adopt changes by a three-fourths majority vote on the system of exploitation and exploration of the Area's resources. The amendments so adopted will have to be ratified by three-fourths of the state parties twelve months thereafter. If an amendment fails to be ratified by three-fourths of the state parties between the twentieth and twenty-first years, the review conference provision will lapse. If a state party opposes such a conference amendment that is ratified without its consent, it would have the option of either withdrawing with one year's notice or denouncing the entire 1982 LOS Convention, in accordance with Article 317. When this situation develops, a thorny legal question arises as to whether the opposing state could continue mining in the area. Several legal experts argue that withdrawing from the entire Convention does not necessarily ''void a contract concluded prior to that withdrawal.''[68] Other scholars contend that state parties would most likely insist on the prohibition from mining outside of the international deep seabed regime by any state, under Article 137(2).[69] (Also see separate section in this chapter on Preparatory Commission.)

Significance. The most important, if not most controversial, aspect of the review conference on the deep seabed mining operation of the international regime (Part XI) has been the legal status and rights of a contractor if and when the review conference recommends and approves changes to any provisions in Part XI of the 1982 LOS Convention without a participating state's consent. For under Article 155, the review conference may very well determine that contracts entered into between the Authority and the sponsoring states of the consortia have not fulfilled the requirements of paragraph 1(a) [benefits for mankind as a whole], paragraph 1(c) [fostering healthy world economy], or paragraph 1(f) [equitable sharing of benefits to meet the interests of developing states]. It may be argued that Article 155(5) makes it clear that ''Amendments adopted by the review conference pursuant to this article shall not affect rights acquired under existing contracts.''[70] Thus, a contractor's rights and investment decision approved prior to the end of the review conference would remain intact or inviolable by any subsequent changes enacted and ratified by three-fourths of the state parties. It has been argued that the provision in Article 155(5) ''compares favorably with that in many developing country mining agreements'' which are subject to expropriation.[71]

The provision in Article 155(5) on inviolability of contracts for deep-seabed mining in the Area even offers ''a stable investment climate'' when compared with mining on land in developed nations where taxes and regulations often impose ''unpredictable changes.''[72] On the other hand, the paramount interest of the Third World nations for a ''New International Economic Order,'' based on the concepts of benefits for mankind and equitable sharing, is inherently in conflict with the contractual rights of a deep-seabed miner to the extent that these can be altered.[73] Reading President Reagan's statement of January 29, 1982, it becomes obvious that one of the United States's objections to the Law of the Sea Convention has been the concern that amendments to the Convention could come into force without approval by the participating states.[74] There has been the suggestion that the analogy of the United States bankruptcy law might be applicable in the case of a "politically failed essential industry," namely the International Seabed Authority, in resolving the troublesome controversy under Article 155 with respect to a deep-seabed miner's legal status and rights in the light of amendments to Part XI of the Convention.[75] It is suggested in that analogy that in the event of reorganization, holders of claims must be permitted to receive cash compensation equal to any fixed liquidation or fixed price the debtor may redeem.[76]

SETTLEMENT OF SEABED DISPUTES IN THE AREA

The 1982 LOS Convention provides detailed procedures for the settlement of disputes concerning seabed mining operations. Section 5, Part XI (Articles 186–191) and Section 4 of Annex VI (Articles 35–40) contain the major provisions governing the settlement of seabed disputes in the Area.

First, the Seabed Disputes Chamber—established by Article 14, Annex VI (Statute of the International Tribunal for the Law of the Sea) and Article 35, Section 4 of Annex VI—is composed of eleven members, to be selected by a majority of the twenty-one elected members of the International Tribunal for the Law of the Sea. The Chamber's membership is based on the established practice of representation by the principal legal systems of the world, plus equitable geographical distribution, in the absence of general recommendations from the Assembly of the Authority. Each of the eleven-member Chamber is to serve for a three-year term and may be selected for a second term.

Second, the Seabed Disputes Chamber has jurisdiction over a wide variety of disputes that may arise over the mining activities in the Area. Article 187 in Section 5, Part XI, lists at least six categories of disputes over which the Chamber has jurisdiction:

Article 187: Jurisdiction of the Sea-Bed Disputes Chamber

The Sea-Bed Disputes Chamber shall have jurisdiction under this Part and the Annexes relating thereto in disputes with respect to activities in the Area falling within the following categories:

(a) disputes between States Parties concerning the interpretation or application of this Part and the Annexes relating thereto;

(b) disputes between a State Party and the Authority concerning:

(i) acts or omissions of the Authority or of a State Party alleged to be in violation of this Part or the Annexes relating thereto or of rules, regulations and procedures of the Authority adopted in accordance therewith; or

(ii) acts of the Authority alleged to be in excess of jurisdiction or a misuse of power;

(c) disputes between parties to a contract, being States Parties, the Authority or the Enterprise, state enterprises and natural or juridical persons referred to in article 153, paragraph 2(b), concerning:

(i) the interpretation or application of a relevant contract or a plan of work; or

(ii) acts or omissions of a party to the contract relating to activities in the Area and directed to the other party or directly affecting its legitimate interests;

(d) disputes between the Authority and a prospective contractor who has been sponsored by a State as provided in article 153, paragraph 2(b), and has duly fulfilled the conditions referred to in Annex III, article 4, paragraph 6, and article 13, paragraph 2, concerning the refusal of a contract or a legal issue arising in the negotiation of the contract;

(e) disputes between the Authority and a State Party, a state enterprise or a natural or juridical person sponsored by a State Party as provided for in article 153, paragraph 2(b), where it is alleged that the Authority has incurred liability as provided in Annex III, article 22;

(f) any other disputes for which the jurisdiction of the Chamber is specifically provided in this Convention.

In disputes between state parties concerning the interpretation or application of Part XI and the appropriate annexes to the 1982 LOS Convention, the rules of law applicable are governed by Article 293, which states that "a court or tribunal having jurisdiction under this section shall apply this Convention's and other rules of international law not incompatible with this Convention," as well as the rules and regulations of the Authority under Article 38(a), Section 4, Annex VI for the Statute of the International Tribunal for the Law of the Sea. This is further reinforced by Articles 21 and 32(1), Annex VI. In addition, as provided in Article 22, the state parties may agree to refer any disputes concerning the interpretation or application of any treaty or convention already in force to the International Tribunal for the Law of the Sea. However, the decision of the Seabed Disputes Chamber of the Tribunal shall be binding upon the state parties in accordance with Article 296, and specifically Article 33(1), Annex VI, which states that "the decision of the Tribunal is final and shall be complied with by all parties to the dispute."

Under Article 187(b), disputes may also be brought to the Seabed Disputes Chamber involving allegations of the Authority's or state parties' excess use or misuse of power or acts or omissions in violation of Part XI. This implies alleged violation concerning rules and regulations to be adopted by the Preparatory Commission for the Authority's operation in deep-seabed mining. However, it should be noted here that Article 308(4) specifically states that "the rules, regulations and procedures drafted by the Preparatory Commission shall apply provisionally pending their formal adoption by the Authority in accordance with Part XI." Under Article 16(8), the Council must approve these rules, regulations and procedures for the Authority by consensus or unanimity.

Under Article 187(c) and (d), the Seabed Disputes Chamber has jurisdiction over mining contract disputes. Brown lists the following types of contractual disputes:[77]

1. Disputes between parties in contract interpretation involving the state parties, the Authority or the Enterprise, State enterprises, or multinational consortia. However, Article 190(2) in Section 5, Part XI, on dispute settlement, stipulates that if a sovereign state is being sued by a multinational consortium, or by a natural or juridical person, "the responding state may request the state sponsoring that person to appear in the proceedings on behalf of that person" and "failing such appearance, the respondent state may arrange to be represented by a juridical person of its nationality."
2. Disputes that may arise between a contractor and the Authority over financial matters.
3. Disputes that involve the performance of a contract in the form of "acts or omissions of a party to the contract relating to the activities in the Area and directed to the other party or directly affecting its legitimate interests."
4. Disputes between the Authority and a prospective contractor on contract refusal or on a legal issue arising in the negotiation of the contract.
5. Disputes between the Authority and a state party, state enterprise or a natural or juridical person on allegations of the Authority's liability for damages as a result of wrongful acts, including industrial secret disclosure as provided in Article 22, Annex II and Article 168(2).

Third, it is not necessary to refer most contractual and other disputes to the Seabed Disputes Chamber exclusively. Other remedies are also provided in the various articles of the Convention. Article 188 provides three other options or alternatives for dispute settlement:

Article 188: Submission of disputes to a special chamber of the International Tribunal for the Law of the Sea or an ad hoc chamber of the Sea-Bed Disputes Chamber or to binding commercial arbitration

1. Disputes between States Parties referred to in article 187, subparagraph (a), may be submitted:

(a) at the request of the parties to the dispute, to a special chamber of the International Tribunal for the Law of the Sea to be formed in accordance with Annex VI, articles 15 and 17; or

(b) at the request of any party to the dispute, to an *ad hoc* chamber of the Sea-Bed Disputes Chamber to be formed in accordance with Annex VI, article 36.

2.

(a) Disputes concerning the interpretation or application of a contract referred to in article 187, subparagraph (c)(i), shall be submitted, at the request of any party to the dispute, to binding commercial arbitration, unless the parties otherwise agree. A commercial arbitral tribunal to which the dispute is submitted shall have no jurisdiction to decide any question of interpretation of this Convention. When the dispute also involves a question of the interpretation of Part XI and the Annexes relating thereto, with respect to activities in the Area, that question shall be referred to the Sea-Bed Disputes Chamber for a ruling.

(b) If, at the commencement of or in the course of such arbitration, the arbitral tribunal determines, either at the request of any party to the dispute or *proprio motu*, that its decision depends upon a ruling of the Sea-Bed Disputes Chamber, the arbitral tribunal shall refer such question to the Sea-Bed Disputes Chamber for such ruling. The arbitral tribunal shall then proceed to render its award in conformity with the ruling of the Sea-Bed Disputes Chamber.

(c) In the absence of a provision in the contract on the arbitration procedure to be applied in the dispute, the arbitration shall be conducted in accordance with the UNCITRAL Arbitration Rules or such other arbitration rules as may be prescribed in the rules, regulations and procedures of the Authority, unless the parties to the dispute otherwise agree.

Furthermore, ad hoc chambers of the Seabed Disputes Chamber are also provided for in Article 36(4), Annex VI (The Statute of the International Tribunal for the Law of the Sea):

Article 36: Ad hoc chambers

1. The Sea-Bed Disputes Chamber shall form an *ad hoc* chamber, composed of three of its members, for dealing with a particular dispute submitted to it in accordance with article 188, paragraph 1(b). The composition of such a chamber shall be determined by the Sea-Bed Disputes Chamber with the approval of the parties.

2. If the parties do not agree on the composition of an *ad hoc* chamber, each party to the dispute shall appoint one member, and the third member shall be appointed by them in agreement. If they disagree, or if any party fails to make an appointment, the President of the Sea-Bed Disputes Chamber shall promptly make the appointment or appointments from among its members, after consultation with the parties.

3. Members of the *ad hoc* chamber must not be in the service of, or nationals of, any of the parties to the dispute.

Then, under Article 188(2)(a), binding commercial arbitration may have the jurisdiction over a dispute at the request of any party. These disputes must be concerned with the interpretation or application of contractual provisions for mining operations in the Area as stated in Article 187(c)(i). Notice that Article 188(2)(c) states that in the absence of a contractual provision for arbitration procedure, UNCITRAL arbitration rules or other arbitration rules may be prescribed in the Authority's rules and regulations.

Brown seems to suggest that in reading both Articles 188(2) and 187(c)(i), one gets the feeling that disputes of that nature would have to be submitted for commercial arbitration unless the parties choose other agreed upon alternatives of settlement. Brown maintains that in disputes involving interpretation of the

1982 LOS Convention, commercial arbitration is not appropriate and that the Seabed Disputes Chamber must be the body for a ruling.[78] (Also see separate sections in this chapter on the Area, Arusha Understanding, Consortia, International Seabed Authority, Pioneer Investors, Preparatory Commission, Reciprocating States Agreement and Unilateral National Legislation.)

Significance. It is expected that the key organs established by the 1982 LOS Convention—the Seabed Disputes Chamber and the ad hoc chambers discussed here—will play an important role in the future development of international law with respect to seabed mining activities. Dispute settlement procedures among the miners and between the mining contractors and the states, multinational consortia and the Authority are now available in the provisions of the Convention. The Seabed Disputes Chamber, a specialized organ created to deal exclusively with seabed disputes, would have compulsory jurisdiction on some matters between the state parties and the Authority. While it is true that the jurisdiction of the Seabed Disputes Chamber and its ad hoc chambers represent compromises between the industrialized states and the Group of 77, the dispute settlement system envisioned in the Convention has been expanded to be comprehensive enough to be able to deal with both the contractual questions and those that deal with the interpretation and application of the Convention. In essence, commercial arbitration must be applied on contractual questions at the request of any party, if the parties have not agreed otherwise in the contract itself. On disputes that deal with the interpretation of the Convention, commercial arbitration may not be considered competent to resolve the case. However, if the question does involve the interpretation of Part XI of the Convention, then the case must be ruled upon by the Seabed Disputes Chamber. The dispute settlement machinery established for deep seabed mining activities ''may prove to be the cornerstone of the Convention.''[79] Both the International Tribunal for the Law of the Sea and its subsidiary, the Seabed Disputes Chamber, could be ''moulders of international law of the sea for the foreseeable future'' and the ''norms and rules'' so formulated could most likely be recognized in all national courts.''[80]

From the procedures standpoint, there is not a doubt that the power of the Authority is enhanced by limiting jurisdiction of dispute settlement in the Seabed Disputes Chamber, but not in terms of decisions made by the Authority; for the Seabed Disputes Chamber cannot rule on questions as to whether the Authority's action is in accordance with the Convention. In her critique of the dispute settlement system provided by Articles 187 and 188, Marianne Gaertner offers several other limitations of the Seabed Disputes Chamber.[81] One shortcoming is the lack of jurisdiction by the Chamber over the Authority's ''discretionary powers'' not defined by the Convention itself, but which may refer to the negotiation of contracts, the selection of contract applications, or even ''the refusal to conclude contracts.''[82] Limitation of the Seabed Disputes Chamber's jurisdiction hinders states parties' ability to challenge the acts of the Authority and thus provides no check on ''arbitrary and capricious behavior of the Authority.''[83] And, finally, the Authority may block a move to use other forms of dispute settlement as outlined in Article 188 by forcing the case into the Seabed Disputes Chamber for resolution. Taken as a whole, these built-in limitations reinforce "a strong bias in favor of the developing countries," which dominate the Authority's Assembly, and, as a consequence, leave doubt as to the "fair and equitable nature of the Tribunal."[84]

TRANSFER OF TECHNOLOGY

One of the most beneficial bargains struck by the Group of 77 representing the Third World developing nations at the UNCLOS III negotiations was the acquisition of deep-seabed mining technology possessed by potential miners from the industrialized countries. It is really meaningless for the developing states to participate in mining activities in the Area if they do not have the know-how in seabed mining venture. Therefore, ways must be found through which deep-seabed mining technology can be transferred not only to those developing states that need it, but to the Enterprise as well. Article 144 states:

Article 144: Transfer of technology

1. The Authority shall take measures in accordance with this Convention:

(a) to acquire technology and scientific knowledge relating to activities in the Area; and

(b) to promote and encourage the transfer to developing States of such technology and scientific knowledge so that all States Parties benefit therefrom.

2. To this end the Authority and States Parties shall co-operate in promoting the transfer of technology and scientific knowledge relating to activities in the Area so that the Enterprise and all States Parties may benefit therefrom. In particular they shall initiate and promote:

(a) programmes for the transfer of technology to the Enterprise and to developing States with regard to activities in the Area, including, *inter alia*, facilitating the access of the Enterprise and of developing States to the relevant technology, under fair and reasonable terms and conditions;

(b) measures directed towards the advancement of the technology of the Enterprise and the domestic technology of developing States, particularly by providing opportunities to personnel from the Enterprise and from developing States for training in marine science and technology and for their full participation in activities in the Area.

The basic intent of Article 144 is further spelled out by Article 148, which makes the developing states active participants, rather than passive recipients, for the benefits derived from seabed resources exploitation and exploration:

Article 148: Participation of developing States in activities in the Area

The effective participation of developing States in activities in the Area shall be promoted as specifically provided for in this Part, having due regard to their special interests and needs, and in particular to the special need of the landlocked and geographically disadvantaged among them to overcome obstacles arising from their disadvantaged location, including remoteness from the Area and difficulty of access to and from it.

In Annex III of the Final Act on prospecting, exploiting and exploring the seabed in the Area, a detailed procedure has been worked out under Article 5(1–3)(e) to facilitate technological transfer:

1. When submitting a plan of work, every applicant shall make available to the Authority a general description of the equipment and methods to be used in carrying out activities in the Area, and other relevant non-proprietary information about the characteristics of such technology and information as to where such technology is available.

2. Every operator shall inform the Authority of revisions in the description and information made available pursuant to paragraph 1 whenever a substantial technological change or innovation is introduced.

3. Every contract for carrying out activities in the Area shall contain the following undertakings by the contractor:

(a) to make available to the Enterprise on fair and reasonable commercial terms and conditions, whenever the Authority so requests, the technology which he uses in carrying out activities in the Area under the contract, which the contractor is legally entitled to transfer. This shall be done by means of licenses or other appropriate arrangements which the contractor shall negotiate with the Enterprise and which shall be set forth in a specific agreement supplementary to the contract. This undertaking may be invoked only if the Enterprise finds that it is unable to obtain the same or equally efficient and useful technology on the open market on fair and reasonable commercial terms and conditions;

(b) to obtain a written assurance from the owner of any technology used in carrying out activities in the Area under the contract, which is not generally available on the open market and which is not covered by subparagraph (a), that the owner will, whenever the Authority so requests, make that technology available to the Enterprise under license or other appropriate arrangements and on fair and reasonable commercial terms and conditions, to the same extent as made available to the contractor. If this assurance is not obtained, the technology in question shall not be used by the contractor in carrying out activities in the Area;

(c) to acquire from the owner by means of an enforceable contract, upon the request of the Enterprise and if it is possible to do so without substantial cost to the contractor, the legal right to transfer to the Enterprise any technology used by the contractor, in carrying out activities in the Area under the contract, which the contractor is otherwise not legally entitled to transfer and which is not generally available on the open market. In cases where there is a substantial corporate relationship between the contractor and the owner of the technology, the closeness of this relationship and the degree of control or influence shall be relevant to the determination whether all feasible measures have been taken to acquire such a right. In cases where the contractor exercises effective control over the owner, failure to acquire from the owner the legal right shall be considered relevant to the contractor's qualification for any subsequent application for approval of a plan of work;

(d) to facilitate, upon the request of the Enterprise, the acquisition by the Enterprise of any technology covered by subparagraph (b), under license or other appropriate arrangements and on fair and reasonable commercial terms and conditions, if the Enterprise decides to negotiate directly with the owner of the technology;

(e) to take the same measures as are prescribed in subparagraphs (a), (b), (c) and (d) for the benefit of a developing State or group of developing States which has applied for a contract under article 9 of this Annex, provided that these measures shall be limited to the exploitation of the part of the area proposed by the contractor which has been reserved pursuant to article 8 of this Annex and provided that activities under the contract sought by the developing State or group of developing States would not involve transfer of technology to a third State or the nationals of a third State. The obligation under this provision shall only apply with respect to any given contractor where technology has not been requested by the Enterprise or transferred by that contractor to the Enterprise.

Article 5(8), Annex III defines technology as

8. For the purposes of this article, "technology" means the specialized equipment and technical know-how, including manuals, designs, operating instructions, training and technical advice and assistance, necessary to assemble, maintain and operate a viable system and the legal right to use these items for that purpose on a non-exclusive basis.

In short, the entire technological system associated with the recovery and processing of seabed resources in the Area must be made available to the developing states. The International Seabed Authority, through its operating arm, the Enterprise, must obtain such technology under Article 5(3)(a), Annex III, by commercial and reasonable terms on the open market. As set forth in Article 5(7) of Annex III, a contractor is obligated to provide technological transfer within a time limit:

7. The undertakings required by paragraph 3 shall be included in each contract for the carrying out of activities in the Area until 10 years after the commencement of commercial production by the Enterprise, and may be invoked during that period.

In addition, Article 5(3)(e) makes it obligatory for the contractor to provide transfer of technology to developing states on the condition that such technology "has not been requested by the Enterprise or transferred by that contractor to the Enterprise." (Also see separate sections in this chapter on the Area, Consortia, the Enterprise, International Seabed Authority and Parallel System.)

Significance. It must be pointed out that it has been a common practice by developed nations in extending technical aid to developing countries to provide technological transfer as well. However, in the case of deep-seabed mining there seems to be some reluctance to provide technological transfer to the developing Third World nations. An example is illustrated by the United States's objection to Article 5, Annex III, which requires contractors to submit to the Authority, along with the work approval, "a general description of the equipment and methods used" in deep-seabed mining operations, plus "other relevant non-proprietary information" about the technology's characteristics and its availability. Article 5 in Annex III also requires that information concerning the technology used by a miner in this case must or shall be made available to the Enterprise on reasonable commercial terms in the form of a license agreement or some other method of negotiation. It may be argued that the objection is valid, for the mandatory provision in Article 5 reduces the competitiveness of the miner under contract to the Authority. It is true that the Enterprise can acquire the needed technology in the open market, but in practice if there is such technology available in the open market, it most likely would not be comparable to what is actually being used by the miner. Provision is also made to enable the Enterprise to acquire the needed technology through joint venture (Article 11, Annex III) with a qualified miner, as it is again currently a rather common practice in international economic relations.

Also, objection has been raised with respect to the confidentiality of data provided by a miner to the Authority or the Enterprise under Article 15 of Annex III and Article 144(2). There is fear of inadequate protection to be exercised by the international staff under the Authority or possible "industrial espionage."

These concerns expressed by the developed states seem to be valid. Yet they can also be remedied by the Preparatory Commission, which must draft rules, regulations and procedures for the operation of the Authority and its Enterprise. These reservations do not seem to be so paramount as to serve as a stumbling block to ratification of the 1982 LOS Convention, as argued so convincingly by Jon M. Van Dyke and David Teichmann.[85]

UNILATERAL NATIONAL LEGISLATION ON DEEP-SEABED HARD MINERALS

The 1980 Deep Seabed Hard Mineral Resources Act (DSHMRA) (Public Law 96–283) for continued development in deep-seabed mining, was passed by the United States Congress and signed into law by President Jimmy Carter after a postponement of more than fourteen years. The influence of the 1980 Deep Seabed Hard Mineral Resources Act was quite evident on the passage of Resolution II, Annex I, of the Final Act for the 1982 LOS Convention. Resolution II provides a compromise between the contending developed and developing states in the form of guaranteed access and contract security for the "pioneer investors," a sort of "grandfather clause" for those multinational deep seabed mining consortia which had already made heavy investment in ocean mining.

After a period of impasse at the UNCLOS III negotiations, the deadlock was broken—influenced by the passage of the 1980 United States domestic deep-seabed mining legislation. Section 201 of the United States DSHMRA expressed the need for guarantees for the investment already made by the mining industry if an international seabed regime were to be established. Within a year of the passage of the 1980 DSHMRA by the United States, three other Western industrialized states followed suit by enacting similar unilateral domestic legislation: Deep Sea Mining Law of 1981 by the United Kingdom; the Law on the Exploration and Exploitation of Mineral Resources of the Deep Seabed (Law 81–1135) by France; and the Act of Interim Regulation of Deep Seabed Mining by the Federal Republic of Germany (1981). The common aim of these unilateral domestic laws on deep-seabed mining was to provide an alternate regime under which a license and fee system could be authorized so as to allow the multinational mining consortia to begin deep-seabed mining operations without having to wait for the UNCLOS III to come up with an international regime for deep seabed mining in the Area. All four pieces of unilateral domestic legislation maintained that the arrangements contained in the laws were temporary or interim measures pending the emergence of an agreed upon international seabed regime from the UNCLOS III negotiations. But the implication seems to be that if there is no international legal regime for deep-seabed mining, or if the Conference on the Law of the Sea fails to reach an agreement, then these unilateral domestic laws on deep-seabed mining would become the alternative legal regimes. Under these domestic laws, only licensed exploration of deep-seabed mineral resources could be permitted by obtaining a license from an authorized governmental agency specified in the laws, for instance, the Secretary of State for the United States in the 1980 Deep Seabed Hard Mineral Resources Act. All these unilateral domestic laws require the levying of permit fees on licenses, based on the value of recovery of hard minerals from the seabed. The permit fees so collected by the various national treasuries would eventually be transferred to the International Seabed Authority to be established by the Law of the Sea Convention. A person or corporation engaged in deep-seabed mining operations under these unilateral domestic laws is not subject to dual licensing by other nations if and when their laws are similar. While the United Kingdom Deep Seabed Mining Law of 1981 does not require proof of technical expertise and financial stability by a miner for a license or permit, both the United States and the Federal Republic of Germany do insist on presentation of evidence to that effect. The latter's domestic laws on deep seabed mining also provide a statutory limit on mine sites so as to avoid monopolistic operation by a few powerful mining concerns. The French law permits licensing for exploitation and exploration by French nationals only.[86] However, European Economic Community nationals may join the French for such purposes. (Also see separate sections in this chapter on Fundamental Principles, International Seabed Authority, Maltese Initiative, Moratorium Resolution, Reciprocating States Agreement.)

Significance. These unilateral domestic laws on deep-seabed mining raise a number of questions. First, the passage of these unilateral domestic laws on deep-seabed mining beyond the limits of national jurisdiction has deepened the ideological or philosophical gulf between the developed and developing states. These enactments revive the debate over whether the 1982 LOS Convention permits authorization of private mining firms to engage in mining activities in the Area on grounds of freedom of the high seas. If so, it has been argued by the developed industrialized nations, then how can the action be considered as not violating the common heritage principle endorsed by the 119 nations in consensus at the UNCLOS III—a consensus that declares that the deep-seabed resources beyond the limits of national jurisdiction are not subject to expropriation by anyone, be it a state or a juridical person (a multinational corporation)?

Leaving aside the question as to whether the United Nations declaration that the deep seabed beyond national jurisdiction remains a common heritage of mankind is already a part of customary international law, the very enactment of these unilateral national laws on deep-seabed mining can create chaos, conflict and tension in the orderly and peaceful development of the Law of the Sea. Unilateral domestic legislation raises the important question of the relationship of these domestic laws to the 1982 LOS Convention, if and when it enters into force. Is a mining license granted by a national legislation in the Area, but not recognized internationally, a license? Common sense seems to indicate that a mining license in the Area must have a secure legal standing in an industry that is full of risks and uncertainties. A suggestion has been made that license under unilateral legislation be "recognized internationally in the framework of mutually agreed reciprocity."[87] This can be accomplished only through negotiations. As a final comment, in view of the questions posed by unilateral domestic legislation on deep-seabed mining in the Area, it may be appropriate for the Preparatory Commission to negotiate with the parties—the Federal Republic of Germany, the United Kingdom, and the United States—so that agreements can be reached or arrangements be made that are designed to resolve these questions.

Meantime, what we have in the world today are two separate regimes for mining the deep seabed resources: an international regime provided by the 1982 LOS Convention and a system of unilateral domestic ocean regimes. How the two ocean regimes can exist alongside of each other without explosive confrontation is hard to imagine, unless there are accommodation and cooperation. Maybe the changing minerals market conditions and the need for updating international rules can serve as an impetus for renegotiating the international deep seabed mining regime.[88] If international cooperation and renegotiation on deep-seabed mining regimes are not possible, then the "Mini-Treaty" or the reciprocal states agreement would have to be the only "viable alternative with a chance to materialize."[89]

NOTES

1. Theodore G. Kronmiller and G. Wayne Smith, eds. *The Lawfulness of Deep Seabed Mining*, vol. 1 (New York: Oceana Publications, 1981), pp. 108–125.

2. Ibid., p. 126.

3. J.R.V. Prescott, *The Maritime Political Boundaries of the World* (London: Methuen, 1985), p. 124.

4. Kronmiller and Smith, eds., *The Lawfulness of Deep Seabed Mining*, p. 130.

5. United National Convention on the Law of the Sea: Understanding of the Preparatory Commission for the International Seabed Authority and for the International Tribunal for the Law of the Sea for Proceeding with Deep Seabed Mining Applications and Resolving Disputes of Overlapping Claims of Mine Sites [Reached during Meeting of August 11–September 5, 1986] UN Document LOS/PCN/L.41/Rev.1, Annex, September 11, 1986. Text can also be found in *International Legal Material* 25, no. 5 (September 1986): 1326–1330.

6. J. M. Broadus and Porter Hoagland III, "Conflict Resolution in the Agreement of Area Entitlements for Seabed Mining," *San Diego Law Review* 21, no. 3 (June 1984): 541–574.

7. *Law of the Sea Bulletin*, no. 10, November 1987, p. 116.

8. See *Seabed Mineral Resources Development* (ST/ESA/107 and Add. 1), United Nations Publication, 1982.

9. Ambassador Elliot L. Richardson, speech to the National Press Club, as reprinted in *The Honolulu Star-Bulletin*, 14 March 1979, p. A–12.

10. See E. D. Brown, *Seabed Energy and Mineral Resources and the Law of the Sea*, vol. 2 (London: Graham & Trotman, 1986), 5.24.

11. Ibid., p. 4.40.

12. See UN Document, *Third United Nations Conference on the Law of the Sea*, vol. 10, "Reports of the Committees and Negotiation Groups," Seventh Session, pp. 61–65.

13. Ibid., p. 66; and also see Brown, *Seabed Energy and Mineral Resources*, 4.41.

14. Brown, *Seabed Energy and Mineral Resources*, 5.20.

15. Ibid., 5.23; and UN Documents, *Third United Nations Conference on the Law of the Sea*, vol. 14, "Summary Records of Meetings, Documents," Resumed Seventh Session, p. 116.

16. Lance N. Atrim and James K. Sebenius, "Incentives for Ocean Mining under the Convention," in Bernard H. Oxman, ed., *Law of the Sea: U.S. Policy Dilemma* (San Francisco, Calif.: ICS Press, 1983), p. 88.

17. Ibid.

18. Ibid.

19. Elisabeth Mann Borgese, "The Law of the Sea: Its Potential for Generating International Revenue," in Elisabeth Mann Borgese and Norton Ginsburg, eds. *Ocean Yearbook 4* (Chicago: The University of Chicago Press, 1983), p. 24.

20. Ibid. For details, see J. D. Nyhart, *A Cost Model of Ocean Mining and Associated Regulatory Issues*, MIT Sea Grant Report (MITSG), 78–4 (Cambridge, Mass.: Massachusetts Institute of Technology, 1978). Also see Oxman, ed., *Law of the Sea*, p. 89; and Brown, *Seabed Energy and Mineral Resources*, 4.45–46.

21. Borgese, "The Law of the Sea," p. 24.

22. Ibid., p. 25.

23. Ibid., p. 26–27.

24. For the historical development of the concept, see Kronmiller and Smith, *The Lawfulness of Deep Seabed Mining*, pp. 106–348. For negotiation on the drafting of the concept, see Brown, *Seabed Energy and Mineral Resources*, 3.5–3.6.

25. "President's Note in the Law of the Sea Conference on the Relationship between the Convention and the 1970 Declaration of Principles on the Seabed," UN Doc. A/62/L.49/ADD.1, 29 March 1980. UN Documents, Official Records, *Third United Nations Conference on the Law of the Sea*, vol. 13, Ninth Session, p. 79.

26. Steven J. Molitor, "The Provisional Understanding Regarding Deep Seabed Matters: An Ill-conceived Regime for U.S. Deep Seabed Mining," *Cornell International Law Journal*, 20, no. 1 (Winter 1987): 228.

27. Kronmiller and Smith, *The Lawfulness of Deep Seabed Mining*, pp. 345–346.

28. Brown, *Seabed Energy and Mineral Resources*, 2.41.

29. David D. Caron, "Reconciling Domestic Principles and International Cooperation," in Oxman, ed., *Law of the Sea*, p. 8.

30. Elisabeth Mann Borgese, "The Law of the Sea," *Scientific American* (March 1983): pp. 42–49.

31. Jonathan I. Charney, "The International Regime for the Deep Seabed: Past Conflicts and Proposals for Progress," *Harvard International Law Journal* 17, no. 1 (Winter 1976): 4–8 and 30.

32. Bernard H. Oxman, "The Third United Nations Conference on the Law of the Sea: The Ninth Session (1980)," *American Journal of International Law* 75, no. 2 (April 1981): 218–219. Also see Kathryn E. Yost, "The International Seabed Authority Decision-making Process: Does It Give a Proportionate Voice to the Participant's Interests in the Deep Sea Mining?" *San Diego Law Review* 20, no. 3 (April 1983): 673.

33. UN Doc. A/6695(XXII), 18 August 1967.

34. *The New York Times*, 14 July 1966, p. 10.

35. See UN Doc. A/RES/2340(XXII), 18 December 1967.

36. See Ann L. Hollick, *U.S. Foreign Policy and the Law of the Sea* (Princeton, N.J.: Princeton University Press, 1981), p. 225.

37. UN Document A/C.1/PV.1709, 12 December 1967, pp. 5 and 15.

38. UN Document A/C.1/PV.1708, 11 December 1967, p. 8.

39. Kronmiller and Smith, *The Lawfulness of Deep Seabed Mining*, pp. 233–234.

40. UN Document A/Conf. 62/WP.8/Rev.1, 8 May 1976. Also see UN Document, Official Records, *Third United Nations Conference on the Law of the Sea*, vol. 5, "Summary of Records of Meetings, Documents," Fourth Session, p. 125. Also see excerpts from speech made by Elliot L. Richardson at the meeting of the National Press Club as reprinted in *The Honolulu Star-Bulletin*, March 14, 1979, p. A–12.

41. Brown, *Seabed Energy and Mineral Resources*, 7.6; and UN Documents A/Conf.62/L/132, 23 April 1982; A/Conf.62/L.139, 28 April 1982; and A/Conf.62/L.141, 29 April 1982.

42. See UN Document LOS/PCN/L.13, 4 September 1984.

43. Brown, *Seabed Energy and Mineral Resources*, 7.13.

44. Ibid., 7.10–11.

45. "Registration of Pioneer Investors in the International Seabed Area in Accordance with Resolution II of the UNCLOS III," *Law of the Sea Bulletin*, Special Issue II, Office for Ocean Affairs and the Law of the Sea, April 1988, p. 8.

46. *Law of the Sea Bulletin*, Special Issue II, Office for Ocean Affairs and the Law of the Sea, April 1988, pp. 40–42.

47. Ibid., p. 57.

48. Ibid., p. 120.

49. "Registration of Pioneer Investors in the International Seabed Area," p. 6.

50. Ibid. Also see UN Documents LOS/PCN/56, 12 March 1985, p. 3, and LOS/PCN/L.27, 3 September 1985, pp. 3–4.

51. For a detailed study of the history of the first group of ''pioneer investors'' see Moritaka Hagashi, ''Registration of the First Group of Pioneer Investors by the Preparatory Commission to the International Seabed Authority and for the International Tribunal for the Law of the Sea,'' *Ocean Development and International Law* 20, no. 1 (1989): 1–34.

52. ''Synopsis,'' *San Diego Law Review* 20, no. 3 (1983): 698.

53. UN Document A/Conf.62/L.30, 1982.

54. See *Law of the Sea Bulletin*, no. 4, December 1989, pp. 88–93. Also see ''Special Report: The Preparatory Commission,'' Council on Ocean Law, September 1989, pp. 1–6.

55. *Oceans Policy News*, April 1990, p. 2.

56. Oxman, ed., *Law of the Sea*, p. 160.

57. ''Agreement Concerning Interim Arrangements Relating to Polymetallic Nodules of the Deep Seabed,'' 2 September 1982, signed by the Federal Republic of Germany, United Kingdom and the United States, as reprinted in *International Legal Materials*, vol. 21, no. 5, September 1982, p. 950.

58. Department of State, *Current Policy*, no. 371, January–February 1982.

59. See document reprinted in *International Legal Materials*, vol. 23, no. 6, 3 August 1984, pp. 1354–1365.

60. Steven J. Molitor, ''The Provisional Understanding Regarding Deep Seabed Matters: An Ill-Conceived Regime for U.S. Deep Seabed Mining,'' *Cornell International Law Journal*, 20 (Winter 1987): 243.

61. ''Provisional Understanding Regarding Deep Seabed Matters,'' *International Legal Materials*, vol. 23, no. 6 (3 August 1984): 1359–1360.

62. Molitor, ''The Provisional Understanding Regarding Deep Seabed Mining,'' p. 245.

63. Jon M. Van Dyke, ed., *Consensus and Confrontation: The United States and the Law of the Sea Convention* (Honolulu: The Law of the Sea Institute, University of Hawaii, 1985), p. 253.

64. Brown, *Seabed Energy and Mineral Resources*, 8.40.

65. ''Freedom and Opportunity: Foundation for a Dynamic Oceans Policy,'' *The Department of State Bulletin* 84, no. 2093 (December 1984): 79.

66. Brown, *Seabed Energy and Mineral Resources*, 3.9–14.

67. *U.S. Department of State Bulletin*, 75 (1976): 395.

68. Bradley Larschan, ''The International Legal States of the Contractual Rights of Contractors under the Deep Seabed Mining Provision, Part XI of the Third UNCLOS,'' *Denver Journal of International Law and Politics* 14, nos. 2–3 (Winter–Spring 1986): 209, no. 101. Also see Bernard H. Oxman, ''Summary of the Law of the Sea Convention,'' in Oxman, ed., *Law of the Sea*, pp. 160–161.

69. John Norton Moore, ''Charting a New Course in the Law of the Sea Negotiations,'' *Denver Journal of International Law and Policy* (1981): 207 and 215.

70. Lance N. Antrim and James K. Sevenius, ''Centuries for Ocean Mining under the Convention,'' in Oxman, ed., *Law of the Sea*, p. 94.

71. Ibid.

72. Ibid.

73. Larschan, "The International Legal Status of the Contractors," pp. 221–223 and 229.

74. Department of State, *Current Policy*, no. 371, January–February 1982.

75. Larschan, "The International Legal Status of the Contractors," p. 229.

76. Ibid., pp. 226–227.

77. Brown, *Seabed Energy and Mineral Resources*, 6.17–21.

78. Ibid., 6.19.

79. Euripides L. Evriniades, "The Third World's Approach to the Deep Seabed," *Ocean Development and International Law* 11, nos. 3–4 (1982): 238–239.

80. Ambassador William B. Jones, "The International Seabed Authority without U.S. Participation," *Ocean Development and International Law* 12, nos. 3–4 (1983): 167.

81. Marianne P. Gaertner, "The Dispute Settlement Provisions of the Convention on the Law of the Sea: Critique and Alternatives to the International Tribunal for the Law of the Sea," *San Diego Law Review* 19, no. 3 (April 1982): 590–591.

82. Ibid., p. 591.

83. Ibid.

84. Ibid., p. 592.

85. Jon M. Van Dyke and David L. Teichmann, "Transfer of Seabed Mining Technology: A Stumbling Block to U.S. Ratification of the Law of the Sea Convention?" *Ocean Development and International Law* 13, no. 4 (1983): 427–456.

86. Denis G. Touret, "The French Deep-Sea Mining Legislation of 1981," *Ocean Development and International Law* 13, no. 1 (1982): 117.

87. Jochen Martin, "Deep-Sea Mining between Convention and National Legislation," *Ocean Development and International Law* 10, nos. 1–2 (1981): 183. For a discussion on leasing issues and claims or patent problems, see Robert H. Nelson, "Guiding the Ocean Search Process: Applying Public Land Experience to the Design of Leasing and Permitting Systems for Ocean Mining and Ocean Shipwrecks," *Ocean Development and International Law* 20, no. 6 (1989): 577–600.

88. See Francisco Orrego Vicuña, "The Deep Seabed Mining Regime: Terms and Conditions for Its Renegotiation," *Ocean Development and International Law* 20, no. 5 (1989): 531–540.

89. Federico Foders, "International Organizations and Ocean Use: The Case of Deep-Sea Mining," *Ocean Development and International Law* 20, no. 5 (1989): 528. For some somber reflections on the deep seabed mining regime, see two recent articles: Giulio Pontecorve, "Musing about Seabed Mining, or Why What We Don't Know Can Hurt Us," *Ocean Development and International Law* 21, no. 1 (1990): 117–118; and Mark W. Zacher and James G. McConnell, "Down to the Sea with Stakes: The Evolving Law of the Sea and the Future of the Deep Seabed Regime," *Ocean Development and International Law* 21, no. 1 (1990): 71–103.

CHAPTER 8

Marine Pollution and Environmental Impact

Since the 1960s the development of global marine environmental principles has assumed an ever-increasing importance in the evolution of the law of the sea. As marine pollution problems have become more acute and as signs of deterioration have appeared more frequently in the marine environmental system, the need for new international rules to protect the marine environment have emerged as a major concern for the world community of nations. This chapter provides a brief look at the evolution of that new and growing body of international law on the prevention and control of marine pollution in its varied manifestations.

The chapter begins with a discussion of the problem of hazardous waste disposal of industrial organic substances that, because of their toxicity, have serious environmental impacts on marine life. Modern industries also use rivers and oceans for the disposal of synthetic organic chemicals. Toxic metals, such as cadmium, mercury, lead and zinc, have been known to contaminate fisheries and cause fatal illness to human beings. Most, if not all, toxic metals enter the marine environment as waste disposed of through land-based sources. From a scientific data-gathering perspective, while it is difficult to compile a definitive list of toxic metals disposed of in the marine environment as industrial waste, as a reference the chapter presents some sample lists of heavy metals and some organic industrial substances that affect the marine environment. The chapter concludes with a brief discussion on the issue of the ocean serving as "waste space" or acting as "a waste receptacle" based on environmental and technical criteria versus the more popular view that the oceans have become the "ultimate sink" for waste disposal.

Next, by focusing on the activities of one such organization, the Intergovernmental Maritime Consultative Organization (IMCO)—since 1982, the International Maritime Organization (IMO)—the chapter discusses the role of international organizations in attempting to regulate marine pollution. Long before the negotiations began on the law of the sea, the IMCO was the only international organization within the framework of the United Nations system that served both as a forum and as an instrument for setting internationally acceptable rules and standards for marine environmental protection.

Since its entry into force in 1958, the IMCO has been responsible for sponsoring more than thirty international conventions, from the 1954 International Convention for the Prevention of Pollution of the Sea by Oil to the 1972 London Dumping Convention. It was also responsible for the entry into force in 1983 of the International Convention for the Prevention of Pollution from Ships (MARPOL).

All the world's industrialized, and many of the developing, nations must now face the enormous problem of land-based solid waste disposal. And until there is an effective land-based solid waste management system, the oceans would continue to be pressured as the convenient receptacle for waste dumping. Added to the problem of land-based solid waste disposal is the question of how to exercise control over transboundary airborne pollution from fossil-burning industries and automobile exhaust—commonly known as acid rain—that eventually enters into the ocean. Reference is made in this chapter as to why there is no general multilateral convention for the control of land-based pollution, except for Article 207 of the 1982 LOS Convention, which places on the states the general obligation to regulate such pollutants. Brief mention is also made of the various regional efforts to prevent and control land-based pollution in the regions of the northeast Atlantic, the Mediterranean, the Kuwait-Persian Gulf, and West Africa. More detailed information and analysis are given concerning the 1972 Convention on the Prevention of Marine Pollution by Dumping of Wastes (the London Convention). A glaring weakness of the London Dumping Convention has been the lack of effective enforcement measures for violators.

As dramatic as are oil spills by tankers due to accidents and offshore well blowouts that dominate the news whenever these occur, only a small portion of hydrocarbon pollution in the ocean is the result of such accidents. In this chapter discussion of marine pollution based on vessel source provides basic reference and analysis about (1) the 1954 Convention for the Prevention of Pollution by oil and its amendments—the first major international effort made to control marine pollution; and (2) the 1973 International Convention for Prevention of Pollution from Ships (MARPOL) and its 1978 Protocol.

Reference is also made to the various liability and compensation schemes for marine pollution damage to injured parties. Liability and compensation schemes are designed to encourage ship owners to conform to standards established by the various international agreements, sponsored by the IMO. While, under these schemes, ship owners can assume liability for damage to the marine environment as a result of pollution, stricter observance to the rules and standards most likely could be better enforced if marine insurers would insist on a higher premium rate for frequent violators.

The problem of ocean burial as an option for disposing of the rapidly accumulating hazardous high-level radioactive or nuclear substances is becoming a major international concern. In addition, systematic dumping of low-level radioactive material into the sea, on an annual basis, has been adopted by the United States and a number of European nations. A summary review is given here on the types of international treaties for regulating the disposal of low-level nuclear wastes. Since disposal of nuclear wastes is one of the new uses of the oceans, existing international agreements, including the 1982 LOS Convention, are not very clear or precise on the question of whether dumping high-level nuclear waste is legally prohibited.

As a conclusion to the introduction to this chapter on marine environmental protection, several pertinent remarks may be made about this extremely important and complex subject. First, international attempts have been made to provide acceptable rules which are designed to control ocean dumping of solid toxic wastes, as well as the liability and compensation schemes for ship owners. There is no compulsory enforceable obligation for states to comply and observe these rules and standards. In other words, coastal states still must face vessel-source pollution and the ever-increasing threat to their marine environment by the failure to eliminate dumping of hazardous toxic waste in the oceans. To a large extent, as well as in practice, enforcement power rests with the flag states, except in the territorial waters of the coastal states.

Second, since a vast majority of marine pollution originates from land-based sources, overall international control is still lacking. There is some doubt as to whether the 1982 LOS Convention has provided the legal machinery and structure to protect the marine environment. It seems that the only area in the ocean commons where the 1982 LOS Convention can enforce marine pollution regulation is in the International Seabed Area. (It is still uncertain whether the coastal states can exercise their regulatory power to protect their marine environment in the newly established Exclusive Economic Zone.)

Third, nevertheless, several significant trends have taken place due to the adoption of the 1982 LOS Convention. One such trend is the comprehensive treatment of marine environment protection by drawing together in one international legal instrument all the existing principles on the subject. International principles on marine environmental protection have been formulated by a host of multilateral agreements among nations to deal with a specific narrowly defined problem.

Another trend is that collectively all international agreements on marine environmental protection to be discussed in this chapter—and the next on regional arrangement—must be viewed in their totality as representing the changing aspect of the law of the sea: that is, there is a shift from the traditional stance by nations of treating the rules and standards for marine environment protection as merely a responsibility to be assumed, to the acceptance of an obligation for regulation. Under the comprehensive 1982 LOS Convention nations now have a duty to protect and preserve the "ocean commons" beyond their national jurisdiction. And, more significant is the fact that their citizens are held responsible for violations against the marine environmental system.

HAZARDOUS WASTE DISPOSAL: A MARINE POLLUTION PROBLEM

Article 1(4) of the 1982 Law of the Sea Convention defines marine pollution as follows:

> "Pollution of the marine environment" means the introduction by man, directly or indirectly, of substances or energy into the marine environment, including estuaries, which results or is likely to result in such deleterious effects as harm to living resources and marine life, hazards to human health, hindrance to marine activities, including fishing and other legitimate uses of the sea, impairment of quality for use of the sea water and reduction of amenities.

There are four ways by which pollutants enter the ocean: discharge of oil by vessels through normal operations or accidents, discharges of harmful and hazardous substances by vessels as a deliberate action for disposal, run-off from land, and deposit of pollutants from the atmosphere such as rainfall into the ocean.[1] In short, sources of marine pollution consist of land-based pollution, ocean dumping, vessel source pollution, and airborne pollution. Marine pollutants are also classified into degradable and nondegradable categories. Discharges from degradable substances, such as sewage sludges and effluents, generally pose no serious harmful effect to the marine environment if they are in "reasonable quantities" and are treated.[2] However, nondegradable pollutants, such as pesticides and metals, constitute a hazardous threat to the marine environment that must be regulates and controlled through international cooperative efforts.

Luc Cuyvers discusses in detail the nature and effects of disposal of industrial organic and inorganic waste in the marine environment.[3] Organic industrial wastes can be harmful because of the toxicity and reduction of oxygen supply they cause in bays and estuaries into which discharges are made. A list of the origin of some organic industrial waste is provided in Table 8.1.

The extent of eventual damage to the marine environment by numerous synthetic organic chemicals is difficult to estimate at the moment. A list of some of the more important products and their harmful effects on the marine environment has been assembled by the Joint Group of Experts on the Scientific Aspects of Marine Pollution (GESAMP). It is presented in Table 8.2 as a reference.

Inorganic industrial wastes discharged into the marine environment consist of hazardous chemicals such as acids, alkalis, cyanides and metals. Biological effects on North Sea fish with tumors and diseases have been attributed to acid wastes discharged in coastal waters. The most dangerous of all inorganic industrial wastes, in terms of toxic contamination and nondestructibility or persistence, discharged into the marine environment have been the heavy metals: cadmium, mercury, lead and zinc. Contaminated fish consumed by humans have

Table 8.1
Some Organic Industrial Wastes of Natural Origin

Compound	Source
Tannins	Dye industry
Lignin	Pulp and paper mills
Carbohydrates	Pulp and paper mills, brewers, distilleries, sugar production
Proteins, peptides, amino acids, fatty acids, lipids	Slaughterhouses, dairies, fish processing plants
Pyrenthrines	Insectides
Terpenes	Flotation of ore

Source: Luc Cuyvers, *Ocean Uses and Their Regulation* (New York: Wiley, 1984), p. 171. Copyright © 1984 by Luc Cuyvers. Reprinted by permission of John Wiley & Sons, Inc.

been known to cause fatal illness. The effect of consuming shellfish contaminated by mercury, discharged by a chemical fertilizer factory near the coastal city of Minamata on the island of Kyushu, Japan, in the 1950s brought death to over one hundred people and inflicted upon others the bone-aching Minamata or *itai-itai* disease.[4]

Then there is also the cadmium problem. Cadmium is a metallic chemical element belonging to the zinc and mercury family. It is generally used as an alloy for plating corroded metals such as iron and steel. It is also used in the control rods for nuclear reactors, automobile enamels, vinyl plastics, phosphorous for color television tubes, and as a component of storage batteries. It has also been widely used in phosphate fertilizer manufacture for agriculture. It is extremely poisonous.

The bulk of cadmium compounds is deposited as waste in landfills; some of the cadmium element is being burned and thereby released as ash into the atmosphere. Disposal of cadmium waste into the water and marine system poses a serious threat to human and marine life.

The disposal of cadmium waste has been considered a public health problem in Japan and Western Europe. Estimated data on the dissemination of cadmium in the environment that could eventually be introduced into the foodstuffs of the European Common Market countries can be seen in Table 8.3.

Synthetic chemicals, generally classified as chlorinated hydrocarbons, widely used by industries and agriculture, can accumulate in fish in high concentrations. Insecticides such as DDT, fumigants, hydraulic fluids, and solvents, as well as PCBs (polychlorinated biphenyls) used industrially in electrical equipment and the manufacture of paints, coating compounds and plastics, are examples of chlorinated hydrocarbons that are mostly insoluble in water. For instance, DDT residue interferes with calcium metabolism causing seabird egg shells to be thin. PCBs are found to cause weakening reproductive and ovulation function in birds

Table 8.2
Some Organic Industrial Substances and Their Effects on the Marine Environment

Compound	Formula	Use	Pathways	Toxicity (LC 50)	Characteristics & Effects
Acetone	Ch_3COCH_3	Solvent, delustrant, decreasing agent	Rivers, direct discharges	100-1000 ppm	Readily degradable, nonpersistent
Acrolein	$CH_2{=}{=}CH{\cdot}CHO$	In production of acrylic and other plastics		<1 mg/l	Unstable and polymerizes rapidly to give disacryl; sub-lethal effects (decreased shell growth in oysters) reported at less than 0.1 mg/l; repellent to fish
Acrylonitrile	$H_2C{=}{=}CHCN$	Intermediate in synthesis of acrylic fibers		25-50 ppm	One of the more oxidation resisting nitriles; relatively short residence time; high cumulative or chronic toxicity to marine organisms
Benzene	C_4H_4	Serves as basic substrate of numerous chemical intermediates in production of petrochemicals and plastics	Ocean dumping, operational discharges, atmosphere, seepage	10-100 ppm	Degrades very slowly; will bioaccumulate and cause tainting
Carbon disulfide	CS_2	Production of rayon, cellulose films, manufacture of tetrachloride and xanthates		<1 ppm	Decomposes in the sea by oxidation; very toxic
Cresol	$CH_3C_4H_4OH$	Manufacture of disinfectants and synthetic resins, tricresyl phosphate, herbicides		1-10 ppm	Biodegradable, breakdown products are less toxic; will taint fish and shellfish at very low concentrations

Crotonaldehyde	$CH_3CH:CHCHO$	Production of acetate solvents	Industrial effluents; leakage	1-10 ppm	Biodegradable and not accumulated; breakdown products are less toxic
Cumene	$C_4H_5CH(CH_3)_2$	Intermediate in production of phenol and acetone; manufacture of plastics; solvent	Evaporation	10-100 ppm	Degradable
Ethyl alcohol	C_2H_5OH	Solvent; production of alcoholic beverages; many minor uses		10-100 ppm	Rapidly biodegraded and not accumulated
Ethyl benzene	$C_6H_5C_2H_5$	Solvent; production of styrene monomer	Industrial effluents; possibly atmosphere	10-100 ppm	Degradable; breakdown products are less toxic; not accumulated
Naphthenic acid	Mixture of carboxylic acids	Production of metal naphthenates		1-10 ppm	Likely to be biodegraded; breakdown products possible with same toxicity; results in tainting of fish and shellfish
Phenol	C_6H_5OH	Chemical intermediate in production of resins, pharmaceuticals, disinfectants, herbicides	Present in most domestic and industrial effluents	10-100 ppm	Although chemically stable, phenol is biodegradable, but the speed of this process in the sea is not known; will react with proteins, but action on marine life has not been studied; tainting may occur at very low levels
Styrene monomer	$C_6H_5CH:CH_2$	Production of polystyrene and other plastics, rubbers, resins	Chemical tanker washings	10-100 ppm	Degrades very slowly; degradation products of the polymer and monomer in the marine environment are not fully known, but are unlikely to be more toxic than the parent compound

Table 8.2 (Continued)

Compound	Formula	Use	Pathways	Toxicity (LC 50)	Characteristics & Effects
Phthalate esters	Plasticizers in production of PVC, polyvinyl acetate and other plastics; solvent, insect repellents, cosmetics			Varies w/ alcohol used; usually low	Rate of breakdown varies between esters; several phthalates are accumulated by fish and invertebrates by factors ranging from 1400-3600
Tetramethyl lead	$Pb(CH_3)_4$	Antiknock additives	Atmosphere	1 ppm (TEL)	Short-term bioaccumulation
Tetraethyl lead	$Pb(C_2H_5)_4$			n.a. (TML)	
Toluene	$C_6H_5CH_3$	Solvent; chemical intermediate	Industrial effluents	10-100 ppm	Biological properties are not well known
Toluene diisocyanate	$CH_3C_4H_3(NCO)_2$	Production of polyurethane foams		1-10 ppm	Will react with seawater to produce solid phenyl ureas
Xylene	$C_6H_4(CH_3)_2$	Solvent in manufacture of paints and surface coatings; synthesis of organic chemicals	Spills, tank washings, some via atmosphere	n.a.	Relatively stable, slow breakdown process; will not bioaccumulate

Source: Cuyvers, *Ocean Uses and Their Regulation*, pp. 74–76. Reprinted by permission of John Wiley & Sons, Inc.

Table 8.3
Current Cadmium Inputs to the Environment of European Common Market Countries

Source	Compartment		
	Air	Land	Water
Volcanic action	20.0	ND	ND
Non-ferrous metal production			
Zinc and cadmium	20.0	200.0	50
Copper	6.0	15.0	ND
Lead	7.0	40.0	20
Production of cadmium-containing materials	3.0	90.0	108
Iron and steel production	34.0	349.0	ND
Fuel combustion			
Coal and lignite	8.0	390.0	ND
Oil and gas	0.5	14.5	--
Waste disposal	31.0	1,434.0	ND
Sewage sludge disposal	2.0	130.0	33
Phosphate fertilizers	--	346.0	62
Totals	132.0	3,009.5	273

Source: Edward D. Goldberg, "The Oceans as Waste Space," in *Ocean Yearbook 5*, Elisabeth Mann Borgese and Norton Ginsburg, eds. (Chicago: University of Chicago Press, 1985), p. 157. Used by permission.

and mammals (seals). In 1968 rice oil contaminated with PCBs caused *yaslo* disease in Japan when thousands of people affected had darkening of the skin or an appearance of skin acne.[5]

In subsequent sections of this chapter we will discuss the prohibition by international conventions of ocean dumping of mercury, cadmium and other dangerous substances. In March 1989 the international conference on movement of hazardous wastes attended by 116 nations produced a convention that prohibits shipping of toxic hazardous wastes to and through a third nation without its specific consent and authorization—the Convention on Transboundary Movement of Hazardous Wastes.[6]

Oil has been a major source of marine pollution. This subject will be discussed in a separate section of this chapter: vessel-source oil pollution.

The oceans have become the receptacle of plastic litter discarded by people. It has been estimated that 1.1 to 2.6 kilograms per person per day of plastic waste has been generated, and most of it has ended up in the ocean. There have been estimates that the world's merchant ships have dumped 450,000 plastic containers per day. Plastic containers (mostly made of polyethylene) are not biodegradable; they are durable, lasting in the sea for as long as three years. Floating plastics have been found to be lodged in the stomachs of large fish; they cover the seabed as "polyethylene sheeting" that poses problems for fisheries.[7] Drift gill fishing nets made of nylon have entangled fish, seabirds diving for fish, and mammals such as seals and whales. Clark reports that the Danish salmon drift net fishery killed an estimated 250,000 to 500,000 seabirds each year from 1965 to 1975.[8] Japanese salmon fishermen using drift gill nets in the north Pacific and the Bering Sea killed an estimated 350,000 to 450,000 seabirds in 1975–1978.[9] In the 1989 session of the Hawaii State Legislature a bill was proposed to prohibit the use of drift gill fishing nets in Hawaiian waters, making it unlawful to use netting for fishing that is made of plastic which is not portable or is more than ten feet in length and six feet in height or width.[10] In 1946 twelve European nations (Belgium, Denmark, Eire, France, Iceland, the Netherlands, Norway, Poland, Portugal, Spain, Sweden and the United Kingdom) concluded a convention for the regulation of the meshes of fishing nets and the size of fish caught in parts of the Atlantic and Arctic Oceans. Article 5 and Annex I of the convention limited the lengthwise measurement of the net to "a flat gauge of 80 mm broad and 2 mm thick."[11] The U.S. National Marine Fisheries Service reported, as revealed by Washington State representatives to Congress, that Japanese drift nets, stretching as long as thirty miles, in 1989 unintentionally snagged millions of fish, thousands of seabirds and hundreds of dolphins. The U.S. Commerce Department in July 1990, based on an international team observation, reported that the Japanese squid fleet in the north Pacific snagged 914 dolphins, 59,060 tuna, 58,100 shark and 9,173 seabirds along with 3 million squid caught during the last six months of 1989.[12] In July 1989 the fifteen nations of the South Pacific Forum signed the Tarawa Declaration, which sought to ban the use of drift nets, an action that forced Japan to reduce its drift net fleet in the south Pacific from the normal sixty to a maximum of about twenty. Likewise, Taiwan has reduced its drift net fleet in the South Pacific and will ban its operation after July 1, 1991.[13] The United Nations General Assembly passed a drift net moratorium resolution on December 22, 1989, which recommended banning the use of drift net fishing on the high seas by 1992. Taiwan announced in June 1990 that it would ban its drift net fleet from fishing in the South Pacific by July 1991. Japan suspended drift net fishing in the South Pacific in the coming 1990–1991 season, a year before the date set by the United Nations moratorium resolution.

Significance. The oceans have become the receptacle not only for the disposal of solid waste (at a rate of 3 billion tons per year) and carbon dioxide (more than 20 billion tons) from fossil fuels and biomass, but also a place for dumping hazardous industrial toxic waste, including low-level radioactive substances. In addition, as pointed out by researchers of an international conference on marine debris held in Honolulu in April 1989, the oceans are choking with debris consisting mainly of synthetic plastic products discarded by human users that bring injury and death to marine life.[14]

While international cooperative efforts, mostly under the auspices of the IMO, for setting procedures and standards regulating the harmful effects that waste disposal at sea can cause, two main problems seem to have impeded the progress of attempts to protect the marine environment. One is the difficulty of instituting enforcement measures for implementing the objectives and goals of the various international convention provisions. The other is the ongoing debate among some scientists and most of the environmentalists on the issue of whether oceans can serve as "waste space" or act as "a waste receptacle."[15] While environmental purists, the so-called "Cousteau Mystique," insist on strict international rules and regulations to police ocean disposal operations, the "ocean as waste space" marine scientists have developed rudimentary models "to determine the assimilative capacities of specific waters on the basis of unacceptable impacts on marine organisms," so that the oceans can become "the most rational disposal site on the basis of environmental, technical and economic criteria."[16]

INTERGOVERNMENTAL MARITIME CONSULTATIVE ORGANIZATION

Originally established as a body for technical cooperation on maritime regulation, practices and safety at sea, the 1948 United Nations Maritime Conference drafted the Convention of the Intergovernmental Maritime Consultative Organization for signature. The organization came into being in 1958, a decade later, when twenty-one nations ratified the convention. The membership included the world's seven major maritime states, each with a total tonnage at the time of at least 1 million gross tons of shipping.[17] The IMCO was intended to be a consultative and advisory body to the contracting governments in the drafting of agreements and conventions, as well as serving the purpose of convening international conferences to achieve these purposes:[18]

1. to provide machinery for cooperation among governments in the field of governmental regulation and practices relating to technical matters, including those concerning safety at sea
2. to encourage the removal of discriminatory action and of unnecessary restrictions by governments
3. to consider matters concerning unfair restrictive practices by shipping concerns
4. to consider any matters concerning shipping that might be referred to it by any organ or specialized agencies of the United Nations
5. to provide for the exchange of information among governments on matters under consideration by the organization

On May 22, 1982, the IMCO changed its name to the International Maritime Organization after the entry into force in 1975 of amendments to the 1958 convention that formed IMCO. The IMO has now expanded its functions to include the prevention and control of marine pollution from vessels and to establish a permanent committee on marine environment protection in its constitution.[19]

IMCO began in 1958 with a total membership of twenty-seven.[20] Since then its membership has grown steadily until there were 102 member states in 1977 and 113 in the 1980s. IMCO's membership growth pattern can be seen in Table 8.4.

Decision making in the IMCO has always been dominated by the major shipowning nations and the major trading countries within the organization's membership.[21] While the IMCO's Assembly, the supreme governing organ for the maritime organization, representing all members, meets only once every two years, its Council of twenty-four members serves as the governing body between the sessions of the Assembly. The Council is, in essence, the "central policy organ" of the IMCO.[22] The Council approves recommendations to the Assembly, which are not binding on members, but may eventually be incorporated into members' national legislation or become provisions in treaties later on.[23]

In 1973, upon the recommendation made by the United States for an expanded role, not only in maritime safety, but in marine environmental protection, the IMCO established the Marine Environmental Protection Committee (MEPC). In fact, the MEPC has adopted a "quasi-legislative" approach in making technical changes to the 1973 International Convention for the Prevention of Pollution from Ships (MARPOL).

Despite its advisory and consultative function on technical matters, IMCO has been instrumental in drafting two major pollution control conventions: the 1954 International Convention for the Prevention of Pollution of the Sea by Oil (amended in 1962 and 1969) and the 1973 International Convention on Pollution from Ships, which are discussed separately in this chapter. IMCO debate after

Table 8.4
List of IMCO Members as of April 2, 1982

Algeria**
Angola
Argentina*
Australia*
Austria
Bahamas
Bahrain
Bangladesh
Barbados**
Belgium*
Benin
Brazil*
Bulgaria**
Burma**
United Republic of Cameroon**
Canada*
Cape Verde
Chile*
China**
Colombia*
Congo
Costa Rica
Cuba*
Cyprus**
Czechoslovakia**
Denmark*
Djibouti
Dominica
Dominican Republic*
Ecuador**
Egypt*
El Salvador
Equatorial Guinea**
Ethiopia
Finland*
France*
Gabon
Gambia
German Democratic Republic
Germany, Federal Republic of
Ghana**
Greece*
Guinea
Guinea-Bissau
Guyana
Haiti**
Honduras**
Hong Kong** (Associate Member)
Hungary**
Iceland**
India*
Indonesia**
Iran**
Iraq**
Ireland*
Israel**
Italy*
Ivory Coast**
Jamaica
Japan**
Jordan**
Kampuchea
Kenya**
Korea, Republic of
Kuwait**
Lebanon*
Liberia**
Libyan Arab Jamahiriya**
Madagascar**
Malaysia**
Maldives**
Malta**
Mauritania**
Mauritius
Mexico**
Morocco**
Mozambique
Nepal
Netherlands*
New Zealand*
Nicaragua
Nigeria**
Norway*
Oman**
Pakistan*
Panama*
Papua New Guinea
Peru*
Philippines**
Poland*
Portugal*
Qatar
Romania**
Saint Lucia
Saint Vincent and the Grenadines
Saudi Arabia**
Senegal**
Seychelles
Sierra Leone**
Singapore**
Somalia
Spain**
Sri Lanka**
Sudan**
Surinam
Sweden*
Switzerland*
Syrian Arab Republic**
United Republic of Tanzania**
Thailand**
Trinidad and Tobago**
Tunisia**
Turkey*
United Arab Emirates
United Kingdom*
United States*
Uruguay**
Union of Soviet Socialist Republics**
Venezuela
Yemen Arab Republic
Yemen, Democratic Republic
Yugoslavia**
Zaire**

* Founding members
** Members having acceded as of 1975
Source: Wilhelm H. Lampe, "The 'New' International Maritime Organization and Its Place in Development of International Maritime Law," *Journal of Maritime Law and Commerce*, 14, no. 3 (July 1983): 307. Used by permission.

the 1967 *Torrey Canyon* oil spill disaster led to many other international agreements on marine pollution control, liabilities and compensation for damages resulting from oil pollution by tankers, and maritime safety, as seen in Table 8.5.

Significance. Since its entry into force in 1954, IMCO (now IMO) has become responsible for tackling problems created by ship-generated marine pollution. In the past forty years, there have been as many as thirty international conventions

Table 8.5
List of International Conventions and Agreements on Marine Pollution and Maritime Safety Sponsored by IMCO (IMO)

	Responsible Organization	In Force
A. General Conventions : Global		
1. Geneva Convention on the Terroritorial Sea and the Contiguous Zone, 1958	U.N.	10 Sept. 1964
2. Geneva Convention on the High Seas, 1958	U.N.	30 Sept. 1962
3. Geneva Convention on Fishing and Conservation of the Living Resources of the High Seas, 1958	U.N.	20 March 1966
4. Geneva Convention on the Continental Shelf, 1958	U.N.	10 June 1964
5. Stockholm Declaration and Action Plan on the Human Environment	UNEP	----
6. United Nations Convention on the Law of the Sea, 1982	U.N.	Not in force
B. Marine Pollution: Global		
7. International Convention for the Prevention of Pollution of the Sea by Oil, 1954 (OILPOL '54) Amended in 1962 and 1969	IMO	26 July 1958
a) 1971 (Great Barrier Reef) Amendment	IMO	Not in force
b) 1971 (Tanks) Amendment	IMO	Not in force
8. International Convention Relating to Interventions on the High Seas in Cases of Oil Pollution, 1969 (INTERVENTION 1969)	IMO	6 May 1975
a) 1973 (Substances other than Oil) Protocol. (INTERVENTION PROT 1973)	IMO	30 March 1983
9. International Convention on the Dumping of Wastes át Sea, 1972 (LDC 1972)	IMO	30 Aug. 1975
10. International Convention for the Prevention of Pollution from Ships, 1973 (MARPOL 1973)	IMO	2 Oct. 1983
i. Annex I: Regulations for the Prevention of Pollution by Oil	IMO	2 Oct. 1983
ii. Annex II: Regulations for the Control of Pollution by Noxious Liquid Substances in Bulk.	IMO	Not in force
iii. Annex III: Regulations for the Prevention of Pollution by Harmful Substances carried by Sea in Packaged Forms, or in Freight Containers, Portable Tanks on Road and Rail Tank Wagon.	IMO	Not in force

Table 8.5 (continued)

	Responsible Organization	In Force
iv. Annex IV: Regulations for the Prevention of Pollution by Sewage from Ships	IMO	Not in force
v. Annex V: Regulations for the Prevention of Pollution by Garbage from Ships	IMO	Not in force
a) 1978 (Tanker Safety and Pollution Prevention) Protocol (MARPOL PROT 1978)	IMO	2 Oct. 1983
C. Marine Pollution: Regional		
11. Agreement for Co-operation in dealing with Pollution of the North Sea by Oil, 1969 (The Bonn Agreement)	FRG Govt	Adopted 1969
12. Agreement between Denmark, Finland, Norway and Sweden concerning Co-operation in Measures to deal with Pollution by the Sea by Oil, 1971 (The Copenhagen Agreement)	Danish Govt	Adopted 1971
13. Convention for the Prevention of Marine Pollution by Dumping from Ships and Aircraft, 1972 (Oslo Convention on Dumping)	Norwegian Govt	Adopted 15 Feb. 1972
14. Convention on the Protection of the Environment between Denmark, Finland, Norway and Sweden, 1974 (Stockholm Convention)	Swedish Govt	Adopted 19 Feb. 1974
15. Convention on the Protection of the Marine Environment of the Baltic Sea Area, 1974 (Helsinki Convention)	UNEP	Adopted 22 March 1974
16. Convention for the Protection of the Mediterranean Sea against Pollution, 1976 (Barcelona Convention)	UNEP	12 Feb. 1978
a) Protocol for the Prevention of Pollution of the Mediterranean Sea by Dumping from Ships and Aircraft	UNEP	12 Feb. 1978
b) Protocol concerning Co-operation in Combating Pollution of the Mediterranean Sea by Oil and other Harmful Substances in Cases of Emergency	UNEP	12 Feb. 1978
17. The Kuwait Regional Convention for Co-operation on the Protection of the Marine Environment from Pollution, 1978 (The Kuwait Convention)	UNEP	30 June 1979
a) Protocol concerning Regional Co-operation in Combating Pollution by Oil and Other Harmful Substances in Cases of Emergency	UNEP	30 June 1979
18. Convention for Co-operation in the Protection and Development of the Marine and Coastal		

Table 8.5 (continued)

		Responsible Organization	In Force
	Environment of the West and Central African Region.	UNEP	Not in force
a)	Protocol concerning Co-operation in Combating Pollution in Case of Emergency	UNEP	Not in force
19.	Convention for the Protection and Development of the Marine Environment of the Wider Caribbean Region	UNEP	Not in force
a)	Protocol Concerning Co-operation in Combating Pollution in Cases of Emergency	UNEP	Not in force
20.	Convention for the Protection of the Marine Environment and Coastal Areas of the South-East Pacific (The Lima Convention)	UNEP	Not in force
a)	Agreement on Regional Co-operation in Combating Pollution of the South-East Pacific by Hydrocarbons and Other Harmful Substances in Cases of Emergency	UNEP	Not in force
b)	Complementary Protocol to the Agreement on Regional Co-operation in Combating Pollution in Cases of Emergency	UNEP	Not in force
21.	Regional Convention for the Conservation of the Marine Environment of the Red Sea and the Gulf of Aden (The Jeddah Convention)	UNEP	Not in force
a)	Protocol concerning Regional Co-operation in Combating Marine Pollution by Oil and other Harmful Substances in cases of Emergency	UNEP	Not in force
22.	Convention for the Protection and Development of Natural Resources and Environment of the South Pacific Region	UNEP	Not in force
a)	Protocol for the Protection of the South Pacific Region by Dumping	UNEP	Not in force
b)	Protocol concerning Co-operation in Combating Oil Pollution Emergencies in the South-Pacific Region	UNEP	Not in force
23.	Memorandum of Understanding on Port State Control	Netherlands Govt	1 July 1982
D.	**Liability & Compensation Schemes: Intergovernmental**		
24.	International Convention Relating to the Limitation of the Liability of Owners of Sea-going Ships, 1957	Govt of Belgium	1957
a)	Amending Protocol 1979	Govt of Belgium	Not in force

Table 8.5 (continued)

	Responsible Organization	In Force
25. International Convention on Civil Liberty for Oil Pollution Damage, 1969 (CLC 1969)	IMO	19 Jan 1975
26. International Convention on the Establishment of an International Fund for Compensation for Oil Pollution Damage 1971 (FUND 1971)	IMO & IOPC Fund	16 Oct. 1978
a) Protocol 1976 (Unit of Account Revision)	IMO & IOPC Fund	Not in force
27. Convention Relating to Civil Liability in the Field of Maritime Carriage of Nuclear Material 1971 (NUCLEAR 1971)	IMO	19 July 1975
28. Liability for Maritime Claims, 1976 (LLMC 1976)	IMO	Not in force
29. Protocol of 1984 to Amend the International Convention on Civil Liability for Oil Pollution Damage, 1969	IMO	Not in force
30. Protocol of 1984 to Amend the International Convention on the Establishment of an International Fund for Compensation for Oil Pollution Damage, 1971	IMO	Not in force
E. Liability & Compensation Schemes: Industry		
31. Tanker Owners' Voluntary Agreement Concerning Liability for Oil Pollution, 1969 (TOVALOP) as revised to 1978	ITOPF	18 Sept. 1969
32. Contract Regarding and Interim Supplement to Tanker Liability for Oil Pollution, 1971 (CRISTAL), as revised to 1978	CRISTAL	14 Jan. 1971
33. Pollution Liability Agreement among Tanker Owners (PLATO), 1985	ITOPF/ PLATO	Not in force
F. General Maritime Safety		
34. International Convention for the Unification of Certain Rules of Law Relating to Assistance and Salvage at Sea, 1910	Govt Belgium	Adopted 23 Oct. 1910
35. International Convention for the Safety of Life at Sea, 1960 (SOLAS 1960) 1960)	IMO	Adopted 26 May 1965
a) Amendments of: 1966, 1967, 1968, 1969, 1971 & 1973	IMO	Not in force
36. International Convention on Load Lines 1966 (LL 1966)	IMO	Adopted 21 July 1968

Table 8.5 (continued)

	Responsible Organization	In Force
a) Amendments of: 1971, 1975 & 1979	IMO	Not in force
37. Convention on the International Regulations for Preventing Collisions at Sea, 1972 (COLREG 1972)	IMO	Adopted 15 July 1977
a) Amendment 1981	IMO	Adopted 1 June 1983
38. International Convention for Safe Containers, 1972 (CSC 1972) as amended	IMO	Adopted 6 Sept. 1977
a) Amendment of 1983	IMO	Adopted 1 Jan. 1984
39. International Convention for the Safety of Life at Sea, 1974 (SOLAS 1974)	IMO	Adopted 25 May 1980
a) 1978 Protocol (SOLAS PROT 1978)	IMO	Adopted 1 May 1981
b) Amendment of 1981	IMO	Adopted 1 Sept. 1984
c) Amendment of 1983	IMO	Adopted 1 July 1986 (expected)
40. International Convention on Standards of Training, Certification and Watch-keeping for Seafarers, 1978 (STCW 1978)	IMO	Adopted 28 April 1984

Source: Edgar Gold, "The Control of Marine Pollution from Ships: Responsibilities and Rights," in *The Law of the Sea: What Lies Ahead?* Thomas A. Clingan, ed. (Honolulu: The Law of the Sea Institute, University of Hawaii, 1987), pp. 292–96. Used by permission.

regulating maritime affairs sponsored by the IMCO. It has served as the secretariat for the 1972 London Convention on Ocean Dumping. It is an established fact that a majority of the existing international machinery, standards and procedures for marine environmental protection are the result of the work of the IMCO in calling for and helping to draft the various international conventions and agreements of marine pollution from vessels. IMCO conventions and agreements tend to be more flexible in consensus building, particularly in its procedure of "tacit acceptance" if a no more than fixed required number of states representing one-half of the world's merchant tonnage object within a certain period.[24]

IMCO (IMO) has often been accused of being a tool that is manipulated and influenced by the shipping interests and oil companies, or "the maritime states club." It nevertheless provides an instrument and a useful forum for international cooperation in marine pollution control. The role of IMO can be expanded to enable it to become "the central source of information on the observance of its own standards," to conduct research on prevention of marine pollution, and to engage in the formulation of regulations for the protection of the marine environment.[25] Its constitution (Article I) has now entrusted it with the prevention and control of marine pollution by ships as one of its functions. However, in the final analysis, the IMO is basically an advisory and consultative organization and possesses no regulatory power despite its sponsorship of a significant number of international conventions in the area of marine environmental protection.

INTERVENTION IN POLLUTION ON THE HIGH SEAS

The 1967 spill of 100,000 tons of oil into the sea, caused by the accidental grounding of the tanker *Torrey Canyon*, raised the legal question of the coastal states' power to intervene promptly to prevent major oil pollution damage to the shorelines by a vessel that was outside the territorial sea or on the high seas. This occurred at the time when the concept of Exclusive Economic Zone was beginning to take shape at the United Nations. In the *Torrey Canyon* case, the British authorities bombed the vessel by setting fire to the oil cargo in order to reduce pollution damage. The IMO (then IMCO) was instrumental in the drafting of the 1969 International Convention Relating to Intervention on the High Seas in Case of Oil Pollution Casualties (The Intervention Convention), which was adopted by the international conference at Brussels and opened for signature from November 29, 1969, to December 31, 1970. The 1969 Intervention Convention entered into force May 6, 1975.

Article I(1) of the 1969 Intervention Convention on the high seas states:

> Parties to the present Convention may take such measures on the high seas as may be necessary to prevent, mitigate or eliminate grave and imminent danger to their coastlines or related interests from pollution or threat of pollution of the sea by oil, following upon a maritime casualty or acts related to such a casualty, which may reasonably be expected to result in major harmful consequences.[26]

Significance. However, before a coastal state takes such measures, it must seek consultation with other affected states and post due notice unless it is a case of "extreme urgency" (Article III). "Maritime casualty" is defined in Article II(1) as "a collision of ships, stranding or other incident of navigation, or other occurrence on board a ship or external to it resulting in material damage or imminent threat of material damage to a ship or cargo." Measures taken by the coastal state for intervention on the high seas must be proportionate to the damage, actual or threatened, to it (Article V). The Annex to the 1969 Convention provides procedures for conciliation in cases of dispute.

In 1973 a Protocol was adopted to expand intervention against casualties caused by oil and pollution by substances other than oil.[27] Substances other than oil are listed in the Annex to the Protocol (see Table 8.6). In addition, Article I(2)(b) added "those other substances which are liable to create hazards to human health, to harm living resources and marine life, to damage amenities or to interfere with other legitimate uses of the sea."

LAND-BASED POLLUTION

About 25 percent of all marine pollution can be attributed to land-based sources: from agricultural runoff of fertilizers and pesticides in top soil to sewage outfalls to industrial waste, including discharges into the atmosphere of automobile exhaust which eventually settles on rivers, lakes or ocean waters as "acid rain" and "acid snow." Article 207(1) of the 1982 LOS Convention makes it an obligation on the part of states to adopt rules and regulations "to prevent, reduce and control pollution of the marine environment land-based sources, including rivers, estuaries, pipelines and outfall structures."

There are four types of land-based pollution: airborne, such as acid rain, toxic waste from landfills, discharge from land into rivers and coastal waters, and erosion or agricultural runoff. Most difficult to regulate has been the transboundary airborne pollution.

Acid rain and any airborne pesticides that fall into the rivers and oceans have been the worst type of "transboundary pollution."[28] When this happens the substances or the acid deposition stimulate algae growth, which prevents sunlight from penetrating to the submerged marine plants and/or suffocate marine life to death. Acid precipitation of airborne pollutants from land-based fossil-burning industries and automobile exhaust have been blamed by the United States Environmental Defense Fund as the cause of destruction of marine life, including spawning grounds of fisheries, in bays, estuaries and lakes in Canada and the United States.[29] Nitrogen oxide emissions contaminate coastal waters of New York and North Carolina. Chesapeake Bay has been contaminated by acid rain and by agricultural runoff and waste disposal from factories. The dispute between the United States and Canada over acid rain pollution illustrates the problem in the control of transboundary land-based pollution, for, as pointed out by John W. Kindt, "polluting countries argue, however, that there is no provable nexus between a 'specific' instance of acid precipitation and an alleged polluter."[30] Control of acid rain must begin at the source as in the case of the controversy between the United States and Canada, the coal-burning industries in the Ohio River Basin.[31] Of course, Canada contributes its share of acid rain for the United States across the border.

In general terms, the 1982 LOS Convention (Article 112[1]) states about pollution from or through the atmosphere:

> States shall adopt laws and regulations to prevent, reduce and control pollution of the marine environment from or through the atmosphere, applicable to the air space under

Table 8.6
List of Substances Established by the Marine Environment Protection Committee of the Organization in Accordance with Paragraph 2(a) of Article I

1. Oil (when carried in bulk)
   - Asphalt Solutions
     - Blending stocks
     - Roofers flux
     - Straight run residue
   - Oil
     - Clarified
     - Mixtures containing crude oil
     - Road oil
     - Aromatic oil (excluding vegetable oil)
     - Blending stocks
     - Mineral oil
     - Penetrating oil
     - Spindle oil
     - Turbine oil
   - Distillates
     - Straight run
     - Flashed feed stocks
   - Gas Oil
     - Cracked
   - Gasoline Blending Stocks
     - Alkylates - fuel
     - Reformates
     - Polymer - fuel
   - Gasolines
     - Casinghead (natural)
     - Automotive
     - Aviation
     - Straight run
   - Jet Fuels
     - JP-1 (kerosene)
     - JP-3
     - JP-4
     - JP-5 (kerosene, heavy)
     - Turbo fuel
     - Mineral spirit
   - Naphtha
     - Solvent
     - Petroleum
     - Heartcut distillate oil
2. Noxious Substances
   - Acetic anhydride
   - Acetone
   - Acetone cyanohydrin
   - Acrolcin
   - Acrylonitrile
   - Aldrin
   - Allyl isothiocyanate
   - Arsenic compounds
   - Atrazine
   - Azinphos methyl (Guthion)
   - Barium azide
   - Aluminium phosphide
   - Ammonia (28% aqueous)
   - Ammonium phosphate
   - Amyl mercaptan
   - Aniline
   - Aniline hydrochloride
   - Antimony compounds
   - Dinitrophenols
   - Endosulphan (Thiodan)
   - Endrin
   - Epichlorohydrin

Table 8.6 (continued)

2. <u>Noxious Substances</u>

Barium cyanide
Barium oxide
Benzene
Benzene hexachloride isomers (Lindane)
Benzidine
Beryllium powder
Bromine
Bromobenzyl cyanide
n-Butyl acrylate
Butyric acid
Cacodylic acid
Cadmium compounds
Carbaryl (Sevin)
Carbon disulphide
Carbon tetrachloride
Chlorodane
Chloroacetone
Chloroacetophenone
Chlorodinitrobenzene
Chloroform
Chlorohydrins (crude)
Chloropicrin
Chromic acid (Chromium trioxide)
Cocculus (solid)
Copper compounds
Cresols
Cupriethylene diamine
Cyanide compounds
Cyanogen bromide
Cyanogen chloride
DDT
Dichloroanilines
Dichlorobenzenes
Dieldrin
Dimethoate (Cygon)
Dimethyl amine (40% aqueous)
Dinitroanilines
4,6 Dinitroorthocresol
Ethyl bromoacetate
Ethylene chlorohydrin (2-Chloro-ethanol)
Ethylene dichloride
Ethyl parathion
Fentin acetate (dry)
Fluosilicic acid
Heptachlor
Hexachlorobenzene
Hexaethyl tetraphosphate
Hydrocyanic acid
Hydroflouric acid (40% aqueous)
Isoprene
Lead compounds
Lindane (Cammexane, BHC)
Malathion
Mercuric compounds
Methyl alcohol
Methylene chloride
Molasses
Napthalene (molten)
Naphthylthiourea
Nitric acid (90%)
Oleum
Parathion
Paraquat
Phenol
Phosphoric acid
Phosphorus (elemental)
Polyhalogenated biphenyls
Sodium pentachlorophenate (solution)
Styrene monomers
Toluene
Toluene diisocyanate
Toxaphene
Tritolyl phosphate (Tricresyl phosphate)
2,4,5-T

3. <u>Liquified Gases</u> (when carried in bulk)

Acetaldehyde
Anhydrous ammonia
Butadiene
Butane
Butane/Propane mixtures
Butylenes
Chlorine
Dimethylanine
Ethyl chloride
Ethane
Ethylene
Ethylene oxide
Methane (LNG)
Methyl acetylene propadiene mixture
Methyl bromide
Methyl chloride
Propane
Propylene
Vinyl chloride monomer
Anhydrous hydrogen chloride
Anhydrous hydrogen flouride
Sulphur dioxide

Table 8.6 (continued)

4. Radioactive Substances

Radioactive substances, including, but not limited to, elements and compounds the isotopes of which are subject to the requirements of Section 835 of the Regulations for the Safe Transport of Radioactive Materials, 1973 Revised Edition, published by the International Atomic Energy Agency, and which may be found to be stored or transported as substances and/or materials in Type A packages, Type B packages, as fissile materials or materials transported under special arrangements, such as:

^{60}Co ^{137}Cs ^{226}Ra ^{239}Pu ^{235}U

Source: *United States Treaties and Other International Agreements*, TIAS 10561 (Washington, D.C.: U.S. GPO, 1982), pp. 9–12.

their sovereignty and to vessels flying their flag or vessels or aircraft of their registry, taking into account internationally agreed rules, standards and recommended practices and procedures and the safety of air navigation.

Then Article 112(3) urges states to establish "global and regional rules" for the reduction and control of such pollution.

However, the 1979 United Nations Convention on Long-Range Trans-boundary Air Pollution is more specific in at least two respects.[32] One, the convention provides two definitions on airborne pollution. "Air pollution" is defined in Article I of the convention as

the introduction by men, directly or indirectly, of substances or energy into the air resulting in deleterious effects of such a nature as to endanger human health, harm living resources and ecosystems and material property and impair or interfere with amenities and other legitimate uses of the environment, and "air pollutants" shall be construed accordingly.

Then the 1979 convention on air pollution defines long-range transboundary air pollution as "air pollution whose physical origin is situated wholly or in part within the area under the national jurisdiction of another state at such a distance that it is not generally possible to distinguish the contribution of individual emission sources or groups of sources." The other specific aspect of the 1979 convention on air pollution is its call for signatory states to exchange scientific data and monitor airborne pollution.

In the recent United States–Canada controversy over acid rain pollution, in August 1988 President Reagan agreed to freeze emission levels of nitrogen oxide at the 1987 levels, or at 19 million tons, for seven years, to 1995. Canada has complained that emission of nitrogen oxide from the United States has acidified more than 700,000 of its lakes, damaged forests and created health problems for its citizens.[33] Canada was a party to the ten-nation (Austria, Canada, Denmark, Finland, France, Federal Republic of Germany, Netherlands, Norway,

Sweden, Switzerland) declaration at the ministerial conference held on March 21, 1984, in Ottawa. The declaration called for the signatories to reduce national annual sulphur emissions by at least 30 percent by 1993, using 1980 emission levels as the basis for calculation. Negotiations, including the United States and the Soviet Union, continued in 1988–1989 on the sixteen-nation treaty for reduction of emission of sulfur dioxide.

An earlier negotiation, the Trail Smelter Arbitration (1935) between Canada and the United States, was a landmark arbitration case dealing with indemnity for damage to the United States caused by a smelter on the Canadian side of the border.[34] The final decision of the tribunal stated that it was the responsibility of a state to prevent its territory being polluted by the operation of a smelter, thus causing damage to persons and property from another state. The arbitration ruling established the liability for airborne pollution damage in the development of international law.[35]

There is no general multilateral convention for the control of land-based pollution except the general provisions in the 1982 LOS Convention mentioned earlier. However, there have been a number of regional conventions negotiated for the control of land-based pollution:

1. the 1974 Convention on the Prevention of Marine Pollution from Land-Based Sources (the Paris Convention) that applies to the northeast Atlantic and the North Sea
2. the 1980 Protocol to the 1976 Mediterranean Convention
3. the Baltic Convention
4. the Kuwait Convention
5. West African Convention

While detailed provisions contained in the regional conventions will be discussed in Chapter 9, it is sufficient to say here that most of these regional conventions for the control of land-based pollution contain specific lists or categories of noxious pollutants whose discharge into the marine environment is to be limited or prohibited.

Significance. There are a number of factors associated with the difficulties in obtaining international cooperation in the control of land-based sources of marine pollution.[36] One is that land-based pollution is "the most 'national' source of marine pollution."[37] Unlike other forms of marine pollution, responsibility rests on the "territorial state" to legislate and seek international and transboundary cooperation in the prevention and control of land-based sources of pollution. Added to the factor of national sovereignty is the difficulty in achieving agreement among states with uniform emission standards.[38] Also, there is the large number of sources of land-based pollutants to be identified and monitored, creating disagreement among states in negotiating a multilateral convention on land-based sources of marine pollution.

A significant step has been taken recently in the adoption of the Basel Convention on the Control of Transboundary Movements of Hazardous Wastes and Their Disposal, passed on March 22, 1989. Article 6 requires notification of transboundary movement of hazardous wastes between parties. Annex I of the Basel Convention provides a list of wastes to be controlled. Other annexes cover lists of hazardous characteristics, such as explosives or flammable solids and disposal operations.

LIABILITY AND COMPENSATION SCHEMES FOR MARINE POLLUTION DAMAGE

It has been pointed out that it is necessary to have liability and compensation schemes for those who have suffered damage resulting from marine pollution. This is deemed necessary in order "to encourage shipowners to take more care in observing the standards which are designed to prevent pollution."[39] The following is a summary of the various liability and compensation schemes now in force, which have been adopted by a number of international conventions.

The International Convention on Civil Liability for Oil Pollution Damage, 1969

Known as the Civil Liability Convention (CLC), it came into force on January 19, 1975. Traditionally, damage can be awarded only when it is proven in a judicial proceeding that a ship owner is at fault; and the damage for a ship owner may be limited in accordance with the 1957 convention on the limitation of liability for ship owners and the subsequent Convention on Civil Liability for Oil Spills, concluded in 1976. This Convention was participated in by nine European nations (Belgium, Denmark, France, The Federal Republic of Germany, Ireland, the Netherlands, Norway, Sweden and the United Kingdom) for those who suffered from damage caused by the exploration of seabed mineral resources.[40] The CLC of 1969 changed "the damage liability base from one of proven or negligence to one of strict liability."[41] Needless to say, this change was motivated by the 1967 *Torrey Canyon* oil spill off the southwest coast of England. Under the Civil Liability Convention of 1969, ship owners flying the flag of the contracting parties to the convention must show evidence of strict financial responsibility to pay for damage to a territory, including the territorial sea of a contracting state, plus the cost for preventing further occurrences of oil discharge or spill (escape). The financial liability, as amended by its 1976 Protocol, is now limited to 133 Special Drawing Rights (SDR) of the International Monetary Fund, the equivalent of $175.39 per ton,[42] or for a total of $18.5 million (about 14 million SDRs), whichever is less (the 1980 rates). In 1984 the upper limit for liability was set at $300 million per accident, still considered insufficient for large spills.[43]

There are only three exceptions for which the ship owner is exempt from liability: an act of war or God, an act done by a third party intended to cause damage, and negligence on the part of the government or authority for maintenance of navigational aids. It is further required by the 1969 CLC, under Article VII, that a registered ship in a state party to the convention must be insured or have sufficient funds available if it is carrying an oil cargo of more than 2,000 tons—demonstrated by a certificate issued by the flag state (Article VII–1). Regardless of whether the flag state is a party to the convention, every ship carrying more than 2,000 tons of oil must be insured if it wishes to use port facilities of a state contracting to the convention. However, victims of the oil pollution must institute suits for damage compensation only in the courts of the contracting state in whose jurisdiction the incident occurred (Article IX–1), and such suit must be brought against the ship owner within three years.

International Convention on the Establishment of an International Fund for Compensation for Oil Pollution Damage, 1971

The Fund Convention, which came into force in October 1978, is an effort to take care of the situations whereby either the ship owner is not liable due to an act of God or war, or is liable but is not able to finance the compensation for damages incurred. It is also an attempt to relieve ship owners of the financial burden imposed by the 1969 CLC. The Fund is financed by a contribution or levy by the contracting states in proportion to the amount of oil imported. The total amount for the Fund is limited to between $62 and $79 million, or, in the language of the convention, 675 million Pointcaré francs. However, the Fund cannot be provided to relieve a ship owner's financial burden if the damage is done as a result of ''wilful misconduct'' or the owner's failure to observe safety provisions of the various IMCO conventions.[44] In addition, the oil companies and tanker owners have also established two compensation schemes for liability in cases of oil pollution.

Tanker Owners' Voluntary Agreement Concerning Liability for Oil Pollution (TOVALOP), 1969

The agreement came into force on September 18, 1969, and is intended to cover oil pollution damage to the territory of a state that is not a party to the 1969 CLC. It is a very significant agreement in two respects. One, the agreement by oil tanker owners covers 90 percent of all oil tankers plying the waters of the oceans. It provides costs for towing a vessel that is in distress as a means of preventing oil spills. More important, the agreement encourages owners to clean up oil spills speedily by making available financial resources regardless of who is at fault. It also compensates governments for the cost involved in their own cleanup.[45]

Contract Regarding and Interim Supplement to Tanker Liability for Oil Pollution (CRISTAL), 1971

This agreement came into force swiftly in 1971 as an interim and supplementary compensation scheme to the 1969 CLC, the 1971 Fund, and the TOVALOP. For one thing, only about one-half of the states are parties to the Civil Liability Convention; for another thing, TOVALOP extends the liability and compensation ceiling considerably. (The claims in the case of the Amoco *Cadiz* exceeded $1 billion.)[46]

Significance. The existence of an elaborate system of compensation for marine pollution damage caused by vessels is attributable to the work of underwriters who provide marine insurance to oil tankers. In many ways it is a matter of good business sense, as well as the tradition that is associated with the world's marine insurance industry. However, despite these liability compensation and insurance schemes for damages caused by vessels, problems remain for ensuring strict compliance with provisions contained in the international conventions for the protection of the marine environment. One is the failure of marine insurance companies to distinguish in terms of rate setting between those ship owners who adhere to high standards of operation and observance of international rules and those who are considered flagrant violators. Elliot Richardson argued that frequent offenders should be levied a higher rate of insurance as an effective way of making them comply with accepted rules of operation at sea.[47]

NUCLEAR WASTE DISPOSAL AND POLLUTION

There has been considerable environmental concern about disposal of nuclear waste into the sea, along with concern for the fallout of radioactive substances into the ocean from nuclear weapon testing and nuclear explosions under the ocean.[48] It may be argued that nuclear fallout from weapon testing—a total of 4.5 million tons of fissionable material was produced by nuclear tests in the period from 1952 to 1958—was "fairly evenly" distributed throughout the oceans and concentrated only in the areas near the testing sites.[49] After the test ban treaty was signed in 1963, only China and France continued to conduct nuclear tests. Nonetheless, nuclear weapons contain enriched uranium and plutonium; when they explode under water, they in turn yield more than 200 fissionable products and isotopes, which circulate the globe as dust and finally settle down as fallout on earth and in surface waters.[50]

Radioactive substances may also enter the oceans from nuclear power plants, and there is an increased concern about the disposal of spent nuclear fuel from power reactors. As of the mid–1980s, there were more than 500 nuclear power plants in the world, in addition to about sixty-five nuclear reactors in operation in thirty-nine countries. Low-level radioactive wastes have been deposited in the ocean along the coasts of the United States and in the Bay of Biscay, affecting western European nations.[51] Water used for cooling nuclear power plants in the form of thermal pollution—the result of discharging the contaminated water into the sea—has caused mortalities in larvae and adult animals. Human consumption of seafood exposed to radioactive substance may be hazardous to human health.[52]

Another source of radioactive contamination on the sea is the release of long-lived gamma radioactivity within twelve miles of the coastline under the United States Navy's nuclear propulsion program. In testimony before Congress, it was revealed that for the ten-year period from 1971 to 1981, a total amount of less than .002 curies of gamma radioactivity was released within twelve miles of the coast.[53] Total long-lived radioactivity (in liquid waste) released more than twelve miles from shore by the United States Navy's nuclear ships was estimated at 0.4 curies per year between 1974 and 1981.[54] There has been some controversy over accidental discharge of "hot" radioactive water from coolant systems in the nuclear submarines in naval shipyards in the United States.[55]

The problem of radioactive disposal is basically finding a suitable site on land, or in the ocean, as a waste receptacle for such a substance. The ocean is said to possess the "cleansing mechanisms" of dilution and is thus an option for disposal of radioactive waste.[56] This view has since been held incorrect by studies that show that the ocean's capacity to dilute and disperse radioactive waste is limited and finite.[57] As John W. Kindt has pointed out, in the early nuclear development stage, the United States packaged the low-level wastes in fifty-five-gallon drums with concrete as fillers and dumped them offshore. From 1946 to 1970 a total of 86,758 containers, or 94,673 curies of low-level waste, were licensed by the United States Atomic Energy Commission for dumping on sites offshore from San Francisco and the Maryland-Delaware coasts.[58] On an annual basis since 1971 joint cooperative dumping—totaling 82,910 tons of radioactive waste, or 867,083 curies of radiation between 1967 and 1981—was carried out by member states (United Kingdom, Belgium, the Netherlands, Switzerland, France, Italy, Sweden and West Germany) of the Organization for Economic Cooperation and Development (OECD).[59]

Since 1974 discussion and studies have focused on the feasibility of burying high-level nuclear waste, such as spent fuel rods of a reactor, which contain about 95 percent uranium oxide, beneath the ocean floor or sub-seabed. The Carter administration had discussed the matter with a number of nations with a view to establishing the burial sites on the ocean floor for storing nuclear wastes. One of a number of options, including a possible Pacific sub-seabed site 2,500 miles from Hawaii, brought out anger and opposition from the late Senator Spark Matsunaga on environmental grounds—the contamination of the lower strata of the food chain.[60] At one time a British royal commission considered drilling holes 2.5 miles deep on the ocean floor for burying spent nuclear fuel in casks sealed with cement and covered with sediment. Studies have been made for selecting a type of canister (the Ticode 12–20) with a 500-year endurance rate in a seabed environment.[61] Also, it has been pointed out that seabed disposal offers (1) "generic barriers" (water depth, geologic stability and sparse biology), and (2) "stepwise barriers" (low leach and corrosion rate, low permeability and slow current).[62]

There have been a number of treaties that contain regulations on the disposal of nuclear waste in the ocean, as well as civil liability for nuclear damage. Table 8.7 represents a summary of the treaty provisions dealing with nuclear waste disposal.

There seems to be some controversy with respect to the legality of disposing of (dumping) high-level radioactive waste on the seabed.[63] The debate centers on the interpretation of the meaning of "disposal at sea" in the 1972 London Dumping Convention, under Article III(1): Does it include or exclude seabed disposal of high-level radioactive waste? The contracting parties to the 1972 London Dumping Convention held consultative meetings in 1983 and 1984 to resolve the controversy over the legal interpretation of Article III.[64] This led to the adoption of a resolution that called for a global moratorium on ocean dumping of low-level radioactive wastes for two years (1983–1985) pending the completion of scientific studies on the matter. Curtis takes the position that seabed disposal of high-level radioactive waste in the marine environment is prohibited under the 1972 London Dumping Convention.[65]

Significance. Since the advent of nuclear energy in the 1950s disposal of high-level radioactive waste is one of the new uses of the oceans. That ocean dumping of such harmful substances presents risks to the marine environment has been a global concern for some time. There are a number of international conventions, as well as national legislation, such as the United States Marine Protection Research and Sanctuaries Act of 1972, that have devised procedures and standards for ocean dumping of packaged low-level radioactive wastes. But neither the 1972 London Dumping Convention, nor the 1982 LOS Convention, is clear or precise on ocean disposal of high-level radioactive waste as a form of dumping that is covered by the legal meaning of Article II, under the former, and Article 1(5), for the latter. However, it is quite clear that disposal of radioactive wastes in the International Seabed Area beyond national jurisdiction must be regulated by the International Seabed Authority under Articles 137 and 145 of the 1982 LOS Convention. Only Article 25 of the 1958 Convention on the High Seas (a convention which came into force in 1962 and was ratified as of July 1988 by fifty-nine states) makes specific reference to pollution of the marine environment by "radioactive materials."

OCEAN DUMPING

Dumping[66] is defined in Article 1(5)(a) as:

(i) any deliberate disposal of wastes or other matter from vessels, aircraft, platforms or other man-made structures at sea;

Table 8.7
International Conventions Dealing with Nuclear Waste Disposal

Convention and Year	Specific Articles of Regulation
1) Convention on the High Seas	Article 25 on national legislation to prevent pollution of the seas from dumping of radioactive waste, and standard-setting by international organizations
2) 1960 Third Party Liability in the Field of Nuclear Energy and 3) 1963 Civil Liability for Nuclear Damage	Designation of the operator of a nuclear installation as the person liable for damage caused by a nuclear incident
4) 1971 Convention Relating to Civil Liability in the Field of Maritime Carriage of Nuclear Material	Any person shall be held liable for damage caused by a nuclear accident except the operator of a nuclear installation held liable under the 1960 and 1963 civil liability conventions
5) 1972 Convention on the Prevention of Marine Pollution by Dumping of Wastes and Other Matter (London Dumping Convention)	"Disposal at sea" may mean prohibition of dumping high-level wastes at sea. Annex I: Standards set by International Atomic Energy Agency (IAEA) to delimit and regulate high-level radioactive waste dumping at sea Annex II: Requirement for permit for disposal of radioactive waste not included in Annex I Annex III: Guidelines for permit issuance
6) 1982 LOS Convention (Part XII: Area)	Article 145: General principle for marine environment protection Article 162: Emergency power to International Seabed Authority (Council) to suspend deep seabed mining operation in case of damage to seabed. Article 209: Requires all marine vessels to establish rules, procedures and standards to reduce pollution in the Area

Source: Based primarily on John Warren Kindt, *Marine Pollution and the Law of the Sea*, vol. 2 (Buffalo, N.Y.: William S. Hein, 1986), pp. 843–846; and Clifton E. Curtis, "Legality of Seabed Disposal of High-Level Radioactive Wastes under the London Dumping Convention," *Ocean Development and International Law* 14, no. 4 (1985): 391–404. Used by permission.

(ii) any deliberate disposal of vessels, aircraft, platforms or other man-made structures at sea.

The first international convention (the Convention for the Prevention of Marine Pollution by Dumping from Ships and Aircrafts, or Oslo Convention) to control dumping of wastes—sewage, chemicals and other industrial wastes—into the ocean was adopted for the northeast Atlantic and the North Sea in February 1972 by twelve European states.[67] While the 1972 Oslo Convention does not prohibit dumping per se, under Article 5 it does require signatory states not to dispose of dangerous toxic wastes in the ocean and sets certain approved conditions for other substances. The 1972 Oslo Convention pioneered the system of listing specific categories of dangerous substances and materials to be prohibited or dumped under special care or special permit.

The 1972 Oslo Convention set the stage and served as a model for a comprehensive multilateral ocean dumping convention: the 1972 Convention on the Prevention of Marine Pollution by Dumping of Wastes and Other Matters, or the London Convention.[68] Its definition of dumping became Article 1(5)(a) of the 1982 LOS Convention. The 1972 London Convention does not include the normal operations of vessels, aircraft, platforms or other man-made structures at sea; nor does it include, under Article II(c), disposal of wastes for the purpose of deep seabed exploitation. Similar to the 1972 Oslo Convention, the 1972 London Convention on ocean dumping instituted the system of classifying dumped substances and material into three categories in terms of harmfulness as annexes to the Convention. Annex I, known as the "black list," prohibits, under Article IV(a), the dumping of any of these harmful and toxic substances into the sea:

Annex I*

1. Organohalogen compounds.

2. Mercury and mercury compounds.

3. Cadmium and cadmium compounds.

4. Persistent plastics and other persistent synthetic materials, for example, netting and ropes, which may float or may remain in suspension in the sea in such a manner as to interfere materially with fishing, navigation or other legitimate uses of the sea.

5. Crude oil, fuel oil, heavy diesel oil, and lubricating oils, hydraulic fluids, and any mixtures containing any of these, taken on board for the purpose of dumping.

6. High-level radio-active wastes or other high-level radio-active matter, defined on public health, biological or other grounds, by the competent international body in this field, at present the International Atomic Energy Agency, as unsuitable for dumping at sea.

7. Materials in whatever form (*e.g.* solids, liquids, semi-liquids, gases or in a living state) produced for biological and chemical warfare.

8. The preceding paragraphs of this Annex do not apply to substances which are rapidly rendered harmless by physical, chemical or biological processes in the sea provided they do not:

*Texts for Annexes I, II and III are to be found in G. J. Timagenis, *International Control of Marine Pollution*, vol. 2, Appendix I, pp. 665–671; and *Treaties and Other International Acts Series* (TIAS), 8165, pp. 2405–2468.

(i) make edible marine organisms unpalatable, or

(ii) endanger human health or that of domestic animals.

The consultative procedure provided for under Article XIV should be followed by a Party if there is doubt about the harmlessness of the substance.

9. This Annex does not apply to wastes or other materials (*e.g.* sewage sludges and dredged spoils) containing the matters referred to in paragraphs 1–5 above as trace contaminants. Such wastes shall be subject to the provisions of Annexes II and III as appropriate.

Annex II to the 1972 London Convention on ocean dumping (the "grey list") contains a list of less noxious substances, such as lead, zinc and pesticides, which can be dumped into the ocean by prior special permits issued by the national authority of the contracting party. Annex II also includes radioactive waste not listed in Annex I, if dumping of such material is permitted upon the recommendation of the International Atomic Energy Agency (IAEA).

Annex II

The following substances and materials requiring special care are listed for the purposes of Article VI(1)(a).

A. Wastes containing significant amounts of the matters listed below:

arsenic
lead
copper
zinc
} and their compounds

organosilicon compounds

cyanides

fluorides

pesticides and their by-products not covered in Annex I.

B. In the issue of permits for the dumping of large quantities of acids and alkalis, consideration shall be given to the possible presence in such wastes of the substances listed in paragraph A and to the following additional substances:

beryllium
chromium
nickel
vanadium
} and their compounds

C. Containers, scrap metal and other bulky wastes liable to sink to the sea bottom which may present a serious obstacle to fishing or navigation.

D. Radio-active wastes or other radio-active matter not included in Annex I. In the issue of permits for the dumping of this matter, the Contracting Parties should take full account of the recommendations of the competent international body in this field, at present the International Atomic Energy Agency.

Annex III contains the general list of waste not in either the "black" or "grey" lists, which may be dumped if a permit is obtained. This permit, in turn, must conform to the criteria established under Annex III in terms of composition of the waste matter, dumping site characteristics and methods of deposit:

Annex III

Provisions to be considered in establishing criteria governing the issue of permits for the dumping of matter at sea, taking into account Article IV(2) include:

A. CHARACTERISTICS AND COMPOSITION OF THE MATTER

1. Total amount and average composition of matter dumped (*e.g.* per year).

2. Form, *e.g.* solid, sludge, liquid, or gaseous.

3. Properties: physical (*e.g.* solubility and density), chemical and biochemical (*e.g.* oxygen demand, nutrients) and biological (*e.g.* presence of viruses, bacteria, yeasts, parasites).

4. Toxicity.

5. Persistence: physical, chemical and biological.

6. Accumulation and biotransformation in biological materials or sediments.

7. Susceptibility to physical, chemical and biochemical changes and interaction in the aquatic environment with other dissolved organic and inorganic materials.

8. Probability of production of taints or other changes reducing marketability of resources (fish, shellfish, etc.).

B. CHARACTERISTICS OF DUMPING SITE AND METHOD OF DEPOSIT

1. Location (*e.g.* co-ordinates of the dumping area, depth and distance from the coast), location in relation to other areas (*e.g.* amenity areas, spawning, nursery and fishing areas and exploitable resources).

2. Rate of disposal per specific period (*e.g.* quantity per day, per week, per month).

3. Methods of packaging and containment, if any.

4. Initial dilution achieved by proposed method of release.

5. Dispersal characteristics (*e.g.* effects of currents, tides and wind on horizontal transport and vertical mixing).

6. Water characteristics (*e.g.* temperature, pH, salinity, stratification, oxygen indices of pollution—dissolved oxygen (DO), chemical oxygen demand (COD), biochemical oxygen demand (BOD)—nitrogen present in organic and mineral form including ammonia, suspended matter, other nutrients and productivity).

7. Bottom characteristics (*e.g.* topography, geochemical and geological characteristics and biological productivity).

8. Existence and effects of other dumpings which have been made in the dumping area (*e.g.* heavy metal background reading and organic carbon content).

9. In issuing a permit for dumping, Contracting Parties should consider whether an adequate scientific basis exists for assessing the consequences of such dumping, as outlined in this Annex, taking into account seasonal variations.

C. GENERAL CONSIDERATIONS AND CONDITIONS

1. Possible effects on amenities (*e.g.* presence of floating or stranded material, turbidity, objectionable odour, discolouration and foaming).

2. Possible effects on marine life, fish and shellfish culture, fish stocks and fisheries, seaweed harvesting and culture.

3. Possible effects on other uses of the sea (*e.g.* impairment of water quality for industrial use, underwater corrosion of structures, interference with ship operations from floating materials, interference with fishing or navigation through deposit of waste or solid objects on the sea floor and protection of areas of special importance for scientific or conservation purposes).

4. The practical availability of alternative land-based methods of treatment, disposal or elimination, or of treatment to render the matter less harmful for dumping at sea.

Two other aspects of the 1972 London Convention on ocean dumping need to be mentioned: record keeping by contracting parties, and incineration of wastes.

Record Keeping on Dumping

Article VI(1)(c) requires the contracting party to "keep records of the nature and quantities of all matter permitted to be dumped and the location, time and method of dumping." Such information must also be reported to the secretariat (Intergovernmental Marine Consultative Organization) and to other parties whenever appropriate. Records must also be kept on incineration at sea.

Incineration at Sea

At the third consultative meeting of the contracting parties to the 1972 London Convention on ocean dumping, held in October 1978, amendments were adopted that were designed to regulate incineration of the toxic waste materials listed in Annexes I and II. In the first place, the amendments provide for emergency situations under which human life and the safety of ships is threatened, a special permit for incineration at sea. Then there is a set of regulations for the control of incineration of toxic substances listed in Annex II. Incineration is defined in the amendment as "the deliberate combustion of wastes or other matters on marine incineration facilities for the purpose of their thermal destruction."[69]

Regulation 2(2) provides that prior to permission for incineration of toxic substances at sea the applicant must first consider "the practical availability or alternative land-based methods of treatment, disposal or elimination."[70]

Because of the emissions of poison from waste burning at sea, European environmentalists have been concerned since 1969 that ships were permitted to burn liquid waste in the North Sea to the detriment of marine life. At the eleventh consultative meeting of the contracting parties to the London Convention, held in London from September 26 to October 7, 1988, delegates from sixty-five nations adopted two resolutions on incineration at sea.[71] One was to impose a worldwide ban on chemical waste incineration at sea by 1994, instead of 1991.[72] The resolution states that "Incineration at sea, as a means of disposal of wastes containing highly toxic substances, is considered to represent subsequent risks of marine and atmospheric pollution."[73] The other resolution called for the immediate halt to the export by developed nations of noxious liquid wastes for burning at sea by incineration facilities built in Third World nations. The 1972 London Convention on ocean dumping came into force on August 30, 1975, and as of January 1989 it had been ratified by sixty-one states, as seen in Table 8.8.

Significance. There are several weaknesses in the 1972 London Convention on ocean dumping. One is the lack of enforcement provisions in the convention, which places compliance in national or coastal state control.[74] Another problem has been the import and export of hazardous wastes from one nation to another, or the "trans-frontier shipment of hazardous waste."[75] On December 6, 1984, the Council of the European Communities agreed upon a directive that requires the shipper or holder of waste to post notification to the state of destination outside of the European community.[76] And it is the responsibility for the holder of waste to notify "the state of dispatch when waste has reached its proper destination."[77] There is a need to develop rules and procedures for liability assessment for dumping and the application of these rules as specific obligations for states parties to the London Convention; these rules must be made a distinct liability regime for all ocean dumping.[78] Article 195 of the 1982 LOS Convention mandates states "not to transfer, directly or indirectly, damage or hazards from one area to another or transform one type of pollution into another."

When the London Convention on ocean dumping was concluded in 1972 the question of maritime jurisdiction with respect to the territorial sea was not yet resolved at the law of the sea negotiations. Thus, a void was left in the treaty concerning area of jurisdiction for enforcement purposes. However, the 1982 LOS Convention filled the void by the provisions in Articles 210 and 216. Article 210(5) states that:

> Dumping within the territorial sea and the exclusive economic zone or onto the continental shelf shall not be carried out without the expressed prior approval of the coastal

Table 8.8
Ratification of the London Dumping Convention (as of January 22, 1986)

Government	Date of Ratification or Accession	Date of Entry into Force
Afghanistan	April 2, 1975	August 30, 1975
Argentina	September 11, 1979	October 11, 1979
Australia	August 21, 1985	September 20, 1985
Belgium	June 12, 1985	July 12, 1985
Brazil	July 26, 1982	August 25, 1982
Byelorussian SSR	January 29, 1976	February 28, 1976
Canada	November 13, 1975	December 14, 1975
Cape Verde	May 26, 1977	June 25, 1977
Chile	August 4, 1977	September 3, 1977
China, People's Republic of	October 22, 1985	November 21, 1985
Cuba	December 1, 1975	January 1, 1976
Denmark[a]	October 23, 1974	August 30, 1975
Dominican Republic	December 7, 1973	August 30, 1975
Finland	February 3, 1977	March 5, 1977
France	February 3, 1977	March 5, 1977
Gabon	February 5, 1982	March 7, 1982
German Democratic Republic	August 20, 1976	September 19, 1976
Germany, Federal Republic of	November 8, 1977	December 8, 1977
Greece	August 10, 1981	September 9, 1981
Guatemala	July 14, 1975	August 30, 1975
Haiti	August 28, 1975	September 27, 1975
Honduras	May 2, 1980	June 1, 1980
Hungary	February 5, 1976	March 6, 1976
Iceland	May 24, 1973	August 30, 1975
Ireland	February 17, 1982	March 19, 1982
Italy	April 30, 1984	May 30, 1984
Japan	October 15, 1980	November 14, 1980
Jordan	November 11, 1973	August 30, 1975
Kenya	January 7, 1976	February 6, 1976
Kiribati	May 12, 1982	June 11, 1982
Libyan Arab Jamahiriya	November 22, 1976	December 22, 1976
Mexico	April 7, 1975	August 30, 1975
Monaco	May 16, 1977	June 15, 1977
Morocco	February 18, 1977	March 20, 1977
Nauru	July 26, 1982	August 25, 1982
Netherlands[b]	December 2, 1977	January 2, 1978
New Zealand	April 30, 1975	August 30, 1975
Nigeria	March 19, 1976	April 18, 1976
Norway	April 4, 1974	August 30, 1975
Oman	March 13, 1984	April 12, 1984
Panama	July 31, 1975	August 30, 1975
Papua New Guinea	March 10, 1980	April 9, 1980
Philippines	August 10, 1973	August 30, 1975
Poland	January 23, 1979	February 22, 1979
Portugal	April 14, 1978	May 14, 1978
Saint Lucia	August 23, 1985	September 22, 1985
Seychelles	October 29, 1984	November 28, 1984

Table 8.8 (Continued)

Government	Date of Ratification or Accession	Date of Entry into Force
Solomon Islands	March 6, 1984	April 5, 1984
South Africa	August 7, 1978	September 6, 1978
Spain	July 31, 1974	August 30, 1975
Suriname	October 21, 1980	November 20, 1980
Sweden	February 21, 1974	August 30, 1975
Switzerland	July 31, 1979	August 30, 1979
Tunisia	April 13, 1976	May 13, 1976
Ukranian SSR	February 5, 1976	March 6, 1976
United Arab Emirates	August 9, 1974	August 30, 1975
USSR	December 30, 1975	January 29, 1976
United Kingdom[c]	November 17, 1975	December 17, 1975
United States	April 29, 1974	August 30, 1975
Yugoslavia	June 25, 1976	July 25, 1976
Zaire	September 16, 1975	October 16, 1975

[a] Extended to be effective in respect of the Faroe Islands as of November 15, 1976.

[b] Ratification by The Netherlands was declared to be effective in respect of the Netherlands Antilles.

[c] Ratification by the United Kingdom was declared also to be effective, as of November 17, 1975, in respect of: Bailiwick of Guernsey, Isle of Man, Belize (now an independent state), Bermuda, British Indian Ocean Territory, British Virgin Islands, Cayman Islands, Falkland Islands, and dependencies, Hong Kong, Montserrat, Pitcairn, Henderson, Ducie and Oeno Islands, Saint Helena and dependencies, Turks and Caicos Islands, Tuvalu (independent), U.K. Sovereign Base, and the areas of Akrotiri and Dhekelia on the Island of Cyprus. Effective in the Bailiwick of Jersey as of April 4, 1976.

Source: Maxwell Bruce, "The London Dumping Convention, 1972: First Decade and Future," in *Ocean Yearbook 6*, Elisabeth Mann Borgese and Norton Ginsburg, eds. (Chicago: University of Chicago Press, 1986), pp. 300–301. Used by permission.

state, which has the right to permit, regulate and control such dumping after due consideration of the matter with other states which by reason of their geographical situation may be adversely affected thereby.

Article 216(1)(a) specifies the coastal states' right to enact laws and regulations on dumping "within its territorial sea or its exclusive economic zone or onto its continental shelf."

As for the future, to summarize the report of the Task Force 2000 of the London Convention, it seems that it may not be possible to eliminate ocean dumping of hazardous wastes as an ultimate goal as long as there are present in the world the constant twin pressures of rapid population growth and increased demand for resources to fuel industries. These pressures ultimately come into conflict with the need to protect the marine environment. A global cooperative effort endeavored by the 1972 London Convention on ocean dumping and the procedures established under the said convention are of great value, for

If the sea is to continue to be a viable part of the human environment under all the conflicting pressures which it will receive in the future, measures must be taken to effectively manage the use of marine resources so as to mitigate short-range damage leading to long-range degrading.[79]

OFFSHORE OIL PLATFORM POLLUTION DAMAGE AND LIABILITY PROBLEMS

The 1973 International Convention for the Prevention of Pollution from Ships removed any doubt as to whether the definition of ''ship'' includes offshore platforms for oil exploration. Article 2(4) defined ''ship'' to mean ''a vessel of any type whatsoever operating in the marine environment and includes hydro-air-cushioned vehicles, submersibles, floating craft and fixed or floating platforms.''[80]

However, as G. J. Timagenis pointed out, the legislative history for the drafting of the 1973 convention and the definition of ''discharge'' contained in the convention raises the problem of making a distinction between the platform as a ''normal ship'' and a platform erected for the purpose of engaging in the exploration of seabed resources when discharge or dumping of harmful substances occurs. This distinction became necessary because the 1973 convention, in Article 2(3)(b)(ii) defines discharge to exclude ''the release of harmful substances directly arising from the exploration, exploitation and associated offshore processing of seabed mineral resources.''[81] In fact, the IMCO conference record showed that a number of delegations to the 1973 conference preferred a separate definition for offshore stationary platforms.[82] In any event the inclusion of ''platform'' in the definition of ''ship'' was adopted by a vote of fifty-six in favor, none against and seven abstentions.[83] However, there is a matter of interpretation that ''some provisions of the Convention may not apply to platforms in some or all the circumstances.''[84] Thus, the confusion remains, for the 1982 LOS Convention is equally lacking in consistency and clarity. Article 1(1)(5)(a) defines ''dumping'' to mean

> (i) any deliberate disposal of wastes or other matter from vessels, aircrafts, platforms or other man-made structure at sea;
>
> (ii) any deliberate disposal of vessels, aircraft, platforms or other man-made structures at sea.

But, in Article 1(5)(b)(i) it states that ''dumping'' does not include ''the disposal of wastes or other matters incidental to, or derived from the normal operations of vessels, aircraft, platforms or other man-made structures at sea.''

There have been only a few cases of accidental ''blowouts'' among thousands of offshore exploration and production wells. In one case, on April 22, 1977, an oil and gas explosion occurred on the Bravo platform in the Ekofish field southwest of the Norwegian coast in the North Sea. It caused spillage of 22,500 tons of crude oil and 1.7 million Nm^3 gas,[85] and was considered to be the first major offshore blowout in the North Sea.

In another case, on June 3, 1977, the Ixtoc I oil well accidentally exploded in the Bay of Campeche northwest of the Yucatán Peninsula in the Gulf of Mexico. There was a discharge of about 3 million gallons of oil into the Gulf of Mexico with oil slicks 180 kilometers in length and 80 kilometers wide extending to the coast and beaches of Texas, endangering the rich shrimp-fishing grounds. The United States attempted to bring a lawsuit for damages against the owner of the offshore oil drilling company, then under contract with Petróleos Mexicanos (Pemex). The suit was not successful. Mexico refused to accept any liability for the offshore explosion and the resultant oil spill on the grounds that there was no existing international law applicable in the case.[86] In a more recent case, in February 1991, Iraqi troops deliberately set fire to 500 of Kuwait's 1,000 oil wells before withdrawing into Iraq under attack from U.S.-led coalition forces.

Significance. The Ixtoc I case points to the problem of "the lack of effective international law for offshore oil explosions producing transnational damage.[87] However, it may be noted here that the 1976 Convention on Civil Liability for Oil Pollution Damage from Offshore Operations for nations bordering the North Sea, Baltic Sea and North Atlantic Ocean made it a "strict liability" of operators of offshore installations for damages caused by oil spills. There is also the regional treaty for northwest Europe, the 1977 Convention on Civil Liability for Oil Pollution Damage Resulting from Exploration for the Exploitation of Seabed Mineral Resources, not yet in force, that requires strict but limited liability. For the northwest European waters, the oil industry also provided a liability scheme, the 1975 Offshore Pollution Liability Agreement (OPOL), paralleling the basic provisions and principles in TOVALOP and CRISTAL.[88] However, one observer advocated the need for a single international convention on a wider geographic basis modeled on the concepts and schemes of the regional treaties, as well as the 1971 Convention on International Liability for Damage Caused by Space Objects, which is based on the doctrine of strict liability.[89]

OIL AND VESSEL-BASED POLLUTION

There are at least four major ways that ships cause marine pollution. Most of this vessel-based pollution is operational and intentional. First, as a standard operation, all ships discharge fumes, since they run on oil-burning diesel engines. Fumes as pollutants eventually settle on the sea. Second, also as standard marine operation, oil is discharged when bilge water is cleaned from the cargo tanks. Tank washing is considered a major vessel source of marine oil pollution.[90] Third, oil is discharged routinely when ballasting takes place. Ballasting is a procedure used by cargo ships and oil tankers to take on board water as additional weight or cargo to stabilize the vessel for a return voyage and to provide maneuverability under conditions of rough seas. Ballast water is mixed with oil residuals and pumped out after unloading. In the deballasting process the dirty or oil ballast becomes the pollutant. It needs to be pointed out

Table 8.9
Sources and Volume of Ship-Generated Oil Discharges, 1973

	Million Metric Tons	Percentage
Operational Discharges from Tankers		
LOT tankers	0.31	14.5
Non-LOT tankers	0.77	36.2
Drydocking	0.25	11.7
Accidental discharges from tankers		
Terminal operations	0.003	0.1
Tanker accidents	0.2	9.4
Operational discharges from nontankers		
Bilges, deballasting fuel tanks	0.5	23.5
Accidental discharges from nontankers		
Nontanker accidents	0.1	4.7
Total	2.13	100.1

Source: Reprinted from "Petroleum in the Marine Environment," 1975, with permission from the National Academy of Sciences, Washington, D.C.

that tankers now adopt the "Load on Top" (LOT) procedure whereby oily, dirty ballast water is placed in special slop tanks so that the heavier seawater settles to the bottom and is then released; then fresh oil is loaded on the oil residue in the slop tanks.[91] LOT is considered not "effective on short hauls, or in heavy seas which prevent settling."[92] Finally, ships dispose of their garbage and discharge their sewage into the sea—it has been estimated that merchant ships dump close to half a million plastic containers per day.

One needs to note that a vast majority of hydrocarbon (oil) pollution in the oceans is the result of intentional or standard operational discharge.[93] Only a small portion of hydrocarbon pollution in the ocean is the result of accidental discharge.[94] Table 8.9 indicates that only 9.4 percent of all vessel-based pollution is attributable to tanker accidents.

However, oil pollution is visible and dramatic as these accidents occur, starting with the March 1967 accidental spill of 40,000 tons of Kuwait crude oil by the ship-wrecked *Torrey Canyon* on the beaches of Cornwall and Brittany. Then, in April 1977 an offshore well blowout in the North Sea (Ekofish field) discharged more than 20,000 tons of oil into the ocean. In March 1978 the Amoco *Cadiz*, a supertanker carrying Iranian crude oil, ran aground off the coast of Brittany and spilled its entire cargo of 210,000 tons of oil, polluted the Brittany coast for two weeks and damaged marine life and recreational beaches.[95] The worst accidental oil spill in the United States—involved the Exxon-owned oil tanker *Valdez*, which, while carrying 1.2 million barrels of Alaskan crude oil, ran into a reef off the coast of the pristine waters of Prince William Sound in the Gulf of Alaska on March 25, 1989. The accident spilled about 10 percent of its cargo, or 240,000 barrels of Alaskan crude oil that endangered marine life and the fishermen's economic well-being. The accident occurred at the harvesting season for herring roe and the release of salmon from the hatcheries into the streams.

The *Valdez* oil spill formed an oil slick—spilled liquid oil spread over the surface of the seawater to form a thin film—about 1,000 meters wide extending five miles toward Prince William Sound. The composition of the oil then changed through what is known as emulsification to form on shore a "viscid mass," or the appearance of "chocolate mousse," thick and sticky pancake masses. Then the residues of the mixture of hydrocarbons turned into tar balls near the beaches and rocks on shore. Seabirds and mammals such as sea lions, seals and otters were smeared with the sticky masses and perished if not rescued.[96] The worst *deliberate* oil spill happened in February 1991 when Iraqi troops released approximately three million barrels (originally estimated closer to eleven million) of crude into the Persian Gulf. Table 8.10 is a summary of the top ten oil spills since 1977.

The 1954 Convention for the Prevention of Pollution of the Sea by Oil and Its Amendments

The first international conference was called by President Harding in June 1926, advocating the prohibition of oil discharge within fifty miles from the coast, a measure endorsed later by seven major maritime powers.[97] In 1934 the League of Nations, under pressure from the United States and Great Britain, circulated a draft convention for international control of oil pollution, but nothing came of that effort as Germany and Italy boycotted the conference. The next major effort for international cooperative action on oil pollution was not undertaken until 1952–1953 when the British government released the Faulkner Report,[98] which advocated the enactment of a number of recommendations to be negotiated at an international conference.[99]

The first postwar conference on oil pollution met in April 1954. Some thirty-two states, representing more than 90 percent of the world's total shipping tonnage at that time, participated. The conference produced the 1954 Convention for the Prevention of Pollution of the Sea by Oil, which established the basic international legal framework for the prevention and control of oil discharge from ships; it came into effect in 1958. The convention did not agree to a general prohibition against discharge from ships bound for port with reception facilities, a proposition opposed by major shipping states and a number of developing states. Instead, a compromise was agreed upon in the 1954 convention prohibiting a ship of over 500 tons from discharging oil in concentration greater than 100 parts per million (ppm) of oil within fifty miles from the nearest land. Exceptions were made in special areas, such as the North Sea and the Adriatic, and the Australian zones (Article III), and for nontankers without port facilities, "a necessary loophole."[100] The 1954 convention also required oily-water separation equipment for bilge discharge. Signatory states to the convention were required to provide adequate shore facilities for oil substances that could not be dumped in the fifty-mile prohibitive zone.

There were several main defects in the 1954 convention. First, Article I(1)

Table 8.10
Top Ten Oil Spills Worldwide Since 1977

Location	Description	Date	Millions of Gallons
Ixtoc I, Mexico	well blowout	June 3, 1979 - March 24, 1980	140.0
Nowruz Oil Field Arabian Gulf	well blowout	Feb. 4, 1983 - end of 1983	80.0
Castillow de Bellver South Africa	tanker	Aug. 6, 1983	78.5
Amoca Cadiz Brittany	tanker	March 16, 1978	68.7
Aegean Captain (6.1 million) & Atlantic Empress (42.7 million) Trinidad and Tobago	collision	July 19, 1979	48.8
D-103 Libya Well Libya	well blowout	August 1980 - January 1981	42.0
Atlantic Empress	tanker	August 2, 1979	41.5
Irenes Serenade Greece	tanker	Feb. 23, 1980	36.6
Kuwait National Petrol Tank Kuwait	storage tank collapse	August 29, 1981	31.2
Independenta Istanbul	tanker	Nov. 15, 1979	28.9

Source: *Oil Spill Intelligence Report*, Arlington, Mass.; as reprinted in *The Christian Science Monitor*, 31 March 1989, p. 8. By permission of the publisher.

of the convention applied restrictions for oil pollution from ships to discharges of crude oil, fuel oil, diesel and lubricating oil, thus excluding all refined oils. Second, the 100 parts per million of oil not prohibited within the fifty-mile zone was considered by environmentalists and scientists as too high a content to be permitted, for marine life would not tolerate more than three parts per million. The acceptance of 100 ppm was evidence that many governments that participated at the 1954 conference "were not aware of (or, at least, concerned about) pollution problems."[101] Third, the convention provided no regulation concerning a vessel's activities outside of the fifty-mile prohibitive zone, probably on the assumption that the ocean had the ability to assimilate a large amount of such substances. In short, the 1954 convention was basically concerned with intentional or operational discharge from tankers by prohibiting these activities in a prohibitive area—while it was common practice for tankers to ballast oily water and clean tanks in the high seas before arriving in port.

Subsequent attempts were made to provide remedies to some of the defects or deficiencies contained in the 1954 Convention on Prevention of Pollution of

Oil from Ships; these were amendments to the convention in 1962, 1969 and 1971. The 1962 conference was convened in London to reconsider some aspects of the 1954 convention on oil pollution; it was led by the British Advisory Committee on Oil Pollution of the Sea (ACOPS). The conference, attended by thirty-eight states, but dominated numerically by states from Western Europe and those from the Soviet bloc, considered a number of proposed changes to the 1954 convention which centered on the need by the maritime powers to extend the prohibitive zones for disposal of oily wastes. Article III and Annex A(3) of the 1954 convention prohibitive zones were amended to provide larger zones—located mostly in developed and more polluted parts of the oceans in Western Europe and North America—from fifty miles to one hundred miles. Under the 1962 amendment, the prohibitive zones extended to one hundred miles were as follows:[102]

1. the Pacific Ocean and the Canadian Western Zone
2. the North Atlantic–North Sea–Baltic Sea Zone
3. the Mediterranean–Adriatic Seas Zone
4. the Black Sea and the Sea of Azov Zone
5. the Red Sea Zone
6. the Persian Gulf–Kuwait–Saudi Arabian Zone
7. the Arabian Sea–Indian Ocean Zone
8. the Australian Zone

At the insistence of the British, but opposed by the United States and Japan, the 1962 amendments also included the provision to prohibit discharges for new vessels over 20,000 tons, which in turn required larger reception facilities at loading ports for larger tankers to dispose of the oil residues. However, Article III(c) still required the discharge rule of 100 ppm outside of the one hundred mile coastal prohibitive zones.

The 1969 amendments centered on the adoption of a new technology, developed by British Shell Oil in 1963, known as the load-on-top (LOT), or retention of oil on board system.[103] By 1965 major oil companies and independent ship owners had adopted the new LOT system to prevent oil pollution in standard operations. Oil industry representatives in the Intergovernmental Maritime Consultative Organization proposed the initiative, with strong support from the British government, for adoption of an effective oil monitoring and separation system, the LOT. (The oily water from tank cleaning is pumped separately into a special slop tank. When it settles, the water at the bottom of the tank is pumped into the ocean before fresh oil is loaded on top of the oil residue remaining in the tank.) The 1969 amendments permitted the total amount of oil to be discharged for ballasting not to exceed 1/15,000 of total cargo capacity of the tanker.

Following the disastrous oil spill by the *Torrey Canyon* in 1967, the 1971 amendments to the 1954 convention on oil pollution addressed mainly the problems resulting from oil-tanker accidents. Within the IMCO and its Maritime Safety Committee the central concern was the need to limit cargo tank size or the "hypothetical oil flow" resulting from damage to ships or tankers.[104] It was finally agreed to limit the size of tankers to 400,000 deadweight tonnage (dwt) and rate of oil escape in case of an accident to about 30,000 cubic meters regardless of size. However, these measures were not binding upon signatory states to the 1954 convention. These amendments were approved by the IMCO Assembly as resolutions.

The 1973 International Convention for the Prevention of Pollution from Ships (MARPOL) and the 1978 Protocol

This convention superseded the 1954 Convention for the Prevention of Pollution of the Sea by Oil and its amendments. The 1973 MARPOL Convention was the product of the International Conference on Marine Pollution attended by seventy-one states. It came into force when fifteen nations ratified it on October 2, 1983, a decade after its adoption. The merchant fleets of the fifteen contracting parties represented 50 percent of the world's total tonnage; they were:

Colombia	Italy	Tunisia
Denmark	Liberia	United Kingdom
France	Norway	United States
Federal Republic of Germany	Peru	Uruguay
Greece	Sweden	Yugoslavia

The 1973 MARPOL Convention reflected the new realities that existed in the world's maritime transport of oil by tankers and the rising concern, as expressed by the 1972 Stockholm conference on human environment, about control and prevention of marine pollution. Consideration was given not only to oil pollution, but also to ocean dumping in general and land-based sources of ocean pollution. More significant was the rapid technological development in the design of large-sized oil tankers which required constant rule changes. By 1973 it was evident that the 1954 convention provisions were inadequate or outdated, and by then the likelihood of the 1954 convention coming into force was rather doubtful. It finally entered into force in January 1978. The 1973 MARPOL contained twenty articles dealing with general obligations under the convention—prohibition of violation of requirements, rules for ship inspection, enforcement, reporting on incidents involving harmful substances, and most importantly, five technical annexes or regulations on

1. oil pollution
2. control of noxious liquid substances in bulk

3. harmful substances carried by sea in package forms or in portable tanks or by rail
4. pollution prevention by sewage from ships
5. pollution by garbage from ships[105]

Significance. The 1973 MARPOL convention, together with the 1978 Protocol must be treated legally as one instrument. A major change in the 1978 Protocol was the requirement that all new tankers of 20,000 deadweight tonnage and above must have segregated ballast tanks (Regulations 1 and 13 to Article 8(b) of the 1973 MARPOL convention), a scaling down from the original 70,000 deadweight tonnage.[106] Another important change in the 1978 Protocol was the adoption of the newly advanced technique of tank washing by oil or the cargo itself, known as ''crude oil washing'' or COW (Regulation 13b). Oil and water mixture was found to be the contributor for much of the operational (intentional) pollution, and the use of COW would in the end terminate operational pollution by tankers.

The 1978 Protocol to the 1973 MARPOL is separate from the 1978 Protocol to the IMCOs 1974 Convention for Safety of Life at Sea (SOLAS). The 1978 Protocol to the 1974 SOLAS was approved at the 1978 Tanker Safety and Pollution Prevention Conference which was concerned with requirements for preventing oil explosions at sea, for navigational safety equipment, and the need for increased inspection of tankers as the number of oil spills increased.[107] At any rate, the 1973 MARPOL convention was considered then to be a major international instrument for ending marine pollution of oil by ship, a rather over-optimistic assessment nevertheless.[108]

Article 211 of the 1982 LOS Convention provides the general guidelines for vessel-source pollution. Article 211(3) does require the port state to notify others, through the IMO, of requirements to be met before a vessel is permitted to enter the port state's territorial waters.

POLLUTION IN THE INTERNATIONAL SEABED AREA

At present there are three known techniques used for dredging the manganese nodules from the deep seabed: air-lift pumping, hydraulic-lift dredging and the continuous line bucket system (see Figure 8.1). All of these techniques for deep-seabed mining involve disturbing the surrounding sediment and water and lifting it to the ocean surface while moving the nodules.[109] Thus, there is no question that these mining activities or disturbances will mostly affect the sediment on the ocean floor and currents. It is not now certain to what extent these mining activities affect the ocean ecosystem. One environmentalist points out that deep-seabed mining can have a far-reaching effect on the benthic clams by reducing their reproductive capacities.[110] John W. Kindt also points out the environmental problems that may be created by nodule processing on board ship, since the ''tailing'' or wastes in the form of mud and ''manganese tracings'' would be

Figure 8.1
Three Systems Proposed for Mining Nodules

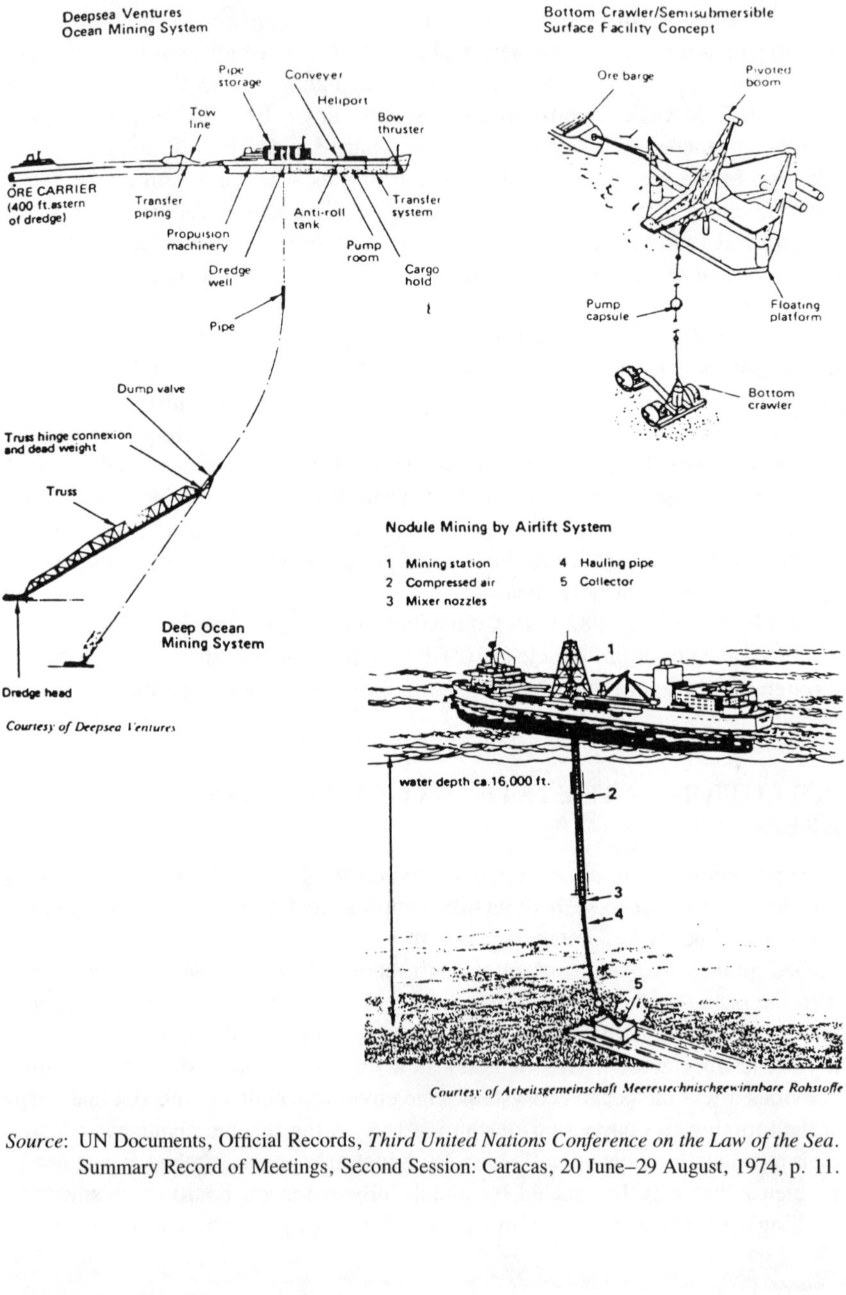

Source: UN Documents, Official Records, *Third United Nations Conference on the Law of the Sea*. Summary Record of Meetings, Second Session: Caracas, 20 June–29 August, 1974, p. 11.

discarded either on land or back into the sea, along with the chemicals used in the nodule extracting process.[111]

Article 145 of the 1982 LOS Convention provides the fundamental principle for marine environmental protection for the International Seabed Area:

Article 145: Protection of the marine environment

Necessary measures shall be taken in accordance with this Convention with respect to activities in the Area to ensure effective protection for the marine environment from harmful effects which may arise from such activities. To this end the Authority shall adopt appropriate rules, regulations and procedures for *inter alia*:

(a) the prevention, reduction and control of pollution and other hazards to the marine environment, including the coastline, and of interference with the ecological balance of the marine environment, particular attention being paid to the need for protection from harmful effects of such activities as drilling, dredging, excavation, disposal of waste, construction and operation or maintenance of installations, pipelines and other devices related to such activities;

(b) the protection and conservation of the natural resources of the Area and the prevention of damage to the flora and fauna of the marine environment.

And in addition, in accordance with Article 211, the Authority may have to share its regulatory power with the International Maritime Organization (IMO) in case of vessel-source pollution generated by the processing ships engaged in deep seabed mining. Article 162(2)(t–w) of the 1982 LOS Convention gives the Council of the Authority the emergency power to suspend deep-seabed mining operations in the Area in order to prevent serious harm caused by such activities to the marine environment:

(t) make recommendations to the Assembly concerning suspension of the exercise of the rights and privileges of membership pursuant to article 185;

(u) institute proceedings on behalf of the Authority before the Sea-Bed Disputes Chamber in cases of non-compliance;

(v) notify the Assembly upon a decision by the Sea-Bed Disputes Chamber in proceedings instituted under subparagraph (u), and make any recommendations which it may find appropriate with respect to measures to be taken;

(w) issue emergency orders, which may include orders for the suspension or adjustment of operations, to prevent serious harm to the marine environment arising out of activities in the Area;

Article 162(2)(x) grants the Authority's Council power to create "marine sanctuaries" or "wilderness areas" in the Area, and to even disapprove any mining activities by any contractor or the Enterprise in the Area that would do harm to the marine environment: "disapprove areas for exploitation by contractors or the Enterprise in cases where substantial evidence indicates the risk of serious harm to the marine environment."

While implying implicitly the lack of experience and knowledge about the environmental impact of the actual operational aspects of deep seabed mining in the Area or outside of it, in Articles 204 to 206 the 1982 LOS Convention provides, nevertheless, that responsibilities be placed on the states to monitor, provide reports and assess the potential effects of such activities on the marine environment. More significant is Article 209, which requires mining vessels, as well as the International Seabed Authority, to establish rules, procedures and standards to reduce marine pollution in the Area. This is required even though questions may be raised as to whether the article specifically mandates all deep seabed mining vessels in the Area to follow the general provisions on the protection of marine environment (Part XII of the 1982 LOS Convention):[112]

Article 209: Pollution from activities in the Area

1. International rules, regulations and procedures shall be established in accordance with Part XI to prevent, reduce and control pollution of the marine environment from activities in the Area. Such rules, regulations and procedures shall be re-examined from time to time as necessary.

2. Subject to the relevant provisions of this section, States shall adopt laws and regulations to prevent, reduce and control pollution of the marine environment from activities in the Area undertaken by vessels, installations, structures and other devices flying their flag or of their registry or operating under their authority, as the case may be. The requirements of such laws and regulations shall be no less effective than the international rules, regulations and procedures referred to in paragraph 1.

On the other hand, Articles 215 and 216 place the enforcement responsibility for marine pollution with these rules, regulations and procedures established for the Area and the Authority:

Article 215: Enforcement with respect to pollution from activities in the Area

Enforcement of international rules, regulations and procedures established in accordance with Part XI to prevent, reduce and control pollution of the marine environment from activities in the Area shall be governed by that Part.

Article 216: Enforcement with respect to pollution by dumping

1. Laws and regulations adopted in accordance with this Convention and applicable international rules and standards established through competent international organizations or diplomatic conference for the prevention, reduction and control of pollution of the marine environment by dumping shall be enforced:

(a) by the coastal State with regard to dumping within its territorial sea or its exclusive economic zone or onto its continental shelf;

(b) by the flag State with regard to vessels flying its flag or vessels or aircraft of its registry;

(c) by any State with regard to acts of loading of wastes or other matter occurring within its territory or at its off-shore terminals.

2. No State shall be obliged by virtue of this article to institute proceedings when another State has already instituted proceedings in accordance with this article.

Under Part XI of the 1982 LOS Convention for the Area there are only a few general provisions concerning marine pollution, as pointed out by John W. Kindt.[113] The more detailed provisions under Article 211 for prevention and control and reduction of vessel-based marine pollution would have to be applied in the Area. Thus, Articles 208, 213 and 214 are said to be more applicable to marine pollution in the Area:

Article 208: Pollution from sea-bed activities subject to national jurisdiction

1. Coastal States shall adopt laws and regulations to prevent, reduce and control pollution of the marine environment arising from or in connection with seabed activities subject to their jurisdiction and from artificial islands, installations and structures under their jurisdiction, pursuant to articles 60 and 80.

2. States shall take other measures as may be necessary to prevent, reduce and control such pollution.

3. Such laws, regulations and measures shall be no less effective than international rules, standards and recommended practices and procedures.

4. States shall endeavour to harmonize their policies in this connection at the appropriate regional level.

5. States, acting especially through competent international organizations or diplomatic conference, shall establish global and regional rules, standards and recommended practices and procedures to prevent, reduce and control pollution of the marine environment referred to in paragraph 1. Such rules, standards and recommended practices and procedures shall be re-examined from time to time as necessary.

Article 213: Enforcement with respect to pollution from land-based sources

States shall enforce their laws and regulations adopted in accordance with article 207 and shall adopt laws and regulations and take other measures necessary to implement applicable international rules and standards established through competent international organizations or diplomatic conference to prevent, reduce and control pollution of the marine environment from land-based sources.

Article 214: Enforcement with respect to pollution from sea-bed activities

States shall enforce their laws and regulations adopted in accordance with article 208 and shall adopt laws and regulations and take other measures necessary to implement applicable international rules and standards established through competent international organizations or diplomatic conference to prevent, reduce and control pollution of the marine environment arising from or in connection with sea-bed activities subject to their jurisdiction and from artificial islands, installations and structures under their jurisdiction, pursuant to articles 60 and 80.

Significance. In drafting Part XI for the International Seabed Area, considerable care and concern seem to have been taken with regard for the need for prevention and control of marine pollution if and when deep-seabed mining commences in the Area beyond national jurisdiction. In addition to setting forth the general principles in Article 145 for protection of the marine environment, enforcement power can be exercised by the Authority over mines and their operation in the Area—including suspension of any mining operation and disapproval of sites for exploitation by contractors, as well as the Enterprise, the operating arm of the Authority. The Authority does have the power to establish rules, regulations and standards for the purpose of preventing and reducing environmental pollution in the Area. For marine environmental protection, there is a stronger legal basis for the International Seabed Area, even though much of the detailed or specific application is not available until deep-seabed mining commences.

NOTES

1. See Luc Cuyvers, *Ocean Uses and Their Regulations* (New York: Wiley, 1984), p. 68.
2. Ibid.
3. Ibid., pp. 71–82.
4. Bob Dunham, "Japan's Collision Course with Ocean Pollution," *Oceans* (November–December 1976): pp. 58–61.
5. See R. B. Clark, *Marine Pollution* (Oxford: Clarendon Press, 1986), pp. 124–126.
6. See *Oceans Policy News*, March 1989, p. 1.
7. Clark, *Marine Pollution*, p. 151.
8. Ibid., p. 152.
9. Ibid.
10. Senate Bill No. 1840 (Hawaii State Legislature, 15th session), 3 February 1989. Also, *The Honolulu Advertiser*, 5 April 1989, p. A–1.
11. Convention for the Regulation of the Meshes of Fishing Nets and the Size Limits of Fish (Signed at London 5 April 1946), United Nations Series, No. 3221, pp. 200–216.
12. See *The Honolulu Star-Bulletin* News Service, 2 July 1990, p. A–4.
13. *Wall Street Journal*, 27 June 1990, p. A–8.
14. See entries on marine debris in James C.F. Wang, *Ocean Politics and Law: An Annotated Bibliography* (Westport, CT: Greenwood Press, 1991).
15. Edward D. Goldberg, "The Oceans as a Waste Space," Elisabeth Mann Borgese and Norton Ginsburg, eds. *Ocean Yearbook 5* (London: University of Chicago Press, 1985), p. 154.
16. Ibid., p. 160.
17. For the formation of the IMCO, see the following: R. M. M'Gonigle and Mark W. Zacher, *Pollution, Politics and International Law* (Berkeley, Calif.:University of

California Press, 1979), pp. 39–44; *Yearbook of the United Nations, 1948–1949* (New York: United Nations Publications, 1950), pp. 1113–1115; *Yearbook of International Organizations* (London: Union of International Associations, 1974), p. 1117.

18. *Yearbook of the United Nations, 1948–1949*, p. 1114.

19. See *Yearbook of the United Nations, 1982*, vol. 36, p. 1585. Also see Wilhelm H. Lampe, "The New International Maritime Organization and Its Place in Development of International Maritime Law," *Journal of Maritime Law and Commerce* 14, no. 3 (July 1983): 305–329; and C. P. Srivastava, "IMO and the Law of the Sea," *The United Nations Convention and the Law of the Sea: Impact and Implementation* (Honolulu: Law of the Sea Institute, University of Hawaii, 1987), pp. 419–425.

20. Zacher, *Pollution, Politics and International Law*, pp. 54–55.

21. Ibid., pp. 52–58.

22. Ibid., p. 46.

23. Ibid., p. 44.

24. Allen L. Springer, *The International Law of Pollution: Protecting the Global Environment in a World of Sovereign States* (Westport, Conn.: Quorum Books, 1983), pp. 107–108.

25. Elliot L. Richardson, "Prevention of Vessel-Source Pollution: Part I and II," *Oceans* 13, no. 3 (May–June 1980): 61.

26. Text of the convention can be found in *U.S. Treaties and Other International Agreements*, 26, pp. 767–831.

27. For text of the 1973 Protocol, see *Treaties and Other International Acts Series* (TIAS), 10561, pp. 3–13.

28. See John Warren Kindt, "International Environmental Law and Policy: An Overview of Transboundary Pollution," *San Diego Law Review* 23, no. 3 (May–June 1986): pp. 583–604. Also see Chapter 11 of his *Marine Pollution and the Law of the Sea* 4 vols. (Buffalo, N.Y.: William S. Hein, 1985), pp. 1034–1973. For an overview and policy analysis of the development of contemporary international law on land-based marine pollution, see Meng Qing-Nan, *Land-Based Marine Pollution: International Law Development* (London: Graham & Trotman, 1987). For a more detailed discussion on transboundary pollution see Constance O'Keefe, "Transboundary Pollution and the Strict Liability Issue: The Work of the International Law Commission on the Topic of International Liability for Injurious Consequences Arising out of Acts Not Prohibited by International Law," *Denver Journal of International Law and Policy* 18, no. 2 (Winter 1990): 146–208.

29. For the joint U.S.–Canada work on pollution control for the Great Lakes and their connecting waterways, see Jennifer Woodward, "International Pollution Control: The United States and Canada—The International Joint Commission," *New York Law School Journal of International and Comparative Law* 9, nos. 2–3 (1988): 325–344. An earlier study of the policy problems raised by acid rain in the United States and Canada can be found in Jurgen Schmandt and Hilliard Roderick, eds., *Acid Rain and Friendly Neighbors: The Policy Dispute between Canada and the United States* (Durham, N.C.: Duke University Press, 1985).

30. Kindt, "International Environmental Law and Policy," p. 592.

31. Ibid.

32. TIAS, no. 10541, November 13, 1979. The convention was undertaken under the auspices of the United Nations Economic Commission for Europe, a regional organization established by the United Nations Economic and Social Council.

33. See *The New York Times*, 7 August 1988, pp. 1 and 21. Also see for background of the controversy, *The New York Times*, 30 April 1988, p. 30; 27 April 1988, p. 45; and 25 April 1988, p. A–10.

34. "Claims: Damages Resulting from Operation of Smelter at Trail, British Columbia," *Treaties and Other International Agreements of the United States of America*, vol. 6, Department of State Publication 8549, pp. 60–64. For an analysis of the case, see Alfred P. Rubin, "Pollution by Analogy: The Trail Smelter Arbitration," *Oregon Law Review* 70 (1971): 259–282.

35. Rubin, "Pollution by Analogy," pp. 259 and 269.

36. R. R.Churchill and A. V. Lowe, *The Law of the Sea* (Manchester, England: Manchester University Press, 1983), pp. 245–249.

37. Ibid., p. 245.

38. Ibid.

39. Ibid., p. 234.

40. See Carl August Fleisher, "Oil Spills: Convention to Limit Liability," *Environmental Policy and Law* 3 (1977): 76–78. Text of the convention is found on pp. 93–95.

41. Edgar Gold, "The Control of Marine Pollution from Ships: Responsibilities and Rights," Thomas A. Clingan, Jr., ed., *The Law of the Sea: What Lies Ahead?* (Honolulu: The Law of the Sea Institute, University of Hawaii, 1988), p. 277.

42. See Churchill and Lowe, *The Law of the Sea*, p. 235; and Elliot L. Richardson, "Prevention of Vessel-Source Pollution, Part II," *Oceans* 13, no. 3 (May 1980): 58.

43. Gold, "The Control of Marine Pollution from Ships," p. 278.

44. Churchill and Lowe, *The Law of the Sea*, p. 235.

45. Gold, "The Control of Marine Pollution from Ships," p. 278.

46. Richardson, "Prevention of Vessel-Source Pollution," p. 59.

47. Ibid., p. 58.

48. Charles D. Hollister, D. Richard Anderson and G. Ross Heath, "Sub-Seabed Disposal of Nuclear Waste," *Science* 13, no. 4514 (18 September 1981): 1321–1326; Clifton E. Curtis, "Legality of Seabed Disposal of High-Level Radioactive Wastes under the London Dumping Convention," *Ocean Development and International Law* 14, no. 4 (1985): 383–416; Kenneth S. Kamlet, "The Oceans as Waste Space: The Rebuttal," *Oceanus* 24, no. 1 (Spring 1981): 10–17; International Atomic Energy Agency, *Site Investigations for Repositories for Solid Radioactive Wastes in Deep Continental Geological Formations (1982)* (Technical Reports Series No. 215); Gregorio J. Timagenes, "Disposal of Nuclear Wastes: A National and International Perspective," *Radioactive Waste Management*, January 1981.

49. Cuyvers, *Ocean Uses and Their Regulation*, p. 91.

50. Clark, *Marine Pollution*, p. 131.

51. Cuyvers, *Ocean Uses and Their Regulation*, p. 93.

52. Clark, *Marine Pollution*, pp. 141–142.

53. Naval Nuclear Propulsion Program—1982: Hearing on H.R. 6151 before Subcommittee on Procurement and Military Nuclear Systems of the House Committee on Armed Forces, 97th Congress, 2nd session 66 (1982), as summarized in Kindt, *Marine Pollution and the Law of the Sea*, vol. 2, pp. 839–840.

54. Kindt, *Marine Pollution and the Law of the Sea*, vol. 2, p. 840.

55. See David E. Kaplan, "When Incidents Are Accidents: The Silent Saga of the Nuclear Navy," *Oceans* 16, no. 4 (July–August 1983): 26–33; and the Navy's response

in "The Navy Defends the Nuclear Navy," *Oceans* 16, no. 5 (September–October 1983): 62–63.

56. Kindt, *Marine Pollution and the Law of the Sea*, vol. 2, p. 828.

57. See Charles D. Hollister, "The Seabed Option," *Oceanus* 20, no. 1 (Winter 1977): 18; and Kenneth S. Kamlet, "The Oceans as Waste Space," p. 10.

58. Kindt, *Marine Pollution and the Law of the Sea*, vol. 2, p. 837.

59. Ibid., p. 838.

60. "Ocean Burial for N-Wastes Pushed," Associated Press release as reprinted by *The Honolulu Star-Bulletin*, 21 April 1977, p. A–10; "Pacific Sub-Seabed Possible for Nuclear Waste Site," *Hawaii Tribune-Herald*, 24 September 1981, p. 14; and "Matsunaga Blasts U.S. Plans for Pacific N-Waste Storage," *The Honolulu Advertiser*, 19 February 1982, p. A–8; and text of his speech to the Pacific and Asian Affairs Council in Honolulu as reprinted in *The Honolulu Star-Bulletin*, 23 March 1982, p. A–16.

61. Hollister, Anderson and Heath, "Sub-Seabed Disposal of Nuclear Waste," p. 1323.

62. Kindt, *Marine Pollution and the Law of the Sea*, vol. 2, pp. 868–869.

63. See Curtis, "Legality of Seabed Disposal of High-Level Radioactive Wastes under the London Dumping Convention," pp. 383–416. Also see Kindt, *Marine Pollution and the Law of the Sea*, vol. 2, p. 873.

64. Curtis, "Legality of Seabed Disposal of High-Level Radioactive Wastes under the London Dumping Convention," pp. 385–386.

65. Ibid., pp. 403–404.

66. The following books represent basic works on ocean dumping: Kindt, *Marine Pollution and the Law of the Sea*, vol. 2, pp. 1085–1141; G. J. Timagenes, *International Control of Marine Pollution*, 2 vols. (Dobbs Ferry, N.Y.: Oceana Publications, 1980); Clark, *Marine Pollution*; M'Gonigle and Zacher, *Pollution, Politics and International Law*; and K. Hakaopää, *Marine Pollution in International Law* (Helsinki: *Annales Academiae Scienterium*, 1981).

67. Text can be found in Timagenes, *International Control of Marine Pollution*, vol. 2, Appendix I, pp. 665–671.

68. Ibid., pp. 673–686. For the text of the treaty also see TIAS, 8165, pp. 2405–2468.

69. Ibid., p. 689.

70. Ibid., pp. 218, 227 and 690.

71. The author is indebted to the information provided by Professor Jon Van Dyke of the Richardson Law School of the University of Hawaii at Manoa, who attended the eleventh consultative meeting as the legal advisor for the Republic of Nauru. Also see Maxwell Brace, "The London Dumping Convention, 1972: First Decade and Future," in Elisabeth Mann Borgese and Norton Ginsburg, eds., *Ocean Yearbook 6* (Chicago: The University of Chicago Press, 1986), pp. 312–313.

72. *The Guardian* (London), 7 October 1988, p. 1.

73. *The Daily Telegraph* (London), 7 October 1988, p. 2.

74. Kindt, *Marine Pollution and the Law of the Sea*, p. 1128.

75. Brace, "The London Dumping Convention, 1972," pp. 305–306.

76. Ibid., p. 305.

77. Ibid.

78. See George C. Kasoulides, "State Responsibility and Assessment of Liability

for Damage Resulting from Dumping Operations,'' *San Diego Law Review* 26, no. 3 (August–September 1989): 497–523.

79. The quote comes from the annex to the Task Force Team 2000 Report and is taken from Brace, ''The London Dumping Convention, 1972,'' p. 318.

80. See text of the 1973 International Convention for the Prevention of Pollution from Ships, in Timagenes, *International Control of Marine Pollution*, vol. 2, p. 700.

81. Ibid., and vol. 1, p. 369.

82. Ibid., vol. 1, pp. 369–370.

83. Ibid., p. 373.

84. Ibid.

85. R. P. Barston and Patricia Birnie, eds. *The Maritime Dimension* (London: Allen and Unwin, 1980), p. 120.

86. See Bath, ''Mexico, the United States and Selected Law of the Sea Issues,'' *Inter-American Affairs* 34 (1981): 19. Also see Handl, ''The Case for Mexican Liability for Transnational Pollution Damage Resulting from the Ixtoc I Oil Spill,'' *Houston Journal of International Law* 2 (1979): 227. Also see text of Agreement Concerning Settlement of Claims Arising from the 1979 Oil Well Blowout and Oil Spill in the Gulf of Mexico, *International Legal Materials* 22, no. 3 (May 1983): 578–586.

87. See Melisa B. Cates, ''Comments, Offshore Oil Platforms which Pollute the Marine Environment: A Proposal for an International Treaty Imposing Strict Liability,'' *San Diego Law Review* 21, no. 3 (June 1984): 693.

88. Churchill and Lowe, *The Law of the Sea*, p. 243.

89. Cates, ''Comments, Offshore Oil Platforms which Pollute the Marine Environment,'' pp. 698–701 and 708.

90. Charles S. Pearson, *International Marine Environment Policy: The Economic Dimension* (Baltimore: The Johns Hopkins University Press, 1975), p. 87.

91. Clark, *Marine Pollution*, pp. 34–35.

92. Ibid.

93. See Kindt, ''International Environmental Law and Policy: An Overview of Transboundary Pollution,'' p. 601; and Kindt's other article, ''Marine Pollution and Hydrocarbons: The Goal of Minimizing Damage to the Marine Environment,'' *California Western International Law Journal* 14 (1984): 245–246. Also see M'Gonigle and Zacher, *Pollution, Politics and International Law*, pp. 15–16. Also see Kindt, *Marine Pollution and the Law of the Sea*, vol. 2, pp. 775–783.

94. Kindt, *Marine Pollution and the Law of the Sea*, vol. 2, pp. 775–783.

95. See a brief summary of the Amoco *Cadiz* case in Barston and Birnie, *The Maritime Dimension*, p. 118. Also see *The Amoco* Cadiz *Oil Spill: A Preliminary Scientific Report (NOAA/EPA Special Report)*, U.S. Department of Commerce and Environmental Protection Agency, August 1978.

96. For a detailed assessment of the Exxon *Valdez* oil spill in Alaska in 1989, see Art Davison, *On the Wake of the Exxon* Valdez *: The Devastating Impact of the Alaska Oil Spill* (San Francisco: Sierra Club Books, 1990).

97. M'Gonigle and Zacher, *Pollution, Politics and International Law*, pp. 81–82.

98. Ibid., pp. 84–85. Also see Ministry of Transport, *Report of the Committee on the Prevention of Pollution of the Sea by Oil* (London: Her Majesty's Stationery Office, 1953).

99. M'Gonigle and Zacher, *Pollution, Politics and International Law*, p. 85.

100. Ibid., p. 88. Also see Churchill and Lowe, *The Law of the Sea*, p. 219.

101. M'Gonigle and Zacher, *Pollution, Politics and International Law*, p. 89.

102. Timagenes, *International Control of Maritime Pollution*, vol. 1, p. 325 (footnote 23) and pp. 350–356. Also see M'Gonigle and Zacher, *Pollution, Politics and International Law*, p. 93.

103. M'Gonigle and Zacher, *Pollution, Politics and International Law*, pp. 96–100.

104. Ibid., pp. 102–105.

105. Text of the 1973 MARPOL Convention and Annexes I–V are to be found in Timagenes, *International Control of Marine Pollution*, vol. 2, pp. 699–804. Also see Churchill and Lowe, *The Law of the Sea*, pp. 220–221 for a summary. Also see "MARPOL 73/78: The International Convention for the Prevention of Marine Pollution from Ships, 1973, as modified by its Protocol of 1978," in Borgese and Ginsburg, eds., *Ocean Yearbook 6*, pp. 576–578.

106. Text can be found in Timagenes, *International Control of Marine Pollution*, vol. 2, pp. 811–812.

107. Elliot L. Richardson, "Prevention of Vessel-Source Pollution: An Attainable Goal," *Oceans* 13, nos. 2 and 3 (March–April 1980): 2–5; and (May–June 1980): 58–61.

108. Steven I. Kern, "No Dumping in This Ocean: Nearing the End of Ship-Generated Pollution," *New York University Journal of International Law and Politics*, Winter 1974, p. 545.

109. Kindt, *Marine Pollution and the Law of the Sea*, vol. 2, pp. 1537; and Scott C. Whitney, "Environmental Regulation of U.S. Deep Seabed Mining," *William and Mary Law Review* 19 (Fall 1977): 78–79.

110. Richard A. Frank, "Environmental Aspects of Deep Seabed Mining," *Virginia Journal of International Law* 15, no. 4 (Summer 1975): 818–819. Also, summary in Kindt, *Marine Pollution and the Law of the Sea.*

111. Kindt, *Marine Pollution and the Law of the Sea*. vol. 2, pp. 1537–1538.

112. Ibid., p. 1582.

113. Ibid.

CHAPTER 9

Regional Arrangements for Marine Environmental Protection and Pollution Control

There is a strong case in support of a regional approach for solutions to marine environmental protection and pollution control problems. It has been considered by many a logical choice between the unilateral (national) and the global (international) approaches. Advocates for the regional approach to marine environment protection methods advance the argument that marine pollution is transboundary and that there are special needs and interests for nations in a physical or geographic region that can best be met by regional arrangements.[1] This is particularly so for many areas of the world which are semi-enclosed seas, for example, the Arabian Sea, Baltic Sea, Caribbean Sea, Mediterranean Sea, North Sea, Persian Gulf and the Red Sea. As summarized by John Warren Kindt, regional arrangements are more suitable for marine pollution regulation because:[2]

1. the differences in types of pollution in various parts of the world require different approaches.
2. technology and facilities can be made more readily accessible to deal with accidents in areas within the region where they are likely to occur.
3. there can be maximum participation by states not directly involved with a given type or area of marine pollution.
4. regional arrangements can be used as forums for consultation or confrontation.

Also, the regional arrangements have the definite advantage of serving as the legal framework for data collection and management planning.[3]

The negotiation history for the pertinent provisions in the 1982 LOS Convention seems to indicate that the regional approach is preferred in the protection and preservation of the marine environment.[4] Article 197 states that:

> States shall cooperate on a global basis and, as appropriate, on a regional basis, directly or through competent international organizations, in formulating and elaborating inter-

national rules, standards and recommended practices and procedures consistent with this Convention, for the protection and preservation of the marine environment, taking into account characteristic regional features.

Furthermore, Articles 198 and 199 of the 1982 LOS Convention obligate the states to develop contingency plans to combat marine pollution:

Article 198: Notification of imminent or actual damage

When a State becomes aware of cases in which the marine environment is in imminent danger of being damaged or has been damaged by pollution, it shall immediately notify other States it deems likely to be affected by such damage, as well as the competent international organizations.

Article 199: Contingency plans against pollution

In the cases referred to in article 198, States in the area affected, in accordance with their capabilities, and the competent international organizations shall co-operate, to the extent possible, in eliminating the effects of pollution and preventing or minimizing the damage. To this end, States shall jointly develop and promote contingency plans for responding to pollution incidents in the marine environment.

One of the purposes of this chapter is to demonstrate the cooperation among nations that has already been developed through a number of regional conventions for the protection of the marine environment. Many of these regional arrangements have been made with the assistance of the United Nations Environment Program (UNEP), established by the General Assembly in 1972, with instructions that the UNEP's Governing Council serve as a catalyst for developing regional arrangements to combat pollution and to provide the needed technical assistance in these endeavors. Since then, under its Regional Seas Program, the UNEP has provided the impetus and assistance to the formation of eleven regional arrangements. This chapter provides a brief summary and analysis of these regional agreements or conventions for the Baltic Sea, Caribbean region, East Africa (Indian Ocean), European Project on Pollution, Kuwait and the Persian Gulf, the Mediterranean, the Nordic Convention, the North Sea, the Red Sea, South Pacific and West and Central Africa. The following is a brief comparative study of these regional arrangements in terms of membership, structure and function.

The largest regional arrangement for marine environmental protection is the twenty-two-member South Pacific region, followed by the Caribbean, Mediterranean and West and Central African regions, with a membership participation in the regional conventions of sixteen to seventeen states. The Baltic and the North Sea arrangements involve seven and eight participating states, respectively. The smallest is the Nordic Convention on oil pollution prevention with four contracting parties.

With the exception of the East Africa Action Plan, the Nordic Agreement, the North Sea Convention, which are primarily concerned with oil pollution, and all other regional arrangements discussed in this chapter require the contracting parties to provide regulatory measures to combat pollution from land-based sources, vessels, dumping and airborne sources. A number of these conventions require monitoring and reporting of incidents, and some form of co-operative effort in organizing contingency plans to meet emergencies. The Kuwait and Mediterranean conventions provide for dispute settlement by negotiation and arbitration. For many of these regional arrangements there are present a number of ''disintegrative forces''—political, ideological and cultural differences, as well as unequal costs and benefits—which tend to prevent their growth as effective instruments for marine environment protection and pollution control.

BALTIC SEA: CONVENTION ON THE PROTECTION OF MARINE ENVIRONMENT (1974)

The Baltic is a semi-enclosed sea, 360,000 square kilometers (125,000 square miles) in area. It is bordered by six riparian states (Denmark, Federal Republic of Germany, Finland, Poland, the Soviet Union and Sweden). One hydrographic feature needs to be considered as an important factor that affects pollution of the Baltic. This is the fact that the Baltic Sea receives drainage from a land area that is four times greater than its own. Thus, land-based pollution constitutes the main threat to its marine environment. Waste disposal of toxic substances created by human activities and oil pollution make the Baltic one of the most polluted seas on earth. Vast amounts of industrial and agricultural waste, in addition to an equally large amount of sewage waste, have been discharged into the Baltic. The increased use of detergents in urban centers of the area contribute to an excess accumulation of phosphates that further cause de-oxygenation of the bottom layers of water in the Baltic. Boleslaw A. Boczek points out that in 1970 the bulk of sewage discharged into the Baltic was untreated.[5] Discharge of toxic substances, such as DDT, polychlorinated biphenyls (PCBs), heavy metals and mercury poses another source of threat to the Baltic Sea—disposal of such wastes mainly by Sweden, Germany (eastern portion) and Poland.[6]

The Convention on the Protection of the Marine Environment of the Baltic Sea Area (hereafter referred to as the Baltic Convention) was the result of the Helsinki diplomatic conference convened by the then seven Baltic states (including East and West Germany) in March 1973 and 1974. It was signed by the seven signatory states on March 22, 1974, and came into force in 1976. The Baltic Convention is designed to protect the marine environment in the ''Baltic Sea Area,'' defined by the 1973 MARPOL Convention (Convention for the Prevention of Pollution from Ships; see Chapter 8), as covering all marine life both in the territorial waters of the signatory states and on the high seas (Article 4.1).[7] Unfortunately, the Baltic Convention has no jurisdiction over the internal waters of the signatory states through which most of the land-based pollutants are discharged into the sea (Article 4.3). However, the signatory states to the

Baltic Convention may, and are encouraged to, promulgate rules and regulations governing pollution from vessels, air and dumping within their own territorial and internal waters. Oil discharge from vessels of 400 or more gross tons is prohibited, and sewage disposal by ships is prohibited within twelve miles of land. Dumping of plastics is strictly banned. Under Article 12(1) of the Baltic Convention a permanent organ, the Baltic Marine Environment Commission, is established with limited regulatory powers. It is operated under the rule of unanimity to recommend to the signatory states measures for pollution prevention and control in the Baltic.

Significance. The Baltic Convention is the only regional arrangement designed to achieve international cooperation for prevention of pollution in an area that has been characterized by political and ideological diversity from Poland and the Soviet Union to Denmark and Sweden. The signatory states to the Baltic Convention are all industrialized states and are keenly aware of the need for regional cooperation for marine pollution control, despite political differences, which, in the view of one observer, may be "a potential disintegrative element" that could prevent effective regional cooperation in the Baltic.[8] Finally, similar to many other international cooperative arrangements, the Baltic Convention lacks enforcement power to implement the rules agreed upon for marine environmental control. It may be noted that general obligations imposed on the states are supplemented and implemented by rules and standards in the annexes to the convention through a commission.

CARIBBEAN REGION: CONVENTION FOR THE PROTECTION AND DEVELOPMENT OF MARINE ENVIRONMENT OF THE WIDER CARIBBEAN REGION (THE CARTAGENA CONVENTION, 1983)

The Caribbean region, as defined by Article 2 of the 1983 Convention for the Protection and Development of the Marine Environment of the Wider Caribbean Region (hereafter, the Cartagena Convention), encompasses the marine environment of the Gulf of Mexico, the Caribbean Sea and the adjacent waters of the Atlantic Ocean (within 200 nautical miles of the Atlantic coasts of states).[9] In reality the region as defined includes a total of thirty states of varying size, language, culture and systems of government. A physical characteristic of the region has been that the area consists of basins (Yucatán Basin, Colombia Basin and Venezuela Basin), which are bordered by submarine sills. Some of the sills are shallower than the basins and thus contribute to the phenomenon of making the water in the Caribbean deeper than sill depth.[10] This results in not very much flushing in the Caribbean with the consequence that pollutants (carried by river sediments) tend to stay in the waters for years without being washed away.[11] There are eighteen rivers that affect the wider Caribbean region.

According to a report by two experts for the UNEP, since most of the states in the wider Caribbean region are developing nations, pollution of the marine environment comes from four main sources: sewage waste and some industrial waste disposal; oil pollution caused by spills and offshore oil well explosions (Ixtoc, on the Gulf of Mexico, and Bahía de Campeche); pollution caused by sugar industries in the disposal of high biological oxygen (BOD) and industrial solid wastes; and discharge of chemical wastes from larger urban or industrial centers, such as Kingston, Jamaica.

In March 1983, a conference on the protection of the marine environment for the Caribbean region was convened in Cartagena, Colombia, by the Executive Director of the UNEP. It was attended by seventeen states (Colombia, Costa Rica, Cuba, France, Grenada, Guatemala, Honduras, Jamaica, Mexico, Netherlands, Nicaragua, Panama, Saint Lucia, Trinidad and Tobago, the United Kingdom, the United States and Venezuela), plus representatives of the Caribbean Community and the European Economic Community (EEC). Article 4 of the Cartagena Convention imposes general obligations on the contracting parties to take appropriate measures to prevent, reduce and control pollution in the wider Caribbean area. In the next five articles, the Caribbean Convention imposes specific obligations on the parties to prevent, reduce and control pollution from ships (Article 5), dumping of wastes at sea from ships, aircraft and man-made structures at sea (Article 6), coastal disposal or by discharges from rivers, estuaries, coastal establishments, outfall structures (Article 7), from seabed activities (Article 8) and discharge from the atmosphere (Article 9). Contracting parties are required to notify other concerned states at once of any emergency pollution incidents and inform other states and "competent international organizations of measures it has taken to minimize or reduce pollution or the threat thereof" (Article 11). An environmental impact statement on the potential effects of any development project on the marine environment must be made as a part of the pollution management policies of the contracting states (Article 12).

Significance. While regional cooperation is stressed by the Caribbean Convention on the need to prevent, reduce and control pollution of the marine environment for the wider Caribbean area, major responsibility for individually or jointly enacting the appropriate measures among the contracting parties rests with the coastal states. Similar to many international arrangements on marine environmental protection, enforcement for discharging the general or specific obligations is woefully lacking or nonexistent. However, the Cartagena Convention was designed to be an "umbrella" agreement under which it is hoped that subsequent specific protocols may be developed to strengthen the legal responsibilities of the contracting parties which represent a diverse array of economic development and cultural differences.

EAST AFRICA AND THE INDIAN OCEAN

The East African Action Plan is a part of the UNEP's Regional Seas Program. It encompasses eight eastern African states: Somalia, Kenya, Tanzania, Mozambique, Malagasy, Comoro Islands, Mauritius and Seychelles. The regional plan came out of UNEP's visiting mission to East Africa in 1980–1981, which assessed the environmental problems of the region.[12] On the whole, these East African states are basically agricultural with expanding populations. Environmental concerns center on waste disposal, both domestic and agricultural, that would primarily affect the fisheries that provide much of the food protein for the region's population. Residues of oil spills in the form of tar balls are common on the beaches in East Africa, the consequence of oil spillage by tankers that use the heavily traveled routes from the Persian Gulf to European ports. At any given time more than 200 oil tankers ply the East African waters, resulting in more than 33,000 metric tons of oil discharge in a given year.[13] Coastal and coral reefs where local fishing takes place have been damaged by silting (due to deforestation and soil erosion), dynamite fishing, and dynamiting for lime along the coasts of Kenya, Madagascar, Comoros Islands and Tanzania. Untreated domestic wastes are released into the Indian Ocean as a matter of common practice for the whole region.

The UNEP-prepared action plan for the eastern African region contains an overall assessment of the environmental conditions, an environmental management plan with guidelines for the control of waste disposal, and a section on draft regional conventions and protocols to establish environmental standards. With the assistance from UNEP and the IMCO/IMO negotiations began in 1983 for a regional convention dealing with environmental marine protection for East Africa.

Significance. As of this writing there is no concrete regional convention for the protection of the marine environment for the eastern African region. This is a vital area for navigation and transport of crude oil from the Persian Gulf; any damage to the marine environment would affect the long-term welfare of the people of the region. Marine pollution is transboundary and global in character. A regional agreement for the control and prevention of pollution could contribute considerably to the effective implementation of related regional plans in the Persian Gulf (the Kuwait Convention) and in West and Central Africa.

While there is no legal framework or a regional convention for East Africa, it is entered here as an example of the many other "action plans" under the auspices of the UNEP's Regional Seas Program.

EUROPEAN PROJECT ON POLLUTION (SEWAGE SLUDGE PROCESSING) AND PORT STATE CONTROL IN IMPLEMENTING AGREEMENTS ON MARINE SAFETY AND MARINE ENVIRONMENTAL PROTECTION

Two European agreements are entered here as examples of regional cooperation for the protection of the marine environment—agreements which are not considered to be within the framework or auspices of the EEC.

The first is a ten-nation (Denmark, Federal Republic of Germany, France,

Italy, Netherlands, Norway, Sweden, Switzerland, United Kingdom and Yugoslavia) agreement signed on November 23, 1971, dealing with the processing and disposal of sewage sludge.[14] The agreement between Denmark, France, Norway, Sweden, Switzerland and the United Kingdom came into force on August 1, 1972. As outlined in the annex to the agreement, the first stage of the project consisted of laboratory work on improving methods for processing and disposal of sewage sludge and the evaluation of industrial plants for incineration of sludges and household refuse, as well as a comparative study of sewage disposal methods in different countries.

The second is the fourteen-power memorandum of understanding on port state control in implementing agreements for maritime safety and protection of the marine environment.[15] The agreement had its origin in the December 2, 1980, Regional European Conference on Maritime Safety, which placed emphasis on maritime safety on board ship as well as the protection of the marine environment. The conference was held with the assistance of IMCO (IMO) and the European Economic Community. Under the memorandum of understanding, all relevant international instruments or agreements on safety at sea and the 1973 International Convention for the Prevention of Pollution from Ships are valid instruments for the parties to observe and enforce. A special feature of implementing international agreements on maritime safety and protection of the marine environment is the inspection procedure and right of detention by port states parties to the memorandum of understanding for checking out the certificates and documents and complaints for violation by ships (Section 3 and Annex 1 of the memorandum).

Significance. While many, if not all, European states have been parties to many international conventions on marine environmental protection, broader continental cooperative efforts in the form of distinct European projects for enforcing implementation of the treaty provisions are illustrated by the two agreements included here. Through cooperative sharing of expenses by the contracting parties, the agreement on processing and disposal of sewage sludge would establish some standard criteria for assessing the methods employed by many European nations—an increasing environmental concern for the more industrialized and urbanized parts of Europe and elsewhere. These are examples of the effort needed to formulate standards for enforcement.

KUWAIT REGIONAL CONVENTION FOR COOPERATION ON THE PROTECTION OF THE MARINE ENVIRONMENT FROM POLLUTION (1978)

With the UNEP's Regional Seas Program as the catalyst, eight states (Bahrain, Iran, Iraq, Kuwait, Oman, Qatar, Saudi Arabia, and the United Arab Emirates) bordering the Persian Gulf convened the Kuwait Regional Conference on the Protection and Development of the Marine Environment and the Coastal Areas in April 1978. This conference produced the Kuwait Regional Convention for

Cooperation on the Protection of the Marine Environment from Pollution (hereafter, the Kuwait Convention), signed on April 24, 1978, by six of the eight Persian Gulf states.[16] The contracting parties agreed to take appropriate measures to combat pollution from ships in accordance with applicable international law with respect to load-on-top, ballast, and crude oil washing procedures for tankers (Article IV). As is the case in many regional seas programs, the Kuwait Convention obligates the contracting parties to take measures to combat pollution caused by dumping from ships and aircraft (Article V), from land-based sources, including waterborne, airborne, or outfalls and pipelines from the coast (Article VI), and from exploration and exploitation of the "bed of the territorial sea and the continental shelf" (Article VII). The convention also requires the contracting parties to make an environmental impact assessment in any planning activity or coastal project that may cause pollution risks in the region (Article XI). Procedures and rules must be established to determine civil liability and compensation for damage resulting from pollution of the marine environment (Article XIII). A permanent regional organization, consisting of a council and a secretariat, for marine environment protection is provided under the Kuwait Convention. For dispute settlement, under Article XVI(b)(iii), the Kuwait Convention provides for a judicial commission as an integral part of the regional organization, to which disputes that cannot be resolved by negotiation may be referred for settlement (Article XXV).

There is also a protocol to the Kuwait Convention on meeting "marine emergencies" of substantial pollution or threat of substantial pollution to the marine environment, such as oil spills, collisions and strandings that involve ships and tankers, or possible emergencies caused by offshore oil well blowouts.[17] Article III of the protocol establishes the Marine Emergency Mutual Aid Centre to assist the contracting parties in developing their own national capabilities for combating pollution by oil.[18]

Significance. Because the Persian Gulf is rather shallow from a geological point of view, the offshore area in particular has been easily exploited for natural gas and oil. This industrial development has accelerated the rapid deterioration of the already fragile natural environment of the coastal sectors of the states bordering the Persian Gulf. Not only is the region the most polluted part of the world, but it is also referred to by the World Wildlife Fund as being in a rapidly dying state. The 1978 Kuwait Convention has somewhat retarded this process because the states have pledged to cooperate for the protection of the marine environment. The Iran–Iraq War interrupted efforts in the control of oil spills, estimated to be at least 4,500 barrels of crude per day, spilled into the Persian Gulf.[19] In addition, the Persian Gulf War in 1991 created unprecedented environmental damage. Deliberate oil spills, estimated at anywhere from three to ten million barrels, and the setting ablaze of hundreds of oil wells has resulted in an emergency far beyond the capacity of the parties to the Kuwait Regional Convention. The convention and its protocol on emergencies, as well as the permanent regional organization established under it, should provide a framework for control of any further pollution of this vital waterway for oil transport, but at present help is needed from many nations.

MEDITERRANEAN REGION: CONVENTION FOR THE PROTECTION OF THE MEDITERRANEAN SEA AGAINST POLLUTION (1976)

The Convention for the Protection of the Mediterranean Sea against Pollution (hereafter, the Mediterranean Convention) was the final result of a Conference of Plenipotentiaries of the Coastal States of the Mediterranean Region for the Protection of the Mediterranean Sea, which met in Barcelona February 2–16, 1976. It was attended by representatives from sixteen states bordering the Mediterranean Sea (Cyprus, Egypt, France, Greece, Israel, Italy, Lebanon, Libya, Malta, Monaco, Morocco, Spain, Syria, Tunisia, Turkey and Yugoslavia). The focus of the Barcelona Conference was the examination and adoption of a draft convention for marine protection and a draft protocol to prevent dumping from ships and aircraft in the Mediterranean. The preparatory work for the drafting of the convention and the protocol was done by the UNEP.[20] The Mediterranean Convention provided the lead or pattern for subsequent regional marine environmental protection conventions by obligating the contracting parties to take all appropriate measures to prevent pollution caused by dumping from ships and aircraft (Article 5), by oil discharge from ships (Article 6), by seabed and continental shelf exploration and exploitation (Article 7), and by land-based sources, such as discharges from rivers and coastal outfalls (Article 8). Primarily because of the nature of the region as a semi-enclosed sea with limited sea space and the intensity of maritime traffic, Article 9 and a special protocol of the Mediterranean Convention also took the lead in obligating the contracting parties to cooperate in taking timely and necessary measures for dealing with pollution emergencies in the region. One of the responsibilities of the contracting parties is to notify the UNEP and the Regional Oil Combating Center for the Mediterranean and other parties affected. A pollution monitoring system, to be established at bilateral or multilateral levels, is encouraged by Article 10. The contracting parties are also asked to develop procedures for compliance control in the application of the convention provisions (Article 21). Dispute settlement methods are by negotiation or through arbitration if negotiation fails to produce a peaceful settlement (Article 22). Annex A to the Mediterranean Convention provides an eight-article arbitration procedure which includes a three-member arbitral tribunal to decide, in accordance with international law, disputes arising from the interpretation and application of the convention provisions.

Two protocols form an integral part of the Mediterranean Convention: one concerns dumping from ships and aircraft, and the other deals with emergency combating of oil pollution and pollution by other harmful substances. Annex I to the protocol on dumping, defined as any deliberate disposal at sea of wastes from ships and aircraft, provides a list of prohibited substances and materials. This list includes mercury compounds, cadmium, plastics, hydrocarbons, all levels of radioactive waste and acid/alkaline compounds. In accordance with Article 5 and Annex II to the protocol on dumping of arsenic, lead, copper, zinc, beryllium, chromium, nickel, and other minerals, a prior special permit issued by competent national authorities is required. In establishing criteria, Article 7 and Annex III to the protocol on dumping provide a list of factors to be taken into consideration in the issuance of permits for dumping: characteristics of the substances to be disposed of in the sea, the site and method of deposit, and conditions governing the permissible dumping.

In cases of emergency, the protocol for cooperation in combating pollution by oil and other harmful substances requires the contracting parties to develop contingency plans for equipment and personnel needs and systems for monitoring activities that cause grave and imminent danger to the Mediterranean marine environment. Under Annex I to the protocol, each contracting party must instruct ship masters flying its flag and aircraft pilots registered in its territory to report in the speediest fashion identification of the source of pollution, time, position, date of incident, as well as the types of harmful substances discharged.

A third protocol, the Protection of the Mediterranean Sea against Pollution from Land-based Sources, concluded at the Conference of Plenipotentiaries of the Coastal States of the Mediterranean Region, was held in Athens from May 12 to 17, 1980. Fifteen states (Algeria, Cyprus, France, Greece, Israel, Italy, Lebanon, Libya, Malta, Monaco, Morocco, Spain, Tunisia, Turkey and Yugoslavia), plus the European Economic Community, were represented.[21] The protocol applies to pollution caused by discharges from land-based sources, particularly from coastal outfalls, rivers, canals or other water courses, including underground runoffs (Article 4). It also applies to airborne pollutants and discharges from man-made offshore structures in the exploitation and exploration of mineral resources on the continental shelf and in the seabed (Article 4.2). The protocol requires the parties to work toward the elimination of land-based pollution by harmful substances of heavy metals (mercury, cadmium), lubricating oils, persistent synthetics, and radioactive material.

Significance. The Mediterranean region has been plagued by oil pollution and deterioration of the marine environment caused by discharges of industrial and domestic waste along the coastal areas. Sewage dumping along some of the Mediterranean coastline has been epidemic resulting in the depletion of the sea's oxygen supply through de-oxidation and in the breeding of infectious diseases, in addition to the accumulation of sediments from industrial waste that prevents the growth of sea floor organisms. The Mediterranean Convention and its protocols on marine environmental protection and pollution control presented here do provide a large measure of anti-pollution regulation on a regional basis, despite the inherent complexity of implementation and enforcement of convention provisions by a diverse collection of industrialized and developing nations in the region. For the first time in the region's long civilization these attempts, in the form of regional cooperation to control the marine environment for the Mediterranean, represent human awareness not to tamper with the Mediterranean's delicate and fragile ecosystem. Even more significant is the willingness of the sixteen contracting parties to the Barcelona Convention to make financial commitments in endorsing the Mediterranean regional cooperation for pollution control, particularly in critical areas of monitoring and research programs.

NORDIC REGION: CONVENTION ON THE PROTECTION OF THE ENVIRONMENT (1974)

In a convention concluded in Stockholm on February 19, 1974, four Nordic nations—Denmark, Finland, Norway, Sweden—agreed to undertake joint responsibility to protect the marine environment and prevent pollution caused by oil and discharges from land-based sources into water courses, lakes or the sea, as well as air and noise pollution. A unique provision of this regional convention is the right of any person to bring before the appropriate court of the contracting parties a request for a ruling on "the question of the permissibility" of environmentally harmful activities, and to sue for compensation for damages (Article 3). The convention also calls for the appointment in each state of a special supervisory authority to institute legal proceedings for safeguarding the general environmental interests (Article 4). Under the convention the cost for activities of the special supervisory authority is shared by the contracting Nordic states.

Significance. The Nordic Convention limits its concern to pollution by oil. Several aspects of the convention set it apart from other regional conventions. First, it empowers a special supervisory authority within each participating state with the right to institute judicial proceedings before a competent court of another contracting party with regard to the "permissibility" of harmful activities and the question of measures to prevent damage. Second, based on agreed instructions by the contesting parties, on-site inspection can be undertaken. However, there is no mention in the Nordic Convention of the specific geographic area of the convention's jurisdiction, except Article 13, which states that the convention shall apply to "the continental shelf areas" of the contracting parties.

NORTH SEA: AGREEMENT CONCERNING POLLUTION OF THE NORTH SEA BY OIL (1969)

Eight North Sea nations—Belgium, Denmark, France, Federal Republic of Germany, the Netherlands, Norway, Sweden and the United Kingdom—concluded an agreement at Bonn on June 9, 1969, for cooperation in the prevention and control of pollution by oil in the North Sea, including the English Channel and Skagerrak.[22] Article 5 of the North Sea agreement mandates the contracting parties to report "a casualty or the presence of oil slicks in the North Sea area" that would be likely to create a serious marine environmental threat to the coast of any other contracting party. At the same time the contracting parties must request masters of all flag ships to report without delay (1) all casualties causing or likely to cause oil pollution of the sea, and (2) the presence and nature of oil slicks on the North Sea (Article 5). A zonal system for assigning responsibilities is delineated in the annex to the convention. A contracting state must make an assessment of the nature, extent and location and speed of any oil slicks found in its zone of responsibility (Article 6). A contracting party to the agreement may call for help from other parties to dispose of the floating oil slick on the sea (Article 7). The North Sea agreement came into force on August 9, 1969, and in 1982 extended pollution concern to cover other harmful substances in addition to oil. The Third International Conference on the Protection of the North Sea convened in The Hague on March 7, 1990. Among the goals endorsed by the participants were the support for low-waste processes and nonhazardous products, promotion of the use of best available technology in reducing emissions and improvement in response procedures to accidents in the North Sea. The conference also called for complete suspension of industrial waste dumping by 1992.

Significance. The North Sea Convention made an important regional breakthrough in combating oil pollution when it established the assessment or evaluation component of the causes, location and extent of oil spills as a basis for the parties to map out appropriate strategy for minimizing the environmental damage that might endanger marine life and human health. The convention mandates ship masters and aircraft pilots to report without delay any oil slick or disposal of harmful substances found in the region; a definite monitoring and reporting system is a prerequisite for coordinated action to combat accidents that are likely to cause marine pollution. The zonal arrangement is an innovative and effective method for assigning cooperative responsibility to the contracting parties to inform, gather and assess damage.

SOUTH PACIFIC REGION: CONVENTION FOR THE PROTECTION OF THE NATURAL RESOURCES AND ENVIRONMENT

On November 24–25, 1986, in Noumea, New Caledonia, twenty-two nations and territories (American Samoa, Australia, Figi, French Polynesia, Guam, Kiribati, Marshall Islands, Nauru, New Caledonia, New Zealand, Niue, Northern Mariana Islands, Palau, Papua New Guinea, Pitcairn Islands, Solomon Islands, Tokelau, Tonga, Tuvalu, Vanuatu, Wallis and Futuna Islands, and Western Samoa) agreed to the adoption of the Convention for the Protection of the Natural

Resources and Environment of the South Pacific Region.[23] The convention area is defined to comprise

1. the 200-nautical-mile zone of the twenty-two South Pacific nations and territories
2. those areas of the high seas that are enclosed by all sides of the 200-nautical-mile zones
3. areas of the Pacific Ocean that have been included and specified by Article 3: any additional areas under the jurisdiction of any contracting parties ''within the Pacific Ocean between the Tropic of Cancer and 60° south latitude, and between 130° east longitude and 120° west longitude to the convention area.''

Similar to many other regional conventions assisted by the UNEP, the South Pacific Convention obligates the contracting parties to take all appropriate measures to prevent, reduce and control pollution from vessels (Article 6), from land-based sources of discharges from rivers and estuaries (Article 7), from seabed activities (Article 8), from airborne pollution (Article 9), and to prohibit the dumping of radioactive wastes (Article 10). In addition, storage of toxic and hazardous wastes in the South Pacific convention area is prohibited (Article 11).

Significance. Unfortunately in this convention there are only mildly worded provisions dealing with pollution caused by the testing of nuclear devices (Article 12) and with coastal erosion caused by mining activities, such as sand removal, reclamation and dredging (Article 13). Contracting parties are required to develop and promote individual or joint contingency plans to respond to emergency cases or incidents involving pollution or threat to the natural resources and marine environment in the South Pacific region by notifying and reporting to other countries and territories (Article 15). Each contracting party must make an environmental impact statement to assess the potential effects of any development project that might affect the marine environment (Article 16). Provision for the standard dispute settlement is also included, as in many other regional conventions for marine environment protection: negotiation by peaceful means and then by procedures of arbitration, using a system of a single arbitrator agreed between the disputing parties, or the choice of the three-member panel (Article 26 and Annex on Arbitration).

There are, in addition to the convention, two protocols: one on dumping in the South Pacific region and the other on combating pollution emergencies. Under Article 4 and Annex I to the protocol, on prevention of dumping of toxic waste, the protocol prohibits dumping in the South Pacific region of organohalogen, mercury and cadmium compounds, persistent plastics, crude oil, and materials produced for biological and chemical warfare.

Prior special permits must be obtained for dumping of wastes such as arsenic, lead, copper and zinc compounds. Prior general permits can be granted for dumping of all wastes or other matter not listed in the Annexes to the dumping protocol.

The protocol on combating pollution in case of emergency or "pollution incident," defined as "a discharge or significant threat of a discharge of oil or other hazardous substance" that presents an imminent threat to marine and coastal environment, requires the contracting parties to enact domestic legislation that would contain contingency plans for responding to the incident (Article 3 of the protocol). The protocol stresses the importance for establishing a rapid information communication system for reporting pollution incidents in the South Pacific region. Upon request by a contracting party, other parties must give assistance based on the agreement in combating hazardous substances other than oil. Parties are pledged to facilitate the movement of technical personnel, equipment and material into, out of, and through their territories for combating pollution incidents.

UNITED NATIONS ENVIRONMENTAL PROGRAM: REGIONAL SEAS PROGRAMS

The Regional Seas Programs of the United Nations Environmental Program were initiated as a direct response to the 1972 United Nations Conference on the Human Environment (Stockholm Conference), which advocated a regional approach for solving global pollution problems. The 1975 Mediterranean Convention was one of its first regional action plans. The UNEP's Regional Seas Program has helped to launch "action plans" for marine environmental protection and pollution control in ten geographic regions of the world, with 120 coastal states participating (see Figure 9.1).[24]

A key consideration in the Regional Seas Programs, many of which resulted in the concluding of regional multilateral conventions, is that the marine environmental and coastal protection programs are designed to meet regional needs by linking the quality of the marine and coastal environment and the causes for pollution with "action-oriented" activities. There are four basic objectives in the UNEP Regional Seas Program: to promote regional conventions for pollution control; to assess the impact of pollution on health and the marine ecosystem; to coordinate regional efforts in the management of marine resources; and to provide support for training and education in marine resources management.[25]

Significance. Although UNEP Regional Seas Program plays a limited role in the development of action plans designed to combat marine pollution in many regions of the world, it has been able to provide technical assistance and a regional framework to the various governments for commencement of planning a coordinated management program for protection of their marine and coastal environments. Much of the impetus for the formation of regional organizations

Figure 9.1
Geographic Coverage of UNEP Regional Seas Program

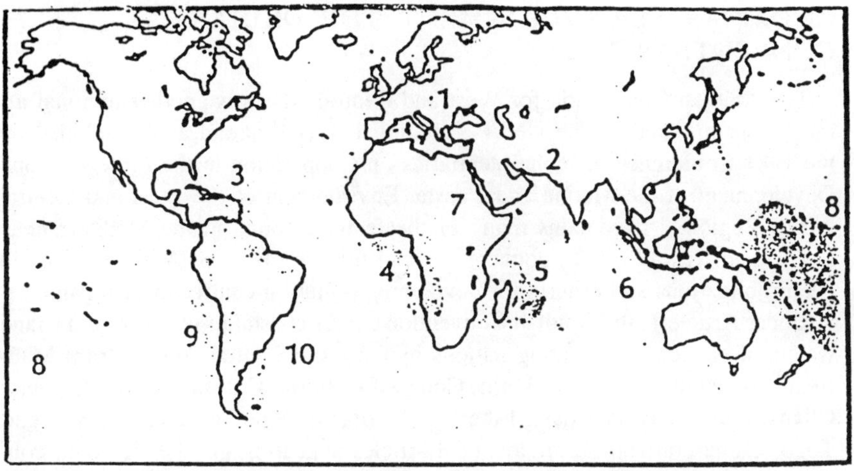

1. Mediterranean Region (Action Plan adopted 1975; Regional Convention signed 1976)
2. Kuwait Region (Action Plan adopted 1978; Regional Convention signed 1978)
3. Caribbean Region (Action Plan adopted 1981; Regional Convention in preparation)
4. West and Central African Region (Action Plan adopted 1981; Regional Convention signed 1981)
5. East African Region (Action Plan preparation initiated)
6. East Asian Region (Action Plan adopted 1981)
7. Red Sea and Gulf of Aden Region (Action Plan adopted 1981; Regional Convention signed 1982)
8. South-West Pacific Region (Action Plan adopted 1982)
9. South-East Pacific Region (Action Plan adopted 1981)
10. South-West Atlantic Region (Action Plan preparation initiated)

Source: Peter S. Thacher, "UNEP, An Update on the Regional Seas Program," in *Ocean Yearbook 4*, Elisabeth Mann Borgese and Norton Ginsburg, eds. (Chicago: University of Chicago Press, 1984), p. 451. Used by permission.

for marine environment protection and pollution control comes from these initiatives originated by the UNEP. It serves in many ways as a catalyst for developing regional approaches and action. As of 1989, the ten Regional Seas Programs—Mediterranean, Kuwait–Persian Gulf, Wider Caribbean, West-Central Africa, East Asian Seas, Southeast Pacific, Southwest Pacific, Red Sea, East Africa, Southwest Atlantic—have established a pattern of cooperation and coordination for pollution control at the regional level, which relies on a three-pronged strategy for action: scientific assessment, environmental management and legal components.

WEST AND CENTRAL AFRICA: CONVENTION FOR THE PROTECTION AND DEVELOPMENT OF MARINE AND COASTAL ENVIRONMENT (THE ABIDJAN CONVENTION, 1981)

The Abidjan Convention for West and Central Africa is another regional arrangement initiated by the UNEP's Regional Seas Program and concluded by the 1981 Conference of Plenipotentiaries on Cooperation in the Protection and Development of the Marine and Coastal Environment of the West and Central Africa Region.[26] It contains many of the features found in the Mediterranean (1976) and Kuwait (1978) conventions and the use of protocols to spell out in detail obligations and criteria for developing pollution control mechanisms.

Under Article 1, the Abidjan Convention covers coastal jurisdiction and island waters of sixteen participating nations in West and Central Africa, from Mauritania to Namibia: Angola, Benin, Congo, Equatorial Guinea, Gabon, Gambia, Ghana, Guinea, Ivory Coast, Liberia, Mauritania, Namibia, Nigeria, Senegal, Togo, Cameroon and Zaire. Identical articles appearing in other regional conventions are included in the Abidjan Convention. They are concerned with pollution from ships (Article 5), pollution caused by dumping from ships and aircraft (Article 6), pollution from land-based sources (Article 7), pollution from seabed activities (Article 8), pollution from or through the atmosphere (Article 9), and control of coastal erosion (Article 10). Similarly, there are also identical provisions on environmental impact statements (Article 13) and dispute settlement (Article 24).

Attached to the convention is the Protocol Concerning Cooperation in Combating Pollution in Case of Emergency in accordance with Article 16 of the Abidjan Convention. It includes cases or incidents which involve collisions by oil tankers, offshore oil-well blowouts, and the presence of oil or other harmful substances. It calls for Marine Emergency Contingency Plans to be drawn up nationally, bilaterally and multilaterally to deal with incidents that could adversely affect the marine and coastal environment for the West and South Africa region. These emergency contingency plans must provide for rapid reports or information to other contracting parties on the presence, characteristics and extent of oil spillage or blowouts or collision by tankers. Aid in the form of reinforcement of personnel, material and equipment must be provided to the party requesting such assistance.

Significance. The Abidjan Convention provides the legal framework under which nations from South and Central Africa can seek cooperation in combating marine pollution along their coastal areas. Pollution in the coastal waters where oil tankers carry crude oil to European ports around the Cape of Good Hope is the top item for regional action. Equally important is the disposal of untreated sewage into the coastal waters in this region, which is generally considered to be developing economically and industrially.

LOCAL ARRANGEMENT: U.S. WESTERN LEGISLATIVE CONFERENCE RECOMMENDATION (JANUARY 1988)

The Ocean Resources Committee for the United States Western Legislative Conference (WLC) was created in the fall of 1985, comprised of the five western states bordering the Pacific (Alaska, California, Hawaii, Oregon and Washington) and three United States Pacific islands (American Samoa, the Commonwealth of the Northern Mariana Islands, and Guam). Legislators from the eight jurisdictions met and discussed their coastal concerns. From these discussions, a series of policy papers on some key ocean problems were issued as a report.[27] The portion of the report on marine environmental quality is included here for reference as an example of possible local action or remedy to the problems.

State and federal environmental laws regulate pollution according to which natural resource—air, land, or fresh or marine waters—is receiving the wastes. This ''medium-based'' approach to waste disposal results in the shifting of wastes to the least regulated medium.

Today, there is enormous pressure to make the ocean the next frontier of waste disposal. The vastness of the ocean and its appearance of great assimilative capacity belies fragile ecosystems which support commercial and recreational fishing, as well as other activities that rely on the scenic and aesthetic values of an environmentally healthy ocean. Current disposal practices are already endangering portions of our coastal waters. The U.S. Congressional Office of Technology Assessment (U.S. Congress 1987) reports that approximately one-third of all shellfish beds in near-shore ocean waters are closed at a given time because of significant environmental damage and potential public health threats. Pollution pressure on marine environments will increase in the future as the coastal population increases and more demands are made for the disposal of sewage sludge and dredge materials, as urban and agricultural run-off increases, and if practices such as the disposal of marine debris and sewage overflows continue unabated.

Findings

- As Pacific States experience rising populations and urban development, marine pollution from nonpoint sources poses an increasing threat to human health, recreation and commercial use. This type of pollution is extremely difficult to regulate since it is generally the cumulative product of sources spread over a large geographic region.
- Federal guidelines under the Clean Water Act have allowed coastal communities to continue to discharge wastewater from households and industries into marine waters. However, recent decreases in federal grant funding have made it increasingly difficult for these communities to meet federal and state mandates for secondary treatment. As a result, state and local governments will need to develop programs to compensate for the federal government's reduced funding.
- Even where sewage treatment facilities and their pipeline networks are built oversized to accommodate storm water run-off, the capacity of the system is occasionally ex-

ceeded, and raw sewage is discharged into marine waters. Discharges of this nature present a direct threat to human health and living marine resources.

- Contaminated sediments and dredge spoils have been identified as problems in many coastal harbors and other locations of previous industrial processes, dumping and accidents. Some of these contaminated sites, which can contain hazardous materials, are affecting the health of bottom-dwelling fish and plants. While the sites may not require dredging for commercial purposes, certain regulatory programs may call for sediment removal or isolation to prevent continued contamination. This type of removal can be very expensive and can resuspend contaminants in the water column.
- Most of the ocean dumping sites in the Pacific States will be evaluated for final site designation using new criteria requiring EPA to consider the costs of land-based disposal alternatives in determining whether the ocean will be unreasonably degraded by use of a particular dump site.

Recommendations

- *Nonpoint Source Pollution*—Pacific States should review existing state programs to control nonpoint source pollution to determine which agency has control responsibility for each type of nonpoint pollution, and to evaluate the adequacy of regulatory authorities. States should also provide guidelines and funding for local government efforts to control nonpoint source pollution.
- *Wastewater*—Pacific States should assist in planning, funding and siting waste water treatment facilities and outfalls by coastal communities—especially where cooperative efforts can achieve economies of scale and reduce multiple discharges.
- *Ocean Dumping*—Ocean dumping must be carefully evaluated before its use is accelerated. The new EEZ is a pristine resource, and its economic development potential must be weighed carefully against the exploitation of the ocean's environment and resources. Pacific States should individually or collectively review proposed changes in EPA ocean dumping regulations. States should also consider the effects of the proposed changes on the decision-making process for approval of ocean disposal of wastes not previously disposed of on the West Coast, such as sewage sludge. In addition, Pacific States should express support of continued funding of the Marine Protection, Research, and Sanctuaries Act's research provisions to enhance understanding of how marine pollution affects the environment.
- *Marine Debris*—Pacific States can aid in the fight against marine debris by promoting beach cleanups, contributing to the education of involved groups, limiting the production of lifetime plastics and encouraging plastics recycling. Pacific States should increase their enforcement of state littering laws in the territorial sea. Pacific States should also participate in international efforts to curb marine pollution by urging Congress to approve international agreements to end ocean disposal of shipboard wastes and assist ports in their preparation to handle these wastes.

Significance. The case used here serves as an illustration of local agencies which are interested in providing regulatory programs in the management of ocean resources. Local concern expressed here has been influenced by a lack of comprehensive programs in those western states of the United States bordering the Pacific for the conservation and management of ocean resources. More important, the 1983 United States proclamation for a twelve-nautical-mile sea has created an opportunity for these coastal states on the Pacific to exercise and assert more fully their responsibility regarding the protection, conservation and development of living and nonliving resources under the national jurisdiction.

NOTES

1. Lewis Alexander, ''Regionalism at Sea: Concept and Reality,'' in Douglas M. Johnston, ed., *Regionalization of the Law of the Sea*, (Cambridge, Mass.: Ballinger Publishing Company, 1978), pp. 3–16; and ''Regional Arrangement in the Oceans,'' *American Journal of International Law* 71 (1977): 140; C. O. Okidi, ''Toward Regional Arrangements for Regulation of Marine Pollution,'' *Ocean Development and International Law* 4, no. 1 (1977): 1–25; W. M. Janis, ''The Roles of Regional Law of the Sea,'' *San Diego Law Review* 16, no. 3 (1975): 553–568; and John Warren Kindt, *Marine Pollution and the Law of the Sea*, vol. 1 (Buffalo, N.Y.: William S. Hein, 1985), pp. 190–193.

2. Kindt, *Marine Pollution and the Law of the Sea*, pp. 193–194.

3. Alexander, ''Regionalism at Sea: Concept and Reality,'' p. 5.

4. Kindt, *Marine Pollution and the Law of the Sea*, pp. 200–201.

5. Boleslaw A. Boczek, ''International Protection of the Baltic Sea Environment against Pollution: A Study in Marine Regionalism,'' *American Journal of International Law* 72, no. 4 (October 1978): 788.

6. Ibid., p. 789.

7. Text of the convention is found in *International Legal Materials* 13 (1974), pp. 546–547.

8. Boczek, ''International Protection,'' p. 814. Also see Bengt Lundholm, ''The Oceans: Their Production and Pollution with the Baltic as a Case Study,'' in Elisabeth Mann Borgese, ed., *Pacem in Maribus* (New York: Dodd Mead, 1972), pp. 25–31. Also see Guenther Jaenicke, ''Cooperation in the Baltic Area,'' in Choon-ho Park, ed., *The Law of the Sea in the 1980s* (Honolulu: Law of the Sea Institute, University of Hawaii, 1983), pp. 500–504.

9. For the text of the Caribbean Convention see *International Legal Materials* 22, no. 2 (March 1983): 227–235.

10. See a study commissioned by FAO and the UN Environment Program (UNEP) in D. K. Atwood, ''Regional Oceanography as It Relates to Present and Future Pollution Problems and Living Resources: Caribbean,'' *Collected Contributions of Invited Lecturers and Authors to the IOC/FAO/UNEP International Workshop on Marine Pollution in the Caribbean and Adjacent Regions*, IOC Workshop Report no. 11, Supplement (Paris: UNESCO, 1977), pp. 47–79. Also see Peter S. Thacher and Nikki Meith, ''The Caribbean Example,'' in Elisabeth Mann Borgese and Norton Ginsburg, eds., *Ocean Yearbook 3* (Chicago: University of Chicago Press, 1982), pp. 226–227. Also see John D. Negroponte, ''Caribbean Marine Science,'' *Oceanus* 30, no. 4 (Winter 1987–88): 3–8; and D. K. Atwood et al., ''Petroleum Pollution in the Caribbean,'' *Oceanus* 30, no. 4 (Winter 1987–88): 25–32.

11. Thacher and Meith, ''The Caribbean Example,'' pp. 230–231.

12. Elisabeth Mann Borgese and Norton Ginsburg, eds., *Ocean Yearbook 4* (Chicago: University of Chicago Press, 1983), pp. 460; and *Ocean Yearbook 5* (Chicago: University of Chicago Press, 1985), pp. 178–180.

13. See Meera Pathmarajah and Nikki Meith, "A Regional Approach to Marine Environmental Problems in East Africa and the Indian Ocean," in Borgese and Ginsburg, eds., *Ocean Yearbook 5*, p. 173.

14. For the text of the agreement see *International Legal Materials* 12, no. 1 (January 1973): 9–15.

15. For the text of the Memorandum of Understanding, see *International Legal Materials* 21, no. 1 (January 1982): 1–15.

16. For the text of the Kuwait Convention, see *International Legal Materials* 17, no. 3 (May 1978): 511–526.

17. Ibid., p. 527.

18. Ibid., p. 528.

19. See Abdel Majid Farid, ed., *The Red Sea: Prospects for Stability* (New York: St. Martin's Press, 1984), pp. 86–87. Also see Mordechai Abir, *Oil, Power and Politics: Conflict in Arabia, the Red Sea and the Gulf* (London: Frank Case, 1974), pp. 119–120.

20. For a summary on the proceeding of the Barcelona Conference, see "UN Environmental Programme: Activities for the Protection and Development of the Mediterranean Region," in Elisabeth Mann Borgese, ed. *Ocean Yearbook 1* (Chicago: University of Chicago Press, 1978), pp. 584–585; and "Conference of Plenipotentiaries of the Coastal States of the Mediterranean Region for the Protection of the Mediterranean Sea," in Borgese, ed., *Ocean Yearbook 1*, pp. 702–713. Also see Baruch Boxer, "Mediterranean Pollution: Problem and Response," *Ocean Development and International Law* 10, nos. 3–4 (1982): 315–356.

21. See *International Legal Materials* 19, no. 4 (July 1980): 863–878.

22. See *International Legal Materials* 11, no. 2 (March 1970): 359–364.

23. See *The Law of the Sea Bulletin*, no. 10 (New York: United Nations Office for Ocean Affairs and the Law of the Sea, November 1987), pp. 59–77.

24. Peter S. Thacher, "UNEP: An Update on the Regional Seas Programme," in Borgese and Ginsburg, eds., *Ocean Yearbook 4*, pp. 450–461. Also see Peter S. Thacher and Nikki Meith, "Approaches to Regional Marine Problems: A Progress Report on UNEP's Regional Seas Program," in Elisabeth Mann Borgese and Norton Ginsburg, eds., *Ocean Yearbook 2* (Chicago: University of Chicago Press, 1980), pp. 153–182.

25. Thacher, "UNEP: An Update on the Regional Seas Programme," p. 453.

26. Text of the Abidjan Convention can be found in Borgese and Ginsburg, eds., *Ocean Yearbook 4*, pp. 533–542.

27. A Leadership Agenda: State Management of Ocean Resources: Report and Recommendation of the Ocean Resource Committee, Western Legislative Conference, January 1988. The author is indebted to state Senator Richard M. Matsuura, Hawaii, for making it possible to obtain a copy of this report.

CHAPTER 10

Military Uses of the Ocean Space: Legality, Prohibitions and Restrictions

A maritime nation, large or small, must use its seapower for these related purposes: to obtain access to the seas; to control the seas for unimpeded navigation, which in turn is essential for commerce or the acquisition of resources; and finally, to provide national security both in terms of self-defense and the ability to project military force overseas in times of war and peace. For major seapowers such as the United States and the Soviet Union, naval presence and mobility in the world's oceans are indicative of global influence and dominance.[1] Two recent developments have had some impact on the traditional uses of military power on the seas. First is the "creeping jurisdiction" of national claims over the ocean space that resulted in the establishment by the 1982 Law of the Sea Convention of new ocean regimes, which tend to reduce naval mobility. The second is the rapid development in modern naval strategy and weaponry that has made military uses of the oceans no longer limited to surface activities. Military activities in the oceans are now increasingly and inextricably linked to strategic nuclear warfare and the anti-submarine activities of underwater detection, identification and surveillance of nuclear-powered submarines capable of firing ballistic missiles with nuclear warheads—submarine-launched ballistic missiles (SLBMs).

Peacetime anti-submarine warfare conducted underneath the ocean surface, as well as the traditional military uses of warships on the ocean water, raises first the question of the legality of these military uses in the context of the new law of the sea convention. Then there is the need for the world community to find ways by which the use and testing of explosive nuclear devices on and under the oceans may be regulated, if not prohibited, by international or regional consensus. This consideration is predicated by the overall necessity for maintaining the existing power balance and guaranteeing "international stability and state security."[2]

As a part of the introduction to this chapter, we will discuss briefly the legal principles established by the 1982 LOS Convention for the peacetime military uses of the ocean.[3] First, the coastal state has complete sovereignty in its internal waters and territorial sea. Therefore, no other state's vessels, including warships, can enter the internal waters, the airspace above and the seabed underneath without the explicit permission of the coastal state, except for the purpose of transit passage. In peacetime it is not permissible for another state to deploy underwater anti-submarine surveillance devices, such as sonobuoys. Such activities constitute a violation of international law, and the coastal state can remove such emplacements from its internal waters. However, David Larson estimated that Soviet submarines had committed a total of 122 "underwater penetrations" or incursions between 1969 and 1982 in Swedish and Norwegian internal waters.[4] Article 19(2) of the 1982 LOS Convention specifies the types of activities in which a foreign state engages in internal waters or the territorial sea that are "prejudicial to the peace, good order or security" of a coastal state. These are: the use of force against the sovereignty, territorial integrity, or political independence of the coastal state; any exercise or practice with weapons of any kind; any act of propaganda; and the launching, landing or taking on board of any aircraft or any military devices. Articles 17–45 of the 1982 LOS Convention provide the coastal states with the right to control and regulate their territorial seas and transit through their straits with respect to innocent passage (see Chapter 3). The March and April 1986 United States military actions involving air strikes against Libya and the show of force and missile exchange around the Gulf of Sidra were incidents of aberration that pose questions of legality in the military uses of the ocean.

On the high seas there is considerable uncertainty about the right of states to engage in military activities in the area beyond the limits of national jurisdiction. While the high seas are open for use by all nations with guarantees of the basic freedoms to navigation, overflight, fishing, cable laying and scientific research, Articles 88 and 89 of the 1982 LOS Convention stipulate that "the high seas shall be reserved for peaceful purposes." Also, "no state may validly purport to subject any part of the high seas to its sovereignty." The language of Article 88 is rather ambiguous, for it does not clearly define between nonmilitary uses and nonaggressive uses of the high seas.[5] If for nonmilitary purposes, then navigation by warships on the high seas surely must not be prohibited; but, if for nonaggressive purposes, then any nation's navy may use the high seas for any military purpose only if such activities are not considered aggressive in nature.[6] Zedalis takes the position that warships must use the high seas as guaranteed by the established freedom-of-navigation principle, so long as such military activities are "reasonable in nature" and do not prevent other nations and their warships from transiting, or so long as a nation does not claim exclusive jurisdiction over others in the high seas area.[7] David L. Larson feels that the provisions of the 1982 LOS Convention do not themselves restrict the use of naval weapons in the high seas. Thus, in Larson's view, with the exception of specific prohibitions by other treaty arrangements, all naval weaponry, including strategic nuclear ballistic missile submarines and strategic nuclear attack submarines, is permitted.[8] As for the contiguous zone and the exclusive economic zone, it is permissible to consider the former a part of the high seas for military purpose, so long as the use is "reasonable." Under Article 73 of the 1982 LOS Convention, the coastal state has the right to enact enforcement laws and regulations in the exclusive economic zone for economic exploitation, navigation and security. Thus the deployment of limited range anti-submarine devices in the zone is permitted. Article 2(1) of the 1958 Convention on the Continental Shelf and Articles 77 and 79 of the 1982 LOS Convention grant "sovereign rights" to the coastal states for the purpose of exploring and exploiting the natural resources on the continental shelf.

The interpretation of these provisions, as well as state practice, seems to indicate that military uses on the continental shelf are specifically prohibited. Thus, in the exercise of the "sovereign rights" of the coastal states, military uses can be permitted so long as they do not interfere with (1) the exercise of navigational freedoms of other states, including laying submarine cables and pipelines, and (2) the coastal state's right to explore and exploit resources on the continental shelf. However, the continental shelf is the prime area for placing anti-submarine detection and surveillance devices. The legality of placing such electronic and acoustic devices on the continental shelf is a matter of debate. One scholar argues, "It may be permissible to emplace the anti-submarine detecting devices beyond the 200 nautical miles with or without the coastal state's approval."[9] But another state's placement on the continental shelf of anti-submarine electronic devices that would interfere with a coastal state's exploration and exploitation of the continental shelf resources is questionable at best.[10] In the context of superpower competition, military and strategic considerations often outweigh the question of legal permissibility. Such has been the case of the emplacement of the sound surveillance system (SOSUS) off the Kuriles and Aleutians in the Pacific, and off the North Cape between Iceland, Greenland and the United Kingdom.

As in the case of the high seas, it is generally accepted as permissible to place strategic ballistic nuclear submarines and other naval weaponry on the deep seabed—if there are no specific prohibitions by treaty arrangements. However, Article 141 of the 1982 LOS Convention states, "The Area shall be open to use exclusively for peaceful purposes by all states, whether coastal or landlocked, without discrimination and without prejudice to the other provisions of this Pact."

Again, if the term "peaceful purposes" means the absence of aggressive uses in the deep seabed area, then military activities are permitted. But, if the term refers to all military activities, then such uses are in violation of Article 141. Aside from the continuous debate among scholars as to whether the Area (deep seabed) is *res communis* or *res nullius* (see Chapter 3), there is really no clear or specific prohibition of the placement of detecting surveillance devices on the seabed so long as there is no exclusive use and it is reasonable. In the future, the deep seabed will become a prime area for anti-submarine activities, for, as pointed out by David L. Larson, "the world ocean is largely a legal vacuum" and the use of naval weaponry is "unrestricted and unrestrained."[11] This chapter focuses the discussion on the military uses of the ocean space in two aspects: naval weaponry, particularly anti-submarine warfare, and prohibitions and restrictions on the use of nuclear weapons in the ocean, including the multilateral arrangements for nuclear free zones.

Entries, alphabetically arranged, on military uses and weaponry, provide discussion and analysis of anti-submarine warfare (ASW), naval weaponry, and mine warfare at sea, including the Persian Gulf "tanker war." Prohibition of the use and placement of nuclear weapons in the oceans is discussed in these entries: the Antarctic Treaty; the placement and the prohibition of nuclear weapons testing by the 1963 Nuclear Test Ban Treaty; the Treaty of Tlatelolco for Latin America; and the 1972 Treaty on the Prohibition of the Emplacement of Nuclear Weapons and Other Weapons of Mass Destruction on the Seabed. In addition, this chapter discusses pollution caused by military uses of the ocean, particularly the disposal at sea of unwanted explosives. As an attempt to demilitarize the ocean areas on a regional basis, the nuclear-free-zone movement is discussed by reviewing briefly the declaration of the Indian Ocean as a zone of peace and the nuclear-free zone for the South Pacific. Finally, the agreement between the United States and the Soviet Union for the prevention of nuclear war incidents on the high seas is analyzed as an attempt to prevent the outbreak of a nuclear war due to naval accidents between the superpowers.

The issue of military uses of the ocean has been neglected at the United Nations Law of the Sea Conferences. As potential conflicts develop between the claims of the coastal states and the need for the sea to be accessible to the world's navies, there are many issues concerning the military uses of the ocean that need clarification. Will the high seas and the deep seabed continue to be used for peaceful purposes in the future against the trend of naval weaponry becoming more sophisticated and more destructive?

There is a deadly game of hunt-and-be-hunted under the ocean waters being engaged in by the superpowers and their submarines, which can slip through the waters of each other's coasts. It is now technologically possible for the Soviet skipper to hear his pursuer under water before he is detected by the United States Navy's listening devices. The balance of power under the ocean waters is changing as new technology develops. The key question to be posed now is, "Can the changing developments in the law of the sea run parallel with arms control schemes that attempt to place limits and restraints on military uses in the oceans in the future" as these had been maintained in the 1960s and 1970s? It may be reasonable to ask that the issue of military uses in the ocean should be a key item for negotiation at the future (the fourth) law of the sea conference.

THE ANTARCTICA TREATY: A DEMILITARIZED ZONE

In the spirit of international cooperation under the framework of the International Geophysical Year (IGY) of 1957–1958, and in the spirit of Antarctic scientific research, the United States and the Soviet Union concluded and signed the Antarctic Treaty in Washington, D.C., on December 1, 1961. By 1986 some thirty-two nations had signed and ratified the Antarctic Treaty.

Article I of the Antarctic Treaty prohibits in the regions around the South Pole any military use, such as the establishment of military bases, fortifications, the carrying out of military maneuvers, and the testing of any type of weapons. Antarctica is designated for peaceful purposes and the only military personnel or equipment permitted in the Antarctic are for scientific research. Article V bans any nuclear explosions and the disposal of radioactive waste material in Antarctica. The treaty thus spares the Antarctic as a nuclear proving ground and as a dumping site for radioactive wastes.

A unique feature established by this treaty is the formation of the Antarctic Treaty Consultative Parties (ATCPs), which may dispatch observers to inspect, including by aerial observation, all areas of Antarctica—stations, installations, equipment and personnel—to ensure that provisions of the treaty are being observed by parties to the treaty. Members of the ATCPs hold regular meetings and make recommendations on all aspects of Antarctic matters. Their concerns are not limited only to keeping the region demilitarized and nuclear free, but they also keep tabs on matters relating to scientific research, conservation of resources, and environmental protection.[12] At present there are sixteen members of the ATCPs, consisting of the original twelve signatories to the treaty (Argentina, Australia, Belgium, Chile, France, Japan, New Zealand, Norway, the Union of South Africa, the United Kingdom, the Soviet Union and the United States), plus those admitted to consultative status (Brazil, Federal Republic of Germany, India and Poland). In addition, fifteen nations have acceded to the Antarctic Treaty: Czechoslovakia (1962), Denmark (1965), Netherlands (1967), Romania (1971), German Democratic Republic (1974), Bulgaria (1978), Uruguay (1980), Italy, Papua New Guinea and Peru (1981), Spain (1982), People's Republic of China (1983), Hungary, Finland and Sweden (1984).

Finally, Article VII of the treaty requires that each of the contracting parties must inform the other parties by advance notice of all expeditions to Antarctica, all stations in Antarctica by its nationals, and any military personnel or equipment to be introduced by it into Antarctica.

Significance. The demilitarization of Antarctica as a nuclear-free zone has this important significance: only 15 percent of Antarctica is unclaimed, and there are a number of territorial disputes in the region that may degenerate into serious armed conflicts. For instance, there are the overlapping claims for portions of Antarctica between Argentina, the United Kingdom and Chile.[13] Of the original twelve signatories to the Antarctica Treaty, only five (Belgium, Japan, South Africa, the Soviet Union and the United States) do not recognize any claims over the region, but reserve the right to make similar claims of their own.[14]

Innovative thinking is needed to provide international cooperation in establishing a global Antarctic regime. A first step in that direction is the demilitarization of Antarctica. Also, as an initial step, the Antarctica Treaty has in fact "frozen" all territorial claims of sovereignty—there is no renunciation of previously claimed territory in the region; in addition there are to be no new claims either.

ANTI-SUBMARINE WARFARE (ASW)

Two interrelated developments in the nuclear missile calculus have thrust the submarine into the forefront of military strategy known as anti-submarine warfare (ASW). One of these developments is the vulnerability of land-based missiles, such as the intercontinental ballistic missile (ICBM), in the case of a first preemptive strike launched by the enemy. Obviously, the second is the consequence of the first development: the advancement of arming the submarine with sophisticated nuclear-powered missiles (the SSBNs)—for example, the *Polaris, Poseidon* and *Trident* (United States) and the *Delta* and *Typhoon* (Soviet Union). These missiles could be aimed at a target thousands of miles away, both as an early warning strategy and to satisfy the need for providing the offensive or attack capability. Anti-submarine warfare was thus born as a powerful naval strategy and a formidable deterrent against an enemy's nuclear attack. Estimated by the United States Navy, 40 percent of all naval aviators and aircraft will be involved in anti-submarine warfare by 1990.[15] Anti-submarine warfare is generally considered to consist of the following activities or phases under the ocean:[16]

1. detecting the presence and movement of concealed enemy submarines which can now remain submerged for a long period of time and hide anywhere "in the upper ten percent of the ocean volume"[17]
2. identification and classification of the suspected submarine detected
3. localizing or positioning the detected submarine for continued surveillance
4. attacking the detected submarine with the appropriate weapons from the ocean surface, from the air, and from under the ocean water

The key to ASW is the use of an array of sophisticated devices for detecting submarines. The Stockholm International Peace Research Institute (SIPRI) has published a list of the following available detecting devices:[18]

1. electromagnetic detection by optical, field, radar, infrared and laser devices
2. acoustic detection, the principal method of finding submarines below the ocean surface: high-powered sonar ("sound, navigation and ranging") mounted on the hull of surface destroyers, submarines; VDS (variable depth sonar) using cable, hovering helicopters and sonar buoys as listening posts
3. a highly sensitive magnetometer, known as magnetic anomaly detector (MAD), which can be used by aircraft, helicopters and underwater cable on the seabed to a depth of 3,000 feet or 1,000 meters

According to the SIPRI report, antisubmarine warfare may involve a coordinated task force of ASW carriers, aircraft, destroyers and "hunter-killer" attack submarines vying against one single enemy submarine. Weapons used could be a combination of torpedoes, anti-submarine rockets (ASROC), air-dropped depth charges, and mines (cable-controlled bottom mines, pressure mines in shallow waters, magnetic mines, acoustic mines, and deep ocean mines or encapsulated torpedoes with nuclear warheads).[19]

Significance. Anti-submarine warfare, engaged in by the world's major naval powers—particularly the United States and the Soviet Union—demands free access to the oceans, freedom of transit and the ability to place under the seas a vast array of sophisticated listening and electronic devices. These freedoms are necessary for the purpose of continuously detecting, identifying and locating suspected submarines in order to provide the essential early warning of a possible nuclear missile attack. Anti-submarine warfare is basically a silent surveillance war game conducted below the surface of the oceans, a matter of watching "the archer" before he fires the "arrow." As a very important military use of the ocean, anti-submarine warfare provides us with the understanding, more vividly than any other aspect, of the importance of the maritime powers' insistence on freedom of navigation and the universal guarantee of the rights of innocent passage and transit (see Chapter 3). Under Article 59, the 1982 LOS Convention does not really clarify the accepted rules in international law for major naval powers to emplace military electronic listening devices on the continental shelf and on the seabed. (It is now possible to use sophisticated computerized undersea robots for detecting and locating submarines on any part of the ocean floor.)

CONTAMINATION AND POLLUTION CAUSED BY MILITARY USE OF THE OCEAN

Ocean pollution or contamination caused by military or naval activities comes from these sources: underwater explosions; radioactive contamination by nuclear weapon manufacturing, testing, routine emissions from nuclear-powered submarines, and accidents involving nuclear naval vessels at sea.[20]

Underwater explosions by the military, either in time of war, for military/naval training exercises in peacetime, or disposal of unwanted explosives at sea, can have harmful effects on marine life due to shock or the release of toxic chemicals. Conventional explosive filler in depth charges used against submarines is a mixture of ammonium picrate and powdered aluminum. According to a number of studies, underwater explosions cause shock waves that can rupture a marine animal's air bladder; and depth charge explosions can be lethal to most marine animals within a radius of seventy-seven miles.[21] TNT is a chemical that sinks to the sea bottom and dissolves slowly; it is also known as a harmful, if not lethal, contaminant to freshwater microorganisms and toxic to mammals. Another source of chemical contamination released into the ocean is caused by the sinking or scuttling of munition ships loaded with unwanted and undetonated explosives.[22] Casings around the sealed explosive munitions begin to deteriorate and release ammonium picrate and powdered aluminum chemicals that are lethal to fish.[23]

Nuclear weapon manufacturing, emissions from nuclear-powered naval ships and testing have been the principal causes of radioactive pollution in the sea. It has been estimated that for the three-decade period, 1945 to 1976, the United States, the Soviet Union, China, France and Britain detonated a total of 1,000 nuclear bombs of less than one megaton, and over 100 hydrogen bombs of greater than one megaton magnitude. And of this total, 6 were exploded under the ocean, 35 on the ocean's surface, and 373 in the atmosphere.[24]

Arthur W. Westing points out that nuclear-powered ships constitute another major source of radioactive ocean contamination. He estimates that the routine release from a total of 266 nuclear-powered ships (mostly submarine and some surface) belonging to the Soviet Union, the United States, the United Kingdom, France, China, West Germany and Japan "might contribute 107 μg of mixed fission products disintegrating, after 100 days, at the rate of about 65 m Ci to the ocean each year."[25] This does not include the large amount of radioactive releases due to accidental sinking of nuclear-powered vessels.[26] A nuclear-powered submarine releases about 23.8 μg of mixed fissional products of short-lived isotopes, the equivalent of a 0.42 kiloton atomic bomb.[27] Before 1960, both the United States and the United Kingdom routinely dumped radioactive wastes of military origin into the ocean, but since then this practice has terminated.[28] No one knows the environmental effects as a result of the loss of two nuclear submarines (*Thresher* in 1963 and *Scorpion* in 1968) by the United States, and the estimated four Soviet submarines lost during 1968 to 1971.

Significance. While military uses contribute only a small fraction (about 6 percent of the amount caused by overall human activities) of ocean pollution, a much larger proportion of the ocean's radioactive contamination can be traced to military origin. Restricting, if not controlling these military uses of the ocean will be a supreme challenge to mankind. Unfortunately, the issue of military uses of the ocean was neglected by those who were formulating laws at the Third UN Conference on the Law of the Sea.

DECLARATION OF THE INDIAN OCEAN AS A ZONE OF PEACE

Superpower rivalry in the Indian Ocean region intensified in the late 1960s due to a number of unfolding world events: the closing of the Suez Canal in 1967 during the Israeli-Egypt conflict; the withdrawal by the British from the Red Sea–Indian Ocean area in 1968; the growing importance of oil in the Persian Gulf; and the emergence of a number of Third World nations—from India and Pakistan, Iran and Iraq to Kuwait, Oman, Yemen, Somalia, Tanzania, Comoros, Mozambique, Madagascar and the mid-ocean states of Malines, Mauritius and Seychelles, which are nonaligned in the rivalry between the superpowers.[29]

By the time Britain declared its withdrawal from the Indian Ocean (1968), the United States and Britain had concluded negotiations that had begun in the early 1960s. This agreement gave the United States use of the strategic island of Diego Garcia in the Indian Ocean to conduct naval operations, which recently consisted of a carrier task force, including nuclear submarines (and served as one of the staging areas for the U.S. dispatch of forces to the Persian Gulf War). Concurrently, in 1968, for the first time, the Soviet Union established its naval presence in the Indian Ocean both for political and strategic reasons. Its naval force was rather small, consisting primarily of seven surface warships and three submarines.[30]

As a response to the superpower naval rivalry in the Indian Ocean, at the Heads of State summit meeting in Lusaka in 1970, led by Sri Lanka, nonaligned countries in the region developed the concept of making the Indian Ocean a "zone of peace."[31] This concept was debated in the 1971 General Assembly; it resulted in a resolution (GA Res. 2832–XXXVI) declaring the Indian Ocean a "zone of peace" by a vote of sixty-one in favor, none against, but fifty-five abstentions from the Western states, the Soviet bloc and a sizable Third World coalition (mostly Latin America).[32] From 1972 to 1980 ten similar General Assembly resolutions were adopted with abstentions, except in 1980; it was passed without a vote.[33] All these resolutions contained three basic elements for a "zone of peace": halting the military presence of the superpowers in the Indian Ocean, eliminating military installations and nuclear weapons in the Indian Ocean and formulating rules to prohibit the use of warships and military aircraft as a threat against any littoral state in the Indian Ocean. Pressure exerted by the nonaligned states in the Indian Ocean and Red Sea region intensified as the United States facilities at Diego Garcia expanded, as the Central Treaty Organization (CENTO) conducted naval exercises in the Indian Ocean and as the Soviet Union acquired the use of facilities at Berbera, Somalia. On the basis of President Carter's 1977 proposal for a demilitarized Indian Ocean, the so-called Naval Arms Limitation Talks between the United States and the Soviet Union began in June 1977, but were interrupted as local wars broke out (with Soviet intervention) in the Horn of Africa between Ethiopia and Somalia. Finally, the December 1979 Soviet invasion of Afghanistan, a hinterland state of the Indian Ocean, led to the United States expansion of military operations in the Indian Ocean and a countermilitary response from the Soviet Union.

Significance. The concept of a peace zone for the Indian Ocean illustrates the classical case of military escalation in the use of oceans for achieving military and political objectives of the superpowers. It is also illustrative of the contest between the naval powers' interests and local littoral interests in stabilizing the tension by reducing or eliminating external power rivalries' military use of the ocean. More importantly, the concept of an IOZP points to the incongruous situation that existed in the 1982 LOS Convention, which reaffirmed the freedoms of navigation on the one hand, but on the other, was rather vague concerning restrictions on the major maritime and naval powers in their use of warships, as distinct from other vessels, in power rivalry in the absence of war. This incongruity can be seen in Articles 19, 39 and 88. Finally, despite its vagueness, the concept of the Indian Ocean as a "zone of peace" presents a challenge to the long-held right of warships at sea and the related issue of demilitarization of the ocean.

PLACEMENT AND PROHIBITION OF THE USE OF NUCLEAR WEAPONS ON THE SEABED

There are three multilateral treaties that contain provisions for the purpose of prohibiting the placement or the use of nuclear weapons and other weapons of mass destruction on the seabed and ocean floor: the 1963 Test Ban Treaty, the 1967 Treaty for the Prohibition of Nuclear Weapons in Latin America (Treaty of Tlatelolco), and the 1972 Treaty on the Prohibition of the Emplacement of Nuclear Weapons and Other Weapons of Mass Destruction on the Seabed and the Ocean Floor and in the Sub-soil Thereof (Seabed Arms Control Treaty).

Nuclear Test Ban Treaty, 1963

Article 1 of the 1963 Treaty Banning Nuclear Weapons Tests in the Atmosphere, in the Outer Space and Underwater—signed in Moscow on August 5, 1963 by the original signatories (the United Kingdom, the United States and the Soviet Union)—provides the following important provision:[34]

Article 1

1. Each of the parties to this treaty undertakes to prohibit, to prevent, and not to carry out any nuclear weapon test explosion, or any other nuclear explosion, at any place under its jurisdiction or control:

> (a) In the atmosphere; beyond its limits, including outer space; or under water, including territorial waters or high seas; or
>
> (b) In any other environment if such explosion causes radioactive debris to be present outside the territorial limits of the State under whose jurisdiction or control such explosion is conducted. It is understood in this connexion that the provisions of this sub-paragraph are without prejudice to the conclusion of a treaty resulting in the permanent banning of all nuclear test explosions, including all such explosions underground, the conclusion of which, as the parties have stated in the preamble to this treaty, they seek to achieve.

The 1963 Test Ban Treaty came into force on October 19, 1963, when 105 nations signed it. France and China, two of the five major nuclear powers, refused to sign the treaty. However, it must be noted that, although the test ban treaty prohibits any nuclear weapon testing in the atmosphere or in outer space, or underwater within territorial waters and on the high seas, it in no way limits the authority of the signatory nations to use nuclear weapons for defense.

Treaty for the Prohibition of Nuclear Weapons in Latin America, 1967

On February 14, 1967, in Tlatelolco, Mexico, twenty-one Latin American states signed a multilateral Treaty for the Prohibition of Nuclear Weapons in Latin America (the Tlatelolco Treaty). The agreement prohibits the testing, placement and use of nuclear weapons on the seabed in Latin America or in that part of the Western Hemisphere south of 35° north latitude, but it excludes the continental part of the United States of America and its territorial waters (Article 4). Under Article 1, the treaty prohibits the testing, use, manufacture, production or acquisition of any nuclear weapons "by the parties themselves, by anyone on their behalf, or in any other way." Article 7 establishes the Agency for the Prohibition of Nuclear Weapons (OPANAL) in Mexico City for the purpose of consultation and supervision of compliance as mandated by the treaty. However, Articles 17 and 18 would permit explosions of nuclear devices for peaceful purposes, but subject to prior notification of the International Atomic Energy Agency (IAEA).

There are two protocols to the Tlatelolco Treaty. Additional Protocol I requests that France, the Netherlands, the United Kingdom and the United States apply the nuclear-free status in their territories that are situated within the treaty zone. On May 26, 1977, the Netherlands, the United Kingdom and the United States signed the Additional Protocol I, and France agreed in March 1979. Additional Protocol II requests that the nuclear powers—China, France, the United Kingdom, the United States and the Soviet Union—respect the nuclear-free status in Latin America and pledge nonuse or threat-to-use nuclear weapons against the contracting parties to the Tlatelolco Treaty. The United Kingdom and the United States signed the Additional Protocol II on May 12, 1971; France, on July 18, 1973; China, on August 21, 1973; and the Soviet Union, on May 18, 1978. As of now the Tlatelolco Treaty has not come into force.

Treaty on the Prohibition of the Emplacement of Nuclear Weapons and Other Weapons of Mass Destruction on the Seabed and the Ocean Floor and in the Subsoil Thereof, 1972

In response to a United Nations General Assembly resolution for prevention of a nuclear arms race on the seabed, a conference of the Committee on Disarmament reported out a draft treaty for the prohibition of placing nuclear weapons on the seabed. On December 7, 1970, by a vote of 104 for, 2 against, and 2 abstentions (Ecuador and France), the General Assembly requested the signing and ratification of the Treaty on the Prohibition of the Emplacement of Nuclear Weapons and Other Weapons of Mass Destruction on the Seabed and the Ocean Floor and in the Subsoil Thereof (the Seabed Arms Control Treaty). As of 1986, eighty-three nations had ratified the treaty.

Article I requires that states parties to the treaty ''undertake not to emplant or emplace on the seabed and the ocean floor and in the subsoil thereof beyond the outer limits of a seabed zone'' (defined in Article II as coterminous with the twelve-mile territorial sea) ''any nuclear weapons or any other types of weapons of mass destruction'' that include ''structures, launching installations or facilities especially designed for storing, testing or using the weapons.'' ''Weapons of mass destruction'' include all biological and chemical weapons. States parties to the treaty also pledge not to assist, encourage or induce another state to carry out any activities of emplacement of nuclear weapons on the seabed and the ocean floor.

Article III is the key operative section of the treaty. It prescribes a five-step monitoring procedure for verification, identification and compliance:

1. Any state party to the treaty has the right to verify by observation any activities of other signatory parties regarding the placement of nuclear weapons or other weapons of mass destruction on the seabed and on the ocean floor beyond a coastal state's twelve-mile territorial sea.
2. If there is any doubt by an observing or monitoring state party to the treaty that such prohibited activities may have been undertaken by another state party to the treaty, the former must notify the latter and the two must then cooperate and consult with each other for the purpose of establishing further agreed upon procedures for verification, including inspection to determine compliance to the treaty provisions. A report of the consultation must be circulated to other signatories by the party which initiated the observation and inspection.
3. If upon observation and monitoring of the structure and installations, it is possible to identify which state has undertaken these prohibited activities on the seabed or the ocean floor, the state party which initiated the investigation has the right to notify and make inquiries of other states parties in the region of the activities. If, through these inquiries, identification is ascertained, then the two states must consult and cooperate in establishing further agreed upon procedures for inquiry, verification and compliance. If identification is not possible, then the inquiring state can invite other states, including any coastal state, in the region of the activities prohibited by the treaty, to seek cooperation and compliance.
4. If, after having entered into consultation with the suspected state about the existence of these prohibited activities, there is further doubt on the part of the initiating state concerning compliance, then the initiating state can bring the matter to the attention of the United Nations Security Council for appropriate action in accordance with the United Nations Charter.
5. A state party to the treaty may undertake verification and identification of the activities on its own or with assistance from any other state, or through ''appropriate international procedures within the framework of the United Nations.''

Significance. Concern about testing and placement of nuclear weapons led to the signing of three main multilateral treaties that limit the right of the nuclear powers to test and use nuclear weapons on the seabed and the ocean floor. The

1963 Nuclear Test Ban Treaty is most significant simply because it binds all the major nuclear powers not to conduct nuclear testing in the atmosphere and under water. The ban has been observed by three of the major nuclear powers (the United Kingdom, the United States and the Soviet Union). China and France have refused to be bound to the testing ban. Their refusal most likely has given impetus to the nuclear-free zone movement, of which the Treaty of Tlatelolco for Latin America is an example. Both China and France signed the Additional Protocol II to this treaty, which requests the recognition by all nuclear powers of the nuclear-free status for Latin America. The 1972 Seabed Arms Control Treaty is the only treaty designed to prohibit placement on the seabed and the ocean floor, not only of nuclear weapon structures and installations, but biological and chemical weapons of mass destruction as well. Verification and enforcement are the two major problems in the implementation of the 1972 Seabed Arms Control Treaty.

MINE WARFARE AT SEA

The placing of sea mines in the Persian Gulf in 1990 by Iraq, the 1984 placing of mines in the Persian Gulf and Red Sea by Iran in its war with Iraq, and the United States mining of Nicaraguan ports in 1982, renewed the world's interest and concern about mines at sea during times of war, peace and tension. The matter of mines at sea has been a subject of international concern dating to the 1907 Hague Peace Conference. At that time certain legal rules were delineated for laying automatic contact mines against submarines. Article 2 of the Hague Convention (VIII) states, "It is forbidden to lay automatic contact mines off the coast and ports of the enemy, with the sole object of intercepting commercial shipping." This means that it is legal to lay mines, so long as the weapon used at sea is not for the sole purpose of intercepting commercial shipping and navigation. Then Article 3 of the convention places a certain amount of responsibility or limitation on the belligerents in laying automatic contact mines so as to insure "the security of peaceful shipping":

> the belligerents undertake to do their utmost to render these mines harmless within a limited time, and, should they cease to be under surveillance, to notify the danger zones as soon as military exigencies permit, by a notice addressed to ship owners, which must also be communicated to the Governments through the diplomatic channel.

Practices in both world wars indicated the legal right to lay mines of whatever type so long as these were not "indiscriminatory" and notification had been issued to neutrals about the areas or operational zones where they had been placed.

Two post-World War II developments seem to have complicated the understanding concerning the rules laid down by the Hague Convention of 1907.[35] One is the tendency for nations to go to war without a declaration, or the prevailing situation of varying degrees of tension that has existed in international relations. The other postwar development is the technological advancement in the manufacture of more lethal mines (including nuclear) for placement at sea, including on the continental shelf. Thus, once again, as pointed out by Captain Thorpe, the same fundamental questions are raised: Is it lawful to use mines as weapons at sea, and if it is lawful, what are the restraints? A brief summary is given here of the complex legal and technical problems of today's mine warfare at sea.

The traditional rules provided by the 1907 Hague Convention (VIII) are still applicable in modern mine warfare, namely the legal right to place mines and the requirements for notification by the belligerents to keep the sea lanes secure for innocent passage. In addition, the 1958 Convention on the Territorial Sea and Contiguous Zone permits belligerents to mine their own internal waters and territorial sea, for Article 16 grants coastal states the right to take "the necessary steps" in their territorial seas to prevent passage which is not innocent. Captain Thorpe offers the interpretation that, even though the same article gives the coastal state the right to temporarily suspend a foreign ship's innocent passage in the specified areas of its territorial sea, such right is not recognized when it applies to passage through international straits under Article 22 of the 1982 LOS Convention.[36] Article 22 of the 1982 LOS Convention states that:

Article 22: Sea lanes and traffic separation schemes in the territorial sea

1. The coastal State may, where necessary having regard to the safety of navigation, require foreign ships exercising the right of innocent passage through its territorial sea to use such sea lanes and traffic separation schemes as it may designate or prescribe for the regulation of the passage of ships.

2. In particular, tankers, nuclear-powered ships and ships carrying nuclear or other inherently dangerous or noxious substances or materials may be required to confine their passage to such sea lanes.

3. In the designation of sea lanes and the prescription of traffic separation schemes under this article, the coastal State shall take into account:

(a) the recommendations of the competent international organization;

(b) any channels customarily used for international navigation;

(c) the special characteristics of particular ships and channels; and

(d) the density of traffic.

4. The coastal State shall clearly indicate such sea lanes and traffic separation schemes on charts to which due publicity shall be given.

In the 1949 Corfu Channel case, the International Court of Justice ruled that:

1. The right of warships to innocent passage through an international strait cannot be prohibited in time of peace.
2. A coastal state has the right to mine its territorial sea so long as such action does not

> close off the international strait, and provided that due warning or notification has been given to other states and ships.

This customary international law is implicit in both the 1958 Convention on the Territorial Sea and the 1982 LOS Convention.

Since Article 88 of the 1982 LOS Convention makes it clear that the high seas are reserved for peaceful purposes and nations are free to lay cables and pipelines, and to fish, it is unlikely or intolerable to permit mine laying in peacetime. Although the exclusive economic zones (EEZs) are not part of the high seas under Article 86 of the LOS Convention, nevertheless it is permissible for coastal states to establish "security zones," not to exceed 500 meters, around their artificial islands and to mine within the zones with due warning (see Chapter 3 for further discussion). There is no justification in customary international law for laying mines along another state's coast within the territorial sea in time of peace. The Central Intelligence Agency (CIA) directed mining of Nicaragua Harbor in 1982 was ruled by the International Court of Justice to be illegal in peacetime.

By invoking Article 51 of the United Nations Charter for purposes of self-defense, mining a coastal state's harbor by another state in time of peace, but during a state of tension in their relations, seems to be justified, though debatable. The mining of Haiphong Harbor in North Vietnam by the United States in 1972 and the laying of mines in the waters off Stanley Island by Argentina in the 1982 Falkland conflict were undertaken with self-defense justification.

The Protocol Additional to the Geneva Conventions of August 12, 1949, and Relating to the Victims of International Armed Conflict does not prohibit the use of low-yield nuclear tactical mines. But Article 1 of the 1971 Treaty on the Prohibition of the Emplacement of Nuclear Weapons and Other Weapons of Mass Destruction on the Seabed and the Ocean Floor in the Subsoil Thereof states otherwise when applied to the seabed area (defined as an area coterminous with the twelve-nautical-mile outer limit for the territorial sea):

> The state parties to this Treaty undertake not to emplant or emplace on the seabed and the ocean floor and in the subsoil thereof beyond the outer limits of a seabed zone . . . any nuclear weapon or any other types of weapons of mass destruction or structures, launching installations or any other facilities specifically designed for storing, testing or using such weapons.

Significance. There is general acceptance by nations that in time of war a belligerent nation does have the right to lay mines in its internal waters and the territorial sea regime, provided due warning and notification have been given to neutrals. These fundamental rules are designed to ensure freedom of navigation and free transit through international straits. In situations of undeclared war and tension, the right to mine parts of the high seas leading to ports may be justified as a self-defense measure, but such action is subject to debate. While placement of nuclear-charged mines outside the territorial sea is considered illegal, technological innovation in the design of mines to be used at sea may alter these generally accepted international rules. For instance, the continental shelf mine could be "tethered" with a rocket-propelled warhead. The mine can remain a long time on the continental shelf and can be remotely activated or deactivated—thus making it a discriminatory weapon designed for anti-submarine warfare, which would not threaten the right of freedom of navigation by nonbelligerent ships. As argued by Captain Thorpe, since the continental shelf mine is not illegal, the traditional concerns for warning and notification and safe passage for ships may not even be necessary.

NAVAL WEAPONRY

The concept of naval weaponry is most complex and broad in the range of instruments available for deployment in different areas or regions by the various naval powers of the world.[37] The following is a list of the major naval weapons available to the world's major naval powers:

1. Aircraft carriers of these types:[38] conventionally powered carrier (CV); conventionally powered attack carrier (CVA); nuclear-powered attack carrier (CVN); auxiliary carrier (CVE); light carrier (CVL).
2. Anti-submarine warfare (ASW) system—this includes not only ballistic missile submarines, such as the United States *Polaris* and the Soviet *Union Golf* or *Yankee*, but also underwater acoustic detection systems.
3. amphibious assault ship (LAA)
4. destroyer with missile (DD)
5. fast attack craft with missile (FAC-M) and with torpedo (FAC-T)
6. light airborne multipurpose system helicopter (LAMPS)
7. mine countermeasures (MCM)
8. submarine-launched ballistic missile (SLBM)
9. submarine-launched cruise missile (SLCM)
10. submarine cruise missile (SSG)
11. submarine cruise missile, nuclear (SSGN)
12. submarine, nuclear attack (SSN)
13. surface-to-air missile (SAM)
14. thermo-nuclear (TN)
15. underwater-to-surface missile (USM)

Submarine missile attack systems have now become the most important deterrent in the nuclear calculus.

Significance. The proliferation of advanced sophisticated naval weaponry used by the world's major powers demonstrates two significant developments that concern the law of the sea. First, except for the prohibition of nuclear weapon placement on the seabed and the ocean floor and the nuclear-free zones in Latin America and the Pacific, there is really no limitation or restriction on the use of nuclear weapons in international law. This means that there is an urgent need for management and demilitarization of the oceans, particularly on the seabed beyond any national jurisdiction. Second, as argued by David L. Larson, there is also the need for calling a third Hague Conference on naval warfare law.[39] Or, as an alternative, military uses of the ocean should be a topic in the Fourth United Nations Conference on the Law of the Sea, if it is held. The subject was neglected at the previous conference, which concluded in 1982, as has been pointed out throughout this chapter on military use of the ocean space.

NUCLEAR-FREE ZONE FOR THE SOUTH PACIFIC (THE RARATONGA TREATY)

A movement that has gathered some momentum within the United Nations for demilitarizing the oceans from the use of the nuclear weapons is the nuclear-free zone established for a particular region of the world. Under nuclear-free zonal arrangements, states are voluntarily assuming the obligation not to station nuclear weapons in their region. The nuclear-free zone-movement had the encouragement of and was sanctioned by General Assembly Resolution 3472B (XXX), adopted December 11, 1975. It states that:

I: Definition of the concept of a nuclear-weapon-free zone

1. A "nuclear-weapon-free zone" shall, as a general rule, be deemed to be any zone, recognized as such by the General Assembly of the United Nations, which any group of States in the free exercise of their sovereignty, has established by virtue of a treaty or convention whereby:

(a) The statute of total absence of nuclear weapons to which the zone shall be subject, including the procedure for the delimitation of the zone, is defined;

(b) An international system of verification and control is established to guarantee compliance with the obligations deriving from that statute.

II: Definition of the principal obligations of the nuclear-weapon States toward nuclear-weapon-free zones and towards the States included therein

2. In every case of a nuclear-weapon-free zone that has been recognized as such by the General Assembly, all nuclear-weapon States shall undertake or reaffirm, in a solemn international instrument having full legally binding force, such as a treaty, a convention or a protocol, the following obligations:

(a) To respect in all its parts the statute of total absence of nuclear weapons defined in the treaty or convention which serves as the constitutive instrument of the zone;

> (b) To refrain from contributing in any way to the performance in the territories forming part of the zone of acts which involve a violation of the aforesaid treaty or convention;
>
> (c) To refrain from using or threatening to use nuclear weapons against the States included in the zone.

While the Treaty of Tlatelolco (1967) was the first such regional arrangement for a ban on the use of nuclear weapons, this nuclear-free-zone agreement goes several steps further in making the region free of nuclear weapons and pollution. The South Pacific Nuclear Free Zone Treaty (SPNFZ) was signed August 6, 1985, in Raratonga, Cook Islands, by members of the South Pacific Forum, comprising thirteen independent and self-governing nations in the southwest Pacific region. A summary of the treaty provisions is provided here.[40]

Article 3 of the SPNFZ treaty prohibits the manufacture, possession or control over any nuclear explosive device defined as ''any nuclear weapon or other explosive device capable of releasing energy, irrespective of the purpose for which it could be used,'' by any means anywhere inside or outside the South Pacific Nuclear-Free Zone. It is also prohibited to seek, receive or encourage any assistance from any state in the manufacture or acquisition of any nuclear explosive device. Article 6 prohibits the testing of, or any action to assist or encourage the testing of, any nuclear explosive device by any state. Article 5 obligates the parties to the treaty to undertake to prevent in their territory, internal waters, territorial sea and archipelagic waters, the seabed and subsoil beneath, the land territory and the air space above them the ''stationing'' (implantation, emplacement, transportation on land or inland waters, stockpiling, storage, installation, and deployment) of any nuclear explosive device. Article 7 imposes the obligation on parties to the treaty not to dump or to take any action or encourage the dumping of radioactive waste and other radioactive matter at sea anywhere in their zone. It also prohibits the dumping of radioactive wastes in the territorial sea.

Article 4 prohibits transporting even special fissionable material designed or prepared for the processing, use or production of such materials for peaceful purposes into any non-nuclear-weapon state, except when specific safeguards are met. These safeguards are defined under Article III.1 of the Non-proliferation Treaty or are subject to applicable agreements with the International Atomic Energy Agency (IAEA). Articles 8 and 9 provide a control system for compliance verification that includes reports and exchange of information, consultation or application to the IAEA for meeting safeguards for peaceful uses. However, Article 5(2) places responsibility on each individual party to the treaty for the sovereign right to decide for itself whether to permit visits by foreign ships and aircraft to its ports and airfields, transit of its airspace by foreign aircraft, or navigation by foreign ships in its territorial sea or archipelagic waters. New Zealand and Vanuatu are the only two states that have prohibited port calls by nuclear-powered ships—a bone of contention between the United States and New Zealand.

There are three protocols to the SPNFZ.[41] The treaty would be incomplete without acceptance by the world's major nuclear powers. Protocol 1 establishes prohibitions on the manufacture, stationing and testing of "explosive nuclear devices" within the treaty territories. It is open for signature by the three nuclear weapon states that have territories within the area of the South Pacific Nuclear-Free Zone: France, the United Kingdom and the United States. As of now, none of these has become a party to Protocol 1.

Protocol 2 prohibits member nations instigating any action in the use or threat to use any nuclear explosive devices against parties or territories within the zone. Protocol 3 prohibits any nation from undertaking nuclear testing in the zone. Both Protocols 2 and 3 are open for signature by the five nuclear weapon states of China, France, the United Kingdom, the Soviet Union and the United States. On December 15, 1986, the Soviet Union signed Protocols 2 and 3; and on February 10, 1987, China signed Protocols 2 and 3 with reservations.

Significance. The signing of the Raratonga Treaty, in addition to the demilitarization treaties for Antarctica and the seabed, signals a decisive gain for those who advocate nuclear-weapon-free zones as a rightful step toward world nuclear disarmament. In fact, this is the only nuclear-free zone to cover a vast area of ocean space, from Africa to South America and from the equator to the South Pole. However, the treaty has created a rift between the United States, the leading nuclear-weapon power in the area, and New Zealand and Vanuatu, which adhere to a nuclear-weapon-free policy. This includes the prohibition of visits in their ports by vessels with nuclear capability. Endorsement of the treaty by thirteen members in the South Pacific region was facilitated because there is no nuclear-weapon nation in the region and there is no nuclear-power rivalry in the South Pacific.

A suggestion has been made recently that both the Raratonga Convention for the South Pacific and the Treaty of Tlatelolco for Latin America, discussed earlier, should be employed as a "vehicle" for nuclear contamination and pollution resulting from nuclear weapon tests.[42]

PERSIAN GULF "TANKER WAR": NAVAL CONVOY AND MINE CLEANSWEEP

During the course of the eight-year war between Iran and Iraq in the 1980s, more than 400 vessels of some thirty neutral states were attacked. This section briefly discusses the actions taken by the United States in 1987–1988 in providing military-escort protection for oil tankers in the Persian Gulf and its minesweeping effort in 1984 in the Persian Gulf and the Red Sea.

United States naval minesweeping activities were undertaken in 1984 in the Red Sea and the Gulf of Suez after mines had damaged sixteen ships. In August 1984 United States forces, accompanied by four RH–53D Sea Stallion helicopters, arrived in the Gulf of Suez, reinforced by an international task force made up of vessels from the United Kingdom, France, Egypt, Saudi Arabia and North Yemen. The operation involved placing hydrofoil sleds and cable rigs for locating and destroying acoustic, magnetic or pressure-sensitive mines. These mines were sowed by the Islamic Holy War group. They were small and planted in water 200 feet deep in the Red Sea channels.

The technique of minesweeping involved three stages of operation. First, minesweeping helicopters towed wire with floats, depressors and explosive charges at both ends of the Red Sea. The wire towed by the helicopter would snag and cut cables on moored mines to permit the mine to float on the ocean surface. When spotting the mine on the surface, naval vessels and helicopters exploded it with gunfire. Or a sled was dragged across mined waters detonating the mines by magnetic field. Also, an acoustic device could be used, pulled behind the sled, emitting fake engine noise that caused the mines to explode.[43]

As the tanker war in the Persian Gulf escalated in the summer of 1987, the United States was providing convoy escorts to Kuwaiti-owned oil tankers, and thus placed its naval forces under a threat from the Iranians and the Iraqis. The U.S.S. *Stark* was attacked by an Iraqi fighter plane, using air-to-surface missiles; thirty-seven of its crew were killed.

Significance. The U.S. naval minesweeping activities in the Red Sea and the convoy escort for oil tankers in the Persian Gulf are illustrations of military use in the "tanker war." These examples raise the old question in international law about the neutral nation's right of legal immunity from belligerent attack. Are the rights of neutral nations no longer recognized and enforceable as in the case of the Persian Gulf "tanker war"?

Military confrontation in the Persian Gulf erupted again in August 1990 between Iraq and the United States, plus other nations, over Iraq's invasion and annexation of Kuwait. The response to the UN Security Council resolution for an economic embargo placed the United States navy in the position of monitoring tankers and freighters in the Persian Gulf and the Red Sea by shadowing their movements—this monitoring function involved firing across the bows of ships.[44] There is some debate with respect to the possible violation of international law by these actions on the high seas. However, the issue became moot as the UN Security Council authorized "the use of force" as a "necessary measure" on November 30, 1990 in order to compel Iraq to withdraw from Kuwait.

PREVENTION OF NUCLEAR WAR INCIDENTS ON THE HIGH SEAS (1972)

In an attempt to prevent the outbreak of a nuclear war by accident, the two superpowers—the United States and the Soviet Union—concluded the 1972 Agreement on Prevention of Incidents on and over the High Seas. It was signed in Moscow on May 25, 1972, and entered into force on the same day.[45]

Article II of the agreement obligates the parties to "take measures to instruct commanding officers of their respective ships to observe strictly the letter and spirit of the International Regulations for Preventing Collision at Sea and the principles with respect to conducting operations on the ocean as recognized in the 1958 Geneva Convention on the High Seas. Specifically, Article III of the agreement provides the following guidelines for preventing accidents on the high seas while conducting naval operations:

1. Ships operating in proximity of each other must stay clear.
2. Naval or military formations and maneuvers must stay away from areas of heavy traffic where internationally recognized traffic separation schemes are in effect.
3. Ships engaged in military surveillance of other ships on the high seas must stay at a distance or avoid executing maneuvers that might endanger or embarrass the ships under surveillance.
4. When engaged in maneuvers, naval vessels must follow the International Code of Signals for signaling operations and intentions.
5. When conducting simulated attacks during naval maneuvers, naval vessels must not aim their weapons—missile launchers, torpedo tubes and other weapons—in the direction of a passing ship of the other party.
6. Submarines engaged in the maneuvers must warn other ships by signals of the presence of submarines in the area.

Article IV mandates the commanders of aircraft engaging in military operations on the high seas to use "the greatest caution and prudence" in approaching ships and aircraft of another party operating on and over the high seas, particularly when launching aircraft. Under Article IV, it prohibits "simulated attacks by the simulated use of weapons against aircraft and ships, or performance of various aerobatics over ships, or dropping various objects near them in such a manner as to be hazardous to ships or to constitute a hazard to navigation." Prior notice or warning (not less than three to five days) must be given through radio broadcasts of any military action on the high seas that represents a danger to navigation or aircraft in flight (Article VI). When instances of collision occur, the navies of the United States and the Soviet Union shall provide each other with the appropriate information.

Significance. The treaty on the prevention of nuclear war incidents on the high seas is of dubious value if recent "bumping" incidents on the high seas by the naval vessels of the two superpowers are any indication. As claimed by the United States, on February 12, 1988, inside the twelve-nautical-mile limits claimed by the Soviet Union as its territorial sea, two Soviet warships deliberately "bumped" two United States navy ships transiting the Black Sea. The collisions occurred within nine nautical miles of the Crimean coast. The U.S. ships were evidently testing the right of innocent passage. Such deliberate activities on the part of both sides could have caused damage and injuries or catastrophe if nuclear-powered warships had been involved. These incidents illustrate the importance of observing the 1972 Agreement on Preventing Incidents on and over the High

Seas. However, in a joint statement by the United States and the Soviet Union on September 23, 1989, the two governments reaffirmed that all ships, including warships, should enjoy the right of innocent passage through territorial sea; if a coastal state questions such a passage the ship concerned must be informed of the reasons why by the coastal states.[46]

NOTES

1. See Elliot L. Richardson, "Power, Mobility and the Law of the Sea," *Foreign Affairs* 58, no. 4 (Spring 1980): 902–919; John Temple Swing, "Who Will Own the Oceans?" *Foreign Affairs* 54, no. 3 (April 1976)): 527–546; Thomas A. Clingan, Jr., "The Next Twenty Years of Naval Mobility," *Proceedings: Naval Review* (1980), pp. 82–93; and George Modelski and William R. Thompson, *Seapower in Global Politics, 1494–1993* (Seattle: University of Washington Press, 1988).

2. See Rex J. Zedalis, "Military Uses of the Ocean Space and the Developing International Law of the Sea: An Analysis in the Context of Peacetime ASW," *San Diego Law Review* 16, no. 13 (April 1979): 591–596; Kenneth Booth, "The Military Implications of the Changing Law of the Sea," John King Gamble, Jr., ed. *Law of the Sea: Neglected Issues* (Honolulu: Law of the Sea Institute, University of Hawaii, 1979), pp. 328–421; and Vaughan Lowe, "The Impact of the Law of the Sea on Naval Warfare," *Syracuse Journal of International Law and Commerce* 14, no. 4 (1988): 657–698.

3. Discussion is based primarily on articles by Zedalis, "Military Uses of the Ocean Space and the Developing International Law of the Sea"; and David L. Larson, "Naval Weaponry and the Law of the Sea," *Ocean Development and the Law of the Sea* 18, no. 2 (1987): 125–190. The same article also appeared in E. D. Brown and R. R. Churchill, eds., *The UN Convention on the Law of the Sea: Impact and Implementation* (Honolulu: Law of the Sea Institute, University of Hawaii, 1987), pp. 41–84.

4. Larson, "Naval Weaponry and the Law of the Sea," p. 135. Also see Finn Laursen, "Security Aspects of Danish and Norwegian Law of the Sea Policies," *Ocean Development and International Law* 18, no. 1 (1987): 199–233.

5. Zedalis, "Military Uses of the Ocean Space and the Developing International Law of the Sea," p. 613. Also see Boleslaw A. Boczek, "Peaceful Purposes Provisions of the United Nations Convention on the Law of the Sea," *Ocean Development and International Law* 20, no. 4 (1989): 371–372.

6. Zedalis, "Military Uses of the Ocean Space and the Developing International Law of the Sea," p. 613.

7. Ibid., p. 615.

8. Larson, "Naval Weaponry and the Law of the Sea," p. 152; and Boczek, "Peaceful Purposes Provisions in the United Nations Convention on the Law of the Sea," pp. 372–373.

9. Larson, "Naval Weaponry and the Law of the Sea," p. 150.

10. Zedalis, "Military Uses of the Ocean Space and the Developing International Law of the Sea," p. 647.

11. Larson, "Naval Weaponry and the Law of the Sea," p. 156.

12. John Warren Kindt, *Marine Pollution and the Law of the Sea*, vol. 4 (Buffalo, N.Y.: William S. Hein, 1985), pp. 1931–1958. Also see Lee Kimball, "Antarctic Issues Today," in Choon-ho Park and Jae Kyu Park, eds., *The Law of the Sea: Problems from*

the East Asian Perspective, (Honolulu: The Law of the Sea Institute, University of Hawaii, 1987), pp. 524–535. See also other bibliographic entries on Antarctica cited in Chapter 1 of this handbook and the annotated bibliography on ocean law and politics published by Greenwood Press.

13. See Michael A. Morris, ''Southern Zone Maritime Security after 1984 Argentine-Chilean Treaty of Peace and Friendship,'' *Ocean Development and International Law* 18, no. 2 (1987): 235–254; and his ''The 1984 Argentine-Chilean Pact of Peace and Friendship,'' *Oceanus* 28, no. 3(1985): 93–96.

14. Kindt, *Marine Pollution and the Law of the Sea*, vol. 4, pp. 1936–1942.

15. See Burl Burlingame, ''U.S. Ferrets Out Soviet Subs,'' *The Honolulu Star-Bulletin*, 26 September 1988, p. A–1.

16. The 1969–1970 Stockholm International Peace Research Institute Report (Stockholm: Almgriest and Wiksell, 1970); portions reprinted in Elisabeth Mann Borgese and Norton Ginsburg, eds. *Ocean Yearbook 1* (Chicago: University of Chicago Press, 1978), pp. 380–385. Also see Robert C. Spindel, ''Antisubmarine Warfare,'' *Oceanus* 28, no. 2 (Summer 1985): 34–36; Owen Wilkes, ''Ocean-based Nuclear Deterrent Forces and Antisubmarine Warfare,'' in Borgese and Ginsburg, eds., *Ocean Yearbook 2* (Chicago: University of Chicago Press, 1980), pp. 226–249; and C. F. Barnaby, ''Superpower Military Activities in the World's Oceans,'' in Borgese and Ginsburg, eds., *Ocean Yearbook 5* (Chicago: University of Chicago Press, 1985), pp. 223–239.

17. The 1969–1970 Stockholm International Peace Research Institute Report, p. 380.

18. Ibid., pp. 381–383.

19. *Ocean Yearbook 1*, pp. 383–385.

20. Summary of these causes of ocean pollution by military uses comes from Arthur H. Westing (Stockholm International Research Institute), ''Military Impact on Ocean Ecology,'' in Borgese and Ginsburg, eds., *Ocean Yearbook 1*, pp. 442–463.

21. See J. A. Aphin, ''Effect of Explosives on Marine Life,'' *California Fish and Game* 33 (1947): 23–30; J. N. Gowanloch and J. E. McDougall, ''Biological Effects on Fish, Shrimp and Oysters of the Underwater Explosion of Heavy Charges of Dynamite,'' *Transactions of the North American Wildlife Conference* 11 (1946): 213–219; and C. M. Coker and E. H. Hollis, ''Fish Mortality Caused by a Series of Heavy Explosions in Chesapeake Bay,'' *Journal of Wildlife Management* 14 (1950): 435–444. Summary of these studies is found in Westing, ''Military Impact on Ocean Ecology,'' pp. 442–446.

22. *Ocean Dumping: A National Policy* (Washington, D.C.: Council on Environmental Quality, 1970), p. 15.

23. Ibid. The case of the Japanese ammunition ship sunk in the Truk lagoon during World War II is summarized in Westing, ''Military Impact on Ocean Ecology,'' p. 446.

24. Westing, ''Military Impact on Ocean Ecology,'' p. 449.

25. Ibid., p. 452.

26. Ibid.

27. Ibid., p. 453.

28. Ibid., p. 453. Also see *Ocean Dumping*, pp. 6–7; and N. Turner, ''Nuclear Waste Drop in the Ocean,'' *New Scientist* 68 (1975): 290.

29. See Alvin J. Cottrell et al., *Sea Power and Strategy in the Indian Ocean* (Beverly Hills, Calif.: Sage Publications, 1981); and Abdel Majid Farid, *The Red Sea: Prospects for Stability* (New York: St. Martin's Press, 1984), pp. 90–93.

30. See Mordechai Abir, *Oil, Power and Politics: Conflict in Arabia, the Red Sea and the Gulf* (London: Frank Case, 1974), p. 148; and Farid, *The Red Sea*, p. 91.

31. See K. P. Misra, ''Developments in the Indian Ocean Area: The Littoral Response,'' *International Studies*, no. 16, July–December 1977, pp. 17–22.

32. General Assembly Resolution 2832 (XXVI), 1971.

33. In 1977 the Soviet Union voted for the General Assembly resolution on the Indian Ocean as a zone of peace as local conflicts escalated that involved superpower intervention.

34. Treaty Banning Nuclear Weapons Tests in the Atmosphere, in Outer Space and Under Water; in 14 U.S.T. 1313, TIAS No. 5433, 480 UNTS 43.

35. See Captain A.G.Y. Thorpe, Royal Navy (United Kingdom), ''Mine Warfare at Sea: Some Legal Aspects of the Future,'' *Ocean Development and International Law* 18, no. 2 (1987): 259–272. The same article appears in Brown and Churchill, eds., *The UN Convention on the Law of the Sea*, pp. 96–108.

36. Thorpe, ''Mine Warfare at Sea,'' p. 259.

37. See Larson, ''Naval Weaponry and the Law of the Sea,'' pp. 125–199. This article also appears in Brown and Churchill, eds., *The UN Convention on the Law of the Sea*, pp. 41–84. Also see C. F. Barnaby, ''Superpower Military Activities in the World's Oceans,'' in Borgese and Ginsburg, eds., *Ocean Yearbook 5*, pp. 223–239.

38. Larson, ''Naval Weaponry and the Law of the Sea,'' pp. 190–197.

39. Ibid., p. 156.

40. Text of the treaty is found in *International Legal Materials* 24, no. 5 (September 1985): 1140–1153. For further discussion on the South Pacific nuclear-free zone, see Paul F. Power, ''The South Pacific Nuclear-Weapon-Free Zone,'' *Pacific Affairs* 59, no. 3 (February 1986): 455–475; and Ramesh Thakur, ''Nuclear-Free South Pacific: A New Zealand Perspective,'' *Pacific Affairs* 58, no. 2 (Summer 1985): 216–238.

41. ''Entry into Force of the South Pacific Nuclear-Free Zone Treaty on December 11, 1986,'' *Law of the Sea Bulletin*, no. 9, April 1986, p. 66. (New York: United Nations Office of the Special Representative of the Secretary-General of the Law of the Sea). Text of the Protocols in *Law of the Sea Bulletin*, no. 6, October 1985, pp. 24–39.

42. See Arthur M. Rieman, ''Creating a Nuclear Free Zone Treaty That Is True to Its Name: The Nuclear Free Zone Concept and a Model Treaty,'' *Denver Journal of International Law and Policy* 18, no. 2 (Winter 1990): 209–278.

43. See ''Fighting the Mines of August,'' *Newsweek*, 20 August 1984, pp. 48–49.

44. See the transcript of the news conference by President George Bush, Defense Secretary Richard Cheney and General Colin L. Powell, *The New York Times*, 23 August 1990, p. A–11.

45. Text is to be found in *U.S. Treaties and Other International Agreements*, vol. 23, pp. 1108–1114.

46. See ''Uniform Interpretation of Norms of International Law Governing Innocent Passage,'' *Law of the Sea Bulletin*, no. 14, December 1989, p. 13.

CHAPTER 11

Navigation, Communication and Shipping

Navigation denotes freedom of the seas, which generally implies the freedom of movement over the oceans by merchant fleets for commerce and trade, and by navies for security and strategic purposes. Freedom to navigate also implies overflight above ocean waters. The 1982 LOS Convention contains approximately one-hundred articles dealing with the rights, as well as restrictions, of international navigation. Some of the salient aspects concerning navigation in that Convention include Articles 17–26 on rules for all ships engaged in innocent passage in the territorial sea, Articles 27–28 on rules applicable to merchant ships and government ships operated for commercial purposes and Articles 29–31 on rules applicable to warships for noncommercial purposes. Twelve articles in the 1982 LOS Convention specifically deal with rules on international navigation through straits. Articles 34–36 provide the legal status of straits used for navigation, and Articles 37–44 spell out the right of transit passage, the duties of ships and aircraft during transit passage, and sea lanes and traffic separation schemes in straits used for navigation. Articles 52 and 53 provide rules on rights of innocent passage in archipelagic waters and the rights of archipelagic states to designate sea lanes and traffic separation schemes for vessels using the archipelagic waters. Article 58 gives other states the right to enjoy freedom of the high seas. Article 78 prohibits coastal states' (there are a total of 140) claims to the continental shelf that infringe or interfere with navigation rights. Article 87 deals with high seas freedoms, in addition to fishing, cable and pipeline laying, engaging in scientific research, and the freedom of navigation and overflight. Article 90 grants every state, whether coastal or landlocked (total of thirty) the right to sail ships flying its flag on the high seas. Finally, Article 125 provides the right of access to and from the sea and the right to freedom of transit using all means of transport by landlocked states through the territory of transit states.

While Chapter 3 discusses the legal status and meaning of the various ocean regimes—internal waters, territorial seas, continental shelf, exclusive economic zone, archipelagic waters and the seabed beyond national jurisdiction—this chapter centers discussion and analysis on the increasing coastal state jurisdiction as compared with the traditional international navigation regime of flag-state responsibilities.

Article 21(1) of the 1982 LOS Convention grants the coastal state the right to enact laws regulating innocent passage in the territorial sea. Article 42 grants the coastal state bordering the straits the right to regulate navigational safety and pollution control, as well as the right of loading or unloading goods in port. As discussed in Chapters 8 and 9, vessels are now subject to many restrictions in environmental protection agreements. The new zonal arrangements or regimes established by the 1982 LOS Convention have given rise to an increase in coastal-state powers over navigation. One traditional navigation right that has not been diminished by the new rules in the law of the sea is the right to lay submarine cables and pipelines, a principle that has been established and universally accepted since 1885.

A persistent problem in commercial navigation, the movement of goods at sea, has been a matter of flag-state responsibility, as provided in Article 94 of the 1982 LOS Convention, and the increased use of "flags of convenience" for international navigation. The problem of not providing a "genuine link" between the ship owner and the flag state has arisen because of the former's desire to make economic gains at the expense of ship safety and international navigation standards.

Interdiction at sea concerns the international community as well as constitutional scholars in the United States because of the conflict this operation has created, not only with the basic established principle of freedom of navigation, but also the constitutional guarantee against unreasonable search and seizure on land, as well as at sea. Does domestic legislation, in this case a United States statute, deviate from freedom of navigation when it authorizes seizure, search and arrest of drug smugglers on the high seas?

The section on safety at sea discusses international efforts, mostly under the auspices of the IMO and the ILO, for providing rules and regulations for ship operation and international standards required of ship masters, officers and crew who staff the ships at sea. This is an area in which the traditional international navigation regime still prevails—that is, there is an established body of rules that require the flag states to observe and comply with at sea.

While Article 22 grants the archipelagic states the right to designate sea lanes and traffic separation schemes, neither the Philippines nor Indonesia has worked out plans for such designation. In the meantime, potential controversy may surface as unconventional baselines for measuring the territorial sea and archipelagic waters have been drawn for the Azores, Faroes, Svalbard and Galápagos, providing mandatory routes that would keep ships at an unreasonable distance from the islands.[1]

While there are uncertainties, as well as restrictions, in the new law of the sea and through the practice of states, navigational freedom within the framework of the overall freedom of the seas will most likely continue in the future. However, with the expansion of state claims for resources over the ocean space, freedom of the seas, of which international navigation is an integral concept, may be "lost in a welter of coastal state jurisdictions."[2]

COASTAL-STATE RIGHTS: THE NEW RULES IN NAVIGATION

In the traditional navigation regime under which the maritime powers relied heavily on the principle of a ship's ability to sail with as little interference as possible on the sea, rules for navigation were basically concerned with unimpeded passage to the ocean waters and the safety of ships and crew. With the advent of expanded coastal nations' claims over the ocean space beyond their narrow belt of territorial waters (see Chapter 3) and the international concern over marine pollution and the environment (see Chapters 8 and 9), coastal states' rights over navigation have increased. The ascendancy of coastal state jurisdiction over navigation is reflected, first of all, in the various provisions contained in the 1982 LOS Convention that constitute in the aggregate the basic rights of navigation. Article 21(1) grants the coastal states the right to enact laws for the purpose of regulating innocent passage in the territorial sea (now with a width of twelve nautical miles) on matters of safety and maritime traffic, protection of navigational aids and facilities, cables and pipelines, fishery regulations, marine scientific research, and marine pollution.[3]

Article 21: Laws and regulations of the coastal State relating to innocent passage

1. The coastal State may adopt laws and regulations, in conformity with the provisions of this Convention and other rules of international law, relating to innocent passage through the territorial sea, in respect of all or any of the following:

(a) the safety of navigation and the regulation of maritime traffic;

(b) the protection of navigational aids and facilities and other facilities or installations;

(c) the protection of cables and pipelines;

(d) the conservation of the living resources of the sea;

(e) the prevention of infringement of the fisheries laws and regulations of the coastal State;

(f) the preservation of the environment of the coastal State and the prevention, reduction and control of pollution thereof;

(g) marine scientific research and hydrographic surveys;

(h) the prevention of infringement of the customs, fiscal, immigration or sanitary laws and regulations of the coastal State.

While unimpeded transit passage is guaranteed under the 1982 LOS Convention, as specified in Article 41, the coastal states that border international straits or waterways may designate sea lanes and traffic separation schemes.

Article 42: Laws and regulations of States bordering straits relating to transit passage

1. Subject to the provisions of this section, States bordering straits may adopt laws and regulations relating to transit passage through straits, in respect of all or any of the following:

(a) the safety of navigation and the regulation of maritime traffic, as provided in article 41;

(b) the prevention, reduction and control of pollution, by giving effect to applicable international regulations regarding the discharge of oil, oily wastes and other noxious substances in the strait;

(c) with respect to fishing vessels, the prevention of fishing, including the stowage of fishing gear;

(d) the loading or unloading of any commodity, currency or person in contravention of the customs, fiscal, immigration or sanitary laws and regulations of States bordering straits.

2. Such laws and regulations shall not discriminate in form or in fact among foreign ships or in their application have the practical effect of denying, hampering or impairing the right of transit passage as defined in this section.

3. States bordering straits shall give due publicity to all such laws and regulations.

4. Foreign ships exercising the right of transit passage shall comply with such laws and regulations.

5. The flag State of a ship or the State of registry of an aircraft entitled to sovereign immunity which acts in a manner contrary to such laws and regulations or other provisions of this Part shall bear international responsibility for any loss or damage which results to States bordering straits.

Article 42 empowers the coastal states bordering the straits not only to provide regulations for safety of navigation and prevention and control of pollution, but to regulate loading and unloading of any commodity. Under Article 53, in archipelagic waters, the archipelagic state may also designate sea lanes and prescribe traffic separation schemes. While a vessel is guaranteed freedom of navigation beyond the limits of the territorial sea, that right is now limited to laws and regulations that may be enacted by the coastal state for its contiguous zone in relation to customs, immigration and sanitation. In the exclusive economic zone, coastal state jurisdiction over the fishery and other resources may restrict the exercise of a ship's navigation and fishing freedom. Even on the high seas, the exercise of freedom of navigation must pay "due regard for the interests of other states." As mentioned in Chapters 8 and 9, vessels are subject to many restrictions in the exercise of their navigational rights by the various international agreements on pollution control and environmental protection.

Significance. Two major forces contributed to the increase in power of coastal states over international navigation. One was the influence exerted by the Group of 77 at the UNCLOS III negotiations in demanding more power for coastal states. The other was concern by many coastal states regarding the increased threat to the marine environment by oil spills and tanker accidents at sea (see Chapter 8). Environmental concerns compel all maritime powers to accept coastal states' rights and responsibilities to regulate international navigation along with some of the traditional flag-state responsibility. On the whole the 1982 LOS Convention has brought changes in international navigation by establishing new zonal arrangements of the archipelagic waters and states, the regime of international straits, and the expanded territorial sea. All these new regimes or zonal arrangements have provided increased power for the coastal states.

The world's increasingly internationalized merchant fleet, now over 400 million tons, will be under constant pressure from the coastal states, which acquired more power under the 1982 LOS Convention, for environmental protection and interference in traditional navigational rights. As pointed out by Edgar Gold, navigation is only one of the many "competing ocean uses in a more complex maritime world."[4]

COMMUNICATIONS AND SATELLITES

Submarine Cables

Under the 1884 Convention on the Protection of Submarine Cables, one of the oldest established navigational rules was the right to lay, and the obligation to protect, submarine cables. The convention came into force on March 14, 1886. Article 1 of the convention states:

> The present Convention shall be applicable, outside of the territorial waters, to all legally established submarine cables landed in the territories, colonies or possessions of one or more of the High Contracting Parties.

Under Article 2, it is a punishable offense to break or injure a submarine cable that would result in either total or partial interruption of telegraphic communication. The only exception to this rule is when lives or vessels must be saved. In these instances, the owners of the cable are required to pay for the cost of repairs. The convention also requires the observance of adopted signals in laying or repairing submarine cables, in order that other vessels can keep a distance of at least one nautical mile from the vessel engaged in such operations (Article 5). The same is required for fishing boats towing gear and nets, provided a twenty-four hour notice has been given to fishing vessels. The owner of the cable must compensate for any anchor or fishing implements damaged while avoiding injuries to a submarine cable (Article 7). As outlined in Articles 5 and 7, prosecution of violation of the convention's provisions must be instituted by the state in a court of law. And, under Article 12, the contracting parties are encouraged to enact domestic legislation to secure the execution of the convention.

The right to lay submarine cable has been upheld by the 1982 LOS Convention in Articles 51(2), 58(1), 79(2), 87(1), and 112–115. Article 51(2) mandates that the archipelagic states respect existing submarine cables laid by other states "passing through its waters without making a landfall," and permit repair and replacement of such cables. States which claim a 200-nautical-mile exclusive economic zone must respect the right of laying submarine cables and pipelines as a lawful use of the sea. Under Article 79 (1) and (2), all states are entitled to lay submarine cable and pipelines on the continental shelf, and a coastal state may not impede the laying or maintenance of such cables and pipelines. Article 87 lists the freedom of submarine cable and pipeline laying as one of the high seas freedoms. Articles 112–115 of the 1982 LOS Convention express the basic principles contained in Articles 4 and 5 of the 1884 Convention on the Protection of Submarine Cables:

Article 112: Right to lay submarine cables and pipelines

1. All States are entitled to lay submarine cables and pipelines on the bed of the high seas beyond the continental shelf.
2. Article 79, paragraph 5, applies to such cables and pipelines.

Article 113: Breaking or injury of a submarine cable or pipeline

Every State shall adopt the laws and regulations necessary to provide that the breaking or injury by a ship flying its flag or by a person subject to its jurisdiction of a submarine cable beneath the high seas done wilfully or through culpable negligence, in such a manner as to be liable to interrupt or obstruct telegraphic or telephonic communications, and similarly the breaking or injury of a submarine pipeline or high-voltage power cable, shall be a punishable offence. This provision shall apply also to conduct calculated or likely to result in such breaking or injury. However, it shall not apply to any break or injury caused by persons who acted merely with the legitimate object of saving their lives or their ships, after having taken all necessary precautions to avoid such break or injury.

Article 114: Breaking or injury by owners of a submarine cable or pipeline of another submarine cable or pipeline

Every State shall adopt the laws and regulations necessary to provide that, if persons subject to its jurisdiction who are the owners of a submarine cable or pipeline beneath the high seas, in laying or repairing that cable or pipeline, cause a break in or injury to another cable or pipeline, they shall bear the cost of the repairs.

Article 115: Indemnity for loss incurred in avoiding injury to a submarine cable or pipeline

Every State shall adopt the laws and regulations necessary to ensure that the owners of ships who can prove that they have sacrificed an anchor, a net or any other fishing gear, in order to avoid injuring a submarine cable or pipeline, shall be indemnified by the owner of the cable or pipeline, provided that the owner of the ship has taken all reasonable precautionary measures beforehand.

Satellite Communication for Navigation of Ships

In 1976, under the auspices of the IMO (then the IMCO), an agreement was reached to provide a worldwide maritime satellite communication system by establishing the International Maritime Satellite Organization (INMARSAT). The convention under that name became operative in February 1982.

The purpose of the convention is to improve the link in maritime communications between ships and their owners, and between crew or passengers on board and persons on shore in a distress situation. Space segment technology—tracking, telemetry, command, control and monitoring facilities—uses satellites orbiting the earth. Under Article 7 of the INMARSAT Convention, communication facilities must be maintained by the organization and made available to all ships.

The organizational structure for INMARSAT consists of an assembly, a council and a secretariat. Functions of the assembly include establishing space segment facilities to provide radio-determination, distress or safety services, reviewing policies, and deciding formal relationships between the states and the organization and with other international organizations. The council serves as an executive organ for determining maritime satellite telecommunications requirements and construction of space segment needs and services. The director for the secretariat serves as the chief (managerial) executive with a support staff. Finances for the organization are provided by contributions from signatories to the convention. Disputes must be settled by an arbitral tribunal of three members governed by a detailed set of procedures delineated in the annex to the convention.

Significance. There are two important aspects for considering laying submarine cables and pipelines as an acceptable "right of immersion." One is the obvious importance of cables as a key communication aid for navigation. While the 1982 LOS Convention has expanded coastal state rights in many areas, the right of states to lay submarine cables, as pointed out in this section, has been guaranteed by numerous articles. Articles 113–115 mandate every state to enact laws and regulations to make it a punishable offense to break or cause injury to undersea cables or telephone communication lines.

The other aspect is that the need to protect submarine cables goes even to the extent of compensating ship owners or fishing boat owners who might have to lose an anchor or a net in order to avoid damage or injury to the cables. Freedom to lay submarine cables and pipelines is one of the enumerated freedoms of the high seas (Article 87).

With the establishment of the satellite communication system for navigation of ships in 1982, there is now an instantaneous link between ships and owners and between crew and passengers with shore facilities and personnel in a distress situation. Maritime communications have now kept pace with advanced technological development.

FLAG-STATE RIGHTS: "FLAG OF CONVENIENCE" AND OPEN REGISTRY

By definition, ''flag state'' refers to the state that grants a vessel the right to sail under its flag. Article 92 of the 1982 LOS Convention states that ships must sail under the flag of one state only and are subject to its exclusive jurisdiction on the high seas. Article 94 of the LOS Convention provides a list of specific duties of the flag state:

Article 94: Duties of the flag State

1. Every State shall effectively exercise its jurisdiction and control in administrative, technical and social matters over ships flying its flag.

2. In particular every State shall:

(a) maintain a register of ships containing the names and particulars of ships flying its flag, except those which are excluded from generally accepted international regulations on account of their small size; and

(b) assume jurisdiction under its internal law over each ship flying its flag and its master, officers and crew in respect of administrative, technical and social matters concerning the ship.

3. Every State shall take such measures for ships flying its flag as are necessary to ensure safety at sea with regard, *inter alia*, to:

(a) the construction, equipment and seaworthiness of ships;

(b) the manning of ships, labour conditions and the training of crews, taking into account the applicable international instruments;

(c) the use of signals, the maintenance of communications and the prevention of collisions.

4. Such measures shall include those necessary to ensure:

(a) that each ship, before registration and thereafter at appropriate intervals, is surveyed by a qualified surveyor of ships, and has on board such charts, nautical publications and navigational equipment and instruments as are appropriate for the safe navigation of the ship;

(b) that each ship is in the charge of a master and officers who possess appropriate qualifications, in particular in seamanship, navigation, communications and marine engineering, and that the crew is appropriate in qualification and numbers for the type, size, machinery and equipment of the ship;

(c) that the master, officers and, to the extent appropriate, the crew are fully conversant with and required to observe the applicable international regulations concerning the safety of life at sea, the prevention of collisions, the prevention, reduction and control of marine pollution, and the maintenance of communications by radio.

5. In taking the measures called for in paragraphs 3 and 4 each State is required to conform to generally accepted international regulations, procedures and practices to take any steps which may be necessary to secure their observance.

6. A State which has clear grounds to believe that proper jurisdiction and control with respect to a ship have not been exercised may report the facts to the flag State. Upon receiving such a report, the flag State shall investigate the matter and, if appropriate, take any action necessary to remedy the situation.

7. Each State shall cause an inquiry to be held by or before a suitably qualified person or persons into every marine casualty or incident of navigation on the high seas involving a ship flying its flag and causing loss of life or serious injury to nationals of another State or serious damage to ships or installations of another State or to the marine environment. The flag State and the other State shall co-operate in the conduct of any inquiry held by that other State into any such marine casualty or incident of navigation.

It seems obvious from this enumeration of duties of the flag state that the nationality of a ship is important in determining which state is legally responsible for the vessel's observance of rules of navigation at sea, as well as for extending diplomatic protection for the vessel. Nationality for ships is identified by registration and by granting the right to fly a state's flag. Under the so-called open registry system, for some period of time a sovereign state could decide at will which ships would be permitted to fly its flag. By this practice a state could derive revenue by allowing other nations and nationals to register their vessels under its flag without assuming the duties and responsibilities for the management and operation of the vessels at sea. However, in the 1955 case of the *Nottebohm*, the ICJ ruled that there must be a "genuine link" between the state and the nationality of a ship for the former to exercise diplomatic and consular protection for the latter.[5] It was the ICJ judgment that influenced the drafters of the 1958 Convention on the High Seas to adopt specific rules in Article 5, which states:

1. Each State shall fix the conditions for the granting of its nationality to ships, for the registration of ships in its territory, and for the right to fly its flag. Ships have the nationality of the State whose flag they are entitled to fly. There must exist a genuine link between the State and the ship; in particular, the State must effectively exercise its jurisdiction and control in administrative, technical and social matters over ships flying its flag.

2. Each State shall issue to ships to which it has granted the right to fly its flag documents to that effect.

The concept of "genuine link" in Article 5 of the 1958 Convention on the High Seas is repeated almost word for word in Article 91 of the 1982 LOS Convention. The problem has been that the requirement imposed by Article 5 of the 1958 Convention on the High Seas in practice has had no effect or has been merely a "paper restraint."[6] Only a small number of states—France, Norway, the United Kingdom and the United States, for instance—insist on implementation of the "genuine link" requirement; many other states ignore it in most instances. These are the "flag of convenience" or "open registry" states that are not parties to the 1958 Convention on the High Seas. Under such a system ship owners abide by international navigation standards as little as possible and pay lower wages to crew on board, thus reducing total operating costs. Major flag-of-convenience states are Bermuda, Cyprus, Liberia, Panama, Singapore and Somalia. In 1987 about 34.2 percent of the world's shipping was represented by open registry fleet.[7]

The move to attack the "open registry" or "flag of convenience" system, initiated under the auspices of the United Nations Conference on Trade and Development (UNCTAD) in 1981, eventually produced on February 7, 1986, the Convention on the Conditions of Registration of Ships seeking to give meaning to the "genuine link" concept in ship registration.[8] Article 7 of the convention requires that a state of registration must comply with the provision in Article 8, which in turn requires participation of the flag state or its nationals as owners of ships flying its flag. Under Article 8, flag states are encouraged to enact laws and regulations that "should be sufficient to permit the flag state to effectively exercise its jurisdiction and control over ships flying its flag." Article 9 stipulates that a state of registration "shall observe the principle that a satisfactory part of the complement consisting of officers and crew of ships flying its flag be nationals or persons domiciled or lawfully in permanent residence in that state." Article 11 provides that the state supply information in establishing a register of ships flying its flag: ship's name, port of registration, international call sign of the ship, name of the builders, description of the main technical features, and name, address and nationality of the owner or owners. Effective implementation of these provisions is a matter of doubt.[9] A list of merchant fleet tonnage registered under the various flag states is provided in Table 11.1.

The tonnage distribution of the world's merchant fleets has been in favor of the less developed nations. Major trading nations such as the United States, Canada, France and the United Kingdom have smaller merchant fleets as compared to developing nations, such as Liberia, Panama, Chile and Cyprus. This trend will most likely continue in the future.

Significance. The continued practice of "flags of convenience" for ship registration is significant in international navigation in that it separates financial control of the vessel from control over safety and the observance of navigational rules at sea. A large part of the traditional maritime regime is based on flag-state jurisdiction as provided in Article 94 of the 1982 LOS Convention. Continued use of "flags of convenience" weakens considerably the flag-state responsibilities and obligations, particularly on matters of safety at sea and liability of ship owners relating to tanker accidents that can pose a threat to the marine environment.

Another reason for tightening or doing away with the open registry—"flag

Table 11.1
Merchant Fleets of the World (Ships of 500 Gross Registered Tons and above as of July 1, 1985)

	Gross Registered Tons
Albania	52,698
Algeria	1,332,863
Angola	71,581
Argentina	2,227,252
Australia	1,877,560
Austria	134,225
Bahamas	3,852,385
Bahrain	26,646
Bangladesh	300,151
Barbados	4,034
Belgium	2,247,571
Benin	2,999
Bolivia	14,913
Brazil	5,935,899
Bulgaria	1,191,419
Burma	94,380
Cameroon	67,057
Canada	841,048
Cape Verde	8,765
Chile	371,468
China	10,167,450
Colombia	357,668
Comoros	649
Costa Rica	12,616
Côte d'Ivoire	124,706
Cuba	784,664
Cyprus	8,134,083
Czechoslovakia	184,299
Democratic Kampuchea	998
Democratic Yemen	4,229
Denmark	4,677,360
Djibouti	2,066
Dominica	500
Dominican Republic	35,667
Ecuador	417,372
Egypt	835,995
Equatorial Guinea	6,412
Ethiopia	54,499
Faeroe Islands	39,333
Fiji	20,145
Finland	1,894,485
France	7,864,931
Gabon	92,687
Gambia	1,597
German Democratic Republic	1,235,840

Table 11.1 (continued)

	Gross Registered Tons
Germany, Federal Republic of	5,717,767
Ghana	99,637
Greece	30,751,092
Guatemala	15,569
Guinea	598
Guyana	3,888
Honduras	301,786
Hungary	77,182
Iceland	69,460
India	6,324,145
Indonesia	1,604,427
Iran (Islamic Republic of)	2,172,401
Iraq	882,715
Ireland	161,304
Israel	541,035
Italy	8,530,108
Jamaica	7,473
Japan	37,189,376
Jordan	47,628
Kenya	1,168
Kiribati	1,480
Korea, Democratic People's Republic of	470,592
Korea, Republic of	6,621,898
Kuwait	2,311,813
Lebanon	461,525
Liberia	57,985,747
Libyan Arab Jamahiriya	832,450
Madagascar	63,115
Malaysia	1,708,599
Maldives	125,958
Malta	1,836,948
Mauritania	1,581
Mauritius	32,968
Mexico	1,282,048
Monaco	3,268
Morocco	377,702
Mozambique	17,013
Nauru	64,829
Netherlands	3,628,871
New Zealand	266,285
Nicaragua	15,869
Nigeria	396,525
Norway	14,567,326
Oman	10,939
Pakistan	429,973

	Gross Registered Tons
Panama	39,366,187
Papua New Guinea	10,671
Paraguay	38,440
Peru	640,968
Philippines	4,462,291
Poland	2,966,534
Portugal	1,280,065
Qatar	339,725
Romania	2,769,937
Saint Vincent and the Grenadines	220,490
Samoa	25,644
Saudi Arabia	2,868,689
Senegal	19,426
Singapore	6,385,919
Solomon Islands	1,018
Somalia	22,802
South Africa	501,386
Spain	5,650,470
Sri Lanka	617,628
Sudan	92,700
Suriname	11,181
Sweden	2,951,227
Switzerland	341,972
Syrian Arab Republic	40,506
Tanzania, United Republic of	43,471
Thailand	550,585
Togo	52,677
Tonga	13,381
Trinidad and Tobago	9,370
Tunisia	274,170
Turkey	3,532,350
Uganda	3,394
Union of Soviet Socialist Republics	16,767,526
United Arab Emirates	805,318
United Kingdom of Great Britain and Northern Ireland	13,260,290
Bermuda	969,081
British Virgin Islands	1,939
Cayman Islands	313,755
Gibraltar	568,247
Hong Kong	6,820,100
Montserrat	711
Saint Helena	3,150
Turks and Caicos Islands	513
United States of America	13,922,244
Uruguay	144,907

Table 11.1 (continued)

	Gross Registered Tons
Vanuatu	132,979
Venezuela	900,305
Viet Nam	277,486
Yugoslavia	2,648,415
Zaire	70,127
Unallocated	4,201,669
World total	383,533,262

Notes: Types of ships included: Oil tankers; Oil/chemical tankers; Chemical tankers; Miscellaneous tankers (trading); Liquified gas carriers; Bulk/oil carriers (including ore/oil); Ore and bulk carriers; General cargo ships; Container ships (fully cellular and lighter carriers); Vehicle carriers; Ferries and passenger ships and passenger/cargo ships; and Livestock carriers.

Excludes the reserve fleet of the United States of America and the United States and Canadian Great Lakes fleets.

Source: Compiled on the basis of data supplied by Lloyd's Shipping Information Services (London); reprinted in *Law of the Sea Bulletin*, No. 7, April 1986, pp. 103–106.

of convenience''—practice is aimed at the possible transfer of open-ship registry to the expanding national fleets of the developing nations. The 1986 UN Convention on the conditions for ship registration does not even use the term ''genuine link''; it upholds the status quo of the flag state's right to maintain open registry and provide the option for establishing the ''genuine link'' in ship ownership and crew recruitment.

INTERDICTION AT SEA AND FREEDOM OF NAVIGATION

Interdiction at sea deals with suppression of smuggling of dutiable goods, a problem around which a good portion of international customary law is built. Modern interdiction copes with the smuggling of drugs and of persons for illegal immigration. While interdiction at sea involves the issue of human rights and the constitutional debate on the application of the Fourth Amendment in the United States Constitution with respect to foreign search and seizure outside of the United States shores,[10] also it has implications for freedom of the high seas and navigational rights.[11]

Interdiction is an enforcement search and seizure measure that includes boarding, examination of ship documents, questioning of crew and passengers, and the escorting of the vessel to the port of departure. Since the late 1970s the United States Coast Guard has increased its interdiction operations to curtail the lucrative maritime smuggling of cocaine and marijuana into the mainland United States by foreign or American vessels with foreign crews.[12] These interdiction operations and court prosecution of drug trafficking have raised questions of Fourth Amendment protection for those seized on the high seas.[13]

The United States courts have upheld the criterion of "reasonable suspicion" for interdiction operations in international waters, defined under the statutes as all waters beyond the territorial sea (twelve nautical miles) of the United States and beyond the territorial sea of any foreign nation. For instance, 14 U.S.C., Section 89(a)(1982) states:

> The Coast Guard may make inquiries, examinations, inspections, searches, seizures, and arrests upon the high seas and waters over which the United States has jurisdiction, for the prevention, detention, and suppression of violations of the laws of the United States. For such purposes, commissioned, warrant and petty officers may at any time go on board any vessel subject to the jurisdiction or to the operation of any law of the United States, address inquiries to those on board, examine, inspect and search the vessel and use all necessary force to compel compliance.

However, a recent case, *United States* v. *Peterson* (812 F.2nd 486, 9th Circuit, 1987) involved the United States Coast Guard intent to board a Panamanian vessel one-hundred miles from Cabo San Lucas in the Philippines after obtaining telephone approval from a Panamanian narcotics official. At the moment of boarding by the Coast Guard, the crew set fire to the ship and threw the marijuana overboard. The Coast Guard recovered some of the marijuana before the ship sank. Court defense of the arrested crew was that the recovery was illegal, that the search was conducted without a warrant, and that the Fourth Amendment of the United States Constitution did not permit searches by foreign powers in their own countries involving Americans on board. The Ninth Circuit Court ruled that the search did not comply with Philippine law and was not reasonable under the Fourth Amendment.

Significance. Interdiction at sea by the United States Coast Guard and the court decisions in these cases of drug smuggling on the high seas present a conflict between the principles of freedom of navigation provided in the 1958 Convention on the High Seas and domestic legislation. Article 6(1) of the 1958 Convention on the High Seas, to which the United States has been a party since 1962, states:

> Ships shall sail under the flag of one state only and save in exceptional circumstances expressly provided for in international treaties or in the articles, shall be subject to its exclusive jurisdiction on the high seas. (see Annex B to Chapter 2)

Article 22(1) states:

> Except where acts of interference derive from powers conferred by treaty, a warship which encounters a foreign merchant ship on the high seas is not justified in boarding her unless there is reasonable ground for suspecting:

(a) that the ship is engaged in piracy; or

(b) that the ship is engaged in slave trade; or

(c) that, though flying a foreign flag or refusing to show its flag, the ship is, in reality, of the same nationality as the warship.

Then Article 22(2) states that under these conditions, the officers of the warship may board the suspected vessel and examine the documents of its officers and crew. The United States Court of Appeals has "denied the self-executing character" of the 1958 Convention on the High Seas.

It may be argued that the domestic legislation discussed above does not deviate from the freedom of navigation principles in international law and thus interdiction at sea is permissible within the meaning of Article 22 of the 1958 Convention on the High Seas.[14] On the other hand, it has also been argued that the United States court decisions must protect the individual within the meaning of the Fourth Amendment to the United States Constitution.[15]

One scholar argues that the United States statutes on which court decisions permitting interdiction at sea are based give too much latitude in these operations, for if read literally they "allow random stops of any vessel any place and at any time" and search and seizure of vessels in violation of the Fourth Amendment.[16] John P. Craven points out that the interdiction operations at sea and the courts in the United States have created pressures on freedom of navigation on the high seas, which could "impinge on the non-negotiable minimum" which may be demanded by maritime states.[17]

SAFETY AT SEA

International concern for safety at sea while transporting goods, and avoidance of collision by ships, has been addressed legally in a number of multilateral conventions. First, there was the 1948 International Convention for the Safety of Life at Sea, which was superseded by the 1960 Convention with the same name. Then it, in turn, was replaced by the 1974 International Convention for the Safety of Life at Sea (known as the SOLAS Convention), which entered into force on May 25, 1980. The 1974 SOLAS Convention and its predecessors were drafted and negotiated under the auspices of the IMCO (now IMO). Second, safety at sea was a major concern at the UNCLOS I, which produced the 1958 Convention on the High Seas. Article 10 of that convention provides the following guidelines for flag states on matters of safety of life at sea:

1. Every State shall take such measures for ships under its flag as are necessary to ensure safety at sea with regard *inter alia* to:

(a) The use of signals, the maintenance of communications and the prevention of collisions:

(b) The manning of ships and labor conditions for crews taking into account the applicable international labor instruments;

(c) The construction, equipment and seaworthiness of ships.

2. In taking such measures each State is required to conform to generally accepted international standards and to take any steps which may be necessary to ensure their observance.

Word for word, the 1982 LOS Convention incorporates Article 10 of the 1958 Convention on the High Seas in Article 94(3)(a–c). In addition, Article 94(4) requires ships to be equipped with navigational instruments for the safety of the ship and to be staffed with qualified crew.

International navigation standards are provided not only by the 1974 SOLAS Convention, but also by the 1972 International Regulations for Preventing Collision at Sea. The 1974 SOLAS Convention and its 1978 Protocol provide detailed regulations for ship owners and flag states on inspection and certification of ships for their seaworthiness, life-saving appliances and equipment of cargo ships, machinery and electrical installation on board ships (tankers of 10,000 tons or more now must install two remote steering gear control systems that comprise two or more identical power units) and fire safety measures for tankers. Chapter V of the 1974 SOLAS Convention, as amended by the 1978 Protocol, provides international standards for navigational safety that include: installation of two radars for all ships of 10,000 gross tons (Regulation 12); requirements for more than one steering gear power unit in operation in areas where navigation demands special caution (Regulation 19–1); testing of steering gear twelve hours before departure (Regulation 19–2); and the requirement for a safety construction certificate for cargo ships, as well as a safety equipment certificate.

The "proper rules of the road" in navigation are provided by the 1972 Convention on the International Regulations for Preventing Collision at Sea.[18] The original convention on prevention of collision at sea dated from 1960. In October 1972, the IMCO held a conference to revise these 1960 regulations. These new regulations are designed to address several navigation problems which stemmed from new technological development. One deals with the traffic separation schemes (Rule 10) to be observed in order to avoid collision in congested sea lanes. Others concern the matter of safe speeds at sea, which require radar to detect the number, location and movement of vessels (Rule 6); proper conduct for ships in restricted visibility (Rule 19); specific regulations with regard to the visibility range for lights for ships with varying length and the type and color of the lights required (Rules 21 and 22). Also, there are specific requirements for sound signals and warning signals (Rules 32–37). Annex I provides rules dealing with positioning and technical details of lights and shapes. Annex III provides technical details of sound signal appliances (whistles). Annex V concerns specific rules for distress signals using a gun or other explosive signal fired at intervals of about a minute; rockets of red stars; the continuous sounding of fog-signal apparatus; or a signal sent by radiotelephone consisting of the spoken words "May Day."

The International Labor Organization (ILO) has helped to draft and negotiate more than twenty conventions concerning working conditions and welfare of sailors while on board vessels at sea. Subject matter covered by these agreements range from medical examinations for seafarers (ILO Convention No. 73, 1946), to food catering for crew on board ship (ILO Convention No. 68, 1946), to certification of cooks on ships (ILO Convention No. 69, 1946), to social security for seamen (ILO Convention No. 70, 1946), to minimum age for employment as seamen (ILO Convention No. 112, 1959 and No. 138, 1973), to minimum standards for merchant ships (ILO Convention No. 147, 1976). In 1978 the IMO assisted in the convention on standards of training certification and watchkeeping for seafarers, which delineates strict requirements for certification of masters and officers on merchant vessels.

Also, mention must be made of two recent international conventions that deal with the safety of navigation. One is the 1988 Convention for the Suppression of Unlawful Acts against the Safety of Maritime Navigation, which is aimed at international terrorism or terrorist acts threatening the safety and the security of passengers and crews.[19] Article 3 states that

Article 3

1. Any person commits an offence if that person unlawfully and intentionally:
   (a) Seizes or exercises control over a ship by force or threat thereof or any other form of intimidation; or
   (b) Performs an act of violence against a person on board a ship if that act is likely to endanger the safe navigation of that ship; or
   (c) Destroys a ship or causes damage to a ship or to its cargo which is likely to endanger the safe navigation of that ship; or
   (d) Places or causes to be placed on a ship, by any means whatsoever, a device or substance which is likely to destroy that ship, or cause damage to that ship or its cargo which endangers or is likely to endanger the safe navigation of that ship; or
   (e) Destroys or seriously damages maritime navigational facilities or seriously interferes with their operation, if any such act is likely to endanger the safe navigation of a ship; or
   (f) Communicates information which he knows to be false, thereby endangering the safe navigation of a ship; or
   (g) Injures or kills any person, in connection with the commission or the attempted commission of any of the offences set forth in subparagraphs (a) to (f).
2. Any person also commits an offence if that person:
   (a) Attempts to commit any of the offences set forth in paragraph 1; or
   (b) Abets the commission of any of the offences set forth in paragraph 1

perpetrated by any person or is otherwise an accomplice of a person who commits such an offence; or

(c) Threatens, with or without a condition, as is provided for under national law, aimed at compelling a physical or juridical person to do or refrain from doing any act, to commit any of the offences set forth in paragraph 1, subparagraphs (b), (c) and (e), if that threat is likely to endanger the safe navigation of the ship in question.

The convention applies if a ship is navigating, or about to navigate, into, through or from waters beyond the outer limits of the territorial sea of a single state, or the lateral limits of its territorial sea with adjacent states (Article 4). The flag state's ship master may deliver to the authorities of any other state party to the convention any suspected person believed to have committed one of the offenses listed in Article 3. In Article 11, a prosecution guideline is provided for extradiction of the offender. The other convention, 1988 Protocol for the Suppression of Unlawful Acts against the Safety of Fixed Platforms Located on the Continental Shelf, deals with unlawful acts by terrorists against fixed platforms on the continental shelf, or acts of offense listed in the 1988 Convention on Unlawful Acts against the Safety of Navigation.

Article 2 of this Protocol lists the categories of offenses which are unlawful under the agreement.[20]

Article 2

1. Any person commits an offence if that person unlawfully and intentionally:

    (a) Seizes or exercises control over a fixed platform by force or threat thereof or any other form of intimidation; or

    (b) Performs an act of violence against a person on board a fixed platform if that act is likely to endanger its safety; or

    (c) Destroys a fixed platform or causes damage to it which is likely to endanger its safety; or

    (d) Places or causes to be placed on a fixed platform, by any means whatsoever, a device or substance which is likely to destroy that fixed platform or likely to endanger its safety; or

    (e) Injures or kills any person in connection with the commission or the attempted commission of any of the offences set forth in subparagraphs (a) to (d).

2. Any person also commits an offence if that person:

    (a) Attempts to commit any of the offences set forth in paragraph 1; or

    (b) Abets the commission of any such offences perpetrated by any person or is otherwise an accomplice of a person who commits such an offence; or

    (c) Threatens, with or without a condition, as is provided for under national law, aimed at compelling a physical or juridical person to do or refrain

> from doing any act, to commit any of the offences set forth in paragraph 1, subparagraphs (b) and (c), if that threat is likely to endanger the safety of the fixed platforms.

Significance. Rules and regulations for safety at sea have been the responsibility of the flag state, and only to a lesser extent are these the responsibility of the port state (navigational aids and facilities, for example). In this connection, two specialized agencies of the United Nations have played an important role in initiating and drafting the various conventions which provide international standards for safety in navigation: the IMO and the International Labor Organization. The IMO must be credited with the adoption of the 1974 SOLAS and the 1972 Convention on Preventing Collision at Sea. The ILO has been primarily responsible for the adoption of a host of international agreements concerning sailors' welfare and standards or requirements for certification to work in the world's merchant fleets. The effective implementation and observance of these safety-at-sea rules and standards are dependent upon willingness on the part of ship owners and flag states. It is ironic that practically all "flag-of-convenience" states are not parties to many of these international conventions. By permitting the owners to use "flags of convenience," the maritime nations have abrogated their jurisdiction as flag states, which are traditionally responsible for safety at sea. Safety rules and standards are more necessary now than ever before, simply because of the increased number of ships at sea, their enormous size and carrying capacity, and the dangerous goods they carry from one ocean to another.

A number of bilateral agreements and joint declarations have been reached concerning safety of navigation at sea: (1) the Federal Republic of Germany and the Soviet Union on ship collision and signals (October 1988); (2) the United States and the Soviet Union on uniform interpretation about innocent passage (September 1989); (3) the United Kingdom and France on a specific regime of navigation over the Straits of Dover (May 1989); and (4) agreements between the Soviet Union and France and Italy on prevention of incidents at sea outside the territorial sea (July and September 1989). (See also Appendix III.)

SEA LANES AND TRAFFIC SEPARATION SCHEMES FOR NAVIGATION

Navigation at sea began with trade routes that are used for transporting goods from one part of the ocean to another. As trade flourished, it was necessary to designate sea routes or paths used by ships across the oceans—the so-called sea lanes of communications, or SLOC.[21] However, it was not until 1967 that flag states were encouraged to observe traffic separation schemes voluntarily. Then it was the obligation of the flag states to follow traffic separation schemes in accordance with Rule 10 of the 1972 International Regulations for Preventing Collisions at Sea, which came into force in 1977. As stated in Rule 10, the regulations are imposed on ship masters and the flag states as a way of avoiding collisions at sea:

Rule 10: Traffic separation schemes

(a) This Rule applies to traffic separation schemes adopted by the Organization.

(b) A vessel using a traffic separation scheme shall:

(i) proceed in the appropriate traffic lane in the general direction of traffic flow for that lane;

(ii) so far as practicable keep clear of a traffic separation line or separation zone;

(iii) normally join or leave a traffic lane at the termination of the lane, but when joining or leaving from the side shall do so at as small an angle to the general direction of traffic flow as practicable.

(c) A vessel shall so far as practicable avoid crossing traffic lanes, but if obliged to do so shall cross as nearly as practicable at right angles to the general direction of traffic flow.

(d) Inshore traffic zones shall not normally be used by through traffic which can safely use the appropriate traffic lane within the adjacent traffic separation scheme.

(e) A vessel, other than a crossing vessel, shall not normally enter a separation zone or cross a separation line except:

(i) in cases of emergency to avoid immediate danger;

(ii) to engage in fishing within a separation zone.

(f) A vessel navigating in areas near the terminations of traffic separation schemes shall do so with particular caution.

(g) A vessel shall so far as practicable avoid anchoring in a traffic separation scheme or in areas near its terminations.

(h) A vessel not using a traffic separation scheme shall avoid it by as wide a margin as is practicable.

(i) A vessel engaged in fishing shall not impede the passage of any vessel following a traffic lane.

(j) A vessel of less than 20 metres in length or a sailing vessel shall not impede the safe passage of a power-driven vessel following a traffic lane.

It was reported by the IMCO/IMO that the effect of Rule 10 has been an appreciable reduction in the number of collisions at sea—in the northwest European waters, collisions decreased from 156 during 1956 to 1961 to about 45 during 1976 to 1981.[22] In Article 22 of the 1982 LOS Convention the coastal states are granted the right to designate sea lanes and traffic separation schemes:

Article 22: Sea lanes and traffic separation schemes in the territorial sea

1. The coastal State may, where necessary having regard to the safety of navigation, require foreign ships exercising the right of innocent passage through its territorial sea to use such sea lanes and traffic separation schemes as it may designate or prescribe for the regulation of the passage of ships.

2. In particular, tankers, nuclear-powered ships and ships carrying nuclear or other

inherently dangerous or noxious substances or materials may be required to confine their passage to such sea lanes.

3. In the designation of sea lanes and the prescription of traffic separation schemes under this article, the coastal State shall take into account:

(a) the recommendations of the competent international organization;

(b) any channels customarily used for international navigation;

(c) the special characteristics of particular ships and channels; and

(d) the density of traffic.

4. The coastal State shall clearly indicate such sea lanes and traffic separation schemes on charts to which due publicity shall be given.

However, under Article 41 of the 1982 LOS Convention, in designating sea lanes and traffic separation schemes, states bordering international straits must ensure that these regulations "conform to generally accepted international standards." The proposals for such sea lanes must be submitted to the IMO, as the competent international organization, "with a view to their adoption."

The 1982 LOS Convention establishes not only a new ocean regime of archipelagic waters, but the specific right of archipelagic states to designate sea lanes for passage through their archipelagic waters. Article 53 stipulates that:

Article 53: Right of archipelagic sea lanes passage

1. An archipelagic State may designate sea lanes and air routes thereabove, suitable for the continuous and expeditious passage of foreign ships and aircraft through or over its archipelagic waters and the adjacent territorial sea.

2. All ships and aircraft enjoy the right of archipelagic sea lanes passage in such sea lanes and air routes.

3. Archipelagic sea lanes passage means the exercise in accordance with this Convention of the rights of navigation and overflight in the normal mode solely for the purpose of continuous, expeditious and unobstructed transit between one part of the high seas or an exclusive economic zone and another part of the high seas or an exclusive economic zone.

4. Such sea lanes and air routes shall traverse the archipelagic waters and the adjacent territorial sea and shall include all normal passage routes used as routes for international navigation or overflight through or over archipelagic waters and, within such routes, so far as ships are concerned, all normal navigational channels, provided that duplication of routes of similar convenience between the same entry and exit points shall not be necessary.

5. Such sea lanes and air routes shall be defined by a series of continuous axis lines from the entry points of passage routes to the exit points. Ships and aircraft in archipelagic sea lanes passage shall not deviate more than 25 nautical miles to either side of such axis lines during passage, provided that such ships and aircraft shall not navigate closer to the coasts than 10 per cent of the distance between the nearest points on islands bordering the sea lane.

6. An archipelagic State which designates sea lanes under this article may also prescribe traffic separation schemes for the safe passage of ships through narrow channels in such sea lanes.

7. An archipelagic State may, when circumstances require, after giving due publicity thereto, substitute other sea lanes or traffic separation schemes for any sea lanes or traffic separation schemes previously designated or prescribed by it.

8. Such sea lanes and traffic separation schemes shall conform to generally accepted international regulations.

9. In designating or substituting sea lanes or prescribing or substituting traffic separation schemes, an archipelagic State shall refer proposals to the competent international organization with a view to their adoption. The organization may adopt only such sea lanes and traffic separation schemes as may be agreed with the archipelagic State, after which the archipelagic State may designate, prescribe or substitute them.

10. The archipelagic State shall clearly indicate the axis of the sea lanes and the traffic separation schemes designated or prescribed by it on charts to which due publicity shall be given.

11. Ships in archipelagic sea lanes passage shall respect applicable sea lanes and traffic separation schemes established in accordance with this article.

12. If an archipelagic State does not designate sea lanes or air routes, the right of archipelagic sea lanes passage may be exercised through the routes normally used for international navigation.

The key point in Article 53 is that, as stated in paragraph 3, archipelagic sea lane passage is identical with that of transit passage through straits, as defined in Article 38(2):

> The rights of navigation and overflight are solely for the purpose of innocent passage or ''continuous, expeditious and unobstructed transit'' between a part of the high seas or an EEZ and another part of the high seas or an EEZ. Such transit passage shall be non-suspendable or ''unobstructed.''

Some scholars, however, point out that there seems to be a distinction between the archipelagic sea lane passage under Article 53(3) and that of transit passage through straits under Article 38(2)—that is the difference between freedom of navigation and overflight and the freedom of the high seas.[23] Article 53(4) stipulates that ships have the right to use ''all normal passage routes used for international navigation and overflight through or over archipelagic waters.'' In designating sea lanes for its archipelagic waters, the archipelagic state must submit the routing proposals to the IMO ''with a view to their adoption.'' It is not clear whether it is mandatory for the archipelagic states to designate sea lanes and traffic separation schemes. If the archipelagic state does not designate the sea lanes in its waters, then the ships must use normal or traditional navigational routes. Designation of sea lanes can be seen in the proposed Indonesian archipelagic sea lanes pictured in Figure 11.1.

Figure 11.1
Proposed Indonesian Archipelagic Sea Lanes

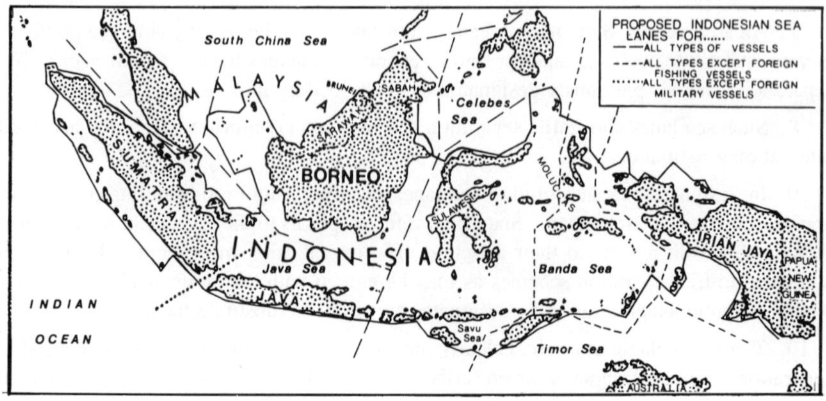

Source: J. R. Morgan and M. J. Valencia, eds., *Atlas for Marine Policy in Southeast Asian Sea* (1983), in *International Navigation: Rocks and Shoals Ahead?*, Jon M. Van Dyke, Lewis M. Alexander and Joseph R. Morgan, eds. (Honolulu: Law of the Sea Institute, University of Hawaii, 1988), p. 195. Used by permission.

Article 53(5) establishes some specific requirements for sea lanes in the archipelagic waters: "Such sea lanes and air routes shall be defined by a series of continuous axis lines from the entry points of passage routes to the exit points." And ships and aircraft traversing the archipelagic sea lanes passage "shall not deviate more than twenty-five nautical miles to either side of such axis lines during passage." Nor shall ships and aircraft "navigate closer to the coasts than 10 percent of the distance between the nearest points on islands bordering the sea lane." Ships and aircraft, under Articles 54 and 39, are required not to use force or threat of force and must comply with "generally accepted international regulations, procedures and practices" in the avoidance of collision and pollution control.

These articles are silent with respect to what happens in cases of noncompliance during passage in sea lanes in archipelagic waters. Indonesia takes the view that, as an archipelagic state, it has the right to take appropriate measures.[24] Because of Indonesia's geographical and historical background, it has been argued that the rights of the archipelagic state are not limited only to designating sea lanes and traffic separation schemes. Thus, in designating archipelagic sea lanes, Indonesia has the right to take into account the factors of traffic concentration, navigation safety, economic development, exploration and exploitation of living and nonliving resources, and geographic realities.[25]

Significance. Through the efforts of the IMO, there are now more than ninety sea lanes and traffic separation schemes in operation for international navigation. The main purpose for designating sea lanes and traffic separation schemes is to prevent collision by ships at sea. In this sense, it is perhaps appropriate to state that international navigation is regulated for reasons of maritime safety, potential ship accidents at sea that cause property damage, loss of life and damage to the marine environment. Sea lanes and traffic separation schemes represent but one of the more important regulatory measures for the control of navigation. Taken together, the 1972 International Regulations for Preventing Collisions at Sea, and the various provisions in the 1982 LOS Convention, provide "an international legal umbrella" for a system of vessel traffic and safety control for international navigation. As vessel traffic becomes more congested, and as tankers cause more oil spills, future shipping transit at sea will be increasingly subject to new systems of control and regulation, particularly in vessel traffic and routing by coastal states and competent international organizations such as the IMO, designated by the 1982 LOS Convention. Thus, vessel traffic management is a timely key to future regulated navigation at sea, a topic discussed at the nineteenth Law of the Sea Institute Conference in 1985.[26]

However, there is some doubt as to whether use of sea lanes is legally binding on all ships in straits and archipelagic waters as it is in territorial waters. Thus, the right to designate sea lanes and traffic separation schemes remains the primary issue for shipping and navigation at sea. The role to be played by the IMO in sea lane designation is also uncertain. In short, together with the various maritime zonal claims, navigational routes and sea lanes will continue to pose problems and affect the freedom of navigation for many trading nations.[27]

NOTES

1. Lewis M. Alexander, "Uncertainties in the Aftermath of UNCLOS III: The Case for Navigational Freedoms," *Ocean Development and International Law* 18, no. 3 (1987): 334–342.

2. John D. Negroponte, "Who Will Protect the Freedom of the Seas?" Thomas A. Clingan, Jr., ed., *The Law of the Sea: What Lies Ahead?* (Honolulu: The Law of the Sea Institute, University of Hawaii, 1988), p. 127.

3. See P. J. Slot, "The International Legal Regime for Navigation," *Ocean Development and International Law* 15, no. 1 (1985): 89–98. Also see R. P. Anand, "Transit Passage and Overflight in International Straits," in Jon M. Van Dyke, Lewis M. Alexander and Joseph R. Morgan, eds., *International Navigation: Rocks and Shoals Ahead?* (Honolulu: Law of the Sea Institute, University of Hawaii, 1988), pp. 125–149; and L. V. Speranokaya, "Marine Environmental Protection and Freedom of Navigation in International Law," in Elisabeth Mann Borgese and Norton Ginsburg, eds., *Ocean Yearbook 6* (Chicago: University of Chicago Press, 1986), pp. 197–202.

4. "International Shipping and the New Law of the Sea: New Directions for a Traditional Use?" *Ocean Development and International Law* 20, no. 5 (1989): 437.

5. R. R. Churchill and A. V. Lowe, *The Law of the Sea* (Manchester, England: University of Manchester Press, 1983), p. 180.

6. Ibid., p. 181; and also see William T. Burke, "Contemporary Developments Affecting Navigation Rights in the Law of the Sea," in Clingan, ed., *The Law of the Sea*, p. 141.

7. George C. Kasoulides, "The 1986 United Nations Convention on the Condition

for Registration of Vessels and the Question of Open Registry,'' *Ocean Development and International Law* 20, no. 6 (1989): 547. Also see G. S. Egiyan, '' 'Flag of Convenience' or 'Open Registration' of Ships,'' *Marine Policy* 14, no. 2 (March 1990): 106–111.

8. See *Law of the Sea Bulletin*, no. 7, April 1986, pp. 81–100. For commentary on the convention, see Burke, ''Contemporary Developments Affecting Navigation Rights in the Law of the Sea,'' pp. 141–142; and Kasoulides, ''The 1986 United Nations Convention,'' pp. 543–576.

9. Burke, ''Contemporary Developments Affecting Navigation Rights,'' p. 142; and Kasoulides, ''The 1986 United Nations Convention,'' p. 566.

10. See Louis B. Sohn, ''International Law of the Sea and Human Rights Issues,'' and Irwin P. Stozky, ''Interdiction at Sea and the Fourth Amendment,'' in Clingan, ed., *The Law of the Sea*, pp. 51–71 and 72–109.

11. See Stefan A. Riesenfeld, ''High Seas and Navigational Rights: What Are They and Who May Assert Them in U.S. Courts?'' in Clingan, ed., *The Law of the Sea*, pp. 41–50.

12. See Andrew W. Anderson, ''In the Wake of the Dauntless: The Background and Development of Maritime Interdiction Operations,'' in Clingan, ed., *The Law of the Sea*, pp. 13–32. For the period of 1978 to the fall of 1980, the United States Coast Guard seized 316 vessels, about 15 percent of which lacked clear flag nationality identity; 70 percent of all vessels seized were American.

13. See Kimberly A. Strang, ''Foreign Search and Seizure: The Fourth Amendment at Large,'' *San Diego Law Review* 25, no. 3 (August–September 1988): 609–630. Also see ''High on the Seas: Drug Smuggling, the Fourth Amendment, and Warrantless Searches at Sea,'' *Harvard Law Review* 725 (1980).

14. See Riesenfeld, ''High Seas and Navigational Rights,'' pp. 46–47.

15. Strang, ''Foreign Search and Seizure,'' pp. 629–630.

16. Stozky, ''Interdiction at Sea and the Fourth Amendment,'' p. 77.

17. John P. Craven, ''Freedom of Navigation for War, Commerce and Piracy,'' in Van Dyke, Alexander and Morgan, eds., *International Navigation*, p. 34.

18. Slot, ''The International Legal Regime for Navigation,'' p. 91.

19. Text can be found in *Law of the Sea Bulletin*, no. 11, July 1986, pp. 14–23.

20. Ibid., pp. 24–27.

21. See Bernhard J. Abrahamsson, ''Commercial Sea Lanes of Communications,'' in Van Dyke, Alexander and Morgan, eds., *International Navigation*, pp. 39–48.

22. See *IMCO News*, no. 4, 1981, p. 3; and Churchill and Lowe, *The Law of the Sea*, p. 187.

23. See Nugroho Wisnumurti, ''Archipelagic Waters and Archipelagic Sea Lanes,'' in Van Dyke, Alexander and Morgan, eds., *International Narigation*, pp. 204–205. Also see Bernard Oxman, ''The Regime of Warships under the United Nations Law of the Seas,'' *Virginia Journal of International Law* 24, no. 809 (1984): 858–861; and Slot, ''The International Legal Regime for Navigation,'' pp. 93–96.

24. Wisnumurti, ''Archipelagic Waters and Archipelagic Sea Lanes,'' p. 211.

25. Atje Misbach Muhjiddin, ''Some Aspects that Should Be Considered in Designating Indonesia's Sea Lanes,'' in Van Dyke, Alexander, and Morgan, eds., *International Navigation*, pp. 212–219.

26. See articles by Edgar Gold, ''Marine Hazards and Casualties: The Need for Vessel Traffic Management''; Thomas A. Mensah, ''The International Regulation of Maritime

Traffic: IMO Approaches''; and R. O. Gross and J. E. Halliday, ''The Cost and Benefits of Navigational Safety''; in E. D. Brown and R. R. Churchill, eds., *The UN Convention on the Law of the Sea: Impact and Implementation* (Honolulu: Law of the Sea Institute, University of Hawaii, 1987), pp. 477–513. Also, Gold, ''Ocean Shipping and the New Law of the Sea: Toward a More Regulatory Regime,'' pp. 92–96.

27. See Lewis M. Alexander, *Navigational Restrictions within the New LOS Context: Geographical Implications for the United States* (Peace Dale, R.I.: Offshore Consultants, December 1986).

CHAPTER 12

Marine Scientific Research and Technological Transfer

Since the end of World War II marine scientific research, which may be defined as any systematic study whose objective is to increase knowledge about the marine environment, has assumed an ever-increasing role in the development of ocean uses. Without a scientific understanding and knowledge of the geological formation of the continental shelf, there would probably be no discovery of offshore resources such as oil and gas. The study of the physical features of the seabed led to the discovery of mineral resources such as manganese nodules. Scientific study and monitoring of the size and recruitment of fishery stocks made it possible to regulate the harvest of a particular stock at a level that would not lead to overfishing. Ongoing scientific research is crucial to devising methods of controlling damage to the marine environment caused by pollution from land-based and vessel sources. And, finally, scientific research has contributed enormously to the uses of military weaponry and highly advanced military technology on the ocean.

This chapter begins with an examination of the key issue of access to and consent for marine scientific research by coastal states under the different regimes provided in the 1982 LOS Convention. From the outset, it must be pointed out that marine scientific research depends on access to the continental shelf where 90 percent of the ocean's living resources and most of the nonliving resources (oil and gas) are found. Thus, the requirement for a coastal state's consent in order to conduct marine scientific research on the continental shelf became an acceptable practice in international law under the 1958 Convention on the Continental Shelf (Article 5).

Restrictions on marine scientific research proliferated at the time when UNCLOS III was convened as the developing Third World nations, organized as the Group of 77, demanded their share of benefits to be derived from the exploration and exploitation of living and nonliving resources of the seas. As they struck their bargains at the UNCLOS III negotiation sessions, concessions and compromises were made by the world's traditional maritime powers. As soon as World War II ended in 1945, marine scientific research and technological advancement led to the rapid discovery of the ocean's natural resources. In the new ocean regime of archipelagic waters and the traditional territorial waters, under Article 245 of the 1982 LOS Convention, the coastal states have the exclusive right to grant or withhold access for conducting marine scientific research. In the new ocean regimes of the continental shelf and the exclusive economic zone (EEZ), Article 246 created for the coastal states the "full consent regime" with discretionary power to withhold consent for marine scientific research conducted by another state.

While Article 87 of the 1982 LOS Convention recognizes the freedom to engage in marine scientific research as one of the freedoms of the high seas, Article 257 nevertheless restricts the freedom to all scientific research "in the water column beyond the limits of the exclusive economic zone," and thus excludes the seabed and the subsoil thereof where the continental shelf extends beyond the exclusive economic zone. Under Article 143, for the International Seabed Area, all states and competent international organizations are granted the right to conduct marine scientific research on these conditions: for peaceful purposes, for the benefit of technology-poor developing states, for the training of personnel of developing nations and of the Authority, and for disseminating the results of the research.

One of the effects of the coastal states' power to grant or withhold consent for conducting marine scientific research in regimes for which they have jurisdiction is that freedom for such research is rather limited, or practically nonexistent. The coastal states' "full consent regime" in marine scientific research will inevitably generate more bureaucratic paperwork in the processing of requests. And the requirements for fulfillment of the detailed conditions contained in the 1982 LOS Convention will most likely increase the cost for conducting these research projects.

One of the primary reasons for granting coastal states control over marine scientific research is the difficulty in distinguishing with any degree of certainty between genuine marine research and those projects designed or disguised for military purposes. This has been the cause for suspicion on the part of the developing Third World nations. (The celebrated cases of the *Pueblo* and Howard Hughes's *Glomar Explorer* were illustrations of research vessels used for military intelligence purposes.) It is against this background that, in Article 240, the 1982 LOS Convention, after lengthy debate and negotiation, laid down a set of general principles for the conduct of marine scientific research, among which is the tenet that such research "shall be conducted exclusively for peaceful purposes." However, for practical purposes there is no legal basis on which to prohibit military research for which consent has been given from being conducted within a coastal state's continental shelf or EEZ.

Under the 1982 LOS Convention only states, regardless of their geographic location, and competent international organizations have the right to conduct marine scientific research, but not scientific institutions. The latter must work through or under the authority of a state or a competent international organization. All states are entitled to conduct marine scientific research—this includes landlocked and geographically disadvantaged states (Article 254). (The practical application of Article 254 may present some problems, including the proviso that the consent-seeking coastal state must notify all concerned landlocked and geographically disadvantaged states.) Thus, as experienced by Sir C. Wyville Thomson's *Challenger* in 1877 under the auspices of the University of Edinburgh, the free and unimpeded exploration on the oceans is no longer possible in this day and age. The coastal state's jurisdiction over ocean space and ocean activities has been expanded and become more restrictive—all under Article 246 of the 1982 LOS Convention which establishes the "consent regime" for marine scientific research on the continental shelf and in the exclusive economic zone.

The restrictive nature of conducting marine scientific research on the continental shelf and in the EEZ can be seen in the procedures outlined by Article 248, 249, 252 and 253 of the 1982 LOS Convention concerning consent requirements with respect to notification, application and eventual consent by the coastal state. While the procedure calls for six-month's advance notification, bureaucratic delay is inevitable in such cases. Despite the Group of 77 opposition, the concept of "implied consent" was endorsed by UNCLOS III in Article 252 to allow adequate time for a coastal state to decide whether consent is to be given or withheld. By acceding to "implied consent," the developing Third World, in another aspect, seems to have gained the imposition of certain conditions to which the research requesting state must comply: to ensure their participation in the research project and to provide the consenting coastal state access to all data and scientific samples, as well as results and conclusions of the project. Under Article 253, the consenting coastal state's discretionary power to order cessation or suspend a marine scientific research project is almost absolute. Here may lie the seed for possible disputes over a very important new use of the ocean.

A very complex procedure has been provided in Articles 264 and 287 for dispute settlement involving marine scientific research, generally a costly undertaking. Article 287(1) offers four alternatives for dispute settlement: the International Court of Justice (ICJ), the Law of the Sea Tribunal, an arbitral tribunal or a special arbitral tribunal. The process becomes more complicated if no settlement can be reached by use of the above alternatives, the application of Annex V (Section 2) or Article 297(2): compulsory submission to conciliation must then be enforced. One sees only a long tedious legal process in the settlement of marine scientific research disputes.

This chapter ends its discussion with the topic of marine technology transfer about which the 1982 LOS Convention devotes a total of thirteen articles. While these provisions are designed to promote technological transfer from industrialized technology-rich nations to the developing technology-poor Third World nations, a glaring deficiency in the convention has been the lack of agreed criteria and standards for technology transfer. One would hope that specialized agencies in the United Nations system, such as the UNCTAD and the World Intellectual Property Organization, might eventually work out a code of conduct for the transfer of technology which would be generally acceptable to all states.

In conclusion, the 1982 LOS Convention has established a "consent regime" for marine scientific research, which empowers the coastal states with a great deal of prerogatives for control. To what extent these powers of control over marine scientific research are to be exercised by the coastal states will be dependent in the future upon the degree of mutual trust that can be cultivated between the consenting coastal states and the researching states. Bilateral and international/regional arrangements for cooperation in marine scientific research can supplement and enhance the full realization of some of the basic objectives in the 1982 LOS Convention. In the final analysis, a coastal state's restriction on scientific marine research may be lessened if there is an increase in the coastal state's incentive to allow such research in its jurisdiction without having to convene a new international conference to reinstate the principle of free access for scientific research.

ACCESS TO AND CONSENT OF COASTAL STATES FOR MARINE SCIENTIFIC RESEARCH AT SEA

One of the contentious issues in marine scientific research has been the need for marine scientists to have access to ocean areas free of governmental interference. That situation prevailed before World War II when the attitude of governments was toward no restriction and, to a large extent, marine research was limited to practical application.[1] With the rapid technological development in exploitation and exploration of living and nonliving resources, plus the emergence of developing Third World nations eager for the acquisition of technology for resources development, governmental control over marine scientific research first surfaced as an issue in the 1958 UNCLOS I. It then expanded into an important concern (Part XIII) of the 1982 LOS Convention.

Even though a comment by the International Law Commission, which prepared the various drafts for the UNCLOS I, did refer to the "freedom to engage in scientific research" as another freedom of the high seas recognized by the general principles of international law, the 1958 Convention on the High Seas did not include freedom of marine scientific research in Article 2 as one of the specified freedoms of the high seas.[2] However, the topic did come up for debate in the drafting of the Convention on the Continental Shelf. The subject of marine scientific research was discussed in relation to the continental shelf, since continental shelf and the coastal zone are the most important areas for marine scientific research. Ninety percent of the world's fishery and mineral resources of the sea come from this area and the waters above it. To a large extent marine scientific research depends on access to the continental shelf and the coastal area. Thus, Article 5(1) of the 1958 Convention on the Continental Shelf provides the broad principle that:

Article 5

1. The exploration of the continental shelf and the exploitation of its natural resources must not result in any unjustifiable interference with navigation, fishing or the conservation of the living resources of the sea, nor result in any interference with fundamental oceanographic or other scientific research carried out with the intention of open publication.

However, Article 5(8) modifies the general principle of marine scientific research on the continental shelf with the restriction that

8. The consent of the coastal State shall be obtained in respect of any research concerning the continental shelf and undertaken there. Nevertheless, the coastal State shall not normally withhold its consent if the request is submitted by a qualified institution with a view to purely scientific research into the physical or biological characteristics of the continental shelf, subject to the proviso that the coastal State shall have the right, if it so desires, to participate or to be represented in the research, and that in any event the results shall be published.

With regard to Article 5(8), scholars have pointed out the many interpretations of the phrase, "any research concerning the continental shelf and undertaken there." Consent is required on any research conducted on the continental shelf and the seabed, or consent is not required if research is conducted in the superjacent waters only.[3]

By the time the UNCLOS III had concluded negotiations and prepared its final draft on a comprehensive law of the sea convention, considerable restrictions had been placed on marine scientific research in the various ocean regimes. The following is a summary of the 1982 LOS Convention requirements for a coastal state's consent to conduct scientific research.

Archipelagic Waters and Territorial Sea

Coastal states have the "exclusive right" over marine scientific research conducted in the territorial sea. Article 245 stipulates:

Article 245: Marine scientific research in the territorial sea

Coastal States, in the exercise of their sovereignty, have the exclusive right to regulate, authorize and conduct marine scientific research in their territorial sea. Marine scientific research therein shall be conducted only with the express consent of and under the conditions set forth by the coastal State.

This means that a coastal state may prohibit the engagement in marine scientific research in the territorial sea by any other state or its nationals. Or, it may, if consent is given, impose conditions for the conduct of scientific research in the territorial sea. Also, the article implies that it is not permissible to conduct marine scientific research when the research vessel is exercising innocent passage, for such activities conducted without a coastal state's consent are noninnocent.[4] The same would apply with respect to transit passage in archipelagic waters and sea lanes, for under Article 49 of the 1982 LOS Convention, the archipelagic state has full sovereignty over its archipelagic waters.

Continental Shelf and Exclusive Economic Zone

Coastal states have the right to control and regulate marine scientific research on the continental shelf and in the exclusive economic zone (EEZ), as governed by Article 246:

Article 246: Marine scientific research in the exclusive economic zone and on the continental shelf

1. Coastal States, in the exercise of their jurisdiction, have the right to regulate, authorize and conduct marine scientific research in their exclusive economic zone and on their continental shelf in accordance with the relevant provisions of this Convention.

2. Marine scientific research in the exclusive economic zone and on the continental shelf shall be conducted with the consent of the coastal State.

3. Coastal States shall, in normal circumstances, grant their consent for marine scientific research projects by other States or competent international organizations in their exclusive economic zone or on their continental shelf to be carried out in accordance with this Convention exclusively for peaceful purposes and in order to increase scientific knowledge of the marine environment for the benefit of all mankind. To this end, coastal States shall establish rules and procedures ensuring that such consent will not be delayed or denied unreasonably.

4. For the purposes of applying paragraph 3, normal circumstances may exist in spite of the absence of diplomatic relations between the coastal State and the researching State.

5. Coastal States may however in their discretion withhold their consent to the conduct of a marine scientific research project of another State or competent international organization in the exclusive economic zone or on the continental shelf of the coastal State if that project:

(a) is of direct significance for the exploration and exploitation of natural resources, whether living or non-living;

(b) involves drilling into the continental shelf, the use of explosives or the introduction of harmful substances into the marine environment;

(c) involves the construction, operation or use of artificial islands, installations and structures referred to in articles 60 and 80;

(d) contains information communicated pursuant to article 248 regarding the nature and objectives of the project which is inaccurate or if the researching State or competent international organization has outstanding obligations to the coastal State from a prior research project.

6. Notwithstanding the provisions of paragraph 5, coastal States may not exercise their discretion to withhold consent under subparagraph (a) of that paragraph in respect of marine scientific research projects to be undertaken in accordance with the provisions of this Part on the continental shelf, beyond 200 nautical miles from the baselines from which the breadth of the territorial sea is measured, outside those specific areas which coastal States may at any time publicly designate as areas in which exploitation or detailed exploratory operations focused on those areas are occurring or will occur within a reasonable period of time. Coastal States shall give reasonable notice of the designation of such areas, as well as any modifications thereto, but shall not be obliged to give details of the operations therein.

7. The provisions of paragraph 6 are without prejudice to the rights of coastal States over the continental shelf as established in article 77.

8. Marine scientific research activities referred to in this article shall not unjustifiably interfere with activities undertaken by coastal States in the exercise of their sovereign rights and jurisdiction provided for in this Convention.

In Article 76, the 1982 LOS Convention defines the continental shelf as "the seabed and subsoil of the submarine area that extends beyond the territorial sea throughout the natural prolongation of its land territory to the outer edge of the continental margin, or to a distance of 200 nautical miles from the baseline from which the breadth of the territorial sea is measured." As pointed out in Chapter 3, that definition comprises the entire continental margin to include the shelf proper (averaging about one-hundred meters), the slope (about 1,500–3,000 meters), and the rise (descent to the level of the seabed at about 3,500–5,000 meters).

For the coastal states, Article 246(2) creates a "full consent regime" for both the continental shelf and the EEZ.[5] For marine scientists, Article 246 endeavors to differentiate between applied and pure research on the continental shelf and in the EEZ. Paragraph (3), or the rather vague phrase "in normal circumstances," implies that the coastal state would ordinarily give consent for marine scientific research "exclusively for peaceful purposes" and for increased "scientific knowledge of the marine environment for the benefit of all mankind."[6] But paragraph 5(a) states that consent may be withheld by a coastal state at its discretion for any research project of another state or competent international organization which "is of direct significance for the exploration and exploitation of natural resources, whether living or non-living." Then, in paragraphs (b), (c) and (d), it expands the coastal state's discretionary power to withhold consent on marine research projects that involve drilling on the continental shelf with the use of explosives, the use of artificial islands and installations, or contain inaccurate information or for failure to meet the obligations to the coastal state.

The coastal state's discretionary power to give or withhold consent for marine research on its continental shelf and in the EEZ is tantamount to being absolute, for Article 297(2)(a)(i) exempts any dispute arising from interpretation of the applicability of Article 264 from a compulsory dispute settlement procedure. It should be pointed out that the United States, in proclaiming the establishment of the EEZ on March 10, 1983, announced its decision not to place restrictions on other states for marine scientific research in the EEZ as a demonstration of its interest "in encouraging marine scientific research and avoiding any unnecessary burdens," but at the same time recognizing the jurisdiction of other coastal states over marine scientific research within their 200 nautical mile EEZ.

On the High Seas and Seabed Area

Several key provisions in the 1982 LOS Convention govern marine scientific research on the high seas. One, Article 87 defines freedom of the high seas to comprise not only the traditional freedoms of navigation, overflight, cable laying, and fishing, but also freedom of scientific research and to construct artificial islands and platforms. The inclusion of the freedom to engage in marine scientific research as one of the freedoms of the high seas has finally corrected the deficiency of the 1958 Convention on the High Seas—a matter of considerable concern to the world's marine scientists. Article 87, in essence, refers not only to marine scientific research, but to all scientific research in the water column, seabed and subsoil thereof and the air space above.

During the various negotiation sessions at the committee level, the concept of freedom for marine scientific research on the high seas was contained in the proposals of several delegations, particularly those of Canada, the United States, Malta, the landlocked states and the nine eastern European states.[7] As early as 1976, at the fourth session of the UNCLOS III, informal meetings seemed to favor a general consensus on the right of all states, regardless of their geographic location, to conduct marine scientific research. This agreement became Article 238 of the 1982 LOS Convention. But, more important is Article 257, which specifically limits freedom to do scientific research to the high seas area only:

> All states, irrespective of their geographic location, and competent international organizations, have the right, in conformity with this Convention, to conduct marine scientific research in the water column beyond the limits of the exclusive economic zone.

Thus, it excludes the seabed and subsoil thereof or when the continental shelf extends beyond the EEZ and the Area, since the right to conduct marine scientific research is governed by Articles 246, as discussed earlier.

Two key articles of the 1982 LOS Convention govern the access to and the right of marine scientific research in the Area (International Seabed Area). Article 143 stipulates:

Article 143: Marine scientific research

1. Marine scientific research in the Area shall be carried out exclusively for peaceful purposes and for the benefit of mankind as a whole, in accordance with Part XIII.

2. The Authority may carry out marine scientific research concerning the Area and its

resources, and may enter into contracts for that purpose. The Authority shall promote and encourage the conduct of marine scientific research in the Area, and shall co-ordinate and disseminate the results of such research and analysis when available.

3. States Parties may carry out marine scientific research in the Area. States Parties shall promote international co-operation in marine scientific research in the Area by:

(a) participating in international programmes and encouraging co-operation in marine scientific research by personnel of different countries and of the Authority;

(b) ensuring that programmes are developed through the Authority or other international organizations as appropriate for the benefit of developing States and technologically less developed States with a view to:

(i) strengthening their research capabilities;

(ii) training their personnel and the personnel of the Authority in the techniques and applications of research;

(iii) fostering the employment of their qualified personnel in research in the Area;

(c) effectively disseminating the results of research and analysis when available, through the Authority or other international channels when appropriate.

Article 256 grants all states, regardless of their geographic location, and competent international organizations the right to conduct marine scientific research in the Area, so long as it is in conformity with the various provisions dealing with the Area or in Part XI of the LOS Convention. For instance, Article 143 requires that marine scientific research in the Area be for peaceful purposes and for the benefit of all mankind.

Significance. Two important developments concerning marine scientific research emerged from the 1982 LOS Convention. One is the prerogative of the coastal states in deciding whether or not to grant a request for a marine scientific research project. From this point of view, under the 1982 LOS Convention, there is a considerable erosion of the rights and freedom for marine scientific research. Article 246(5) gives the coastal states many grounds on which a request for conducting marine scientific research could be granted or denied. Thus, it is now difficult to maintain that there is such a concept as ''unlimited and uncontrolled freedom'' of scientific research on the ocean.

Second, coastal states' prerogatives with respect to access for marine scientific research have been enlarged not only to the exclusive economic zone, but also extended to the continental shelf beyond the 200 nautical miles. This amounts to a total of about 42 percent of the ocean. As discussed earlier, this is the area that is most important to marine scientists and where most research projects would be conducted.

State practice in giving consent or denial for requests to engage in marine scientific research can be seen in part from Table 12.1 of requests to the United States Department of State for research clearance in waters of coastal

Table 12.1
Summary of Clearance Experience

Country	Requests						Total	Total
	1979	1980	1981	1982	1983	1984	Requests	"Denials"
Antigua					1	1	2	0
Argentina	1		3			3	7	0
Australia	2					1	3	0
Bahamas	3	4	5	4	5	7	28	0
Bahrain					1		1	1
Barbados	1	1	3	1	5	5	16	1
Belize			1			1	2	0
Brazil	4			5	3	4	16	2
Canada	14	22	14	16	27	35	128	0
Chile	4	1	2	2	5	6	20	0
China		1					1	0
Costa Rica	1	1	1	1		1	5	1
Colombia					1		1	1
Cuba	3	1					4	4
Denmark			1		3	1	5	0
Dominica	2		1			2	5	0
Dominican Republic	2	4		1		6	13	1
Ecuador				3	3	1	7	0
Egypt					1	4	5	0
Fiji							3	0
France	2	2	1	3	4		12	0
French Guiana					1		1	0
Granada	1					2	3	0
Guatemala			2			1	3	0
Guyana	1					1	2	0
Haiti	1	1	2	2	2	5	13	1
Honduras			1	1	1	3	6	0
Iceland					3		3	0
Indonesia	1	1					2	1
Ivory Coast					1		1	0
Jamaica	1	1	1	1	3	1	8	0
Japan						3	3	0
Kiribati						1	1	0
Mexico	33	19	26	12	11	13	114	28
Morocco	1		1	1	2		5	0
Netherlands	1			1	1		3	0
New Zealand	1				1	1	3	0
Nicaragua	1		1				2	1
Norway					5	3	8	0
Panama	2				2	3	7	1
Papua New Guinea	1					2	3	0
Peru	1	1	2	4	4	3	17	0
Philippines	2	2					4	0

Table 12.1 (Continued)

Country	Requests 1979	1980	1981	1982	1983	1984	Total Requests	Total "Denials"
Portugal						6	6	0
Romania						1	1	0
Saudi Arabia					2	2	4	1
Saint Lucia	2	1	2	2		3	10	0
Saint Vincent	1	1	1	1		4	9	0
Solomon Is.				2		1	3	0
Somalia	1		1			1	3	0
South Africa					1	1	2	0
Spain			2	2	2		6	2
Suriname	1					1	2	0
Tonga				1		1	2	0
Trinidad and Tobago	1					1	2	1
Turkey						1	1	0
United Arab Emirates						1	1	0
United Kingdom	3	3	2	3	5	10	26	0
Uruaguay						2	2	0
U.S.S.R.	2					2	4	3
Vanuatu				1		1	2	0
Venezuela	2	1	1	1	2	2	9	2
Requests	100	68	78	72	109	162	589	53
Countries	34	19	24	25	31	48	62	18

Source: John A. Knauss and Mary Hope Katsouros, "The Effect of the Law of the Sea on Marine Scientific Research in the United States: Recent Trends," in *The UN Convention on the Law of the Sea: Impact and Implementation*, E. D. Brown and R. R. Churchill, eds. (Honolulu: The Law of the Sea Institute, University of Hawaii, 1987), pp. 377–378. Used by permission.

state jurisdiction. It needs to be pointed out that 41 percent of the 589 clearance requests by U.S. marine scientists were sought from Canada and Mexico. Of the total of 589 requests, 53 were refusals that consisted of outright denial, delay, no response and unacceptable conditions—all seemed to have stemmed from the coastal states' more rigid application of the 1982 LOS Convention provisions discussed here. If the experience of the scientists is an example, it seems that there have been denials, delays and many opportunities lost.

DEFINITION: PRINCIPLES AND RIGHTS TO MARINE RESEARCH

The question of what constitutes marine scientific research was raised in a subcommittee discussion as early as 1971 when the Seabed Committee of the

United Nations General Assembly was debating on the possible establishment of a deep-seabed regime. Different versions were offered, all purporting to indicate the nature and objective of marine scientific research. Definitions ranging from ''any study . . . intended to increase knowledge about the marine environment'' (Canadian),[8] to the acquisition of ''knowledge of all aspects of the natural processes and phenomena occurring in ocean space, on the seabed and in the subsoil thereof'' (East European),[9] and to ''any systematic investigation . . . the primary aim of which is to increase knowledge of the marine environment for peaceful purpose'' (Maltese).[10] In the 1975–1976 negotiation sessions, the question of definition was simply omitted in the committee report. It was not until the summer of 1978 that the U.S. delegation revived the informal discussion by reintroducing their draft in the Informal Single Negotiation Text (ISNT): ''Marine scientific research means any study or related experimental work designed to increase man's knowledge of the marine environment.'' The 1982 LOS Convention provides no definition of ''marine scientific research'' on the grounds that it is really not necessary, for any applied research dealing with resources exploration and exploitation is covered by those sections of the convention which grant sovereign rights to coastal states. (Exploration and exploitation of deep seabed resources for commercial purposes are the sole jurisdiction of the International Seabed Authority.)

However, the 1982 LOS Convention does provide a set of general principles for conducting marine scientific research regardless of location, on the high seas or in the coastal states' zonal arrangements established by the convention. Article 240 stipulates:

Article 240: General principles for the conduct of marine scientific research

In the conduct of marine scientific research the following principles shall apply:

(a) marine scientific research shall be conducted exclusively for peaceful purposes;

(b) marine scientific research shall be conducted with appropriate scientific methods and means compatible with this Convention;

(c) marine scientific research shall not unjustifiably interfere with other legitimate uses of the sea compatible with this Convention and shall be duly respected in the course of such uses;

(d) marine scientific research shall be conducted in compliance with all relevant regulations adopted in conformity with this Convention including those for the protection and preservation of the marine environment.

The first general principle of conducting marine scientific research exclusively for peaceful purposes seems to be the only one that is controversial. The application of this general principle may be interpreted as a prohibition against marine scientific research for military purposes, on the basis that any form of military use could be considered as ''nonpeaceful'' or incompatible with the United

Nations Charter. However, under Article 246, if a coastal state consents to a marine scientific research project that might have military implications, to be conducted within its zonal jurisdiction, there is no way, from a practical point of view, to stop such activity. Of course, offensive weapon testing might not be considered marine scientific research.

Alfred Soons of the Netherlands provides the following interpretation: If a state wishes to conduct marine scientific research for military purposes on the continental shelf or the EEZ of another state, it must have the consent of that coastal state, in accordance with Article 246; and, under Article 252, must make the results of such research generally available. The other alternative is to carry out the research without consent, and this violates the coastal state's rights.[11] Marine scientific research for military purposes in the archipelagic waters, international sea, high seas and the Area must be governed by Article 244, which requires publication of the research results.[12]

There is another question related to that of whether marine scientific research is one of the specified freedoms of the high seas: Who does, in fact, have the right to conduct marine scientific research in the ocean space? In the early stages of the UNCLOS III negotiation sessions, the general consensus among the delegations seemed to be in favor of endowing all coastal states the right to conduct marine scientific research. The exception was the proposal submitted by the Group of 77, which favored only the coastal states and the International Seabed Authority.[13] In the end, the version proposed by the landlocked and geographically disadvantaged states was adopted as Article 238, which states:

Article 238: Right to conduct marine scientific research

All States, irrespective of their geographical location, and competent international organizations have the right to conduct marine scientific research subject to the rights and duties of other States as provided for in this Convention.

As interpreted by one authority, "competent international organizations" refers to those international or intergovernmental organizations that are authorized by their own charter or constitution or enabling instrument to conduct marine scientific research, in addition to having the qualifications to engage in these scientific activities.[14] Under Article 238, no natural or juridical person—scientific institution, for instance—has the right to conduct marine scientific research except through or under the authority of a state or a competent international organization.[15]

Significance. The importance of Article 238 lies in these areas:

1. It is the legitimate right for all states to conduct marine scientific research, so long as the research is subject to the interests and duties of other states, as explicitly provided in the 1982 LOS Convention.
2. The right to conduct marine scientific research must be governed by a set of general principles as laid down in Article 240(a–d).

3. A competent international organization also has the right to conduct marine scientific research—that is, an intergovernmental organization whose constitution empowers it to engage in scientific research in the ocean.
4. No natural or juridical person—a scientific institution, for example—has the right to conduct marine scientific research; it can do so only under the sponsorship or authority of a state or competent international organization.

DUTY TO PROVIDE INFORMATION AND KNOWLEDGE TO THE CONSENTING STATE: THE PROCESS FOR OBTAINING CONSENT OR REVOCATION

While Article 246 provides the consent regime for marine scientific research on the continental shelf and within the EEZ, Article 248 outlines a set of application procedures for consent by the research-requesting state to the coastal state:

Article 248: Duty to provide information to the coastal State

States and competent international organizations which intend to undertake marine scientific research in the exclusive economic zone or on the continental shelf of a coastal State shall, not less than six months in advance of the expected starting date of the marine scientific research project, provide that State with a full description of:

(a) the nature and objectives of the project;

(b) the method and means to be used, including name, tonnage, type and class of vessels and a description of scientific equipment;

(c) the precise geographical areas in which the project is to be conducted;

(d) the expected date of first appearance and final departure of the research vessels, or deployment of the equipment and its removal, as appropriate;

(e) the name of the sponsoring institution, its director, and the person in charge of the project; and

(f) the extent to which it is considered that the coastal State should be able to participate or to be represented in the project.

The procedure provides an important time element in the application for a coastal state's consent: "no less than six months in advance of the expected starting date of the marine scientific research project." The starting date refers to the day on which the project is planned to begin operation on the continental shelf or within the EEZ. Article 252 states that "States or competent international organizations may proceed with a marine scientific research project six months after the date upon which the information required pursuant to Article 248 was provided to the coastal state." Of course, the application may be submitted to the consenting coastal state earlier to allow ample time for evaluation and for making arrangements to participate in the project. Article 248(f) stipulates: The researching state shall provide a full description on "the extent to which it is considered that the coastal state should be able to participate or to be represented in the project."

The question arises when a researching state follows the application requirements, as laid down in Article 248, but does not receive a reply from the consenting coastal state for some time: Can it then presume that such consent has been given, or must there be prior explicit consent before research activities can commence?[16] In the early 1970s when a proposal was presented at the Seabed Committee debate in the General Assembly to assume consent under the circumstance, the Group of 77 countered with a proposal that called for advanced explicit consent.[17] At the UNCLOS III, a procedure of implied consent was accepted to become the substance of Article 252:

Article 252: Implied consent

States or competent international organizations may proceed with a marine scientific research project six months after the date upon which the information required pursuant to article 248 was provided to the coastal State unless within four months of the receipt of the communication containing such information the coastal State has informed the State or organization conducting the research that:

(a) it has withheld its consent under the provisions of article 246; or

(b) the information given by that State or competent international organization regarding the nature or objectives of the project does not conform to the manifestly evident facts; or

(c) it requires supplementary information relevant to conditions and the information provided for under articles 248 and 249; or

(d) outstanding obligations exist with respect to a previous marine scientific research project carried out by that State or organization, with regard to conditions established in article 249.

The specific provisions of Article 252 may be interpreted as follows:[18] One, the timetable is considered adequate for the consenting coastal state to reach a decision after having evaluated the information provided in the application as outlined in Article 248. Second, implied consent under Article 252 applies to both pure research under Article 246(3) and applied research under paragraph (5). Third, the requirement for supplementary information about the project can be read either as another way for the consenting coastal state to delay its final approval, or a real need for additional information in order to facilitate consent.

In order to enable the consenting coastal state to participate in the project and to have access to the results, the research-requesting state must comply with additional conditions as provided in Article 249 of the 1982 LOS Convention:

Article 249: Duty to comply with certain conditions

1. States and competent international organizations when undertaking marine scientific research in the exclusive economic zone or on the continental shelf of a coastal State shall comply with the following conditions:

(a) ensure the right of the coastal State, if it so desires, to participate or be represented in the marine scientific research project, especially on board research vessels and other craft or scientific research installations, when practicable, without payment of any remuneration to the scientists of the coastal State and without obligation to contribute towards the costs of the project;

(b) provide the coastal State, at its request, with preliminary reports, as soon as practicable, and with the final results and conclusions after the completion of the research;

(c) undertake to provide access for the coastal State, at its request, to all data and samples derived from the marine scientific research project and likewise to furnish it with data which may be copied and samples which may be divided without detriment to their scientific value;

(d) if requested, provide the coastal State with an assessment of such data, samples and research results or provide assistance in their assessment or interpretation;

(e) ensure, subject to paragraph 2, that the research results are made internationally available through appropriate national or international channels, as soon as practicable;

(f) inform the coastal State immediately of any major change in the research programme;

(g) unless otherwise agreed, remove the scientific research installations or equipment once the research is completed.

2. The article is without prejudice to the conditions established by the laws and regulations of the coastal State for the exercise of its discretion to grant or withhold consent pursuant to article 246, paragraph 5, including requiring prior agreement for making internationally available the research results of a project of direct significance for the exploration and exploitation of natural resources.

In paragraph (a) of Article 249(1), representation or participation in the field work implies more than the boarding of a research vessel or aircraft as observers from the consenting coastal state. It may also involve participation in the evaluation of the data. It is the duty of the researching scientists to provide the consenting coastal state with the preliminary report, free of charge, that contains final results and conclusions of the scientific investigation (paragraph b). It is also the duty of the researching scientists to provide direct access to ''all data and samples derived from the marine scientific research project'' (paragraph c). The exact details on methodology for furnishing the data and samples to the consenting coastal state may be arranged by specific agreement between the parties concerned. A potential troublesome point may be paragraph (f) in which the researching state must immediately inform the consenting state of "any major change" in the project. This paragraph must be read in conjunction with Article 246(5)(a–d), discussed earlier, which empowers the consenting coastal state to withhold its consent if any of the project's basic characteristics are not met. Under Article 253, the consenting coastal state also has the right to suspend or call for the cessation of any marine scientific research activities in progress:

Article 253: Suspension or cessation of marine scientific research activities

1. A coastal State shall have the right to require the suspension of any marine scientific research activities in progress within its exclusive economic zone or on its continental shelf if:

(a) the research activities are not being conducted in accordance with the information communicated as provided under article 248 upon which the consent of the coastal State was based; or

(b) the State or competent international organization conducting the research activities fails to comply with the provisions of article 249 concerning the rights of the coastal State with respect to the marine scientific research project.

2. A coastal State shall have the right to require the cessation of any marine scientific research activities in case of any non-compliance with the provisions of article 248 which amounts to a major change in the research project or the research activities.

3. A coastal State may also require cessation of marine scientific research activities if any of the situations contemplated in paragraph 1 are not rectified within a reasonable period of time.

4. Following notification by the coastal State of its decision to order suspension or cessation, States or competent international organizations authorized to conduct marine scientific research activities shall terminate the research activities that are the subject of such a notification.

5. An order of suspension under paragraph 1 shall be lifted by the coastal State and the marine scientific research activities allowed to continue once the researching State or competent international organization has complied with the conditions required under articles 248 and 249.

Article 253, read in its entirety, grants the coastal state considerable power in enforcing its rights at various stages in the conduct of the marine scientific research activities for which it has given consent. Under these conditions, the research vessel must either suspend or cease its activities, but need not immediately depart the continental shelf or the EEZ area, for it still by then enjoys the freedom of navigation as guaranteed by Articles 58 and 87 (freedom of scientific research as one of the high seas freedoms).

Significance. The articles discussed here that deal with notification, application and consent for conducting marine scientific research are controversial and in the end will be determined by state practices between now and the time when the 1982 LOS Convention becomes effective. One controversial question has been: What constitutes the expected starting date of the marine scientific research project: the date when the research plan commences, or the date the research vessel departs, or the date the actual research operation begins in a coastal state's jurisdictional water? Article 252(c), on submitting supplementary information, may be abused for the purpose of preventing a research project from ever being operational.

However, as a whole, Articles 248, 249, 252 and 253 constitute a workable consent regime for marine scientific research. Article 253 grants the consenting coastal states enormous discretionary power in ordering cessation and suspension of a marine scientific research project.

INTERNATIONAL COOPERATION IN MARINE SCIENCE RESEARCH

The exchange and publication of scientific data generated by marine science research is one area where there can be no disagreement. Thus, there is a need for international cooperation in both the exchange and dissemination of scientific information and knowledge. In fact, the basic purpose of the Intergovernmental Oceanographic Commission (IOC), established in 1960 within the UNESCO, is promotion of scientific ocean research for gaining more knowledge about the nature and resources of the ocean. At the nongovernmental level, the Scientific Committee on Ocean Research (SCOR) was formed in 1957 by the International Council of Scientific Unions (ICSU). There has been a long-established tradition among the world's marine scientists of international cooperation in marine research, as evidenced by the number of nongovernmental organizations established for the exchange of information on ocean matters (see Appendix VII).

At UNCLOS III, in addition to Article 143 (discussed earlier), three specific articles were incorporated into the 1982 LOS Convention dealing with the need for promoting international cooperation in marine scientific research. First, there is Article 242 for the promotion of international cooperation:

Article 242: Promotion of International co-operation

1. States and competent international organizations shall, in accordance with the principle of respect for sovereignty and jurisdiction and on the basis of mutual benefit, promote international co-operation in marine scientific research for peaceful purposes.

2. In this context, without prejudice to the rights and duties of States under this Convention, a State, in the application of this Part, shall provide, as appropriate, other States with a reasonable opportunity to obtain from it, or with its co-operation, information necessary to prevent and control damage to the health and safety of persons and to the marine environment.

The important point of Article 242 is in paragraph (2), which mandates that a state which is conducting marine scientific research must provide other states access to information "necessary to prevent and control damage to the health and safety of persons and to the marine environment." Thus, scientific information about underwater volcanic eruptions, or tsunamis, or hurricanes, as well as ocean pollution control and prevention measures, must be shared with other states on a reciprocal basis.

As a way of promoting international cooperation in marine scientific research, Article 243 encourages the creation of favorable conditions, through bilateral or multilateral agreements, for scientists to conduct joint investigations on the ocean environment.

Article 243: Creation of favorable conditions

States and competent international organizations shall co-operate, through the conclusion of bilateral and multilateral agreements, to create favourable conditions for the conduct of marine scientific research in the marine environment and to integrate the efforts of scientists in studying the essence of phenomena and processes occurring in the marine environment and the interrelations between them.

It goes without saying that making research information available to others, or the publication of the research results or findings in a marine scientific research project, is very important. Article 244 then proceeds to outline the methodology for promoting such scientific exchange:

Article 244: Publication and dissemination of information and knowledge

1. States and competent international organizations shall, in accordance with this Convention, make available by publication and dissemination through appropriate channels information on proposed major programmes and their objectives as well as knowledge resulting from marine scientific research.

2. For this purpose, States, both individually and in co-operation with other States and with competent international organizations, shall actively promote the flow of scientific data and information and the transfer of knowledge resulting from marine scientific research, especially to developing States, as well as the strengthening of the autonomous marine scientific research capabilities of developing States through, *inter alia*, programmes to provide adequate education and training of their technical and scientific personnel.

First, it requires publication and dissemination of the proposed research project to be undertaken. Then it calls for making available such research information to developing states, as well as efforts that can be made to strengthen the scientific research capabilities of the developing states. It may mean assistance in the training of scientific personnel and the promotion of such cooperation through the establishment of institutional arrangements. For a discussion of regional cooperation in marine scientific research for fisheries, see Chapter 5; and in pollution control, see Chapter 9.

Significance. Article 244 is one of the most important provisions dealing with global and regional cooperation in marine scientific research, for it places the obligation on all states and competent international organizations "to make available by publication and dissemination" information, data, and results of research projects, so as to increase mankind's knowledge about the marine environment. However, under Article 249(2), if it is not in its own interest to do so, the coastal state may at its discretion refuse to make significant research results available to others.

LEGAL STATUS AND LIABILITIES OF RESEARCH INSTITUTIONS

Marine scientific research employs not only research vessels or aircraft, but also a variety of fixed structures or platforms, known as the ocean data acquisition system (ODAS). These include submersibles, buoys, fixed bottom-bearing installations or devices that can be connected by cables for recording data on shore. The IOC produced a report in 1969 about the legal problems associated with the ODAS.[19] The report was intended to be the basis for a draft convention by an IMO-sponsored conference, but it never came to fruition.[20] However, the 1982 LOS Convention incorporated many of the original key plans concerning the legal status of the ODAS as they had been contained in the IOC report.

First, is Article 258, which states:

Article 258: Deployment and use

The deployment and use of any type of scientific research installations or equipment in any area of the marine environment shall be subject to the same conditions as are prescribed in this Convention for the conduct of marine scientific research in any such area.

The phrase, "subject to the same conditions as are prescribed in this Convention" for conducting marine scientific research, means that:

1. Expressed consent from the coastal state must be obtained for deployment of any ODAS in the territorial sea and archipelagic waters.
2. Coastal consent must be obtained in the manner as governed by Articles 246 and 252 for the continental shelf and the EEZ.
3. Deployment of an ODAS in the area beyond national jurisdiction does not require consent from any coastal state, but is subject to specific conditions provided in Articles 259–262. (These will be discussed shortly.)[21]

Article 258 does not provide clear answers to questions about free-floating buoys, which are unpredictable as to whose coastal state's jurisdiction they might enter or drift into without advance notification. Article 258 does not cover artificial islands, which are governed by Articles 60 and 80—that is, deployment of these structures is the exclusive jurisdiction of the coastal state. The legal status of artificial islands is explained by Article 259:

Article 259: Legal status

The installations or equipment referred to in this section do not possess the status of islands. They have no territorial sea of their own, and their presence does not affect the delimitation of the territorial sea, the exclusive economic zone or the continental shelf.

A key question not addressed by Article 259 is: Which state exercises jurisdiction over these installations and equipment? An answer to the question is provided in Article 262:

Article 262: Identification markings and warning signals

Installations or equipment referred to in this section shall bear identification markings indicating the State of registry or the international organization to which they belong and shall have adequate internationally agreed warning signals to ensure safety at sea and the safety of air navigation, taking into account rules and standards established by competent international organizations.

Thus, if the installations must be registered in a state, then jurisdiction lies in the state of registry, as in the case of a ship by a flag state.

From Chapter 3, it will be recalled that under Article 60(4)–(5) the coastal state is responsible for establishing "a reasonable safety zone" around the artificial islands in its exclusive economic zone, and that the breadth of the safety zone shall not exceed a distance of 500 meters in radius. Article 260 also calls for the establishment of a safety zone around the installations for marine scientific research whose breadth must not exceed 500 meters:

Article 260: Safety zones

Safety zones of a reasonable breadth not exceeding a distance of 500 metres may be created around scientific research installations in accordance with the relevant provisions of this Convention. All States shall ensure that such safety zones are respected by their vessels.

In Article 261, it is also stipulated that the deployment or installation of equipment for marine scientific research must not interfere with normal navigation or "constitute an obstacle to established international shipping routes."

A state or an international organization must be responsible and liable for any action taken while conducting marine scientific research that violates the provisions of the 1982 LOS Convention or causes pollution damage to the marine environment. Article 263 stipulates:

Article 263: Responsibility and liability

1. States and competent international organizations shall be responsible for ensuring that marine scientific research, whether undertaken by them or on their behalf, is conducted in accordance with this Convention.

2. States and competent international organizations shall be responsible and liable for the measures they take in contravention of this Convention in respect of marine scientific research conducted by other States, their natural or juridical persons or by competent international organizations, and shall provide compensation for damage resulting from such measures.

3. States and competent international organizations shall be responsible and liable pursuant to article 235 for damage caused by pollution of the marine environment arising out of marine scientific research undertaken by them or on their behalf.

Paragraph 1 of Article 263 refers to all public research institutions or departments, as well as private groups contracting with a state or a competent international organization. Since, under Articles 248 and 250, all communication with respect to the application for a coastal state's consent is conducted through the researching state, it is then the responsibility of the researching state to assume all liability for violations and damages while conducting marine scientific research activities. This is particularly true for environmental damage caused by pollution, pursuant to Article 235.

In case of dispute, the compulsory procedure is provided in Part XV of the 1982 LOS Convention. It is available for the disputing parties involved, with respect to differences in the interpretation of the various provisions covering marine scientific research, as stipulated by Article 264:

Article 264: Settlement of disputes

Disputes concerning the interpretation or application of the provisions of this Convention with regard to marine scientific research shall be settled in accordance with Part XV, sections 2 and 3.

Part XV, Section 2, particularly Article 287(1), offers a choice of several means for dispute settlement:

1. the International Tribunal of the Law of the Sea
2. the International Court of Justice at The Hague
3. an arbitral tribunal established in the Annex VII to the 1982 LOS Convention
4. a special arbitral tribunal of five members under Annex VIII to the Convention

However, while the dispute is pending for a settlement, the marine scientific research project cannot be continued without the coastal state's consent:

Article 265: Interim measures

Pending settlement of a dispute in accordance with Part XV, sections 2 and 3, the State or competent international organization authorized to conduct a marine scientific research project shall not allow research activities to commence or continue without the express consent of the coastal State concerned.

Significance. Disputes that raise questions about the coastal state's right to grant or withhold consent for conducting marine scientific research must be settled by conciliation in accordance with the general provisions for peaceful settlement of disputes (Articles 279 and 280 of the 1982 LOS Convention). In addition, all other disputes concerning marine scientific research must be settled in accordance with Articles 264 and 287. If not, then under Article 297(2) or Section 2, Annex V, such disputes must be presented for compulsory submission to a conciliation procedure. Under the above provision, parties (states) are obligated to take part in the conciliation proceedings. In short, dispute settlement arising from marine scientific research is elaborate and complex.

RIGHTS OF NEIGHBORING LANDLOCKED AND GEOGRAPHICALLY DISADVANTAGED STATES TO CONDUCT MARINE SCIENTIFIC RESEARCH

As mentioned in Chapter 2, the landlocked and geographically disadvantaged states played an influential role at the UNCLOS III negotiation sessions. One clear piece of evidence of their influence was their ability to exact a concession from the coastal states for certain preferential rights on the continental shelf and in the EEZ with respect to benefits derived from the exploration and exploitation of the resources in these areas. But more important was the need for these states (which border coastal states declaring exclusive fishery zones) to obtain living resources essential for the nutritional demands of their people. The end result of these negotiations was the granting of special rights for access to marine scientific research information from projects performed by a research state or an international organization in the waters of a neighboring coastal state.

Article 254: Rights of neighbouring land-locked and geographically disadvantaged States

1. States and competent international organizations which have submitted to a coastal State a project to undertake marine scientific research referred to in article 246, paragraph 3, shall give notice to the neighbouring land-locked and geographically disadvantaged States of the proposed research project, and shall notify the coastal State thereof.

2. After the consent has been given for the proposed marine scientific research project by the coastal State concerned, in accordance with article 246 and other relevant provisions of this Convention, States and competent international organizations undertaking such a project shall provide to the neighbouring land-locked and geographically disadvantaged

States, at their request and when appropriate, relevant information as specified in article 248 and article 249, paragraph 1(f).

3. The neighbouring land-locked and geographically disadvantaged States referred to above shall, at their request, be given the opportunity to participate, whenever feasible, in the proposed marine scientific research project through qualified experts appointed by them and not objected to by the coastal State, in accordance with the conditions agreed for the project, in conformity with the provisions of this Convention, between the coastal State concerned and the State or competent international organizations conducting the marine scientific research.

4. States and competent international organizations referred to in paragraph 1 shall provide to the above-mentioned land-locked and geographically disadvantaged States, at their request, the information and assistance specified in article 249, paragraph 1(d), subject to the provisions of article 249, paragraph 2.

Article 254 delineates the following procedure for providing the neighboring landlocked and geographically disadvantaged state with information concerning a particular application by a researching state for conducting marine scientific research on the continental shelf or EEZ of a consenting coastal state. First, soon after communicating with the consenting coastal state in accordance with Article 246, the researching state or international organization must give notice of the project to be performed. Then, if requested by the neighboring landlocked or geographically disadvantaged state, and if appropriate, the researching state or the international organization must provide information concerning the nature and objectives of the project, methods to be used, the precise geographic areas, the dates of appearance and departure of the research vessel, and other data. Third, the landlocked or geographically disadvantaged state must be given the opportunity to participate in the proposed marine research project, as well as be provided with data, samples and research results or "assistance in their assessment or interpretation."

Significance. On the one hand, it is only fair to grant the landlocked and coastal states which are geographically disadvantaged (bordering enclosed or semi-enclosed seas, as defined in Article 70(2) of the 1982 LOS Convention) these preferential rights to living resources and access to marine scientific information, for these states are dependent upon exploitation of the living resources of another state's exclusive economic zone. On the other hand, at UNCLOS III, the position of these landlocked and geographically disadvantaged states, *vis-à-vis* other coastal states, was that a concession was made possible in Article 254. However, Article 254(1) does limit the rights of the landlocked and geographically disadvantaged states to those marine scientific research projects in the exclusive economic zone or on the continental shelf. This means that any information on marine scientific research projects dealing with exploitation and exploration of other natural resources cannot be provided by the coastal states when they are engaged in such research projects in their own EEZ.

Article 254 may also present another problem to marine scientists: A consent-seeking research state must give notice and deal with a host of landlocked and geographically disadvantaged states bordering the consenting coastal state—in practice, a bureaucratic nightmare. For instance, if a research project is planned on the eastern part of the Persian Gulf, states involved would be not only Iran, but Iraq, Afghanistan and the Soviet Union.

MARINE TECHNOLOGY TRANSFER

This section deals with only the transfer of marine scientific technology information in general and does not discuss those aspects of technology transfer for deep-seabed mining, which has already been discussed in Chapter 7.

For the Third World nations, marine scientific technology transfer is indispensable to their economic development; it serves as the most efficient and effective method of bridging the technology gap between the industrialized and less developed countries. At the negotiation sessions of the UNCLOS III, the demand for marine technology transfer was a very important part of the New International Economic Order (NIEO).[22] In Part XIV, the 1982 LOS Convention contains a total of thirteen articles on the development and transfer of marine technology information. Article 266 calls on all states to promote the development and transfer of marine science and technology in all areas on a fair, reasonable and equitable basis:

Article 266: Promotion of the development and transfer of marine technology

1. States, directly or through competent international organizations, shall cooperate in accordance with their capabilities to promote actively the development and transfer of marine science and marine technology on fair and reasonable terms and conditions.

2. States shall promote the development of the marine scientific and technological capacity of States which may need and request technical assistance in this field, particularly developing States, including land-locked and geographically disadvantaged States, with regard to the exploration, exploitation, conservation and management of marine resources, the protection and preservation of the marine environment, marine scientific research and other activities in the marine environment compatible with this Convention, with a view to accelerating the social and economic development of the developing States.

3. States shall endeavour to foster favourable economic and legal conditions for the transfer of marine technology for the benefit of all parties concerned on an equitable basis.

The basic operational objectives for the promotion and development of marine technology transfer are given in Article 268:

Article 268: Basic objectives

States, directly or through competent international organizations, shall promote:

(a) the acquisition, evaluation and dissemination of marine technological knowledge and facilitate access to such information and data;

(b) the development of appropriate marine technology;

(c) the development of the necessary technological infrastructure to facilitate the transfer of marine technology;

(d) the development of human resources through training and education of nationals of developing States and countries and especially the nationals of the least developed among them;

(e) international co-operation at all levels, particularly at the regional, subregional and bilateral levels.

In accordance with this article, states or Third World nations can negotiate through bilateral arrangements or through an international organization for access to marine technology information and data. More important is the objective of training and education of nationals from technology-poor states to develop the needed human resources. These operational goals are to be achieved by the following methods:

Article 269: Measures to achieve the basic objectives

In order to achieve the objectives referred to in article 268, States, directly or through competent international organizations, shall endeavour, *inter alia*, to:

(a) establish programmes of technical co-operation for the effective transfer of all kinds of marine technology to States which may need and request technical assistance in this field, particularly the developing land-locked and geographically disadvantaged States, as well as other developing States which have not been able either to establish or develop their own technological capacity in marine science and in the exploration and exploitation of marine resources or to develop the infrastructure of such technology;

(b) promote favourable conditions for the conclusion of agreements, contracts and other similar arrangements, under equitable and reasonable conditions;

(c) hold conferences, seminars and symposia on scientific and technological subjects, in particular on policies and methods for the transfer of marine technology;

(d) promote the exchange of scientists and of technological and other experts;

(e) undertake projects and promote joint ventures and other forms of bilateral and multilateral co-operation.

In Part IV, Section 3, the 1982 LOS Convention also contains articles for the establishment of national and regional marine scientific and technological centers to stimulate marine scientific research in developing coastal states (Articles 275–277). Under Article 277, functions of regional centers include: educational and training programs in all aspects of marine scientific and technological research; management studies; study programs for marine environmental protection; data acquisition and processing; and studies on marketing of technology and on contracts concerning patents. Here UNCTAD has pioneered promotion of regional cooperation in the transfer of technology by establishing centers in Asia, Africa, Latin America and the Middle East.[23]

Significance. The criteria and standards for technology transfer are key issues which have not been clearly delineated by the 1982 LOS Convention. Article 271 merely asks states to promote the establishment of generally accepted guidelines for the transfer of technology through bilateral arrangements or through the framework of an international organization. The problem here is essentially that of the inability of both the industrialized and Third World nations—the Group of 77—to agree on a set of generally accepted and legally binding criteria. In 1978, the UNCTAD drafted an International Code of Conduct on the Transfer of Technology, but it progressed no further than a proposal primarily because some nations wanted only voluntary guidelines.[24] Technology transfer also involves patent rights and the protection of patent rights. Here again, the United Nations specialized agency, the World Intellectual Property Organization (WIPO), has held several meetings to revise the 1983 International Convention for the Protection of Industrial Property. However, as yet no concrete results have been produced.

NOTES

1. R R. Churchill and A. V. Lowe, *The Law of the Sea* (Manchester, England: University of Manchester Press, 1983), p. 255.

2. See Alfred H. A. Soons, *Marine Scientific Research and the Law of the Sea* (The Hague: T.M.C. Asser Instituut, 1982), pp. 49–55.

3. Churchill and Lowe, *The Law of the Sea*, p. 256. Also see Bernard H. Oxman, "The Third United Nations Conference on the Law of the Sea: The 1977 New York Session," *American Journal of International Law* 72, no. 1 (January 1978): p. 76.

4. Churchill and Lowe, *The Law of the Sea*, p. 258. Also see Soons, *Marine Scientific Research*, pp. 146–153.

5. Soons, *Marine Scientific Research*, p. 164.

6. As explained by the original United States proposal, the term "normal circumstances" can exist between two nations when there are no diplomatic relations; thus Article 246(4). What is not "normal circumstances" may be a situation where hostility exists in the relationship between a coastal state and a requesting state. For more discussion, see Soons, *Marine Scientific Research*, pp. 167–169; Churchill and Lowe, *The Law of the Sea*, p. 260; Gerard J. Mangone, "The Effect of Extended Coastal State Jurisdiction over the Seas and Seabed upon Marine Science Research," *Ocean Development and International Law* 9, nos. 3–4 (1981): pp. 207–209; and Bernard H. Oxman, "The Third United Nations Conference on the Law of the Sea: The Eighth Session (1979)," *American Journal of International Law* 74, no. 1 (January 1980): 25–26.

7. See UNCLOS III documents: A/AC.138/SC.III/L.18 (Canada); A/AC.138/SC.III/L.44 (U.S.A.); A/AC.138/SC.III/L.34 (Malta); A/Conf.62/C.3/L/19 (landlocked nations); and A/Conf.62/C.3/L.26 (nine eastern European states: Bulgaria, Byelorussia S.S.R. Czechoslovakia, German Democratic Republic, Hungary, Mongolia, Poland, Ukrainian S.S.R., and U.S.S.R.).

8. A/AC.138/SC.III/L.18.

9. A/AC.138/SC.III/L.31.

10. A/AC.138/SC.III/L.34.

11. Soons, *Marine Scientific Research*, p. 135.

12. Ibid.

13. For granting all coastal states the general right to marine scientific research, see A/Conf.62/C.3/L.19 (by landlocked states); A/Conf.62/C.3/L.29 (Colombia, Mexico and Nigeria); A/Conf.62/C.3/L.26. The Group of 77 proposal is contained in A/Conf.62/C.3/L.13.

14. Soons, *Marine Scientific Research*, p. 130.

15. Ibid.

16. Ibid., pp. 188–189.

17. See A/C.138/SC.III/L.50 and the Group of 77 reaction in A/AC.138/SC.III/L.55.

18. These points of interpretation come from Soons, *Marine Scientific Research*, pp. 198–201.

19. See Intergovernmental Oceanographic Commission (IOC) Technical Series No. 5 (1969).

20. Churchill and Lowe, *The Law of the Sea*, p. 262.

21. Soons, *Marine Scientific Research*, p. 234.

22. See Elisabeth Mann Borgese, "The Role of the International Seabed Authority in the 1980s," *San Diego Law Review* 18, no. 3 (1981): 395–407; Alan G. Friedman and Cynthia A. Williams, "The Group of 77 at the United Nations: An Emergent Force in the Law of the Sea," *San Diego Law Review* 16, no. 3 (1979); 555–574; Boleslaw A. Boczek, *The Transfer of Marine Technology to Developing Nations in the International Law* (Honolulu: The Law of the Sea Institute, University of Hawaii, 1982), pp. 1–3 and 24–26; Churchill and Lowe, *The Law of the Sea*, p. 265.

23. UNCTAD Document TD/B/C.6/9 (1975) for the Establishment of Centers for the Transfer and Development of Technology.

24. For the code see *International Legal Materials* 19, no. 2, (1980): 773–774. Also see Churchill and Lowe, *The Law of the Sea*, p. 266.

CHAPTER 13

Major Players at UNCLOS III: Summary of Positions on Selected Issues

The 1982 LOS Convention was the product of compromises and "package deals" negotiated by many players, individual influential nations and groups of power blocs. To a large extent the convention was shaped and hammered out through bargaining and trade-offs by various individual nations and caucusing groups during the eleven sessions of UNCLOS III from 1973 to 1982. Politics of major players in terms of their support base and goals or special interests can be seen in Table 13.1. This chapter attempts to reconstruct the role played by some individual nations and caucusing groups at the UNCLOS III negotiations by presenting a summary of their respective positions on selected issues.

The chapter begins with the small but influential mid-ocean states known as the archipelagic group, consisting of Fiji, Indonesia, Mauritius and the Philippines, later joined by the Bahamas. Their definition of the high seas not only excluded the territorial sea, but added the novel concept of archipelagic waters surrounding a large group of islands. Their success as a bargaining group lay in the linkage of their issue with that of free transit through straits, a priority goal of the maritime powers. By 1975–1976, a bargain was struck by which they obtained from the United States a concession in return for their support of an international guarantee for navigation of the right of free transit through, over and under straits.

The most influential and certainly the most complex group in the law of the sea negotiations has been the Group of 77: the developing African, Asian and Latin American nations. Although their numerical strength, a total of 120 to 130 nations, was overwhelming when it came to voting, the group was diverse and troubled at times by inner group dissension based on regional differences. Nevertheless, the Group of 77 was successful in obtaining compromises from its main adversary, the maritime powers of the world, on many law of the sea issues. The Group's push for universal acceptance of such revolutionary concepts as the common heritage and expanded coastal state jurisdiction over the exclusive

Table 13.1
Politics of Major Players at the Third United Nations Law of the Sea Conference

Country/Group	Basic Support From	Active Nations	Goals/Interests
1) Archipelagic States	Oceanic/Island States	Fiji, Indonesia Mauritius, Philippines	Archpelagic waters by strait baseline and 200-mile economic zone
2) Group of 77	Afro-Asian and Latin-American states		International regime for seabed mining; common heritage; production limits and price control on seabed mining
3) Japan	N/A	N/A	Opposed to expanded claims on territorial sea and fishery zone; Access to deep seabed mining
4) Landlocked/ Geographically Disadvantaged (LL/GDS)	A mixed group of forty-eight developing and developed states from all regions		Revenue sharing; living and non-living resource exploitation; right to participate in research; 12-mile territorial sea
5) Patrimonialists and	Latin-American and Caribbean	Colombia, Haiti, Jamaica, Mexico, Trinidad, Venezuela	200-mile zone over renewable resources
Territorialist	Latin-American	Chile, Ecuador, Peru, Panama	200-mile territorial sea
6) United States of America	N/A	N/A	Free navigation; guaranteed free transit through straits, free access to deep seabed mining
7) Soviet East European Bloc	USSR	Albania, Hungary, Czechoslovakia, Poland, Romania, Yugoslavia	Seabed mining; 200-mile EEZ; continental shelf; territorial sea; fisheries transit
8) Western Europe (EEC) and Group of 11	European Community, plus Scandinavians	EEC and Scandinavians, plus Australia, Austria, Canada, Ireland, New Zealand	Coastal jurisdiction over fisheries; free access to deep seabed mining.

Source: A modified version based on Ann L. Hollick, *U.S. Foreign Policy and the Law of the Sea* (Princeton, N.J.: Princeton University Press, 1981), pp. 250–256; and Edward L. Miles, "The Structure and Effects of the Decision Process in the Seabed Committee and the Third United Nations Conference on the Law of the Sea," *International Organization* 31, no. 2 (1977): 161–166. Used by permission.

economic zone must be considered as its chief contribution to a new international regime for the oceans. Its willingness to accept the "parallel system" offered by the United States made it possible to break the deadlock over the core issue in deep seabed mining: access to the Area. Since then, the Group of 77 has become an important force in international politics.

Next to the Group of 77 in terms of numerical strength and influence were the landlocked and geographically disadvantaged states (LL/GDS)—a bloc of forty-eight votes. Not only did the group consist of developed as well as developing states, it also included several members of the Soviet bloc (Byelorussian S.S.R., Czechoslovakia, German Democratic Republic, Hungary, Mongolia and Poland). Despite the ideological differences, the LL/GDS had been an effective caucusing group in negotiating draft articles by obtaining support from the Organization of African Unity, a subgroup of the Group of 77, for their right to free and unrestricted access to and from the high seas, as well as fishery access in the exclusive economic zone of neighboring states.

The third influential group at UNCLOS III negotiation sessions was the Latin American group of states, which advocated the concept of a patrimonial sea, the outgrowth of the Montevideo, Lima and Santo Domingo declarations of 1970 and 1972. The group's greatest contribution, in cooperation with the LL/GDS, was to lobby for a definition which would place limits not to exceed 200 nautical miles on continental shelf claims. Support of the Latin American and Caribbean block was crucial in drafting Article 82 dealing with revenue sharing for resources exploited beyond the 200 nautical mile limit, a proposal originally made by the United States.

At first, the Soviet Bloc as a group played the role of a leading promoter for the "package deal" with the United States on securing an international guarantee for free strait transit and freedom of navigation. Once these concerns were taken care of, the Soviet Bloc sought alliance with the developing state members of the Group of 77 over the core issue of deep-seabed mining. While the Soviet Union gained by supporting the common heritage concept and the "parallel system," which enabled it to be registered as a "pioneer investor" in seabed mining in the Area, its acceptance of the 200-nautical-mile EEZ served to reduce the activities of its distant water fleets. Throughout the UNCLOS III negotiations, the Soviet bloc adhered to the "package deal," originally formulated with the United States in 1967. It insisted that its acceptance and recognition of the 200-nautical-mile economic zone was contingent upon the acceptance by developing Third World nations of other issues, such as free transit through straits, freedom of navigation and the outer limits of the continental shelf to which the Soviet Union made a significant contribution.

The last caucusing group in the law of the sea negotiations was Western Europe, through the European Economic Community (EEC). The EEC had taken a pronounced stand reflecting regional concern over fishery issues. Its members stressed the need for reliance on established regional regulatory commissions for fisheries and conservation management, as well as their own qualifications as an appropriate regional arrangement for fishery regulation. While the EEC had taken the position that manganese nodule mining from the seabed was part of the freedom of the high seas and was critical about the deep seabed mining provisions in the 1982 LOS Convention, it nevertheless signed the Convention and took an active role in the Preparatory Commission.

This chapter designates two individual countries for their role in the UNCLOS

III negotiations: Japan and the United States. They are selected here only as illustrations of the complex pattern of the negotiation process at the law of the sea conferences, not necessarily because of their unique contributions as players.

Japan, a major maritime power and user of the oceans, had stubbornly fought against expanded coastal state claims in 1958 and 1960. By the 1970s Japan fought alone, but eventually had to capitulate under pressure to accept the twelve-nautical-mile territorial sea and the 200-nautical-mile fishery zone for conservation and management. It was a combination of a world oil crisis in the mid–1970s and its dispute with South Korea, which forced Japan to alter it long-held policy of opposing extension of coastal state jurisdiction over continental shelf resources. However, Japan vigorously pursued its interests in deep-seabed mining and shared the views of most industrialized states on the questions of access and conditions of exploration. Japan, like France, signed the 1982 LOS Convention and participated actively in the Preparatory Commission. At the risk of being criticized by the developing nations organized under the framework of the Group of 77, nevertheless it joined the United States and other Western nations in 1982 and 1984 for a unilateral regime on deep-seabed mining. This was an expression both of its need to cooperate with the Western industrialized states and its dependency on imported mineral resources.

The United States played a key role in the UNCLOS III negotiations. In the pages to follow its positions on a number of key law of the sea issues are analyzed as evidence of the effort, time and thinking that went into the negotiating and drafting process. One need not cast doubt as to the United States' intent for an orderly comprehensive ocean regime to emerge from the UNCLOS III. With the exception of Part XI on deep-seabed mining, the United States was willing to apply its prestige and influence by working with other caucusing groups to search for workable compromises on some of the most complex law of the sea issues. Unfortunately, it was its objections to the deep seabed portion that caused the United States to refuse to sign the 1982 LOS Convention (see Chapter 7). However, the United States has pledged that it accepts and acts in accordance with the rest of the Convention provisions which have been agreed to by the vast majority of the world.

As a final concluding remark concerning major players at the law of the sea conferences: bloc or group negotiations have evolved into the only possible negotiation mechanism available, given the context of more than 150 nations divided on the basis of their stage of economic development.

ARCHIPELAGIC GROUP

As discussed in Chapter 1, led by two mid-ocean island states (Indonesia and the Philippines), the 1958 UNCLOS I worked unsuccessfully to persuade the world's maritime powers to accept the new concept of a special archipelagic regime. The effort for recognition and acceptance of the archipelagic regime was renewed at UNCLOS III—this time the Philippines and Indonesia were joined in their negotiation stance by several other newly emerged mid-ocean island states. Their concept of the archipelagic state was contained in their joint draft proposal dated August 9, 1974:[1]

Article 1

1. These articles apply only to archipelagic States.

2. An archipelagic State is a State constituted wholly by one or more archipelagos and may include other islands.

3. For the purpose of these articles an archipelago is a group of islands, including parts of islands, interconnecting waters and other natural features which are so closely interrelated that such islands, waters and other natural features form an intrinsic geographical, economic and political entity, or which historically have been regarded as such.

Article 2

1. An archipelagic State may employ the method of straight baselines joining the outermost points of the outermost islands and drying reefs of the archipelago in drawing the baselines from which the extent of the territorial sea, economic zone and other special jurisdictions are to be measured.

2. The drawing of such baselines shall not depart to any appreciable extent from the general configuration of the archipelago.

3. Baselines shall not be drawn to and from low-tide evaluations unless lighthouses or similar installations which are permanently above sea level have been built on them or where a low-tide elevation is situated wholly or partly at a distance not exceeding the breadth of the territorial sea from the nearest island.

4. The system of straight baselines shall not be applied by an archipelagic State in such a manner as to cut off the territorial sea of another State as determined under article . . . of chapter . . . of this Convention.

In a further effort to make their point, Fiji, Indonesia, Mauritius and the Philippines defined the term "high seas" to mean "all parts of the sea that are not included in the territorial sea or in the internal waters of a State, or, in the case of an archipelagic State, its archipelagic waters."[2] Then the Bahamas joined the negotiation process by introducing a separate resolution with identical expression on the rights of an archipelagic state in the archipelagic regime.[3]

Significance. In subsequent negotiation sessions at the UNCLOS III, the archipelagic group of states not only persisted and held firm their position, but, beginning in the 1975 sessions, the issue was linked with that of free transit through the international straits, a question of paramount importance to the world's maritime powers such as the United States. This linkage provided the advocates of the archipelagic regime with the needed bargaining power at the negotiations. Throughout the 1975–1976 negotiation sessions, the United States made concessions to the archipelagic states in exchange for their support of the United States insistence that guarantees be made for the right of free transit through, over and under straits used for international navigation which would be overlapped by extension of the territorial sea from the traditional three to twelve nautical miles. This was a part of the so-called "package deal."[4]

In the first draft of a comprehensive law of the sea treaty, the Informal Single Negotiating Text (ISNT), Part VII, Articles 117–130, contained practically all of the demands made by the archipelagic states for a special archipelagic regime, including the right to claim the 200-nautical-mile economic zone beyond the straight baselines linking the outermost islands and reefs as archipelagic waters.[5] This claim would enormously expand their control over the ocean (see Chapter 3 for further discussion). According to one observer, the bargain struck between the United States and the archipelagic states isolated the coastal strait states of Spain, Iran, Oman, Morocco, Yemen and Egypt.[6]

GROUP OF 77 AND THE AFRICAN STATES

"Group of 77" refers to one of the principal voting and negotiating blocs of developing Third World nations that participated and engaged actively in negotiations at the Third United Nations Law of the Sea Conference from 1974 in Caracas to the concluding session in New York in 1982. The voting bloc had its debut in the 1964 United Nations Conference on Trade and Development held in Geneva. Since then, it has become a vehicle through which developing nations in the Third World have amassed their numerical strength to influence and direct discussions and negotiations in multilateral conference diplomacy. By 1978, at the Law of the Sea Conferences in Geneva and New York, the numerical strength of the Group of 77 had reached a total of 119 developing nations.

Membership and geographic distribution for the Group of 77 can be seen in Figure 13.1.

The Group of 77 played a crucial role in the adoption of the Maltese proposal (the Pardo proposal), which formed the basis for passage in the United Nations General Assembly of the key resolutions dealing with the establishment of an international regime for the seabed beyond the limit of national jurisdiction,[7] particularly Resolution 2574D (XXIV), 1967, on moratorium of seabed activities; Resolution 2574C (XXIV) on the establishment of an international regime for the seabed; and Resolution 2749 (XXV), 1970, on declaration of principles governing the seabed and the ocean floor.[8] Also the Group of 77 has projected itself at international forums as champion for a new international economic order aimed at redressing or reducing the economic disparity in the world. It has become a formidable antagonist to the affluent and technologically endowed developed states.[9] The Group's stand on an international regime for seabed exploitation and exploration, with benefits derived from these activities to be shared by the developing states, revealed both its strengths and weaknesses.[10]

The Group's strength has been in the large bloc of votes it could command at various international forums. With a solid bloc of sixty votes in the Ad Hoc Committee on the Seabed debates in the 1960s and 1970s, it controlled both the

Figure 13.1
Group of 77

The Group of 77 (G-77) is the Third World's economic advocate. More loosely organized than the Nonaligned Movement, the group had more than 120 members in 1980, comprising virtually all developing countries. The term originated with the 77 nations supporting a common program at the first meetings of the UN Conference on Trade & Development (UNCTAD) in 1964. Meeting as the G-77, developing countries prepare common positions for international economic negotiations. Like the Nonaligned Movement, the G-77 urges changes in the world economic system to promote faster growth in the Third World.

Members: Afghanistan, Algeria, Angola, Antigua and Barbuda, Argentina, The Bahamas, Bahrain, Bangladesh, Barbados, Belize, Benin, Bhutan, Bolivia, Botswana, Brazil, Burma, Burundi, Cameroon, Cape Verde, Central African Republic, Chad Chile, Colombia, Comoros, Congo, Costa Rica, Cuba, Cyprus, Djibouti, Cominica, Dominican Republic, Ecuador, Egypt, El Salvador, Equatorial Guinea, Ethiopia, Fiji, Gabon, The Gambia, Ghana, Grenada, Buatemala, Buinea, Guinea-Bissau, Guyana, Haiti, Honduras, India, Indonesia, Iran, Iraq, Ivory Coast, Jamaica, Jordan, Kampuchea, Kenya, Kiribati, North Korea, South Korea, Kuwait, Laos, Lebanon, Lesotho, Liberia, Libya, Madagascar, Malawi, Malaysia, Maldives, Mali, Malta, Mauritania, Mauritius, Mexico, Morocco, Mozambique, Nepal, Nicaragua, Niger, Nigeria, Oman, Pakistan, Panama, Papua New Guinea, Paraguay, Peru, Philippines, Qatar, Romania, Rwanda, St. Lucia, St. Vincent and the Grenadines, Sao Tome and Principe, Saudi Arabia, Senegal, Seychelles, Sierra Leone, Singapore, Solomon Islands, Somalia, Sri Lanka, Sudan, Suriname, Swaziland, Syria, Thailand, Togo, Trinidad and Tobago, Tunisia, Uganda, United Arab Emirates, Tanzania, Upper Volta, Uruguay, Vanuatu, Venezuela, Vietnam, Western Samoa, Yemen (Aden), Yemen (Sanaa), Yugoslavia, Zaire, Zambia, Zimbabwe

Note: Boundary representation is not necessarily authoritative.
Source: *Atlas of U.S. Foreign Relations*, U.S. Department of State, June 1983, p. 31.

direction and the substance of the discussions. For instance, the United Nations General Assembly resolution on the declaration of principles governing the seabed was adopted by a vote of 108, with 14 abstentions; and Resolution 2750 (XXV) on the United Nations decision to convene UNCLOS III was adopted by a vote of 106 to 7, with 6 abstentions. The group's weakness has been its difficulty in developing a consensus when regional and coastal states' interests on boundary limits were in conflict with the overall concerns about the seabed development.[11]

In most instances, however, Group of 77 has been able to provide direction in the course of the Law of the Sea negotiations, even though the Group lacked both technical knowledge and experience on seabed exploitation. It made up that deficiency by ''exploiting'' the United Nations Secretariat or the Secretary General in numerous resolutions for studies.[12]

The Group's position was weakened somewhat after the Caracas sessions of the UNCLOS III. There were inner group dissent and divergent views with the landlocked and geographically disadvantaged states whose main concerns on the right of transit were legion; but the issue generated little enthusiasm among the Group's dominant nonlandlocked coastal states, particularly the bloc's subgroup which consisted of Latin American states.

The initial insistence by the Group of 77 at the UNCLOS III negotiation sessions in New York was that the International Seabed Authority be responsible exclusively for control over seabed exploitation in the Area. This position ran counter to the developed states' position, particularly that of the United States, which insisted on open access to seabed resources by privately organized multinational consortia sponsored by the states parties to the Convention. The UNCLOS III conference was deadlocked by the summer of 1978, and the impasse was not broken until a compromise was reached on the ''parallel system,'' a concession made by the United States (see Chapter 7). The parallel system became an integral part of Annex II to the Final Act on ''Basic Conditions for Prospecting, Exploration, and Exploitation.'' However, when unilateral national legislation on mining deep-seabed hard minerals was enacted by a number of Western industrialized states, along with the reciprocating-states regime, or ''mini-treaty'' arrangement (see Chapter 7), the Group of 77 reacted indignantly as seen in the following official statement:[13]

> Consequently, any unilateral act or mini-treaty is unlawful in that it violates these principles, for the legal régime, whether provisional or definitive, can only be established with the consent of the international community as the sole representative of mankind and in conformity with the system determined by the international community.
>
> The adoption of unilateral measures, draft legislation and limited agreements would merely be an event without international legal effect and hence incapable of being invoked vis-à-vis the international community.
>
> The great majority of States would not admit the validity of such legislation, nor could such legislation constitute valid grounds for any juridical claim to explore or exploit the area. Furthermore, if such unilateral legislation or mini-treaty should be put into operation,

the international responsibility of the States concerned would be engaged in respect of damage caused by such activities incompatible with the principles applicable in the area.

It should be stressed that no investor would have any legal guarantee for his investments in such activities, for he would likewise be subject to individual or collective action by the other States in defence of the common heritage of mankind, and no purported diplomatic protection would carry any legal weight whatsoever.

Then, in August 1979 the Chairman of the Group of 77, M. Carias of Honduras, fired off another protest statement and reiterated the illegal status of the unilateral domestic legislation on deep-seabed mining:[14]

(1) Neither the Geneva Convention on the High Seas, 1958, nor customary international law deals with or regulates this exploration and exploitation of the resources of the international sea-bed area. These are not covered by the freedoms of the high seas.

(2) The international sea-bed area beyond the limits of national jurisdiction, as well as its resources, are the common heritage of mankind.

No State shall claim or exercise sovereignty or sovereign rights over any part of the international sea-bed area or its resources, nor shall any State or person, natural or juridical, appropriate any part thereof. No such claim or exercise of sovereignty or sovereign rights, nor such appropriation, shall be recognized. All rights in the resources of the area are vested in mankind as a whole. The exploitation of minerals from these resources shall be organized, regulated and controlled by an international machinery, such as the proposed International Sea-Bed Authority.

The above principles are imperative rules of international law, the derogation of which is allowed neither by unilateral legislation nor by restricted treaties. Any unilateral legislation adopted while these negotiations are going on will not only violate the rule of good faith in negotiations but, as I said on 19 March 1979, may also have wider impact on economic co-operation between developing and developed States.

(3) Unilateral mining legislation not only will not be recognized by the international community, but also will entail international responsibility to other States.

In view of the grave consequences which such unilateral mining legislation may entail for the enacting States and their contractors, for the future of the Conference, and for peace, co-operation and orderly economic development of the world community as a whole, the Group of 77 reiterates its request and urges all States to make every effort to bring this Conference to an early and successful conclusion and to the adoption of a Convention which is fair and acceptable to all sections of the world community.

As seen in the position paper given in 1974 at the Caracas session, the Organization of African Unity (OAU), a subgroup within the Group of 77, laid out its initial positions on the various law of the sea issues: the right of access to and from the sea by the landlocked states and the regime of innocent passage, the right to establish an exclusive economic zone not to exceed 200 nautical miles, an international fishery regime for the high seas fishing, training and assistance in technology transfer and marine scientific research, and coastal obligation in the control and prevention of marine pollution.[15]

The African States Regional Seminar on the Law of the Sea, which met in

Yaoundé, Cameroon, in June 1972, helped to solidify the African states' regional position on the 200-nautical-mile economic zone.[16] This was further refined in 1974:[17]

Article 1

A coastal State has the right to establish beyond its territorial sea an exclusive economic zone which shall not exceed 200 nautical miles from the applicable baselines for measuring the territorial sea.

Article 2

1. In the exclusive economic zone a coastal State shall have sovereignty over the living and non-living resources. It shall have sovereign rights for the purpose of regulation, control, exploration, exploitation, protection and preservation of all living and non-living resources therein.

2. The resources referred to in paragraph 1 of this article, shall encompass the living and non-living resources of the water column, the sea-bed and the subsoil.

3. . . . no other State has the right to explore and exploit the resources therein without the consent or agreement of the coastal State.

Article 3

A coastal State shall also have exclusive jurisdiction within the exclusive economic zone, *inter alia*, for the purposes of:

(a) Control, regulation and preservation of the marine environment including pollution control and abatement;

(b) Control, authorization and regulation of scientific research;

(c) Control and regulation of customs and fiscal matters related to economic activities in the zone.

Significance. The success of the Group of 77 at UNCLOS III lay in the Group's ability to make trade-offs that cut across regional boundaries and, in the end, to reach significant compromises on a number of key provisions in the 1982 LOS Convention, particularly those controversial aspects dealing with the international seabed regime under Part XI. For instance, it was at the Group's insistence that the Authority for the seabed resources beyond national jurisdiction was designed as an international monopoly with effective control over the production of mineral resources in order not to adversely affect the prices and markets of the land-based supplies among the Group's members.

Group of 77 has had its internal problems and is by no means monolithic. But it has exerted its influence on the outcome of the Law of the Sea conference negotiations. By the Group's action, it has not only forced the Western industrialized states to compromise, but at times it has put them on the defensive. The defensive stance taken by the Western developed nations has created an alternative regime, the reciprocal states regime, in competition with the Authority for deep seabed mining. Unless the present dual seabed mining regimes come to an accommodation, we may expect the renewal of Group of 77 militancy vis-à-vis the Western industrialized states over deep-seabed mining development.

JAPAN

As the leading maritime power in Asia, Japan fought stubbornly in 1958 and 1960 at the UNCLOS I and II against any change in a territorial sea limit from the traditional three miles to any distance beyond. They emphasized the necessity for preserving the freedom of the high seas.[18]

Japan became a party to only two of the four 1958 UNCLOS I conventions: the territorial sea convention without specific delimitation, and the high sea convention. They refused to become a party to the 1958 convention on fishery conservation and the continental shelf convention. At the time of negotiation in 1958 and 1960, the Japanese delegation had frustrated the United States–Canadian effort to reach a compromise on the territorial sea issue by casting its vote of abstention to kill the compromise.[19]

Under the combined pressure of world consensus for an expanded twelve-nautical-mile territorial sea, which had developed by the 1970s, and Japan's concern over the Soviet Union and South Korean increased fishing activities in Japanese waters, Japan's original position against an expanded territorial sea and the coastal state's preferential fishing rights began to be modified. By the time UNCLOS III convened in Caracas in 1974, Japan began to reassess its policy regarding the breadth of the territorial sea and its opposition to the new 200-mile economic zone for fishery conservation and management. Although Japan's foreign affairs officials and the domestic industries concerned had barely begun to reexamine the nation's status quo positions on the law of the sea, this reassessment was reflected in Japan's acceptance of the twelve-nautical-mile territorial sea as contained in the Informal Single Negotiating Text (ISNT, May 7, 1975). The new proposal ruled out any foreign fishing (particularly by Soviet fishing fleets) within the territorial sea, a condition demanded by the Japanese fishing industry.

Because of the complexities in Japanese domestic politics, the territorial sea issue was temporarily referred to fishery claims and jurisdiction pending a final law of the sea conference decision. It was not until May 2, 1977 (effective July 1, 1977) that a Japanese law was enacted to declare the territorial sea of Japan as an area of the sea extending from the baseline to twelve-nautical-miles seaward. However, at the same time, Japan designated five straits (the Soga, the Tsugaru, Tsushima Channel East, Tsushima Channel West, and the Osumi) with a three-nautical-mile limit—an action which created conflict with the 1982 LOS Convention regime over passage through straits.

At first, Japan fought the introduction of the concept for a 200-nautical-mile economic zone. At Caracas, it was obvious that Japan was fighting a lone battle against the overwhelming pressure exerted by the Group of 77, which advocated an exclusive economic zone for fishery and mineral resources. Most important of all, the plea by Japan at Caracas was for freedom of access to fishery resources as a means of protecting its distant water fleets.

> Freedom of access to fishery resources, if it was retained only beyond 200 miles, would become practically meaningless. Except for highly migratory ocean species, fish lived close to the shore, mostly within areas that would be covered by a 200-mile zone, and they were also unevenly distributed, tending to live in great abundance off the coasts of a rather limited number of countries. If the proposed 200-mile economic zone was adopted, the major fertile fishing grounds of the world would come under the exclusive jurisdiction of several coastal States, including some highly developed countries. That fact showed, as other representatives had observed, that acceptance of the exclusive economic zone as currently conceived would accentuate rather than reduce existing inequities.

Again faced with pressure from the Group of 77 for acceptance of the 200-nautical-mile economic zone at the subsequent sessions of UNCLOS III and the declaration by the United States and the Soviet Union for a 200-nautical-mile economic zone in 1976–77, Japan had to accede by May 2, 1977 to the establishment of the 200-nautical-mile fishery zone via an order of the cabinet. However, Japan has not yet declared a 200-nautical-mile EEZ claiming sovereign rights over the exploitation of living as well as nonliving resources.

For over two decades, from the 1950s to the 1970s, Japan opposed the continental shelf concept as embodied in the 1958 Convention on the Continental Shelf, which it refused to sign. This reluctance for acceptance of the continental shelf concept was partly due to the long debate within the bureaucratic politics of its governmental agencies and partly because of the low level of oil and gas exploration on the Japanese continental shelf, little of which is under shallow water. The 1974 worldwide oil crisis, and Japan's dispute with South Korea over the continental shelf, forced Japan to rethink its status quo position into devising a formula for reducing the coastal state's claim over continental shelf resources. This was reflected in its draft proposal dealing with the continental shelf which was submitted at Caracas in 1974:

DOCUMENT A/CONF.62/C.2/L.31/Rev.1
Japan: revised draft article on the continental shelf

[*Original: English*]
[*16 August 1974*]

1. The coastal State exercises sovereign rights over the continental shelf (the coastal sea-bed area) for the purpose of exploring it and exploiting its mineral resources.

2. The outer limit of the continental shelf (the coastal sea-bed area) shall not exceed a maximum distance of 200 nautical miles from the baseline for measuring the breadth of the territorial sea as set out in . . .

3.

(a) Where the coasts of two or more States are adjacent or opposite to each other, the delimitation of the boundary of the continental shelf (the coastal sea-bed area) appertaining to such States shall be determined by agreement between them, taking into account the principle of equidistance.

(b) Failing such agreement, no State is entitled to extend its sovereign rights over the continental shelf (the coastal sea-bed area) beyond the median line, every point of which is equidistant from the nearest points of the baselines, continental or insular, from which the breadth of the territorial sea of each State is measured.

4. Nothing provided herein shall prejudice the existing agreements between the coastal States concerned relating to the delimitation of the boundary of their respective continental shelf (coastal sea-bed area).

This draft proposal referred to continental shelf resources as ''coastal seabed resources,'' implying only mineral resources, but not living or biological resources. In addition, Japan provided the criterion that the outer limits of the continental shelf shall not exceed 200 nautical miles, measured from the baseline where the territorial sea is measured.

Even though Japan's vain attempt to limit the continental shelf concept as applicable only to mineral resources represented a lone battle that attracted hardly any converts at UNCLOS III, its position on the deep-seabed mining issue was considered to be in line with that of the technologically advanced industrialized Western states. For by 1974, Japan had, through the Ministry of International Trade and Industry (MITI), consulted with the multinational corporation known as Deep Ocean Minerals Association (DOMA) of Sumitomo Metal Mining Company, Mitsubishi Corporation and Mitsui Corporation regarding deep-seabed mining.[20] Behaving as a member of the most industrialized states of the world, Japan's concern over deep-seabed mining focused on the procedures by which the International Seabed Authority must regulate and manage the exploitation and exploration of seabed resources. Its working paper submitted at Caracas in 1974 was an example of Japan's attitude toward deep seabed mining:

DOCUMENT A/CONF.62/C.1/L.9
Japan: working paper on conditions of exploration and exploitation

[*Original: English*]
[*19 August 1974*]

Basic rules and regulations regarding the conditions of exploration and exploitation

1. *Activities to be regulated*

All activities of exploration and exploitation shall be carried out through either registration or contracts with the Authority in conformity with the provisions of this Convention and the rules and regulations contained herein (hereinafter referred to as the ''Rules''). Such activities shall be divided into three phases:

1. General survey;
2. Development activities;

(a) Evaluation;

(b) Exploitation

II. *Eligible entities*

Only the following entities may register or conclude contracts with the Authority for the purpose of conducting general survey, evaluation and exploitation:

(a) Contracting Parties;

(b) Group of Contracting Parties; and,

[(c) Natural or juridical persons of such a Party or Parties.]

At the UNCLOS III negotiations Japan's position on the deep-seabed mining issue generated criticism from the subgroup of the Group of 77, the landlocked and geographically disadvantaged states. The criticism and alienation from the Group of 77 did not in the end deter Japan from signing in 1982 the Provisional Understanding Regarding Deep Seabed Matters, otherwise known as the ''Mini-Treaty'' of seven other Western nations (see Chapter 7). At the same time, Japan participated in the Preparatory Commission (see Chapter 7) and has been granted status as a ''pioneer investor'' for deep-sea mining in the Area.[21] Japan has negotiated with the Group of 77 at meetings of the Preparatory Commission for the purpose of writing deep-seabed mining rules and regulations that will be palatable enough for the United States and other Western industrialized nations to sign the 1982 LOS Convention.

Significance. Japan's eventual acceptance of the 200-nautical-mile territorial sea and the 200-nautical-mile fishery zone represented a significant departure from its traditional ocean policy, established in 1870—a policy that had been dedicated to keeping the seas as open as possible with very limited enclosure by coastal states.

To a large extent Japan's adherence to these new ocean regimes has been necessitated by the realities of a changing world, in particular the expansion of Soviet fishing activities near the northern islands. As a result of declaring and recognizing a 200-nautical-mile fishery zone, Japan must constantly seek new access to fishery resources by entering bilateral agreements with other coastal states or through offshore joint ventures for fishery exploitation. It must also face rising import costs for fishery products as Japanese fishing access is reduced by coastal jurisdiction over the 200-nautical-mile fishery zones. On the other hand, by its signing in 1984 of the 1982 LOS Convention and its participation in the Preparatory Commission for the international seabed regime, Japan's position on deep-seabed mining has placed it in a much more favorable light.

LANDLOCKED AND GEOGRAPHICALLY DISADVANTAGED STATES (LL/GDS)

The second principal negotiating group, or voting bloc, at UNCLOS III was the coalition of forty-eight landlocked and geographically disadvantaged states

Table 13.2
Landlocked and Geographically Disadvantaged States*

Afghanistan**	Lesotho**
Austria**	Liechtenstein**
Bahrain	Luxembourg**
Belgium	Malawi**
Bhutan**	Mali**
Bolivia**	Mongolia**
Botswana**	Nepal**
Burundi**	Netherlands
Byelorussian SSR**	Niger**
Central African Republic**	Paraguay**
Chad**	Poland
Czechoslovakia**	Qatar
Ethiopia	Rwanda**
Finland	San Marino**
Gambia	Singapore*
German Democratic Republic	Sudan
Germany, Federal Republic of	Swaziland**
Holy See**	Sweden
Hungary**	Switzerland**
Iraq	Uganda**
Jamaica	United Arab Emirates
Jordan	Upper Volta**
Kuwait	Zaire
Laos**	Zambia**

* Lists of "geographically disadvantaged" states vary considerably, depending on the preparer and the criteria used. The above is the official U.S. Department of State listing.
** 100 percent landlocked.
Source: Hollick, *U.S. Foreign Policy and the Law of the Sea*, p. 398. Used by permission.

(hereafter LL/GDS). A landlocked state is defined under Article 124(1)(a) of the 1982 LOS Convention as "a state which has no sea-coast." Geographically disadvantaged states are defined by Article 70(2) as

> coastal states, including states bordering enclosed or semi-enclosed seas, whose geographical situation makes them dependent upon the exploitation of the living resources of the exclusive economic zones of other states in the sub-region or region for adequate supplies of fish for the nutritional purposes of their populations or parts thereof, and coastal states which can claim no exclusive economic zones of their own.

While a fundamental objective of the landlocked group was to ensure its access to the sea, the geographically disadvantaged states sought access to the living resources in the economic zones of the neighboring coastal states that claimed the EEZ. A list of LL/GDS is given in Table 13.2.

As early as the spring of 1974 the LL/GDS, now comprising about one-third of the states at the conference, formulated some of its basic negotiation positions at Kampala (Uganda). The Kampala Declaration presented a nine-point set of principles representing the essential rights and interests of the developing LL/ GDS:[22]

1. the right of landlocked states for free and unrestricted access to and from the sea
2. the right of GDS for free and unrestricted access to and from the high sea
3. the right of landlocked states to transit rights and facilities from the transit states
4. the right of LL/GDS for free access to and from the area of the seabed
5. the right of landlocked states to use, on an equal basis, facilities, equipment and all other installations in the ports
6. the right to be exempt from duties or taxes while in transit, except service charges in connection with traffic in transit
7. the right of representation by LL/GDS in the organs of international seabed machinery, the decisions of which shall be made with due regard to their special needs and problems
8. the right of LL/GDS to deep seabed resources, and the exploitation of such resources shall be governed by the concept of common heritage
9. the LL/GDS shall have equal rights with other states in the exercise of jurisdiction over resources in areas adjacent to the territorial sea.

The Kampala Declaration was endorsed by seventeen landlocked states from Asia (Afghanistan, Bhutan, Laos, Mongolia and Nepal), Latin America (Bolivia and Paraguay), Africa (Botswana, Burundi, Lesotho, Mali, Swaziland, Uganda, Upper Volta, Zambia) and Eastern Europe (Czechoslovakia and Hungary).[23]

Significance. The LL/GDS group negotiated and lobbied vigorously on the issue of their right to the living resources in the proposed 200-nautical-mile economic zone. Since 1973 some forty delegation chairmen, dominated by many coastal states, had met as semi-official negotiators known as the Evensen Group of judicial experts, headed by Norway's Jen Evensen. The Evensen Group drafted a number of articles dealing with the economic zone. When the draft was circulated, the LL/GDS objected to a number of these draft articles. Their opposition had the support of the OAU, which endorsed the concept of the right of LL/ GDS for free and unrestricted access to and from the high seas. Frank X. Njenga of Kenya, who served as the leader of the contact group for the Group of 77, presented several drafts which would provide the LL/GDS the right to access to fisheries in the economic zone, but his efforts were met with strong opposition from the coastal states.[24] The issue of LL/GDS right to fishery access in the economic zone was not resolved until the seventh session (1978) when the conference resorted to a system of seven negotiation groups; Negotiating Group 4 was able to produce the acceptable draft that eventually became Articles 69 and 70 in the 1982 LOS Convention:[25]

Article 69: Right of land-locked States

1. Land-locked States shall have the right to participate, on an equitable basis, in the exploitation of an appropriate part of the surplus of the living resources of the exclusive

economic zones of coastal States of the same subregion or region, taking into account the relevant economic and geographical circumstances of all the States concerned and in conformity with the provisions of this article and of articles 61 and 62.

2. The terms and modalities of such participation shall be established by the States concerned through bilateral, subregional or regional agreements taking into account, *inter alia*:

(a) the need to avoid effects detrimental to fishing communities or fishing industries of the coastal State;

(b) the extent to which the land-locked State, in accordance with the provisions of this article, is participating or is entitled to participate under existing bilateral, subregional or regional agreements in the exploitation of living resources of the exclusive economic zones of other coastal States;

(c) the extent to which other land-locked States and geographically disadvantaged States are participating in the exploitation of the living resources of the exclusive economic zone of the coastal State and the consequent need to avoid a particular burden for any single coastal State or a part of it;

(d) the nutritional needs of the populations of the respective States.

Article 70: Right of geographically disadvantaged States

1. Geographically disadvantaged States shall have the right to participate, on an equitable basis, in the exploitation of an appropriate part of the surplus of the living resources of the exclusive economic zones of coastal States of the same subregion or region, taking into account the relevant economic and geographical circumstances of all the States concerned and in conformity with the provisions of this article and of articles 61 and 62.

2. For the purposes of this Part, "geographically disadvantaged States" means coastal States, including States bordering enclosed or semi-enclosed seas, whose geographical situation makes them dependent upon the exploitation of the living resources of the exclusive economic zones of other States in the subregion or region for adequate supplies of fish for the nutritional purposes of their populations or parts thereof, and coastal States which can claim no exclusive economic zones of their own.

The right of LL/GDS to participate in fishery exploitation in neighboring economic zones is subject to limitations designated in Article 71 which prevent the LL/GDS participation "in the case of a coastal state whose economy is overwhelmingly dependent on the exploitation of the living resources of its exclusive economic zone." Their right is also subject to Articles 61 and 62 which preserve the coastal state's right to determine the allowable catch and the surplus, if any, within their exclusive economic zone.

The landlocked states also won the issue over freedom of transit and related rights. Article 125 of the 1982 LOS Convention is the result of the group's negotiation at the 1977–1978 sessions:

Article 125: Right of access to and from the sea and freedom of transit

1. Land-locked States shall have the right of access to and from the sea for the purpose of exercising the rights provided for in this Convention including those relating to the

freedom of the high seas and the common heritage of mankind. To this end, land-locked States shall enjoy freedom of transit through the territory of transit States by all means of transport.

2. The terms and modalities for exercising freedom of transit shall be agreed between the land-locked States and transit States concerned through bilateral, subregional or regional agreements.

3. Transit States, in the exercise of their full sovereignty over their territory, shall have the right to take all measures necessary to ensure that the rights and facilities provided for in this Part for land-locked States shall in no way infringe their legitimate interests.

THE LATIN AMERICAN GROUP: THE "PATRIMONIAL SEA"

As a group with diverse interest in the law of the sea, the Latin American and Caribbean nations had formulated their basic positions in a number of regional conferences before the UNCLOS III was to convene in Caracas in 1974. Two of these need to be discussed.

First were the 1970 Montevideo and Lima declarations, which extended the coastal states' right to all resources of the sea, including the seabed and the subsoil thereof. The Montevideo Declaration recognized the 200-nautical-mile zone for exercising such coastal states' rights; but the Lima Declaration gave the coastal state the right to designate any limit for the zone.[26] These declarations provided the basis for the evolution of the movement for a ''patrimonial sea,'' or ''patrimonio,'' led by Argentina, Brazil, Chile, Ecuador, El Salvador, Nicaragua, Panama, Peru, Uruguay and joined by Mexico, the Dominican Republic, Colombia, Guatemala and Honduras.[27]

The ''patrimonial sea'' concept finally took shape in the 1972 Specialized Conference of the Caribbean Countries and Problems of the Sea (thereafter known as the Santo Domingo Declaration), attended by Barbados, Colombia, Costa Rica, the Dominican Republic, El Salvador, Guatemala, Guyana, Haiti, Honduras, Jamaica, Mexico, Nicaragua, Panama, Trinidad, Tobago and Venezuela. The Santo Domingo Declaration advocated a new zone, added to the 12-nautical-mile territorial sea, known as the ''patrimonial sea,'' not to exceed 200 nautical miles (or 12 plus 188 nautical miles) as its limit.[28] The ''patrimonial sea'' was not to be a part of the territorial sea or the high sea, but the coastal states would have sovereignty over all resources from surface to seabed. However, the ''patrimonial sea'' was not to affect the traditional rights of free navigation, overflight and cable laying. Under the Santo Domingo Declaration, seabed resources beyond the limits of the ''patrimonial sea'' would be governed by the common heritage principle.

Significance. The Latin American group drafted (by Mexico) Article 59 of the 1982 LOS Convention for conflict resolution with respect to questions of rights or jurisdiction of the coastal states in the exclusive economic zone on the basis of equity and interests of parties. However, it also joined other members of the Group of 77 to limit the EEZ to not more than 200 nautical miles, as originally embodied in the Santo Domingo Declaration.[29] As pointed out by Andrés Aguilar: "no doubt, without the active participation by a number of Latin American states and the support by the group as a whole, neither the archipelagic states, nor the LL/GDS group could have secured their demands in the UNCLOS III."[30] Without the Latin American/Caribbean group's support on the need for defining the limits of the continental shelf, UNCLOS III would have found it difficult to adopt Annex 2 (Commission on the Limits of the Continental Shelf) and Article 82 (revenue sharing of resources beyond the 200-nautical-mile limit) as parts of the comprehensive treaty on the law of the sea.

One major confrontation occurred. The government of UNCLOS III conference President Amerasinghe had undergone change back home in Sri Lanka. Eighteen Latin American states voted not to retain Amerasinghe as conference president—an action taken by some of the Latin American group members because they feared that Amerasinghe would reduce coastal-state rights in the exclusive economic zone.

THE UNITED STATES: A LEAD PLAYER

In early 1975, following the Caracas session the year before, in their testimonies before the United States Senate Foreign Relations Committee and the House Committee on the Judiciary, John R. Stevenson, Special Representative of the President for the Law of the Sea Conference, and his deputy, John Norton Moore, outlined the United States positions on the eight major issues for negotiation at UNCLOS III.[31] These United States positions on some of the issues for negotiation are summarized here as background information for understanding the United States's role in the UNCLOS III negotiations.

Territorial Sea and Free Transit through Straits

The United States position on the territorial sea was formulated in 1967 in a joint initiative undertaken by the United States and the Soviet Union. It called for the two superpowers to promote as a "package deal" the twelve-mile territorial sea with a guarantee for free navigation through the straits, coupled with their willingness to consider preferential fishery rights for coastal states beyond the territorial sea.[32] By 1970, public pronouncements were made by both President Nixon and John R. Stevenson that the United States government was willing to accept the twelve-mile territorial sea, provided that there be free transit through straits.[33] As pointed out in Chapter 3, the United States' basic concern about free passage through straits was the need to keep these international waterways open and accessible to all. More important, as argued by the United States, the application of the innocent-passage principle to straits in customary international law was not sufficient to permit "submerged transit by submarines or overflight by aircraft," leaving aside the "subjective interpretation of 'innocence' " by coastal states.[34] Thus, the United States' position on the breadth of the territorial sea was linked with the issue of free transit through international straits.

The United States then proposed in 1975 that the law of the sea treaty must contain:

1. the right of unimpeded navigation through and over international straits by vessels or aircraft (it had, by 1972, dropped the linkage of coastal state fishery rights as part of the "package deal" originally developed in 1967)[35]
2. as a recognition of straits states' concern over safety and pollution, the United States proposed that surface ships observe traffic separation schemes of IMCO and air regulations by ICAO
3. the application of strict liability for damages caused by nonobservance of IMCO and ICAO rules[36]

It was not until 1979 that Elliot L. Richardson, Special Representative of the President for the Law of the Sea Conference, was able to announce the resolution of the territorial sea issue linked with free transit through straits:

> Delegates have solved the incendiary problem of "creeping jurisdiction" by reaching consensus on a 12-mile territorial sea. . . . We, as well as the Soviet Union, have adhered unequivocally to the position that our commercial and military vessels and aircraft have the right to traverse on, over and under international straits and the waters beyond the territorial sea. Formal affirmation of this right was a priority second to none. The world community, through the conference, has accorded us that recognition.[37]

The Exclusive Economic Zone

The United States' position on the establishment of a regime for the 200-nautical-mile exclusive economic zone for the coastal states was a policy decision made as early as 1970. It made a distinction between the exploitation of fisheries and the exploration of mineral resources on the continental margin, which includes the continental shelf.

On fishery exploitation, the United States advocated coastal state control over coastal (haddock) and anadromous (salmon) stocks and "international management" of highly migratory species (tuna).[38] In addition to the coastal state's broad power to control these fishery stocks, the United States' position with respect to the exclusive economic zone would grant "preferential harvesting rights" within the allowable catch and share the surplus with other nations. The coastal state must have the "management jurisdiction" and "preferential rights" over anadromous stocks (salmon) since they spawn in the coastal state's fresh waters:

> This stock can be properly conserved and managed only if caught when returning to the fresh waters of its origin in the internal waters, territorial sea, or economic zone of

the host state. Taking salmon on the high seas would be banned except with the consent of the host state.[39]

For highly migratory species such as tuna, the United States' original position was to call for coastal state cooperation in the formulation of "equitable" international and regional conservation and allocation of these species,[40] as well as the requirement for entering into international management arrangements with the aid of FAO.[41] By the spring of 1976, Henry Kissinger was able to announce publicly:

> Therefore, we are gratified that the conference is ready to settle upon a 200-mile economic zone. . . . The coastal states will control fisheries, mineral, and other resources activities. At the same time freedom of navigation and other freedoms of the international community must be retained; in this sense the economic zone remains part of the high seas. In addition the treaty must protect certain international interests, such as insuring adequate food supply, conserving highly migratory species, and accommodating the concerns of states—including the landlocked—that otherwise would derive little benefit from the economic zone.[42]

However, as pointed out in Chapter 3, negotiation on the EEZ spent considerable time over the drafting languages to answer questions on the coastal state's jurisdiction, rights, duties and the legal status of the EEZ. The problem over the EEZ was complicated by the respective negotiation positions and power of many other negotiating groups. The coastal states insisted on exclusive rights over fisheries; the major fishing states and distant-water fishing fleets wanted to grant only preferential rights to the coastal states; the LL/GDS wanted the access on an equal basis and the right to participate in the surplus; and the European Economic Community preferred the regional approach based on their experiences in the Atlantic. Thus, Articles 61–74 on the exclusive economic zone represent a composite of compromises, aided by the contribution made by the Evensen Group.

The Issue of Continental Shelf and Continental Margin Resources

The United States linked the establishment of a 200-nautical-mile economic zone to a resolution on other issues, such as free navigation and free transit through straits. In addition, the United States would require that the area be subject to appropriate standards for marine environmental preservation, protection of investment already made in resource development on the continental shelf and the margin, compulsory dispute settlement, and revenue sharing for areas extending beyond the 200-nautical-mile limit.[43]

Considerable controversy at the conference centered on coastal states' right to the mineral resources on the continental margin extending beyond 200 nautical miles, a claim demanded by those coastal states that have an extended margin.

In contrast, the African subgroup of the Group of 77 and the LL/GDS preferred a limit of 200 nautical miles for the continental shelf and margin. In 1975 the United States offered the compromise of a reasonable limit for the outer edge of the continental margin and a revenue-sharing formula "of the well-head value of petroleum and natural gas production with the international community."[44] Contained in the United States continental margin compromise proposal was the suggestion that a coastal state be permitted to claim an additional sixty miles beyond the foot of the continental slope (the so-called "Hedberg formula," after Hollis Hedberg), instead of the continental rise or the "depth of sediment formula (the Irish formula)." (See Chapter 1 for these features.)

By 1978, at the Seventh Session of UNCLOS III, the "depth of sediment" or "Irish formula," combined with the Soviet proposal, was included in the informal Composite Negotiation Text (ICNT) by Negotiating Group 6; the formula was the consensus, accepted by the LL/GDS if revenue sharing was included. However, the United States expressed its willingness to accept either of the formulas.[45] The implications of Article 76 of the 1982 LOS Convention on the continental shelf and margin are discussed in Chapter 3.

Deep Seabed

In 1975 the United States was interested in an international agreement for "an effective international regime" for deep seabed resources development, a regime that would create a stable investment climate for deep seabed mining. The United States then was in favor of "revenue-sharing" to produce assistance for developing nations.[46] But the United States also admitted the "ideological gap" that existed between the developed and developing nations over the type and nature of a deep-seabed authority: whether there should be established an exclusive international authority to control all deep-seabed mining and to be the exclusive operator as well. The United States wanted "a legal order which permits access to the resources of the deep seabed under reasonable conditions that will facilitate investment," and recognized the necessity for establishing via an international treaty a "predictable environment" for protecting "investment, access and profit" of the deep-seabed-mining industry.[47]

In April 1976, Henry Kissinger outlined for the United States the following proposal on deep seabed mining:[48]

1. An international seabed resource authority with an equitable decision-making system under which an assembly of all member states could negotiate on general policy guidance, an executive council for decision making, and a tribunal for resolving disputes
2. Nondiscriminatory access for states and their nationals to deep-seabed resources under reasonable conditions
3. An "Enterprise" to serve as the international deep-seabed authority's operating arm under the same conditions as apply to all mining

4. The offer by the United States of a system of prime mining sites reserved exclusively by the ''Enterprise'' directly for the developing nations
5. A revenue-sharing system for the poorer nations to be supervised by the international deep seabed authority
6. Technology transfer in order to enhance the skills and access of developing nations to advance deep-seabed mining and training of personnel

By the time the Informal Composite Negotiating Text (ICNT) was released in the spring of 1977 at the conference's Sixth Session, the United States considered the provisions on deep-seabed mining to be unsatisfactory and unacceptable.[49] Primary objections by the United States to the deep-seabed provisions in the ICNT were as follows:[50]

1. Exploitation of deep seabed resources was reserved for an international monopoly without assurance of access by qualified contractors.
2. Artificial production limitation through price fixing and market regulation of deep seabed resources
3. The decision-making process, the governance issue, of the international deep seabed authority on a one-nation-one-vote basis without taking into account the production, investment and consumption interests of others
4. The financial burden to be imposed on contractors. (For specifics, see Chapter 7).

The deadlock over the deep seabed mining issue was broken in 1978–1979 when the ''parallel system,'' proposed as a compromise by the United States, was accepted by the Group of 77 and other groups and incorporated into the revised version of the Informal Composite Negotiating Text.[51] Elliot Richardson hailed the compromise as a milestone:

> In essence, we offered to split the difference. On one side would be the private corporations and state enterprises of the industrialized countries, mining under license of the Authority with a share of revenue earmarked for that body. On the other would be the Authority's own operating arm—called the Enterprise—mining for Third World financial advantage.[52]

The ''parallel system,'' as a basic element in the compromise, was subject to review after twenty years; this became part of Article 155 of the 1982 LOS Convention on the Review Conference (for discussion, see Chapter 7).

Significance. There was no question that the United States played a key role in the UNCLOS III negotiations. Yet, its role or its ability to negotiate at the law of the sea conference was restricted. The more than one-hundred nations, representing a variety of world interests, had in the main compelled the United States to make compromises in order to accommodate the Group of 77 (most important of all) and other caucusing groups such as the geographically disadvantaged states, for the sake of helping to establish a new comprehensive law of the sea.

On most of the non-seabed-mining issues, the United States was able and willing to apply its prestige and influence, coupled with adroit diplomatic maneuvering, to accomplish its goals. Freedom of navigation and free strait transit–priority objectives at the Law of the Sea Conference for the United States and other major maritime powers—were guaranteed by trade-offs in the "package deal": a 12-nautical-mile territorial sea and coastal states' rights in the 200-nautical-mile exclusive economic zone. The United States' initiative and its willingness to compromise on the continental margin, particularly the suggestion for revenue sharing of resources exploitation in the continental margin beyond the 200 nautical miles, paved the way for the subsequent consensus on a contentious issue.

The deadlock over the seabed issue could have paralyzed the Law of the Sea Conference. But the stalemate was broken by the United States' willingness to negotiate and to seek a solution to the core ocean problem by offering the "parallel system" for deep-seabed exploitation and exploration. To Elliot Richardson, a former United States Chief Negotiator at the Law of the Sea Conference, it was unfortunately during the last two sessions of UNCLOS III that the United States had been unable "to grasp the procedures of international institutions and forums and then use them to channel decisions to the best national advantage."[53]

SOVIET UNION AND EAST EUROPEAN GROUP

The participation of the Soviet Union and the Eastern European countries in UNCLOS III is briefly presented here on the following selected issues of the law of the sea.

Territorial Sea

Under the framework of the United States–Soviet 1967 agreement to promote a "package deal" of a 12-nautical-mile territorial sea and international guarantee for free navigation through straits, two early proposals from the Soviet Group on the territorial sea and international straits, may be summarized briefly. A joint draft resolution on the territorial sea submitted by Bulgaria, the German Democratic Republic, Poland and the Soviet Union supported the maximum breadth of a 12-nautical-mile territorial sea.[54] The proposal attempted to add five draft articles to the 1958 Convention on the Territorial Sea and Contiguous Zone concerning rights and rules, applicable to all ships, for innocent passage through the territorial sea. The Soviet bloc wanted to define more precisely the concept of innocent passage to include a list of activities considered not innocent, such as the use of weapons and launching of missiles.[55]

In another early draft proposal the Soviet bloc proposed a set of six rules for freedom of navigation through straits. These included

1. prohibition of any threat to the coastal state's territorial inviolability or political independence not to engage in military exercise, and the launching or landing of aircraft
2. the right of the coastal state to designate traffic separation schemes
3. precaution against marine pollution
4. liability for damages to coastal states of the straits
5. nonsuspension of transit of ships through straits
6. noninstallation in straits by coastal states of any structure that could interfere with or hinder the transit of ships[56]

Exclusive Economic Zone

The Soviet Union and the East European socialist nations of Bulgaria, Byelorussia S.S.R., the German Democratic Republic, Poland and Ukrainian S.S.R. submitted a joint proposal concerning the economic zone.[57] Their support for a 200-nautical-mile economic zone was conditioned upon the acceptance of a "package deal" for all other interrelated law of the sea issues, such as the 12-nautical-mile territorial sea, free transit through straits, freedom of navigation, outer limits of the continental shelf, marine pollution and the seabed regime.[58] While the Soviet Union would recognize the right of the coastal states to regulate fishery conservation within the 200-mile zone, it argued that special treatment must be given to LL/GDS and recognition must be given to the rights of those states that had traditionally engaged in fishing in the area. In the end, in exchange for support on the issues of the territorial sea and free transit through straits, the Soviet bloc lent its support to the LL/GDS states in their claim for rights to living resources in the 200-mile economic zone.

Continental Shelf and Continental Margin

The issue that caused prolonged debate and negotiation at UNCLOS III was the question of the outer limit of the continental margin. For both the 1978 seventh session and the 1979 eighth session there emerged two proposals for determining the outer edge of the continental shelf extending into the continental margin—the Irish formula and the Soviet formula. The Soviet formula was intended to refine the Irish formula in establishing the outer edge of the continental margin. First, the Irish formula was an amendment to Article 76 of the Informal Composite Negotiating Text (ICNT). It contained these provisions:

> the coastal state shall establish the outer edge of the continental margin wherever the margin extends beyond 200 nautical miles from the baseline from which the breadth of the territorial sea is measured, by either:
>
> (a) A line delineated in accordance with paragraph 4 by reference to the outermost fixed points at each of which the thickness of sedimentary rocks is at least 1% of the shortest distance from such point in the foot of the continental slope; or

(b) A line delineated in accordance with paragraph 4 by reference to fixed points not more than 60 nautical miles from the foot of the continental slope.[59]

At first, there was no consensus on the Irish formula because the Arab states group wanted to limit continental margin jurisdiction to 200 nautical miles. At this point, the Soviet Union offered its amendment, or formula, which in essence suggested the following:

(1) Where the continental margin does not extend beyond the confines of the 200-mile economic zone, the edge of the continental shelf will lie along the outer limit of the economic zone.

(2) In cases where the edge of the continental margin extends less than 100 miles beyond the outer limit of the 200-mile economic zone, the continental shelf of the coastal state will be determined on the basis of scientifically-sound geological and geomorphological data. . . .

(3) Where the continental margin extends beyond the 100-mile strip adjacent to the 200-mile economic zone, the edge of the continental shelf will be fixed at a distance of 100 miles from the outer limit of the economic zone.[60]

Thus, the Soviet proposal made no reference to the thickness of sediment in determining the outer edge of the continental margin. It also provided that continental shelf jurisdiction should not extend more than 100 nautical miles from the outer limit of the 200-mile economic zone. According to Bernard Oxman, the Soviet proposal seemed to receive support from some nations because "it is easier to apply" and it would reduce disputes.[61] Its defects were that it ignored the "geological basis" of the continental shelf and "failed" to take into account the coastal state interest in the hydrocarbon resources of its coast.[62]

Not until the eighth session of UNCLOS III in 1979 was it decided to combine the Irish and the Soviet formulas. Eventually, through more negotiations, this compromise became the essence of Article 76 of the 1982 LOS Convention, which permits the continental shelf to be extended to a distance of 200 nautical miles from the coast, even if the outer edge of the continental margin is at a lesser distance from the baseline (coast). In addition, the fixed points for the outer edge of the continental shelf may not exceed 350 nautical miles from the coast or 100 nautical miles from the 2,500-meter isobath, whichever is farther seaward.

Deep-Seabed Mining

The basic Soviet position on the whole range of issues related to deep-seabed mining was outlined in 1974.[63] First, it accepted the common heritage principle for the exploration and exploitation of the seabed and its subsoil beyond the continental shelf. Second, it recognized that the right of every state to exploit deep-seabed resources must be ensured. Third, it wanted to guarantee that deep seabed activities did not infringe on the basic freedoms of navigation, fishing, scientific research and cable and pipeline laying. Fourth, the Soviet Union favored a system of licensing exclusively by an international organization. And, finally, the Soviet Union supported the right of the landlocked states for free access to the international seabed area and the right to participate in the exploitation of deep seabed resources. In the negotiating process, the Soviet Union and the Eastern European socialist nations fairly consistently adhered to the end to these basic positions. This group joined the Group of 77 in opposing the unilateral exploitation of deep-seabed resources which, through national legislation, had been declared by a number of Western industrialized states, including the United States. The Soviet group argued that deep-seabed mining is not a part of the high seas freedom; therefore, any unilateral exploitation system established outside the framework of an international seabed authority would be incompatible with the common heritage principle.[64]

Significance. On the one hand, as key promoters along with the United States of the "package deal," the Soviet Union and its Eastern European socialist allies played a dual role of supporting the basic objectives of the maritime powers on matters of the 12-nautical-mile territorial sea and the 200-nautical-mile exclusive economic zone. But, on the other hand, the bloc lent its support to the demands of the Group of 77 or the Third World nations on the core ocean problem—deep-seabed mining. In so doing, the bloc, particularly the Soviet Union, stood to benefit from the outcome of the UNCLOS III. For instance, the "parallel system" for deep-seabed mining enhanced the Soviet position in that it would enable it to qualify and register for "pioneer status" along with France, Japan and India. Once the overlap claim with France in the Clarion-Clipperton mining area was settled, it would then receive an allocation from the Preparatory Commission of a Pacific pioneer site in the Area not to exceed 300,000 square kilometers (see Chapter 7). The promotion and recognition of the 200-nautical-mile EEZ may be considered a loss to the Soviet Union, for in the end, the new ocean regime would reduce the activities of its distant-water fleet of trawlers and factory ships.

WESTERN EUROPE AND THE "GROUP OF 11"

On a number of law of the sea issues, the European Economic Community had taken joint positions reflecting regional concerns and interests, even though several EEC members were also members of the LL/GDS group (Belgium, the Federal Republic of Germany, Luxembourg and the Netherlands). This regional approach was especially pronounced on the fishery issue. In their joint proposal regarding fisheries, Belgium, Denmark, France, the Federal Republic of Germany, Ireland, Italy, Luxembourg and the Netherlands emphasized the need for the coastal state, in fixing its total allowable catch, to submit the figures to the appropriate regional organization.[65] This regional authority would be empowered to adopt regulatory measures for fishery conservation and management. Thus, the matter of allocation of allowable catch within the 200-nautical-mile economic zone would be an internal matter for the community to decide—including whether nonmember states could fish in EEC waters. (After the EEC signed the 1982 LOS Convention on December 10, 1984, it then declared itself as the appropriate organ to adopt relevant rules and regulations on matters of fishery conservation and management.)[66]

The EEC supported the contention that deep-seabed mining of mineral resources, such as manganese nodules, in waters beyond the limits of national jurisdiction fell within the purview of the freedoms of the high seas. This position was adhered to also by most of the industrialized states of the West, plus Japan. On signing the 1982 LOS Convention in 1984, the EEC declared that "significant provisions of Part XI of the Convention are not conducive to the development of the activities" in the International Seabed Area (Part XI).[67] While it is critical of the provisions contained in Part XI, the EEC has signed the convention and is a member of the Preparatory Commission for the International Seabed Authority.

The "Group of 11" (Australia, Austria, Canada, Denmark, Finland, Iceland, Ireland, New Zealand, Norway, Sweden and Switzerland) became visible or identifiable only when efforts were made at the last session to bring together the United States and the Group of 77 to renegotiate Part XI. This portion of the 1982 LOS Convention, on the issue of deep seabed mining, contained provisions objectionable to the United States. This effort failed, for the Group of 77 perceived that the United States had rejected any possible negotiation on any compromise proposals.

In the early stages of negotiation at UNCLOS III, Canada's main concerns were the protection of its fishery resources along its coast, particularly the anadromous species (salmon), and marine environmental protection. At the Caracas session Canada submitted a working paper on the subject of management of salmon, which, because of the anadromous spawning nature of the salmon, advocated a regime which "assures for the state of origin the fruits of its effort and so encourages it to continue to bear the cost."[68] It then proposed the curtailment of salmon fishing in the high seas outside the limits of national jurisdiction; also, that there must be "cooperation with the state of origin by other salmon fishing states through whose zones the salmon must migrate."[69] Thus, with strong United States support, Canada's "salmon provision" became Article 66 of the 1982 LOS Convention. It accorded the state of origin the right to manage salmon species and, at the same time, prohibited taking of salmon on the high seas.[70]

Related to salmon fishery was Canada's concern for the 200-nautical-mile exclusive economic zone, particularly the problem of overlapping fishery resources located beyond the limit—or specifically, the Grand Banks of Newfoundland. Canada was successful in drafting and achieving acceptance of Article 63(2):

2. Where the same stock or stocks of associated species occur both within the exclusive economic zone and in an area beyond and adjacent to the zone, the coastal State and the States fishing for such stocks in the adjacent area shall seek, either directly or through appropriate subregional or regional organizations, to agree upon the measures necessary for the conservation of these stocks in the adjacent area.

On the issue of protection for the marine environment, Canada joined other states (Fiji, Ghana, Guyana, Iceland, India, Iran, New Zealand, the Philippines and Spain) in a draft resolution that contained articles recommending a zonal or regional approach to the preservation of the marine environment.[71]

One of Canada's most interesting roles at the UNCLOS III was its position, as a major land-based mineral supplier of nickel, on production control of seabed mining. Canada joined and worked closely with other land-based mineral suppliers, such as Zaire, Zambia, Indonesia and Zimbabwe, for the imposition of a restrictive production limitation on deep-seabed mining. Canada also parted company with the United States by criticizing the latter's policy of enacting unilateral domestic deep-seabed mining legislation, labeling it as "undesirable" and "unnecessary."[72] In addition, Canada developed differences with the Group of 77 which, under the leadership of Nandan from Fiji, proposed a formula of a 3 percent floor for deep-seabed production control and complete safeguards for deep-seabed miners to produce minerals beyond the level of the total mineral market.[73] (However, Canada did play an influential role in organizing mixed middle-power coastal states, such as Australia, Iceland, New Zealand and Norway, during the Caracas session, by seeking support from the Group of 77 and the Latin American group for a 200-nautical-mile economic zone.)[74]

Significance. The EEC's position on deep-seabed mining can be explained by the interests of European businesses concerning oil and minerals. Their interests are evidenced by the formation of national and international consortia in Europe: The AFERNOD (*Association Française pour L'Étude de Recherche des Nodules*), DORD (Deep Ocean Development Company), KCON (Kennecott Consortium), British Petroleum, Union Seas (Belgium) and Ocean Minerals. As mentioned in Chapter 7, four European nations—France, the Federal Republic of Germany, Italy and the United Kingdom—have enacted domestic legislation for deep-seabed mining. By signing the 1982 LOS Convention, the EEC has made a strong commitment to the world at large that it considers a paramount priority to be the establishment of a new, orderly ocean regime for governing the uses of the oceans.

As Linda Filardi argued, Canada could have played its role as a middle power between the Group of 77 and the Western industrialized powers by "bridging the gap," or as "harmonizer." But, in fact, it alienated the United States and almost antagonized the Group of 77.[75] Its efforts, as a member of the middle-power Group of 11, to find some grounds for compromise over the deep-seabed mining issue were too late (in the summer of 1982) to be of any real consequence.

Table 13.3
UNCLOS III Committee System

UNCLOS III Committee System		
Committee	Subject Jurisdiction	Chairman
I	Seabed exploitation system	Paul Engo (Cameroon)
II	Offshore issues: EEZ, territorial sea, continental shelf, strait transit	Andres Aguilar (Venezuela)
III	Marine environment and scientific research	Alexander Yankov (Bulgaria)

* At first, chairmanship was rotated between Galindo Pohl of El Salvador and Andrés Aguilar of Venezuela.

Source: Information on the UNCLOS III committee system is based on Hollick, *U.S. Foreign Policy and the Law of the Sea*, pp. 290–299; and "Synopsis: Recent Developments in the Law of the Sea, 1978–1979," *San Diego Law Review* 17, no. 3 (April 1980): 694–700. Used by permission.

THE NEGOTIATING GROUPS

A major device employed by the chairmen for the three primary conference committees at the UNCLOS III was the use of negotiating groups. The process placed an inordinate amount of discretionary power into the hands of the committee chairmen for drafting acceptable language on the various law of the sea issues. Thus, collectively, the primary conference committee chairmen and the seven official negotiating groups constituted the most influential, if not decisive, body in the decision-making process for the Third United Nations Law of the Sea Conference. Subject jurisdiction and chairmanship for the conference's main committees are given in Table 13.3.

In April 1978 the conference general (steering) committee decided to permit the formation of negotiating groups, which would have to report to and consult with the appropriate main committee chairmen and then to the conference president concerning compromises reached and for disposal of the issues assigned to them.[76] Each negotiating group would have the right to form smaller groups for the purpose of expediting the negotiation process. Seven official negotiating groups were designated to expedite the many hard core law of the sea issues.[77]

Negotiating Group 1:	System of exploration and exploitation and resource policy (chaired by Francis X. Njenga of Kenya)

Negotiating Group 2:	Financial arrangements for the Authority and the Enterprise, and terms of contracts for exploration (chaired by Tommy T. B. Koh of Singapore)
Negotiating Group 3:	Organs and decision-making power of the Authority (chaired by Paul B. Engo of Cameroon)
Negotiating Group 4:	Right to access to living resources in the EEZ for LL/GDS (chaired by Satya N. Nanda of Fiji)
Negotiating Group 5:	Dispute settlement in the EEZ (chaired by Constantin A. Stavropoulos of Greece)
Negotiating Group 6:	Definition of the outer limits of continental shelf, and revenue sharing (chaired by Andrés Aguilar of Venezuela)
Negotiating Group 7:	Delimitation of maritime boundaries between adjacent and opposite states (chaired by E. J. Manner of Finland)

Significance. Despite criticisms about the conference negotiating style, the system yielded compromises that, in the end, led to acceptance of the language for agreement. The objections revolved around the power that had been placed in the hands of the main committee chairmen and the negotiating groups, subgroups, or informal groups in conducting meetings often in secrecy and with arbitrary exclusion of other interested states. There is no denying that the power of negotiation was entrusted to the hands of a few personalities from the African-Asian-Latin American groups who significantly shaped the 1982 LOS Convention text and the final outcome for the conference.

NOTES

1. Text of the proposal, UN Document A/Conf.62/C.2/L.49, August 9, 1974, can be found in *Third United Nations Conference on the Law of the Sea*, Official Records, vol. 3, Documents of the Conference, 1st and 2nd Sessions (New York: United Nations, 1975), pp. 226–227.
2. Ibid., p. 235 in UN Document A/Conf.62/C.2/L.69, August 19, 1974.
3. Ibid., p. 236 in UN Document A/Conf.62/C.2/L.70, August 20, 1974.
4. See State Department, Special Report, No. 1 (revised): "UN Law of the Sea Conference 1975," February 1975, pp. 1–2 (based on statement made by John R. Stevenson, Special Representative of the President for the Law of the Sea Conference, before the Senate Foreign Relations Committee and the House Committee on the Judiciary); *GIST*, Public Affairs, Department of State, August 1975, p. 1; Henry Kissinger, "The Law of the Sea: A Test of International Cooperation," Bureau of Public Affairs, April 8, 1976 (speech before the Foreign Policy Association, U.S. Council of International Chambers of Commerce, and the UN Association of the U.S.A. in New York City),

pp. 3–4; and George H. Aldrich, Acting Special Representative of the President for the Law of the Sea Conference before the National Association of Manufacturers in San Francisco on December 9, 1980, "Seabed Resources: Law of the Sea," Current Policy No. 255, Department of State, December 9, 1980, p. 3.

5. For the text see UN Document A/Conf.62/WP.8, May 7, 1975, in *Third United Nations Conference on the Law of the Sea*, Official Records, vol. 4, 3rd Session, Geneva, March 17 –May 9, 1975, pp. 168–170.

6. See Ann L. Hollick, *U.S. Foreign Policy and the Law of the Sea* (Princeton, N.J.: Princeton University Press, 1981), p. 305.

7. *Third United Nations Conference on the Law of the Sea*, Official Records, vol. 3, pp. 172–173.

8. For a summary of these resolutions, see E. D. Brown, *Seabed Energy and Mineral Resources and the Law of the Sea*, vol. 2 (London: Graham & Trotman, 1986), pp. 2, 16–35.

9. *Third United Nations Conference on the Law of the Sea*, vol. 11, p. 82.

10. Barry Buzan, *Seabed Politics* (New York: Praeger, 1976), pp. 120–130.

11. Allan G. Friedman and Cynthia A. Williams, "The Group of 77 at the United Nations: An Emergent Force in the Law of the Sea," *San Diego Law Review* 16, no. 3 (April 1979): 570–572.

12. Buzan, *Seabed Politics*, pp. 129–130; 159–160.

13. See UN Document A/Conv.62/77, April 24, 1979, *Third United Nations Conference on the Law of the Sea*, Official Records, vol. 11, p. 82.

14. *Third United Nations Conference on the Law of the Sea*, Official Records, vol. 12, pp. 70–71.

15. Ibid., pp. 240–241.

16. For an account of the Yaoundé meeting see Frank X. Njenga, "Historical Background of the Evolution of the Exclusive Economic Zone and the Contribution of Africa," in Giulio Pontecorvo, ed. *The New Order of the Oceans: The Advent of a Managed Environment* (New York: Columbia University Press, 1986), pp. 125–127.

17. *Third United Nations Conference on the Law of the Sea*, Official Records, vol. 3, pp. 240–241.

18. See Tsuneo Akah, *Japan in Global Ocean Politics* (Honolulu: The Law of the Sea Institute, University of Hawaii, 1985), pp. 24–58; and Haruhiro Fukui, "How Japan Handled UNCLOS Issues: Does Japan Have an Ocean Policy?" Robert Friedheim et al., eds., *Japan and the New Ocean Regime* (Boulder, Colo.: Westview Press, 1984), pp. 21–66. Also see Tadao Kuribayashi, "The United Nations Convention on the Law of the Sea and the Japanese Municipal Laws," in Choon-ho Park and Jae Kyu Park, eds., *The Law of the Sea: Problems from the East Asian Perspective* (Honolulu: The Law of the Sea Institute, University of Hawaii, 1987), pp. 316–322.

19. Fukui, "How Japan Handled UNCLOS Issues," p. 37; and Akah, *Japan in Global Ocean Politics*, pp. 34–38.

20. Fukui, "How Japan Handled UNCLOS Issues," pp. 29–31.

21. See Moritaka Hayashi, "Japan and Deep Seabed Mining," *Ocean Development and International Law* 17, no. 4 (1986): 357–365; and Takeo Iguchi, "Japan and the New Law of the Sea: Facing the Challenge of Deep Seabed Mining," *Virginia Journal of International Law* 273 (Spring 1987): 535–541.

22. For the text of the Kampala Declaration, see UN Document A/Conf.62/23, May

2, 1974, *Third United Nations Conference on the Law of the Sea*, Official Records, vol. 2, p. 3.

23. UN Document A/Conf.62/C.2/L.29, July 30, 1974, *Third United Nations Conference on the Law of the Sea*, Official Records, vol. 3, pp. 206–210.

24. See Njenga, "Historical Background of the Evolution of the Exclusive Economic Zone and the Contribution of Africa," pp. 143–146; and Hollick, *U.S. Foreign Policy and the Law of the Sea*, pp. 317 and 394.

25. See Hollick, *U.S. Foreign Policy and the Law of the Sea*, p. 328; and Bernard Oxman, "The Third United Nations Conference on the Law of the Sea: The Seventh Session (1978)," *American Journal of International Law* 73, no. 1 (January 1979): 6 and 16–18.

26. David L. Larson, ed., *Major Issues of the Law of the Sea* (Durham, N.H.: University of New Hampshire, 1976), p. 47.

27. Hollick, *U.S. Foreign Policy and the Law of the Sea*, pp. 103–252; and Andrés Aguilar Mawdsley, "Law of the Sea: The Latin-American View," in Pontecotvo, ed., *The New Order of the Oceans*, pp. 175–177.

28. Mawdsley, "The Law of the Sea: The Latin-American View," pp. 178–179. Also see UN Document A/AC.138/SC.II/L.21, June 7, 1972, as a joint proposal at the UN Seabed Committee debate.

29. Mawdsley, "The Law of the Sea: The Latin-American View," p. 190.

30. Ibid., pp. 190–193.

31. "Special Report: U.N. Law of the Sea Conference 1975," Department of State, Bureau of Public Affairs, February 1975.

32. See "Special Report: U.N. Law of the Sea Conference 1975." Also see Hollick, *U.S. Foreign Policy and the Law of the Sea*, p. 234. For a recent case study of the United States role in the negotiation of the Law of the Sea treaty, see Steven R. David and Peter Digeser, *The United States and the Law of the Sea Treaty* (Lanham, Md.: University Press of America, February 1990).

33. *Department of State Bulletin* 62, no. 1602 (March 9, 1970): 329–330; and 62, no. 1603 (March 16, 1970): 339–343.

34. "Special Report: U. N. Law of the Sea Conference 1975," p. 3.

35. Hollick, *U.S. Foreign Policy and the Law of the Sea*, p. 271. Also see H. Gary Knight, "The 1971 United States Proposals on the Breadth of the Territorial Sea and Passage through International Straits," *Oregon Law Review* 51 (Summer 1972): 759–787.

36. "Special Report: U.N. Law of the Sea Conference 1975," p. 4.

37. Elliot L. Richardson, Special Representative of the Law of the Sea Conference, Speech before the Washington Press Club, March 14, 1979, "Law of the Sea: A Test for the United Nations," *Current Policy*, no. 60, March 1979, Bureau of Public Affairs, Department of State, pp. 2–3.

38. "Special Report: U.N. Law of the Sea Conference 1975," p. 4.

39. Ibid.

40. Ibid.

41. Hollick, *U.S. Foreign Policy and the Law of the Sea*, p. 357.

42. "Special Report: U.N. Law of the Sea Conference 1975," p. 5 and also see Bernard H. Oxman, "The United Nations Conference on the Law of the Sea: The 1977 New York Session," *American Journal of International Law* 22, no. 1 (January 1978): 67–75.

43. "Special Report: U.N. Law of the Sea Conference 1975," p. 5.

44. U.S. Department of State news release, Status Report on Law of the Sea Negotiation after Geneva, statement by John R. Stevenson before the Senate Foreign Relations Committee, Subcommittee on Oceans and International Environment, May 22, 1975, p. 2.

45. See Bernard H. Oxman, "The United Nations Conference on the Law of the Sea: The Seventh Session (1978)," *American Journal of International Law* 73, no. 1 (January 1979): 19–22; and "The Third United Nations Conference on the Law of the Sea: The Eighth Session (1979)," *American Journal of International Law* 74, no. 1 (January 1980): 20–22.

46. "Special Report: U.N. Law of the Sea Conference 1975," p. 5. Also see statement by Secretary of State Henry Kissinger in "The Law of the Sea: A Test of International Cooperation," p. 5.

47. "Special Report: U.N. Law of the Sea Conference, 1975," p. 5.

48. Kissinger, "The Law of the Sea: A Test for International Cooperation," pp. 6–7.

49. Text of Elliot Richardson speech before the Seapower Symposium of the Cincinnati Council of the Navy League of the United States in "Bulletin Reprint: Law of the Sea Conference," Bureau of Public Affairs, Department of State, January 18, 1978, p. 1.

50. Ibid., pp. 1–3. Also see *The Department of State Bulletin* 77 (1977): 389.

51. The text is to be found in UN Document A/Conf.62/WP.10/Rev.1, April 28, 1979. Also see "Law of the Sea: A Test for the United Nations," speech by Elliot Richardson.

52. Kissinger, "Law of the Sea: Test for the United Nations," p. 3.

53. See Elliot L. Richardson's letter to the editor of *Foreign Policy* in response to an article by James L. Malone, "Who Needs the Sea Treaty?" *Foreign Policy* no. 54 (Spring 1984): p. 179.

54. See UN Document A/Conf.62/C.2/L.26, July 29, 1974, in *Third United Nations Conference on the Law of the Sea*, Official Records, vol. 3, p. 203.

55. Ibid. And also see *Third United Nations Conference on the Law of the Sea*, Official Records, vol. 2, Summary of Records, 2nd Session, Caracas, June 20–August 29, 1974, pp. 105 and 116–117.

56. See UN Document A/Conf.62/C.2/L.11, July 17, 1974, in *Third United Nations Conference on the Law of the Sea*, Official Records, vol. 3, pp. 189–190.

57. UN Document A/Conf.62/C.2/L.38, August 5, 1974. Text is found in *Third United Nations Conference on the Law of the Sea*, Official Records, vol. 3, pp. 214–216.

58. See statement by the Soviet delegate at the twenty-eighth meeting of the Second Committee at Caracas, *Third United Nations Conference on the Law of the Sea*, Official Records, vol. 2, p. 217.

59. See Negotiation Group 6/1, as provided in Oxman," The Third United Nations Conference on the Law of the Sea: The Seventh Session (1978)," pp. 19–20.

60. Informal meeting of Committee 2 (C.2/Informal/14, April 27, 1978) as provided in Oxman, "The United Nations Conference on the Law of the Sea: The Seventh Session (1978)," p. 20. Also see statement by the Soviet delegate at the twentieth meeting of the Second Committee at the 1974 Caracas session, *Third United Nations Conference on the Law of the Sea*, Official Records, vol. 2, pp. 160–161, for an earlier official position on the outer edge of the continental shelf.

61. Oxman, "The Third United Nations Conference on the Law of the Sea: The Seventh Session (1978)," p. 20.

62. Ibid., p. 21.

63. See UN Document A/Conf.62/C.1/L.12, March 12, 1975, in *Third United Nations Conference on the Law of the Sea*, Official Records, vol. 4, pp. 182–185; and statement by the Soviet delegate at the eighth meeting of the First Committee at the Caracas session, *Third United Nations Conference on the Law of the Sea*, Official Records, vol. 2, pp. 38–40.

64. Oxman, "The Third United Nations Conference on the Law of the Sea: The Seventh Session (1978)," p. 35.

65. See UN Document A/Conf.62/C.2/L.40 and ADD.1, 5 & 28, August 1974, in *Third United Nations Conference on the Law of the Sea*, Official Records, vol. 3, pp. 217–218.

66. See Michael Hardy, "The Law of the Sea and the Prospects for Deep Seabed Mining: The Position of the European Community," *Ocean Development and International Law* 17, no. 4 (1986): 311–313 and 318–319 (for text of the declaration).

67. Ibid., p. 321.

68. See UN Document A/Conf.62/C.2/L.81, August 23, 1974, in *Third United Nations Conference on the Law of the Sea*, Official Records, vol. 3, p. 240.

69. Ibid.

70. See Ted L. McDorman, "Will Canada Ratify the Law of the Sea Treaty?" *San Diego Law Review* 25, no. 3 (August–September 1988): 537.

71. UN Document A/Conf.62/C.3/L.6, July 31, 1974, in *Third United Nations Conference on the Law of the Sea*, Official Records, vol. 3, p. 249.

72. See Linda Filardi, "Canadian Perspectives on Seabed Mining: The Case of the Production Limitation Formula," *Ocean Development and International Law* 13, no. 4 (1983): 472.

73. Ibid., p. 473.

74. Edward L. Miles, "The Structure and Effects of the Decision Process in the Seabed Committee and the Third United Nations Conference on the Law of the Sea," *International Organization* 31, no. 2 (Spring 1977): 231.

75. Filardi, "Canadian Perspectives on Seabed Mining," pp. 457 and 476–477. For a recent study of the Canadian marine policy and its role in the law of the sea negotiations, see Donald McRae and Gordon Munro, *Canadian Ocean Policy: National Strategies and the New Law of the Sea* (Vancouver, B.C.: University of British Columbia Press, 1989).

76. UN Document A/Conf.62/61, April 1978, in *Third United Nations Conference on the Law of the Sea*, Official Records, vol. 10, p. 2.

77. Ibid. Also see Oxman, "The Third United Nations Conference on the Law of the Sea: The Seventh Session (1978)," pp. 8–24; and UN Document A/Conf.62/121, October 27, 1982.

APPENDIX I

Chronological Listing of Treaties on the Law of the Sea*

1884

14 March 1884	PARIS	Convention on the Protection of Submarine Cables
		PARIS - Declaration of 1 December 1886 relating to the Convention on the Protection of Submarine Cables
		PARIS - Protocol of 7 July 1887 relating to the Convention on the Protection of Submarine Cables

1888

29 October 1888	CONSTANTINOPLE	Convention respecting the Free Navigation of the Suez Maritime Canal

1910

23 September 1910	BRUSSELS	Convention for the Unification of Certain Rules of Law respecting Assistance and Salvage at Sea
		BRUSSELS - Protocol of 27 May 1967 to amend the Convention for the Unification of Certain Rules of Law relating to Assistance and Salvage at Sea
23 September 1910	BRUSSELS	Convention for the Unification of Certain Rules of Law respecting Collisions between Vessels (with Optional Protocol)

1920

9 February 1920	PARIS	Treaty relating to the Status of Spitzbergen (Svalbard), with Annex

*The Law of the Sea: Multilateral Treaties Relevant to the United Nations Convention on the Law of the Sea (United Nations: Office of the Special Representative of the Secretary-General for the Law of the Sea. 1985).

15 June 1920	GENOA	Convention for Establishing Facilities for Finding Employment for Seamen
15 June 1920	GENOA	Convention concerning Unemployment Indemnity in Case of Loss or Foundering of the Ship
15 June 1920	GENOA	Convention Fixing the Minimum Age for Admission of Children to Employment at Sea

1921

20 April 1921	BARCELONA	Convention and Statute on Freedom of Transit
20 April 1921	BARCELONA	Convention and Statute on the Régime of Navigable Waterways of International Concern
		BARCELONA - Additional Protocol of 20 April 1921 to the Convention on the Régime of Navigable Waterways of International Concern
20 April 1921	BARCELONA	Declaration recognizing the Right to a Flag of States having no Sea-coast
21 October 1921	GENEVA	Convention fixing the Minimum Age for the Admission of Young Persons to Employment as Trimmers and Stokers
25 October 1921	GENEVA	Convention concerning the Compulsory Medical Examination of Children and Young Persons Employed at Sea

1923

9 December 1923	GENEVA	Convention and Statute on the International Régime of Maritime Ports

1924

25 August 1924	BRUSSELS	International Convention for the Unification of Certain Rules relating to the Limitation of the Liability of Owners of Seagoing Vessels
25 August 1924	BRUSSELS	International Convention for the Unification of Certain Rules relating to Bills of Lading
		BRUSSELS - Protocol of 23 February 1968 to Amend the International Convention for the Unification of Certain Rules relating to Bills of Lading
		BRUSSELS - Protocol of 21 December 1979 amending the International Convention for the Unification of Certain Rules of Law relating to Bills of Lading

1925

19 February 1925	GENEVA	International Opium Convention
		LAKE SUCCESS - Protocol of 11 December 1946 amending the International Opium Convention

1926

10 April 1926	BRUSSELS	International Convention for the Unification of Certain Rules relating to Maritime Liens and Mortgages
10 April 1926	BRUSSELS	International Convention for the Unification of Certain Rules relating to the Immunity of State-owned Vessels
		BRUSSELS - Additional Protocol of 24 May 1934 to the International Convention for the Unification of Certain Rules concerning the Immunity of State-owned Vessels
23 June 1926	GENEVA	Convention concerning the Repatriation of Seamen
24 June 1926	GENEVA	Convention concerning Seamen's Articles of Agreement
25 September 1926	GENEVA	Slavery Convention
		NEW YORK - Protocol of 7 December 1953 amending the Slavery Convention

1930

23 October 1930	LISBON	Agreement Concerning Maritime Signals

1932

9 December 1932	MADRID	International Telecommunication Convention for the Establishment of the International Telecommunication Union (ITU) (with Annex)

1934

16 April 1934	WARSAW	Convention relating to the Tonnage Measurement of Merchant Ships

1936

26 June 1936	GENEVA	Convention for the Suppression of the Illicit Traffic in Dangerous Drugs
		LAKE SUCCESS - Protocol of 11 December 1946 amending the Convention for the Suppression of the Illicit Traffic in Dangerous Drugs
20 July 1936	MONTREUX	Convention regarding the Régime of Straits (with Annexes and Protocol)
24 October 1936	GENEVA	Convention Fixing the Minimum Age for the Admission of Children to Employment at Sea
24 October 1936	GENEVA	Convention concerning the Minimum Requirement of Professional Capacity for Masters and Officers on Board Merchant Ships
24 October 1936	GENEVA	Convention concerning Sickness Insurance for Seamen
29 October 1936	GENEVA	Convention concerning the Liability of the Shipowner in case of Sickness, Injury or Death of Seamen

1938

28 September 1938	BRUSSELS	International Convention for the Unification of Certain Rules relating to Assistance and Salvage of Aircraft or by Aircraft at Sea

1944

7 December 1944	CHICAGO	International Civil Aviation Organization: Provisional Organization
7 December 1944	CHICAGO	International Civil Aviation Organization: Interim Agreement
7 December 1944	CHICAGO	Convention on International Civil Aviation

MONTREAL - Protocol of 14 June 1954 relating to Certain Amendments to the Convention on International Civil Aviation

MONTREAL - Protocol of 21 June 1961 relating to an Amendment of Article 50(a) of the Convention on International Civil Aviation to Increase Membership of the Council From Twenty-One to Twenty-Seven

ROME - Protocol of 15 September 1962 relating to an Amendment of Article 48(a) to the Convention on International Civil Aviation to increase the number of parties which may request holding an extraordinary meeting of the Assembly

BUENOS AIRES - Protocol of 24 September 1968 on the Authentic Trilingual Text of the Convention on International Civil Aviation (with Annex and Proces-verbal of Rectification of 8 April 1969)

WASHINGTON - Proces-verbal of 8 April 1969 of Rectification to the Protocol of 24 September 1968 on the Authentic Trilingual Text of the Convention on International Civil Aviation

NEW YORK - Protocol of 12 March 1971 relating to the Amendment of Article 50(a) of the Convention on International Civil Aviation to Increase Membership of the Council From Twenty-Seven to Thirty

VIENNA - Protocol of 7 July 1971 relating to the Amendment of Article 56 to the Convention on International Civil Aviation to Enlarge the Membership of the Air Navigation Commission

1946

27 June 1946	SEATTLE	Convention concerning Food and Catering for Crew on Board Ship
27 June 1946	SEATTLE	Convention concerning the Certification of Ships' Cooks
28 June 1946	SEATTLE	Convention concerning Social Security for Seafarers
28 June 1946	SEATTLE	Convention concerning Seafarers' Pensions
29 June 1946	SEATTLE	Convention concerning the Medical Examination of Seafarers
29 June 1946	SEATTLE	Convention concerning the Certification of Able Seamen
22 July 1946	NEW YORK	Constitution of the World Health Organization
2 December 1946	WASHINGTON	International Convention for the Regulation of Whaling (with annexed Schedule)
		WASHINGTON - Protocol of 19 November 1956 to the International Convention for the Regulation of Whaling
		WASHINGTON - Schedule of 25 June 1971 to the International Whaling Convention of 1946 revised to include the Amendments adopted at the 23rd Meeting of the International Whaling Commission (schedule amended annually)

1947

10 June 1947	OSLO	Convention for a Uniform System of Tonnage Measurement of Ships

1948

26 February 1948	BAGUIO	Agreement for the Establishment of the Indo-Pacific Fisheries Council
		KARACHI - Amendments of 20 January 1961 to the Agreement for the Establishment of the Indo-Pacific Fisheries Council
6 March 1948	GENEVA	Convention on the International Maritime Organization

Amendments:

1. IMO Res. A.69(ES.II) of 15 September 1964
2. IMO Res. A.70(IV) of 28 September 1965
3. IMO Res. A.315(ES.V) of 17 October 1974
4. IMO Res. A.358(IX) of 14 November 1975
5. IMO Res. A.371(X) of 9 November 1977
6. IMO Res. A.400(X) of 17 November 1977
7. IMO Res. A.450(XI) of 15 November 1979

10 June 1948	LONDON	International Convention for the Safety of Life at Sea

<u>1949</u>

31 May 1949	WASHINGTON	Convention for the Establishment of an Inter-American Tropical Tuna Commission
18 June 1949	GENEVA	Convention concerning Vacation Holidays with Pay for Seafarers
18 June 1949	GENEVA	Convention concerning Crew Accommodation on Board Ship
24 September 1949	ROME	Agreement for the Establishment of a General Fisheries Council for the Mediterranean
		ROME - Amendments of 22 May 1963 to the Agreement for the Establishment of a General Fisheries Council for the Mediterranean

<u>1951</u>

25 May 1951	GENEVA	International Sanitary Regulations

<u>1952</u>

7 March 1952	OSLO	Agreement between the Governments of Norway, Denmark, and Sweden concerning measures for the Protection of the Stocks of Deep-Sea Prawns (*Pandalus borealis*), European Lobsters (*Homarus vulgaris*), Norway Lobsters (*Nephrops norvegicus*) and Crabs (*Cancer pagurus*)
		OSLO - Protocol of 14 October 1959 between the Governments of Norway, Denmark and Sweden amending Article 4 of the Agreement concerning measures for the Protection of Stocks of Deep-Sea Prawns, European Lobsters, Norway Lobsters and Crabs
9 May 1952	TOKYO	International Convention for the High Seas Fisheries of the North Pacific Ocean (with Annex and Protocol)
		SEATTLE - Amendments of 17 November 1962 to the Annex to the International Convention for the High Seas Fisheries of the North Pacific Ocean *and* Recommendations relating to Halibut and Herring adopted at the Ninth Annual Meeting of the International North Pacific Fisheries Commission
		TOKYO - Protocol of 25 April 1978 amending the International Convention for the High Seas Fisheries of the North Pacific Ocean
10 May 1952	BRUSSELS	International Convention on Certain Rules concerning Civil Jurisdiction in Matters of Collision
10 May 1952	BRUSSELS	International Convention for the Unification of Certain Rules relating to Penal Jurisdiction in Matters of Collision or other Incidents of Navigation
10 May 1952	BRUSSELS	International Convention for the Unification of Certain Rules relating to the Arrest of Sea-going Ships

1954

12 May 1954	LONDON	International Convention for the Prevention of Pollution of the Sea by Oil (with Annexes) 1. 1962 Amendments to OILPOL 1954 Amendments to articles I to X, XIV, XVI and XVIII and to Annexes A and B to the Convention done at London on 11 April 1962 2. 1969 Amendments to OILPOL 1954 Done at London on 21 October 1969 3. 1971 Amendments to OILPOL 1954 Great Barrier Reef done at London on 12 October 1971 4. 1971 (Tanks) Amendments to OILPOL 1954 Concerning Tanks Arrangements and Limitation of Tank Size done at London on 15 October 1971
4 December 1954	LIMA	Agreements signed at the Second Conference on the Exploitation and Conservation of the Maritime Resources of the South-Pacific

1955

19 March 1955	STOCKHOLM	Agreement between Denmark, Norway and Sweden to Facilitate the Sanitary Control of Traffic between those Countries

1956

7 September 1956	GENEVA	Supplementary Convention on the Abolition of Slavery, the Slave Trade, and Institutions and Practices Similar to Slavery

1957

9 February 1957	WASHINGTON	Interim Convention on Conservation of North Pacific Fur Seals (with Schedule) WASHINGTON - Protocol of 8 October 1963 Amending the Interim Convention on Conservation of North Pacific Fur Seals WASHINGTON - Protocol of 7 May 1976 Amending the Interim Convention on Conservation of North Pacific Fur Seals WASHINGTON - Protocol of 14 October 1980 Amending the Interim Convention on Conservation of North Pacific Fur Seals
25 March 1957	ROME	Treaty Establishing the European Economic Community (with Annexes and Protocols)
10 October 1957	BRUSSELS	International Convention relating to Stowaways
10 October 1957	BRUSSELS	International Convention relating to the Limitation of the Liability of Owners of Sea-going Ships LONDON - Protocol of 21 December 1979 amending the International Convention relating to the Limitation of the Liability of Owners of Sea-going Ships

<u>1958</u>

29 April 1958	GENEVA	Convention on the Territorial Sea and the Contiguous Zone
29 April 1958	GENEVA	Convention on the High Seas
29 April 1958	GENEVA	Convention on Fishing and Conservation of the Living Resources of the High Seas
29 April 1958	GENEVA	Convention on the Continental Shelf
14 May 1958	GENEVA	Convention concerning Wages, Hours of Work on Board Ship and Manning
30 May 1958	GENEVA	Convention concerning Seafarers' National Identity Documents

<u>1959</u>

24 January 1959	LONDON	North-East Atlantic Fisheries Convention (with Annex) LONDON - Procès-verbal of 24 January 1959 concerning modifications to Article 7(1) of the North-East Atlantic Fisheries Convention
19 June 1959	GENEVA	Convention concerning the Minimum Age for Admission to Employment as Fishermen
19 June 1959	GENEVA	Convention concerning the Medical Examination of Fishermen
19 June 1959	GENEVA	Convention concerning Fishermen's Articles of Agreement
7 July 1959	VARNA	Convention concerning fishing in the Black Sea (as amended)
1 December 1959	WASHINGTON	The Antarctic Treaty

<u>1960</u>

17 June 1960	LONDON	International Convention for the Safety of Life at Sea

<u>IMO Resolutions amending the International Convention on Safety of Life at Sea, 1960:</u>

1. <u>1966 Amendments to the Convention</u>
   Done at London on 30 November 1966
2. <u>1967 Amendments to the Convention</u>
   Done at London on 25 October 1967
3. <u>1968 Amendments to the Convention</u>
   Done at London on 26 November 1968
4. <u>1969 Amendments to the Convention</u>
   Done at London on 21 October 1969
5. <u>1971 Amendments to the Convention</u>
   Done at London on 12 October 1971
6. <u>1973 (General) Amendments</u>
   Done at London on 20 November 1973
7. <u>1973 (Grain Amendment)</u>
   Done at London on 20 November 1973

17 June 1960	LONDON	International Regulations for Preventing Collisions at Sea
29 June 1960	PARIS	Convention on Third-Party Liability in the Field of Nuclear Energy
		BRUSSELS - Supplementary Convention of 31 January 1963 to the Paris Convention on Third-Party Liability in the Field of Nuclear Energy
		PARIS - Additional Protocol of 28 January 1964 to the Convention on Third-Party Liability in the Field of Nuclear Energy
1961		
30 March 1961	NEW YORK	Single Convention on Narcotic Drugs
		GENEVA - Protocol of 25 March 1972 amending the Single Convention on Narcotic Drugs
29 April 1961	BRUSSELS	International Convention for the Unification of Certain Rules relating to the Carriage of Passengers by Sea
1962		
20 February 1962	LONDON	International Agreement regarding the Maintenance of Certain Lights in the Red Sea
25 May 1962	BRUSSELS	Brussels Convention on the Liability of Operators of Nuclear Ships
28 June 1962	WARSAW	Agreement concerning Co-operation in Marine Fishing
18 September 1962	HELSINKI	Agreement between Denmark, Finland, Norway and Sweden concerning Uniform Rules for the Marking of Navigable Waters
20 December 1962	STOCKHOLM	Agreement concerning the Protection of the Salmon Population in the Baltic Sea
1963		
21 May 1963	VIENNA	Vienna Convention on Civil Liability for Nuclear Damage
		VIENNA - Optional Protocol of 21 May 1963 concerning the Compulsory Settlement of Disputes (to the Vienna Convention on Civil Liability for Nuclear Damage)
7 June 1963	MOSCOW	Agreement concerning the Load Lines for Ships sailing under the Flags and between the ports of the German Democratic Republic, the Polish People's Republic and the Union of Soviet Socialist Republics on the Baltic Sea (with Annexes)
5 August 1963	MOSCOW	Treaty Banning Nuclear Weapon Tests in the Atmosphere, in Outer Space and Under Water

1964

20 August 1964	WASHINGTON	Agreement Establishing Interim Arrangements for a Global Commercial Communications Satellite System, and Special Agreement (with Annex) WASHINGTON - Supplementary Agreement of 4 June 1965 on Arbitration to the Agreement establishing Interim Arrangements for a Global Communications Satellite System
12 September 1964	COPENHAGEN	Convention for the International Council for the Exploration of the Sea COPENHAGEN - Protocol of 13 August 1970 to the Convention for the International Council for the Exploration of the Sea

1965

22 January 1965	STRASBOURG	European Agreement for the Prevention of Broadcasts transmitted from Stations outside National Territories
9 April 1965	LONDON	Convention on Facilitation of International Maritime Traffic (with Annex) 1. 1969 Amendments to the Annex Cruises and cruise passengers. Done at London on 28 November 1969 2. 1971 Amendments to the Annex Passengers in transit and ships in scientific services. Done at London on 27 April 1971 3. 1973 Amendments to the Annex Cargo handling equipment. Done at London on 31 January 1973 4. 1973 Amendments to the Annex Shore leave for crew members. Done at London on 2 August 1973 5. 1973 Amendments to the Convention Amendment to Article VII. Done at London on 19 November 1973 6. 1974 Amendments to the Annex Upgrading of recommended practices to standards. Done at London on 26 February 1974 7. 1977 Amendments to the Annex Done at London on 10 November 1977
8 July 1965	NEW YORK	Convention on Transit Trade of Land-locked States
12 November 1965	MONTREUX	International Telecommunication Convention

<u>1966</u>

5 April 1966	LONDON	International Convention on Load Lines (with Annexes) 1. <u>1971 Amendments to the Convention</u> Done at London on 12 October 1971 2. <u>1975 Amendments to the Convention</u> Done at London on 12 November 1975 3. <u>1979 Amendments to the Convention</u> Done at London on 15 November 1979 4. <u>1983 Amendments to Annex II</u> Done at London on 17 November 1983
14 May 1966	RIO DE JANEIRO	International Convention for the Conservation of Atlantic Tunas
21 June 1966	GENEVA	Convention concerning Fishermen's Certificates of Competency
21 June 1966	GENEVA	Convention concerning Accommodation on Board Fishing Vessels

<u>1967</u>

14 February 1967	MEXICO CITY	Treaty for the Prohibition of Nuclear Weapons in Latin America (Treaty of Tlatelolco) (with Additional Protocols I and II)
3 May 1967	MONACO	Convention on the International Hydrographic Organization
27 May 1967	BRUSSELS	International Convention for the Unification of Certain Rules relating to Carriage of Passenger Luggage by Sea
27 May 1967	BRUSSELS	International Convention for the Unification of Certain Rules relating to Maritime Liens and Mortgages
27 May 1967	BRUSSELS	Convention relating to Registration of Rights in Respect of Vessels under Construction
1 June 1967	LONDON	Convention on Conduct of Fishing Operations in the North Atlantic
28 December 1967	BANGKOK	Agreement Establishing the South-East Asian Fisheries Development Centre BANGKOK - Protocol of 13 January 1968 amending the Agreement Establishing the South-East Asian Fisheries Development Centre

1968

22 April 1968	WASHINGTON, LONDON, MOSCOW	Agreement on the Rescue of Astronauts, the Return of Astronauts and the Return of Objects Launched into Outer Space
1 July 1968	WASHINGTON, LONDON, MOSCOW	Treaty on the Non-Proliferation of Nuclear Weapons
13 December 1968	PARIS	European Convention for the Protection of Animals during international transport
		STRASBOURG - Additional Protocol of 10 May 1979 to the European Convention for the Protection of Animals during international transport

1969

6 May 1969	LONDON	European Convention on the Protection of the Archaeological Heritage
9 June 1969	BONN	Agreement for Co-operation in Dealing with Pollution of the North Sea by Oil (with Annex)
23 June 1969	LONDON	International Convention on Tonnage Measurement of Ships, 1969
25 July 1969	BOSTON	International Health Regulations
23 October 1969	ROME	Convention on the Conservation of the Living Resources of the South-East Atlantic
29 November 1969	BRUSSELS	International Convention on Civil Liability for Oil Pollution Damage
		LONDON - Protocol of 19 November 1976 to the International Convention on Civil Liability for Oil Pollution Damage
		LONDON - Protocol of 25 May 1984 to the International Convention on Civil Liability for Oil Pollution Damage
29 November 1969	BRUSSELS	International Convention relating to Intervention of the High Seas in Cases of Oil Pollution Casualties

1970

30 October 1970	GENEVA	Convention concerning Crew Accommodation on Board Ship (Supplementary Provisions)
30 October 1970	GENEVA	Convention concerning the Prevention of Occupational Accidents to Seafarers

1971

11 February 1971	LONDON, MOSCOW, WASHINGTON	Treaty on the Prohibition of the Emplacement of Nuclear Weapons and other Weapons of Mass Destruction on the Sea-bed and the Ocean Floor and in the Subsoil Thereof
21 February 1971	VIENNA	Convention on Psychotropic Substances (with list of substances)
20 August 1971	WASHINGTON	Agreement relating to the International Telecommunications Satellite Organization "INTELSAT" (with Operating Agreement and Annexes)
16 September 1971	COPENHAGEN	Agreement between Denmark, Finland, Norway and Sweden concerning Co-operation in Measures to Deal with Pollution of the Sea by Oil
6 October 1971	LONDON	Special Trade Passenger Ships Agreement
3 December 1971	BUDAPEST	Agreement on Co-operation with regard to Maritime Merchant Shipping
17 December 1971	BRUSSELS	Convention relating to Civil Liability in the Field of Maritime Carriage of Nuclear Material
18 December 1971	BRUSSELS	International Convention on the Establishment of an International Fund for Compensation for Oil Pollution Damage
		LONDON - Protocol of 19 November 1976 to the International Convention on the Establishment of an International Fund for Compensation for Oil Pollution Damage
		LONDON - Protocol of 25 May 1984 to amend the International Convention on the Establishment of an International Fund for Compensation for Oil Pollution Damage, 1971

1972

11 February 1972	LONDON	Convention for the Conservation of Antarctic Seals
15 February 1972	OSLO	Convention for the Prevention of Marine Pollution by Dumping from Ships and Aircraft
20 October 1972	LONDON	Convention on the International Regulations for Preventing Collisions at Sea
		1981 Amendments to the Convention Done at London on 19 November 1981
23 November 1972	PARIS	Convention concerning the Protection of the World Cultural and Natural Heritage

2 December 1972	GENEVA	Customs Convention on Containers
2 December 1972	GENEVA	International Convention for Safe Containers 1. 1981 Amendments to Annex I Done at London on 2 April 1981 2. 1983 Amendments to Annexes I and II Done at London on 13 June 1983
29 December 1972	LONDON, MEXICO CITY, MOSCOW AND WASHINGTON	Convention on the Prevention of Marine Pollution by Dumping of Wastes and Other Matter 1. 1978 Amendments to the Convention (concerning Settlement of Disputes) Done at London on 12 October 1978 2. 1978 Amendments to the Annex (Incineration) Done at London on 12 October 1978 3. 1980 Amendments to the Annexes Done at London on 24 September 1980

1973

3 March 1973	WASHINGTON	Convention on International Trade in Endangered Species of Wild Fauna and Flora
26 June 1973	GENEVA	Convention concerning Minimum Age for Admission to Employment
13 July 1973	LONDON	Protocol on Space Requirements for Special Trade Passenger Ships
13 September 1973	GDANSK	Convention on Fishing and Conservation of the Living Resources in the Baltic Sea and the Belts WARSAW - Protocol of 11 November 1982 to the Convention on Fishing and Conservation of the Living Resources in the Baltic Sea and the Belts
25 October 1973	MALAGA-TORREMOLINOS	International Telecommunication Convention on Compulsory Settlement of Disputes (with Final Protocols I through VI and Optional Additional Protocol)
2 November 1973	LONDON	Protocol relating to Intervention on the High Seas in Cases of Pollution by Substances Other than Oil
2 November 1973	LONDON	International Convention for the Prevention of Pollution from Ships LONDON - Protocol of 17 February 1978 relating to the International Convention for the Prevention of Pollution from Ships 1984 Amendments to the Annex Done at London in September of 1984
15 November 1973	OSLO	Agreement on Conservation of Polar Bears
18 December 1973	COPENHAGEN	Arrangement relating to Fisheries in Waters surrounding the Faroe Islands

1974

19 February 1974	STOCKHOLM	Convention on the Protection of the Environment between Denmark, Finland, Norway and Sweden (with Protocol)
22 March 1974	HELSINKI	Convention on the Protection of the Marine Environment of the Baltic Sea Area
6 April 1974	GENEVA	Convention on a Code of Conduct for Liner Conferences
4 June 1974	PARIS	Convention for the Prevention of Marine Pollution from Land-based Sources
1 November 1974	LONDON	International Convention for the Safety of Life at Sea
		1. 1981 Amendments to the Convention Done at London in November of 1981
		2. 1983 Amendments to the Convention Done at London in June of 1983
		LONDON - Protocol of 17 February 1978 relating to the International Convention for the Safety of Life at Sea
		1981 Amendments to the Protocol Done at London in November of 1981
13 December 1974	ATHENS	Athens Convention relating to the Carriage of Passengers and their Luggage by Sea
		LONDON - Protocol of 19 November 1976 to the Athens Convention relating to the Carriage of Passengers and their Luggage by Sea

1976

16 February 1976	BARCELONA	Convention for the Protection of the Mediterranean Sea against Pollution
		BARCELONA - Protocol of 16 February 1976 concerning Co-operation in Combating Pollution of the Mediterranean Sea by Oil and Other Harmful Substances in Cases of Emergency
		BARCELONA - Protocol of 16 February 1976 for the Prevention of Pollution of the Mediterranean Sea by Dumping from Ships and Aircraft
		ATHENS - Protocol of 17 May 1980 for the Protection of the Mediterranean Sea against Pollution from Land-based Sources
		GENEVA - Protocol of 3 April 1982 concerning Mediterranean Specially Protected Areas
10 May 1976	MONACO	Agreement concerning the Protection of the Waters of the Mediterranean Shores
12 June 1976	APIA	Convention on Conservation of Nature in the South Pacific

16 June 1976	SANTIAGO	Convention on the Protection of the Archaeological, Historical, and Artistic Heritage of the American Nations
3 September 1976	LONDON	Convention on the International Maritime Satellite Organization (INMARSAT)
		LONDON - Operating Agreement of 3 September 1976 on the International Maritime Satellite Organization (INMARSAT)
28 October 1976	GENEVA	Convention concerning Continuity of Employment of Seafarers
29 October 1976	GENEVA	Convention concerning Annual Leave with Pay for Seafarers
29 October 1976	GENEVA	Convention concerning Minimum Standards in Merchant Ships
19 November 1976	LONDON	Convention on Limitation of Liability for Maritime Claims
10 December 1976	NEW YORK	Convention on the Prohibition of Military or Any Other Hostile Use of Environmental Modification Techniques

1977

2 April 1977	TORREMOLINOS	Torremolinos International Convention for the Safety of Fishing Vessels
1 May 1977	LONDON	Convention on Civil Liability for Oil Pollution Damage Resulting from Exploration For and Exploitation of Seabed Mineral Resources
7 September 1977	WASHINGTON	Panama Canal Treaty
7 September 1977	WASHINGTON	Treaty concerning the Permanent Neutrality and Operation of the Panama Canal

1978

31 March 1978	HAMBURG	United Nations Convention on the Carriage of Goods by Sea, 1978
24 April 1978	KUWAIT	Kuwait Regional Convention for Co-operation on the Protection of the Marine Environment from Pollution
		KUWAIT - Protocol of 24 April 1978 concerning Regional Co-operation in Combating Pollution by Oil and Other Harmful Substances in Cases of Emergency
7 July 1978	LONDON	International Convention on Standards of Training, Certification and Watchkeeping for Seafarers
24 October 1978	OTTAWA	Convention on Future Multilateral Co-operation in the North-West Atlantic Fisheries

1979

27 April 1979	HAMBURG	International Convention on Maritime Search and Rescue
13 November 1979	GENEVA	Convention on Long-Range Transboundary Air Pollution

1980

20 May 1980	CANBERRA	Convention on the Conservation of Antarctic Marine Living Resources (with annex for an arbitral tribunal)
18 November 1980	LONDON	Convention on Future Multilateral Co-operation in the North-East Atlantic Fisheries

1981

23 March 1981	ABIDJAN	Convention for Co-operation in the Protection and Development of the Marine and Coastal Environment of the West and Central African Region
		ABIDJAN - Protocol of 23 March 1981 concerning Co-operation in Combating Pollution in Cases of Emergency
12 November 1981	LIMA	Convention for the Protection of the Marine Environment and Coastal Area of the South-East Pacific
12 November 1981	LIMA	Agreement on Regional Co-operation in Combating Pollution of the South-East Pacific by Oil and Other Harmful Substances in Cases of Emergency
		QUITO - Protocol of 22 July 1983 for the Protection of the South-East Pacific Against Pollution from Land-based Sources

1982

14 February 1982	JIDDAH	Regional Convention for the Conservation of the Red Sea and Gulf of Aden Environment
		JIDDAH - Protocol of 14 February 1982 concerning Regional Co-operation in Combating Pollution by Oil and other Harmful Substances in Cases of Emergency
2 March 1982	REYKJAVIK	Convention for the Conservation of Salmon in the North Atlantic Ocean
10 December 1982	MONTEGO BAY	United Nations Convention on the Law of the Sea

The entries from 1983 to 1989 have been compiled by the author of this handbook:

1983

		Eastern Pacific Ocean Tuna Fishing Agreement
24 March 1983	CARTAGENA	Convention for the Protection and Development of the Marine Environment of the Wider Caribbean Region
		CARTAGENA - Protocol of 24 March 1983 concerning Cooperation in Combating Oil Spills in the Wider Caribbean Region
23 August 1983	OTTAWA	Agreement to Track Air Pollution across Eastern North American between Canada and the United States (Acid Rain Research)
26 August 1983	COPENHAGEN	Canada-Denmark: Agreement for Cooperation relating to the Marine Environment

1984

		Provisional Understanding Regarding Deep Seabed Matters
21 March 1984	OTTAWA	Canada-Europe Minsterial Declaration on Acid Rain
28 September 1984	GENEVA	Protocol to the 1979 Convention on Long-Range Transboundary Air Pollution, on Financing the Monitoring and Evaluation of Air Pollution in Europe
18 October 1984		Treaty of Peace and Friendship between Argentina and Chile

1985

6 August 1985	RARATONGA, COOK ISLAND	South Pacific Forum: The South Pacific Nuclear Free Zone Treaty

1986

7 February 1986		United Nations Convention on Conditions for Registration of Ships
24-25 November	NOUMEA, NEW CALEDONIA	Convention for the Protection of the Natural Resources and Environment of the South Pacific Region
25 November 1986		Protocol for the Prevention of Pollution of the South Pacific Region by Dumping

26 November 1986		Protocol concerning Cooperation in Combating Pollution Emergencies in the South Pacific Region

1987

2 April 1987	PORT MORESBY	Treaty on Fisheries between the Governments of Certain Pacific Island States and the Government of the United States of America
28 May 1987	HARARE, ZIMBABWE	Botswana-Mozambique-Tanzania-Zambia-Zimbabwe: Agreement on the Action Plan for the Environmentally Sound Management of the Common Zambezi River System
14 August 1987		Belgium-Canada-Italy-Netherlands-USSR: Agreement on the Resolution of Practical Problems with Respect to Deep Seabed Mining Area, and Exchange of Notes between the United States and the Parties to the Agreement
8 October 1987	GENEVA	Convention concerning Health Protection and Medical Care of Seafarers
9 October 1987	GENEVA	Convention concerning Social Security for Seafarers (Revised)
9 October 1987	GENEVA	Conventon concerning the Repatriation of Seafarers (Revised)
16 October 1987	GENEVA	Convetnion concerning Seafarers' Welfare at Sea and in Port

1988

		Protocol to the 1979 Convention on Long-Range Transboundary Air Pollution on Long-Term Financing of the Co-operative Programme for Monitoring and Evaluation of of the Long-Range Transmission of Air Pollutants in Europe
		Protocol to the 1979 Convention on Long-Range Transboundary Air Pollution on the Reduction of Sulphur Emissions or Their Transboundary Fluxes by at least 30 Percent
		Amendments to the Convention and Operating Agreement of INMARSAT of 1985
	LONDON	Second International Conference on the Protection of the North Sea: Ministerial Declaration Calling for Reduction of Pollution

1988

10 March 1988	ROME	Convention and Protocol from the International Conference on the Suppression of Unlawful Acts against the Safety of Maritime Navigation
		Protocol for the Suppression of Unlawful Acts against the Safety of Fixed Platforms Located on the Continental Shelf
26 March 1988	PARIS	Contracting Parties to the Convention for the Prevention of Marine Pollution from Land-Based Sources: Protocol Amending the Convention
2 June 1999	WELLINGTON	Final Act on the Regulation of Antarctic Mineral Resource Activities (Antarctic Treaty Special Consultative Meeting on Antarctic Mineral Resources

1989

22 March 1989	BASEL	Convention on the Control of Transboundary Movements of Hazardous Wastes and Their Disposal
		Final Act of the Conference of Plenipotentiaries on the Global Convention on the Control of Transboundary Movements of Hazardous Wastes
28 April 1989		International Convention on Salvage, 1989
11 July 1989	TARAWA	Tarawa Declaration
21 September 1989		Protocol for the Conservation and Management of Protected Marine and Coastal Areas of the Southeast Pacific
21 September 1989		Protocol for the Protection of the Southeast Pacific against Radioactive Pollution
23 November 1989		Convention for the Prohibition of Fishing with Long Drift Nets in the South Pacific
24 November 1989	ST. LUCIA	The Castries Declaration

APPENDIX II

Status of the United Nations Convention on the Law of the Sea

A. Table of signatures and ratifications as of 3 May 1990

STATES	FINAL ACT SIGNATURE	CONVENTION SIGNATURE a/	CONVENTION RATIFICATION
Afghanistan		18/3/83	
Albania			
Algeria * b/	x	x	
Angola *	x	x	
Antigua and Barbuda		7/2/83	2/2/89
Argentina *		5/10/84	
Australia	x	x	
Austria	x	x	
Bahamas	x	x	29/7/83
Bahrain	x	x	30/5/85
Bangladesh	x	x	
Barbados	x	x	
Belgium *	x	5/12/84	
Belize	x	x	13/8/83
Benin	x	30/8/83	
Bhutan	x	x	
Bolivia *		27/11/84	
Botswana	x	5/12/84	2/5/90
Brazil * ** c/	x	x	22/12/88
Brunei Darussalam d/		5/12/84	
Bulgaria	x	x	
Burkina Faso	x	x	
Burundi	x	x	
Byelorussian SSR *	x	x	
Cambodia e/		1/7/83	
Cameroon	x	x	19/11/85
Canada	x	x	
Cape Verde * **	x	x	10/8/87
Central African Republic		4/12/84	
Chad	x	x	

STATES	FINAL ACT SIGNATURE	CONVENTION SIGNATURE	CONVENTION RATIFICATION
Chile *	x	x	
China	x	x	
Colombia	x	x	
Comoros		6/12/84	
Congo	x	x	
Costa Rica *	x	x	
Côte d'Ivoire	x	x	26/3/84
Cuba * **	x	x	15/8/84
Cyprus	x	x	12/12/88
Czechoslovakia	x	x	
Democratic People's Rep. of Korea	x	x	
Democratic Yemen **	x	x	21/7/87
Denmark	x	x	
Djibouti	x	x	
Dominica		28/3/83	
Dominican Republic	x	x	
Ecuador	x		
Egypt **	x	x	26/8/83
El Salvador		5/12/84	
Equatorial Guinea	x	30/1/84	
Ethiopia	x	x	
Fiji	x	x	10/12/82
Finland *	x	x	
France *	x	x	
Gabon	x	x	
Gambia	x	x	22/5/84
German Democratic Republic *	x	x	
Germany, Federal Republic of	x		
Ghana	x	x	7/6/83
Greece *	x	x	
Grenada	x	x	
Guatemala		8/7/83	
Guinea *		4/10/84	6/9/85
Guinea-Bissau **	x	x	25/8/86
Guyana	x	x	
Haiti	x	x	
Holy See	x		
Honduras	x	x	
Hungary	x	x	
Iceland **	x	x	21/6/85
India	x	x	
Indonesia	x	x	3/2/86
Iran (Islamic Republic of) *	x	x	
Iraq *	x	x	30/7/85
Ireland	x	x	

STATES	FINAL ACT SIGNATURE	CONVENTION SIGNATURE	CONVENTION RATIFICATION
Israel	x		
Italy *	x	7/12/84	
Jamaica	x	x	21/3/83
Japan	x	7/2/83	
Jordan	x		
Kenya	x	x	2/3/89
Kiribati			
Kuwait **	x	x	2/5/86
Lao People's Democratic Republic	x	x	
Lebanon		7/12/84	
Lesotho	x	x	
Liberia	x	x	
Libyan Arab Jamahiriya	x	3/12/84	
Liechtenstein		30/11/84	
Luxembourg *	x	5/12/84	
Madagascar		25/2/83	
Malawi		7/12/84	
Malaysia	x	x	
Maldives	x	x	
Mali *		19/10/83	16/7/85
Malta	x	x	
Mauritania	x	x	
Mauritius	x	x	
Mexico	x	x	18/3/83
Monaco	x	x	
Mongolia	x	x	
Morocco	x	x	
Mozambique	x	x	
Myanmar f/	x	x	
Namibia g/	x	x	18/4/83
Nauru	x	x	
Nepal	x	x	
Netherlands	x	x	
New Zealand	x	x	
Nicaragua *		9/12/84	
Niger	x	x	
Nigeria	x	x	14/8/86
Norway	x	x	
Oman * **	x	1/7/83	17/8/89
Pakistan	x	x	
Panama	x	x	
Papua New Guinea	x	x	
Paraguay	x	x	26/9/86
Peru	x		
Philippines * **	x	x	8/5/84

STATES	FINAL ACT SIGNATURE	CONVENTION SIGNATURE	CONVENTION RATIFICATION
Poland	x	x	
Portugal	x	x	
Qatar *		27/11/84	
Republic of Korea	x	14/3/83	
Romania *	x	x	
Rwanda	x	x	
Saint Kitts and Nevis h/		7/12/84	
Saint Lucia	x	x	27/3/85
St. Vincent and the Grenadines	x	x	
Samoa	x	28/9/84	
San Marino			
Sao Tome and Principe *		13/7/83	3/11/87
Saudi Arabia		7/12/84	
Senegal	x	x	25/10/84
Seychelles	x	x	
Sierra Leone	x	x	
Singapore	x	x	
Solomon Islands	x	x	
Somalia	x	x	24/7/89
South Africa *		5/12/84	
Spain *	x	4/12/84	
Sri Lanka	x	x	
Sudan *	x	x	23/1/85
Suriname	x	x	
Swaziland		18/1/84	
Sweden *	x	x	
Switzerland	x	17/10/84	
Syrian Arab Republic			
Thailand	x	x	
Togo	x	x	16/4/85
Tonga			
Trinidad and Tobago	x	x	25/4/86
Tunisia **	x	x	24/4/85
Turkey			
Tuvalu	x	x	
Uganda	x	x	
Ukrainian SSR *	x	x	
Union of Soviet Socialist Republics *	x	x	
United Arab Emirates	x	x	
United Kingdom	x		

STATES	FINAL ACT SIGNATURE	CONVENTION SIGNATURE	CONVENTION RATIFICATION
United Republic of Tanzania **	x	x	30/9/85
United States of America	x		
Uruguay *	x	x	
Vanuatu	x	x	
Venezuela	x		
Viet Nam	x	x	
Yemen *	x	x	
Yugoslavia **	x	x	5/5/86
Zaire	x	22/8/83	17/2/89
Zambia	x	x	7/3/83
Zimbabwe	x	x	
TOTAL STATES	141	156	43

OTHERS (Art. 305 (1) (c),(d),(e) and (f))	FINAL ACT SIGNATURE	CONVENTION SIGNATURE	CONVENTION RATIFICATION
Cook Islands	x	x	
European Economic Community *	x	7/12/84	
Niue		5/12/84	
Trust Territory of the Pacific Islands	x		
West Indies Associated States			
TOTAL STATES AND OTHERS	144	159	43

OTHER ENTITIES WHICH SIGNED THE FINAL ACT OF THE CONFERENCE

African National Congress
Netherlands Antilles
Palestine Liberation Organization i/
Pan Africanist Congress of Azania
South West Africa People's Organization

a/ Those States which signed the Final Act and/or the Convention on 10 December 1982 are indicated by an "x". Those which signed at a later date are indicated by that date.

b/ Those States which made declarations at the time of signature of the Convention are indicated by an asterisk (*).

c/ Those States which made declarations at the time of ratification of the Convention are indicated by a double asterisk (**).

d/ Became a Member of the United Nations on 18 September 1984.

e/ The name of Democratic Kampuchea was officially changed to "Cambodia" as of 3 February 1990.

f/ The name of Burma was officially changed to "Myanmar" as of 18 June 1989.

g/ Namibia became an independent State as of 21 March 1990 and the 160th State Member of the United Nations as of 23 April 1990. The instrument of ratification was deposited by the United Nations Council of Namibia on behalf of Namibia on 18 April 1983.

h/ Became a Member of the United Nations on 23 September 1983. Formerly Saint Christopher and Nevis.

i/ In accordance with General Assembly resolution 43/177 of 15 December 1988, as of that date, the designation "Palestine" should be used in place of the designation "Palestine Liberation Organization".

B. Chronological order of ratifications of the Convention, giving ratifying State's regional group

	Date	State	Regional group
1.	10 December 1982	Fiji	Asian
2.	7 March 1983	Zambia	African
3.	18 March 1983	Mexico	Latin Am./Carib.
4.	21 March 1983	Jamaica	Latin Am./Carib.
5.	18 April 1983	Namibia	African
6.	7 June 1983	Ghana	African
7.	29 July 1983	Bahamas	Latin Am./Carib.
8.	13 August 1983	Belize	Latin Am./Carib.
9.	26 August 1983	Egypt	African
10.	26 March 1984	Côte d'Ivoire	African
11.	8 May 1984	Philippines	Asian
12.	22 May 1984	Gambia	African
13.	15 August 1984	Cuba	Latin Am./Carib.
14.	25 October 1984	Senegal	African
15.	23 January 1985	Sudan	African
16.	27 March 1985	Saint Lucia	Latin Am./Carib.
17.	16 April 1985	Togo	African
18.	24 April 1985	Tunisia	African
19.	30 May 1985	Bahrain	Asian
20.	21 June 1985	Iceland	Western European and Other States
21.	16 July 1985	Mali	African
22.	30 July 1985	Iraq	Asian
23.	6 September 1985	Guinea	African
24.	30 September 1985	United Rep. of Tanzania	African
25.	19 November 1985	Cameroon	African
26.	3 February 1986	Indonesia	Asian
27.	25 April 1986	Trinidad and Tobago	Latin Am./Carib.
28.	2 May 1986	Kuwait	Asian
29.	5 May 1986	Yugoslavia	Eastern European
30.	14 August 1986	Nigeria	African
31.	25 August 1986	Guinea-Bissau	African

	Date	State	Regional group
32.	26 September 1986	Paraguay	Latin Am./Carib.
33.	21 July 1987	Democratic Yemen	Asian
34.	10 August 1987	Cape Verde	African
35.	3 November 1987	Sao Tome and Principe	African
36.	12 December 1988	Cyprus	Asian
37.	22 December 1988	Brazil	Latin Am./Carib.
38.	2 February 1989	Antigua and Barbuda	Latin Am./Carib.
39.	17 February 1989	Zaire	African
40.	2 March 1989	Kenya	African
41.	24 July 1989	Somalia	African
42.	17 August 1989	Oman	Asian
43.	2 May 1990	Botswana	African

43 ratifications deposited with the Secretary-General

Note: Merging of the People's Democratic Republic of Yemen and the Yemen Arab Republic to form a single state named Yemen, May 22, 1990.

APPENDIX III

Bilateral Agreements and Recent Court Decisions on Maritime Boundary Delimitation and Disputes

A. List of Bilateral Agreements on Maritime Boundary Delimitation and Disputes

1494	Treaty of Tordesillas, 1494 145
1661	Denmark-Sweden. Convention, Naslebacke, 26 October 1661. 6 CTS 495 62
1774	Russia-Turkey. Treaty of Perpetual Peace and Amity, Kucuk Kainardji, 10 July 1774. In force January 1775. 45 CTS 349 87
1857	Treaty for the Redemption of Sound Dues, Copenhagen, 14 March 1857. In force 31 March 1857. Fifteen ratifications.
1868	Convention for Rhine Navigation, Mannheim, October 1868, as amended. In force 17 April 1869. Six ratifications.
1881	Argentine-Chile. Boundary Treaty, Buenos Aires, July 1881. In force 22 October 1881.
1897	Anglo-Venezuelan Treaty.
1903	Panama-USA. Convention for the Construction of a Ship Canal, Washington, 18 November 1903. In force 26 February 1904.
1904	France-Great Britain. Declaration respecting Egypt and Morocco, London, 8 April 1904. In force 8 April 1904.
1927	Great Britain-Johore. Agreement concerning the Johore Strait, 19 October 1927. No information on date of entry into force. Schedule to the Straits Settlement and Johore Territorial Waters (Agreement) Act, 1928.
1932	Denmark-Sweden. Declaration concerning the Boundaries of the Sound, Stockholm, 30 January 1932. In force 30 January 1932.
1952	Declaration on the Maritime Zone by Chile, Ecuador and Peru.

1954 Agreement relating to a Special Maritime Zone among Chile, Ecuador and Peru.

1957 Agreement and Descriptive Protocol between Norway and the Soviet Union relating to the Division of the Continental Shelf in the Varangerfjord.

1958 Agreement between Bahrein and Saudi Arabia on the Delimitation of Adjacent Parts of the Continental Shelf.

1958 Poland-USSR. Protocol concerning the Delimitation of Polish and Soviet Territorial Waters in the Gulf of Gdansk in the Baltic Sea.

1960 Exchange of Notes between France and Portugal regarding the maritime boundary between Senegal and Portuguese Guinea.

1960 Federal Republic of Germany-Netherlands. Treaty concerning Arrangements for Co-operation in the Ems Estuary, The Hague, 8 April 1960. In force 1 August 1963.

Convention on Third Party Liability in the Field of Nuclear Energy, Paris, 29 July 1960. In force 1 April 1968. Number of ratifications not known. 1968 UKTS 69

1961 Argentina-Uruguay. Declaration on the Outer Limit of the River Plate, Montevideo, 30 January 1961. *Limits in the Seas* No. 44 (1972) 42

1962 International Agreement regarding the Maintenance of Certain Lights in the Red Sea, London, 20 February 1962. In force 28 October 1966. Fourteen ratifications.

Convention on the Liability of Operators of Nuclear Ships, Brussels, 25 May 1962. Not in force. Six ratifications. 57 *AJIL* 268 (1963) 237

1964 Treaty between the Federal Republic of Germany and the Netherlands concerning the Lateral Delimitation of the Continental Shelf Near the Coast.

1965 Agreement between the Federal Republic of Germany and Denmark concerning the Delimitation of the Continental Shelf of the North Sea near the Coast.

Protocol to the Agreement between Denmark and Federal Republic of Germany of 9 June 1965, with respect to Baltic Sea continental shelf.

Agreement between Finland and the Soviet Union concerning the Boundaries of the Sea Areas and of the Continental Shelf in the Gulf of Finland.

Agreement between Kuwait and Saudi Arabia relating to Partition of the Neutral Zone.

Agreement between Norway and the United Kingdom relating to the Delimitation of the Continental Shelf.

Agreement between the United Kingdom and the Netherlands relating to the Delimitation of the Continental Shelf under the North Sea between the Two Countries.

1965–74 Agreement between Denmark and Norway on delimitation of the continental shelf.

1966 Agreement between the Netherlands and Denmark concerning the Delimitation of the Continental Shelf under the North Sea.

1966 Agreement between the United Kingdom and Denmark relating to the Delimitation of the Continental Shelf between the Two Countries.

1967 Special Agreement between Denmark and Federal Republic of Germany submitting continental shelf dispute to ICJ.

Special Agreement between Federal Republic of Germany and the Netherlands submitting continental shelf dispute to ICJ.

Agreement between Finland and the Soviet Union concerning the Boundary of the Continental Shelf in the North-Eastern Part of the Baltic Sea.

1968 Declaration of 23 October 1968 by the German Democratic Republic, Poland and the Soviet Union on the Continental Shelf of the Baltic Sea.

Agreement between the German Democratic Republic and Poland.

Agreement between Iran and Saudi Arabia concerning Sovereignty over Al-Arabiyah and Farsi Islands and Delimitation of Boundary Line separating Submarine Areas between the Kingdom of Saudi Arabia and Iran.

Agreement between Italy and Yugoslavia on Delimitation of the Continental Shelf.

Agreement between Norway and Sweden concerning the Delimitation of the Continental Shelf.

1969 Agreement between Abu Dhabi and Qatar on Delimitation of the Continental Shelf.

Agreement Concerning the Boundary Line Dividing the Continental Shelf between Iran and Qatar.

Agreement between Malaysia and Indonesia on the Delimitation of the Continental Shelf between the Two Countries.

Treaty between Poland and the Soviet Union Concerning the Boundary of the Continental Shelf in the Gulf of Gdansk and the South-Eastern Part of the Baltic Sea.

1970 Federal Republic of Germany-Liberia. Treaty on the Use of Liberian Waters and Ports by N. S. *Otto Hahn*, Bonn, 27 May 1970. No information on date of entry into force.

1971 Agreement between Bahrain and Iran Concerning the Delimitation of the Continental Shelf.

Agreement between Denmark and the United Kingdom relating to the Delimitation of the Continental Shelf.

Agreement between the Federal Republic of Germany and the Kingdom of Denmark concerning the Delimitation of the Continental Shelf under the North Sea.

Agreement between Indonesia and Australia establishing Certain Seabed Boundaries.

1971 Agreement among Indonesia, Malaysia and Thailand relating to the Delimitation of the Continental Shelf Boundaries in the Northern Part of the Straits of Malacca.

Agreement between Indonesia and Thailand relating to the Delimitation of a Continental Shelf Boundary in the Northern Part of the Straits of Malacca and the Andaman Sea.

Agreement between Italy and Tunisia relating to the Delimitation of the Continental Shelf.

Treaty between the Netherlands and the Federal Republic of Germany concerning the Delimitation of the Continental Shelf under the North Sea.

Protocol between the Netherlands and the United Kingdom amending the Agreement of 6 October 1965 relating to the Delimitation of the Continental Shelf under the North Sea.

Agreement between Tunisia and Italy on Delimitation of the Continental Shelf.

Agreement between the United Kingdom and the Federal Republic of Germany relating to the Delimitation of the Continental Shelf.

Portugal-Spain. Agreement concerning Oceanographic Co-operation, Lisbon, 27 May 1971. In force 17 May 1971.

Nordic Agreement concerning Co-operation in Measures to Deal with Pollution of the Sea by Oil, Copenhagen, 16 September 1971. In force 16 October 1971. Four ratifications.

1972 Agreement on delimitation between Brazil and Uruguay.

Agreement between Indonesia and Australia Establishing Certain Seabed Boundaries in the Area of the Timor and Arafura Seas, supplementary to the Agreement of 18 May 1971.

Oslo Convention for the Prevention of Marine Pollution by Dumping from Ships and Aircraft.

1972–73 London Convention on the Prevention of Marine Pollution by Dumping of Wastes and Other Matter.

USSR-USA. Agreement on the Prevention of Incidents on and over the High Seas, Moscow, 25 May 1972. In force 25 May 1972.

USSR-USA. Protocol to the Agreement, Washington, 22 May 1973. In force 22 May 1973.

Brazil-Uruguay. Agreement on the Final Establishment of the Chuy River Bank and the Lateral Sea Limit, Montevideo, 21 July 1972. In force 12 June 1975.

1973 Treaty of the Rio de la Plata and its Maritime Limits between Argentina and Uruguay.

Agreement between Canada and Denmark relating to the Delimitation of the Continental Shelf between Greenland and Canada.

1973 Agreement between Indonesia and Australia Concerning Certain Boundaries between Indonesia and Papua New Guinea.

USSR-USA. Agreement relating to the Consideration of Claims resulting from Damage to Fishing Vessels or Gear and Measures to Prevent Fishing Conflicts, Moscow, 21 February 1973. In force 21 February 1973.

Norway-United Kingdom. Agreement relating to the Transmission of Petroleum by Pipeline from the Ekofisk Field and Neighbouring Areas to the United Kingdom, Oslo, 22 May 1973. In force 22 May 1973.

Italy-Yugoslavia. Agreement relating to Fishing by Italian Fishermen in Yugoslav Waters, Belgrade, 15 June 1973. In force 1 October 1974.

International Convention for the Prevention of Pollution from Ships, London, 2 November 1973, as amended by the Protocol, London, 1 June 1978. In force 2 October 1983. Twelve ratifications.

1974 Japan-Korea. Agreement concerning Joint Development of the Southern Part of the Continental Shelf adjacent to the Two Countries, Seoul, 30 January 1974. In force 22 June 1978.

Italy-Yugoslavia. Agreement on Co-operation for the Protection of the Waters of the Adriatic Sea and Coastal Zones from Pollution, Belgrade, 14 February 1974. In force 20 April 1977.

Nordic Convention on the Protection of the Environment, Stockholm, 19 February 1974. In force 5 October 1976. Four ratifications.

Convention on the Protection of the Marine Environment of the Baltic Sea Area, Helsinki, 22 March 1974. In force 3 May 1980. Seven ratifications. *ND* IV, p. 455 217, 222, 233, 239, 241, 248, 250.

Denmark-Sweden. Agreement concerning the Protection of the Sound from Pollution, Copenhagen, 5 April 1974. In force 13 December 1974.

Canada-USA. Agreement relating to the Establishment of Joint Pollution Contingency Plans for Spills of Oil and Other Noxious Substances, Ottawa, 19 June 1974. In force 19 June 1974.

India-Sri Lanka. Agreement on the Boundary in Historic Waters between the Two Countries and Related Matters, New Delhi, 26 June 1974. In force 8 July 1974.

Convention on a Code of Conduct for Liner Conferences, New York, 1 July 1974. Not in force. Fifty-one ratifications.

Agreement between the Federal Republic of Germany and the German Democratic Republic Establishing a Maritime Boundary in Lubeck Bay.

1974 Convention between France and Spain on the Delimitation of the Continental Shelves of the Two States in the Bay of Biscay.

Agreement between India and Indonesia regarding the Delimitation of the Continental Shelf and the Great channel between Nicobar Island and Sumatra.

Agreement between Iran and Oman Concerning Delimitation of the Continental Shelf.

Convention between Italy and Spain on the Delimitation of the Continental Shelf.

Agreement between Korea and Japan concerning the Establishment of the Boundary in the Northern Part of the Continental Shelf Adjacent to the Two Countries.

Agreement between Sudan and Saudi Arabia relating to the Joint Exploitation of the Natural Resources of the Sea-Bed and the Subsoil of the Red Sea in the Common Zone.

1975 Agreement between Colombia and Ecuador on the Delimitation of Marine and Submarine Areas and Maritime Co-operation.

Arbitration Agreement between France and the United Kingdom.

Gambia-Senegal. Agreement delimiting Maritime Boundaries, Banjul, 4 June 1975. In force 27 August 1976.

Colombia-Ecuador. Agreement on Delimiting Marine and Submarine Areas and on Maritime Co-operation, Quito, 23 August 1975. In force 22 December 1975.

1976 India-Sri Lanka. Agreement on the Maritime Boundary between the Two Countries in the Gulf of Mannar and the Bay of Bengal, and related matters, New Delhi, 23 March 1976.

India-Sri Lanka. Supplementary Agreement on the Extension of the Maritime Boundary in the Gulf of Mannar to the Trijunction Point.

Agreement relating to the Protection of the Waters of the Mediterranean Coast, Monaco, 10 May 1976. In force 1 January 1981. Three ratifications.

Norway-United Kingdom. Agreement relating to the Exploitation of the Frigg Field Reservoir and the Transmission of Gas therefrom to the United Kingdom, London, 10 May 1976. In force 22 July 1977.

Special Agreement between Libya and Malta for the Submission to the International Court of Justice of a Continental Shelf Dispute.

Agreement among Sri Lanka, India and the Maldives concerning the Trijunction Point in the Gulf of Mannar.

1976–77 Exchange of Notes between Ireland and the United Kingdom concerning Continental Shelf Delimitation.

1977 Treaty between Colombia and Costa Rica on the Delimitation of Marine and Submarine Areas and Maritime Co-operation.

Agreement between Haiti and Cuba regarding the Delimitation of the Maritime Boundaries between the Two States.

Maritime Boundary Agreement between the United States and Cuba.

Agreement between Italy and Greece establishing Continental Shelf Boundary.

Special Agreement between Tunisia and Libya submitting Continental Shelf question to International Court of Justice.

Denmark-EEC. Agreement on Fisheries, Brussels, 15 March 1977. Not in force.

Colombia-Costa Rica. Treaty on Delimitation of Marine and Submarine Areas and Maritime Co-operation, San José, 17 March 1977.

United Kingdom-USA. Exchange of Notes concerning the Use of the Louisiana Offshore Oil Port by Vessels registered in the United Kingdom, the West Indies Associated States or its other Territories or flying the Flag of the United Kingdom, Washington, 14 and 25 May 1979. In force 25 May 1979.

Denmark-USSR. Agreement on Mutual Fishery Relations between the Faroes and the USSR, Torshavn, 27 November 1977. In force 16 May 1978.

1978 Agreement between Australia and Papua New Guinea concerning sovereignty and maritime boundaries.

Agreement on the Declaration of Marine and Submarine Areas and Maritime Co-operation between the Dominican Republic and Colombia.

Agreement between Colombia and Haiti for the Delimitation of the Marine and Submarine areas of Colombia and the Exclusive Economic Marine Zone and Continental Shelf of Haiti.

Treaty between Mexico and the United States on Maritime Boundaries.

Agreement between Netherlands and Venezuela establishing Continental Shelf Boundary.

Maritime Boundary Agreement between Netherlands Antilles and Venezuela.

Maritime Boundary Treaty between Venezuela and the United States.

Colombia-Haiti. Maritime Limits Agreement, Bogotá, 18 February 1978. No information on date of entry into force.

1979 Treaty on the Delimitation of Marine and Submarine Areas between the Dominican Republic and Venezuela.

1979 Canada-USA. Special Agreement between United States and Canada to Submit to a Chamber of the International Court of Justice the Delimitation of the Maritime Boundary in the Gulf of Maine Area, Washington, 29 March 1979.

Faroes-Norway. Agreement on Mutual Fishery Rights, Torshavn, February 1979. No information on date of entry into force.

1980 France-Tonga. Convention concerning the Delimitation of Economic Zones, Nuku' Alofu, 11 January 1980. In force 11 January 1980.

Mexico-USA. Agreement of Co-operation regarding Pollution of the Marine Environment by Discharges of Hydrocarbons and Other Hazardous Substances, Mexico City, 24 July 1980. In force 30 March 1981.

China-USA. Agreement on Maritime Transport, Washington, 17 September 1980. In force 17 September 1980.

1981 Abidjan Convention for Co-operation in the Protection and Development of the Marine and Coastal Environment of the West and Central African Region and related Protocol.

Brazil-France. Treaty of Maritime Delimitation 30 January 1981.

Iceland and Norway. Agreement on the Continental Shelf between Iceland and Jan Mayen, Oslo, 22 October 1981. In force 2 June 1982.

1983 Australia and France. Entry into force of the Agreement on Maritime Delimitation. Ratification 10 January 1983.

Brazil and France. Entry into force of the Maritime Delimitation Treaty. Ratification 19 October 1983.

Fiji and France. Maritime Delimitation Agreement between the Government of Fiji and the Government of France. Date of signature 13 January 1983.

1984 Maritime Delimitation Agreement between the Government of His Most Serene Highness the Prince of Monaco and the Government of the French Republic. 16 February 1984.

1985 Argentina-Chile. Negotiation and conclusion of Border Dispute Agreement 20 February 1978–14 January 1985.

1986 Agreement between the Government of the United Kingdom of Great Britain and Northern Ireland and the Government of the Union of Soviet Socialist Republics concerning the Prevention of Incidents at Sea beyond the Territorial Sea. 15 July 1986.

Maritime Delimitation Treaty between Colombia and Honduras, 2 August 1986.

Burma-India. Agreement on the Delimitation of the Maritime Boundary in the Andaman Sea, the Coco Channel and the Bay of Bengal, Rangoon, 23 September 1986.

Agreement between the Government of the French Republic and the Government of the Italian Republic on the Declaration of the Maritime Boundaries in the Area of the Strait of Bonifacio, Paris, 28 November 1986.

1987 Maritime Delimitation Agreement between the Government of His Most Serene Highness the Prince of Monaco and the Government of France, Paris, 16 April 1987.

Exchange of Notes between the Government of the United Kingdom of Great Britain and Northern Ireland and the Government of the Union of Soviet Socialist Republics concerning Deep Seabed Mining Areas, Moscow, 14 August 1987.

1988 Sweden-USSR. Agreement on Principles for the Delimitation of Sea Area in the Baltic Sea, Stockholm, 13 January 1988.

Agreement between the Government of Solomon Islands and the Government of Australia Establishing Certain Sea and Sea-Bed Boundaries, 2 October 1988.

Agreement between the Government of the French Republic and the Government of the United Kingdom of Great Britain and Northern Ireland Relating to the Delimitation of the Territorial Sea in the Straits of Dover, 2 November 1988.

Agreement between the Government of the United Kingdom of Great Britain and Northern Ireland and the Government of the Republic of Ireland concerning the Delimitation of Areas of the Continental Shelf between the Two Countries, 7 November 1988.

1989 Agreement between the Government of the Union of Soviet Socialist Republics and the Government of the French Republic concerning the Prevention of Incidents at Sea outside Territorial Waters of 4 July 1989.

Agreement between the Government of the Italian Republic and the Government of the Union of Socialist Republics concerning the Prevention of Incidents at Sea outside Territorial Waters of 30 November 1989.

Joint Statement by the United States of America and the Soviet Union concerning innocent passage, 23 September 1989.

1990 Agreement between the Government of the United States of America and the Government of the Union of Soviet Socialist Republics of Cooperation in Ocean Studies of 1 June 1990.

Agreement on Maritime Delimitation between the Government of the Cook Islands and the Government of the French Republic of 3 August 1990.

Agreement between the United States and the Union of Socialist Soviet Republics on maritime boundary disputes in the North Pacific Ocean, the Bering Sea and the Arctic Ocean, 1 June 1990.

Source: The list is a combined listing of bilateral treaties provided by the following works: R. R. Churchill and A. V. Lowe, *The Law of the Sea* (Manchester, England: Manchester University Press, 1983), pp. xvii–xxix; E. D. Brown, *Sea-Bed Energy and Mineral Resources and the Law of the Sea*, vol. I (London: Graham and Trotman, 1984), pp. xxiii–xxxi; and *The Law of the Sea: Current Developments in State Practices: Declaration on Maritime Jurisdiction and Comments Related Thereto* (United Nations: Office of Special Representative of the Secretary-General for the Law of the Sea, 1987).

B. Recent Court Decisions on Maritime Boundaries Disputes

24 February 1982. ICJ: Case concerning the Continental Shelf (Tunisia/Libyan Arab Jamahiriya).

20 March 1982. ICJ: Libya-Malta. Special Agreement for the Submission to the International Court of Justice of a Continental Shelf Dispute (Valetta, 23 May, 1976. In force 20 March, 1982).

8 March 1984. ICJ: Case concerning Delimitation of the Maritime Boundary in the Gulf of Maine Area (Canada/United States).

12 October 1984. ICJ: Case concerning Delimitation of the Maritime Boundary in the Gulf of Maine area between Canada and the United States of America.

14 February 1985. ICJ: Arbitration Tribunal for the Delimitation of the Maritime Boundary between Guinea and Guinea-Bissau: Award of 14 February 1985.

3 June 1985. ICJ: Case concerning the Continental Shelf between Libyan Arab Jamahiriya and Malta.

10 December 1985. ICJ: Judgment on Appreciation for Revision and Interpretation of the Judgment in the case concerning the Continental Shelf (Tunisia/Libyan Arab Jamahiriya).

24 May 1986. ICJ: El Salvador and Honduras submit Boundary Dispute to the International Court of Justice.

8 May 1987. ICJ: Order constituting a Chamber in the case concerning the land, island and maritime frontier dispute of El Salvador and Honduras.

16 August 1988. Denmark Filed an Application instituting legal proceedings against Norway concerning the delimitation over East Coast of Greenland and the island of Jan Mayan.

31 July 1989. ICJ: Communique concerning arbitral award in the case of maritime boundary between Guinea-Bissau and Senegal.

2 March 1990. ICJ: Order dismissing the request of Guinea-Bissau for the indication of provisional measures concerning the arbitral award for maritime boundary dispute.

APPENDIX IV

National Legislation on the Exclusive Economic Zone, the Economic Zone and the Exclusive Fishery Zone

ANGOLA. Decree No. 12-A/80 of 6 February 1980.

ANTIGUA AND BARBUDA. The Territorial Waters Act, 1982, Act No. 18 of 17 August 1982.

AUSTRALIA.

BAHAMAS. Fisheries Resources (Jurisdiction and Conservation) Act, 1977, No. 13 of 1977.

BANGLADESH.

I. Territorial Waters and Maritime Zones Act 1974, Act No. XXVI of 1974.

II. Notification No. LT-I/3/74 of the Ministry of Foreign Affairs, Dacca, of 13 April 1974.

BARBADOS. Marine Boundaries and Jurisdiction Act, 1978–3, 25 February 1978.

BURMA. Territorial Sea and Maritime Zones Law, 1977, PYITHU HLUTTAW Law No. 3 of 9 April 1977.

CANADA. Fishing Zones of Canada (Zones 4 and 5) Order of 1 January 1977.

CAPE VERDE. Decree Law No. 126/77 of 31 December 1977.

COLOMBIA. Act No. 10 of 4 August 1978 establishing rules concerning the Territorial Sea, the Exclusive Economic Zone and the Continental Shelf and regulating other matters.

COMOROS. Law No. 82–005 relating to the delimitation of the maritime zones of the Islamic Federal Republic of the Comoros of 6 May 1982.

COOK ISLANDS. Territorial Sea and Exclusive Economic Zone Act, Act No. 16 of 14 November 1977.

COSTA RICA. Article 6 of the Constitution as amended by Decree No. 5699 of 5 June 1975.

CÔTE D'IVOIRE. Law No. 77–926 delimiting the Maritime Zones placed under the National Jurisdiction of the Republic of Ivory Coast of 17 November 1977.

CUBA. Legislative Decree No. 2 of 24 February 1977 concerning the establishment of an Economic Zone.

DEMOCRATIC KAMPUCHEA. Statement of the spokesman of the Ministry of Foreign Affairs of Democratic Kampuchea of 15 January 1978.

DEMOCRATIC YEMEN. Act of 1977 concerning the Territorial Sea, Exclusive Economic Zone, Continental Shelf and other Marine Areas, Act No. 45 of 17 December 1977.

DENMARK. Act No. 597 of 17 December 1976 on the Fishing Territory of the Kingdom of Denmark.

DJIBOUTI. Law No. 52/AN/78 concerning the Territorial Sea, the Contiguous Zone, the Exclusive Economic Zone, the Maritime Frontiers and Fishing.

DOMINICA. Territorial Sea, Contiguous Zone, Exclusive Economic and Fishery Zones Act, 1981, Act No. 26 of 25 August 1981.

DOMINICAN REPUBLIC. Act No. 186 of 13 September 1967 on the Territorial Sea, Contiguous Zone, Exclusive Economic Zone and Continental Shelf as amended by Act No. 573 of 1 April 1977.

EQUATORIAL GUINEA. Act No. 15/1984 of 12 November 1984 on the Territorial Sea and Exclusive Economic Zone.

FIJI.

I. Marine Spaces Act, 1977, Act No. 18 of 15 December 1977, as amended by the Marine Spaces (Amendment) Act 1978, Act No. 15 of 6 October 1978.

II. Marine Spaces (Archipelagic Baselines and Exclusive Economic Zone) Order, 1981.

FRANCE.

I. Law No. 76–655 of 16 July 1976 relating to the Economic Zone off the coasts of the territory of the Republic.

II. Decree No. 77–130 of 11 February 1977 on the establishment, pursuant to the law of 16 July 1976 of an Economic Zone off the coasts of the territory of the Republic bordering the North Sea, the English channel and the Atlantic, from Franco-Belgian border to the Franco-Spanish border.

GAMBIA. Fisheries Act of 1977.

GERMAN DEMOCRATIC REPUBLIC.

I. Decree concerning the establishment of a Fishery Zone of the German Democratic Republic in the Baltic Sea of 22 December 1977.

II. Law on Fisheries in the Fishery Zone of the German Democratic Republic of 13 October 1978.

GERMANY, FEDERAL REPUBLIC OF. Proclamation of the Federal Republic of Germany of 21 December 1976 on the establishment of a Fishery Zone of the Federal Republic of Germany in the North Sea.

GRENADA. Marine Boundaries Act, 1978, Act No. 20 of 1 November 1978.

GUATEMALA. Legislative Decree No. 20–76 of 9 June 1976 concerning the breadth of the Territorial Sea and the establishment of an Exclusive Economic Zone.

GUINEA. National Limits of Jurisdiction; Decree No. 336/PRG of 30 July 1980.

GUINEA-BISSAU. Law No. 3/78 on the extension of the Territorial Sea and Exclusive Economic Zone of 19 May 1978.

GUYANA. Maritime Boundaries Act, 1977, Act No. 10 of 30 June 1977.

HAITI. Declaration by the Haitian Government of 6 April 1977 establishing the boundary of the territorial waters of the Republic of Haiti at 12 nautical miles and that of its Economic Zone at 200 nautical miles.

HONDURAS. Decree No. 921 of 13 June 1980 on the utilization of Marine Natural Resources.

ICELAND. Law No. 41 of 1 June 1979 concerning the Territorial Sea, the Economic Zone and the Continental Shelf.

INDIA. The Territorial Waters, Continental Shelf, Exclusive Economic Zone and other Maritime Zones Act, 1976, Act No. 80 of 28 May 1976.

INDONESIA. Act No. 5 of 18 October 1983 on the Indonesian Exclusive Economic Zone.

IRAN (Islamic Republic of). Proclamation of 30 October 1973 concerning the outer limit of the Exclusive Fishing Zone of Iran in the Persian Gulf and the Sea of Oman.

IRELAND. Maritime Jurisdiction (Exclusive Fishery Limits) Order, 1976, Order No. 320 of 22 December 1976.

JAPAN.

I. Law No. 31 of 2 May 1977 on Provisional Measures relating to the Fishing Zone, as amended by Law No. 83 of 29 November 1977.

II. Enforcement Order of 17 June 1977 of Law No. 31 of 2 May 1977 on Provisional Measures relating to the Fishing Zone, as amended in 1977.

KENYA. Presidential Proclamation of 28 February 1979.

KIRIBATI. Proclamation of 10 March 1978.

MALDIVES.

I. Law No. 30/76 relating to the Exclusive Economic Zone of the Republic of Maldives of 5 December 1976.

II. Law No. 32/76 of 5 December 1976 relating to the navigation and passage by foreign warships and aircraft through the airspace, territorial waters and the Economic Zone of the Republic of Maldives.

MAURITANIA. Law No. 78.043 establishing the Code of the Merchant Marine and Maritime Fisheries of 28 February 1978.

MAURITIUS. Maritime Zones Act, 1977, Act No. 13 of 3 June 1977.

MEXICO.

I. Decree of 26 January 1976 adding a new paragraph 8 to Article 27 of the Constitution of the United Mexican States, to provide for Exclusive Economic Zone beyond the Territorial Sea.

II. Decree of 7 June 1976 establishing the outer limit of the Exclusive Economic Zone of Mexico.

III. Mexican Federal Act relating to the Sea of 8 January 1986.

MOROCCO. Act No. 1–81 of 18 December 1980, promulgated by dahir No. 1–81–179 of 8 April 1981, establishing a 200-nautical-mile Exclusive Economic Zone off the Moroccan coasts.

MOZAMBIQUE. Mozambique Council of Ministers; Decree Law No. 31/76 of 19 August 1976.

NAURU. Marine Resources Act 1978 (No. 8 of 1978).

NETHERLANDS (Unofficial translation).

I. Act of 8 June 1977 authorizing the Government to establish a Fisheries Zone of up to a maximum of 200 nautical miles.

II. Implementation Decree of 23 November 1977 laying down that the outer limit of the Dutch Fishing Zone would follow the delimitation of the Dutch section of the Continental Shelf beneath the North Sea.

NEW ZEALAND. Territorial Sea and Exclusive Economic Zone Act 1977, Act No. 28 of 26 September 1977 as amended by Act No. 146 of 1980.

NIGERIA. Exclusive Economic Zone Decree No. 28 of 5 October 1978.

NIUE. Territorial Sea and Exclusive Economic Zone Act 1978.

NORWAY.

I. Act No. 91 of 17 December 1976 relating to the Economic Zone of Norway.

II. Royal Decree of 17 December 1976 relating to the establishment of the Economic Zone of Norway.

OMAN. Royal Decree concerning the Territorial Sea, Continental Shelf and Exclusive Economic Zone of 10 February 1981.

PAKISTAN. Territorial Waters and Maritime Zones Act 1976 of 22 December 1976.

PAPUA NEW GUINEA.

I. Declaration of Fishing Zone of 17 March 1978.

II. National Seas Act 1977, Act No. 7 of 7 February 1977.

III. Offshore Seas Proclamation of 28 March 1978.

PHILIPPINES. Presidential Decree No. 1599 of 11 June 1978 establishing an Exclusive Economic Zone and for other purposes.

PORTUGAL. Act No. 33/77 of 28 May 1977 regarding the juridical status of the Portuguese Territorial Sea and the Exclusive Economic Zone.

QATAR. Declaration by the Ministry of Foreign Affairs of 2 June 1974.

SAMOA. Exclusive Economic Zone Act No. 3 of 25 August 1977, as amended by the Exclusive Economic Zone Amendment Act 1980.

SAO TOME AND PRINCIPE. Decree-Law No. 15/78 of 16 June 1978.

SENEGAL. Act No. 76–89 of 2 July 1976 establishing a Sea Fishery Code as amended by the Law of 8 February 1985.

SEYCHELLES.

I. Maritime Zones Act, 1977, Act No. 15 of 23 May 1977.

II. Exclusive Economic Zone (No.2) Order, 1978.

SOLOMON ISLANDS. Delimitation of Marine Waters Act 1978, No. 32 of 1978.

SPAIN. Act No. 15/1978 on the Economic Zone of 20 February 1978.

SRI LANKA.

I. Marine Zones Law No. 22 of 1 September 1976.

II. Presidential Proclamation of 15 January 1977 in pursuance of Maritime Zones Law No. 22 of 1 September 1976.

SURINAME. Law concerning the extension of the Territorial Sea and the establishment of a Contiguous Economic Zone of 11 June 1978.

TOGO. Ordinance No. 24 delimiting the Territorial Waters and creating a protected Economic Maritime Zone of 16 August 1977.

TONGA. The Territorial Sea and Exclusive Economic Zone Act, Act No. 30 of 23 October 1978.

TUVALU.

I. Fisheries Ordinance No. 1 of 11 May 1978.

II. Proclamation No. 1 of 26 October 1978.

UNION OF SOVIET SOCIALIST REPUBLICS. Decree of the Union of Soviet Socialist Republics on the Economic Zone of 28 February 1984.

UNITED ARAB EMIRATES. Declaration of the Ministry of Foreign Affairs concerning the Exclusive Economic Zone and its Delimitation of 25 July 1980.

UNITED KINGDOM OF GREAT BRITAIN AND NORTHERN IRELAND. An Act to extend British Fishery Limits and make further provision in connection with the Regulation of Sea Fishing of 22 December 1976.

UNITED STATES OF AMERICA. Proclamation 5030, 10 March 1983, by the President of the United States of America.

VANUATU. Maritime Zones Act No. 23 of 1981.

VENEZUELA. Act establishing an Exclusive Economic Zone along the coasts of the Mainland and Islands of 26 July 1978.

VIET NAM. Statement on the Territorial Sea, the Contiguous Zone, the Exclusive Economic Zone and the Continental Shelf of 12 May 1977.

Source: United Nations, Office of the Special Representative of the Secretary-General for the Law of the Sea, 1986.

APPENDIX V

Selected Bilateral Fishery Agreements Concluded as a Result of the New Regime of the Oceans

17 January 1975	Italy/Senegal—Agreement on marine fisheries
31 January 1975	Nigeria/Mauritania—Agreement on fishing
15 February 1975	Mauritania/Soviet Union—Agreement on marine fisheries
25 February 1975	Bulgaria/Mauritania—Agreement on cooperation in the field of marine fisheries
27 February 1975	Benin/France—Convention concerning marine fishing
28 February 1975	Barbados/Brazil—Shrimp agreement
28 February 1975	Brazil/Trinidad & Tobago—Shrimp agreement
14 March 1975	Brazil/USA—Agreement concerning shrimp
18 March 1975	The Gambia/Soviet Union—Agreement on cooperation in the field of fisheries
4 April 1975	Brazil/The Netherlands—Shrimp agreement
11 April 1975	Guinea Bissau/Soviet Union—Agreement on cooperation in the field of fisheries
11 April 1975	Norway/Soviet Union—Agreement on cooperation in the field of fisheries
16 May 1975	Senegal/Spain—Convention on cooperation in the field of fisheries
23 August 1975	Colombia/Ecuador—Convention on delimitation of marine and submarine areas and maritime cooperation

Source: J. E. Carroz and J. Savini, "The New International Law of Fisheries Emerging from Bilateral Agreements," *Marine Policy* 1 (April 1979): 80–82, published by Butterworth-Heinemann Ltd, Oxford, and is reprinted with the kind permission of the publisher.

1 September 1975	Poland/Mauritania—Agreement on cooperation in the field of marine fisheries
28 November 1975	Belgium/Iceland—Fisheries agreement relating to the extension of the Icelandic fishery limits to 200 miles
28 November 1975	Federal Republic of Germany/Iceland—Fisheries agreement relating to the extension of the Icelandic fishery limits to 200 miles
2 December 1975	Canada/Norway—Agreement on mutual fishery relations
February 1976	Republic of Korea/Morocco—Agreement on fisheries cooperation
10 March 1976	Iceland/Norway—Exchange of notes concerning fishing off the coast of Iceland
12 March 1976	Mauritania/Portugal—Agreement on cooperation in the field of marine fisheries
17 March 1976	Poland/Senegal—Convention concerning marine fisheries
20 March 1976	Denmark (Faeroes)/Iceland—Fishery agreement
23 March 1976	India/Sri Lanka—Agreement on the maritime boundary in the Gulf of Mannar and the Bay of Bengal and related matters
25 March 1976	Morocco/Portugal—Agreement concerning marine fishing
27 March 1976	Mauritania/Spain—Fishery agreement
14 April 1976	Mauritania/Morocco—Agreement on economic cooperation for the development of the Saharian recovered territories
15 April 1976	France/Mauritania—Agreement concerning lobster fishing
May 1976	Angola/Soviet Union—Agreement on cooperation in fisheries
5 May 1976	Mauritania/Soviet Union—Agreement on cooperation in the field of fisheries
14 May 1976	German Democratic Republic/Guinea—Protocol of agreement concerning the exploitation of Guinean fishery resources
14 May 1976	Sierra Leone/Soviet Union—Agreement on cooperation in the field of fisheries
14 May 1976	Canada/Poland—Agreement on mutual fisheries relations
19 May 1976	Canada/Soviet Union—Agreement on mutual fisheries relations
1 June 1976	Iceland/United Kingdom—Provisional agreement on fisheries
10 June 1976	Canada/Spain—Agreement on mutual fisheries relations
19 June 1976	Italy/Tunisia—Agreement concerning fishing by Italian vessels in Tunisian waters
July 1976	Republic of Korea/The Gambia—Agreement on fisheries cooperation
26 July 1976	Cuba/Mexico—26 July 1976—Fishery agreement

29 July 1976	Canada/Portugal—Agreement on mutual fisheries relations
2 August 1976	Poland/USA—Agreement concerning fisheries off the coasts of the USA
5 October 1976	German Democratic Republic/USA—Agreement concerning fisheries off the coasts of the USA
11 October 1976	Finland/Soviet Union—Agreement on certain questions relating to fishing in the Finnish fishing zone
15 October 1976	Norway/Soviet Union—Agreement on mutual fishery relations
23 November 1976	Romania/USA—Agreement concerning fisheries off the coasts of the USA
24 November 1976	Mexico/USA—Fisheries agreement
26 November 1976	USA/Soviet Union—Agreement concerning fisheries off the coasts of the USA
9 December 1976	Norway/Sweden—Agreement on fishing
17 December 1976	Agreement concerning fisheries off the coasts of the USA
29 December 1976	Finland/Norway—Agreement concerning fishing
30 December 1976	Brazil/USA—Agreement extending the agreement of March 14, 1975 concerning shrimp
December 1976	Greece/Guinea—Fishery agreement
4 January 1977	Republic of Korea/USA—Agreement concerning fisheries off the coast of the USA
20 January 1977	France/Guinea Bissau—Fishery agreement
26 January 1977	Ivory Coast/Senegal—Agreement in the field of marine fisheries
28 January 1977	German Democratic Republic/Norway—Agreement concerning fisheries
4 February 1977	Denmark (Faeros)/Iceland—Reciprocal fisheries agreement
8 February 1977	Norway/Portugal—Exchange of notes concerning fisheries
10 February 1977	Japan/USA—Exchange of notes concerning fisheries off the coasts of the USA
12 February 1977	Morocco/Spain—Agreement for cooperation in marine fishing
15 February 1977	EEC/USA—Agreement concerning fisheries off the coasts of the USA
16 February 1977	Spain/USA—Agreement concerning fisheries off the coasts of the USA
22 February 1977	Denmark (Faeroes)/Sweden—Fishery agreement
24 February 1977	Canada/USA—Reciprocal fisheries agreement
11 March 1977	Mauritania/Nigeria—Fishery agreement
15 March 1977	EEC/Denmark (Faeroes)—Agreement concerning fisheries

17 March 1977	Colombia/Costa Rica—Agreement on marine cooperation
18 March 1977	Japan/USA—Agreement concerning fisheries off the coast of the USA
21 March 1977	EEC/Sweden—Agreement on fisheries
26 March 1977	Mauritania/Soviet Union—Fishery agreement
28 March 1977	Mauritania/Portugal—Agreement on fisheries
31 March 1977	Brazil/USA—Shrimp agreement
End March 1977	Greece/Mauritania—Agreement for fishing cooperation
15 April 1977	Norway/Spain—Exchange of notes concerning fisheries
25 April 1977	Iceland/Soviet Union—Agreement on scientific cooperation and consultation in the field of fisheries and research with respect to the living resources of the sea
27 April 1977	Cuba/USA—Agreement concerning fisheries off the coasts of the USA
1 May 1977	USA/Brazil—Agreement concerning shrimp
11 May 1977	Iran/Republic of Korea—Agreement on fishery cooperation
12 May 1977	Canada/Cuba—Agreement on mutual fisheries relations
20 May 1977	Guinea-Bissau/Portugal—Agreement on cooperation in fisheries
24 May 1977	Norway/Poland—Agreement concerning fisheries
27 May 1977	Japan/Soviet Union—Agreement concerning fisheries in waters off the Soviet Union in the Northwest Pacific Ocean
7 June 1977	Chile/Spain—Agreement on cooperation in fishing
24 June 1977	United Kingdom/USA—Reciprocal fisheries agreement
July 1977	Japan/Soviet Union—Fishery agreement
27 July 1977	Mauritania/Romania—Fishery agreement
26 August 1977	Mexico/USA—Agreement concerning fisheries off the coasts of the USA
27 September 1977	Bulgaria/Canada—Fishery agreement
20 October 1977	Norway/Soviet Union—Agreement on catch quotas in the Barents Sea
7 December 1977	Japan/South Africa—Fishery agreement
7 December 1977	Denmark (Faeroes)/Norway—Reciprocal fishery agreement
12 December 1977	Iceland/Faeroes—Fishery agreement
16 December 1977	Japan/Soviet Union—Exchange of letters allocating quotas
22 December 1977	Sweden/Soviet Union—Fishery agreement
March 1978	Korea (Republic of)/New Zealand—Fisheries agreement
18 March 1978	Japan/Portugal—Agreement on fisheries
4 April 1978	New Zealand/Soviet Union—Agreement on fisheries

11 April 1978	Canada/USA—Reciprocal fisheries agreement
21 April 1978	Japan/Soviet Union—Fishery cooperation agreement
27 April 1978	Morocco/Soviet Union—Fishery agreement
28 April 1978	Canada/Japan—Fishery agreement
23 June 1978	Seychelles/Soviet Union—Agreement on cooperation in the field of fisheries
1 September 1978	Japan/New Zealand—Agreement on fisheries

The text of most of these agreements was provided to the Food and Agriculture Organization (FAO) by the governments concerned in response to a questionnaire sent by the Secretariat of the Organization, which had been requested by the Committee on Fisheries to prepare FAO Fisheries Circular No. 709.

APPENDIX VI

Coastal State Requirements for Foreign Fishing

ANGOLA

- Agreement with USSR - Information on revenues from joint Soviet/Angolan operations not available.
- Agreement with Cape Verde, 1981 - Allows fishing vessels of Cape Verde to fish in Angolan waters from October to May when there is shortage of tuna in Cape Verde's waters.
- Agreement with Nigeria, 23 February 1982 - Experimental fishing for ninety days; 50% of catch delivered to Angola; Angolan contribution to include fuel and salary of Angolan crew.
- Agreement with Spain, signed end 1984 -

  For crustaceans: Spanish vessels authorized to catch 10,000 tons of crustaceans against payment in kind of 2.1 tons of mixed species fish for each ton of crustaceans; lump sum of US $300,000 payable in quarterly installments.

  For finfish: For first 700 tons lump sum payment of US $40,000 per year; for catches over 700 tons, for each 10% of the additional catch, fees for 95% of the excess catch set at US $520 per ton and remaining 5% at US $930 per ton; Spanish vessels also to hand over by-catch from shrimp operations. Spain to provide 40 scholarships.

  (Entry verified: October 1985)

ARGENTINA

- Under arrangements with certain enterprises in Japan (January 1978), Germany (FDR) (April 1978) and USSR (June 1981) - Experimental fishing by foreign vessels allowed for one year at end of which feasibility studies and proposals for future joint venture fishing operations to be submitted.

AUSTRALIA

- Australia/Japan Agreement on Tuna Longlining, October 1983 valid through end October 1984 - $A 2,275,000 (US$ 1,496,711) for up to 290 Japanese longliners.
- New Agreement with Japan signed 30 October 1984 valid through end October 1985; new level of fees unknown.
- Australia/KKFC Pty Ltd. Agreement, August 1984 valid through end July 1985 - $A 1,447,985 (US$ 952,623) lump sum access fee for up to 30 gillnetters (quota of 5,000 tons of pelagic fish), and 120 pair trawlers (quota of 27,500 tons of demersal finfish).

Source: Gerald K. Moore, *Coastal State Requirements for Foreign Fishing*, Legislative Study No. 21, Rev. 2, Food and Agriculture Organization of the United Nations (Rome, 1985), pp. 34–128.

BENIN

. By virtue of unwritten reciprocal arrangement Nigerian and Benin vessels operate in each other's zones.

BRAZIL

. Framework agreements with Barbados (15 February 1978), and with Trinidad and Tobago (8 May 1978). (Note: New legislation under consideration) - The Brazilian partner must hold at least 60% of the capital and 51% of the voting shares; the joint venture must have its head office in Brazil, but may also be registered as carrying on business in Trinidad and Tobago; joint venture must not interfere with activities of small scale fishermen.

CAMEROON

. Agreement with Equatorial Guinea, 26 November 1981 (valid for two years, renewable unless denounced) - Provides for reciprocal fishing rights. (Entry verified September 1984)

CAPE VERDE

. Agreement with Portugal, 20 April 1980 (valid for three years, renewable unless denounced) - "Fishing conditions" to be agreed upon annually by representatives of both countries.

. Agreement with Spain, 25 September 1981 (valid for three years, renewable for one year unless denounced) - Fees not specified in the agreement; Spanish shipowners to enter into contracts with Capeverdean National Co. providing for the "economic conditions" of fishing operations; Spain to set up an ice plant in Cape Verde, to undertake two scientific research programs into demersal and pelagic stocks and fishing methods, to supply two tuna boat skippers during three years for Capeverdean vessels, to fund a biologist to carry out tuna research, to grant five annual scholarships.

. Agreement with Senegal, 29 March 1985 with implementing annual protocol - National vessels defined as vessels flying the flag of one of the countries which belongs at least 51% to national of Senegal or Cape Verde or to a company of which at least 51% of capital held by Senegalese or Cape Verdeans and having its head office in one of the two countries, a Board of Directors of which the Chairman and the majority of the members are nationals and a manager or director-general who is a national of Senegal or Cape Verde. (Article 4)

CONGO

. Agreement with Gabon, 9 November 1982 - Provides for reciprocal fishing rights; no fees specified.

COSTA RICA

. Agreement with Panama and USA, 14 March 1983 (valid until withdrawal)

Tuna Fishing: For five contracting parties, US$ 60 per article; for additional contracting parties (coastal states), fees increased up to maximum of US$ 100 per article. [Note: Increases to be determined by Council set up under agreement; minimum increase of US$ 10 per article for each additional contracting party (coastal state) as determined by Council down to minimum of US$ 60 per article.] Fees to be paid in full before license issued; Licenses valid until end year in which issued; proceeds of fees less up to 10% for administrative costs, to be distributed to coastal states in proportion to amount of tuna taken in respective 200-mile area. (Note: Agreement not yet in force.)

EQUATORIAL GUINEA

. Agreement with Spain, 31 October 1979, in force from 14 April 1982.
  Freezer Trawlers - License "A" (fishing allowed anywhere in zone) = 1,000,000 pesetas (US$ 2,105) per year; License "B" (fishing only beyond 12 mi. = 600,000 pesetas (US$ 1,263) per vessel per year.
  Fresh Fish - 200,000 pesetas (US$ 421) per vessel per year.
  Tuna Freezer Vessels - 50,000 pesetas (US$ 105) per vessel per year. Spain to provide credit of up to US$ 10,000,000 for implementation of several fishing projects (cold storage, distribution network, etc.)
. Agreement with Republic of Cameroon, signed 1980 (valid for two years, automatically renewed unless denounced)- Reciprocal fishing agreement; no fee.
. Agreement with Nigeria, 27 November 1981 (valid for five years, automatically renewed unless denounced) - 50 tons of fish for each boat per year; 20% of catch by purse seiners per boat per year; license fee of US$ 2,000 per boat per year.
. Agreement with EEC, 1983 (valid through 1986) - ECU 20 (US$ 17.4) per ton of fish caught; ECU 40,000 (US$ 34,800) paid in advance; ECU 180,000 (US$ 156,600) annually for development projects to be increased proportionately if tuna catches exceed 4,000 tons; agreement provides for authorizations for 27 tuna freezer vessels; additional authorizations may be accorded on request of one party on terms to be agreed. (Text published in EC Official Journal No. L 237/13 of 26 August 1983. Entry verified, August 1983)

FRENCH DEPENDENT TERRITORIES

. Agreement with Japan, 14 August 1982 (valid through August 1983) - 0.23 F/kg (US$ 0.02) for New Caledonia
  0.27 F/kg (US$ 0.03) for Wallis and Futuna
  0.36 F/kg (US$ 0.04) for Indian Ocean Islands
  0.32 F/kg (US$ 0.03) for French Polynesia
. Alternative fee formulation
  2,865,000 F (US$ 301,579) for a global quota (10,700 tons)
  1,276,000 F (US$ 134,316) for New Caledonia (5,550 tons)

364,500 F (US$ 38,368) for Wallis and Futuna (1,350 tons)
1,152,000 F (US$ 121,263) for French Polynesia (3,600 tons)
72,000 F (US$ 7,579) for Indian Ocean Islands (200 tons)

. Agreement with Korea (Republic of), November 1981 (valid through 19 January 1983) - Lump sum payment of US$ 481,000 for 300 vessels (in French Polynesia and Wallis and Futuna) (Entry verified, October 1982)

GABON

. Agreement with Congo of 9 November 1982 - Reciprocal fishing rights amendment.
. Agreement with Republic of Korea, December 1984 - 350-ton trawler licensed to fish January to July 1985 against payment of US$ 8,500. (Source: FWI, April 1985; Entry verified, October 1985)

GAMBIA

. Agreement with Senegal, 22 October 1982 (valid for two years, renewable on tacit understanding) - Reciprocal fishing rights agreement; fishing rights for industrial vessels to be determined annually by mixed commission. (Entry verified, September 1984)

GUINEA

. Agreement with Nigeria, 28 August 1981 (valid for five years) - 167 metric tons of fish per trawler per annum and 28% of the catch per purse seiner per annum; each fishing vessel to pay an annual tax of US$ 7,920; for each fishing vessel deposit of a Guarantee Fee of US$ 20,000 to guarantee correct execution of committments.
. Agreement with EEC, August 1982 (valid from 1 January 1982 to 31 December 1985) - Either 100 ECU/GMT/year (US$ 87) or delivery of part of the catch at Conakry (in any case delivery of a minimum of 200 tons per vessel per year) plus non-reimbursable financial compensation of 2,100,000 ECU (US$ 1,827,000) and contribution of 200,000 ECU (US$ 174,000) to a Guinean fish research program.
. Protocol under the Agreement with USSR of 1981, 28 October 1983 (valid for one year) - Licensing of up to 11 Soviet vessels in exchange for sale of 10,000 tons of fish to Guinea; payment by Guinea of US$ 412 per ton of fish.
. Agreement with Spain, 30 April 1984 (valid for three years) - Granting of renewable 3-month fishing licenses for up to 47 vessels; payment in the form of supply of semi-industrial trawlers and seiners of an average length of 13 meters, according to conditions set out in an annex to the Agreement.
. Arrangements concluded with seven private companies for 1984 - Payment of a fee from US$ 200/GRT to US$ 220/GRT per year plus landing of 200 tons of catch per vessel/year; if vessels operate less than one year, landing of 25 tons of

catch per month. (Entry verified, October 1985)

- Framework agreement with Ghana, 18 August 1978 - Provides for joint Ghanean/Guinean fishing operations and formation of one joint venture.

GUYANA [Maritime Boundaries (Fishery Zone Fees) (Amendment) Regulations 1977 Schedule]

- Agreement with USSR - Experimental fishing by two Soviet shrimp trawlers for one year; no fees; all shrimp to be landed locally; by-catch transhipped to Soviet collector vessel; costs of operation Soviet vessels to be met from proceeds of sale of shrimp in hard currency; any profits for Guyana.
- Agreement with Cuba, 1978 (valid one year, renewable) - 12% of total shrimp catch for four to thirty shrimp trawlers, plus locally-based foreign fishing fee and contribution in joint research projects; no examption from taxes.
- Agreement with German Democratic Republic, 1979- Exploratory commercial fishing for one vessel, one fishing trip, no fees. (Entry verified, October 1985)

IVORY COAST

- Agreement with Senegal, 11 June 1979 - Both governments grant reciprocal fishing rights for tuna in their EEZs.
- Liberia-Ivory Coast Cooperation Agreement - Reciprocal fishing rights for three bona fide Liberian and Ivory Coast fishing vessels (shrimp trawlers, approximately 70 ft. 350 M.P., with refrigeration capacity of 25 tons); no fees; other provisions on exchange information, joint studies.

KIRIBATI [Fisheries Ordinance 1977 S.5(4)] (Note: In practice fees set in access agreements)

- Agreement with Japan (Federation of Japan Tuna Fisheries Cooperative Associations), August 1984 (valid 1 September 1984 through 31 August 1985) - Longline and pole and line; Goods and services: Yen 35,000,000+ (US$ 140,000); Registration fee: Y 30,000 (US$ 120) per boat; License fee calculated as follows for longliners:

    Vessels under 100 GRT: Yen 29,382 (US$ 118) per MT estimated fish catch per trip based on historical catch data (39 MT September/October 1984)

    Vessels over 100 GRT: Yen 29,302 (US$ 117) per MT estimated fish catch per trip based on historical catch data (48 MT September/October 1984)

    For Pole and Line Vessels: Yen 6,298 (US$ 25) per MT estimated fish catch per trip based on historical catch data (51 MT September 1984/April 1985)

  Fee levels revised automatically to reflect changes in market prices at "basket" of markets according to formula: Initial license fee per MT x Amount of catch per trip (MT) x (Monthly catch price:initial catch price). Initial prices are: for longline fish - Yen 767 per kg; pole and line fish - Yen 169 per kg.

- Agreement with Republic of Korea, 12 November 1984 (valid through 11 November 1985) - Lump sum payment of US$ 200,000 for up to 60 boats; for any additional vessels over 60, fee: US$ 5,000 per vessel.
- Agreement with Sobryflot (USSR), August 1985 (valid for one year) - Permits to be issued in respect of five large purse-seiners, two small perse-seiners, three small longliners and one processing/factory vessel with 6 catcher boats, for lump sum payment of A$ 2,400,000, payable in three installments.
- Note: Agreement between Government Kiribati, Micronesia Maritime Authority, Palau Maritime Authority, and American Tunaboat Association, 1 January 1983 (valid through 31 December 1984) has now lapsed. (Entry verified, October 1985)

LIBERIA

- Liberia-Ivory Coast Cooperation Agreement - Reciprocal fishing rights for three bona fide Liberian and Ivory Coast fishing vessels (Shrimp trawlers, approximately 70 ft. 350 M.P., with refrigeration capacity of 25 tons); no fees; other provisions on exchange information, joint studies. Entry verified, October 1983)

MADAGASCAR

- Agreement with EEC, 1985 (valid three years, renewable automatically for periods two years unless notice denunciation) - Tuna fishing: licenses to be issued for 27 ocean-going freezer tuna boats (no more than 18 at one time); financial contribution for fisheries development projects: flat-rate fixed at minimum of 900,000 ECU (US$ 783,000) for duration of Protocal, payable in three equal annual installments; if catch exceeds 6,000 tons tuna per year, contribution to be increased accordingly up to maximum of 3,000,000 ECU (US$ 2,610,000) for duration protocol, i.e. 1,000,000 ECU (US$ 870,000) per year; contribution of 350,000 ECU (US$ 304,500) towards financing scientific program; license fee of 20 ECU (US$ 17.4) per ton of fish caught in fishing zone payable by shipowners; 15,000 ECU (US$ 13,050) to be paid as non-reimbursable advance; two Malagasy seamen to be signed on permanently for tuna fleet, failing which payment flat-rate 50% wages to be used for training seamen.

MAURITANIA

- Agreement with Republic of Korea, May 1981 (valid for five years, renewable for 2-year periods unless denounced) with implementing process verbal of May 1983 as subsequently amended - Trawlers fee: US$ 450 per BMT/year; all catch to be landed Naouadhibou; plus US$120 tax per ton of fish caught and exported; total tonnage authorized: 4,500 GRT; financial grant of US$ 1,000,000 per year for three years.
- Agreement with Senegal, 11 August 1983 (valid for two years, renewable unless denounced), with Protocol (valid for one year, renewable unless denounced).

Pelagic trawlers, US$ 200 GRT/year; Sardine vessels, US$ 200 GRT/year; Tuna vessels, US$ 200 GRT/campaign.

. <u>Contracts with French interests of 1985</u>:
    US$ 110/GRT/year for ple and line tuna boats
    US$ 3,500/GRT/year for lobster vessels
    US$ 200/GRT/year for shrimp vessels

. <u>Contracts with Spanish interests for 1985</u>:
    US$ 200/GRT/year for shrimp boats

Note: Most foreign vessels are under time-charter to Mauritanian-based companies. Under normal contracts, about 31% of the demersal catch and between 27% and 31% of the pelagic catch suplied to the Mauritanian companies. (Entry verified, July 1985)

MOROCCO

. <u>Agreement with Spain</u>, 1 August 1983 (valid through 31 July 1987) - Licenses granted for a degressive global tonnage of vessels: 138,602 GRT by 1 August 1983 and $ 1,961 GRT after 1 August 1986. All vessels to pay a progressive annual fee defined in Special Drawing Rights (SDR) per Gross Registered Ton by type of vessel and payable in convertible currency.

<u>North of Cape Noun</u>: For vessels of less than 100 GRT, 87,14 SDR (US$ 87) from 1 July 1984; 96,48 SDR (US$ 96) from 1 January 1985; 181,10 SDR (US$ 105) from 1 January 1986. For vessels of more than 100 GRT, 149,14 SDR (US$ 149) from 1 July 1984; 166,12 SDR (US$ 166) from 1 January 1985; 181,10 SDR (US$ 181) from 1 January 1986.

<u>South of Cape Noun</u>: Sardine vessels: 99,22 SDR (US$ 99) from 1 July 1984; 109,85 SDR (US$ 109) from 1 January 1985; 120,48 SDR (US$ 120) from 1 January 1986; Artisanal vessels: 62,17 SDR (US$ 62) from 1 July 1984; 68,83 SDR (US$ 68) from 1 January 1985; 75,49 SDR (US$ 75) from 1 January 1986; Cephalopoda freezer vessels: 186,23 SDR (US$ 186) from 1 July 1984; 206,18 SDR (US$ 206) from 1 January 1985; 226,13 SDR (US$ 226) from 1 January 1986; Other cephalopoda vessels: 136,33 SDR (US$ 136) from 1 July 1984; 150,93 SDR (US$ 150) from 1 January 1985; 165,53 SDR (US$ 165) from 1 January 1986; Merlusa vessels: 70,53 SDR (US$ 70) from 1 July 1984; 78,09 SDR (US$ 78) from 1 January 1985; 85,65 SDR (US$ 85) from 1 January 1986; plus Spain to supply for the period of the agreement two credits of US$ 400,000,000 and US$ 150,000,000 respectively on conditions defined in the Agreement. (Entry verified, October 1985)

MOZAMBIQUE

. <u>Agreement with Portugal</u>, 1982 (valid through end 1983)- Licenses issued to Portuguese vessels to fish in Mozambique EEZ; no license fees mentioned; quota of 700 tons of shrimp fixed for 1983 for Portuguese market; four study places allocated to Mozambique nationals at Portuguese institutions; one specially equipped Portuguese vessel to carry out scientific and technical survey and train

Mozambique nationals. (Entry verified, May 1983)

NEW ZEALAND DEPENDENT TERRITORIES

. Niue: Agreement between Government Kiribati, Micronesia Maritime Authority, Palau Maritime Authority, and American Tunaboat Association, 1 January 1983 (valid through 31 December 1984) has now lapsed. (Entry verified, October 1985)
Note: No access agreements in force; agreement with Republic of Korea (November 1982, valid through November 1983) now lapsed.
Note: Agreement with Taiwanese Fishermans' Association, 7 October 1981, valid through 6 October 1982, now lapsed. (Entry verified, October 1985)

OMAN

. Agreement with Korean Company - 50% of catch (in kind or equivalence.)

PANAMA

. Agreement with Costa Rica and USA, 14 March 1983 (valid until withdrawal) - Tuna Fishing: For five contracting parties - US$ 60 per artical; for additional contracting parties (coastal states) fees increased up to maximum of US$ 100 per article.
Note: Increases to be determined by Council set up under agreement; minimum increase of US$ 10 per article for each additional contracting party (coastal state) after sixth; fees to be reduced on withdrawal by any contracting party (coastal state) as determined by Council down to minimum of US$ 60 per article; fees to be paid in full before license issued; licenses valid until end of year in which issued; proceeds of fees, less up to 10% for administrative costs, to be distributed to coastal states in proportion to amount of tuna taken in respective 200-mile areas. (Agreement not yet in force) (Entry verified, October 1984)

PAPUA NEW GUINEA

. Japanese/Papua New Guinea Fishing Arrangement (valid 7 August 1981 until three months after either party gives notice of termination) - Fees as above; operation fee determined by formula: (Estimated catch per trip in tons) x (FOB price in Kina per ton) x (Unit Rate in percentage) x (Operation Ratio) x (Duration Ratio for Longliners and group purse-seiners or number of trips per year for single purse-seiners - nothing for pole and liners) x (Factor - for single purse-seiners only); FOB price calculated in accordance with agreed formula from average of Yaisu market prices over previous three months.
. Agreement with American Tunaboat Association, 1982 (valid through 31 December 1982) now lapsed. (Entry verified, October 1985)

SAO TOME and PRINCIPE

- Agreement with Portugal, October 1979 - Portuguese vessels allowed to operate in Sao Tomean waters; fees to be established according to S.T. laws and regulations; parties shall seek to establish fishing joint ventures.
- Agreement with the EEC, 1983 (valid through 1986) - ECU 20 per ton of fish caught (ECU 40,000 paid in advance); ECU 180,000 annually for development projects to be increased proportionately if tuna catches exceed 4,000 tons; agreement provides for authorizations for 27 tuna freezer vessels; additional authorizations may be accorded on request of one party on terms to be agreed. (Text published in EC Official Journal No. L 282/567, 14/10/1983.) (Entry verified, October 1983)

SENEGAL

- Agreement with EEC, 15 June 1979, as amended January 1982 and January 1984 (valid until denounced) - Fees set on following scale:
  - a Trawlers landing their entire catch (licenses to be issued for up to 2,500 GRT): CFA 8,500 (US$ 18) per GRT per year for shrimp boats; CFA 7,500 (US$ 16) per GRT per year for fish boats.
  - b Trawlers not landing their entire catch and fishing throughout the year (up to 5,000 GRT for year): CFA 17,000 (US$ 46) per GRT per year for shrimp boats; CFA 15,000 (US$ 41) per GRT per year for fish boats.
  - c Freezer trawlers not landing their entire catch and fishing for a specific four-month period for each vessel (up to 9,000 GRT additional to the 5,000 GRT referred to under (a): CFA 10,500 (US$ 28).
  - d Tuna boats landing their entire catch (up to 3,000 GRT): CFA 2 (US$ 0.005) per kg of fish caught.
  - e Tuna boats not landing their entire catch (up to 23,300 GRT): CFA 6 (US$ 0.016) per kg of fish caught.

  Plus financial compensation for the period 16 January 1984 to 15 January 1986 of CFA 3,000,000,000 (US$ 6,757,000), plus CFA 100,000,000 (US$ 270,000) contribution towards the financing of a Senegalese scientific program.
- Agreement with Gambia, 22 October 1982 (valid for two years, renewable on tacit understanding) - Reciprocal fishing rights agreement; fishing rights for industrial vessels to be determined yearly.
- Agreement with Ivory Coast, 11 June 1979 - Ivory Coast vessels allowed to fish upon payment of fees laid down by national legislation; Ivory Coast to allow duty-free imports of fishing products from Senegal up to 13,000 tons per year.
- Agreement with Nigeria, 8 November 1982 (valid for two years, renewable on tacit understanding) - Fees and other payments to be agreed upon subsequently through implementing protocols. (Entry verified, August 1985)

SEYCHELLES

- Agreement with EEC (Valid from 1 November 1984 to 1 October

1987) - 27 tuna vessels of which only 18 may fish at any one time; 1,000 GMT of other fishing vessels; Fees of 20 ECU (US$ 17.4) payable by vessel operators [ECU 120,000 (US$ 104,400) paid in advance]; Financial compensation = 300 ECU (US$ 261,000) + 50 ECU (US$ 43) per ton if catch exceeds 6,000 tons per year up to a ceiling of 1,000,000 ECU (US$ 870,000) per year plus 250,000 ECU (US$ 217,500) over three years to finance scientific programs.

- Agreement with 2 private fishing companies, March 1984 (valid 5 years; automatically renewed for further periods of 1 year unless denounced.) - Fishing permits to be given to 2 tuna purse-seiners; fees set at 10% of 50% of total catches in the Western Indian Ocean FOB Victoria; payments to be made six-monthly; vessels to be based preferentially in Victoria and at least 80% of trans-shipments and revictualling to be carried out in Victoria.
- Agreement with Spain, 1 June 1984 (valid for 5 years, renewed automatically for periods of 1 year unless denounced 6/3 months before expiry) - For up to 15 tuna purse-seiners: fees fixed at 10% of landed value of 50% of catch FOB Victoria; payment to be made every six months.
- Agreement with French, Ivorian and Mauritian Companies, indefinite duration; annual fees per vessel not published. (Entry verified, October 1985)

SIERRA LEONE

- Agreement with USSR, 14 May 1976 (valid for 5 years, renewable for 3-year periods on tacit understanding) - Fishing conditions laid down by implementing protocols; under implementing protocol now in force, 12% of catch supplied to Sierra Leone; remaining 88% retained by USSR but the Sierra Leone Fishing Company may buy up to 38% of this amount at a preferential pre-agreed price. (Source: *West Africa*, May/June, 1984, p. 1129); agreement renewed 30 October 1985 (Source: *Marchés tropicaux* 15 November 1985)

SOLOMON ISLANDS

- Agreement with Japanese Tuna Fisheries Co-operative Associations under Japanese Head Agreement of 1978 (January 1984, valid through December 1984; extended thereafter until six months after notice given of intent to terminate)

  Tuna longlining and pole and line fishing operations:

  a Permit fee of Y 27,000 (US$ 108) per vessel (valid one year);

  b Permit Activation fee (valid for one trip); permit activation fee calculated on basis of value of fish to be caught during permit activation period, according to formula: Initial price per metric ton x Catch per trip x Monthly "all tuna" or "skipjack" price, divided by initial "all tuna" or "skipjack" price.

  Longline vessels:

  Initial price - January 1984: Y 21,500 (US$ 86)
  Initial "all tuna" price: Y 590/kg (US$ 2.4)

Pole and line vessels:
Initial price - January 1984: Y 6,500 (US$ 26)
Initial "skipjack" price: Y 209/kg (US$ 0.8)
Note: Price calculated on approximate basis of 5% of market value of catch; maximum allowable catch for Japanese fishing vessels set at 6,000 per year tons for pole and line vessels, and 6,500 tons per year for longline vessels.

- Agreement with Deep-Sea Fisheries Association of Republic of Korea, 1980 (valid from 12 January 1982 through 11 January 1983 - for longliners) NO LONGER IN FORCE.
- Agreement with SPFC - Vanuatu (valid through January 1981- longliners) NO LONGER IN FORCE. (Entry verified, October 1985)

SOMALIA

- Somalia/Republic of Korea Agreement on Fisheries (valid 1 March through 31 May 1985) - Total of twenty boats to be licensed at fee of US$ 4,000 per boat, targeting primarily on tuna. (Source: INFOFISH Trade News, February 1985)

SOUTH AFRICA

- Agreement with Japan, 6 December 1977 - South Africa to collect reasonable fees from Japanese vessels.
- Agreement with Spain, 14 August 1979 - Spanish vessels to pay such fees as the Government of South Africa may impose (Article 4).

SPAIN

- Agreement with EEC, April 1980 (valid five years and further periods of five years each unless renounced) - Reciprocal fishing arrangements; no fees.
  Note: On January 1986 Spain and Portugal will become members of the EEC. As from that date, fishing in Spanish waters will be governed by agreements made by the EEC; licences will be issued by EEC within the common fishing zone; no fees.

TRINIDAD AND TOBAGO

- Agreement with Venezuela, 1978 - Fishing by nationals of Venezuela under conditions of reciprocity; no fees.
- Agreements with Venezuela and Brazil provide for establishment of joint venture companies.

TUVALU

- Agreement with Deep-Sea Fisheries Association of Republic of Korea under Head Agreement with Government of Republic of Korea dated 1980 (valid December 1982 through December 1983) - Lump sum payment of US$ 70,000 for up to sixty vessels (longlining only).
  Note: Agreement renewed 31 January 1984 (valid through 31 January 1986); changes to terms unknown.
  Note: Agreement between Governments of Niue, New Zealand (for Tokelau), Tuvalu and Western Samoa and American

Tunaboat Association, September 1983 (valid through end of 1984) - AGREEMENT NO LONGER IN FORCE. (Entry verified, October 1985)

UNION OF SOVIET SOCIALIST REPUBLICS

- Agreement with Japan concerning salmon quotas in Northwest Pacific, 1983 - Yen 4,250,000 (US$ 17,000) for 42,500 tons of salmon.
- Agreement with Japan, May 1983 - 375 Japanese vessels (45 more than 1982) to exploit seaweeds (Lamimaria) around Kaigara Isle in the Shikotan Islands.

UNITED STATES TRUST TERRITORY

- Federated States of Micronesia
  - Agreement with Japanese Fishing Associations, 25 January 1984 (valid from 10 February 1984 through 9 August 1984) - Longline, pole and line and purse seiner - up to 650 vessels; lump sum payment of Y 285,000,000 (US$ 1,140,000) for six-month period of validity; new agreement signed 16 July 1984, effective from 10 August 1984 and continuing in force thereafter until expiry of 120 days from notice of intent to terminate; fees unknown.
  - Agreement with Kaohsiung Fishery Association, 16 July 1982 (valid through 15 July 1983, extended to 15 July 1984) - Two seiner groups (1 group = 1 purse seiner + 2 carriers) = lump sum of US$ 26,000 for two groups. Note: lump sum based on 5% of estimated value of landed catch.

    NOTE: AGREEMENT APPARENTLY NO LONGER IN FORCE.

    Note: Agreement with Republic of Korea, 14 November 1980 (valid through 13 November 1981); Agreement between Government of Kiribati, Micronesia Maritime Authority, Palau Maritime Authority and American Tunaboat Association (valid 1 January 1983 through 31 December 1984); Agreement with Samyong Enterprise Co. Ltd., 19 October 1982 (valid through 31 December 1983); Agreement with Mar Fishing Co., Inc. (Philippines), 29 December 1982 (valid 1 January 1983 through 31 December 1983) AGREEMENTS NO LONGER IN FORCE (Entry verified, October 1985)
- Marshall Islands
  - Agreement with Japanese Fisheries Associations, May 1985 (valid through April 1986 and thereafter until six months after notice of termination by either party-longline/pole line) - Registration Fee (all vessels): Yen 36,000 (US$ 150); Variable-per-Vessel-per-Trip Fee: For May 1985: Longliners - Yen 801,680 (US$ 3,340); Pole and liners - Yen 544,320 (US$ 2,268). Fees subject to monthly variation thereafter to reflect market fluctuations. (See entry under Solomon Islands for price formula) (Entry verified, December 1985)
- Palau
  - Agreement with Japan, November 1983 (valid 1 January

through 31 December 1984) - Lump sum payment of equipment/aid to value of Y 65,000,000 (US$ 260,000) for up to 290 vessels (longline/pole and line/purse-seine); parties to explore alternative fee systems for next agreement, based on pre-determined fee levels for individual vessels. Agreement renewed through December 1985 by exchange of letters; lump sum payment apparently US$ 263,000. (Source FFA)

- Agreement with Sino-Palau Fishing Co., Ltd. signed 27 July 1982 (valid for one year, automatically renewed for further periods of one year unless notice given of intent to terminate) - Lump sum of US$ 14,800 for one longline vessel under 200 GRT + two longline vessels under 100 GRT + eight small seine fishing vessels under 50 GRT.

  Note: Agreement between Government of Kiribati, Micronesia Maritime Authority, Palau Maritime Authority and American Tunaboat Association (valid 1 January 1983 through 31 December 1984) AGREEMENT NO LONGER IN FORCE (Entry verified, October 1985)

WESTERN SAMOA

Note: Agreement between Governments of Niue, New Zealand (for Tokelau), Tuvalu and Western Samoa and American Tunaboat Association, September 1983 (valid through end 1984) AGREEMENT NO LONGER IN FORCE (Entry verified, October 1985)

YEMEN DEMOCRATIC REPUBLIC

Pro-rata royalty fees based on species, sizes and grades; payments to be made either in kind as percentage of catch, in cash or in delivery of catch at below market prices.

- Agreement with USSR, 1969 (renewed annually) - Licenses granted to USSR trawlers and research vessels; joint expedition in fishing for supply of fish for domestic consumption in the PDRY; Fisheries development projects provided by USSR on soft loans.
- Agreement with Libya - A joint company apparently established in 1982; 60% shares held by Yemen; the Company charters fishing vessels from Yemen and catches are aimed at domestic markets of the two countries, as well as for export.

APPENDIX VII

Directory of Selected Non-Governmental International Organizations Interested in Ocean Affairs

Arab Lawyers Union
13 Arab Lawyers Union Street
Garden City
Cairo, Egypt

Center for Inter-American Relations has been absorbed by:
America's Society
680 Park Avenue
New York, NY 10021

Commission of European Communities
Rue de la Loi 200
B-1049 Brussels, Belgium

Commonwealth Secretariat
Marlborough House
Pall Mall
London, SW1Y 5HX, England

Council of Europe
B.P. 431 B6
F-67006 Strasbourg, France

Friends of the Earth
530 Seventh St., S.E.
Washington, DC 20003

Friends World Committee for Consultation
Drayton House
30 Gordon Street
London WC1H OAX, England

International Air Transport Association
IATA Building
2000 Peel Street
Montreal, P. Q.
Canada H3A 2R4

International Atomic Energy Agency
Vienna International Centre
P.O. Box 100
Wagramerstrasse 5
A-1400 Vienna, Austria

International Bar Association
2 Harewood Place
Hanover Square
London WIR 2HB, England

International Chamber of Commerce
38 Coers Albert
F-75008 Paris, France

International Chamber of Shipping
30/32 St. Mary Axe
London EC3A 8ET, England

International Commission of Jurism
P.O. Box 120
109 Ponte de Chene
Chene-Bougeries
CH-1224 Geneva, Switzerland

International Confederation of Free Trade Unions
Rue Montagne aux Herkes Potageres, 37
B-1000 Brussels, Belgium

International Cooperative Alliance
15, Route des Morillons
Grand-Saconnex
CH-1218 Geneva, Switzerland

International Federation for Human Rights
27 Rue Jean-Dolent
F-75014 Paris, France

International Hotel Association
89, Rue du Faubourg-Saint-Honore
F-75008 Paris, France

International Hydrographic Organization
7 Ave. President J. F. Kennedy
B. P. 345
MC-98000 Monte Carlo, Monaco

International Council of Environmentalists
Adenaueralee 214
D-5300 Bonn,
Federal Republic of Germany

International Council of Scientific Unions
51 Boulevard de Montmorency
F-75016 Paris, France

International Council of Voluntary Agencies
13 Rue Gautier
CH-1201 Geneva, Switzerland

International Council of Women
13, Rue Caumartin
F-75009 Paris, France

International Law Association
Three Paper Buildings, Temple
London EC4Y 7EU, England

International Ocean Institute
P.O. Box 524
Valetta, Malta

Intergovernmental Oceanographic Commission
c/o UNESCO
7 Place de Fontenoy
F-75700 Paris, France

International Organization of Consumers Unions
9 Emmastraat
NL-2595 EG The Hague,
Netherlands

International Telecommunication Union
Place des Nations
CH-1211 Geneva 20, Switzerland

International Union for Conservation of Nature and Natural Resources
CH-1196 Gland, Switzerland

International Youth and Student Movement for the United Nations
c/o Palais des Nations
CH-1211 Geneva 10, Switzerland

National Audubon Society
950 Third Avenue
New York, NY 10022

Organization of the Islamic Conference
Kilo 6, Makkah Al-Murkarramah
P.O. Box 178
Jeddah 21441, Saudi Arabia

Organization of the Petroleum Exporting Countries
Obere-Donaustrasse 93
A-1020 Vienna, Austria

Pax Christi International
Kerkstraat 150
B-2008 Antwerp, Belgium

Society for International Development
Palazzo Civilta del Lavoro, EUR
1-00144 Rome, Italy

Sierra Club
730 Polk Street
San Francisco, CA 94109

United Towns Organisation
1, Rue de Logelbach
F-75017 Paris, France

Women's International League for Peace and Freedom
1 Rue de Varembe
CH-1211 Geneva 20, Switzerland

World Alliance of Young Men's Christian Associations
37 Quai Wilson
CH-1201 Geneva, Switzerland

World Association of World Federalists
21 Leliegracht GR
Amsterdam, Netherlands

World Conservation Center
CH-1196 Gland, Switzerland

World Confederation of Labour
Rue Joseph II, Bet. 2, 71
B-1040 Brussels, Belgium

World Federation of Scientific Workers
6 Endsleigh Street
London WC1H ODX, England

World Federation of United Nations Associations
c/o Palais des Nations
CH-1211 Geneva 10, Switzerland

World Intellectual Property Organization
34, Chemin des Colombettes
CH-1211, Geneva 20, Switzerland

World Young Women's Christian Association
37, Quai Wilson
CH-1201 Geneva, Switzerland

Selected Bibliography

Abir, Mordechai. *Oil, Power and Politics: Conflict in Arabia, the Red Sea and the Gulf*. London: Frank Case, 1974.

Adede, A. O. *The System for Settlement of Disputes under the United Nations Convention on the Law of the Sea: A Drafting History and a Commentary*. Dordrecht, Netherlands: Martinus Nijhoff, 1987.

Ademuni, Odeke. *Protectionism and the Future of International Shipping*. Dordrecht, Netherlands: Martinus Nijhoff; London: Graham & Trotman, 1984.

Akah, Tsuneo. *Japan in Global Ocean Politics*. Honolulu: The Law of the Sea Institute, University of Hawaii, 1985.

Alexander, Lewis. ''Rights to Oceanic Resources: Deciding and Drawing Maritime Boundaries.'' *Marine Policy* 12, no. 1 (January 1988): 70–73.

———. *Navigational Restrictions within the New LOS Context: Geographical Implications for the United States*. Peace Dale, R.I.: Offshore Consultants, 1986.

———. ''The Ocean Enclosure Movement: Inventory and Prospect.'' *San Diego Law Review* 20, no. 3 (April 1983): 561–594.

Alexanderson, G. *The Baltic Straits*. Dordrecht, Netherlands: Martinus Nijhoff; London: Graham & Trotman, 1982.

Allen, Craig H. ''Doctrine of Hot Pursuit: A Functional Interpretation Adaptable to Emerging Maritime Law Enforcement Technologies and Practices.'' *Ocean Development and International Law* 20, no. 4 (1989): 309–342.

Allen, K. Radway. *Conservation and Management of Whales*. Seattle: A Washington Sea Grant Publication, University of Washington Press, 1980.

Allen, S., and L. C. Hanson, eds. *New Developments in Marine Science and Technology: Economic, Legal and Political Aspects of Change*. Honolulu: The Law of the Sea Institute, University of Hawaii, 1989.

Amerasinghe, C. F. ''The Problem of Archipelagos in the International Law of the Sea.'' *International and Comparative Law Quarterly* 23 (1974): 539–575.

Attard, David Joseph. *The Exclusive Economic Zone in International Law*. Oxford: Clarendon Press; New York: Oxford University Press, 1987.

Bandow, Doug. ''UNCLOS III: A Flawed Treaty.'' *San Diego Law Review* 19, no. 3 (April 1982): 475–492.

Baram, Michael S., David Rice, and William Lee. *Marine Mining of the Continental Shelf: Legal, Technical and Environmental Considerations*. Cambridge, Mass.: Ballinger, 1978.

Barkenbus, Jack N. *Deep Seabed Resources: Politics and Technology*. New York: The Free Press, 1981.

Barston, R. P., and Patricia Birnie, eds. Introduction to *The Maritime Dimension*. London: Allen & Unwin, 1980.

Bhatt, J. J. *Oceanography: Exploring the Planet Ocean*. New York: Van Nostrand, 1978.

Blecher, M. D. "Equitable Delimitation of the Continental Shelf." *American Journal of International Law* 73, no. 1 (January 1979): 60–88.

Boczek, Boleslaw. "Law of Warfare at Sea and Neutrality for the Gulf War." *Ocean Development and International Law* 20, no. 3 (1989): 239–271.

———. *The Transfer of Marine Technology to Developing Nations in International Law*. Honolulu: The Law of the Sea Institute, University of Hawaii, 1982.

Booth, Kenneth. "The Military Implications of the Changing Law of the Sea." In *Law of the Sea: Neglected Issues*, edited by John King Gamble, Jr. Honolulu: The Law of the Sea Institute, University of Hawaii, 1979.

Borgese, Elisabeth Mann. *The Mines of Neptune: Minerals and Metals from the Sea*. New York: Harry N. Abrams, 1985.

Boyle, Alan E. "Marine Pollution under the Law of the Sea Convention." *American Journal of International Law* 79, no. 2 (April 1985): 347–372.

Bravender-Coyle, Paul. "The Emerging Legal Principles and Equitable Criteria Governing the Delimitation of Maritime Boundaries between States." *Ocean Development and International Law*. 19, no. 3 (1988): 171–228.

Brill, E. J. *The World of the Whales*. New York: Spencer W. Tinker, 1988.

Brill, Richard. "Disarmament Interests on the Shelf." In *The Law of the Sea: International Rules and Organization for the Sea*, edited by Lewis M. Alexander. Kingston: University of Rhode Island, 1969.

Brittin, Burdick H. *International Law for Seagoing Officers*. 5th ed. Annapolis, Md.: Naval Institute Press, 1986.

Brown, E. D., and R. R. Churchill, eds. *The UN Convention on the Law of the Sea: Impact and Implementation*. Honolulu: The Law of the Sea Institute, University of Hawaii, 1987.

———. *Seabed Energy and Mineral Resources and the Law of the Sea*. 3 vols. London: Graham & Trotman, 1986.

———. "Freedom of the High Seas Versus the Common Heritage of Mankind: Fundamental Principles in Conflict." *San Diego Law Review* 20, no. 3 (April 1983): 521–560.

Burke, C. A., and C. L. Drake. *The Geology of Continental Margins*. New York: Springer-Verlag, 1974.

Butler, William E. *Law of the Sea and International Shipping*. Dobbs Ferry, N.Y.: Oceana, 1985.

———. *Northeast Arctic Passage*. Dordrecht, Netherlands: Martinus Nijhoff; London: Graham & Trotman, 1978.

Buzan, Barry. *Seabed Politics*. New York: Praeger, 1976.

Cafruny, Alan W. *Ruling the Waves: The Political Economy of International Shipping*. Berkeley and Los Angeles: University of California Press, 1987.

Caron, David D. and Charles D. Buderi. *Perspectives on U.S. Policy toward the Law of the Sea*. Honolulu: The Law of the Sea Institute, University of Hawaii, 1982.

Charney, Jonathan I. "The Exclusive Economic Zone and Public International Law." *Ocean Development and International Law* 15, nos. 3–4 (1985): 233–288.

Christie, Donna R. "Georges Bank: Common Ground or Continued Battleground? Comparative Marine Resource Management and Environmental Assessment in the United States and Canada." *San Diego Law Review* 23, no. 3 (May–June 1986): 491–543.

Churchill, R. R. and A. V. Lowe. *EEC Fisheries Law*. Dordrecht, Netherlands: Martinus Nijhoff, 1987.

———. *The Law of the Sea*. Manchester, U.K.: Manchester University Press, 1983.

Clark, R. B. *Marine Pollution*. Oxford: Clarendon Press, 1986.

Clingan, Thomas A., Jr. *The Law of the Sea: What Lies Ahead?* Honolulu: The Law of the Sea Institute, University of Hawaii, 1988.

Commission of the European Communities. *Law and Practice Relating to Pollution Control in the Member States of the European Communities*. London: Graham & Trotman, 1983.

Conforti, Benedetto, Gramprero Francalance, Angelo Labella, and Daniela Romano, eds. *Atlas of the Seabed Boundaries*. Milan: Dott A. Giaffre Editore, 1987.

Cottrell, Alvin J. *Sea Power and Strategy in the Indian Ocean*. Beverly Hills, CA: Sage, 1981.

Cottrell, Alvin J., and R. M. Burrell, eds. *The Indian Ocean: Its Political, Economic and Military Importance*. New York: Praeger, 1972.

Cousteau, Jacques Yves. *The Ocean World*. New York: Abradale Press/Harry N. Abrams, 1985.

Craven, John P. *The Management of Pacific Marine Resources: Present Problems and Future Trends*. Boulder, Colo.: Westview Press, 1982.

Craven, John P., Jan Schneider, and Carol Stimson, eds. *The International Implications of Extended Maritime Jurisdiction in the Pacific*. Honolulu: The Law of the Sea Institute, University of Hawaii, 1989.

Cunha, Derek da. *Soviet Naval Power in the Pacific*. Boulder, Colo.: Lynne Rienner, 1990.

Cuyvers, Luc. *Ocean Uses and Their Regulation*. New York: Wiley, 1984.

Dahmani, M. *The Fisheries Regime of the Exclusive Economic Zone*. Dordrecht, Netherlands: Martinus Nijhoff, 1987.

Dallmeyer, Dorinda G., and Louis Devorsey, Jr. *Rights to Oceanic Resources: Deciding and Drawing Maritime Boundaries*. Dordrecht, Netherlands: Martinus Nijhoff; London: Graham & Trotman, 1989.

Davison, Art. *On the Wake of the Exxon Valdez: The Devastating Impact of the Alaska Oil Spill*. San Francisco: Sierra Club, 1990.

Day, David. *The Whale War*. San Francisco: Sierra Club, 1987.

Doumani, George A. *Ocean Wealth: Policy and Potential*. Rochelle Park, N.J.: Hayden, 1973.

Dupuy, R. J., ed. *The Settlement of Disputes on the New Natural Resources*. Dordrecht, Netherlands: Martinus Nijhoff; London: Graham & Trotman, 1983.

Eckert, Ross D. *The Enclosure of Ocean Resources: Economics and the Law of the Sea*. Stanford, Calif.: Hoover Institution Press, 1979.

Emery, K. O. ''Geological Limits on the Continental Shelf.'' *Ocean Development and International Law* 10, nos. 1–2 (1981): 1–12.

Farid, Abdel Majid. *The Red Sea: Prospects for Stability*. New York: St. Martin's, 1984.

Fenn, Percy Thomas, Jr. ''Origins of the Theory of Territorial Waters.'' *American Journal of International Law* 20 (July 1926): 465–482.

Fieldhouse, Richard, and Shunji Taoka. *Superpowers at Sea: An Assessment of the Naval Arms Race*. London: Oxford University Press, 1989.

Fincham, Charles, and William van Rensburg. *Bread upon the Waters: The Developing Law of the Sea.* Forest Grove, Oreg.: Turtledove, 1980.

Flinterman, Cees, Barbara Kwiatkowska, and John G. Lammers, eds. *Transboundary Air Pollution: International Legal Aspects of the Cooperation of States*. Dordrecht, Netherlands: Martinus Nijhoff, 1986.

Friedman, Norman. *The U.S. Maritime Strategy*. London: Jane's, 1988.

Fu, Kuen-Chen. *Equitable Ocean Boundary Delimitation*. Taipei: National Taiwan University, 1989.

Garwin, Richard L. ''Anti-Submarine Warfare and National Security.'' *Scientific American* 227, no. 1 (July 1972): 14–25.

German, Robert K. ''Nuclear Free Zones: Norwegian Interest, Soviet Encouragement.'' *ORBIS* 26, no. 2 (Summer 1982): 451–476.

Gerstle, M. S. *The Politics of UN Voting: A View of the Seabed from the Glass Palace*. Honolulu: The Law of the Sea Institute, University of Hawaii, 1977.

Gold, Edgar. *A New Law of the Sea for the Caribbean: An Examination of Marine Law and Policy Issues in the Lesser Antilles*. New York: Springer-Verlag, 1989.

———. ''International Shipping and the New Law of the Sea: New Directions for a Traditional Use?'' *Ocean Development and International Law* 20, no. 5 (1989): 433–444.

Grunawalt, Captain Richard Jack. ''New Legal Issues Resulting from the U.S. Global Military Commitment: A Naval Perspective of the Persian Gulf Tanker War.'' In *Proceedings*, from The Law of the Sea Institute Annual Conference, University of Rhode Island, June 1988.

Harrison, Selig S., and K. Subrahmangam. *Superpower Rivalry in the Indian Ocean*. New York: Oxford University Press, 1989.

Henderson, Hamish McN. *Oil and Gas: The North Sea Exploitation*. Dobbs Ferry, N.Y.: Oceana, 1981.

Hollick, Ann L. *U.S. Foreign Policy and the Law of the Sea*. Princeton, N.J.: Princeton University Press, 1981.

Hull, E.W.S. *The International Law of the Sea: A Case for a Customary Approach*. Honolulu: The Law of the Sea Institute, University of Hawaii, 1976.

Huyghe, Patrick. ''Oceans from Comets—New Evidence.'' *Oceans* 21, no. 2 (March-April 1988): 8–11.

Jackson, David C. *World Shipping Laws*. Dobbs Ferry, N.Y.: Oceana, 1979.

Jagota, S. P. *Maritime Boundary*. Dordrecht, Netherlands: Martinus Nijhoff; London: Graham & Trotman, 1985.

Janis, Mark W. *Sea Power and the Law of the Sea*. Lexington, Mass.: D. C. Heath, 1976.

Janis, Mark W., and D.C.F. Daniel. *The USSR: Ocean Use and Ocean Law*. Honolulu: The Law of the Sea Institute, University of Hawaii, 1974.

Jenkins, Raymond W., M. Karl Jugel, Kent M. Keith, and Maurice A. Meylan. *The*

Feasibility and Potential Impact of Manganese Nodule Processing in the Puna and Kohala Districts of Hawaii. State of Hawaii, Department of Planning and Economic Development, in cooperation with the U.S. Department of Commerce and National Oceanic and Atmospheric Administration, November 1981.

Johnston, Douglas M. *The Theory and History of Ocean Boundary Making*. Montreal: McGill-Queen's University Press, 1989.

———. *The International Law of Fisheries: A Framework for Policy-Oriented Inquiries*. Norwell, Mass.: Kluwer Academic, 1987.

Joseph, James, and Joseph W. Greenough. *International Management of Tuna, Porpoise and Billfish: Biological, Legal and Political Aspects*. Seattle: University of Washington Press, 1979.

Joyner, Christopher C., and Sudhir K. Chopra. *The Antarctic Legal Regime*. Dordrecht, Netherlands: Martinus Nijhoff, 1988.

Juda, Lawrence. *The United States without the Law of the Sea Treaty: Opportunities and Costs*. Wakefield, R. I.: Times Press, 1983.

———. *Ocean Space Rights: Developing U.S. Policy*. New York: Praeger, 1975.

Kasoulides, George C. "The 1986 United Nations Convention on the Conditions for Registration of Vessels and the Question of Open Registry." *Ocean Development and International Law* 20, no. 6 (1989): 543–576.

Kent, George. *The Politics of Pacific Island Fisheries*. Boulder, Colo.: Westview, 1980.

Kimball, Lee A. "Antarctica: The Challenges that Lie Ahead." *Journal of Human Environment* 18, no. 1 (1989).

Kindt, John Warren. *Marine Pollution and the Law of the Sea*. 4 vols. Buffalo, N.Y.: William S. Hein, 1985.

Knight, H. Gary. *Managing the Sea's Living Resources: Legal and Political Aspects of High Seas Fisheries*. Lexington, Mass.: Lexington Books, 1977.

Koh, Tommy T. B. "The Exclusive Economic Zone." *Malaya Law Review* 30 (1988): 1–33.

Kronmiller, Theodore G., and G. Wayne Smith, eds. *The Unlawfulness of Deep Seabed Mining*. 3 vols. Dobbs Ferry, N.Y.: Oceana, 1981.

Kwaiatkowska, Barbara. *The 200-Mile Exclusive Economic Zone in the Law of the Sea*. Dordrecht, Netherlands: Martinus Nijhoff; London: Graham & Trotman, 1989.

Lamson, Cynthia, and David L. Vander Zwaag, eds. *Transit Management in the Northwest Passage: Problems and Prospects*. Cambridge, U.K.: Cambridge University Press, 1988.

Larson, David L. "When Will the UN Convention on the Law of the Sea Come into Effect?" *Ocean Development and International Law* 20, no. 2 (1989): 175–202.

———. "Naval Weaponry and the Law of the Sea." *Ocean Development and International Law* 18, no. 2 (1987): 125–199.

Laurila, Simon H. *Islands Rise from the Sea: Essays on Exploration, Navigation and Mapping in Hawaii*. New York: Vintage, 1989.

Laursen, Finn. *Superpower at Sea: U.S. Ocean Policy*. New York: Praeger, 1983.

The Law of the Sea: Pollution by Dumping. A legislative history on the establishment and enforcement of rules and standards. New York: United Nations, 1981.

Livingston, D. *Marine Pollution Articles in the Law of the Sea Single Informal Negotiating Text*. Honolulu: The Law of the Sea Institute, University of Hawaii, 1976.

Lones, Laura. "The Marine Mammal Protection Act and International Protection of

Cetaceans: A Unilateral Attempt to Effectuate Transnational Conservation.'' *Vanderbilt Journal of Transnational Law* 22, no. 4 (1989): 997–1028.

Luard, Evan. *The Control of the Seabed: A New International Issue*. London: Heinemann, 1974.

Lucas, C. E. *International Fishery Bodies in the North Atlantic*. Honolulu: The Law of the Sea Institute, University of Hawaii, 1970.

Mahmoudi, Said. *The Law of Deep Seabed Mining: A Study of the Progressive Development of International Law Concerning the Management of Polymetallic Nodules of the Deep Seabed*. Stockholm: Almquist and Wiksell International, 1987.

Mangone, G. J. *American Strategic Minerals*. New York: Crane Russak, 1984.

May, John. *Antarctica: A New View of the Seventh Continent*. Garden City, N.Y.: Doubleday, 1989.

McDougal, Myres S., and William T. Burke. *The Public Order of the Oceans: A Contemporary International Law of the Sea*. Norwell, Mass.: Kluwer, 1987.

M'Gonigle, R. Michael, and Mark W. Zacher. *Pollution, Politics and International Law: Tankers at Sea*. Berkeley and Los Angeles: University of California Press, 1979.

McNeil, William J. *Salmon Production, Management and Allocation: Biological, Economic and Policy Issues*. Corvalis: Oregon State University Press, 1988.

Meng, Qing-Nan. *Land-Based Marine Pollution: International Law Development*. London: Graham & Trotman, 1987.

Mero, John L. *The Mineral Resources of the Sea*. New York: Elsevier Scientific, 1965.

Miles, Edward L. ''Preparation for UNCLOS IV?'' *Ocean Development and International Law* 19, no. 5 (1988): 421–430.

Miles, Edward L., and John King Gamble, Jr., eds. *Law of the Sea: Conference Outcomes and Problems of Implementation*. Cambridge, Mass.: Ballinger, 1977.

Mining Development Scenario for Cobalt-Rich Manganese Crusts in the Exclusive Economic Zones of the Hawaii Archipelago and Johnston Island. State of Hawaii, Department of Planning and Economic Development, in cooperation with U.S. Department of the Interior Minerals Management Service, January 1987.

Modelski, George, and William R. Thompson. *Seapower in Global Politics, 1494–1993*. Seattle: University of Washington Press, 1988.

Moore, John Norton. ''The Regime of Straits and the Third United Nations Conferences on the Law of the Sea.'' *The American Journal of International Law* 74 (January 1980): 77–121.

Nordquist, Myron H., and Choon-ho Park. *The Reports of the United States Delegation to the Third United Nations Conference on the Law of the Sea*. Honolulu: The Law of the Sea Institute, University of Hawaii, 1983.

Oda, Shigeru. *The International Law of Ocean Development*. 4 vols., 1975–1982. Dordrecht, Netherlands: Martinus Nijhoff; London: Graham & Trotman, 1989.

———. *International Law of the Resources of the Sea*. Dordrecht, Netherlands: Martinus Nijhoff; London: Graham & Trotman, 1976.

Ogley, Roderick C. *Internationalizing the Seabed*. Brookfield, VT: Gower, 1984.

Okidi, C. O. *Regional Control of Ocean Pollution: Legal and Institutional Problems and Prospects*. Dordrecht, Netherlands: Martinus Nijhoff; London: Graham & Trotman, 1978.

Packer, Tim. *Survey of Foreign Development Activities for Offshore Non-Fuel Mineral Resources: Part II*. Waterloo, ONT: University of Waterloo, 1988.

Papadakis, N. *The International Legal Regime of Artificial Islands*. Dordrecht, Netherlands: Martinus Nijhoff; London: Graham & Trotman, 1977.

Park, Choon-ho, and Jae Kyu Park, eds. *The Law of the Sea: Problems from the East Asian Perspective*. Honolulu: The Law of the Sea Institute, University of Hawaii, 1987.

———. *East Asia and the Law of the Sea*. 2d ed. Seoul, Korea: Seoul National University Press, 1985.

Parker, Henry S. *Exploring the Oceans: An Introduction for the Traveler and Amateur Naturalist*. Englewood Cliffs, N.J.: Prentice-Hall, 1985.

Pearson, Charles S. *International Marine Environment Policy: The Economic Dimension*. Baltimore: Johns Hopkins University Press, 1975.

Pharand, D. *Northwest Passage: Arctic Straits*. Dordrecht, Netherlands: Martinus Nijhoff; London: Graham & Trotman, 1984.

Pinkerton, Evelyn, ed. *Cooperative Management of Local Fisheries: New Directions for Improved Management and Community Development*. Vancouver: University of British Columbia, 1989.

Post, Alexander M. *Deepsea Mining and the Law of the Sea*. Dordrecht, Netherlands: Martinus Nijhoff; London: Graham & Trotman, 1983.

Prescott, J. R. Victor. *The Maritime Political Boundaries of the World*. New York: Methuen, 1985.

Price, R. *The Maritime Law of the Arabian Gulf Cooperation Council States*. Dordrecht, Netherlands: Martinus Nijhoff; London: Graham & Trotman, 1986.

Ramazani, R. K. *The Persian Gulf and the Strait of Hormuz*. Dordrecht, Netherlands: Martinus Nijhoff; London: Graham & Trotman, 1979.

Rao, P. Sreenivasa. *The Public Order of Ocean Resources: A Critique of the Contemporary Law of the Sea*. Cambridge: The Massachusetts Institute of Technology Press, 1975.

Raphael, Perl. *The Falkland Islands Dispute in International Law and Politics*. Dobbs Ferry, N.Y.: Oceana, 1983.

Reisman, Michael. "Regime of Straits and National Security: An Appraisal of International Lawmaking." *The American Journal of International Law* 74 (January 1980): 48–76.

Rembe, N. S. *Africa and the International Law of the Sea: A Study of the Contribution of the African States to the Third United Nations Conference on the Law of the Sea*. Dordrecht, Netherlands: Martinus Nijhoff; London: Graham & Trotman, 1980.

Reynolds, Clark G. *History and the Sea: Essays on Maritime Strategies*. Columbia, S. C.: University of South Carolina Press, 1989.

Richardson, Elliot L. "Power, Mobility and the Law of the Sea." *Foreign Affairs* 58, no. 4 (Spring 1980): 902–919.

Richardson, Jacques G., ed. *Managing the Ocean: Resources, Research, Law*. Mt. Airy, Md.: Lomond Publications, 1985.

Ronzitti, N. *The Law of Naval Warfare: A Collection of Agreements and Documents with Commentaries*. Dordrecht, Netherlands: Martinus Nijhoff; London: Graham & Trotman, 1988.

Ross, David A. *Opportunities and Uses of the Ocean*. New York: Springer-Verlag, 1978.

Rozakis, C. L. *The Greek-Turkish Dispute over the Aegean Continental Shelf*. Honolulu: The Law of the Sea Institute, University of Hawaii, 1975.

Saetevik, Sunneva. *Environmental Cooperation between the North Sea States: Success or Failure?* Washington, D.C.: Belhaven Press, 1988.

Samuels, Marwyn S. *Contest for the South China Sea.* New York: Methuen, 1982.

Sauwant, Karl. *Group of 77.* Dobbs Ferry, N.Y.: Oceana, 1981.

Sayed, H. E. *Maritime Regulations in Saudi Arabia.* London: Graham & Trotman, 1987.

Schmandt, Jurgen, and Hilliard Roderick, eds. *Acid Rain and Friendly Neighbors: The Policy Dispute between Canada and the United States.* Durham, N.C.: Duke University Press, 1985.

Schusterich, Kurt Michael. *Resource Management and the Oceans: The Political Economy of Deep Seabed Mining.* Boulder, Colo.: Westview Press, 1982.

Simon, Anne W. *Neptune's Revenge: The Ocean of Tomorrow.* New York: Franklin Watts, 1984.

Sinjela, A. Mpazi A. "Land-Locked States Rights in the Exclusive Economic Zone from the Perspective of the UN Convention on the Law of the Sea." *Ocean Development and International Law* 20, no. 1 (1989): 63–82.

Skinner, Brian J., and Karl K. Turekian. *Man and the Ocean.* Englewood Cliffs, N.J.: Prentice-Hall, 1973.

Slot, P. J. "The International Legal Regime for Navigation." *Ocean Development and International Law* 15, no. 1 (1985): pp. 89–98.

Smith, Brian D. *State Responsibility and the Marine Environment: The Rules of Decision.* Oxford: Clarendon Press, 1988.

Society for Underwater Technology. *Exclusive Economic Zones: Resources, Opportunities and the Legal Regime.* Dordrecht, Netherlands: Martinus Nijhoff; London: Graham & Trotman, 1986.

Sohn, Louis B. "International Law of the Sea and Human Rights Issues." In *The Law of the Sea: What Lies Ahead?*, edited by Thomas A. Clingan, Jr. Honolulu: The Law of the Sea Institute, University of Hawaii, 1988.

Soons, Alfred H. A. *Marine Scientific Research and the Law of the Sea.* Antwerp: Kluwer Law and Taxation Publishers, 1988.

———. *Artificial Islands and Installations in International Law.* Honolulu: The Law of the Sea Institute, University of Hawaii, 1974.

Springer, Allen L. *The International Law of Pollution: Protecting the Global Environment in a World of Sovereign States.* Westport, Conn.: Quorum, 1983.

Sullivan, Jeremiah J. *Pacific Basin Enterprise and the Changing Law of the Sea.* Lexington, Mass.: D. C. Heath, 1977.

Swartztrauber, Sayre A. *The Three-Mile Limit of Territorial Seas.* Annapolis, Md.: Naval Institute Press, 1972.

Szekely, Alberto. *Latin America and the Development of the Law of the Sea: Regional Documents, National Legislation.* Dobbs Ferry, N.Y.: Oceana, 1976.

Thurman, Harold V. *Introductory Oceanography.* 2d ed. Columbus, Ohio: Merrill, 1978.

Tinker, Spencer Wilkie. *The World of Whales.* New York: E. J. Brill, 1988.

Todd, P. *Contracts for the Carriage of Goods by Sea.* Palo Alto, Calif.: Blackwell Scientific, 1988.

Triggs, Gillian D., ed. *The Antarctica Treaty Regime: Law, Environment and Resources.* Cambridge: Cambridge University Press, 1987.

Truver, S. G. *The Strait of Gibraltar and the Mediterranean.* Dordrecht, Netherlands: Martinus Nijhoff; London: Graham & Trotman, 1980.

Twitchell, Marlyn. "Implementing the U.S.-Canada Pacific Salmon Treaty: The Struggle to Move from 'Fish Wars' to Cooperative Fishery Management.'' *Ocean Development and International Law* 20, no. 4 (1989): 409–428.

Tyack, Peter L., and Laela S. Sayigh. ''Those Dolphins Aren't Just Whistling in the Dark.'' *Oceanus* 32, no. 1 (Spring 1989): 80–83.

UN Document, Official Records. *Third United Nations Conference on the Law of the Sea*. Vol. 17. ''Summary Records of Meetings, Documents.'' Resumed Eleventh Session: New York, 22–24 September 1982. Final Part of Eleventh Session and Conclusion of Conference.

UN Office for Ocean Affairs and the Law of the Sea. *The Law of the Sea: National Legislation on the Exclusive Economic Zone, The Economic Zone and the Exclusive Fishery Zone*. New York: United Nations, 1989.

———. *The Law of the Sea: Maritime Boundary Agreements (1970–1984)*. New York: United Nations, 1988.

———. *Registration of Pioneer Investors in the International Seabed Area in Accordance with Resolution II of the Third United Nations Conference on the Law of the Sea*. Special Issue II. *Law of the Sea Bulletin*. New York: United Nations, April 1988.

U.S. Department of Commerce, National Oceanic and Atmospheric Administration. *Report to the Congress on Ocean Pollution, Monitoring and Research, October 1986 through September 1987*. Washington, D.C.: GPO, June 1988.

———. *Summary of Ocean Minerals Activities and Related Research*. Washington, D.C.: GPO, 5 July 1988.

Van Dyke, Jon M., ed. *Consensus and Confrontation: The United States and the Law of the Sea Convention*. Honolulu: The Law of the Sea Institute, University of Hawaii, 1985.

Van Dyke, Jon M., Lewis M. Alexander, and Joseph R. Morgan, eds. *International Navigation: Rocks and Shoals Ahead?* Honolulu: The Law of the Sea Institute, University of Hawaii, 1988.

Varghese, Peter. *Law Enforcement Capabilities in EEZs: Australia and the South Pacific Island States*. Washington, D.C.: Embassy of Australia, 1988.

Von Munch, Ingo. *Internationales Seerecht*. Heidelberg: R. V. Decker's Verlag, G. Schenck, 1985.

Voskuil, C.C.A., and J. A. Wade. *Carriage of Goods by Sea, Maritime Collisions, Maritime Oil Pollution, Commercial Arbitration*. Dordrecht, Netherlands: Martinus Nijhoff; London: Graham & Trotman, 1980.

Walsh, Don, ed. *The Law of the Sea: Issues in Ocean Resources Management*. New York: Praeger, 1977.

Wenk, Edward, Jr. *The Politics of the Ocean*. Seattle: University of Washington Press, 1972.

Westerman, Gayl. *The Juridical Bay*. New York: Oxford University Press, 1987.

Wooster, Warren S. ''Research in Troubled Waters: U.S. Research Vessel Clearance Experience, 1972–1978.'' *Ocean Development and International Law* 9, nos. 3–4 (1981): 219–240.

Wooster, Warren S., ed. *Freedom of Oceanic Research*. New York: Crane, Russak, 1973.

Zacklin, R., and L. Caflisch. *The Legal Regime of International Rivers and Lakes*. London: Graham & Trotman, 1981.

Index

About the Author

JAMES C. F. WANG is Professor of Political Science and International Studies at the University of Hawaii at Hilo. He has published a number of books on contemporary Chinese and Asian politics. He is a member of the Law of the Sea Institute and the Council on Ocean Law.